HANDBOOK ON PUNISHMENT DECISIONS

Handbook on Punishment Decisions: Locations of Disparity provides a comprehensive assessment of the current knowledge on sites of disparity in punishment decision-making. This collection of essays and reports of original research defines disparity broadly to include the intersection of race/ethnicity, gender, age, citizenship/immigration status, and socioeconomic status, and it examines dimensions such as how pretrial or guilty plea processes shape exposure to punishment, how different types of sentencing decisions and/or policy structures (sentencing guidelines, mandatory minimums, risk assessment tools) might shape and condition disparity, and how post-sentencing decisions involving probation and parole contribute to inequalities. The sixteen contributions pull together what we know and what we don't about punishment decision-making, and plow new ground for further advances in the field.

The ASC Division on Corrections & Sentencing Handbook Series publishes volumes on topics ranging from violence risk assessment to specialty courts for drug users, veterans, or people with mental illness. Each thematic volume focuses on a single topical issue that intersects with corrections and sentencing research.

Jeffery T. Ulmer is Professor of Sociology and Criminology and Associate Department Head, Sociology and Criminology, at Pennsylvania State University. He received his Ph.D. and M.A. in Sociology from Pennsylvania State University. His interests include courts and criminal sentencing, racial inequalities in criminal punishment, structural disadvantage and violence, religion and crime, symbolic interactionism, organizations, and the integration of qualitative and quantitative methods. He is the author or co-author of several books and over 65 articles and book chapters. He received the Distinguished Scholar Award from the American Society of Criminology (ASC) Division on Corrections and Sentencing in 2012, and in 2006 (with Darrell Steffensmeier) won ASC's Michael Hindelang Award for Outstanding Book for *Confessions of a Dying Thief: Understanding Criminal Careers and Illegal Enterprise.*

Mindy S. Bradley is Professor in the Department of Sociology and Criminal Justice at the University of Arkansas. Her areas of research include: courts and sentencing, corrections, intersections of mental/behavioral health and justice systems, and deviance. She received her Ph.D. in Sociology and M.A. in Crime, Law, and Justice from Pennsylvania State University. She was a National Institute of Mental Health Postdoctoral Research Fellow at the Cecil G. Sheps Center for Health Services Research at the University of North Carolina, Chapel Hill. She is the author of *Naked Lives: Inside the Worlds of Exotic Dance* (SUNY Press) and co-editor (with Brent Teasdale) of *Preventing Crime and Violence* (Springer), the second volume of the Advances in Prevention Science series.

The ASC Division on Corrections & Sentencing Handbook Series
Edited by Pamela K. Lattimore and John R. Hepburn

The American Society of Criminology's Division on Corrections & Sentencing sponsors a series of volumes published by Routledge on seminal and topical issues that span the fields of sentencing and corrections. The critical essays, reviews, and original research in each volume provide a comprehensive assessment of the current state of knowledge, contribute to public policy discussions, and identify future research directions. Each thematic volume focuses on a single topical issue that intersects with corrections and sentencing research. The contents are eclectic in regard to disciplinary foci, theoretical frameworks and perspectives, and research methodologies.

Short Title: ASC Handbook Series

1 **Handbook on Risk and Need Assessment**
Theory and Practice
Taxman

2 **Punishment Decisions**
Locations of Disparity
Ulmer and Bradley

3 **The Consequences of Sentencing and Punishment Decisions**
Huebner and Frost

Corrections & Sentencing

The nature of justice requires that systematic disparities in the delivery of punishment should be identified and condemned. This important new Handbook goes a crucial step further by also locating the sources of disparity in the hidden processes and policies of criminal justice agents and the legal system. This is essential reading for anyone concerned with making justice more just.

—**Shadd Maruna**, *Professor of Criminology, University of Manchester, UK*

Jeffery Ulmer, leading scholar of disparities in punishment decisions, their structural, institutional, and policy contexts, joined forces with the excellent Mindy Bradley to bring together an exceptional group of contributors to this volume. Its publication is a defining moment. It will have consequences for the future of this field.

—**Joachim J. Savelsberg**, *Professor of Sociology and Law, University of Minnesota, USA*

HANDBOOK ON PUNISHMENT DECISIONS

Locations of Disparity

Edited by Jeffery T. Ulmer and Mindy S. Bradley

Routledge
Taylor & Francis Group
LONDON AND NEW YORK

First published 2018
by Routledge

2 Park Square, Milton Park, Abingdon, Oxfordshire OX14 4RN
52 Vanderbilt Avenue, New York, NY 10017

Routledge is an imprint of the Taylor & Francis Group, an informa business

First issued in paperback 2019

Library of Congress Cataloging-in-Publication Data
A catalog record for this book has been requested

ISBN: 978-1-138-22147-5 (hbk)
ISBN: 978-0-367-40516-8 (pbk)

Typeset in Bembo
by Apex CoVantage, LLC

CONTENTS

CONTRIBUTORS

Michael Adorjan is an Associate Professor in the Department of Sociology at the University of Calgary, and Fellow with the Centre for Criminology, University of Hong Kong. His research and teaching focus on youth crime and cyber-risk, fear of crime, and perceptions of police. He is currently a Principal Investigator (with Rose Ricciardelli, Memorial University) on a Social Sciences and Humanities Research Council funded Insight Development Grant examining youth and cyber-risk in Canada. His first book, co-authored with Wing Hong (Eric) Chui, *Responding to Youth Crime in Hong Kong: Penal Elitism, Legitimacy and Citizenship*, was published in 2014. His second book, co-edited with Rose Ricciardelli, *Engaging with Ethics in International Criminological Research*, has recently been published.

Akilah Alleyne is pursuing a Master's Degree in Sociology at the University of Delaware. She received her B.A. in Social Sciences from the University of Delaware in 2015.

Pauline K. Brennan is Associate Professor and Doctoral Program Coordinator of the University of Omaha School of Criminology and Criminal Justice. She has a Ph.D. in Criminal Justice from the State University of New York at Albany. Her research interests include the disparity in court processing outcomes, correctional issues, female offenders and issues, and race and ethnicity in media depictions of offenders.

Shawn D. Bushway is a Professor of Public Administration and Policy at the Rockefeller College of Public Affairs and Policy with a courtesy appointment in the School of Criminal Justice. He is a graduate of the Heinz School of Public Policy at Carnegie Mellon University. He received the University at Albany (SUNY) Award for Excellence in Research in 2013 and the State University of New York Chancellor's Award for Excellence in Scholarship in 2014. He is a member of New York State's Permanent Commission on Sentencing Reform, and his primary research interests involve criminal justice policy, the desistance process, and the effect of background check policies on employment for individuals with criminal history records. He is an associate editor of the *Journal of the Royal Statistical Society, Series A* and the *Journal of Quantitative Criminology*, and he is on the editorial board for four other journals, including *Criminology* and the *Journal of Policy Analysis and Management.*

Rodney L. Engen is Associate Professor of Sociology at the University of Arkansas. Previously he was Associate Professor of Sociology at North Carolina State University. He specializes in the study of criminology and the criminal justice process.

Jonathan Evans works as a Senior Lecturer at the Centre for Criminology in the School of Humanities and Social Sciences at the University of South Whales. He is a member of the university's Crime and Social Policy Research Institute. His main research and teaching interests are in youth justice, public care, and youth policy.

James Frank received his Ph.D. from Michigan State University in Criminal Justice and Criminology. He is a professor in School of Criminal Justice and the Director of the Center for Criminal Justice Research. Dr. Frank's research primarily focuses on understanding the behavior of street-level police officers, officer decision-making during interactions with the public, and citizen attitudes toward the police. His funded policing research projects have examined officer use of police technology involving gunshot location programs and the use of non-emergency call numbers, the hiring practices of police agencies, the work routines of police officers, the influence of race on traffic stops, citizen attitudes toward the police, and the implementation of problem-solving strategies. He has also been involved in funded studies examining juror understanding of death penalty instructions, sentencing in state and federal courts, and the impact of collateral consequences of conviction in Ohio. He has published articles in *Justice Quarterly, Police Quarterly, Crime and Delinquency, Criminology and Public Policy, the Journal of Criminal Justice*, and *Policing: An International Journal of Police Strategy and Management.* He is a past President of the Academy of Criminal Justice Sciences. He teaches in the areas of policing, legal issues, and criminal justice.

Natalie Goulette is Assistant Professor of Criminology and Criminal Justice at the University of West Florida. Goulette, who holds a Ph.D. in Criminal Justice from the University of Cincinnati, conducts research on judicial matters, examining such questions as whether female defendants receive different treatment than male defendants and what role defense attorneys paly in generating disparities in case dispositions and outcomes.

Richard D. Hartley is an associate professor at The University of Texas at San Antonio. He received his Ph.D. in Criminology and Criminal Justice from University of Nebraska, and his M.A. and B.A. in Criminal Justice from Minot State University. His research interests include disparities in sentencing practices, race/ethnicity and crime, the war on drugs and narcotics violations, and quantitative methods.

Brian D. Johnson is an Associate Professor of Criminology and Criminal Justice at the University of Maryland. He received his Ph.D. in Crime, Law & Justice in 2003 from the Pennsylvania State University. His dissertation was supported by the Forrest Crawford Fellowship for Ethical Inquiry and received the Penn State Alumni Association Dissertation Award. In 2008 Dr. Johnson received the American Society of Criminology Ruth Shonle Cavan Young Scholar Award. His current research interests include contextual variations in sentencing, racial and ethnic relations in society, and the use of advanced statistical modeling techniques to study criminal processes.

Byungbae Kim is currently a fourth-year doctoral student from Seoul, South Korea. Kim worked as a policymaker for the Ministry of Justice, Korea for about six years before coming to Arizona State University (ASU) for his doctoral degree. Mr. Kim's main research interests are sentencing, corrections, and quantitative data analysis. He has just begun his dissertation titled "the impacts of incarcerations and reentry contexts on mental health among serious juvenile delinquents."

Aaron Kupchik received his Ph.D. in Sociology from New York University and is a Professor and the Director of Graduate Studies in the Department of Sociology and Criminal Justice at the University of Delaware. His research focuses on the punishment of youth in schools, courts, and correctional facilities. He is author of *The Real School Safety Problem: The Long-Term Consequences of Harsh School Punishment*, *Homeroom Security: School Discipline in an Age of Fear*, and *Judging Juveniles: Prosecuting Adolescents in Adult and Juvenile Courts*. He is a past recipient of the American Society of Criminology Michael J. Hindelang Book Award and the American Society of Criminology Ruth Shonle Cavan Young Scholar Award. His work has been funded by the National Science Foundation and the National Institute of Justice. He serves on several editorial boards and has held leadership positions within the American Society of Criminology and American Sociological Association's Crime, Law, and Deviance Section.

Megan C. Kurlychek joined the University at Albany, SUNY, faculty at the School of Criminal Justice in the fall of 2007. Her primary research interests include juvenile justice and delinquency, specifically prevention and rehabilitation programming. Megan's current research also encompasses the more general area of offender rehabilitation and reentry. She has published several pieces focusing on the impact of rehabilitative programming offered in correctional bootcamps and aftercare programs. Recently her research has focused on the many obstacles offenders face as they attempt to reenter society and the use of criminal history records in limiting legitimate opportunities. Megan has previously worked as a research analyst for the Pennsylvania Commission on Sentencing, the National Center for Juvenile Justice, and the Pennsylvania State Senate, and retains a major focus on public policy and evaluation research.

James Lant holds an M.A. in Sociology, Criminology, and Statistics from Queens University and a B.A. in Social Sciences and Humanities from the University of Ontario Institute of Technology. He currently works as a Research Scientist at Multi-Health Systems Inc.

Julia A. Laskorunsky is a doctoral candidate in the Criminology program at Penn State University. Her research is in the areas of sentencing and corrections, with a focus on risk prediction and recidivism. She was awarded the 2016 National Institute of Justice Dissertation Fellowship. Her dissertation examines actuarial and clinical risk prediction at sentencing and its effect on racial/ethnic disproportionality. Her work can be seen in the *Journal of Crime and Justice*, *Advancing Criminology and Criminal Justice Policy*, and *Oxford Handbooks Online*.

Rachel Lautenschlager, M.A. is a doctoral student in sociology concentrating in the areas of criminology and race, ethnicity, and immigration. Her research explores how law enforcement and other components of the criminal justice system vary across neighborhoods, and the ways that this results in differential outcomes across racial and ethnic groups. She earned her B.A. in Judaic studies in 2012 at the George Washington University.

Michael J. Leiber is a Professor and Chair in the Department of Criminology at the University of South Florida. He earned his doctorate in criminal justice from the State University of New York at Albany. His main research interests and publications lie in juvenile delinquency, juvenile justice, and race/ethnicity. Over the last twenty years, he has also worked with the Office of Juvenile Justice & Delinquency Prevention (OJJDP) as a consultant dealing with the overrepresentation of minority youth in the juvenile justice system. Since 2010, he has served as Editor of the *Journal of Crime and Justice*.

Sean Maddan is Associate Professor of Criminology and Criminal Justice. Maddan specializes in the advancement of criminological theory, refining both research methods and statistical applications, and applying these to different forms of criminality and the response of the criminal justice system (police, courts, and corrections) to crime in society.

Paul Nieuwbeerta is full Professor of Criminology at the Institute of Criminal Law and Criminology of Leiden University. He is Chair of the Department of Criminology. His research interests include criminal behavior over the life-course, homicide, and the determinants and consequences of imprisonment.

Marisa Omori is Assistant Professor in the Department of Sociology at the University of Miami. She holds a Ph.D. in Criminology, Law, and Society, an M.A. in Social Ecology from the University of California, Irvine, an M.A. in Criminal Justice from the John Jay College of Criminal Justice, The City University of New York, and an A.B. in Economics from Occidental College. Her research interests include criminology, racial stratification within criminal justice institutions, courts and sentencing, drug use and drug policy, and research methods.

Noah Painter-Davis is Assistant Professor in the Department of Sociology at the University of New Mexico. He received a Ph.D. from Pennsylvania State University in 2013. His research interests include crime, law, and social control, and race and ethnicity.

Jennifer H. Peck is an Assistant Professor in the Department of Criminal Justice at the University of Central Florida. She holds her M.A. and Ph.D. in Criminology from the University of South Florida. Her most recent publications appear in *Justice Quarterly, Law and Human Behavior,* and *Crime & Delinquency*. Her research interests include racial/ethnic disparities in juvenile court processing, the treatment of disadvantaged groups in the juvenile justice system, and the causes and correlates of delinquent behavior.

Michelle S. Phelps is an Assistant Professor in the Department of Sociology at the University of Minnesota. She holds an M.A. and Ph.D. in Sociology from Princeton University, and a B.A. in Psychology from the University of California, Berkeley. Phelps' research is in the sociology of punishment, focusing in particular on the punitive turn in the U.S. Her current work focuses on the rise of probation supervision as a criminal justice sanction and its relationship to mass incarceration. She has also examined a variety of criminal justice topics, including changes in rehabilitative programming in U.S. prisons since the 1970s and the recent decarceration trend and its implications for inequality. Together with Professors Joshua Page and Philip Goodman, she is the author of *Breaking the Pendulum: The Long Struggle Over Criminal Justice.*

Allison D. Redlich, a Professor in the Department of Criminology, Law, and Society at George Mason University, was trained as an experimental psychologist but uses multiple methods to conduct her research. To a large degree, her research centers on whether legal decision-making is knowing, intelligent, and voluntary. She examines such decision-making in vulnerable (juveniles and persons with mental health problems) and non-vulnerable defendants, and across several different contexts—in the interrogation room, during the guilty plea process, and in mental health courts. Professor Redlich also studies wrongful convictions, with a particular focus on false confessions and false guilty pleas. In addition to publishing numerous articles on these and related topics, she has co-authored/edited four books, most recently two volumes on the international practices of interviewing victims, witnesses, and suspects. To pursue her research, Professor Redlich has received funding from the National Science Foundation, the National Institute of Justice, the Brain and Behavior Research Association, and the Federal Bureau of Investigation, among others. She especially enjoys working with and mentoring undergraduate and graduate students.

Rose Ricciardelli is an Associate Professor & the Coordinator of Criminology at Memorial University. She is the Inaugural Associate Director, Corrections, for the Canadian Institute of Public Safety Research and Treatment (CIPSRT). Her research is centered on social health, corrections, and gender, including evolving understandings of gender, vulnerabilities, risk, and experiences and issues within different facets of the criminal justice system. Beyond her work on the realities of penal living and community re-entry for federally incarcerated men in Canada, her current work includes a focus on the experiences of correctional officers and police officers given the potential for compromised psychological, physical, and social health inherent to the occupations.

Rebecca Richardson is currently a fourth-year student in the Ph.D. program at the University of Maryland, working as a research assistant for Dr. Brian D. Johnson. Her Master's thesis evaluated gender and the focal concerns theory of sentencing. She earned a B.A. in Psychology and Economics from Wellesley College in 2012. Her interests currently include criminal court decision-making and sentencing, and gender and race disparities in the criminal justice system.

Melanie Valentin Rosa began the University of South Florida Criminology Ph.D. program in the fall of 2015 after completion of a M.S. in Criminal Justice-Research and a B.S. in Psychology at the University of Central Florida. Her research interests focus on program evaluations in correctional facilities, prisoner reentry, sexual offenders, juvenile delinquency, and detention alternatives.

Tayler Shreve holds a B.A from the University of South Florida. She is currently pursuing her Master's Degree in Criminology at the University of South Florida and is working on her thesis that focuses on race/ethnicity, objective decision-making tools, and juvenile justice court outcomes.

Cassia C. Spohn is a Foundation professor and director of the School of Criminology and Criminal Justice at Arizona State University (ASU). She received her Ph.D. in political science from the University of Nebraska-Lincoln in 1978. Prior to joining the faculty at ASU, she was a Professor in the School of Criminology and Criminal Justice at the University of Nebraska at Omaha, where she served as Director of Graduate Studies for 12 years and as Department Chair for 1 year. Spohn is the author of the book *How Do Judges Decide? The Search for Fairness and Justice in Punishment*, and the co-author of several others. She has published more than a hundred articles. Her work has been supported by the National Science Foundation, the National Institute of Justice, and the Robert Wood Johnson Foundation. In 1987 her research was cited by the U.S. Supreme Court in the landmark case *McCleskey v. Kemp*. In 2011 she was named an ASU Foundation Professor and in 2013 she was awarded ASU's Faculty Achievement Award for Defining Edge Research in Social Sciences. She has been the editor of *Justice Quarterly* since 2011.

Darrell Steffensmeier received his Ph.D. in sociology from University of Iowa in 1972. The underlying theme of his research is understanding how stratification (gender, age, race, class, spatial) and culture impact level of crime and social control efforts. He is a fellow of American Society of Criminology and past President of the International Association for Study of Organized Crime (IASOC). In the graduate program, he teaches seminars on criminological theory; gender, crime, and punishment; race-ethnicity, crime, and punishment; and types of crime and criminal organization.

Two of his books have received major awards for outstanding scholarship: *The Fence: In the Shadow of Two Worlds* (from the Society for the Study of Social Problems) and *Confessions of a Dying Thief: Understanding Criminal Careers and Illegal Enterprise* (from the American Society of Criminology). He recently received a major three-year grant from the National Institute of Justice to study the causes of serious forms of white-collar corporate financial crime.

Heather M. Washington is Assistant Professor at Western Virginia University. Washington is primarily interested in understanding the consequences of incarceration for individuals and those who are connected to them by familial ties, with an emphasis on racial and ethnic variation in the outcomes. She explores these issues by integrating perspectives from the disciplines of criminology and family sociology to provide a more complete understanding than previously available as to how and why incarceration detrimentally affects offenders' families and children. Her past and current research in this area uses data from the Fragile Families and Child Wellbeing Study to explore: (1) the consequences of individuals' involvement in crime and history of incarceration for family formation, family dynamics, and youths' behavior; (2) the characteristics and circumstances that might mediate and/or moderate the impact of incarceration on children and families; and (3) whether the effects of incarceration are universal across ethnoracial groups and immigrant backgrounds.

Hilde Wermink is Assistant Professor of Criminology at the Institute of Criminal Law and Criminology at Leiden University in the Netherlands. She obtained a B.A. in Sociology and a M.A. in Sociology and Social Research from Utrecht University. She started as a junior researcher at the Netherlands Institute for the Study of Crime and Law Enforcement (NSCR), and earned her Ph.D. in Criminology from Leiden University. She has been a visiting scholar at Maryland University and at the University of California, Berkeley. Her current research interests include disparities in criminal court decision-making and sentencing, consequences of imprisonment (and other punishments) on criminal behavior, and life-course criminology. Her work has been supported by the Netherlands Organization for Scientific Research, the Council of the Judiciary, the Research and Documentation Centre, and Leiden University Fund.

Johan van Wilsem is head of the Department of Crime, Law Enforcement, and Sanctions at Research and Documentation Centre (WODC), Dutch Ministry of Security and Justice. Formerly, Johan van Wilsem was an Associate Professor of Criminology at Leiden University. He studies patterns of cybercrime victimization (e.g. online consumer fraud, identity fraud), their consequences for adaptive behaviors, and future risks. Using prospective crime victimization data, he also studies the dynamics and shifts between offline and online victimization experiences.

Sigrid van Wingerden is Associate Professor of Criminology at the Institute of Criminal Law & Criminology at Leiden University. She received her Ph.D. in Criminology for her thesis on the role of risk-related offender characteristics at sentencing in the Netherlands. She teaches courses on the legitimacy and effectiveness of sentencing and corrections in the Criminal Justice master. Her current research interests include ethnic disparities in judicial decision-making, risk-based sentencing and public opinion on sentencing.

John Wooldredge is a Professor in the School of Criminal Justice at the University of Cincinnati. He received his Ph.D. in Sociology in 1986 from the University of Illinois. His research and publications focus on institutional corrections (crowding, inmate crimes, and victimizations) and criminal case processing (sentencing and recidivism, and micro- versus macro-level extralegal disparities in case processing and outcomes). He is currently involved in research on neighborhood effects on sentencing, official responses to prison inmate rule violations, prisoner victimization, and factors shaping correctional officer professionalism and morale. In the undergraduate program, he teaches courses on institutional corrections and research methods. His courses in the graduate program include a seminar on institutional corrections, and classes on the general linear model (Statistics II), multilevel modeling, and sampling.

Shi Yan's research focuses on sentencing and plea bargaining. He is particularly interested in modeling the criminal careers of defendants, as well as examining how the properties of the criminal careers predict the case outcomes. He is also investigating measurement issues related to criminal records data. His previous published works include an examination of the use of alternative sanctions in New York State and a description of the trajectories of criminal behaviors before the first prison admission. He received a Ph.D. in criminal justice in 2016 from the University at Albany, SUNY, an M.A. in criminal justice in 2013 from the University at Albany, SUNY, and an LL.B. in law in 2008 from Peking University, Beijing, China.

INTRODUCTION

Jeffery T. Ulmer and Mindy S. Bradley

Established in 1999, The American Society of Criminology's (ASC) Division on Corrections & Sentencing (DCS) aims to facilitate discussion and promote research and theoretical development in the study of punishment, broadly conceived. By bringing together scholars, policymakers, and practitioners, the DCS provides a forum to help promote research on the correlates, costs, and consequences of the punishment of adults and juveniles and defines its scope broadly to include such areas as sentencing, rehabilitation, imprisonment, community corrections, diversionary programs, and diversions and justice alternatives. The ASC Division on Corrections & Sentencing Handbook Series was created as a tool to encourage interaction and dissemination of research among ASC members, practitioners, funding agencies, policymaking bodies, corrections and sentencing organizations, students, and other relevant groups.

Each thematic volume focuses on a topical issue that intersects with corrections and sentencing research. In Volume 1, Faye Taxman provided an in-depth treatment of risk assessment for individuals being considered for parole or probation. Evidence-based approaches to such decisions can provide transparency and consistency, helping to take the emotion and politics out of community corrections. As the U.S. perhaps shifts away from mass incarceration policies, the first volume will likely prove especially useful for those seeking to make evidence-based decisions that help ensure public safety, effective rehabilitation of those on community supervision, and success reentry of offenders.

We believe that the chapters in this volume stake out new claims in the familiar territory of punishment disparity. Disparities and differential impacts of punishment decisions that advantage some types of offenders and disadvantage others may stem from what Bushway and Forst (2013) call "Type A" discretionary decisions by local criminal justice officials during arrest, charging, conviction, and sentencing. Cassia C. Spohn (2015) reviews the multiple waves of sentencing and race research, noting how research questions have become increasingly complex and theoretically sophisticated over time. In the most recent wave of sentencing research, scholars are focusing less exclusively on final sentencing outcome and more on the "life course" of a criminal case and "the ways in which disparities accumulate through the criminal process" (Spohn, 2015: 76). She and others suggest that our focus on individual-level sentencing outcomes after controlling for other "legally-relevant" characteristics does not tell us about racial and ethnic inequalities that may exist in earlier stages, such as charging, pre-trial detention, or plea bargaining decisions (Baumer, 2013). It is important to understand that modest or small disparities at each stage of criminal justice processing can contribute to larger cumulative disadvantage across the system, resulting in substantial disproportional impacts. Most of the chapters in this volume grapple with this kind of Type A discretion in one fashion or another, and several also implicate cumulative disadvantages that can occur across criminal justice stages, especially those chapters in Part II, "Disparities in Pre-Conviction Processes."

In addition, Bushway and Forst (2013) draw attention to "Type B" discretion, in which choices embedded in *criminal justice policies* differentially impact some offenders over others, especially (but not exclusively) racial or ethnic minorities. That is, policy structures can encode racial and ethnic disparity into sentencing by emphasizing punishment criteria that differentially impact certain types of offenders. Type B discretion shapes and provides the "windows" for Type A discretion (see Ulmer, 1997; Ulmer, Painter-Davis, and Tinik, 2016). We are pleased that a number of the chapters to follow also grapple in various ways with Type B discretion and policy-embedded disparities and differential impacts. This is especially true of the chapters in Part I, "Policy Choices and Mass Punishment," and Part IV, "Risk: Race, Age, and Social Class."

Furthermore, a great deal of policy and scholarly discourse has centered on judicial discretion as a key issue relative to disparity and disproportional impact of punishment decisions. Indeed, sentencing structures such as guidelines and mandatory minimums were developed with the aim of controlling such discretion. However, we are proud to present many chapters in this volume that move beyond a focus on judicial discretion to also focus on prosecutors, defense attorneys, probation officers, juvenile court officials, and even school security personnel.

An additional way of thinking about the stages of the criminal justice system and points at which disparity could arise comes from the field of psychiatry. The sequential intercept model envisions a series of points at which an intervention can be made to prevent individuals from entering or penetrating deeper into the criminal justice system (Munetz and Griffin, 2006). In some ways, we approached the creation of this volume with this sequential intercept idea in mind as well, selecting individual chapters that make novel conceptual, theoretical, or analytical contributions to the study of differences in punishment across stages and points of justice processing. We selected chapters while thinking more broadly about how we define, conceptualize, measure, and explain disparity and while thinking across the different actors and decision points involved (policymakers, judges, prosecutors, defense attorneys, probation officers, etc.).

Through invitation and open solicitation, we compiled a group of chapters which, as a whole, provide new comprehensive examinations of punishment decision-making, and highlight both familiar and not-so-easily recognized sources of disparity. Among many excellent potential contributions, we selected these chapters based on their creativity and innovation, overall quality and thoroughness, and thematic contribution. We aimed for a balance of chapters that take new and interesting approaches to investigate familiar sources of disparity, as well as those that shine light on underexplored sources or consequences of disparity. We also are pleased to feature works that suggest new definitions of disparity, focus on different units of analysis, and demonstrate the utility of different analytical choices. Our national and international collection of authors includes established and well-known scholars in in our field, as well as emerging scholars shaping the field.

Chapters

Our first section, "Policy Choices and Mass Punishment," focuses on the causes and correlates of macro-level changes in punishment policies and practices. In Chapter 1, Rodney L. Engen critically examines the role of sentencing policies, and sentencing practices, for explaining mass imprisonment in the U.S. He argues that the conventional wisdom about the importance of "tough on crime" sentencing laws, in fact, rests on very limited empirical evidence. He shows how the analytical strategies typically used in individual-level sentencing research simply are not designed to answer questions about aggregate patterns, such that institutionalized policies and practices may disadvantage minorities in ways that may not appear as "disparity."

In Chapter 2, Michelle S. Phelps builds on her earlier work arguing that the expansion of mass probation through the 1990s and 2000s is a critical and understudied dimension of the carceral state. Phelps examines the race, class, and gender disparities in probation. She investigates competing perspectives on probation, showing how it can be both an "alternative" to imprisonment or "net-widener." Her works finds that probation may more effectively serve as a prison alternative for relatively advantaged probationers, who are more likely to be diverted and complete successfully, whereas for the less advantaged adults it functions more commonly as a net-widener and stepping-stone to further criminal justice control.

The idea that responses to low-level misbehavior can become a pathway for further justice involvement is taken up by Aaron Kupchik and Akilah Alleyne's discussion of the "school-to-prison pipeline." In Chapter 3, they detail the process by which school treatment of children places them at increased risk of future incarceration. The immediate and long-term consequences of exclusion and criminalization of students thus increases the risk that students become involved in the justice system. Studies find that racial minorities are at higher risk of suspension and expulsion. These authors argue how social exclusion and justice system involvement at an early age can have clear ramifications for future punishment decisions

An overwhelming majority of criminal cases in the United States are resolved via guilty pleas in lieu of court trials. Thus the guilty plea process, as well as other pre-conviction and pre-sentencing decision points, are critical areas for revealing disparities in punishment. We devote Part II ("Disparities in Pre-Conviction Processes") to this important area, with chapters devoted to showing how inequalities in pre-conviction decisions may produce greater cumulative inequalities over the entire criminal justice system process. In Chapter 4, Marisa Omori and Rachel Lautenschlager discuss the understudied variation that occurs in the less visible initial filing decisions by prosecutors and plea negotiations. This is particularly relevant in determinate sentencing states with guidelines and mandatory minimums, which many believe have shifted much of the discretion to prosecutors over judges. They also point out the geographic concentration of punishment, noting that criminal justice outcomes are tightly tied to neighborhood characteristics, and neighborhoods remain highly racially segregated.

In Chapter 5, Megan C. Kurlychek and Heather M. Washington take a novel look at a very understudied issue: state and federal criminal record-sealing policies. They discuss how prosecutorial and judicial decision-making in charging and plea bargaining/conviction could produce disparity regarding which individuals are eligible to have their records sealed. Because of the lifelong collateral consequences of a criminal record, including access to housing and employment, these authors propose that the inability to have a record sealed or expunged is indeed another source of potential punishment disparity.

Relatedly, Shi Yan, Shawn D. Bushway, and Allison D. Redlich discuss the power of the prosecutor in charge determinations and how prosecutorial discretion can be an important source of racial disparities in punishment. In Chapter 6, they suggest that researchers focusing on study the sentence at conviction should determine if and how the pattern shifts when controlling for the arraignment and arrest charges instead of the conviction charge. On the other hand, John Wooldredge, James Frank, and Natalie Goulette believe there should also be greater attention paid to defense attorneys given their roles in shaping charge reductions and guilty plea submissions. In Chapter 7, they take a mixed-methods approach, combining court data with interviews to elucidate several ways in which defense attorneys might be just as culpable as prosecutors and judges for shaping case outcomes.

Part III, "Disparities in Punishment Outcomes," focuses on more traditional sentencing outcomes and processes but provides new insights on some familiar themes. The focal concerns perspective is a predominant conceptual framework for explaining sentencing disparities and other criminal justice decision-making, and it is ideally paired with the court community model of court organizational culture. The chapters in this section make new contributions to focal concerns model, expanding its concepts, asking new questions, and employing new methodological strategies. In Chapter 8, Darrell Steffensmeier and Noah Painter-Davis link the focal concerns model to intersectionality theory, with particular focus on how the framework helps to theorize and guide research about the intersection of gender, race, and age effects on the sentencing of criminal defendants.

Other chapters in this section lend further theoretical complexity to the study of disparities in sentencing. In Chapter 9, Cassia C. Spohn, Pauline K. Brennan, and Byungbae Kim apply a critical race feminist approach to test whether sentencing processes are racially and ethnically disparate among female offenders. They note that the vast majority of sentencing studies have focused on male offenders or have merely included offender sex as a control variable in their examinations of data sets comprised largely of male offenders. Using path analysis (an underused approach in sentencing research), they demonstrate how to test for how race can have a direct effect on sentencing and an indirect on sentencing through its impact on other adjudication outcomes, including pre-trial release and sentencing guideline departures.

A key gap in the literature is that almost all of the research on sentencing is limited to the contemporary North American—particularly the U.S. (Ulmer, 2012). In addition, most of the literature on race/ethnicity is focused on black-white comparisons or, in the last decade and half, black-white-Hispanic comparisons. In Chapter 10, Hilde Wermink, Sigrid van Wingerden, Johan van Wilsem, and Paul Nieuwbeerta provide more nuanced distinctions among ethnicity and incorporate measures of social integration to explore ethnic disparities among first- and second-generation immigrants in the Netherlands. Their findings imply that patterns of social stratification, and anti-immigrant biases in punishment, are not limited to the U.S. context but also apply to other contexts where we might otherwise expect lower levels of discrimination.

Another novel theoretical and empirical extension of themes from the focal concerns, court communities, and other models comes from Chapter 11. Michael J. Leiber, Jennifer H. Peck, Melanie Valentin Rosa, and Tayler Shreve draw from feminist theory and public administration literature to explore the possibility of gender differences in probation officer recommendations and actual judicial decision-making in the treatment of male criminal offenders. Their work shows how specific combinations of demographic characteristics of the offender and probation officers influence case outcomes. By examining the effects of probation officer characteristics and recommendations on actual case outcomes, they highlight an understudied potential area of courtroom influence and the importance of asking questions about how other courtroom participants make decisions, how such decisions align with the norms and practices of the courtroom workgroup, and how these decisions may impact sentencing determinations among other court actors.

In Chapter 12, Brian D. Johnson and Rebecca Richardson apply focal concerns concepts of blameworthiness and culpability to examine how race and physical appearance are tied to criminal stereotypes. Using perceptional measures derived from defendant booking photos, they uncover how race and ethnicity, physical appearance characteristics, and criminal trait impressions are related to criminal punishment vis-à-vis focal concerns assessments. Finally, Sean Maddan and Richard D. Hartley attempt to advance the focal concerns' empirical measurement and testability in Chapter 13. Specifically, they review the assumptions and statements about the focal concerns perspective and articulate explicit theoretical propositions and testable hypotheses. A particularly different and promising approach is their application of exploratory and confirmatory factor analysis to create distinct measures of the focal concerns model's concepts.

In Part IV, we revisit the topic of risk assessment raised in Volume 1 of the ASC Division on Corrections & Sentencing Handbook Series, this time through the lens of disparity. The growing popularity of risk assessments in guiding punishment decisions raises important questions about how these instruments are constructed and applied. Chapters in this section, "Risk: Race, Age, and Social Class," critically evaluate the use of risk assessment, highlighting that, despite benefits offered by decision-making driven by systematic, evidence-based, rubric-driven determinations of criminogenic risk, risk assessments have drawbacks. In their development and administration, risk assessments may have the potential to seemingly legitimate and institutionalize disparity. In this last section, we include chapters exploring these issues and the constitutional challenges of using extra-legal variables such as race, gender, and age in structured decision-making instruments. In Chapter 14, Julia A. Laskorunsky puts risk assessment into a broader context of judicial decision-making, sentencing guidelines, and sentencing disparity. She explores the implications for disparity of moving toward sentencing models that build in formal consideration of risk, exemplified by the Pennsylvania's sentencing guidelines future mandate to build risk assessment into sentencing options.

This section, and the volume, close with two more contributions from outside the U.S. context. In Chapter 15, Rose Ricciardelli, Michael Adorjan, and James Lant examine the use of assessment in post-release supervision in Canada, looking at variation in evaluators' subjective assessment of individual scores on motivation to desist, accountability for prior actions, and engagement in correctional plan. They then uncover how these and clinical diagnoses of mental illness impact disparities in clients' assigned level of supervision. Finally, in Chapter 16, Jonathan Evans first of all provides readers with an education in the Public Care and Youth Justice Systems in the United Kingdom. He then problematizes the practice of and utility of risk assessment in the public care and youth justice system. He points out how disparities in assessment and intervention arise from social class inequalities and cultural biases. He then discusses the role of practitioner agency in relation to clinical and actuarial assessments of risk.

Overall, we believe that this handbook provides a broad array of new theoretical, empirical, methodological contributions in the study of punishment disparity, highlighting some of the key current and emerging areas of inquiry in the field of sentencing and corrections. Moreover, in keeping with the "fifth wave" of punishment research (Spohn, 2015) and the sequential intercept approaches (Munetz and Griffin, 2006), it highlights strategic points for intervention, assessment, and reevaluation of punishment policies and practices. As part of the ASC Division on Corrections & Sentencing Handbook series, we hope that this volume can serve as a valuable reference and standalone introduction to punishment decision-making, or as part of a broader review of the diversity of topics in corrections and sentencing research.

References

Baumer, E. P. (2013). Reassessing and redirecting research on race and sentencing. *Justice Quarterly*, *30*(2), 231–261.

Bushway, S., & Forst, B. (2013). Studying discretion in the processes that generate criminal justice sanctions. *Justice Quarterly*, *30*(2), 199–222.

Munetz, M. R., & Griffin, P. A. (2006). Use of the sequential intercept model as an approach to decriminalization of people with serious mental illness. *Psychiatric Services*, *57*, 544–549.

Spohn, C. (2015). Race, crime and punishment in the twentieth and twenty-first centuries. In M. Tonry (Ed.), *Crime and justice: A review of research* (Vol. 44). Chicago: University of Chicago Press.

Ulmer, J. T. (1997). *Social worlds of sentencing: Court communities under sentencing guidelines*. Albany, NY: State University of New York Press.

Ulmer, J. T. (2012). Recent developments and new directions in sentencing research. *Justice Quarterly*, *29*, 1–40.

Ulmer, J. T., Painter-Davis, N., & Tinik, L. (2016). Disproportional imprisonment of black and Hispanic males: Sentencing discretion, processing outcomes, and policy structures. *Justice Quarterly*, 33, 642–681.

PART I

Policy Choices and Mass Punishment

1

WHAT WE KNOW, DO NOT KNOW, AND NEED TO KNOW ABOUT SENTENCING AND MASS INCARCERATION IN THE U.S. AND WHAT "SENTENCING" RESEARCH COULD TEACH US

Rodney L. Engen

In her historic 2016 Presidential Address to the American Society of Criminology (ASC), ASC President Dr. Ruth Peterson called upon scholars to "take stock of what we know, do not know, and need to know" about race, crime, and justice, to seek answers to "looming general questions," and to identify the mechanisms and processes that produce race/ethnic disparities at different levels of analysis (Peterson, 2016, 2017). In the realm of sentencing and sentencing disparity, it is fair to say that scholars have been taking stock of the state of knowledge individually, and as a community, on a more-or-less ongoing basis for many years. As a result, we have several excellent, and still timely, reviews summarizing the evidence and the development of this research over the past thirty years, highlighting the strengths and limitations common to much of the research, and urging scholars to extend the boundaries of our research enterprise. As so much ground has already been covered, I encourage interested readers to study these papers, carefully (e.g., Spohn, 2015; Ulmer, 2012; Baumer, 2013).

For my part, I will take President Peterson's call as an opportunity to do several things. One is to join a growing number of scholars in challenging the conventional wisdom about the *causes of mass incarceration* in the U.S. (e.g., Bushway and Forst, 2013; Pfaff, 2014, 2017; Lynch, 2011; Enns, 2016). Specifically, the general consensus that "tough on crime" sentencing policies—mandatory minimums, three-strikes laws, truth-in-sentencing, abolishing parole, etc.—were instrumental in driving up imprisonment rates rests on *very little*, and *very weak*, empirical evidence. Frequently, the evidence marshaled in support of this narrative entails little more than inferences based on national imprisonment trends and well-known examples of extreme policies, usually California's three-strikes law and the federal mandatory minimums for drug trafficking, which are important but are not representative of the laws or of sentencing practices in most states. This consensus view also fails to fully consider credible alternative explanations, including changes in the behavior of prosecutors, correctional authorities, and even judges.

Regrettably, the extensive research literature on individual-level sentencing decisions and sentencing disparity also does not equip us to answer questions about the effects of sentencing reforms on imprisonment rates, or on racial disproportionality in imprisonment, and offers little to inform current policy debates. The reason for this is simple. "Sentencing" research currently does not include an explicit focus on the effects of sentencing policies, either with respect to changes in the severity of punishment, sentencing disparity, or the process itself (e.g., effects on plea-bargaining) (Engen, 2009). Thus, my second objective is to invite readers, especially scholars with expertise in sentencing and corrections, to think broadly about the *goals and objectives of sentencing research* and to prioritize research that informs our understanding of *how sentencing policies affect sentencing practices* (case processing and severity of punishment) and *how sentencing at the individual-level affects aggregate imprisonment rates*. Toward this end I also highlight some innovative attempts to understand the effects of sentencing policies that others can learn from and build upon.

Third, given the emphasis on sentencing and sentence length for understanding imprisonment rates, I examine the relationship between sentence length and several sentencing reforms (sentencing guidelines, determinate sentencing, mandatory minimums), using data on prison admissions in 26 states in 2000 and 2010 from the National Corrections Reporting Program (NCRP). I use hierarchical linear modeling (HLM) to estimate the relative influence of individual, county, and state characteristics on sentence length and to test interactions between individuals' race and social structural characteristics of the county and the state, between individuals' race and state sentencing policies, and between individuals' race and region of the country. The results reveal important effects at each level of analysis, substantial sentencing policy effects, and significant cross-level interactions with race. The results also draw attention to the geographic distributions of race and ethnicity in the U.S. I discuss some implications of these geographic distributions for understanding disproportionality in imprisonment nationally.

The Effects of Sentencing Policies on Imprisonment

The Consensus View

In 2012, the National Research Council (NRC) of the National Academy of Sciences established a committee of leading scholars to review and summarize the evidence on the causes and consequences of mass incarceration in the United States and to identify implications for public policy. The NRC's final report (Travis et al., 2014) provides an excellent and comprehensive overview of a large body of literature and is probably the best indicator of the consensus view on these issues, if one exists. With respect to the proximal causes of the growth in imprisonment, the NRC is unambiguous and unequivocal:

> The best single proximate explanation of the rise in incarceration is not rising crime rates, but the policy choices made by legislators to greatly increase the use of imprisonment as a response to crime. *Mandatory prison sentences*, intensified *enforcement of drug laws*, and *long sentences* contributed not only to overall high rates of incarceration, but also *especially to extraordinary rates of incarceration in black and Latino communities.*
>
> (p. 3, emphasis added)

> The increase in U.S. incarceration rates over the past 40 years is preponderantly the result of increases both in the likelihood of imprisonment and in lengths of prison sentences—with the latter having been the primary cause since 1990. These increases, in turn, are a product of the proliferation in nearly every state and in the federal system of *laws and guidelines providing for lengthy prison sentences for drug and violent crimes and repeat offenses*, and the enactment in more than half the states and in the federal system of *three strikes* and *truth-in-sentencing* laws.
>
> (p. 70, emphasis added)

> [T]he steady growth in incarceration rates has been significantly fuelled by longer prison sentences. A variety of statutory enactments have driven these results, including laws imposing *truth-in-sentencing*, *life without parole*, and *three strikes*. . . . [States also] *reduced or eliminated the use of discretionary parole release*, increased the level of *returns to prison for parole violations*, *reduced the use of "good time"* [and other early release mechanisms such as halfway houses]. *These policy shifts significantly increased the average time served for a felony conviction.*
>
> (p. 344, emphasis added)

To avoid confusion, I concur that *our response to crime*, not the crime rate, produced the growth in imprisonment, especially once crime began to decline in the early 1990s, and it is highly probable that sentencing policies contributed to this growth.[1] However, I disagree that the available empirical evidence warrants any strong inferences about specific policies, or types of policies, or even that we can assert, as a general conclusion, that "sentencing policy" is a principle reason for the continued growth in imprisonment rates. This is mainly because very little research—almost none—has been undertaken for the purpose of assessing whether these policies affected imprisonment rates and because most of the limited evidence that exists fails to meet even minimal criteria for inferring an association between the enactment of these sentencing policies and states' imprisonment rates.

The Evidence

Much of what we know about mass incarceration, including the disproportionate imprisonment of persons of color, especially African American men, derives from primarily qualitative, macro-historical analyses of changes in the U.S. prison population, and the various social, cultural, and political dynamics that occurred in the same general time frame or that provide its historical context. These include the civil rights movement, rising violent crime rates, "civil unrest," the "Southern Strategy," the politicization of crime, the war on drugs, etc. (e.g., Garland, 2001; Beckett, 1997; Beckett and Western, 2001; Gottschalk, 2006; Alexander, 2010; Clear and Frost, 2014). Likewise, much of the research on race and the drug war centers on describing policy changes, the politics and philosophical arguments related to these changes, and the social consequences of the increase in African American arrest and imprisonment rates (Tonry, 2011). Clearly, this literature is empirically grounded and includes much evidence that our legal institutions changed in fundamental ways, including the expansion of policing powers and the scaling back of 4th Amendment protections that facilitated the War on Drugs (Alexander, 2010; Lynch, 2011), the rise of neo-liberalism and the retrenchment of the welfare state (Wacquant, 2009), and the repudiation of the rehabilitation philosophy in favor of policies emphasizing deterrence, incapacitation, and retribution as the proper goals of punishment (Tonry, 1993; Travis et al., 2014).

However, when it comes to the whether these policies, or other actions, directly produced the growth in imprisonment in the U.S., with the exception of the well-documented increase in street-level drug enforcement (e.g., Tonry, 2011), the evidence is largely indirect and includes large gaps. In this literature, the central questions pertaining to mass incarceration are about its cultural meaning and the causal processes, operating largely at the societal level, that explain *why these policies were enacted*, not whether they actually made a difference (Garland, 2001; Beckett, 1997; Wacquant, 2009). Rather, my impression is that many scholars assumed that the tough on crime policies did exactly what their sponsors promised they would do—put more people in prison, and for longer. David Garland's (2013) acknowledgment that (paraphrasing) "we know mass incarceration is a result of policy choices, we just don't know which ones" seems consistent with this interpretation.

Of course, there is relevant empirical evidence in the form of evaluation research examining mandatory minimums, sentencing guidelines, truth-in-sentencing and three-strikes, at least in California. Of all of the criminal justice "reforms" introduced beginning in the 1970s and 1980s, sentencing guidelines like those in Minnesota, Washington, and Pennsylvania are the most comprehensive and most closely studied. Presumptive guidelines embodied the nation's changing priorities and philosophical rationales for punishment and scholars who reviewed the evidence concluded that the reforms seemed to work (e.g., Blumstein et al., 1983; Von Hirsch, Knapp, and Tonry, 1987; Tonry, 1996; Austin et al., 1996). Judicial "compliance" with presumptive guidelines was generally high and, at least in Minnesota, guidelines did not appear to "displace" racial disparities to the charging stage (Miethe and Moore, 1985; Miethe,

1987). However, concluding that these reforms were working as intended did not mean they were increasing the severity of punishment. Although they required punishment based on the conviction offense and criminal history, the main goals were to make sentencing more predictable, fair, and to reduce racial disparities (Tonry, 2015).[2] Also, in some states (e.g., Minnesota, Washington, and later North Carolina), the goals included controlling their prison populations, and it appeared to work, at least initially (Wright, 2001; Marvell and Moody, 1996).

Studies evaluating mandatory minimums, three-strikes, and truth in sentencing (TIS) vary greatly in quantity and quality. Overall, however, there is little compelling evidence that they significantly increased imprisonment rates, and abundant examples in which these reforms seemed to make little difference (Engen, 2008). Numerous studies find that prosecutors and judges routinely circumvent mandatory minimums for gun violations and drug crimes either through plea bargaining or simply because they believe the punishment to be too severe (Travis et al., 2014). It is possible that they result in more severe punishments, on average, but most studies cannot assess this, and some find no change in the average sentences (Loftin and McDowall, 1981). There is even less evidence that three-strike laws substantially increased imprisonment in the U.S., mainly because most are written fairly narrowly and applied rarely (Travis et al., 2014). Also, they do not all require life without parole (LWOP) or 25 to Life, as in California. If prosecutors use them for leverage in plea bargaining, it is likely that some offenders are receiving longer sentences than they would have otherwise, but in most states, someone who qualifies for sentencing as a "habitual offender" would receive a very long sentence either way. Even in California, the impact on overall imprisonment rates was probably far less than assumed, and varies substantially by county, leading Sutton (2013) to conclude that its effect was largely, but not entirely, symbolic.

Despite the emphasis placed on TIS statutes, and the 1994 Violent Crime Act, which authorized federal funding for prison construction to states that require violent offenders to serve 85 percent of their sentence in prison, evaluation studies have not shown consistently that imprisonment rates or average time served by violent offenders increased in TIS states more than in non-TIS states, or that any differences that appear an be attributed to TIS laws (Sabol et al., 2002; Rosich and Kane, 2005; Turner et al., 2006). Perhaps these policies were instrumental in increasing imprisonment rates, but a common response to the inconsistent evidence of the earlier evaluations is that it was too soon to see the effects of TIS legislation on time served (Travis et al., 2014). If that is true, it suggests we should not place much weight on those studies. Regardless of the time period examined, these evaluations have much more fundamental problems. For example, Turner et al. (2006) compare trends in imprisonment rates, average sentence length, average time served, and the percentage of sentence served in TIS and non-TIS states. They do not control for any other policies that might either explain or obscure the differences observed.

Commitment Rates and Average Time Served

Some of the most persuasive evidence that changes in punishment increased imprisonment, as opposed to crime rates or arrest rates, comes from Blumstein and Beck's (1999) analyses of trends in arrests and in prison admissions and releases. Blumstein and Beck showed that the ratio of prison admissions per arrest (the "commitment" rate) increased markedly in the 1980s and 1990s and that the average time served in prison (calculated as the ratio of the total prison population to the number of people entering prison each year) also increased. Together, these changes accounted for 88 percent of the growth in imprisonment in the period they examined. Parole revocations also increased, adding to the increase in average time spent in prison.

This is important evidence that the severity of *punishment of* crime increased, which they attributed to "sentencing" and sentencing policies. The NRC report presents recently updated analyses provided by Beck and Blumstein (2012), which it describes as differentiating the effects of crime from the effects of "sentencing policy," as do comparable analyses by other researchers. I find this interpretation unpersuasive and, frankly, misleading. An increase in prison commitments per arrest could result for *many* reasons that have *nothing to do with sentencing policies*, such as an increase the proportion of cases prosecuted, prosecutors' willingness to plea bargain, or the quality and legality of evidence provided by police. Likewise, in virtually every state, factors in addition to the court-ordered sentence will affect how long someone is in prison, especially paroling authorities and "good time" policies. Equally important, "sentencing" includes *discretionary* decisions by judges, not only in the majority of states where sentencing is still largely unstructured, but also in most guideline states (Frase, 2013). Thus, any changes in commitments per arrest or in average time served in prison, especially based on nationally aggregated data, will also reflect discretionary decisions of prosecutors, judges, and correctional authorities, as well as institutional policies and practices affecting release (Blumstein and Beck, 1999). Finally, two more-recent studies by Bushway and Forst (2013) and Pfaff (2014) argue that changes in *conviction* rates in the 1990s indicate that prosecutorial discretion probably played the leading role in increasing prison commitments. This is still limited evidence, but it is more evidence than currently exists linking the increase to sentencing policies.

Multivariate Analyses of State Imprisonment Rates

Finally, the most rigorous quantitative evidence relevant to the effects of policies on imprisonment comes from multivariate, multi-state, usually longitudinal, analyses of state imprisonment rates or prison admission rates. These are especially important for several reasons. Although imprisonment rates increased in all states in the U.S. beginning in the mid-1970s, some increased much more than others, and they differ greatly in their overall imprisonment rates (Travis et al., 2014). Garland (2013) suggested there is as much variation between state imprisonment rates within the U.S. as there is between the U.S. and other nations. States also differ greatly in the kinds of sentencing reforms they adopted. Yes, roughly half enacted three-strikes and/or TIS, but half did not. Many also abolished parole, but most, about 60 percent did not (and those that abolished parole did not abolish early release). Analyses of imprisonment rates for the entire U.S. obscure this variation; systematic analyses of states, over time, provide a way to begin to sort out whether any of these policies is associated with the level or growth in imprisonment. Of course, states also differ in social and political characteristics theorized to affect imprisonment rates. These multivariate studies also control for a range of social structural and political characteristics that are related to imprisonment rates.

Specific findings, and methodologies, vary, but the evidence overall indicates that imprisonment rates are related to factors such as crime rates, political conservatism, ideology, racial composition, correctional spending, and region (Greenberg and West, 2001; Jacobs and Carmichael, 2001; Sorensen and Stemen, 2002; Stucky, Heimer, and Lang, 2005; Heimer et al., 2012), but they provide little evidence that the growth in imprisonment is substantially due to sentencing polices. Rather, the most common finding is that determinate and presumptive sentencing guidelines are associated with *lower* imprisonment rates, especially in combination (Marvell and Moody, 1996; Greenberg and West, 2001; Jacobs and Carmichael, 2001; Sorensen and Stemen, 2002; Smith, 2004; Stemen at al., 2005; Zhang, Maxwell, and Vaughn, 2009; Stemen and Rengifo, 2011; Spelman, 2009). Others report mixed results or no significant effects (Stucky, Heimer, and Lang, 2005; Heimer et al., 2012; Harmon, 2013). Of three studies that included measures of TIS, or three-strikes, none found a significant positive effect of three-strikes, but two found positive effects of TIS (Stemen et al., 2005; Spelman, 2009). Only Stemen et al. measured the presence of mandatory minimums, and they found a positive association with imprisonment. However, they also showed that none of the sentencing reforms included in their model explained away the effects of other state characteristics, or of the time trend.

It is unclear what explains the negative effects of determinate sentencing and guidelines, largely because very few studies have tried to explain them. Also, most of the studies listed here only included a single variable indicating whether states had adopted "determinate sentencing," defined as having abolished discretionary parole for most offenders, but many of these states also adopted various types of presumptive sentencing laws to regulate judicial discretion (Marvell and Moody, 1996; Stemen et al., 2005). Thus it is not clear if the negative effects on imprisonment result from eliminating parole boards, or from regulating judges, nor if it is because they affect the sentences ordered or the release date. This is an issue I explore in the analyses to follow.

In short, despite the near consensus that tough on crime laws drove the growth in imprisonment in the U.S., the evidence from state-level analyses does not warrant consensus that the growth in imprisonment is mainly due to sentencing policies. The best evidence is that some of these laws actually slowed the growth of imprisonment, perhaps by design (Marvell and Moody, 1996; Wright, 2001). Also, these studies indicate that sentencing policies *do not explain away the effects of social and political forces* on imprisonment; this may mean they operate mainly through other mechanisms, such as intensive law enforcement, more aggressive prosecution, tougher sentencing, or correctional release and revocation (Sorensen and Stemen, 2002; Stemen et al., 2005). Many questions remain to be answered.

Research on Racial Disproportionality

Unfortunately, every limitation in our understanding of the effects of sentencing laws on imprisonment overall applies equally to our understanding of racial disproportionality. Empirical analyses of race and imprisonment rates are almost entirely limited to studies describing national trends (Tonry, 2011), or comparing the racial makeup of the nation's prison population with the characteristics of people arrested. National rates mask substantial variation between states (Bridges and Crutchfield, 1988; Crutchfield et al., 1994) and tell us nothing about the effects of tough on crime sentencing reforms, most of which operate at the state level.

Only a handful of multivariate studies investigate black versus white imprisonment at the state level in the past 30 years, and sentencing reforms are not usually a focus of the research. Collectively, these studies provide little evidence that sentencing laws (specifically determinate sentencing) are to blame (Bridges and Crutchfield, 1988; Carroll and Cornell, 1985; Yates, 1997; Yates and Fording, 2005). Harmon (2011) finds several significant effects of sentencing reforms in interaction models, both positive and negative, but it is impossible to draw any conclusions given the numerous methodological differences among these studies and the widely varying time periods examined. No research has tested whether state sentencing laws for drug crimes increased racial disproportionality. The federal mandatory minimums for crack and powder cocaine likely did have this effect, but non-experts may be surprised to learn that most states did not adopt anything like the federal laws. The federal laws are important but do not apply to the vast majority of people convicted of drug crimes, and there is no research testing the impact of states' drug sentencing policies, or sentencing practices, on the imprisonment rates of black men. Research using individual-level data from multiple states could potentially assess whether racial disparity is related to the sentencing laws in effect, but very little research of this type exists. One study of sentencing outcomes in a sample of urban counties, in multiple states (State Court Processing Statistics [SCPS] data), finds racial disparity may be conditional on sentencing polices (Wang et al., 2013) but others using these data found little variation in race effects (Weidner et al., 2004). Mitchell's (2005) metanalysis of individual-level sentencing studies also indicated disparities may be smaller in studies in states with sentencing guidelines.

A Role for Research on Sentencing Policies and Practices

In the introduction to this chapter I made a claim that likely struck many readers as hyperbole—that we do not know what effect tough on crime sentencing policies have had on imprisonment rates or disproportionality. Again, I do not claim that the evidence shows that these policies had no effects, simply that there is almost no evidence that they did, mainly because there is very little research designed to answer this question. At this point, I suspect some readers who are intimately familiar with sentencing and corrections, and who share my methodological orientation, need no further convincing. Others, if they are still reading, may be thinking, "What does he not get? It's obvious!" In other words, I suspect I have stumbled upon a fundamental difference in how some groups of scholars understand the relationship between theory and empirical data, how they assess cause and effect, and perhaps fundamental differences in their understanding of the criminal justice process. From my perspective, as a quantitatively trained sociologist who studies sentencing, the incongruity between, on one hand, the *virtual absence* of empirical evidence of a positive association between these policies and imprisonment, much less a non-spurious association, and, on the other hand, the widely held belief (if not consensus) that these policies caused the U.S. prison population to increase from one million to 2.3 million in a little more than a decade is difficult to reconcile. I am equally confident that some exceptionally intelligent people whose work I respect very much, disagree.

Epistemological differences aside, I think we all can agree that a better understanding of the relationship between policy (in this case, laws affecting sentencing) and practice (actual decision-making in the process from charging to prison and parole) would be beneficial. I also believe that research employing techniques common in the literature on sentencing, but applied in some new ways, and with an appreciation of the *centrality of discretion* in the sentencing/corrections process, could substantially advance our understanding of these important issues. Also, I do not mean to imply that sound inferences can only be made on the basis of "rigorous" statistical methods. On the contrary, a well-executed qualitative study assessing the implementation of some policy change, whether designed to get tough on crime or do the reverse, including whether it was followed by a change in the probability of a prison sentence, or in the average sentence length, or affected racial disparities (or whatever objective it was designed to achieve) would be a *significant* contribution to the literature, especially if it provides theoretical insight into why the policy effort did or did not succeed. In fact, the research agenda I envision cannot likely succeed without a combination of methods being brought to bear. Regardless of one's methodological approach, the key, I think, is to approach every research endeavor as an opportunity to investigate fundamental questions about how sentencing policies affect the discretion available to criminal justice actors, and how criminal justice actors exercise discretion in relation to the opportunities and constraints provided by sentencing policies.

To return to Ruth Peterson's call, I think a concerted effort to answer some of these more substantive questions, about which we know little, would be a place to start:

1. **How have major sentencing reforms of the last 40 years affected punishment in the United States?** Did they affect the likelihood of prison admissions, sentence length, or time served in prison? Did they increase or decrease disparities in sentencing? How important are sentencing policies (state laws) for understanding punishment, as opposed to discretionary decisions by prosecutors, judges, and correctional officials?
2. **What is the relationship between racial-ethnic or gender "disparity" in individual-level case outcomes and "disproportionality" in imprisonment rates?** In other words, is disproportionality a product of disparity and does reducing disparity reduce disproportionality? How is decision-making at the individual level related to imprisonment rates at the macro-level?

Next, I use data on prison admissions to explore some of these questions, including the relationship between sentence length and race-ethnicity, social characteristics of the counties in which people were sentenced, and the effects of state characteristics including sentencing laws.

Testing the Effects of Sentencing Polices on Sentence Length and Racial Disparity

I noted above that research has yet to explain the negative effects of determinate sentencing and guidelines on imprisonment rates. One hypothesis is that abolishing parole "insulates" the correctional process from pressure to increase the length of imprisonment (Jacobs and Carmichael, 2001; Stemen and Rengifo, 2011), but studies have not found that these policies, or others, increased time-served in prison (Sorensen and Stemen, 2002; Zhang et al., 2009). Sorensen and Stemen (2002) found that determinate sentencing and presumptive guidelines were *each* negatively related to average sentence lengths imposed, which could reduce incarceration rates, but again, they did not find a relationship with actual time served by people released from prison in 1997. And one study (Weidner et al., 2005) found that states with sentencing guidelines were less likely to sentence convicted offenders to prison.

More recently, Bradley and Engen (2016) found that determinate sentencing is *positively* related to time served by prisoners released in 2004, but only after controlling for sentence length. Supplemental analyses of those data showed that, overall, time served was in fact shorter in determinate sentencing states. This lends some support to the "sentence length" explanation, but also suggests that determinate sentencing affects both sentence length, and release decisions. They also found a significant difference in time served by black and white prisoners, which was partly explained by average sentence length, and partly by the likelihood of conditional release.

Data and Methods

The analyses employ individual level data on people sentenced and admitted to prison from the National Corrections Reporting Program (NCRP), in 2000 and 2010, in twenty-six states, along with publically available data on county and state characteristics from the U.S. Census, the Uniform Crime Reports, and other commonly used sources. The twenty-six states in the NCRP included nearly 73 percent of the total U.S. population, and 75 percent of prisoners in state custody in the U.S., in both 2000 and 2010. They include even larger shares of the total U.S. black and Hispanic populations (81 and 82 percent, respectively), and 78 percent of the black and Hispanic prison populations. Thus, in addition to being larger than the non-reporting states, on average, the sample states are also less "white," accounting for 70 percent of non-Hispanic white residents of the U.S., and 71 percent of non-Hispanic whites in state prisons. In short, the sample is not representative of all 50 U.S. states, but analyses of prison sentences in these states can still inform our understanding of race and punishment in the U.S. I restricted the sample to adult men (89.8 percent of admissions), age 18 or older, identified as white, black, or Hispanic, with sentences of at least 1 year; excluding prison transfers or other administrative admissions and cases missing essential data (around 2 percent, mostly due to missing offense or sentence) ($N = 710{,}908$). Limiting the sample to men facilitates model estimation; the vast majority of counties sentence very few women to prison, especially black and Hispanic women.[3] The full sample included cases from 1,950 counties each year, but 22 percent had zero black admissions. I selected counties with a minimum of 10 black and 10 white persons admitted to prison in 2000 and 2010 ($N = 969$ counties per year), which reduced the final sample to $N = 659{,}717$.

Individual Level—Person and Case Characteristics

The dependent variable is the court-ordered *maximum sentence length* for the current prison admission, in months, logged. For cases with multiple conviction offenses, this represents the total amount of time that a person may be required to serve for all offenses. Taking the natural log (ln) of total months is common practice in sentencing research, and helps to normalize the otherwise highly skewed distribution of sentence lengths. In order to include cases sentenced to death, life imprisonment, or LWOP, I assigned them a value of 1,200 months (100 years). I also recoded a small number of cases with sentences greater than 100 years to 1,200 months.[4] Independent variables at the individual level (L1), include the person's *age* when they were admitted to prison (logged years), two dummy variables indicating if the person was *black* or *Hispanic* (versus white non-Hispanic), and a single measure of *offense seriousness*, which represents the expected sentence, in log months, for the primary conviction offense. This measure of offense seriousness warrants elaboration.

Operationalizing Offense Seriousness

One challenge to conducting analyses of sentencing in multiple states, using a data source like the NCRP, is deciding how to control for differences in the seriousness of offending, which might explain both geographic variation in average sentence length (between counties and states), and differences by race-ethnicity. Sentencing researchers accustomed to analyzing data provided by state agencies, or the U.S. Sentencing Commission, generally use measures provided by those agencies, such as the offense seriousness level/class, or the presumptive sentence based on the conviction offense(s) and criminal history. The NCRP does not collect, or provide, any such measures, but it does assign common offense codes for several hundred different types of crimes. Moreover, if state-specific measures were available, treating them as objective measures of "offending" in a comparative study would not necessarily be preferable. State-specific offense rankings, or presumptive sentences, would result in greater explanatory power, but it would potentially *obscure* differences in punishment between states in much the same way that the different criminal history scoring rules described by Frase et al. (2015) produce harsher punishment, and greater racial disparities, in some states than others.

My goal, therefore, is to construct a measure of seriousness that utilizes information about the relationship between the offense type and the average sentence imposed (and thus will have predictive power), but that is independent of the state in which someone is sentenced, independent of racial-ethnic disparity in sentences imposed for that type of offense, and independent of the racial composition of people sentenced to prison for that offense. One approach is to simply classify offense types in a way that represents the seriousness of the crime, and include a set of dummy variables in regression models. For example, Bradley and Engen (2016) reduced the NCRP offense codes to 16 offense types, ranging from public order and vice to murder. However, this does not work as well with counties as a unit of analysis, some of which have quite small numbers of cases.

For these reasons, I operationalize the seriousness of the primary conviction offense as the *expected sentence* (log months) *for that offense among non-Hispanic white males*. Specifically, I estimate a three-level HLM predicting log-sentence length as a function of the 16 (−1) offense type dummy variables, plus age at admission, with random effects at the state and county levels, using only the data for white men. Then I calculated the predicted sentence for each offense type as the intercept plus the fixed effect for that offense, and assigned these values to the individual cases in the full sample. Thus, for someone whose most serious offense was burglary, "offense seriousness" equals the expected sentence (i.e., the average of the state-specific means) for non-Hispanic whites convicted of burglary.[5] This ensures that the expected sentences are independent of race and independent of the sentencing practices in large states and large counties that account for most of the cases. The expected sentences appear in Table 1.1, along with the frequency of each offense type.

Table 1.1 Expected Sentence by Offense Type for Non-Hispanic White Males

	Expected Maximum Sentence				
	LnMonths	*Months*	*Years*	N	*Percent*
Murder	5.97	605	50.4	14,584	2.2%
Rape/Sexual Asslt	5.01	226	18.9	11,099	1.7%
Kidnapping	4.61	130	10.8	6,044	0.9%
Manslaughter	4.60	121	10.1	6,884	1.0%
Robbery	4.53	109	9.1	64,716	9.8%
Other Sex Offense	4.30	92	7.7	25,739	3.9%
Arson	4.19	78	6.5	5,511	0.8%
Burglary/B&E	4.12	75	6.3	102,256	15.5%
Drug Trafficking	4.13	73	6.1	97,863	14.8%
Aggravated Assault	3.94	61	5.1	47,281	7.2%
Drug Possession	3.74	50	4.2	21,401	3.2%
Other Assault	3.79	51	4.3	24,068	3.6%
Weapons	3.77	52	4.3	110,336	16.7%
Theft/forgery	3.74	49	4.0	63,126	9.6%
Pub. Order/Court	3.53	40	3.4	12,482	1.9%
Other Property	3.55	41	3.4	46,327	7.0%

Note: Expected sentences are based on fixed effects estimated with random intercepts and random slopes by county and state.

County and State Variables

Percent black, percent urban, total population (ln), black and *white poverty rates*, and the difference in *black-white poverty rates* are included at the county and state levels, for theoretical reasons, although poverty and population measures were eventually dropped at the county level because they had no effects. The white non-Hispanic prison admission rate (ln) and the black-white difference in admission rates are included at both the county and state levels primarily to control for the propensity to use imprisonment, and also to explore the relationship between racial disproportionality in prison admission rates and racial disparity in sentence length. The county-level models also include the proportion of prison admissions that were for serious violent crimes, and the proportion drug offenses.[6]

I also examine several social and political characteristics of states that prior theory and research has identified as related to incarceration rates, or to sentence severity. These include having a Republican governor (*GOP gov*), citizen and government *political ideology* (Berry et al., 1998), the *violent crime rate*, *region*, and *Year* (2010 vs. 2000). Social, political, and crime variables are measured in 1999 and 2009 (i.e., lagged 1 year). My main focus though, at the state level, is on the effects of sentencing policies. I include dummy variables indicating whether states adopted *voluntary sentencing guidelines* or *presumptive guidelines*, *determinate sentencing* (i.e., abolishing discretionary parole for most or all cases), and an interaction term representing the combination of determinate sentencing with presumptive sentencing guidelines. I also include the summary of mandatory minimums developed by Stemen et al. (2005).[7] The coding of states' sentencing policies appears in Appendix A. Table 1.2 presents descriptive statistics for the individual, county, and state variables included in the analysis. Some county and state measures were dropped from the final model but were included in prior stages of analyses. Several variables with skewed distributions appear in Table 1.2 in logged and unlogged form.

Table 1.2 Descriptive Statistics

County (Level 2)	*Mean*	*s.d.*	*State-yr (Level 3)*	*Mean*	*s.d.*
Max Sentence months	82.77	153.31	Pct Black	13.47	9.87
Max Sent ence In	3.87	.89	Pct Hispanic	9.40	9.28
White non-Hispanic	.35	.48	Black Poverty Rate	23.74	5.86
Black	.45	.50	White Poverty Rate	10.77	2.78
Hispanic	.20	.40	Blk-Wht Pov rates	12.97	5.35
Age at admission	33.33	10.28	Citizen Ideology	50.52	12.56
Age (ln)	3.46	.31	Govt Ideology	53.41	29.86
Expected Sent (ln)	4.05	.43	GOP Governor	.48	.51
Level 1 N = 659,717			Violent Crime per 10k	44.88	16.92
			White Adm Rate (ln)	2.30	.52
County (Level 2)			Black Adm Rate (ln)	4.03	.45
County pop ln	11.31	1.22	B-W ln Adm Rates	1.73	.46
Pct Black	16.12	14.40	South	.54	.50

(*Continued*)

Table 1.2 (Continued)

County (Level 2)	*Mean*	*s.d.*	*State-yr (Level 3)*	*Mean*	*s.d.*
Pct Black ln	2.45	0.94	West	.19	.40
Pct Urban	58.33	27.80	Northeast	.12	.32
Pct Urban ln	3.86	0.89	Midwest	.15	.36
Pr Serious violent	0.19	0.09			
Pr Drug crimes	0.12	0.32	Pres. Guidelines	.27	.45
Pct Black Poverty	10.45	28.35	Vol. Guidelines	.17	.38
Black Poverty (ln)	3.31	0.41	Determinate	.27	.45
Non-Black Pov	4.65	12.35	P. Guide. × Determ	.15	.36
Non-Black Pov (ln)	2.53	0.37	Mandatory Mins.	9.19	7.48
Pct Blk Male 15–29	2.43	0.32	Truth in Sentencing	.69	.47
White Adm Rate (ln)	2.49	0.65	3-Strikes	.60	.50
Black Adm Rate (ln)	4.12	0.69	Level 3 $N = 52$		
B-W ln Adm Rates	1.63	0.63			
Level 2 $N = 1{,}938$					

Results

I estimated a series of three-level hierarchical linear models (HLMs) of sentence length (log months) as a function of individual (level 1), county (level 2), and state (level 3) effects (see Raudenbush and Bryk, 2002).[8] In addition to a random error term at the individual level, as in ordinary linear regression (OLS), HLM includes random effects of each county, and each state. County (level 2) effects represent deviation of individual counties from the expected value (i.e., the average) within the state and year, and random effects for each state (or simply "state effects") represent deviation of each state from the overall average, or grand mean, for that year (i.e., the average of state means). The effects (coefficients or "slopes") for predictors included in the level 1 equation are allowed to vary between counties and states, and all county-level effects can vary between states.

Individual-Level Effects

To begin, I estimated a "null" model (i.e., random intercepts only) and a model with only level-1 predictors (see Table 1.3). The null model confirms that sentence length varies significantly at both the county and state-year levels. Consistent with prior research, most of the variance (79 percent) is at the individual level (within counties), about 3 percent is variance between counties (within states), and 18 percent of the variance is between states. Offense seriousness clearly has the strongest effect on sentence length, but its interpretation is not straightforward. Multiplying the coefficient by its standard deviation, and taking the exponent ($\exp(.957 \star .43) = 1.51$), indicates that a one standard deviation increase in the expected sentence increases sentence length by about 51 percent. Age also has a strong effect; a one standard deviation increase (about 10 years) increases the average sentence by about 8 percent, which may partly reflect unmeasured effects of criminal history (Bushway and Piehl, 2007).

Table 1.3 Unconditional (Null) Model and Level 1 Model of Max Sentence

			Variance Components		
Null model	*Coeff.*	*s.e.*	*L1*	*L2*	*L3*
Intercept	4.028	.054	.648	.024	.152
L-1 Model	*Coeff.*	*s.e.*	*L1*	*L2*	*L3*
Intercept	4.002	.053	.477	.026	.144
Age (ln)	.259	.029		.019	.041
Black	.061	.011		.006	.005
Hispanic	.031	.022		.003	.016
Offense Seriousness	.957	.033		.029	.058

The significant race effect indicates that, controlling for age and seriousness, black men on average had sentences approximately 6.3 percent longer than similar non-Hispanic whites.[9]

The effects of age, race-ethnicity, and offense seriousness also vary across significantly between counties and states. The variance estimates for each predictor, also shown in Table 1.3, reveal something else potentially very important. Most of the variance appears to be at the state level (i.e., the differences between states are greater than the differences between counties within states), but the county-level variance is also substantial. Most of the variance in sentence length that is not explained by individual level factors is variance between states (86 percent), states account for about two-thirds of the variance in the effects of age and offense seriousness, and state differences account for 84 percent of the variance in Hispanic versus non-Hispanic white sentences. But there is one important exception—just over *half* (50.5 percent) of the variance in the black-white sentence gap is variance between *counties*. It is not clear exactly what this means, but it suggests that state-level factors, perhaps laws, may play an important role in determining sentence severity generally but racial disparity in sentences may depend equally on forces operating at a local level.

Substantive Interpretation

For non-specialists, and students, making sense of these findings can seem daunting, but there are some fairly straightforward interpretations. The variation (differences) between people in the lengths of prison sentences received is explained first and foremost (about 80 percent) by the crime they were convicted and sentenced for (more precisely, by the average sentence for that crime). After differences in offending, the sentence someone receives largely depends on which state they are in, and, to a lesser extent, the county where they were sentenced. Similarly, the difference in the average sentences of blacks relative to white non-Hispanics also depends on the state, but it depends equally on which county within that state.

Interpreting effect sizes (e.g., difference in sentence length for black and white men) as percentage change is convenient, because the percentage change is not dependent on the expected value. However, with nonlinear models, the "real" effect (i.e., the actual difference in months) will depend on the expected sentence for the reference group. In absolute terms, the intercept indicates an expected sentence of (exp(4.002 log-months)), or 54.7 months for white men of average age and average seriousness. The model predicts that blackmen with mean age and offense seriousness have an expected sentence of 4.002 + .061 = 4.063 log-months, which translates to 58.1 months, a difference of approximately 3.5 months.

County and State Effects

The next steps in the analyses involved estimating numerous models testing the effects of county and state characteristics on average sentence severity and on the black-white difference in sentence length. Table 1.4 presents the final model, including direct effects of county and state characteristics, and interactions between race (black) and both county and state characteristics.[10] I provide a brief overview of the findings here, followed by a closer examination of the effects of sentencing policies, and geography. The level-1 effects do not change substantively from those shown in Table 1.3.[11]

Table 1.4 Multilevel Regression of Sentence (log months) on Person, County, and State Characteristics

	Coeff γ	*s.e.*		*Coeff γ*	*s.e.*
Intercept (γ000)	4.173***	.033			
Level-1 Person					
Age (ln)	.258***	.030			
Offense Seriousness	.958***	.034			
Hispanic	.037	.022			
Black	.043**	.012			
Level-2 County Effects					
Prop. Serious Violent	−.001***	.099	× Black	−.030	.091
Prop. Drug	.020*	.068	× Black	.059	.063
Pct Black(ln)	.002	.008	× Black	−.007	.008
Pct Urban (ln)	−.008	.008	× Black	.016*	.008
White Adm Rate (ln)	.005	.014	× Black	.024*	.010
Black-White Adm Rate	−.008	.011	× Black	.022	.012
L-3 State-yr Effects					
Pres. Guidelines (PG)	.174**	.061	× Black	.107***	.023
Vol. Guidelines	.113*	.055	× Black	.032	.019
Determinate (DS)	−.469***	.054	× Black	−.004	.020
PG × DS	−.506***	.098	× Black	−.120*	.037
Mand. Mins. × 10	−.007*	.003	× Black	−.013	.010
White Poverty Rate	−.017	.009	× Black	.015***	.004
Black-White Poverty Rate	.009*	.004	× Black	.002	.002
Citizen Ideology × 10	−.067**	.029	× Black	.002**	.001

	Coeff γ	*s.e.*		*Coeff γ*	*s.e.*
Pct Black × 10	−.268***	.034	× Black	.000	.001
Violent Crime × 10	−.002	.016	× Black	−.008	.001
South	−.185*	.079	× Black	.065*	.031
Northeast	−.124	.116	× Black	.000	.047
Midwest	.261**	.095	× Black	−.012	.041
Year (2010)	−.153*	.063	× Black	.033	.024
White Adm. Rate (ln)	−.229***	.065	× Black	.006	.027
Black-White Adm. Rate	−.517***	.097	× Black	.054	.039
Variance L1	.477				
Components L2	.017				
L3	.036				

Age and Expected Sentence are grand-mean centered. All level-2 variables are group-mean centered.
Level 3 variables are grand-mean centered, except the sentencing system dummy variables.
* $p < .05$, ** $p < .01$, and *** $p < .001$.

Social and Political Factors

I find only two significant effects on sentence length at the county level. The proportion of prison admissions that were for serious violent crimes has a small *negative* effect, and the proportion drug offenses has a significant *positive* effect. Recall that the model controls for offense seriousness (expected sentence length) at the individual level. I also find two significant interactions with race, percent urban (+.016) and the white admission rate (.024). These estimates indicate that a one standard deviation change in either of these variables increases the black coefficient by more than one third (33.5 percent for pct urban and 36 percent for white admissions). In this model the expected sentence is 64.9 months for a 33-year-old man who is white, and 67.8 months for one who is black, a difference of 2.85 months. In a county that is one standard deviation above the mean on percent urban, the predicted black sentence increases by about one month, to 68.8 months. If that county also has a higher prison admission rate (again, one s.d. in the white admission rate), the predicted black sentence increases to 69.8 months. The effects on total months will be larger in more serious cases, and wherever average sentences are longer.

At the state level, average sentence length is significantly related to a number of social structural and political factors. Sentences are significantly *longer* in states where the *black-white poverty gap* is larger, where citizens are more *ideologically conservative*, and in the *Midwest*. Sentences tend to be *shorter* in states with *higher percent black* populations, in states with *higher prison admission rates*, and in the *South*. Many of these effects appear fairly large; sentences are nearly 30 percent longer in the Midwest than in the West, and about 17 percent shorter in the South. Contrary to the racial threat thesis, an increase of 10 percent black in the population is associated with 25 percent *shorter* sentences. Sentence length also decreased by 14 percent from 2000 to 2010.

The black-white "gap" in sentence length is also significantly related to several state level factors. Specifically, the difference in expected sentences for blacks and white non-Hispanics in the South is more than double the average effect (.043 + .065 × South). The race effect is also positively related to the *white poverty rate* (but not black poverty or the black-white difference in poverty rates) and to *citizen ideology*. However, the positive effect of ideology indicates that the race gap is largest in *less* conservative states. The results presented in Table 1.4 were estimated with individuals' age and expected sentence (seriousness) centered at their grand means; thus, it is unlikely that the state and county effects are due to differences in these individual-level case characteristics. However, unmeasured individual-level factors, such as criminal history, may play a role if they differ systematically between states or counties.

The effects of sentencing policies are among the strongest in the model. Compared with states that did not adopt these reforms, mandatory minimums, determinate sentencing (DS), and the combination of DS with presumptive guidelines (PG) are each *negatively* related to average sentence length, whereas voluntary and presumptive guidelines are each significant and *positively* related to sentence length. Sentences are about 19 percent longer in states that only adopted presumptive guidelines, and about 12 percent longer with voluntary guidelines. Alone, determinate sentencing reduces sentence length by about 37 percent (exp(−.469) = .63), and the combination of determinate and presumptive sentencing guidelines reduces sentences even further. Importantly, the black-white "gap" in sentence length is also significantly *larger in states with presumptive guidelines*, but the effect is negated when sentencing guidelines are also determinate, resulting in slightly shorter sentences. I also calculated the combined policy effects on the intercept, and on the race difference in the final model. Presumptive guidelines and determinate sentencing, together, reduce sentence length by 55 percent, and race disparity reduced by about 40 percent, compared with indeterminate sentencing and no guidelines.

These state-level effects are highly robust. The size of coefficients change somewhat, but the regional pattern and policy effects hold *irrespective* of the presence of other state variables. The sentencing system effects on sentence length also remain whether or not I include separate indicators for voluntary versus presumptive guidelines, and whether the model includes the interaction term for determinate and presumptive sentencing or the control for mandatory minimums.[12] The same pattern of regional effects also appears regardless of the inclusion of other state-level predictors in the model, including sentencing policies. The final model reduces the between-state variance in sentence length by about 77 percent, with nearly 70 percent explained by the sentencing policy variables alone.

Implications

In published studies, the presentation of findings generally end here, to be followed by a discussion of the theoretical and substantive relevance of the findings, limitations of the data or analysis, of which there are many, and a call for additional research on questions raised, but not fully answered, by the current study. I will mention a few things that I think are important, here, but I have an additional goal, which is to explore what we can learn from findings like these regarding some of the largely unexamined questions I raised earlier. How important are sentencing policies and practices for understanding imprisonment rates and racial disproportionality in imprisonment?

Perhaps most importantly, the findings show that sentencing laws matter, and in at least two of the ways that a few prior studies have suggested: presumptive and determinate sentencing guidelines seem to reduce sentence lengths, and may provide some protection against racial disparity. The reductions in sentence length may help explain the negative effects of these policies on imprisonment rates. This does not resolve the question about determinate sentencing and guidelines, but if joined with analyses of prison admission rates and time served, could bring us closer to an answer. The unexpected negative effect of mandatory minimums presents another puzzle to be solved. It is easier to explain a non-effect than a negative one, although it does not necessarily indicate an effect of these policies. If the presence of mandatory minimums is, in fact, more symbolic than substantive, perhaps it reflects downward pressure of reduced prison capacity on average length of sentence (i.e., courts adapting to unsustainable imprisonment rates following 30 years of being "tough on crime"). A comparison of the average sentences ordered for different crimes, under different sentencing systems, would also be informative.

The finding that determinate sentencing reduces sentence length is also intriguing, in part because the effect cannot be explained as a consequence of taking parole boards out of the picture. Or can it be? Why would abolishing parole affect decision-making by judges, even in the absence of presumptive sentencing laws? Perhaps it is because determinate sentencing not only affects how people are released from prison, *it also changes the sentencing process.* Under *indeterminate* sentencing, judges typically make "in/out" decisions, and may set a minimum or maximum term, but they are not directly responsible for how long people spend in prison. Under *determinate* sentencing, judges must order a *specific maximum term* of confinement. Most people do not serve the maximum in prison, but their expected time in prison can be predicted accurately, which is the whole point of determinate sentencing. Could it be that this procedural difference alters judges' decision-making in ways that minimized punitiveness, at least in the 2000s? Does making judges responsible for how long someone spends in prison also make them more responsive to concerns about the high cost and/or consequences imprisonment? Are judges reducing sentences in states with determinate sentencing but no guidelines *because they can*? I am not aware of prior scholarship proposing this sort of effect, but perhaps it is worth exploring.

In these ways, the findings seem to say sentencing policies are important, and we still have much to learn about how they affect the process. Are the effects large? Probably most authors reporting effects of this size would say the policy effects are "substantial," and that the effects will be larger for more serious crimes and smaller for less serious crimes. If the average race effect is about three months, most would probably say that it is a substantively meaningful difference. As for the effects of policies on disparity, I reported above that, combined, determinate and presumptive sentencing guidelines reduced the race coefficient by 40 percent, which sounds like a lot. Specifically, the model predicts about a 4.4 percent longer sentence for blacks under indeterminate sentencing and about 2.6 percent under determinate, presumptive guidelines. Presented this way, the policy impact looks pretty small as well—important, no doubt, to those people whose lives are altered, but not likely to have much impact on imprisonment rates for African Americans generally. We could argue that the variance between states and counties shows that "in some places" the effects are larger, and we could calculate the range of effects to demonstrate the point; and of course we can argue that cumulative effects across the process may be substantial.

The Big Picture—What Does It All Mean?

This kind of assessment of the results (in greater depth) may satisfy many academic readers, because that is what they are used to reading, but many non-academic audiences and policymakers would also like more specific answers, and answers to the more concrete questions I posed earlier: *What is the impact of these sentencing policies on imprisonment rates?* and *How much of racial disproportionality in the population is the result of sentencing disparity, or a result of sentencing laws?* And here is a tricky one someone might ask who is paying very close attention: *Considering the geographic distribution of African Americans in the U.S., do these regional and urban/rural effects increase or decrease disproportionality in imprisonment?*

Answering these questions is much harder, if not impossible, because even if the results I presented are "correct," *they do not provide answers to these questions.* The fundamental problem is not that we are using the wrong statistical tests—hierarchical models are the appropriate choice when data are nested (people within counties, within states and years)—but we cannot answer questions about population effects using only regression coefficients, especially the fixed effects estimated in hierarchical models. The very feature that makes HLM useful in this context—that it holds constant the effects of place—means that the intercept does not represent the expected value in the population, it is the average of the state and county means. Likewise, the regression coefficient for race does not represent the overall effect of race in the population, it is the average of the race effects estimated in each county and state. For example, the mean sentence in the full sample is 3.87 ln months, but the intercept in the null model with state and county effects is 4.03 ln months, which translates to about a 5 month difference in the predicted sentence. This makes sense given the results I presented, too. The mean sentence in the population is less than the average of the county and state means, because the majority of prison admissions are from urban counties, and in Southern states, each of which issued shorter sentences.

This leads to the second problem with inferring effects on the population from these coefficients, such as inferring how important "disparity" is for explaining disproportionate imprisonment rates. Holding constant differences in offense seriousness (the one thing we probably do want to hold constant), the total effect of differences by race-ethnicity in sentence length, at the individual level, on the total number of white, black, and Hispanics in prison each year (i.e., total "person years") in the population will depend on the size of the race-ethnicity effects *in the places where blacks, whites, and Hispanics are actually sentenced*, and also on the average sentences in those places. Likewise, if we want to understand the effects of state sentencing policies, or of county characteristics like the percent black, or the poverty rate, we need to know the effects of these variables in specific places, and the characteristics of people sentenced in those places.

To summarize, we need to *predict* the distribution of our dependent variable in the populations of interest, and in the particular contexts that interest us (urban rural, or region, or type of sentencing system). We can use the slopes and intercepts estimated through HLM models to do that, but rather than holding constant all of the important independent variables, we need to include the actual variation that exists in the population, especially the specific state and county effects. These "unit effects" do not appear as regression coefficients, but they are estimated by HLM and other statistical software packages, and we can save and use them in post-estimation analyses. Perhaps most importantly, we also need to factor in *the distributions of groups across states and counties*. As my last hypothetical question implied, above, the effect of "region" on sentence length or on disparity in the population will depend on not only the size of the fixed effect for region, but also on the size and characteristics of the population affected. As a result, a "large" disparity in Iowa will be important to the people who live there, and will affect disproportionality measured at the state level, but may be far less consequential, nationally, than a small disparity—or even no disparity—in a state like Texas, or California, that sentence large numbers of African Americans to prison.

Exploratory Findings

Generating and interpreting the population estimates is beyond the scope of this chapter, but as an exploratory step, I calculated the racial distributions of cases by type of sentencing system, and by region (see Figures 1.1 and 1.2). Given the size of the system effects, groups more likely to be in states with presumptive guidelines and determinate sentencing (MN, NC, OR, WA) would be likely to have the shortest sentence, and determinate sentencing alone (CA, FL, VA) the next shortest. The 4 PG-DS states have only 6 percent of all prison admissions, but white non-Hispanics are the most likely (7.3 percent) to be in these states, and Hispanics least likely (2 percent). Nearly half of white admissions are in a DS state (46 percent), but only about 38 percent of black admissions. However, because most Hispanics are in California, they are the most likely to be in a determinate sentencing state either with or without guidelines (65 percent). Thus, Hispanic persons convicted of crimes appear to be the most likely to benefit from determinate sentencing, and blacks the least. Black men are more likely than white and Hispanic men to be sentenced in the most punitive states, those with sentencing guidelines but indeterminate sentencing (MI, PA, and TN), and fully 50 percent are in states with indeterminate sentencing and no guidelines which are the next-most-punitive, in terms of sentence length.

For all groups, most people being admitted to prison are in the South or the West. Regional effects may benefit African Americans slightly, as they are most likely to be in the south, which had the shortest average sentences. Hispanics are mostly in the

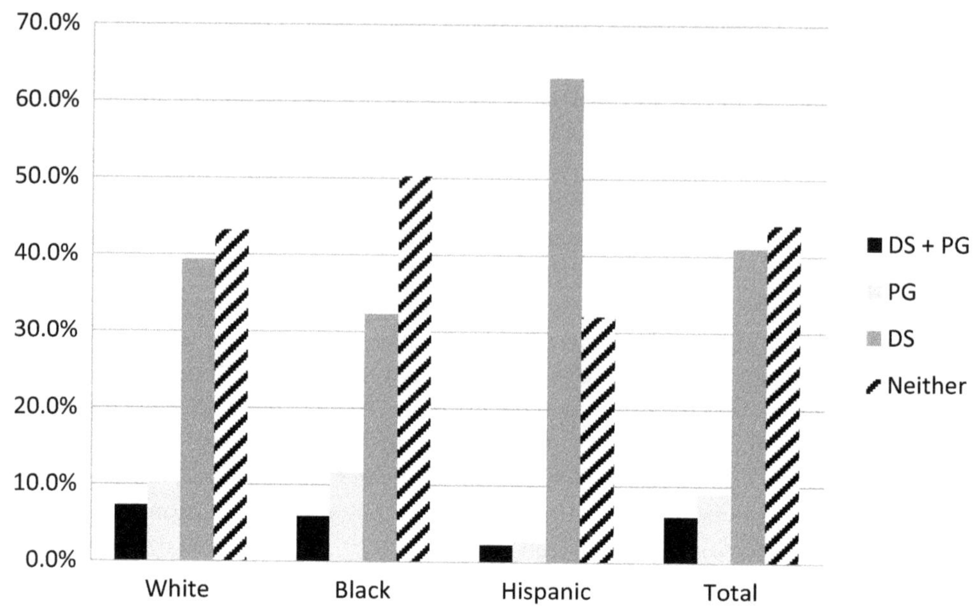

Figure 1.1 Percent Under Determinate or Presumptive Sentencing, by Race-Ethnicity: NCRP Admissions in 26 States (N = 659,717)

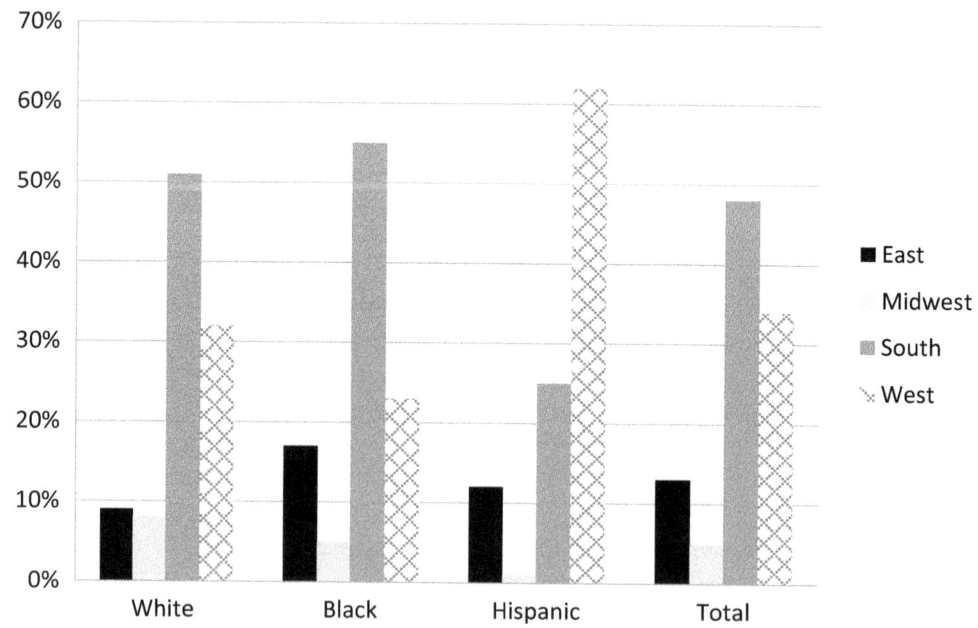

Figure 1.2 Percent Prison Admissions per Region, by Race-Ethnicity: NCRP Sample in 26 States (N = 659,717)

West, which was about in the middle on average sentence. White non-Hispanics are also most likely of each group to be in the Midwest, which had higher than average sentences. In terms of population effects though, percentages are not all that matters. Total numbers do as well. Thus, I prepared Figures 1.3 and 1.4, which present the total numbers of black, white, and Hispanic men and women in prison in each state in 2010. Numbers like these suggest, to me, that we should seriously consider whether it is even meaningful to calculate or interpret the national imprisonment figures as representing the United States, given that the state of Texas held 12 percent of all black men and women in prison in the U.S.—*62,000*—more than the 30 states with the fewest blacks, combined. And as a final observation, Texas is one of four states in this sample that did not adopt any of the reforms I examined, including three-strikes or TIS.

Innovations in Research on Sentencing Policies and Practices

In closing, I want to highlight some studies that present creative ways of thinking about, and examining, the effects of policy changes. They are not all recent, but we can gain much from reviewing past and current efforts. For example, *Criminology & Public Policy* has published at least three sets of research articles and accompanying policy essays (commentaries) dealing directly with how to assess, and how to even think about, the consequences of changes in sentencing policies. Two issues specifically consider the consequence of USSC decisions affecting the constitutionality of presumptive sentencing laws at the federal and state levels. The first includes three

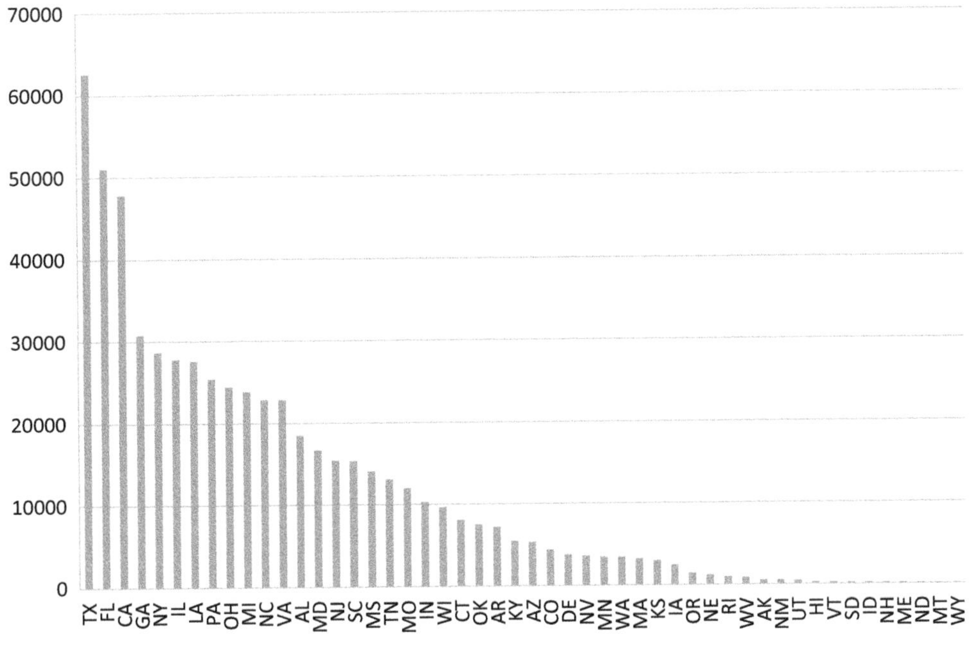

Figure 1.3 Black Prisoners by State, 2010

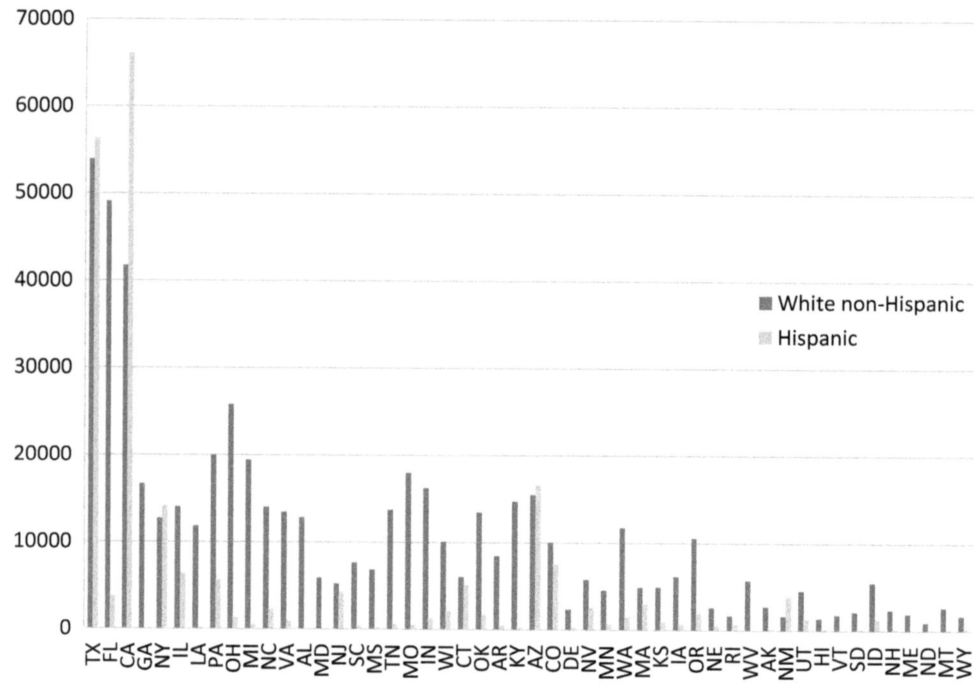

Figure 1.4 Total White and Hispanic Prisoners by State, 2010

research articles (Frase, 2007; Hofer, 2007; Bushway and Piehl, 2007) with two essays (Hunt, 2007; Piquero, 2007). Bushway and Piehl (2007) is unique, however, in that they compared discretion in plea bargaining in Washington versus Maryland, using SCPS data. Others could easily refine and adapt their approach for making other kinds of comparisons between states with different sentencing policies. The second group of papers has one article by Ulmer, Light, and Kramer (2011) and four essays (Spohn, 2011; Scott, 2011; Engen, 2011; Albonetti, 2011). Ulmer et al. (2011) examine race-ethnic sentencing disparity in U.S. federal courts in four time periods corresponding to a series of landmark rulings that alternately reduced, and then increased, the discretion available to federal judges. Those same rulings also resulted in several states changing their presumptive sentencing laws to advisory, which provide additional research opportunities (see Stemen and Rengifo, 2012). In the third set, Wooldredge (2009) examines changes in sentencing related to the adoption of structured sentencing laws in Ohio, with essays by Kramer (2009) and Engen (2009).

One paper by Engen and Steen (2000) examined adaptations to changes in guidelines in Washington state, specifically changes in the severity of punishment for drug offenders. Although less dramatic than, say, switching from presumptive to voluntary guidelines, or abolishing guidelines altogether, these kinds of guideline revisions are extremely common. States like WA and MN changed some sentencing provisions virtually every year, especially in the tough on crime era. These less sweeping kinds of changes provide many opportunities to learn about the effects of sentencing policies on imprisonment, and may be more indicative of the kinds of changes states may consider as ways of reducing imprisonment. Another interesting paper by Sutton (2013) used SCPS data to assess the effects of the introduction of three-strikes in California. He concluded that the law was "largely symbolic," but probably did produce a modest increase in sentence length after its introduction. He also found that the effect was larger in more conservative counties. Sutton's finding is especially interesting given that California's three-strikes law is often described as a definitive example of how tough on crime legislation produced mass incarceration. His analysis could also serve as a model for examining the effects of policy changes, including the adoption of three-strikes or TIS in other states.

Two final examples take a different, and very promising, approach to understanding the effects of sentencing policies—examining the differential effects on white and African Americans of sentencing guideline grids, especially the weight accorded to sentence enhancements and criminal history. Frase (2009) and Bushway and Piehl (2007, 2011) examined the actual distributions of people convicted of felonies across the sentencing guideline grids and estimated the contribution of criminal history and other factors to producing higher recommended sentences for blacks. Frase, using data for Minnesota, found that African Americans were about 45 percent more likely to have a recommended prison sentence under the guidelines, and this difference was largely explained by criminal history, as well mandatory minimums, and trial penalties. Bushway and Piehl (2011), examining data, and the sentencing grid, in Maryland, reached a different conclusion. Blacks sentenced in Maryland did have more criminal history points, but it did not differentially affect their recommended sentences. However, they concluded, based on hypothetical modifications to existing guidelines, that these criteria could have substantially different effects. Frase et al. (2015), comparing the effects of guidelines criminal history scoring on racial differences in multiple states, reached a similar conclusion; racial differences can vary substantially due to differences in the treatment of criminal history. Although much research remains to be done, these initial findings lead Frase to argue "the disparate impact of race neutral criteria [such as criminal history] does not reduce under sentencing guidelines—indeed, it might even increase (2013: 210)." It is too soon to anticipate the full implications of these findings, in part because there is no simple answer to the question of how criminal history *should* be scored, but these findings also imply that much—if not all—of the research on racial disparity in guideline jurisdictions has likely underestimated the full effects of race on punishment.

Notes

1 The report also acknowledges the impact of the sharp increase in arrests and imprisonment for drug crimes in the 1970s and 1980s. The conclusions, however, like much of the discussion, centered on explaining why the imprisonment rate increased every year until 2009, given that the crime rate fell precipitously after 1991.

2 I have used the term "sentencing reform" broadly to refer to legislative changes designed to change sentencing practices. Tonry refers to the 1970s and early 1980s as the "sentencing reform"

era, and the mid-1980s to 1990s as the "tough on crime" era, when the emphasis shifted to making punishment more certain and severe.

3 The NCRP was developed by the Bureau of Justice Statistics (BJS) and the Bureau of the Census. The data used here are from the 2000–2012 "Term Records" file, provided by National Archive of Criminal Justice Data, ICPSR study no. 34984. Data for three states are from the annual admission file for 2000. Several states were excluded either because they did not report in one or both years (nine states never report to NCRP), or because they were missing critical data. American Indian or Alaskan Native (1.2 percent), Asian (.4 percent), and Native Hawaiian or Pacific Islander (.2 percent) are not present in the data in most counties. Comparisons with U.S. total population and total prison population are based on the author's calculations. States represented: AL, AR, CA, CO, FL, GA, IA, KY, LA, MD, MI, MN, NJ, NY, NC, OK, OR, PA, SC, SD, TN, TX, UT, VA, WA, and WV.

4 The treatment of life and death sentences poses a challenge for multi-state analyses. Because states differ greatly in their use of these sentences excluding them could bias estimates of state-level differences. I assigned values of 1,200 months based on several factors, including the distribution of non-life/death sentences, typical minimum time-served requirements for lifers (20 to 40 years), and typical "good time" policies. All things considered, a person sentenced to 100 years would likely serve between 30 and 45 years.

5 This is conceptually similar to Crutchfield et al. (1994), who used offense-specific ratios of white imprisonment per arrest to measure the expected black imprisonment rate. A virtually identical measure to the one used here can be constructed by computing the average sentences, by offense, at the county level, then averaging the county means within states, and finally taking the average of the state means.

6 Population characteristics were obtained from U.S. decennial census (2000 and 2010), and Current Population Surveys. Prison admission rates, and the proportion serious violent and drug admissions were calculated using the NCRP data and census population figures.

7 Don Stemen and Andres Rengifo (2012) provide an excellent survey of determinate and structured sentencing laws through the 2000s, including their effective dates. My coding of sentencing systems is largely consistent with theirs. For an in depth analysis of the structure of sentencing guidelines and their use of criminal history see Richard Frase (2013). Stemen et al.'s (2005) study ended in 2002, so there is no measure of mandatory minimums in effect in 2010. Most of these laws were created in the 1990s, and no state had repealed them as of 2010 (Tonry, 2015), so I use the 2000 measure for 2010 as well.

8 Individual cases (people admitted to prison) are grouped by county, state, and year. Formally, therefore, the level-3 unit of analysis is the state-year (i.e., the state in 2000 is independent of the same state in 2010), and level 2 is the county-year, but for ease of communication I generally refer to levels 2 and 3 as counties and states. Models are estimated using HLM v6 (Raudenbush, Bryk, and Congdon, 2004).

9 Age and seriousness are group-mean centered. Dummy variables for race are un-centered, so the level 2 and level 3 intercepts represent the expected sentences for someone white, not Hispanic, at the mean age and seriousness for the county, state, and year.

10 County-level variables are group-mean centered. Dummy variables for year (2010) and for state policies are un-centered. The remaining state-yr variables are grand-mean centered. Thus, in this model, the fixed effect for the intercept represents the expected sentence (the grand mean) for someone who is white, not Hispanic, in a state with indeterminate sentencing and no sentencing guidelines, in 2000. The fixed effect for race (black) changed because it now represents the difference in sentence lengths of black and white men in an indeterminate, non-guideline, state in 2000. Age and offense seriousness at the individual level are grand-mean centered, so differences between counties and states should not be due to compositional differences in these characteristics.

11 Some theoretically relevant predictors were ultimately dropped from the analysis (e.g., Republican governor, government ideology) because they had no significant effects, and their exclusion

did not alter any other parameter estimates. Non-significant policy variables were retained for the substantive interpretation of the model.

12 When slopes and intercepts are correlated it is preferable to include the same predictors in each equation (Raudenbush and Bryk, 2002). This also greatly simplifies the interpretation.

References

Albonetti, C. A. (2011). Judicial discretion in federal sentencing: An intersection of policy priorities and law. *Criminology & Public Policy, 10*, 1151–1155.

Alexander, M. (2010). *The new Jim Crow: Mass incarceration in the age of colorblindness.* New York: The New Press.

Austin, J., Jones, C., Kramer, J., & Renninnger, P. (1996). *National assessment of structured sentencing.* Washington, D.C.: U.S. Department of Justice Bureau of Justice Assistance.

Baumer, E. (2013). Reassessing and redirecting research on race and sentencing. *Justice Quarterly, 30*, 231–261.

Beck, A. J., & Blumstein, A. (2012). Trends in incarceration rates: 1980–2010. Paper prepared for the National Research Council Committee on the Causes and Consequences of High Rates of Incarceration, Washington, D.C.

Beckett, K. (1997). *Making crime pay: Law and order in contemporary American politics.* New York: Oxford University Press.

Beckett, K., & Western, B. (2001). Governing social marginality: Welfare, incarceration, and the transformation of state policy. *Punishment and Society, 3*, 43–59.

Berry, W. D., Ringquist, E. J., Fording, R. C., & Hanson, R. L. (1998). Measuring citizen and government ideology in the American states, 1960–93. *American Journal of Political Science, 42*, 327–348.

Blackmon, D. A. (2008). *Slavery by another name.* New York: Anchor Books.

Blumstein, A., & Beck, A. J. (1999). Population growth in U.S. prisons, 1980–1996. In M. Tonry & J. Petersilia (Eds.), *Crime and justice: A review of research, vol. 26, Prisons.* Chicago: University of Chicago Press.

Blumstein, A., Cohen, J., Martin, S., & Tonry, M. (Eds.). (1983). *Research on sentencing: The search for reform.* Washington, DC: National.

Bradley, M. S., & Engen, R. L. (2016). Leaving prison: A multilevel investigation of racial and ethnic disproportionality in correctional release. *Crime and* Delinquency, *62*(2), 253–279.

Bridges, G. S., & Crutchfield, R. D. (1988). Law, social standing and racial disparities in imprisonment. *Social Forces, 66*, 699–724.

Bushway, S. D., & Forst, B. (2013). Studying discretion in sentencing. *Justice Quarterly, 30*(2), 199–222.

Bushway, S. D., & Piehl, A. M. (2007). Social science research and the legal threat to presumptive sentencing guidelines. *Criminology & Public Policy, 6*, 461–482.

Bushway, S. D., & Piehl, A. M. (2011). Location, location, location: The impact of guideline grid location on the value of sentencing enhancements. *Journal of Empirical Legal Studies, 8*, 222–238.

Carroll, L., & Cornell, C. P. (1985). Racial composition, sentencing reforms, and rates of incarceration, 1970–1980. *Justice Quarterly, 2*, 473–490.

Clear, T. R. & Frost. N. A. (2014). *The Punishment Imperative: The Rise and Fall of Mass Incarceration in America.* New York: New York University Press.

Crutchfield, R. D., Bridges, G. S., & Pitchford, S. R. (1994). Analytical and aggregation biases in analyses of imprisonment: Reconciling discrepancies in studies of racial disparity. *Journal of Research in Crime and Delinquency, 31*, 166–182.

Ditton, P. M., & Wilson, D. J. (1999). *Truth in sentencing in state prisons.* Washington, DC: U.S. Bureau of Justice Statistics.

Engen, R. L. (2008). Have sentencing reforms displaced discretion over sentencing from judges to prosecutors? In J. L. Worrall & M. E. Nugent-Borakove (Eds.), *The changing role of the American prosecutor* (pp. 73–90). Albany, NY: SUNY.

Engen, R. L. (2009). Assessing determinate and presumptive sentencing—making research relevant. *Criminology & Public Policy, 8*, 323–336.

Engen, R. L. (2011). Racial disparity in the wake of Booker/Fanfan: Making sense of "messy" results and other challenges for sentencing research. *Criminology & Public Policy, 10*, 1139–1149.

Engen, R. L., & Steen, S. (2000). The power to punish: Discretion and sentencing reform in the war on drugs. *American Journal of Sociology, 105*(5), 1357–1395.

Enns, P. K. (2016). *Incarceration nation: How the United States became the most punitive democracy in the world*. New York: Cambridge University Press.

Frase, R. S. (2004). Sentencing guidelines in Minnesota, 1978–2003. In *Crime and justice: A review of research* (Vol. 32, pp. 131–220). Chicago: University of Chicago Press.

Frase, R. S. (2007). The Apprendi–Blakely cases: Sentencing reform counterrevolution? *Criminology & Public Policy, 6*, 403–432.

Frase, R. S. (2009). What explains persistent racial disproportionality in Minnesota's prison and jail populations? In M. Tonry (Ed.), *Crime and justice, a review of research* (Vol. 38). Chicago: University of Chicago Press.

Frase, R. S. (2013). *Just sentencing: Principles and procedures for a workable system*. New York: Oxford University Press.

Frase, R. S., Roberts, J.V., Hester, R., & Mitchell, K. L. (2015). *Criminal history enhancements sourcebook*. University of Minnesota: Robina Institute of Criminal Law and Criminal Justice.

Garland, D. (2001). *The culture of control: Crime and social order in contemporary society*. Chicago, IL: University of Chicago Press.

Garland, D. (2013). The 2012 Sutherland address: Penality and the penal state. *Criminology, 51*(3), 475–517.

Gottschalk, M. (2006). *The prison and the gallows: The politics of mass incarceration in America*. Cambridge: Cambridge University Press.

Greenberg, D., & West, V. (2001). State prison populations and their growth, 1971–1991. *Criminology, 39*, 615–653.

Harmon, M. (2011). The imprisonment race: Unintended consequences of "Fixed" sentencing on people of color over time. *Journal of Ethnicity in Criminal Justice, 9*, 79–109.

Harmon, M. (2013). Fixed sentencing: The effect on imprisonment rates over time. *Journal of Quantitative Criminology, 29*, 369–396.

Heimer, K., Johnson, K. R., Lang, J. B., Rengifo, A. F., & Stemen, D. (2012). Race and women's imprisonment: Poverty, African American presence, and social welfare. *Journal of Quantitative Criminology, 28*, 219–244.

Hofer, P. J. (2007). *United States v. Booker* as a natural experiment: Using empirical research to inform the federal sentencing policy debate. *Criminology & Public Policy, 6*, 433–460.

Hunt, K. S. (2007). Standards of evidence. *Criminology & Public Policy, 6*, 483–492.

Jacobs, D., & Carmichael, J. T. (2001). The politics of punishment across time and space: A pooled time-series analysis of imprisonment rates. *Social Forces, 80*, 61–91.

Kramer, J. H. (2009). Mandatory sentencing guidelines: The framing of justice. *Criminology & Public Policy, 8*, 313–321.

Loftin, C., & McDowall, D. (1981). "One with a gun gets you two": Mandatory sentencing and firearms violence in Detroit. *The ANNALS of the American Academy of Political and Social Science, 455*(1), 150–167.

Lynch, M. (2011). Mass incarceration, legal change, and locale: Understanding and remediating American penal overindulgence. *Criminology & Public Policy, 10*(3), 673–698.

Marvell, T. B., & Moody, C. E. (1996). Determinate sentencing and abolishing parole: The long-term impacts on prisons and crime. *Criminology, 34*, 107–128.

Miethe, T. D. (1987). Charging and plea bargaining under determinate sentencing: An investigation of the hydraulic displacement of discretion. *Journal of Criminal Law and Criminology, 78*, 155–176.

Miethe, T. D., & Moore, C. A. (1985). Socioeconomic disparities under determinate sentencing systems: A comparison of preguideline and postguideline practices in Minnesota. *Criminology, 23*, 337–363.

Mitchell, O. (2005). A meta-analysis of race and sentencing research: Explaining the inconsistencies. *Journal of Quantitative Criminology, 21*, 439–466.

Peterson, R. D. (2016). Presidential address to the American Society of Criminology, November 18, New Orleans, LA.

Peterson, R. D. (2017). 2016 Presidential address to the American Society of Criminology: Interrogating race, crime, and justice in a time of unease and racial tension. *Criminology, 55*(2), 245–272.

Pfaff, J. F. (2014). Escaping from the standard story: Why the conventional wisdom of prison growth is wrong, and where we can go from here. *Federal Sentencing Reporter, 26*, 265–270.

Pfaff, J. F. (2017). *Locked in: The true causes of mass incarceration and how to achieve real reform*. New York: Basic Books.

Piquero, N. L. (2007). What about organizational defendants? They're affected as well. *Criminology & Public Policy, 6*: 493–502.

Raudenbush, S., & Bryk, A. (2002). *Hierarchical linear models: Application and data analysis methods* (2nd ed.). Thousand Oaks, CA: Sage.

Raudenbush, S., Bryk, A., & Congdon, R. (2004). *HLM 6 for Windows [Computer software]*. Lincolnwood, IL: Scientific Software International, Inc.

Rosich, K. J., & Kane, K. M. (2005). Truth in sentencing and state sentencing practices. *NIJ Journal, 252*. Retrieved from www.ojp.usdoj.gov/nij/journals/252/sentencing_print.html.

Sabol, W. J., Rosich, K., Kane, K. M., Kirk, D., & Dubin, G. (2002). The influences of truth-in- sentencing reforms on changes in states' sentencing practices and prison populations. Washington, DC: Urban Institute Press.

Scott, R. W. (2011). Race disparity under advisory guidelines: Dueling assessments and potential responses. *Criminology & Public Policy, 10*, 1129–1138.

Smith, K. B. (2004). The politics of punishment: Evaluating political explanations of incarceration rates. *Journal of Politics, 66*, 925–938.

Sorensen, J., & Stemen, D. (2002). The effect of state policies on incarceration rates. *Crime and Delinquency, 48*, 456–475.

Spelman, W. (2009). Crime, cash, and limited options: Explaining the prison boom. *Criminology and Public Policy, 8*, 29–77.

Spohn, C. (2011). Unwarranted disparity in the wake of the Booker/Fanfan decision: Implications for research and policy. *Criminology & Public Policy, 10*, 1119–1127.

Spohn, C. (2013). The effect of the offender's race, ethnicity, and sex on federal sentencing outcomes in the guidelines era. *Law & Contemporary Problems, 76*, 75–104.

Spohn, C. (2015). Race, crime, and punishment in the twentieth and twenty-first centuries. In M. Tonry (Ed.), *Crime and justice: A review of research* (Vol. 44, No. 1, pp. 49–97). Chicago: University of Chicago Press.

Stemen, D., & Rengifo, A. F. (2011). Policies and imprisonment: The impact of structured sentencing and determinate sentencing on state incarceration rates, 1978–2004. *Justice Quarterly, 48*(1), 174–201.

Stemen, D., & Rengifo, A. F. (2012). Charting the evolution of structure and determinacy in state sentencing and corrections policies 1970–2010. *Justice Research and Policy, 14*(2), 1–31.

Stemen, D., Rengifo, A., & Wilson, J. (2005). *Of fragmentation and ferment: The impact of state sentencing policies on incarceration rates, 1975–2002*. Final report to the National Institute of Justice Grand No.:2002-IJ-CX-0027, Unpublished Report, NCJRS 213003.

Stucky, T. D., Heimer, K., & Lang, J. (2005). Partisan politics, electoral competition, and imprisonment: An analysis of states over time. *Criminology, 43*, 211–248.

Sutton, J. R. (2013). Symbol and substance: Effects of California's three strikes law on felony sentencing. *Law & Society Review, 47*, 37–71.

Tonry, M. (1993). Sentencing commissions and their guidelines. In M. Tonry (Ed.), *Crime and justice: A review of research* (Vol. 17). Chicago: University of Chicago Press.

Tonry, M. (1996). *Sentencing matters*. New York: Oxford University Press.

Tonry, M. (2011). *Punishing race: An American dilemma continues*. New York: Oxford University Press.

Tonry, M. (2015). *Sentencing fragments: Penal reform in America, 1975–2025*. New York: Oxford University Press.

Travis, J., Western, B., & Redburn, S. (Eds.). (2014). *The growth of incarceration in the United States: Exploring causes and consequences*. Committee on Causes and Consequences of High Rates of Incarceration; Committee on Law and Justice; Division of Behavioral and Social Sciences and Education; National Research Council.

Turner, S., Greenwood, P. W., Fain, T., & Chiesa, J. R. (2006). An evaluation of the federal government's violent offender incarceration and truth-in-sentencing incentive grants. *The Prison Journal, 86*, 364–385.

Ulmer, J. T. (2012). Recent developments and new directions in sentencing research. *Justice Quarterly, 29*, 1–40.

Ulmer, J. T., Light, M. T., & Kramer, J. H. (2011). Racial disparity in the wake of the Booker/Fanfan decision: An alternative analysis to the USSC's 2010 report. *Criminology & Public Policy, 10*, 1077–1118.

Von Hirsch, A., Knapp, K., & Tonry, M. (1987). *The sentencing commission and its guidelines*. Boston, MA: Northeastern University Press.

Wacquant, L. (2009). *Punishing the poor: The neoliberal government of social insecurity*. Durham, NC: Duke University Press.

Wang, X., Mears, D. P., Spohn, C., & Dario, L. (2013). Assessing the differential effects of race and ethnicity on sentence outcomes under different sentencing systems. *Crime & Delinquency, 59*, 87–114.

Weidner, R. R., Frase, R., & Pardoe, I. (2004). Explaining sentence severity in large urban counties: A multilevel analysis of contextual and case-level factors. *The Prison Journal, 84*(2), 184–207.

Weidner, R. R., Frase, R. S., & Schultz, J. S. (2005). The impact of contextual factors on the decision to imprison in large urban jurisdictions: A multilevel analysis. *Crime & Delinquency, 51*, 400–424.

Western, B. (2006). *Punishment and inequality in America*. New York: Russell Sage Foundation.

Wooldredge, J. (2009). Short- versus long-term effects of Ohio's switch to more structured sentencing on extralegal disparities in prison sentences in an urban court. *Criminology & Public Policy, 8*, 285–312.

Wright, R. (2001). Counting the cost of sentencing in North Carolina, 1980–2000. In M. Tonry (Ed.), *Crime and justice: A review of research* (Vol. 29, pp. 39–112) Chicago: University of Chicago Press.

Yates, J. (1997). Racial incarceration disparity among states. *Social Science Quarterly, 78*, 1001–1010.

Yates, J., & Fording, R. (2005). Politics and state punitiveness in black and white. *The Journal of Politics, 67*, 1099–1121.

Zhang, Y., Maxwell, C. D., & Vaughn, M. S. (2009). The impact of state sentencing policies on the U.S. prison population. *Journal of Criminal Justice, 37*, 190–199.

Appendix A
SENTENCING POLICIES AND PRISON ADMISSION RATES BY STATE

State	*Policies in Effect, 2000–2010*					*Male Prison Admission Rates, 2010*			
	DS	*PG*	*VG*	*TIS*	*3-strk*	*Total*	*White*	*Black*	*Hispanic*
AL			x			19.6	11.2	44.8	
AR			x		x	26.6	19.5	69.9	9.3
CA	x			x	x	35.1	25.6	161	36
CO					x	15.3	9.6	87.7	27.2
FL	x			x	x	15.5	9.3	52.5	8
GA				x	x	18.7	10.3	41.6	2.3
IA				x		12.3	10.4	120.8	
KY						19.9	14.5	91	13.2
LA				x	x	28.8	12.2	64.7	
MD			x		x	14.8	5.4	40.5	
MI		x		x		12	7.2	44.1	
MN	x	x		x		7.9	4.6	92.5	15.3
NJ				x	x	15.9	4.6	70.7	19.7
NY				x		13.5	4	42.2	23.5
NC	x	x		x	x	13	6.9	35.3	9.3
OK				x		21	18.7	79.4	19.5
OR	x	x		x		4.6	4.1	21.6	10
PA		x		x	x	8.9	3.6	46.4	34
SC				x	x	21.6	10	50	4.6
SD						13	13.7	91.4	
TN		x		x	x	20.3	10.9	68.8	9.6
TX						18.1	13.4	57.9	13.1
UT			x	x	x	13.7	12.3	138.9	21.7
VA	x		x	x	x	7.9	3.4	27.1	1.4
WA	x	x		x	x	9.9	8	69.7	15.2
WV						7.4	6.7	33.8	3.3

Note: Alabama adopted voluntary guidelines in 2006. DS = determinate sentencing, PG = presumptive guidelines, VG = voluntary guidelines, TIS = truth in sentencing, and 3-strk = three-strikes.

2

MASS PROBATION AND INEQUALITY

Race, Class, and Gender Disparities in Supervision and Revocation

Michelle S. Phelps[1]

Introduction

In recent years, there has been growing concern with the tremendously high imprisonment rate in the U.S. and disparities by class, race, and gender in who gets locked up. As Western (2006) documents, the effects of the prison boom were concentrated among young black men without a high school diploma, for whom imprisonment became a routine experience by the 2000s (27). Yet at the same time as imprisonment rates expanded, probation—or supervision in the community in lieu of imprisonment—remained the predominant mode of criminal justice supervision. As I argue elsewhere, this expansion of *mass probation* is a critical and deeply understudied dimension of the penal state (Phelps, 2017). At its peak in 2007, there were nearly 4.3 million Americans under probation supervision, compared to the 1.6 million in state and federal prisons (Kaeble et al., 2015). Yet we know little about how this expansion varied across demographic groups. This chapter evaluates race, class, and gender differences in the experience of probation supervision to build a more complete picture of disparities in the criminal justice system.

Probation is a contested institution. Originally designed and promoted as an "alternative" to imprisonment that would spare promising individuals from the ravages of institutionalization, it has often instead served as a "net-widener" that expands formal supervision for low-level cases (Aebi, Delgrande, and Marguet, 2015; Blomberg, 2003; Morris and Tonry, 1990; Phelps, 2013; Rothman, 2002). In addition, though frequently dismissed as a "slap on the wrist," probation can entail fairly onerous supervision requirements, including frequent reporting and drug testing, expensive fines and fees, and tedious rules and regulations. Probationers frequently fail to meet the multitude of conditions, which can lead to revocation to jail or prison. For these individuals, probation represents a *delayed* path to prison rather than a true diversion or alternative (Klingele, 2013). Phelps (2013) tests these two competing visions of probation (alternative or net-widener) at the state level and finds that probation plays both roles to varying degrees, depending in part on the state's sentencing and supervision practices.

In this chapter, I develop an account of probation as both penal alternative and net-widener at the individual level of analysis, structured by the relative social advantage of probationers. We know from sentencing research that markers of social privilege correlate with more lenient sentences in general, including diversion to probation (see e.g. Kim et al., 2015; Kutateladze et al., 2014; Wooldredge et al., 2015). In addition, researchers have found that adults with more privilege have an easier time completing supervision requirements like reporting at appointments on time, interacting deferentially with their probation officer, and paying fines and fees (Albonetti and Hepburn, 1997; Jannetta et al., 2014; Doherty, 2016). This suggests that probation may more effectively serve as a prison alternative for relatively advantaged probationers, who are more likely to be diverted and complete successfully, whereas for the less advantaged adults it functions more commonly as a net-widener and stepping-stone to further criminal justice control.

To bolster this perspective on probation, I provide the first national demographic portrait of probationers—both in the community and failed probationers incarcerated in the nation's jails and prisons during the peak of the carceral build-up (mid-2000s). As described below, the lack of such basic information about probationers (e.g. prevalence rates by gender, race, and age) is due in large part to scholarly neglect of probation and the limitations of the national data collection efforts on probation (Phelps, 2015). To maneuver around these limitations, I estimate probationer demographics using a national household survey—the Substance Abuse and Mental Health Services Administration's National Survey on Drug Use and Health. I then compare these characteristics to those of inmates in jail or prison who were on probation at the time of arrest using the Bureau of Justice Statistics' Survey of Inmates in Local Jails and Survey of Inmates in State and Federal Correctional Facilities. I also analyze the reasons for probationers' incarceration, evaluating in particular whether they are incarcerated for new crimes or violations of the terms of supervision ("technical" violations).

The results show that while probationers are skewed relative to the U.S. resident adult population along the expected lines of privilege/disadvantage (more likely to be male, non-white, and non-college educated), these disparities are substantially less pronounced than those for prisoners. Thus, compared to prisoners, probationers are more similar to the general population and, accordingly, are more likely to come from higher socioeconomic backgrounds. Yet failed probationers, incarcerated in jail and prison, are nearly indistinguishable from other prisoners. Further, roughly one quarter of these adults are incarcerated for probation violations that do not involve a new arrest (e.g. failure to report, drug use, and non-payment of fines/fees). This pattern of results suggests that probation plays a crucial role in stratifying outcomes in the criminal justice system, providing an off-ramp for some and a conveyor belt toward prison for others. In the conclusion, I sketch out a vision for the sociology of mass probation and highlight the importance of considering privilege alongside disadvantage in explaining criminal justice outcomes.

Literature Review

Mass Incarceration and Inequality

Western's *Punishment and Inequality in America* (2006) stands as the central account of how imprisonment shapes U.S. social stratification patterns. While the overall individual risk of imprisonment for adults remains relatively low (less than 1% in the early 2000s), he argues that the criminal justice system plays a key role in shaping inequality because it is heavily concentrated among the most disadvantaged. In particular, the (direct) effects of the prison boom were largely concentrated among young (aged 20–40 years) black men without a high school diploma, over 30% of whom were in jail or prison on any given day in 2000 (17). By age 34, nearly 60% of black high school dropouts who came of age during the prison boom (born 1965 to 1969) had experienced incarceration, compared to 5% of black men who had attended college and 11% of white high school dropouts (27). Further, the experience of incarceration exacerbates existing social inequalities for these adults post-release (Western, 2006), including deteriorated labor market outcomes, health, family stability, and educational attainment (for a review, see Wakefield and Uggen, 2010).

More recent work has begun to explore the "edge of stigma," exploring how more common low-level contacts with the criminal justice system influence inequality (Uggen et al., 2014). Many more than the estimated 13% of U.S. adult males that have been convicted of a felony (Shannon et al., f.c.) have been stopped by police and, in some cases, convicted of misdemeanor and other low-level offenses (Kohler-Hausmann, 2013; Natapoff, 2011). Criminal justice involvement for these individuals can stretch on for years, often prolonged by the burdens of excessive fines and fees imposed by the court (Harris, 2016). These processes have transformed life in economically marginalized inner-city communities, with residents becoming "cop-wise" (Stuart, 2016; see also Goffman, 2014) "custodial citizens" whose relationship with the state is dominated by criminal justice interactions (Lerman and Weaver, 2014). While probation is often lurking in the background of these studies (serving as the most common form of supervision), research on the direct effects of probation has been sparse, as described below.

The Rise of Mass Probation

Probation in the U.S. initially expanded during the Progressive Era, becoming the "exemplary penal form" of the penal-welfarist model that became dominant in the 1950s and 1960s (Simon, 2013). The core idea was that "promising" cases could be diverted from institutionalization and guided by a mentor (first a member of the community and later a trained professional) within the community (Rothman, 2002). With the decline of the rehabilitative ideal and the shift toward more punitive criminal justice practices (with the prison as the exemplary penal form), many expected probation rolls to empty (Robinson, McNeill, and Maruna, 2013).

Instead, *mass probation* developed right alongside mass imprisonment (Phelps, 2017). The timing and state-level variation in the expansion of these two forms of supervision suggests that rather than diverting cases from prison, probation often "widened the net" of social control (Phelps, 2013). The state and federal probation population soared from 1 million in 1980 to a peak of nearly 4.3 million in 2007. In more recent years, probation populations have (modestly) downsized, dropping to just under 3.9 million by 2014. Probation continues to be the predominant form of formal supervision, comprising 56% of those under correctional control (which includes probation, parole, prison, and jail counts) in 2014 (Kaeble et al., 2015). In addition, the U.S. probation rate remains more than five times the average across European countries (Alper et al., 2016).

Feeley and Simon (1992) argue that the expansion of community supervision was part of a broader shift toward the "new penology" model, which framed probation and parole as "cost-effective" risk-management solutions. As a result, community supervision grew increasingly managerial and punitive, with rising revocation rates (or returns to jail and prison) as the primary indicator of this new "toughness" (Simon, 1993; Caplow and Simon, 1999; Petersilia, 2002). Former Probation Commissioner Ronald Corbett (2015) describes this as "the burdens of leniency," noting that the average probationer now faces between 10 and 20 conditions of supervision, including regular reporting, paying fines and fees, abstaining from drugs and alcohol, avoiding criminal "associates," finding and maintaining employment, and more. This laundry list of conditions requires probationers to "obey all laws and be good," a standard vague enough that probation officers have tremendous discretion over charging supervision violations (Doherty, 2016). In addition, most probationers receive little in the way of treatment, services, or assistance programs that would help them address their (often many) challenges, including addiction, spotty work histories, histories of trauma and abuse, and unstable family and living arrangements (Taxman, 2012).

As a result, many probationers fail to meet the demands of supervision, ending up in jail or prison as a result (Klingele, 2013). Critics thus charge that not only does probation contribute to "front-end net-widening" through the failures of diversion, but it also produces "back-end net-widening" by incarcerating probation violators (Tonry and Lynch, 1996). Probationers are penalized in three ways: they are subject to revocation for behaviors that would not be criminal were they not on supervision (i.e. breaking curfew or drinking alcohol), they face increased risk of incarceration for new crimes (due to greater surveillance and the relative ease of incarceration through the probation revocation process as compared to prosecuting new convictions), and they can be hit with more severe sentences if charged with a new crime because their probation status increases their criminal history score and/or serves as an aggravating factor (Doherty, 2016; Petersilia, 2002; Kingsnorth et al., 2002; Klingele, 2013). As a result of these various pathways, the lines between incarceration for new crimes and technical violations can be very blurry.

In addition to the burdens of supervision, probationers are "marked" with a conviction record and thus face many of the same negative consequences ascribed to imprisonment, including barriers to employment, democratic participation, housing, and public assistance, that likely hinder integration and success (Chiricos et al., 2007; Jacobs, 2015; Pager, 2007). In 2014, 56% of probationers bore the stigma of felony-level offense. We are also learning how misdemeanor offenses—for which 42% of probationers were under supervision in 2014 (Kaeble, Maruschak, and Bonczar, 2015)[2]—negatively impact individuals' life trajectories through disruption, explicit bans on employment and assistance opportunities, and discrimination by employers and others (Kohler-Hausmann, 2013; Natapoff, 2011).

Not surprisingly, research on supervisees suggests that probation is often viewed as a punitive intervention, even in European contexts where social supports are more robust (Fitzgibbon, Graebsch, and McNeill, 2016). Durnescu (2011) outlines the "pains of probation," including deprivation of autonomy, private or family life, and time; financial costs; stigmatization effects; forced rumination over one's crime; and the looming threat of revocation. As a result, surveys of criminal justice populations find that U.S. adults often prefer a shorter prison term over a longer period of probation (Crouch, 1993; May, Wood, and Eades, 2008).[3] In a surprising moment of transparency, a local probation director in Texas recently told reporters that if he were faced with the choice between probation and prison, he would pick prison (Lieber, 2016).

In recent years, states have tried to rein in probation revocations to reduce prison populations, through changing revocation policies and improving supervision according to "evidence-based practices" (Phelps, 2013). These reforms include tailored supervision plans based on risk-needs assessments, concentrating resources on "high-risk" cases (and reducing burdens for "low-risk" cases), alleviating the barriers to employment, implementing graduated sanctions for violations, and shifting the fiscal and administrative burden of revocations to local counties (instead of the state) to incentivize counties to reduce revocations (Taxman, 2012; Klingele, 2013; Vera Institute of Justice, 2013). At the same time, success rates have slowly crept up, with the percentage of exiting probationers successfully completing probation hovering around 65% (and sometimes slightly higher) between 2008 and 2014 (Kaeble, Maruschak, and Bonczar, 2015), compared to a low of just under 60% from 2003 to 2006 (Glaze and Bonczar, 2006, 2009).

Mass Probation and Inequality

As suggested by the term *mass probation*, probation supervision is socially concentrated among economically disadvantaged men of color. At its peak in 2007, an estimated 1 in every 21 black adults (and 1 in 12 black men) was under probation supervision nationally, compared to 1 in 53 adults, 1 in 65 white adults, and 1 in 41 white men (Phelps, 2017). Using data from a household survey, Lerman and Weaver (2014) find that fully 46% of young (24 to 32 years old) black men without a high school degree report having been on probation at some point in the past.

It is less clear, however, if and how probation affects individuals and, more broadly, patterns of inequality. This ambiguity is driven both by neglect in the literature and by the complex role of probation as a penal sanction or *alternative*. In other words, what is the comparison case for probationers? If supervision is simply a treatment-oriented intervention whereby all eligible adults are diverted from prison and connected to social services, then we might expect it to have inequality-ameliorating consequences (as compared to these cases going to prison). In contrast, to the extent that probation widens the "net" of control (diverting low-level cases *up* from no supervision to formal control) and makes success more difficult, we would expect probation to exacerbate patterns of inequality. In addition, in the absence of record sealing and expungement programs, probation automatically comes with a stigmatizing criminal record that can thwart life goals regardless of the quality or orientation of supervision.

High-quality research evaluating these competing visions of probation is limited. The studies that do exist often focus on the effect of imprisonment, using probation as a counter-factual. These studies allow us to compare probation to imprisonment, but not to consider probation versus no formal supervision. The first wave of this research used regression model techniques to compare adults sentenced to prison versus probation and other alternative sanctions, often finding that incarceration had a negative impact on individuals' trajectories (for reviews, see Bushway et al., 2007; Nagin, Cullen, and Jonson, 2009; Loeffler, 2013). However, this research was critiqued as insufficiently controlling for selection into prison, pushing scholars toward quasi-experimental approaches (Apel and Sweeten, 2010).

In perhaps the most exacting published study to date, Loeffler (2013) uses variation in judicial severity to estimate the effect of imprisonment (compared to probation) on later re-arrest[4] and employment rates among felons in Cook County (Chicago). The point estimates suggest that prisoners face somewhat worse outcomes on some dimensions, but these differences are not statistically significant (arguably due to insufficient statistical power).[5] Loeffler attributes the null findings to selection (and the changing social context of increased criminal justice contact), arguing that many of the negative consequences ascribed to imprisonment are simply due to the pre-existing challenges faced by those who are imprisoned.

We might also interpret this evidence to support the hypothesis that conviction with probation is (nearly) as damaging to individuals as imprisonment.[6] Or perhaps the mixed results are a product of the heterogeneity in the experience of supervision for both probationers and prisoners. While some programs may do a better job at assisting probationers in building successful lives, others may be more focused on punitive surveillance and catching violations. As Bushway (2011) argues, "the nature of the treatment (type of program, length of program, etc.) seems fundamentally more important than the program venue (community or prison)" (331).[7] It is also likely that the effects of supervision are heterogeneous across the population of probationers, as calls to tailor supervision practices to individuals' needs and social context highlight (Taxman, 2012).

Stratified Outcomes: Mass Probation Across Privilege/Disadvantage

I hypothesize that probation serves multiple roles in the criminal justice system, stratified by the relative social privilege of probationers. Although the majority of adults involved in the courts and under penal control have lower income and education levels than the average American (Brennan Center for Justice, 2010), there is still relative socioeconomic gradation as well as variation across gender, age, location, and other axes of inequality. For relatively advantaged adults, probation may be more likely to function as a true diversion whereby individuals are shunted away from prison and able to complete probation successfully. For relatively disadvantaged probationers, supervision may more often serve as a "piling on" of sanctions that ultimately ends with imprisonment. Thus, just as research has shown that the role of probation as a diversion or net-widener varies by state policy choices (Phelps, 2013), so too may the interpretation (and likely effects) of probation supervision vary across individuals.

Existing research findings on both sentencing and revocation patterns support this hypothesis. First, a massive (and growing) literature on sentencing disparities outlines the direct and indirect effects of "extralegal" individual characteristics (particularly race, age, gender, and socioeconomic status) as well as their interaction with the "legal" characteristics (including prior record) that affect sentencing severity (for a handful of recent exemplars, see Kim et al., 2015; Kutateladze et al., 2014; Wooldredge et al., 2015; for a qualitative analysis of these dynamics, see Van Cleve, 2016). These studies examine various sites in the sentencing process, from the setting of bail and pre-trial detention, to a guilty plea versus a trial finding guilt, to whether to incarcerate or not, and the sentence length (Baumer, 2013). As Spohn (2015) notes in a recent review essay, research on sentencing disparities has moved away from a simple descriptive account of disparities and, later, regression models that tried to estimate the direct causal effect of status characteristics in sentencing decisions, toward more complex accounts of how the direct and indirect effects of race (and other factors) compound through each stage of the criminal justice system, creating a cumulative disadvantage cascade that is particularly disastrous for young black men.

In addition, research shows that probation revocation is more likely for relatively disadvantaged probationers. Studies of jurisdictions across the country have found that probation revocation is associated with the same characteristics correlated with sentencing outcomes (Albonetti and Hepburn, 1997; Cunniff and Shilton, 1991; Gray et al., 2001; Rodriguez and Webb, 2007; Stevens-Martin et al., 2014). Consistent with disparities in other places in the criminal justice system, women, older adults, those with stable employment, and (in some findings) white adults are the most likely to complete probation successfully. The Urban Institute (Jannetta et al., 2014) recently found that black and Hispanic probationers faced substantially higher revocation rates in the four jurisdictions studied, which were only partially explained by factors like risk assessment scores and probation violation charges. As Albonetti and Hepburn (1997) argue, these characteristics often are mutually constitutive: "social disadvantage may condition the effects of other offender characteristics (such as age, race, and gender), incident offense characteristics, and treatment conditions on probation failure" (126).

Doherty (2016) and Corbett (2015) illustrate several possible mechanisms for the relationship between privilege/disadvantage and revocation, the most obvious of which is that poor people face unique challenges in meeting the requirements of supervision, which include maintaining employment, meeting regularly with the probation officer, and paying fines and fees. Failure to meet these obligations—including financial penalties—can lead to imprisonment, creating a loophole for legal prohibitions against "debtor's prisons" (Harris, 2016). Relatively poorer probationers and racial minorities are also more likely to be rated as "high risk" on actuarial risk assessment instruments and therefore may face greater supervision burdens. Lastly, relatively more disadvantaged probationers may lack the social capital to negotiate with their probation officer and face implicit to explicit discrimination in the officer's supervision style and use of discretion.

A final mechanism through which disadvantage affects revocation is through the likelihood of committing new crimes. Just as differences in criminal offending rates are *partially* responsible for the disparities in incarceration rates (Tonry and Melewski, 2008), so too do crime patterns shape probation admission and revocation. Rather than seeing this as a confounding variable, however, I construe criminal offenses as part of the constellation of behaviors that reflect and shape individuals' social context (Simons et al., 2014), in part because neighborhood conditions play a crucial role in raising or lowering overall crime prevalence and the risk of arrest. Thus, we should be wary of framing incarceration for new convictions (or revocations based on a new arrest) as a "justifiable" result of probationer's misbehavior that is entirely distinct from other kinds of violations.

Data and Methods

The core data collection on probation is the Bureau of Justice Statistics' (hereafter BJS) Annual Probation Survey, which sends questionnaires to local and state agencies identified by the BJS as adult probation agencies. In addition to asking for probationer totals, the survey contains questions about the basic demographic characteristics of agencies' probationer populations (including gender and race/ethnicity, but not socioeconomic markers or age).[8] Due to reporting challenges, even these minimal descriptive characteristics of probationers are unavailable for many jurisdictions (Phelps, 2015). In addition, the BJS surveys miss a non-trivial number of supervising agencies (Tubman-Carbone and Glaze, 2013), particularly local programs for misdemeanor supervision, which provide the majority of probation services for misdemeanants in a small number of states (Phelps, 2017).[9] These data omissions skew both overall rate and demographic composition estimates.

Due to these limitations, I use the Substance Abuse and Mental Health Services Administration's National Survey on Drug Use and Health (hereafter NSDUH), an annual household survey sent to a nationally representative stratified sample of non-institutionalized U.S. residents.[10] In the most recent iteration (2014), the sample size was 67,000 respondents with a weighted interview response rate of 71%. The NSDUH includes a single question about probation, asking respondents to report if they were on probation at any time in the past 12 months. The NSDUH also has a wealth of demographic questions, including race/ethnicity, gender, age, and level of education.

Relying on the NSDUH, I estimate the demographic composition of adults in the community who report having been on probation in the past year during the mid- to late-2000s. I include the following characteristics: race/ethnicity (percent non-Hispanic black, percent Hispanic, percent non-Hispanic white), percent male, age (percent aged

18–29 years), and educational composition (percent high school graduate, percent with some college, percent with college degree) as a proxy measure for socioeconomic status. All NSDUH respondents under 18 years of age are excluded to limit the analyses to U.S. adults. In addition to demographic composition estimates, I provide probation prevalence rates for key demographic groups, comparing these to the estimates of imprisonment rates produced by Western (2006).

Next, I estimate the demographic characteristics of adults behind bars in jail and prison who were on probation at the time of arrest (i.e. failed probationers). For these calculations, I rely on the BJS Survey of Inmates in Local Jails (hereafter SILJ) and Survey of Inmates in State and Federal Correctional Facilities (SISFCF).[11] These surveys include nationally representative stratified random samples of inmates in jails and prisons, respectively. The sample size for the 2002 SILJ was 6,982 inmates, with a response rate of 84%. For the 2004 SISFCF, the statistics are 14,499 and 89% for state inmates and 3,686 and 85% for federal inmates. The SILJ and SISFCF include questions about all of the key demographic characteristics listed above. Inmates are also asked whether they were on probation (and/or parole and other forms of supervision) at the time they were arrested for the charges that led to their current spell of incarceration. In addition, inmates are asked about whether they were charged with and convicted of a new offense and/or had their probation revoked for supervision violations, which are used to categorize the reasons for incarceration. I distinguish between new arrests, convictions, and revocations for new crime; revocations for all other supervision violations (e.g. failure to report, drug use, and unpaid fines and fees); and other reasons for incarceration.

The spatial and temporal scope of study is constrained by the combined limitations of the datasets. None of the series are designed to provide state-level estimates, limiting these analyses to the national level.[12] Due to changes in the survey design, NSDUH data from before 2002 are not comparable to the later years.[13] To produce stable estimates for the key demographic characteristics of adult probationers in the community, it was necessary to aggregate across years.[14] I combine data from the 2002, 2003, 2004, 2005, and 2006 NSDUH surveys to roughly correspond with the most recent iterations of the BJS surveys (2002 for the SILJ and 2004 for the SISFCF). For the prevalence rates, I generate estimates for 2002–2006 and 2010–2014 NSDUH surveys to evaluate whether trends have changed significantly in recent years. For all of these estimates, I use take into account the stratified sampling designs and final sample weights.[15] Cases with missing data on the relevant outcomes are dropped in analyses.[16] Due to the survey differences (described below), I only calculate statistical significance tests within (not across) datasets, using Wald mean tests to compare group means.

There are several additional limitations. First, the three surveys measure individuals' self-reported criminal justice status, requiring that community members and inmates be able to report accurately that they were on probation supervision.[17] Second, the probation questions are not identical. The NSDUH asks respondents to report whether they were under probation supervision in the past year, while the BJS collections ask inmates whether they were on probation at the time of the arrest that led to their current incarceration. On average, probation terms currently last 22 months (Kaeble, Maruschak, and Bonczar, 2015), which suggests that there should be substantial overlap between the population on probation at any given point in time and those who were on probation in the past year.

Third, because the NSDUH is a household survey, it does not include individuals who are homeless, in housing transitions or insecurely housed, or in institutional settings. In addition, since the survey only records the probation status of the primary respondent, it may under-report probation rates among those living in housing arrangements that deviate from the single-family norm (e.g. multiple younger adults in one household). In addition, results may be affected by non-response rates, which are somewhat higher for the NSDUH than for the SILJ and SISFCF. These concerns produce a bias toward under-reporting the most disadvantaged criminal justice-involved populations, most of whom lack stable traditional single-family housing (Western et al., 2016). As a result, some of the estimates for the demographic groups most likely to be insecurely housed may be overly conservative. I return to this concern in the conclusion.

One check on the reliability of the NSDUH data is to compare the estimates of the total probationer population generated from the NSDUH results to the total population reported by agencies to the BJS. As shown in Appendix A, these populations show a rough consistency, although the NSDUH estimates are generally higher than the BJS totals (which is perhaps reflective of the missing misdemeanant probationers in the BJS counts and/or the more expansive question wording of the NSDUH series). Both series also show a decline in the population since 2010, although time trends before this period (2002–2010) are not as consistent. The other comparison we can make is between the race and gender breakdowns reported by agencies to BJS (in 2012) to the NSDUH demographics (for 2010-2014). These estimates show a correspondence for percent non-Hispanic white (54% in BJS and 58% in NSDUH), although the percent identified as non-Hispanic black is much higher in the BJS data (30% vs. 18%) and the percent Hispanic is much lower (13% vs. 19%), perhaps reflecting a hesitation on behalf of probation authorities to categorize supervisees as Hispanic (instead of black or white) and/or an under-reporting of race/ethnicity data in jurisdictions with larger Hispanic populations. The percent female is also lower in the BJS data (24% vs. 30%), which might reflect that the NSDUH data better captures probationers under supervision for lower-level offenses and/or serving shorter terms of supervision. Since both datasets have significant limitations, it is unclear what conclusions to draw from these comparisons. However, the rough correspondence of the two datasets on most dimensions suggests that there is substantial overlap between the administratively reported probation data and the NSDUH survey.

Results

Household Respondents

Among the household resident adult population in the U.S. during the mid-2000s, approximately 2% report having been on probation in the prior year. There are very large differences between all respondents and those reporting probation experience. As summarized in Table 2.1, compared to the total household population, probationers are significantly more likely to be racial/ethnic minorities (57% vs. 70% non-Hispanic white), male (74% vs. 48%), and young (63% vs. 31% aged 18–34 years). In addition, probationers are educationally disadvantaged, with 68% reporting a high school diploma (compared to 83% in the general population) and only 7% (compared to 26%) reporting a college degree. Thus, like the prison population, the probation population is significantly skewed toward young men of color with low levels of formal education.

Another way to visualize these trends is through prevalence rates, which reflect the percent of respondents in particular demographic groups who report having been on probation in the past year. Figure 2.1 displays prevalence rates among non-institutionalized younger adults (aged 20–34),[18] sorted according to race, gender, and educational attainment (with error bars reflecting the 95% confidence interval). I estimate these rates during two periods: the early to mid-2000s (2002–2006) and the period of recent reforms (2010–2014). The results show that, compared to the differential for incarceration rates, probation experience is more evenly distributed, with surprisingly high rates among relatively privileged groups.

As expected, the rate of probation supervision rate is highest among young black men without a high school diploma, standing at an estimated 19% in the early 2000s and 16% in more recent years. This means that nearly one fifth of non-institutionalized black men aged 20 to 34 without a high school diploma were on probation in an average year during the height of the penal boom. Yet young white men without high school diplomas face a prevalence rate of 12% in both periods. This is a statistically and substantively significant difference from the 16%–19% of similarly situated black men

Table 2.1 Demographic Characteristics of U.S. Adults by Penal Status

	All Household Respondents (2002–2006)	*Household Respondents on Probation in Past Year (2002–2006)*	*All Jail Inmates (2002)*	*Jail Inmates on Probation at Time of Arrest (2002)*	*All Prison Inmates (2004)*	*Prison Inmates on Probation at Time of Arrest (2004)*
On probation	2%		33%		23%	
Race/Ethnicity						
NH black	11%	17%	41%	40%	42%	40%
Hispanic	12%	20%	18%	17%	19%	18%
NH white	70%	57%	37%	41%	36%	39%
Male	48%	74%	88%	87%	93%	90%
18–34 years	31%	63%	61%	67%	50%	64%
Education Level						
HS graduate	83%	68%	40%	39%	35%	32%
Some college	51%	30%	15%	15%	15%	13%
College graduate	26%	7%	3%	2%	3%	2%

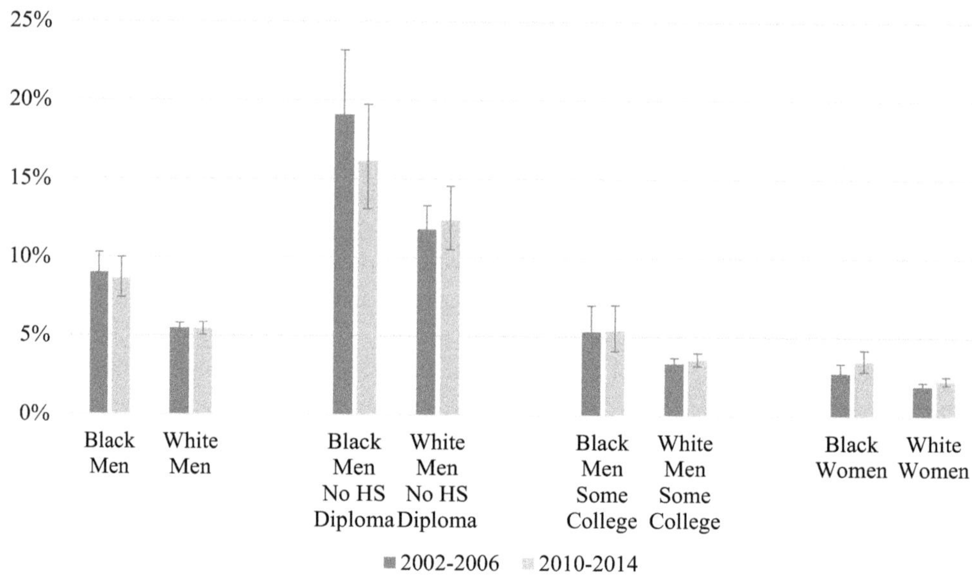

Figure 2.1 NSDUH Prevalence Rates for Probation in Prior Year Among Adults Aged 20–34 Years, 2002–2006 and 2010–2014

under probation supervision, but the disparity (at worst 1.6:1) is far less severe than the 4.8:1 ratio Western (2006: 19) finds for imprisonment rates. Similarly, black young men with some college experience had a prevalence rate of 5% in the two periods, compared to 3%–4% for white college men (a race difference that is statistically significant at $p < .05$ but substantively small). Prevalence rates among women were generally lower, and again we see a small, but statistically significant, difference (3% for black women; 2% for white women).

As documented in Appendix A, both the BJS and NSDUH estimates for the total number of probationers declined between the peak of the probation population in 2007 and 2014. However, this decline is not reflected in the estimates for the demographic group prevalence rates displayed in Figure 2.1 (with the exception of the noticeable, but not statistically significant, decline in rates for young black men without a high school diploma). This is likely due to the relatively small scale of decline (especially in the context of pooled data) and the large standard errors. Thus, these data do not permit us to draw conclusions about changes across the time periods for demographic groups.

Jail and Prison Inmates

Among inmates in jail and prison, many were on probation at the time of their arrest (33% of jail inmates and 23% of prisoners). Returning to Table 2.1, the estimates reveal that prisoners who were on probation at the time of arrest are demographically very similar to other prisoners. For example, the percent identified as non-Hispanic white is estimated as 39% of prisoners who were on probation at the time of arrest, compared to 36% of all prisoners (or 41% vs. 37% for jail inmates). The percent identified as male is also substantially skewed for all incarcerated adults, reaching 87% among failed probationers in jail (compared to 88% of all jail inmates) and 90% of failed probationers in prison (compared to 93% of all prisoners). The percentage aged 18 to 34 years was much higher among institutionalized populations, reaching a high of 67% of jail inmates on probation at arrest (compared to 61% for all jail inmates, 64% of prison inmates on probation at arrest, and 50% for all prison inmates). We can also see this trend across high school dropout rates, which reach 61% among failed probationers in jail and 68% for failed probationers in prison, compared to 60% and 65% of all jail and prison inmates, respectively.

While some of these differences reach statistical significance, they are generally substantively small (with the exception of age, where failed probationers skew much younger than other prisoners). Thus, except for age profiles, failed probationers in jail and prison demographically overlap with all incarcerated adults. This lack of difference is particularly stark when compared to the sizable differences between the demographics of probationers in the community and the broader household population.

Finally, we turn to the reasons probationers are behind bars. Table 2.2 summarizes the most serious legal status of jail and prison inmates who were on probation at the time of arrest. Collapsing across survey questions on arrests, convictions, and revocation reveals that 25% of failed probationers in jail and 70% of failed probationers in jail have been convicted of a new crime, while an additional 32% of jail inmates and 6% of prison inmates' most serious legal status was being charged with a new crime and/or revoked (or facing revocation) for new arrest(s). This means that 55% of jail inmates (and over 75% of prison inmates) are incarcerated for new arrests and convictions. However, one fifth to more than one quarter (27% of jail inmates and 21% of prisoners) of inmates who entered incarceration while on probation are incarcerated for other kinds of supervision violations (including failure to report, drug use,

Table 2.2 Most Serious Legal Status of Jail and Prison Inmates Who Were on Probation at Time of Arrest

Jail Inmates (2002)	
Convicted of New Crime	25%
Charged with New Crime and/or Revocation for New Arrest	32%
Revoked (or Awaiting Hearing) for Other Supervision Violations	27%
Incarcerated for Other Reasons	16%
State and Federal Prisoners (2004)	
Convicted of New Crime	70%
Revoked for New Arrest	6%
Revoked for Other Supervision Violations	21%
Incarcerated for Other Reasons	3%

Note: Categories sum to 100% because only most serious legal status is represented. Many inmates fit multiple categories (e.g. both a new conviction and revocation). Cases with missing data on all legal status variables (and inmates held for supervision violations without revocation or new offense charges filed) are included in the residual category (Incarcerated for Other Reasons).

and non-payment of fines and fees).[19] The remaining 16% of jail inmates and 3% of prisoners are incarcerated without a new arrest/conviction or revocation (or did not report those data).

For comparison purposes, Appendix B replicates these results for parole, the other predominant form of community supervision. Overall, fewer jail and prison inmates were on parole (as compared to probation) at the time of arrest (12% of jail inmates and 18% of prisoners), reflecting the much smaller scale of parole supervision.[20] In terms of the most serious legal status, the results for parole echo those for probation: 64% of failed parolees in jail and 79% of failed parolees in prison were incarcerated for reasons related to a new arrest (including a new criminal charge, conviction, and/or revocation for new arrest). Roughly one fifth of inmates who were on parole at the time of arrest were incarcerated for other kinds of supervision violations (24% of jail and 18% of prison inmates). Another 12% of jail inmates and 3% of prisoners were incarcerated without a new arrest/conviction or revocation (or did not report those data).

Conclusions: Toward a Sociology of Mass Probation

This chapter had a modest goal: to produce descriptive estimates of the probation population in the community and failed probationers behind bars. The results show that disparities in probation supervision rates across race, gender, age, and educational attainment are substantially less pronounced than those for imprisonment rates. Yet when we examine probationers behind bars, they are once again the "usual suspects"—disproportionately young, non-white men with low levels of formal schooling. This supports the hypothesis that probation provides a bifurcated pathway, diverting relatively more privileged defendants toward community supervision (which they can more easily complete) while their less advantaged counterparts are funneled deeper into the criminal justice system.

This bifurcated perspective provides a complex picture of how probation shapes broader inequalities in the criminal justice system. The results suggest that probation supervision contributes to racial disparities in imprisonment, both by diverting more white defendants to probation initially and by revoking black probationers at greater rates. Yet, more broadly, including probation as a measure of punishment reduces racial disparities—revealing that the population under formal supervision is more demographically representative of the U.S. as a whole (as compared to statistics that focus solely on imprisonment). Rather than conceiving of whites in the criminal justice system as simply "collateral damage" (Forman, 2012), the results direct us to ask how and why these multiple forms of control expanded differentially (and to different effects) across demographic groups (for a similar argument at the state level, see Phelps, 2017).

However, one important caveat to these results is that the NSDUH data may systematically under-report the most vulnerable or marginalized populations due to its sampling of the *household* population, as noted above. This means that the demographic portrait of probationers in the community from Table 2.1 may be unduly conservative (i.e. the gap between household residents and probationers should be larger) and that the prevalence rates in Figure 2.1 may be too low for some groups. However, the rough correspondence between the NSDUH estimates of the probation totals and the BJS figures (Appendix A) and the massive demographic differences between those who were on probation in the past year and all household respondents suggests that this likely under-reporting was not large enough to invalidate the pattern of results. In addition, the bias from under-reporting would have to be quite large to alter the conclusion that the demographics of failed probationers are much more skewed than those for probationers in the community, given the substantial differences observed in the results. Finally, such under-reporting would not affect the conclusion that there are surprisingly high rates of probation supervision among those with more educational privilege (as compared to the likelihood of imprisonment), or the conclusions drawn from the SISFCF and SILJ that a substantial percent of jail and prison inmates are incarcerated simply for technical violations that did not involve new arrests.

Looking forward, these results suggest two different avenues of research. First, the overwhelming focus on the ways in which *disadvantage* shapes the criminal justice system has led to a neglect the effect of social advantage or *privilege*. What would it mean to think about the effect of privilege instead of disadvantage in the criminal justice system? For one, it would point our attention to the social contexts in which sentences err on the side of leniency. These examples may provide a model for what a more humane system of justice might look like in the U.S. Second, it provides a new perspective on supervision regimes, prompting us to ask not just why people fail—but how and why they succeed. Again, such a focus may help us to shift policies in a way that acknowledges the challenges of supervision and reduces the burdens of supervision for less privileged probationers (e.g. by decreasing the number and onerousness of conditions or providing alternative ways of satisfying financial obligations).

Third, the results prompt a series of questions about the individual-level effects of probation. We still have very little reliable evidence on the effects of probation supervision on individuals' employment histories, criminal activity, relationship patterns, and overall health and wellbeing—especially compared to those who receive no post-conviction supervision. Critical to this line of research will be defining the counterfactual: what is probation an *alternative* to (and for which individuals)? In what ways does probation help or harm supervisees—and how much of this effect is due simply to pre-existing inequalities and the effects of a criminal record? These questions will require the kind of focused attention and methodological rigor and diversity that has been applied to the question of the effects of imprisonment.

More broadly, what are the consequences of mass probation for families, neighborhoods, and inequality more broadly? We would expect probation to influence families and communities in ways quite different than imprisonment since probationers are usually supervised while living at home. Rather than "missing men" pulled away from (and cycled back into) the community through mass imprisonment (Pettit, 2012), probation instead draws the formal criminal justice system into the community (Cohen, 1985). Several recent analyses provide hints of what we might find. Rios (2011), for example, shows how juvenile probation officers in Oakland, CA, have become ingrained in schools and community centers, fueling a "youth control complex" that criminalizes and stigmatizes young men of color. How does this process work for adults and communities more broadly?

In addition, given the broader spread of the demographics of adults under probation supervision, we would expect probation to be an influence in a more diverse array of neighborhoods. How does probation supervision influence family and neighborhood dynamics across these different contexts? In particular, how does probation operate in relatively more advantaged communities with less of a law enforcement presence? These questions suggest that there is much more to learn about community control. A spotlight on the development of mass probation and its effects on individuals, families, and neighborhoods will help us to develop a fuller picture of U.S. exceptionalism in harsh penal policies and their role in shaping social inequality.

Notes

1 Thanks to Fergus McNeill, Chris Uggen, Matthew DeMichele, Gil Rothschild, and Robert Stewart for helpful comments on this project. Jennifer Chudoba, Michael Eastman, and Veronica Horowitz provided research assistance. Lauren Glaze at the Bureau of Justice Statistics initially directed my attention to the NSDUH data on probation. This work also benefited from the resources of the Minnesota Population Center (NICHD 5R24HD041023). Finally, thanks go to the audience members at the Minnesota Population Center Seminar Series and the 2016 American Society of Criminology meetings who provided helpful comments.

2 There is also substantial variations in terms of probationers' offense categories. In 2014, the breakdown was 19% violent, 28% property, 25% drug, 16% public order (mostly DWI/DUI), and 11% other (Kaeble, Maruschak, and Bonczar, 2015).

3 May, Wood, and Eades (2008) estimate an "exchange rate" that measures the number of months that adults (in Kentucky) would be willing to serve on probation in lieu of twelve months in a medium security prison. By group, the average exchange rate was: 24 months among current probationers and parolees, 27 months among members of the public, 40 among judges, and 44 months among probation and parole officers.

4 One important difference between probationers and prisoners is that probationers are subject to local law enforcement throughout their supervision, whereas prisoners are only "at risk" of re-arrest after release (since most offenses behind prison walls do not lead to a new arrest record). To (partially) respond to this challenge, Loeffler (2013) compares re-arrest rates in the 5 years after indictment.

5 Green and Winik (2010) use a similar design and find no significant effect of imprisonment on recidivism among drug offenders in the District of Columbia. Recent work in the U.K. has used propensity score matching to compare the effects of probation versus imprisonment, finding that incarceration has a small but significant positive effect on reoffending and reincarceration (see e.g. Jolliffe and Hedderman, 2012). Research in progress suggests that, if we compare split sentences of probation and jail to jail without probation, those with probation experience better employment outcomes in the initial post-release period (Nguyen et al., 2016).

6 One mechanism by which probation may have negative effects on individuals' trajectories is that probationers (and parolees) can be subject to short-term custodial stays for smaller supervision violations. New research suggests that even short periods of incarceration can cause enough disruption to destabilize family relationships and employment (Comfort, 2016; Apel, 2016; Harding et al., f.c.).

7 See also Welsh and Rocque (2014) on the complexities of evaluating criminal justice interventions.

8 Although see Cunniff and Shilton (1991).

9 The BJS is now working to address some of these limitations in the latest wave of data collection, including a broader sample of supervising agencies.

10 Results are generated from the public-use version of the NSDUH data for the years 2002–2014. The public-use file is a subsample and provides less detailed information for certain variables. Applications for access to the restricted full sample were put on hold indefinitely as of May 2015. The National Survey on Drug Use and Health public data files are available at the Substance Abuse and Mental Health Data Archive and the Inter-university Consortium for Political and Social Research, which are sponsored by the Office of Applied Studies, Substance Abuse and Mental Health Services Administration. Retrieved from www.icpsr.umich.edu/icpsrweb/ICPSR/series/64.

11 I rely on the restricted access versions of these datasets in order to estimate error terms that account for the stratified sampling design. The data are collected by the United States Department of Justice, Office of Justice Programs, Bureau of Justice Statistics, and are available through a data access request to the Inter-university Consortium for Political and Social Research. The Survey of Inmates in Local Jails, 2002 (ICPSR 4359) is available at www.icpsr.umich.edu/icpsrweb/ICPSR/studies/4359. The Survey of Inmates in State and Federal Correctional Facilities, 2004 (ICPSR 4572) is available at www.icpsr.umich.edu/icpsrweb/ICPSR/studies/4572.

12 In some cases, it is possible to generate state-level estimates for the largest states (if they represent a unique sampling stratum). It is also possible to use small area estimation techniques to create state-level estimates with the NSDUH, but due to the rarity of probation and its wide variance across states, these are unlikely to be reliable.

13 See Appendix C at http://media.samhsa.gov/data/nhsda/2k2nsduh/results/appC.htm.

14 The NSDUH is a large survey, but since probation is a rare experience (2% of the sample), pooling across annual waves is necessary to get reliable estimates.

15 I calculate the results in STATA using the survey proportion and test commands. I use $p < .05$ as the significance level cut-off.

16 The one exception to this rule is the most serious legal status of jail and prison inmates. Here, I utilize all relevant data, even if some of the variables had missing information. Cases with no information on legal status were included in the "other" category. However, the estimates were consistent within 1–2 percentage points even if all cases with any missing data were dropped.

17 It might be particularly challenging for some respondents to distinguish between various types of community supervision. For example, in some locales, the differences between probation and parole are murky, and individuals can be on both forms of supervision simultaneously. In other cases, individuals might be on "paper-only" supervision that requires no reporting and is very similar to a suspended sentence. The NSDUH survey distinguishes between "probation" and "parole, supervised release, or other conditional release from prison." Of those reporting supervision on probation in the years 2002 through 2006, 23% also reported being on parole in the past year.

18 The public-use NSDUH data do not provide age in years but instead generate a categorical variable for years. Since ages 35 to 49 were bundled together in one age bin, I was not able to estimate probation rates for the age category Western (2006) adopts (20–40 years). Instead, I estimated rates for adults aged 20–34 years.

19 These estimates are lower than many other studies of probation violations and revocations (e.g., Clear et al., 1992; Gray et al., 2001; Rodriguez and Webb, 2007; Cunniff and Shilton, 1991), likely in large part because stock (rather than flow) measures of the prison population emphasize more serious offenses (because these individuals remain in jail or prison longer).

20 Jail inmates were allowed to report simultaneous parole and probation supervision at the time of arrest. Prison inmates were forced to choose one category of pre-arrest supervision.

References

Aebi, M. F., Delgrande, N., & Marguet, Y. (2015). Have community sanctions and measures widened the net of the European criminal justice systems? *Punishment & Society*, *17*(5), 575–597. http://doi.org/10.1177/1462474515615694

Albonetti, C. A., & Hepburn, J. R. (1997). Probation revocation: A proportional hazards model of the conditioning effects of social disadvantage. *Social Problems, 44*(1), 124–138.
Alper, M., Corda, A., & Reitz, K. R. (2016). *American exceptionalism in probation supervision*. Minneapolis, MN: Robina Institute of Criminal Law and Criminal Justice.
Apel, R. (2016). The effects of jail and prison confinement on cohabitation and marriage. *The Annals of the American Academy of Political and Social Science, 665*(1), 103–126.
Apel, R., & Sweeten, G. (2010). The impact of incarceration on employment during the transition to adulthood. *Social Problems, 57*(3), 448–479. http://doi.org/10.1525/sp.2010.57.3.448
Baumer, E. P. (2013). Reassessing and redirecting research on race and sentencing. *Justice Quarterly, 30*(2), 231–261. http://doi.org/10.1080/07418825.2012.682602
Blomberg, T. G. (2003). Penal reform and the fate of "Alternatives." In T. G. Blomberg & S. Cohen (Eds.), *Punishment and social control* (2nd ed., pp. 417–432). New York: Aldine de Gruyter.
Brennan Center for Justice. (2010). *Criminal justice debt: A barrier to reentry*. New York, NY: Brennan Center for Justice at New York University School of Law.
Bushway, S. D. (2011). So policy makers drive incarceration—now what? *Criminology & Public Policy, 10*(2), 327–333.
Bushway, S. D., Stoll, M. A., & Weiman, D. (2007). *Barriers to reentry? The labor market for released prisoners in post-industrial America*. New York: Russell Sage Foundation.
Caplow, T., & Simon, J. (1999). Understanding prison policy and population trends. *Crime and Justice, 26*, 63–120.
Chiricos, T., Barrick, K., Bales, W., & Bontrager, S. (2007). The labeling of convicted felons and its consequences for recidivism. *Criminology, 45*(3), 547–581. http://doi.org/10.1111/j.1745-9125.2007.00089.x
Clear, T. R., Harris, P. M., & Baird, S. C. (1992). Probationer violations and officer response. *Journal of Criminal Justice, 20*(1), 1–12.
Cohen, S. (1985). *Visions of social control: Crime, punishment, and classification*. Cambridge: Polity Press.
Comfort, M. (2016). "A Twenty-Hour-a-Day Job": The impact of frequent low-level criminal justice involvement on family life. *The ANNALS of the American Academy of Political and Social Science, 665*(1), 63–79. http://doi.org/10.1177/0002716215625038
Corbett, R. P., Jr. (2015). The burdens of leniency: The changing face of probation. *Minnesota Law Review, 99*(5), 1697–1732.
Crouch, B. M. (1993). Is incarceration really worse? Analysis of offenders' preferences for prison over probation. *Justice Quarterly, 10*(1), 67–88. http://doi.org/10.1080/07418829300091711
Cunniff, M. A., & Shilton, M. K. (1991). *Variations on felony probation: Persons under supervision in 32 urban and suburban counties*. Washington, DC: U.S. Department of Justice: Bureau of Justice Statistics. Retrieved from http://www.ncjrs.gov/App/Publications/abstract.aspx?ID=129490
Doherty, F. (2016). Obey all laws and be good: Probation and the meaning of recidivism. *Georgetown Law Journal, 104*(2), 291–354.
Durnescu, I. (2011). Pains of probation: Effective practice and human rights. *International Journal of Offender Therapy and Comparative Criminology, 55*(4), 530–545. http://doi.org/10.1177/0306624X10369489
Feeley, M. M., & Simon, J. (1992). The new penology: Notes on the emerging strategy of corrections and its implications. *Criminology, 30*(4), 449–474.
Fitzgibbon, W., Graebsch, C., & McNeill, F. (2016). Pervasive punishment: Experiencing supervision. In M. Brown & E. Carrabine (Eds.), *Handbook of visual criminology*. London: Routledge.
Forman, J. J. (2012). Racial critiques of mass incarceration: Beyond the new Jim Crow. *New York University Law Review, 87*, 21.
Glaze, L. E., & Bonczar, T. P. (2006). *Probation and parole in the United States, 2005*. Washington, DC: Bureau of Justice Statistics.
Glaze, L. E., & Bonczar, T. P. (2009). *Probation and parole in the United States, 2008*. Washington, DC: Bureau of Justice Statistics.

Goffman, A. (2014). *On the run: Fugitive life in an American city*. Chicago; London: University of Chicago Press.

Gray, M. K., Fields, M., & Maxwell, S. R. (2001). Examining probation violations: Who, what, and when. *Crime & Delinquency*, *47*(4), 537–557. http://doi.org/10.1177/0011128701047004003

Green, D. P., & Winik, D. (2010). Using random judge assignments to estimate the effects of incarceration and probation on recidivism among drug offenders. *Criminology*, *48*(2), 357–387. http://doi.org/10.1111/j.1745-9125.2010.00189.x

Harding, D. J., Siegel, J. A., & Morenoff, J. D. (f.c.). Custodial parole sanctions and earnings after release from prison. Forthcoming, *Social Forces*.

Harris, A. (2016). *A pound of flesh: Monetary sanctions as punishment for the poor* (1st ed.). New York: Russell Sage Foundation.

Jacobs, J. B. (2015). *The eternal criminal record*. Cambridge, MA: Harvard University Press.

Jannetta, J., Breaux, J., Ho, H., & Porter, J. (2014). *Examining racial and ethnic disparities in probation revocation*. Washington, DC: Urban Institute.

Jolliffe, D., & Hedderman, C. (2012, December 6). Investigating the impact of custody on reoffending using propensity score matching. *Crime and Delinquency*, *5*, 1–27.

Kaeble, D., Glaze, L. E., Tsoutis, A., & Minton, T. (2015). *Correctional populations in the United States, 2014*. Washington, DC: Bureau of Justice Statistics.

Kaeble, D., Maruschak, L. M., & Bonczar, T. P. (2015). *Probation and parole in the United States, 2014*. Washington, DC: Bureau of Justice Statistics.

Kim, B., Spohn, C., & Hedberg, E. C. (2015). Federal sentencing as a complex collaborative process: Judges, prosecutors, judge—prosecutor dyads, and disparity in sentencing. *Criminology*, *53*(4), 597–623. http://doi.org/10.1111/1745-9125.12090

Kingsnorth, R. F., MacIntosh, R. C., & Sutherland, S. (2002). Criminal charge or probation violation? Prosecutorial discretion and implications for research in criminal court processing. *Criminology*, *40*(3), 553–578. http://doi.org/10.1111/j.1745-9125.2002.tb00966.x

Klingele, C. (2013). Rethinking the use of community. *Journal of Criminal Law and Criminology*, *103*(4), 1015–1070.

Kohler-Hausmann, I. (2013). Misdemeanor justice: Control without conviction. *American Journal of Sociology*, *119*(2), 351–393. http://doi.org/10.1086/674743

Kutateladze, B. L., Andiloro, N. R., Johnson, B. D., & Spohn, C. C. (2014). Cumulative disadvantage: Examining racial and ethnic disparity in prosecution and sentencing. *Criminology*, *52*(3), 514–551. http://doi.org/10.1111/1745-9125.12047

Lerman, A. E., & Weaver, V. M. (2014). *Arresting citizenship: The democratic consequences of American crime control*. Chicago; London: University of Chicago Press.

Lieber, D. (2016). Watchdog: Pay-or-go-to-jail policy makes probation officers bill collectors. *The Dallas Morning News*. Retrieved from www.dallasnews.com/investigations/watchdog/20160401-watchdog-pay-or-go-to-jail-policy-makes-probation-officers-bill-collectors.ece

Loeffler, C. E. (2013). Does imprisonment alter the life course? Evidence on crime and employment from a natural experiment. *Criminology*, *51*(1), 137–166. http://doi.org/10.1111/1745-9125.12000

Maruschak, L. M., & Bonczar, T. P. (2013). *Probation and parole in the United States, 2012*. Washington, D.C.: Bureau of Justice Statistics.

May, D. C., Wood, P. B., & Eades, A. (2008). Lessons learned from punishment exchange rates: Implications for theory, research, and correctional policy. *The Journal of Behavior Analysis of Offender and Victim Treatment and Prevention*, *1*(2), 187–201. http://doi.org/10.1037/h0100443

Morris, N., & Tonry, M. H. (1990). *Between prison and probation: Intermediate punishments in a rational sentencing system*. New York: Oxford University Press.

Nagin, D. S., Cullen, F. T., & Jonson, C. L. (2009). Imprisonment and reoffending. *Crime and Justice*, *38*(1), 115–200. http://doi.org/10.1086/599202

Natapoff, A. (2011). Misdemeanors. *Southern California Law Review*, *85*, 1313–1376.

Nguyen, A. P., Harding, D. J., Morenoff, J. D., & Bushway, S. D. (2016). *The effects of community supervision on recidivism and labor market outcomes: Evidence from a natural experiment.* Presented at the American Society of Criminology Annual Meeting, New Orleans, LA.

Pager, D. (2007). *Marked: Race, crime, and finding work in an era of mass incarceration.* Chicago: University of Chicago Press.

Petersilia, J. (2002). *Reforming probation and parole.* Lanham, MD: American Correctional Association.

Pettit, B. (2012). *Invisible men: Mass incarceration and the myth of black progress.* New York: Russell Sage.

Phelps, M. S. (2013). The paradox of probation: Community supervision in the age of mass incarceration. *Law & Policy, 35*(1–2), 51–80. http://doi.org/10.1111/lapo.12002

Phelps, M. S. (2015). The curious disappearance of sociological research on probation supervision. *Criminal Justice and Law Enforcement Annual: Global Perspectives,* 7 *(New Series Volume 2),* 1–30.

Phelps, M. S. (2017). Mass probation: Toward a more robust theory of state variation in punishment. *Punishment & Society, 19*(1), 53–73. http://doi.org/10.1177/1462474516649174

Rios, V. M. (2011). *Punished: Policing the lives of Black and Latino boys.* New York: NYU Press.

Robinson, G., McNeill, F., & Maruna, S. (2013). Punishment in society: The improbable persistence of probation and other community sanctions and measures. In *The Sage handbook of punishment and society* (pp. 321–340). London: Sage. Retrieved from https://us.sagepub.com/en-us/nam/the-sage-handbook-of-punishment-and-society/book233796#features

Rodriguez, N., & Webb, V. J. (2007). Probation violations, revocations, and imprisonment: The decisions of probation officers, prosecutors, and judges pre- and post-mandatory drug treatment. *Criminal Justice Policy Review, 18*(1), 3–30. http://doi.org/10.1177/0887403406292956

Rothman, D. J. (2002). *Conscience and convenience: The asylum and its alternatives in progressive America* (Rev. ed). New York: Aldine de Gruyter.

Shannon, S., Uggen, C., Schnittker, J., Massoglia, M., Thompson, M. & Wakefield, S. (f.c.) The growth, scope, and spatial distribution of people with felony records in the United State. Forthcoming in *Demography.*

Simon, J. (1993). *Poor discipline: Parole and the social control of the underclass, 1890–1990.* Studies in Crime and Justice. Chicago: University of Chicago.

Simon, J. (2013). Punishment and the political technologies of the body. In *The Sage handbook of punishment and society* (pp. 60–89). London: Sage. Retrieved from https://us.sagepub.com/en-us/nam/the-sage-handbook-of-punishment-and-society/book233796#features

Simons, R. L., Burt, C. H., Barr, A. B., Lei, M.-K., & Stewart, E. (2014). Incorporating routine activities, activity spaces, and situational definitions into the social schematic theory of crime. *Criminology, 52*(4), 655–687.

Spohn, C. (2015). Evolution of sentencing research. *Criminology & Public Policy, 14*(2), 225–232. https://doi.org/10.1111/1745-9133.12125

Stevens-Martin, K., Oyewole, O., & Hipolito, C. (2014). Technical revocations of probation in one jurisdiction: Uncovering the hidden realities. *Federal Probation, 78,* 16.

Stuart, F. (2016). Becoming "copwise": Policing, culture, and the collateral consequences of street-level criminalization. *Law & Society Review, 50*(2), 279–313. http://doi.org/10.1111/lasr.12201

Taxman, F. S. (2012). Probation, intermediate sanctions, and community-based corrections. In J. Petersilia & K. R. Reitz (Eds.), *The Oxford handbook of sentencing and corrections* (pp. 363–385). New York: Oxford University Press.

Tonry, M., & Lynch, M. (1996). Intermediate sanctions. *Crime and Justice, 20,* 99–144.

Tonry, M., & Melewski, M. (2008). The Malign effects of drug and crime control policies on Black Americans. *Crime and Justice,* 37(1), 1–44. doi:10.1086/588492.

Tubman-Carbone, H., & Glaze, L. (2013). *Census of adult probation supervising agencies (capsa): A resource for probation research Heather Tubman-Carbone, Westat.* Presented at the American Society of Criminology, Atlanta, GA.

Uggen, C., Vuolo, M., Lageson, S., Ruhland, E., & Whitham, H. K. (2014). The edge of stigma: An experimental audit of the effects of low-level criminal records on employment. *Criminology, 52*(4), 627–654. http://doi.org/10.1111/1745-9125.12051

Van Cleve, N. G. (2016). *Crook county: Racism and injustice in America's largest criminal court*. Stanford, CA: Stanford Law Books.

Vera Institute of Justice. (2013). *The potential of community corrections to improve safety and reduce incarceration*. New York: Vera Institute of Justice.

Wakefield, S., & Uggen, C. (2010). Incarceration and stratification. *Annual Review of Sociology, 36*(1), 387–406. http://doi.org/10.1146/annurev.soc.012809.102551

Welsh, B. C., & Rocque, M. (2014). When crime prevention harms: A review of systematic reviews. *Journal of Experimental Criminology, 10*(3), 245–266. http://doi.org/10.1007/s11292-014-9199-2

Western, B. (2006). *Punishment and inequality in America*. New York: Russell Sage.

Western, B., Braga, A., Hureau, D., & Sirois, C. (2016). Study retention as bias reduction in a hard-to-reach population. *Proceedings of the National Academy of Sciences, 113*(20), 5477–5485. doi:10.1073/pnas.1604138113.

Wooldredge, J., Frank, J., Goulette, N., & Travis, L. (2015). Is the impact of cumulative disadvantage on sentencing greater for black defendants? *Criminology & Public Policy, 14*(2), 187–223. https://doi.org/10.1111/1745-9133.12124

Appendix A
COMPARING BJS AND NSDUH PROBATION ESTIMATES

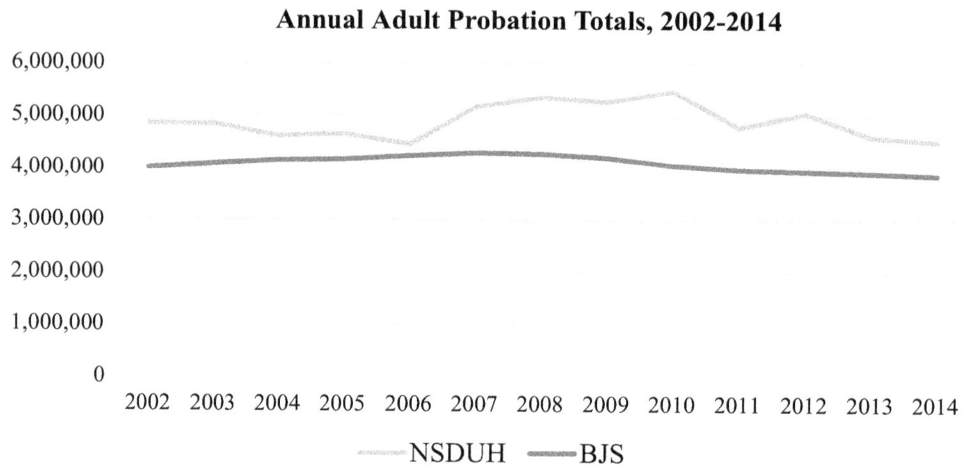

Annual Adult Probation Totals, 2002–2014	*NSDUH (Weighted Average 2010–2014)*	*BJS (2012)*
Black	18%	30%
Hispanic	19%	13%
Non-Hispanic White	58%	54%
Male	70%	76%

Note: The BJS probation population reflects an estimated year-end count for all reporting jurisdictions (as available online through the Corrections Statistical Analysis Tool for Probation, generated June 9, 2017). The NSDUH totals reflect the estimated number of household respondents nationally who report having been on probation during the prior year. Race and gender percentages are only reported by some jurisdictions to the BJS (Maruschak and Bonczar, 2013).

Appendix B

JAIL AND PRISON INMATES ON PAROLE AT TIME OF ARREST

Percent on Parole at Time of Arrest	
Jail Inmates (2002)	12%
State and Federal Prisoners (2004)	18%

Most Serious Legal Status	
Jail Inmates (2002)	
Convicted of New Crime	24%
Charged With New Crime and/or Revocation for New Arrest	40%
Revoked (or Awaiting Hearing) for Other Supervision Violations	24%
Incarcerated for Other Reasons	12%
State and Federal Prisoners (2004)	
Convicted of New Crime	75%
Revoked for New Arrest	4%
Revoked for Other Supervision Violations	18%
Incarcerated for Other Reasons	3%

Note: Categories sum to 100% because only most serious legal status is represented. Many inmates fit multiple categories (e.g. both a new conviction and revocation). Cases with missing data on all legal status variables (and inmates held for supervision violations without revocation or new offense charges filed) are included in the residual category (Incarcerated for Other Reasons).

3

SOWING THE SEEDS OF FUTURE JUSTICE SYSTEM DISPARITIES

School Punishment and the School-to-Prison Pipeline

Aaron Kupchik and Akilah Alleyne

The term "school-to-prison pipeline" refers to a process by which school treatment of children places them at increased risk of future incarceration. This school treatment can include denial of needed services to youth, out-of-school suspension, expulsion, and arrest. As many criminologists and other scholars have pointed out in recent years, school suspensions have significantly increased over the past few decades, as has the placement of police officers in schools and the use of other security practices (Hirschfield and Celinska, 2011; Kupchik, 2016), making school punishment and arrest more likely than in prior eras. This criminalization of students (Hirschfield, 2008) has been grouped together with broader criminal justice trends, such as mass incarceration, as both are symptoms of what Simon calls "governing through crime" (Simon, 2007).

School punishment and policing can have many harmful consequences for students, as we discuss below. When children are excluded from school and/or denied necessary educational and social supports (especially for students with disabilities), they become less likely to benefit from the school's ability to suppress delinquency and are instead given more unsupervised time on the streets. They also build school disciplinary records that can place them at greater risk of harsher school punishments in the future. And, research finds that more police in schools is associated with more arrests, particularly for minor misbehaviors (e.g., Na and Gottfredson, 2013; Nance, 2016). Though the term "school-to-prison pipeline" may be an oversimplification, the term brings attention to an important problem within public schools across the U.S. (see Kupchik, 2014).

School punishment and the school-to-prison pipeline are thus very relevant to our understanding of punishment decisions. Further, because school punishment is disproportionately felt by socially marginalized students (see Skiba, Arredondo, and Williams, 2014; Skiba et al., 2016), it is an important site at which disparity in future punishment decisions is shaped. Indeed, the problem of racial disproportionality in school punishment has received a great deal of attention from scholars as well as policymakers, including the Department of Education's Office of Civil Rights. Yet youth of color are not the only students at heightened risk of experiencing the school-to-prison pipeline; students with disabilities, LGBTQ youth, and others are as well (Skiba et al., 2016). In the pages that follow, we explore this in greater depth. After describing the school-to-prison pipeline and its consequences, we then provide exploratory analyses that consider the extent to which social status relates to school punishment and, as a result, influences disparity in future punishment decisions.

Harms of the School-to-Prison Pipeline

Strict and consistent rule enforcement is important for teaching children behavior standards and managing school environments (Arum, 2003). But since the 1990s, schools across the U.S. have gone well beyond such a standard, with exclusionary punishments (most often, suspension) typically in response to minor forms of misbehavior. Indeed, research finds that suspension is most commonly used to respond to minor behaviors such as defiance of authority or insubordination (Fabelo et al., 2011), behavior that, in prior years, might have resulted only in a trip to the principal's office and afterschool detention.

There is no credible evidence to suggest that growing numbers of suspensions for minor misbehaviors prevent future misbehaviors or school crime. In fact, some scholars suggest that it might cause increases in school misbehavior (see Hemphill et al., 2006). This is because an overly punitive environment can alienate students and disrupt their bonds to the school, deteriorating the school social climate (Fine et al., 2004; Rios, 2011). Given that several prior studies find that schools with more inclusive school social climates—where students feel respected, listened to, and valued as community members—have lower misbehavior rates (see Cook et al., 2010), the overuse of suspension might indeed make school safety worse, not better.

Prior research demonstrates many collateral harms that stem from student criminalization, affecting schools, families, and communities, not just the individual students who are suspended or arrested. Perry and Morris (2014), for example, find that, in schools with relatively high suspension rates, students who are *not* suspended do worse on standardized tests, compared to those in similarly situated schools, demonstrating the corrosive effect of high suspension rates on entire schools. Kupchik and Mowen (2016) illustrate how entire families suffer as a result of children's exclusion from school, including experiences such as loss of work, family conflict, and even physical symptoms, based on a series of interviews with parents whose children have been excluded from schools (Kupchik and Mowen, 2016). And Kupchik and Catlaw (2015) find that entire communities can be impacted by school suspension, since a student's experience with school suspension is predictive of lower probability of voting and volunteering in one's community years later (see also Kupchik, 2016).

But the most important consequences that result from the criminalization of students are felt by the students themselves. These harms include greater potential for exposure to justice system involvement and academic failure. For example, in *Homeroom Security*, Kupchik (2010) notes the irony of school suspension as a response to the many students whose classroom misbehavior is, according to the teachers he spoke to, the result of their academic frustration. In other words, many students who are behind their peers in understanding course material become frustrated and say or do something they shouldn't; in response, schools suspend them from school, causing them to fall even further behind. Research shows that suspended youth are at increased risk of failing courses (Balfanz et al., 2015), being held back a grade, and failing to graduate (Fabelo et al., 2011). Failing to graduate high school in turn diminishes job prospects (Rumberger, 1987), resulting in an indirect effect of school discipline on future financial insecurity. Suspension of students with working parents also means they have more free unsupervised time, which could put them at greater risk of getting in trouble in their communities.

The criminalization of students isn't limited to school suspensions but also includes a greater police presence in schools (Hirschfield, 2008). Though much is still unknown about how the presence of police, commonly known as School Resource Officers (SROs), affects schools, research finds that their presence results in increased arrests for minor offenses (Na and Gottfredson, 2013; Nance, 2016). Other research suggests that the presence of SROs might contribute to the overall criminalization of youth in more subtle ways, increasing the likelihood of criminal behavior as acts of defiance (Rios, 2011).

The criminalization of students thus increases the risk that students become involved in the justice system, in several ways. Most directly, a police presence in schools can increase the risk of arrest at schools. Indirectly, increased risk of school suspension makes it more likely that students fail, academically, and fail to graduate from high school. This, in itself, is an important risk factor for future justice system involvement (Western, 2006). Further, the criminalization of students might make students more likely to commit crimes; this can occur if students respond to school policing and punishment with deviant or criminal identities (Rios, 2011), or if excessive time spent out of school results in decreased supervision and increased criminal activity. When one considers the fact that compulsory attendance laws mean that the vast majority of youth attend public schools, it becomes clear that school policing and punishment, which result in what is called a school-to-prison pipeline, have important effects on risk of justice system involvement at an early age, with clear ramifications for future punishment decisions.

Racial Disproportionality

Recent studies find that students of color, particularly Black students, are more likely to experience exclusionary school discipline such as expulsion and out-of-school suspension (Skiba, Mediratta, and Rausch, 2016; Wallace, Goodkind, and Bachman, 2008). Further, the problem of racial disproportionality seems to be growing; the risk of out-of-school suspension for African American students increased from two times greater than the risk faced by White students in 1970, to three times the risk faced by White students in 2002. Black students are now almost four times more likely to receive one or more out-of-school suspensions or be expelled from school, compared to White students (U.S. Department of Education, 2014). Studies also suggest that Latino/a students have a greater likelihood of experiencing suspension and/or expulsion than White youth (Skiba et al., 2011), even when their levels of misbehavior are less than or equal to those of White students (Peguero and Shekarkhar, 2011). Such instances of racial disproportionality begin as early as *preschool* for students of color (U.S. Department of Education, 2014), and exist even when controlling for self-reported student misbehavior (e.g., Rocque and Paternoster, 2011; Skiba et al., 2014).

Studies examining the intersectionality of race and gender in school punishment find that Black males and females have greater likelihoods of experiencing disproportionate punishments when compared to other races and ethnicities (Anyon et al., 2014; Losen and Skiba, 2010; Morris, 2012; Wallace et al., 2008). For example, Black males have significantly higher likelihoods of being suspended or expelled from school (Darensbourg, Perez, and Blake, 2010; Shollenberger, 2014; Townsend, 2000) than their White counterparts (Bradshaw et al., 2010; Skiba et al., 2014; Wallace et al., 2008). Moreover, scholars find that Black females, too, have significantly higher rates of out-of-school suspension when compared to Latina and White students (Finn and Servoss, 2015; Toldson, McGee and Lemmons, 2015).

There is still limited research on the plight of Black females' experiences with the school-to-prison pipeline. However, Black females are more vulnerable to a variety of risk factors that put them at risk of school punishment (Crenshaw, 2011; Morris, 2012), and such experiences are unique from those of Black males, as well as females from other races/ethnicities (Crenshaw, 2011; Morris, 2012). Scholars find that Black girls and women are victims of exacerbated stereotypical definitions of Black femininity and behavior in ways that cause them to be singled out for punishment for acts such as being "loud" or "aggressive" (Morris, 2012), particularly when they are seen as deviating from White middle-class social norms. Compared to White women, Black women are 6.9 times more likely to have contact with the criminal justice system, while Latina women are 2.5 times more likely (Crenshaw, 2011).

Prior research suggests that the racially disproportionate rates of school punishment are not due to different rates of misbehavior (Kupchik, 2016; Losen and Skiba, 2010; Skiba et al., 2002). Rather, classroom and school-level factors, such as implicit racial bias and stereotypes, and faculty and staffs' subjective perceptions of defiance or disrespect from students of color (Kahn, Goff, and Glaser, 2016; Okonofua and Eberhardt, 2015) appear to be responsible for much of the racial disparities in exclusionary school discipline (Gregory and Weinstein, 2008; Payne and Welch, 2010; Skiba et al., 2002). Teachers and other school staff members demonstrate subtle biases, whereby they may be quicker to view youth of color as defiant and disorderly and are quicker to respond punitively than they might be to White students.

Research finds school-level effects as well. That is, schools with greater proportions of poor students and students of color are more likely to use punitive disciplinary practices such as in- and out-of-school suspension and zero tolerance policies (Nance, 2013; Payne and Welch, 2010; Welch and Payne, 2010, 2012). Schools with more youth of color are also more likely to have metal detectors and rely on police and other forms of rigid control (Irwin, Davidson, and Hall-Sanchez, 2013; Kupchik and Ward, 2014).

Racially disproportionate school discipline thus means that youth of color are more likely to suffer the harms of the school-to-prison pipeline that we describe above, particularly increased contact with police and the criminal justice system (Darensbourg, Perez, and Blake, 2010; Gabbidon and Greene, 2016; New York Civil Liberties Union, 2011; Wolf and Kupchik, 2017). In this way, the education system serves as a disproportionate path to incarceration. Thus, the disproportionate use of discipline on youth of color only exacerbates existing racial inequality in future justice system exposure.

Other Sources of Disparity

Racial disparities in school punishment are perhaps the most studied type of disparity, but race/ethnicity is not the only source of disparity in school punishment. Other student characteristics such as being low-income, having learning or behavioral disabilities, or LGBTQ status, also relate to greater likelihood of harsh school punishment.

Certainly, school administrators have discretion to punish students with disabilities who violate their schools' codes of conduct. But federal law puts restrictions on this discretion through the 2004 IDEA (Individuals with Disabilities Education Act); under certain circumstances, administrators can be limited in the number of days that they exclude disabled students from schools or for what behaviors.[1] Despite the fact that there are more restrictions on the use of school punishment for students with disabilities than for others, students with disabilities are still at greater risk of school punishment than others. Recent research finds that nationally, students with disabilities are nearly twice as likely to receive an out-of-school suspension than non-disabled peers (Losen and Gillespie, 2012), and when disabled students receive suspensions, they tend to be for longer periods of time than received by others (Balfanz, Byrnes, and Fox, 2015). Further, the intersection of disability status and race/ethnicity can put students at even greater risk of school punishment, with African American students who have disabilities at substantially greater risk of punishment than others (Losen and Gillespie, 2012).

Low-income students are also at greater risk of school punishment than middle-class and wealthy students (e.g., Wu et al., 1982). These effects are seen at both the school- and student-levels. At the school level, research finds that schools with larger populations of students receiving free- or reduced-price lunch (an imperfect but available proxy for the size of a school's low-income population) are more likely to have criminal justice-oriented security practices such as the presence of police officers and drug-sniffing police dogs on campus (Kupchik and Ward, 2014), as well as relatively high rates of suspension and student arrests (Ramey, 2015). At the student level, studies find that, even when controlling for measures of student misbehavior, low-income students are at heightened risk of school suspension and expulsion (Rocque and Paternoster, 2011; Skiba et al., 2014; Wu et al., 1982).

Though scholars have only recently turned to sexuality and gender identity as risk factors for school punishment, recent research finds that LGBTQ and gender non-conforming youth are indeed at heightened risk of school punishment. Himmelstein and Bruckner (2011), for example, find that youth who report same-sex attraction are at greater risk than others of being expelled from school, even when controlling for self-reported rates of misbehavior (see also Mitchum and Moodie-Mills, 2014; Snapp et al., 2015).

Prior work also finds that immigration status can shape a student's risk of school punishment. For example, Anthony Peguero et al. (2015) find that Black youth who are children (and grandchildren) of immigrants, as well as Latino/a grandchildren of immigrants, are more likely to be disciplined at school than White youth, despite similar levels of misbehaviors.

This body of research demonstrates how students who occupy socially and economically marginalized positions are at heightened risk of experiencing exclusionary school punishment and suffering the harms of the school-to-prison pipeline. Overall, students of color, low-income students, students with learning and behavioral disabilities, and LGBTQ students occupy a different social space than White, middle-class, non-disabled, heterosexual youth. Each of these statuses can be a social stigma, possibly leading school staff to view them as deviant and deserving of punishment.

Based on this accumulated body of research, we believe that scholars studying school punishment should turn toward a more general view of status. Though race/ethnicity, poverty, sexual orientation/identity, and disabilities are each important in their own right, a more general investigation into how social status influences school punishment seems warranted as well. Such an investigation could help us understand whether these and other markers of lower status tap into broader themes, such as cultural, social, or political capital. That is, are students who occupy stigmatized or marginalized positions at greater risk of punishment in part because of their marginal status, and a corresponding lack of social/political/financial power?

Exploratory Analysis

To further investigate how social status influences punishment, we now turn to exploratory analyses, using data from the High School Longitudinal Study, 2009–2013. HSLS:09 is a longitudinal, nationally representative study of a randomly selected sample of fall-term 9th-graders from 944 eligible public and private high schools. We use the publicly available version of the dataset, obtained from the Inter-University Consortium for Political and Social Research (ICPSR) through the National Center for Education Statistics. The HSLS:09 data explore secondary and post-secondary plans of students by examining factors that influence students' attitudes, behaviors, and decisions towards high school courses and college majors. As part of the core research questions, data on high school students' interests leading into and out of science, technology, engineering, and mathematics (STEM) paths are also collected. Thus, some of the questions in the questionnaires for students, and math and science teachers, are STEM focused as part of the study. The base-year survey was administered in the 2009–10 school year to students who were in 9th grade and collected information on student home life, student and parent background information, school climate, teacher background and preparation, and classroom practices.

There were 25,184 eligible student participants; 21,444 student participants responded and completed the base year survey questionnaire (85.7% weighted, 85.1% unweighted). Students from the 9th grade cohort participated in the first follow-up during their 11th grade year. The response rate for the first follow-up was 82.0%, and 81.8% (unweighted), and included 939 schools that were still eligible from the base year. Students were then randomly selected from the 939 schools; they completed all surveys and the mathematics assessment online using computers in their schools. Surveys were also administered to parents, teachers, and counselors online, in person, or through computer-assisted phone via request. Teacher responses and transfer students associated with ineligible schools were not included in the first follow-up. The total sample size sample was n = 18,623 student respondents. Due to missing values, our final analytical sample size is n = 15,772.

We use these data to explore punishment rates among students who are socially marginalized and economically disadvantaged. School punishment is measured in the first follow-up parent survey. Parents are asked whether their children had ever been suspended or expelled from school. Overall, 12% of students had been suspended or expelled. To consider how social status and disadvantage relates to punishment, we analyze how suspension relates to a number of social status variables, including school bonds, socio-economic status (SES), sex, English language learner status, and race/ethnicity. English language learner status information comes from the first follow-up parent survey; parents were asked whether the students had ever been enrolled in an English learning program during high school. Information on sex and race/ethnicity are self-reported by respondents in the baseline interview.

Our variable for SES is taken from the baseline survey. It is a standardized measure, provided in the HSLS, that is based on parent/guardians' education, occupation, and family income. The SES variable allows us to examine whether there are any differences in suspension or expulsion across socio-economic status. Our variable for school bonds consists of the mean response to three questions asked of students in the baseline student survey: whether they feel *safe* at school, whether they feel *proud* to be part of school, and whether getting *good grades* is important. Each is measured along the scale: 1 = Strongly Agree, 2 = Agree, 3 = Disagree, 4 = Strongly Disagree. All of these items measuring attitudes and feelings towards school were reverse coded, so that higher values represent stronger school bonds. An exploratory factor analysis confirmed that the three questions load highly onto a single factor, and the resulting index has an alpha reliability coefficient of 0.65. School bonds represent a form of social capital; students with stronger bonds are likely to be more central to the school community, whereas students with weaker bonds are somewhat marginalized. Given that we seek to explore a variety of sources of student marginalization, this offers a relevant and novel view into variations in school punishment.

To analyze how school bonds and SES relate to the likelihood of punishment, we consider the proportion of students who are suspended or expelled, by quartile of each of these two continuous measures. These results are presented in Figure 3.1 and

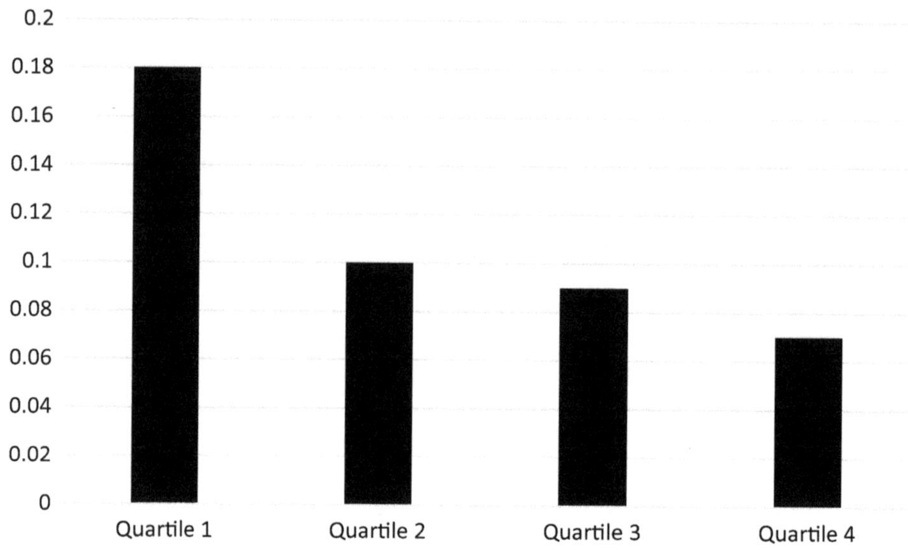

Figure 3.1 Proportion of Students Suspended or Expelled, by School Bonds (Quartiles)

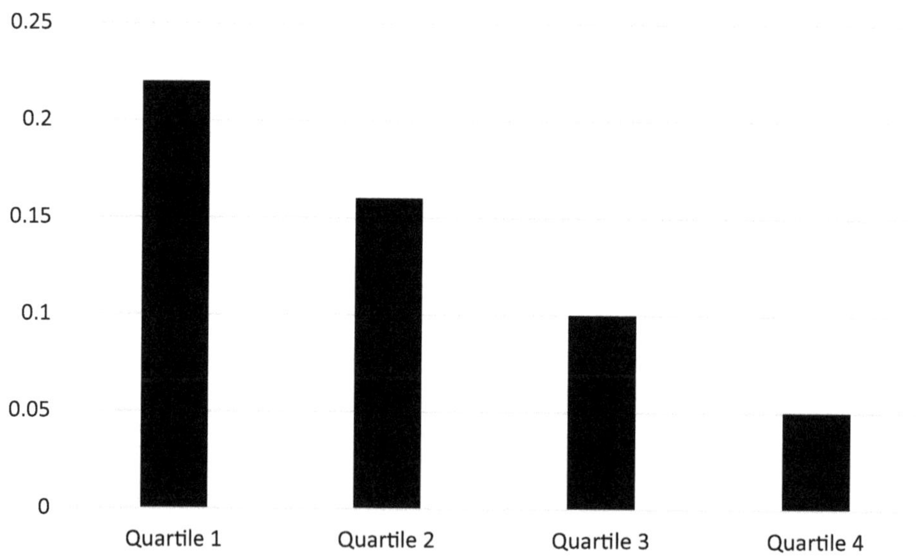

Figure 3.2 Proportion of Students Suspended or Expelled, by SES (Quartiles)

Figure 3.2. We also show the proportion of students of each recorded race/ethnicity who are suspended or expelled in Figure 3.3, and results for English language learner (ELL) status and sex in Figure 3.4. The results show significant differences in suspension/expulsion by sex and for each racial/ethnic group, relative to others. We also find that suspension rates vary significantly by quartile of SES and school bonds, based on ANOVA tests. As we discuss below, the only result that was not statistically significant was our comparison of ELL youth to other youth.

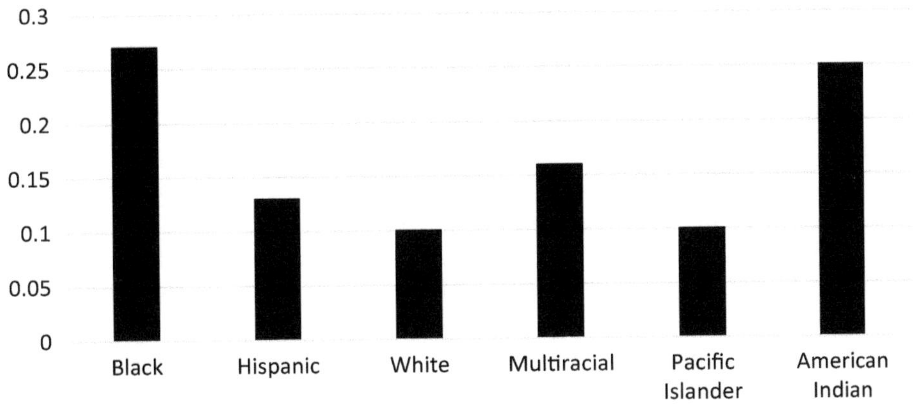

Figure 3.3 Proportion of Students Suspended or Expelled, by Race/Ethnicity

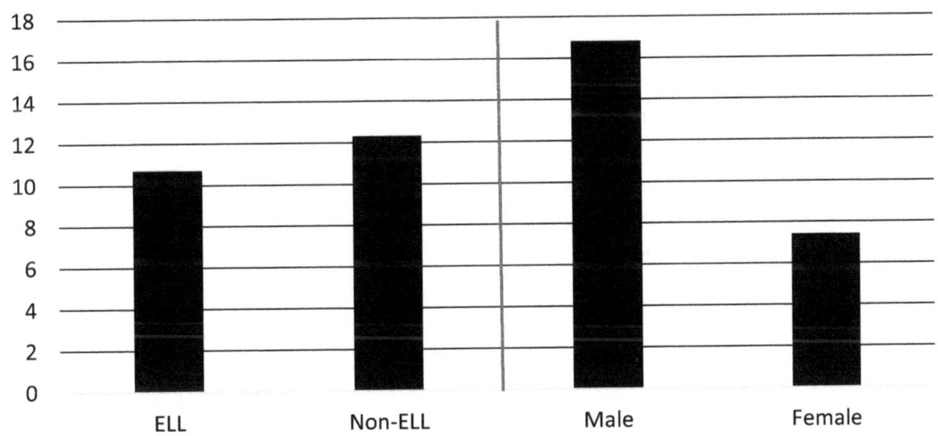

Figure 3.4 Proportion of Students Suspended or Expelled, by English Language Learner Status and by Sex

Figure 3.1 illustrates the proportion of students in each quartile of our school bond measure that were suspended or expelled. The relationship is clear, with 18% of students in the lowest quartile of school bonds having been suspended or expelled, but only 7% of students in the highest quartile. A similar pattern is evident in Figure 3.2, where we show the proportion of students in each quartile of SES who are suspended or expelled. The rate of suspension/expulsion consistently declines with higher levels of SES, ranging from 22% to only 5% in the highest SES quartile.

Figure 3.3 reports the proportion of youth of each racial/ethnic group who were suspended or expelled. As expected, Black youth are much more likely to receive school punishment; 27% of Black youth experienced exclusionary school punishment, as opposed to only 10% of White youth. Though there are far fewer of them in our sample, American Indian youth also show high rates of suspension and expulsion, as 25% report such punishment.

Figure 3.4 includes two separate analyses. The first is a comparison of the rate of exclusionary punishment among youth who have ever been in ELL courses, compared to others. While those in ELL courses have lower rates of exclusionary punishment, this is the only result shown that is not statistically significant at $p < .05$. The second result in Figure 3.4 is a comparison of males to females, where we find that 17% of males report exclusionary punishment as opposed to only 7% of female respondents.

While these are only bivariate, preliminary findings, they both mirror prior results and begin to extend prior work by considering additional avenues of student marginalization. Results for sex, race/ethnicity, and SES are indeed what one would expect based on prior work. But by comparing school punishment rates across students who are well-bonded to schools and those who may be socially marginalized, and also by considering how English language learner status may relate to school punishment, we offer novel analyses of additional ways that marginalized or low status students might be at greater risk of school punishment

Conclusion

Above we review research on school punishment, and how it is an important precursor to justice system involvement. It is very clear that schools across the U.S. are quicker to exclude students than were schools a generation ago, most commonly via out-of-school suspension, for relatively minor offenses. It is also clear that this increased rate and severity of school punishment has the potential to increase the likelihood of future justice system involvement. School suspension can mark students as trouble-makers, set them on a path for increased misbehavior, interrupt their educational paths, make high school graduation less likely, and result in arrest and/or incarceration.

Not only are schools an important precursor of future justice system involvement, they are also a site at which disparities in who becomes entangled with the justice system develop and grow. Prior research has established racial disproportionality in school punishment as a substantial problem on a national scale. As we discuss, other disparities are worth consideration as well. While youth of color are undeniably at greater risk than White students of school punishment, a small but growing body of research finds that other sources of marginalization matter as well, including disability status, gender identity and sexual orientation, immigration status, and socio-economic status. To the extent that school punishment is a response to students who violate social norms or lack social/political/financial capital, other sources of marginalization or disadvantage might similarly serve as risk factors for the harmful effects of exclusionary school punishment.

Our exploratory analysis is intended to both reinforce prior research findings and begin a conversation into other sources of marginalization and school punishment. Our analyses are preliminary; one particularly important limitation is that they do not control for additional influences, such as student misbehavior. But they do find that potential sources of marginalization other than race/ethnicity—including sex, SES, and school bonds—may matter as well. We encourage other researchers to continue to explore understudied sources of student marginalization that may increase their risk of punishment.

Educational achievement is commonly discussed as a means for avoiding poverty and problems such as incarceration (see Kupchik, 2016). Yet, research on school punishment finds that some school practices, such as overuse of exclusionary punishment, place students at increased risk of the future problems that education is intended to help them avoid. Moreover, students of color and other marginalized youth disproportionately feel these harms; thus schools become sites at which future justice system disparities emerge and grow.

We end with a note of optimism. We are encouraged by the fact that a handbook in the ASC Division on Corrections & Sentencing Handbook Series would include a chapter on school punishment. The overuse of harsh school punishment is indeed an important risk factor for future justice system involvement, and we are grateful that it is recognized as such, with attention being paid to the long-term consequences of school punishment. Our hope is that such recognition represents an important step toward effectively addressing this problem.

Note

1 https://sites.ed.gov/idea.

References

Anyon, Y., Jenson, J. M., Altschul, I., Farrar, J., McQueen, J., Greer, E., . . . Simmons, J. (2014). The persistent effect of race and the promise of alternatives to suspension in school discipline outcomes. *Children and Youth Services Review*, *44*, 379–386.

Arum, R. (2003). *Judging school discipline: The crisis of moral authority*. Cambridge, MA: Harvard University Press.

Balfanz, R., Byrnes, V., & Fox, J. (2015). Sent home and put off-track: The antecedents, disproportionalities, and consequences of being suspended in the 9th grade. In D. J. Losen (Ed.), *Closing the school discipline gap: Equitable remedies for excessive exclusion* (pp. 17–30). New York: Teachers College Press.

Bradshaw, C. P., Mitchell, M. M., O'Brennan, L. M., & Leaf, P. J. (2010). Multilevel exploration of factors contributing to the overrepresentation of black students in office disciplinary referrals. *Journal of Educational Psychology*, *102*(2), 508.

Cook, P. J., Gottfredson, D. C., & Na, C. (2010). School crime control and prevention. *Crime and Justice*, *39*, 313–440.

Crenshaw, K. W. (2011). From private violence to mass incarceration: Thinking intersectionally about women, race, and social control. *UCLA Law Review*, *59*, 1418.

Darensbourg, A., Perez, E., & Blake, J. (2010). Overrepresentation of African American males in exclusionary discipline: The role of school-based mental health professionals in dismantling the school to prison pipeline. *Journal of African American Males in Education*, *1*(3), 196–211.

Fabelo, T., Thompson, M. D., Plotkin, M., Carmichael, D., Marchbanks, M. P. III, & Booth, E. A. (2011). *Breaking schools' rules: A statewide study of how school discipline relates to students' success and juvenile justice involvement*. New York: Council of State Governments Justice Center and Public Policy Research.

Fine, M., Burns, A., Payne, Y. A., & Torre, M. A. (2004). Civics lessons: The color and class of betrayal. *Teachers College Record, 106*, 2193–2223.

Finn, J. D., & Servoss, T. J. (2015). Security measures and discipline in American high schools. In D. J. Losen (Ed.), *Closing the school discipline gap: Equitable remedies for excessive exclusion* (pp. 44–58).

Gabbidon, S. L., & Greene, H. T. (2016). *Race and crime* (4th ed.). Thousand Oaks, CA: Sage Publications.

Gregory, A., & Weinstein, R. S. (2008). The discipline gap and African Americans: Defiance or cooperation in the high school classroom. *Journal of School Psychology, 46*(4), 455–475.

Hemphill, S. A., Toumbourou, J. W., Herrenkohl, T. I., McMorris, B. J., & Catalano, R. J. (2006). The effect of school suspensions and arrests on subsequent adolescent antisocial behavior in Australia and the United States. *Journal of Adolescent Health, 39*, 736–744.

Himmelstein, K. E. W., & Bruckner, H. (2011). Criminal-justice and school sanctions against non-heterosexual youth: A national longitudinal study. *Pediatrics, 127*, 49–57.

Hirschfield, P. (2008). Preparing for prison? The criminalization of school discipline in the USA. *Theoretical Criminology*, 12(1), 79–101.

Hirschfield, P., & Celinska, K. (2011). Beyond fear: Sociological perspectives on the criminalization of school discipline. *Sociology Compass*, 5(1), 1–12.

Irwin, K., Davidson, J., & Hall-Sanchez, A. (2013). The race to punish in American schools: Class and race predictors of punitive school-crime control. *Critical Criminology, 21*, 47–71.

Kahn, K. B., Goff, P. A., & Glaser, J. (2016). Research and training to mitigate the effects of implicit stereotypes and masculinity threat on authority figures' interactions with adolescents and non-whites. In R. J. Skiba, K. Mediratta, & M. K. Rausch (Eds.), *Inequality in school discipline* (pp. 189–205). New York: Palgrave Macmillan.

Kupchik, A. (2010). *Homeroom security: School discipline in an age of fear*. New York: NYU Press.

Kupchik, A. (2014). The school-to-prison pipeline: Rhetoric and reality. In F. E. Zimring & D. S. Tanenhaus (Eds.), *Choosing the future for American juvenile justice* (pp. 94–119). New York: NYU Press.

Kupchik, A. (2016). *The real school safety problem: The long-term consequences of harsh school punishment*. Oakland, CA: University of California Press.

Kupchik, A., & Catlaw, T. (2015). Discipline and participation: The long-term effects of suspension and school security on the political and civic engagement of youth. *Youth and Society, 47*, 95–124.

Kupchik, A., & Mowen, T. (2016). Hurting families. In *The real school safety problem: The long-term consequences of harsh school punishment* (pp. 56–72). Oakland, CA: University of California Press.

Kupchik, A., & Ward, G. (2014). Race, poverty, and exclusionary school security: An empirical analysis of U.S. elementary, middle, and high schools. *Youth Violence and Juvenile Justice, 12*, 332–354.

Losen, D. J., & Gillespie, J. (2012). *Opportunities suspended: The disparate impact of disciplinary exclusion from school*. Los Angeles, CA: UCLA Civil Rights Project. Retrieved from http://civilrightsproject.ucla.edu/resources/projects/center-for-civil-rights-remedies/school-to-prison-folder/federal-reports/upcoming-ccrr-research/losen-gillespie-opportunity-suspended-2012.pdf.

Losen, D. J., & Skiba, R. J. (2010). *Suspended education urban middle schools in crisis*. Los Angeles, CA: UCLA The Civil Rights Project. Retrieved from http://escholarship.org/uc/item/8fh0s5dv.

Mitchum, P., & Moodie-Mills, A. C. (2014). *Beyond bullying: How hostile school climate perpetuates the school-to-prison-pipeline for LGBT youth*. Washington, DC: Center for American Progress.

Morris, M. W. (2012). *Race, gender, and the "school to prison pipeline": Expanding our discussion to include Black girls*. African American Policy Forum. http://schottfoundation.org/resources/race-gender-and-school-prison-pipeline-expanding-our-discussion-include-black-girls.

Na, C., & Gottfredson, D. C. (2013). Police officers in schools: Effects on school crime and the processing of offending behaviors. *Justice Quarterly, 30*, 619–650.

Nance, J. (2013). Students, security and race. *Emory Law Journal, 63*, 1–57.

Nance, J. (2016). Students, police and the school-to-prison pipeline. *Washington University Law Review, 93*, 919–987.

New York Civil Liberties Union. (2011). *Education interrupted: The growing use of suspensions in New York city's public schools*. New York: Author.

Okonofua, J. A., & Eberhardt, J. L. (2015). Two strikes race and the disciplining of young students. *Psychological Science, 26*(5), 617–624.

Payne, A. A., & Welch, K. (2010). Modeling the effects of racial threat on punitive and restorative school discipline practices. *Criminology, 48*, 1019–1062.

Peguero, A. A., & Shekarkhar, Z. (2011). Latino/a student misbehavior and school punishment. *Hispanic Journal of Behavioral Sciences, 33*(1), 54–70.

Peguero, A. A., Shekarkhar, Z., Popp, A. M., & Koo, D. J. (2015). Punishing the children of immigrants: Race, ethnicity, generational status, student misbehavior, and school discipline. *Journal of Immigrant & Refugee Studies, 13*, 200–220.

Perry, B. L., & Morris, E. W. (2014). Suspending progress: Collateral consequences of exclusionary punishment in public schools. *American Sociological Review, 79*(6), 1067–1087.

Ramey, D. M. (2015). The social structure of criminalized and medicalized school discipline. *Sociology of Education, 88*, 181–201.

Rios, V. M. (2011). *Punished: Policing the lives of Black and Latino boys*. New York: NYU Press.

Rocque, M., & Paternoster, R. (2011). Understanding the antecedents of the "school-to-jail" link: The relationship between race and school discipline. *The Journal of Criminal Law and Criminology, 101*, 633–665.

Rumberger, R. W. (1987). High school dropouts: A review of issues and evidence. *Review of Educational Research, 57*, 101–121.

Shollenberger, T. L. (2014). Racial disparities in school suspension and subsequent outcomes. In D. J. Losen (Ed.), *Closing the school discipline gap: Equitable remedies for excessive exclusion* (p. 31).

Simon, J. (2007). *Governing through crime: How the war on crime transformed American democracy and created a culture of fear*. New York: Oxford University Press.

Skiba, R. J., Arredondo, M. I., & Williams, N. T. (2014). More than a metaphor: The contribution of exclusionary discipline to a school-to-prison pipeline. *Equity & Excellence in Education, 47*(4), 546–564.

Skiba, R. J., Horner, R. H., Chung, C. G., Rausch, M. K., May, S. L., & Tobin, T. (2011). Race is not neutral: A national investigation of African American and Latino disproportionality in school discipline. *School Psychology Review, 40*(1), 85.

Skiba, R. J., Mediratta, K., & Rausch, M. K. (2016). *Inequality in school discipline: Research and practice to reduce disparities*. New York: Palgrave MacMillan.

Skiba, R. J., Michael, R. S., Nardo, A. C., & Peterson, R. L. (2002). The color of discipline: Sources of racial and gender disproportionality in school punishment. *The Urban Review, 34*(4), 317–342.

Snapp, S., Burdge, H., Licona, A. C., Moody, R., & Russell, S. T. (2015). Students' perspectives on LGBTQ-inclusive curriculum. *Equity and Excellence in Education, 48*, 249–265.

Toldson, I. A., McGee, T., & Lemmons, B. P. (2015). Reducing suspensions by improving academic engagement among school-age Black males. In D. J. Losen (Ed.), *Closing the school discipline gap: Equitable remedies for excessive exclusion* (pp. 107–117).

Townsend, B. L. (2000). The disproportionate discipline of African American learners: Reducing school suspensions and expulsions. *Exceptional Children, 66*(3), 381–391.

U.S. Department of Education Office of Civil Rights. (2014). *Civil rights data collection data snapshot: School discipline*. Issue Brief No. 1. U.S. Government Printing Office, Washington, DC. Retrieved from www.ocrdata.ed.gov.

Wallace, J. M. Jr., Goodkind, S., Wallace, C. M., & Bachman, J. G. (2008). Racial, ethnic, and gender differences in school discipline among US high school students: 1991–2005. *The Negro Educational Review, 59*(1–2), 47.

Welch, K., & Payne, A. A. (2010). Racial threat and punitive school discipline. *Social Problems, 57*, 25–48.
Welch, K., & Payne, A. A. (2012). Exclusionary school punishment: The effect of racial threat on expulsion and suspension. *Youth Violence and Juvenile Justice, 10*, 155–171.
Western, B. (2006). *Punishment and inequality in America.* New York: Russell Sage Foundation.
Wallace, J. M., Goodkind, S., Wallace, C. M., & Bachman, J. G. (2008). Racial, ethnic, and gender differences in school discipline among U.S. high school students: 1991–2005. *Negro Educational Review, 59*, 47–62.
Wolf, K., & Kupchik, A. (2017). School suspension and adverse experiences in adulthood. *Justice Quarterly, 34*(3), 407–430.
Wu, S., Pink, P., Crain, R., & Moles, O. (1982). Student suspension: A critical reappraisal. *Urban Review*, 14, 245–303.

PART II

Disparities in Pre-Conviction Processes

4

CUMULATIVE DISADVANTAGE AND THE GEOGRAPHY OF RACIAL INEQUALITY IN CRIMINAL PUNISHMENT

Marisa Omori and Rachel Lautenschlager

Introduction

Although there has been a softening of the War on Drugs, its policies and practices still drive much of the racial inequality in the criminal justice system today (Provine, 2011; Roberts, 2004). In part, the Drug War and mass incarceration changed the landscape of many communities of color through its increased sentencing policies targeting crack cocaine and broadening proactive policing on enforcement of drug crimes (Lynch, 2012; Reinarman and Levine, 1997), as well as policies that impacted employment opportunities, housing, civic citizenship, and other "collateral consequences" of incarceration (Clear, 2002; Pager, 2008; Manza and Uggen, 2006). While scholars have noted that the high rates of arrests and incarceration have disproportionately impacted Black and Latino communities, we have little understanding of how this disproportionate impact of policing in neighborhoods of color results in inequality in mass criminalization through prosecution and sentencing.

In this chapter, we suggest a twofold approach by which punishment and sentencing researchers may broaden conceptualizations of inequality in the criminal justice system: 1) by examining and capturing the criminal justice process that occurs before sentencing and 2) by moving beyond individual defendants in order to examine neighborhood-level outcomes. In this chapter we explore these two advances with an overview of current research done in cumulative disadvantage in courts and sentencing, as well as neighborhood analyses of racial inequality in policing outcomes. We conclude by investigating the ways in which we can consider them jointly in corrections, sentencing, and punishment broadly. These approaches can help us understand some of the broader mechanisms of racial inequality in the wake of the War on Drugs.

Despite the large racial inequality represented in the criminal justice system, quantitative studies in sentencing frequently find only small direct racial differences in sentence outcomes (Baumer, 2013). Often, racial disparities are conditioned on other factors, such as gender (Spohn, 2009), age, and socioeconomic status. This may be due to sentencing scholars' focus on individual level sentencing outcomes (in particular, the "in/out" prison decision and sentence length) after controlling for other "legally-relevant" characteristics (Baumer, 2013; Starr and Rehavi, 2013; Ulmer, 2012). It is likely that the two analytical choices prevalent in sentencing research—a focus on the final sentencing stage alone and examining individual defendants—may be why scholars continue to find such small racial disparities (or null racial disparities) despite the large inequality in the system.

While scholars have recognized that the treatment of race is relatively narrow in sentencing (Baumer, 2013), methods of reconceptualizing how to include race more broadly have moved slowly. Sentencing research that only examines individual direct "race effects" may overlook how discrimination operates in these more subtle and indirect ways (Zatz, 1987). Greater attention needs to be given to the many ways in which racial power operates in groups and institutions throughout the criminal justice system (Murakawa and Beckett, 2010; Van Cleve and Mayes, 2015). Methods for examining racial inequality must better account for the compounding role of inequality both within the criminal justice system, as well as consider how the criminal justice system is embedded in larger systems of inequality beyond its (metaphorical) institutional walls.

Research on institutional racism is helpful in reorienting the framework on inequality in the criminal justice system. This line of work suggests that racism is a normalized, institutional process that affords advantages to Whites and disadvantages to people of color systematically, rather than an individual prejudice or even coordinated group interests (Alexander, 2010; Bonilla-Silva, 2006; Haney Lopez, 2000). These views focus on revealing how, at the institutional level, the racial structure is maintained through policies and informal practices even while they are color-blind at face value. For example, through the geographic targeting of "hotspots" in Black and Latino communities (Geller and Fagan, 2010) and focus on crack by police (Beckett, Nyrop, and Pfingst, 2006; Beckett et al., 2005); through unequal charging practices of prosecutors (Lynch, 2011a); and through the use of mandatory minimums (Lynch and Omori, 2014) and repeat offenders in sentencing decisions (Farrell and Swigert, 1978). While these decisions are on their face race-neutral, they have all had large racial impacts.

These racially unequal policies and practices may also be compounded through the discretionary decisions made by criminal justice system actors. Steffensmeier, Ulmer, and Kramer (1998) suggest that court actors' have "focal concerns" when considering court and sentencing decisions, including blameworthiness of the defendant, protection of the community, and practical constraints in the organizational environment. Courts are often overburdened with cases that have limited time to be settled, and court actors may (though not always) use racial stereotypes as "perceptual shortcuts" to make decisions about these concerns when they do not have full information about a case (Kramer and Ulmer, 2009; Johnson et al., 2008; Ulmer and Johnson, 2004). This is particularly true in state courts, which have relatively less information, fewer resources, and a higher caseload compared to the federal system. These stereotypes are driven, in large part, by the myth of Black criminality pervasive in American culture (Roberts, 1999). Research suggests that these stereotypes of Black aggression and criminality are deeply embedded in criminal justice actors, such as law enforcement (Agozino, 2000; Eberhardt et al., 2004).

In addition to broadening the framework of inequality within the criminal justice system, sentencing and punishment scholars should consider more broadly how patterns of socioeconomic and racial segregation both contribute to and are perpetuated by mass incarceration and the criminal justice system. Other scholars have discussed how the criminal justice system grew out of patterns of residential segregation (Peterson and Krivo, 2012). The current system of mass incarceration thus serves as a new formation of a long-standing racial caste system, which has always been in place in order to maintain the status quo (Alexander, 2010; Wacquant, 2001). On the back end of the system, the "collateral consequences" of mass criminalization have left entire communities with weakened networks (Clear, Rose, and Ryder, 2001; Roberts, 2004) and structural barriers to employment, housing, public assistance, and civic participation (Manza and Uggen, 2006; Roberts, 2004; Pager, 2008; Wakefield and Uggen, 2010; Western, 2006). Despite this, most scholars only focus on how individual defendants, once in the system, are processed. Racial inequality in sentencing therefore not only requires a look at early stages pre-sentencing but also an examination of where defendants are coming from and how sentencing (and the criminal justice system more broadly) is impacting communities of color on the back end.

Racial Inequality Within the System: Considering Cumulative Disadvantage

Definition and Approaches

While sentencing scholars have commended the body of literature surrounding racial inequality in final sentencing decisions, they have also argued for a greater examination of how earlier stages are racially stratified or how they might impact later stages of sentencing (Baumer, 2013; Ulmer, 2012). Most criminological literature on racial inequality is still limited to a particular stage of the criminal justice system, such as arrest, sentencing, or corrections, but does not examine how smaller inequalities in multiple stages may produce greater cumulative inequalities over the entire criminal justice system process (Kutateladze et al., 2014; Schlesinger, 2007; Sutton, 2013; Zatz, 1987). For example, there is research on racial inequality in policing (Beckett et al., 2005; Buckman and Lamberth, 2001); sentencing (Kautt and Spohn, 2002; Ulmer and Johnson, 2004); and incarceration (Clear, 2007; Mauer, 1999; Western, 2006), but less research on how these institutions work together to produce inequality in the criminal justice system overall.

Some sentencing scholars have recognized this gap in the literature and have started to address it through the framework of cumulative disadvantage. Cumulative disadvantage was originally coined by Merton (1973, 1988) as "cumulative advantage" to explain the relative advantages that recognized scientists have in gaining additional recognition and funding over unknown ones. Based on studies by Zuckerman (1977) examining the careers of Nobel laureates, Merton (1973) noted that awards in science are often given as a result of recognition by fellow scientists and that those already known are therefore at an advantage to being credited (whether accurately or not) for additional scientific contributions. Calling this "The Matthew Effect in Science," Merton (1988) notes that one implication of this reward structure is the social selection process of cumulative advantage:

> [Cumulative advantage] refers to the social processes through which various kinds of opportunities for scientific inquiry as well as the subsequent symbolic and material rewards for the results of that inquiry tend to accumulate for individual practitioners of science, as they do for organizations engaged in scientific work. The concept of cumulative advantage directs our attention to the ways in which initial comparative stages of trained capacity, structural location, and available resources make for successive increments of advantage such that the gaps between the haves and the have-nots in science (as in other domains of social life) widen until dampened by countervailing process.
>
> (p. 606)

Cumulative advantage (or disadvantage) is generally used to explain how general patterns of stratification of an outcome, such as wealth, health, or other outcomes, accumulate over the life course (Dannefer, 2003; DiPrete and Eirich, 2006). The general concept has been used to explain a number of social processes where the initial resources given to a group help that group gain further advantages over time (DiPrete and Eirich, 2006; Sutton, 2013). Cumulative advantage/disadvantage therefore suggests that stratification happens because of the initial structural position of individuals or groups (and the resources allocated to them) rather than merit (Merton, 1988). Moreover, as Dannefer (2003) points out, these processes not only have a selection element, where those with greater initial resources are allocated greater additional resources through selection, but also a socialization element, where those in advantageous positions are taught the norms for navigating their current position to maintain their status.

DiPrete and Eirich (2006) argue that there are two major forms of cumulative advantage. The first is a "strict" form, similar to a model of compound interest, where the two groups have relatively different starting resources, and cumulative advantage or disadvantage is based directly on the differences in the previous stage. This method produces growing, exponentially greater differences between groups over time, even if the "interest rate" at individual stages were the same. The second form of cumulative disadvantage is based on group differences that may persist over time. For example, in Blau and Duncan's (1967) work, compared to Whites, Black Americans had a cumulative disadvantage on socioeconomic outcomes because race had both direct and indirect effects on socioeconomic status at multiple stages in the life course. In contrast to the "strict" form, the group differences model does not necessarily suggest that there are growing differences over time, but rather persistent differences over time due to the constant structural racial disadvantages.

Cumulative advantage has been expanded to many other life-course contexts to explain how socioeconomic status results in unequal health outcomes (Ross and Wu,

1996); race and gender stratification in employment over the course of a person's career (Blau and Duncan, 1967; Fernandez-Mateo, 2009; Tomaskovic-Devey, Thomas, and Johnson, 2005); and educational stratification based on early tracking (Kerckhoff and Glennie, 1999). These studies have generally found that racial differences when examined as a whole are much larger over the life course compared to individual stages. In the context of the courts, Zatz (1987) notes that small racial differences may not even be statistically significant in individual stages but could compound over multiple stages.

Cumulative Disadvantage in Sentencing

Despite the early recognition that more studies needed to examine how defendants flowed through the criminal justice system (Hagan, 1974), where small racial differences at individual stages within the system have compounding effects over the entire process, only a handful of studies have empirically examined cumulative racial inequality in the criminal justice system context (Kutateladze et al., 2014; Schlesinger, 2007; Sutton, 2013; Wooldredge et al., 2015). One reason that cumulative racial inequality has been largely unexplored in the courts is due to the relative lack of pre-conviction data and because scholars tend to focus more narrowly on sentencing decisions (Baumer, 2013; Ulmer, 2012). In some ways, this makes sense. Sentencing is the final and most visible stage of the court process and is the direct driver of incarceration and correctional statistics. The focus on final sentencing, however, masks much of the variation that occurs in preceding decisions, including the less visible initial filing decisions by prosecutors and plea negotiations. This is particularly the case in an era of more determinate sentencing with guidelines and mandatory minimums, which have shifted much of the discretion to prosecutors over judges (Engen, 2008).

Focusing on final sentencing decisions alone may be problematic in terms of uncovering racial inequality. Researchers have found that there is larger racial inequality in earlier pre-sentencing stages compared to sentencing (Omori, 2014; Ulmer, Painter-Davis, and Tinik, 2016). Some researchers have suggested that later court outcomes may "correct" earlier biases in the criminal justice system (Dannefer and Schutt, 1982; Rodriguez, 2007). For example, cases referred by the police are relatively weaker for non-White defendants compared to White defendants and so might be "corrected" at later stages through lower rates of prosecutorial filing and higher rates of dismissals. Moreover, there are multiple ways in which defendants are "selected out" of the system (Zatz, 1987). This selection process may result in selecting out much of the potential racial differences between defendants in pre-sentencing stages, retaining a more homogenous group of convicted defendants in sentencing (Bushway, Johnson, and Slocum, 2007; Zatz, 1987). In part because sentencing is the most visible stage of the court process, this could lead to scholars misrepresenting the inequality in the criminal justice system by focusing just on sentencing for samples of convicted defendants alone.

Although sentencing scholars have only started to adapt the cumulative disadvantage framework formally, they have long recognized that early police and court processing outcomes may act as stratification mechanisms for later decisions in the criminal justice process (Dannefer and Schutt, 1982; Farrell and Swigert, 1978; Johnson, Ulmer, and Kramer, 2008; Liska and Tausig, 1979; Rodriguez, 2010; Spohn, 2009; Zatz, 1984). The bulk of this work has focused on how racial inequality in pretrial detention has contributed to the inequality in final sentencing (Albonetti et al., 1989; Demuth, 2003; Demuth and Steffensmeier, 2004; Kutateladze et al., 2014; Schlesinger, 2005; Spohn, 2009; Wooldredge et al., 2015). For example, Spohn (2009) found that pretrial detention was more likely for Black defendants and that race had an indirect effect on sentence severity through pretrial status but no direct effect on sentence severity. Some scholars have also argued that diversion acts as a "sorting mechanism" for White drug defendants (Albonetti and Hepburn, 1996; Lynch, 2012). Albonetti and Hepburn (1996) found an interactive effect of Black or Latino defendants based on age and previous criminal history on diversionary outcomes, and Schlesinger (2013) found that pretrial diversion was more likely for White defendants compared to Black or Latino defendants.

Relatedly, other early prosecutorial decisions have been less studied, but research has found that they also impact racial inequality in sentencing. In drug sentencing at the federal level, Lynch (2012) argues that many of these early decisions, such as the selection of cases to prosecute, the decision to apply mandatory minimums, career offender enhancements, and the uneven application of the "safety valve" relief from a drug mandatory minimum act as mechanisms of racial inequality, and the sentencing decision represents the end product of these discretionary decisions made in preceding stages. Thus, the uneven application of these prosecutorial decisions may be the primary drivers of racial inequality in sentencing. For example, Bushway and Piehl (2007) found that prosecutors are likely to plea bargain with White defendants compared to Black or Latino defendants. Moreover, early assessments of defendants may have a direct impact on later decision-making stages. Hagan (1975) finds that probation officers disproportionately weigh pre-sentence recommendations against non-White defendants, which are used in final sentencing decisions.

While sentencing studies generally acknowledge that early police and court processing outcomes influence later decisions, fewer have examined how these effects compound over the court process. To date, there are only a handful of empirical studies that have explicitly focused on cumulative disadvantage in sentencing (Kutateladze et al., 2014; Schlesinger, 2007; Stolzenberg, D'Alessio, and Eitle, 2013; Spohn, 2009; Sutton, 2013; Wooldredge et al., 2015). These studies build strongly from the previous literature examining the role of pretrial detention and other previous stages on sentence outcomes. Cumulative disadvantage studies have examined the total effects of inequality based on multiple stages compounding each other (Kutateladze et al., 2014; Stolzenberg et al., 2013; Sutton, 2013), as well as examining the role of race on multiple single stages of court processing, including indirect effects on sentence outcomes (Chen, 2008; Schlesinger, 2007; Wooldredge et al., 2015). Some of these sentencing studies as also consider how early decisions increase racial inequality in sentencing.

Studies of cumulative disadvantage in sentencing tend to focus on the "total effects" of cumulative inequality, generally by looking at conditional probabilities of outcomes given previous stages. Sutton (2013) for example calculates conditional probabilities for pretrial detention, guilty pleas, and sentence severity. He finds about a 26% higher cumulative disadvantage for Black and Latino defendants compared to White defendants for prison, given the probabilities of previous stages. Similarly, Kutateladze et al. (2014) examine cumulative racial disadvantages by modeling the probabilities of different combinations of negative outcomes, including case acceptance, pretrial detention, plea offer, and incarceration. The authors find that Black and Latino defendants receive the most disadvantageous combination of court outcomes compared to White or Asian defendants, including detention, case dismissal, custodial plea offer, and incarceration. Specifically, Black and Latino defendants receive this combination of outcomes 33% and 30% of the time, respectively, compared to White defendants receiving it 28% of the time. These racial gaps were even greater for misdemeanor offenses. Finally, Stolzenberg, D'Alessio, and Eitle (2013) focus on decisions surrounding bail, pretrial detention, adjudication as a felony, and carceral sentences. Using a meta-analysis technique to examine outcomes overall, they find that Black defendants have a 40% increased odds of receiving a severe sanction compared to White defendants.

Some sentencing studies have also articulated how this cumulative disadvantage occurs by examining how racial stratification occurs at multiple stages of the court and sentencing process. In a group-level study of several California counties, Chen (2008) finds accelerating aggregate racial disparities between Black and White defendants but more continuous disparities between Latino and White defendants as they move through stages of the court system. Schlesinger (2007) finds that Black and Latino drug defendants receive more severe sentences compared to White men but finds that these disparities are produced through direct and indirect effects. Examining multiple outcomes including bail decision and amount, adjudication, and sentencing, Schlesinger (2007) finds that, because of beneficial pretrial decisions and the ability to post bail, White drug defendants are much less likely to have pretrial detention. Black and Latino men receive racially disparate processing directly through sentencing decisions and indirectly through pretrial detention and adjudication. Similarly, Wooldredge et al. (2015) find indirect disadvantages for Black defendants on pretrial detention and prior incarceration on final sentencing.

Thus, recent cumulative disadvantage studies have focused on both the total cumulative effects of this racial disadvantage, as well as the process within the criminal justice system's compounding effects. While these studies represent a much-needed contribution to the literature on racial inequality and sentencing, much more work can be done in this area. First, while these studies have identified stages of racial inequality in the criminal justice system, more efforts should be made to link the mechanisms of inequality (and in particular, prosecutorial decisions) with the cumulative inequalities in sentencing outcomes. In other words, this may help identify how different stages such as pretrial detention matter so much for sentencing outcomes. As Starr and Rehavi (2013) have suggested, this may include examining how prosecutorial choices such as charging, plea-bargaining, and fact-finding are also racially disparate. Since prosecutors are present for much of the criminal justice decisionmaking, they dictate much of the process—from negotiating sentences, to influencing law enforcement activity by screening cases, and deciding whether to file charges (Worrall, 2008). This is particularly applicable in lower criminal cases because justice is often mostly exercised during the pretrial process, where cases are resolved by a market-like negotiation between different parties, with different "going rates" for crimes (Feeley, 1979).

Second, many studies have noted how context matters, and there has been a body of research documenting how sentencing varies across places (Johnson, Ulmer, and Kramer, 2008; Kautt, 2002; Lynch, 2012; Lynch and Omori, 2014; Wu and Spohn, 2008). Much of this is driven by prosecutorial practices, which vary widely across districts (Brickley, 1995). For example, at the peak of the war on drugs in the early 1990s, in the Southern District of California, simple possession cases were 14% of the total caseload but were only 2% of cases in the neighboring Central District of California. Recent research has found that even within states, incarceration rates by county differ substantively (Lynch, 2011b; Ulmer and Johnson, 2004). Even though the federal system operates under uniform laws, there are large differences between federal judicial districts (Kautt, 2002; Lynch and Omori, 2014; Wu and Spohn, 2008). Differences between federal jurisdictions may be due to a number of factors, including racial and ethnic makeup of the court actors, differing crime rates, caseload sizes, racial makeup of the caseloads, and idiosyncratic practices around substantial assistance and other departures from the sentencing guidelines (Kautt, 2002; Ward, Farrell and Rousseau, 2009). Given these variations, more research should specify how cumulative disadvantage operates across different frameworks and types of settings. It seems likely that different environmental and organizational pressures may suggest different mechanisms for cumulative disadvantage.

Finally, while the cumulative disadvantage model is helpful to conceptualize inequality endogenous to court decisions, empirical studies in the sentencing literature have done little to examine how the process connects to policing (on the front end), and corrections (on the back end) of the criminal justice system. There have been a handful of studies (e.g. Starr and Rehavi, 2013) examining the federal system process from arrest to sentencing, but much more work should be done in this area. This might be particularly the case with drug cases. Because drug cases require more proactive policing and prosecution compared to many other types of crime, they require closer, more cooperative relationships between criminal justice agencies (Hagan, 1989). For example, narcotics officers must secure otherwise-unwilling informants in order for district attorneys to prosecute cases. Therefore, disparities in drug sentencing must be viewed as a function of relationships and processes spanning multiple stages of the criminal justice system.

In short, the cumulative disadvantage literature is one way to conceptually and empirically broaden how sentencing scholars consider racial inequality within the criminal justice system process. Although the concept of cumulative disadvantage in the criminal justice system is not new (see Zatz, 1987), empirical research on this topic has been relatively recent. Drawing from this model, new research efforts should continue to move in two directions. First, sentencing (as well as policing) scholars should broaden their focus on understanding the whole court process, viewing sentencing as the amalgamation of multiple decisions that start significantly earlier. Not only is the court process punitive in itself (Feeley, 1979), but focusing on sentencing alone misses many people who are "leaked out" of the criminal justice system funnel at earlier stages, including arrest, filing, and early pretrial stages. Using a process approach—such as cumulative disadvantage—to criminal justice system prosecution will help researchers better understand how previous decisions influence later ones, and how racial inequality may be otherwise indirect, subtle, and difficult to detect in sentencing. Second, scholars should expand research beyond individual defendants to consider different mechanisms, court contexts, and criminal justice institutions beyond the courts. Fundamentally, crime, and in particular sociological views on crime, necessitates researchers to examine the larger context in which criminal prosecution occurs. While we have done significant research on causes and theories of criminal behavior, we still have relatively little research on causes and theories of the criminal justice system (Hagan, 1989). Centrally incorporating how courts and other criminal justice institutions operate "on the ground" in context is key to understanding the localized mechanisms of inequality.

Racial Inequality Beyond the System: The Geographic Concentration of Crime and Crime Enforcement

Conceptualizing inequality more broadly also includes an examination of how the criminal justice system is both a product of and contributes to larger patterns of racial inequality in the community (Peterson and Krivo, 2012; Western, 2006). Historical residential racial and economic segregation has left a deep connection between the urban "ghetto" and mass incarceration (Wacquant, 2001). Wacquant (2001) argues that these "peculiar institutions" have served to continue racialized economic control over Black Americans. Courts and sentencing scholars have acknowledged, but done little about, the fact that cases brought into the court system in the first place often occur through geographically concentrated policing practices. The literature on neighborhoods and crime, as well as the geographic concentration of crime enforcement, can help sentencing and punishment scholars better consider how these patterns contribute to racial inequality in the system.

The idea that crime and crime enforcement are geographically oriented phenomenon, tied to local community characteristics, is long-standing and well-established within the discipline of sociology. This spatial understanding of crime patterns is rooted in Park and Burgess's (1925) landmark study, in which they propose an ecological model of social organization and encourage researchers to understand a city as more than an aggregation of individuals. According to this perspective, a city consists of socially distinct geographic areas, each characterized by unique social forces. Notably, Park and Burgess acknowledge the capacity for a city's physical and moral structure to influence the lives of its inhabitants. Shaw and McKay (1942) prescribed a community, rather than an individually oriented, approach to addressing crime in applying social disorganization to the study of urban crime. They discovered that the spatial distribution of juvenile delinquency across a city was strongly related to neighborhood social and economic conditions, including poverty, unemployment, and residential instability. This same pattern was discovered in 20 cities across the country, suggesting a fundamental connection between neighborhood disadvantage and crime. Furthermore, because Shaw and McKay's research spanned two decades during which immigrants arrived and settled in American cities in droves, they were able to demonstrate that high rates of juvenile delinquency persisted in some areas regardless of who lived there. The logical conclusion of this finding was that it was characteristics of the place, rather than the people who resided there, that were criminogenic.

The underlying proposition of Shaw and McKay's theory is not that disadvantaged neighborhood conditions cause crime. Rather, they argue that neighborhood characteristics such as poverty, residential instability, and racial and ethnic heterogeneity disrupt the social processes that normally work to inhibit crime from occurring. Contemporary tests of the theory have provided evidence that measures of social disorganization mediate the relationship between local social conditions and crime as predicted (Sampson and Groves, 1989; Osgood and Chambers, 2000). The mechanisms of this relationship have been elucidated by scholars, proposing that ecological characteristics such as poverty and residential instability negatively impact social networks (Bursik and Grasmick, 1993) and collective efficacy (Sampson, Raudenbush, and Earls, 1997), thus making it more difficult to instigate communal norms and values. While social disorganization theory pivots away from the idea that certain groups of people are inherently inclined towards crime, there remains an underlying assumption that disorganization is intrinsic to the neighborhood itself. Instead of viewing disadvantaged neighborhoods as fundamentally impaired, social disorganization should be framed as the product of resource deprivation and weak institutions that are themselves a result of political, economic, and social decisions linked to the maintenance of racial power. At the same time, the neighborhood conditions associated with social disorganization tend to occur in communities of color. When conceptualized through this lens, Latino and Black communities are depicted as volatile and dangerous, providing the justification for stringent, arguably excessive, criminal justice oversight in these neighborhoods.

Not only do people of color reside in spatially separated spaces from Whites, but the neighborhoods that they live in are socioeconomically incomparable (Peterson and Krivo, 2012). In other words, Black and Latino individuals conduct their daily activities in neighborhoods characterized by greater disadvantage than those frequented by Whites (Krivo et al., 2013). The combined result of persistent residential segregation and the geographic concentration of crime is vast racial and ethnic inequalities in the risk of criminal victimization. The effects of segregation are so detrimental for Black neighborhoods that the extent of geographic isolation of Black communities within a city serves as a barometer for Black crime participation (Shihadeh and Flynn, 1996). While this difference in social proximity to crime is frequently understood as a consequence of structural inequalities, it should simultaneously be viewed as a mechanism driving racial and ethnic inequalities in the criminal justice system.

The Localized Nature of the Criminal Justice System

In this way, scholars have documented the relationship between neighborhood characteristics and crime, which leaves Blacks and Latinos especially vulnerable to victimization. However, they are not only victimized by crime. Although the criminal justice system is often understood as a nationally uniform institution, the everyday processes constituting the system are similarly tied to local conditions. The grip of the criminal justice system is so firm in some places that a neighborhood may become defined by its overwhelming presence (Fagan, 2004). Research in the areas of sentencing, incarceration, and reentry provides insight into how social conditions can influence individual and neighborhood-level outcomes at various stages, which in turn reinforce preexisting disparities across communities.

There is evidence that sentencing decisions vary across court jurisdictions depending on racial/ethnic and economic characteristics (Heydebrand and Seron, 1990; Kautt, 2002; Ulmer and Johnson, 2004; Johnson, Ulmer and Kramer, 2008; Lynch and Omori, 2014). For one, researchers have demonstrated a relationship between the racial and ethnic composition of an area and sentence outcomes and severity. Unsurprisingly, it is Black and Latino individuals and communities that are most negatively affected. While a Black defendant's likelihood of receiving a prison sentence increases along with the size of a county's Black population (Wang and Mears, 2010), defendants of all races and ethnicities received harsher sentences if they were sentenced in counties with larger Latino populations (Johnson, 2005). In Florida, habitual offender status, which can carry with it more severe sentences, is more likely to be applied to Black and Latino defendants in areas with increasing Black and Latino populations, respectively (Caravelis, Chiricos, and Bales, 2011). It is not only who the defendant is that matters in predicting sentencing outcomes, but where the sentencing takes place.

Fewer studies have examined how neighborhood characteristics are related to variation in sentencing outcomes within a jurisdiction. Rodriguez (2007) examined the relationship between community characteristics and court processing decisions in Maricopa County, Arizona, and found that the rate of juvenile detention varied significantly across zip codes. Additionally, the probability of Latino defendants' detention was mediated by measures of community unemployment and poverty. Wooldredge (2007) determined not only that defendants from lower socioeconomic status areas are more likely to receive prison sentences, but also that neighborhood disadvantage is a stronger predictor of prison sentencing than a defendant's race. Examining neighborhood patterns in sentencing, Omori (2016) found that more disadvantaged census block groups in Sacramento had higher rates of conviction as well as longer jail and prison sentences. The enhanced punitiveness that is exercised when processing defendants from poor communities of color suggests that defendants are not only punished for their behavior but also for where they come from. Therefore, differences in sentencing are key factors in perpetuating the racial and ethnic imbalance of mass incarceration.

Driven by patterns of residential segregation, the disproportionate implication of Black and Latino individuals in the criminal justice system has resulted in uneven incarceration rates across neighborhoods (Sampson and Loeffler, 2010). While incarceration is quite rare in some neighborhoods, it is commonplace in others. Specifically, incarceration rates are sky high in the poorest, most disadvantaged neighborhoods (Clear, 2008; Fagan, 2004). Nonetheless, mass incarceration is frequently discussed as a national trend, disregarding the highly localized character of the problem (Lynch, 2011b; Sampson and Loeffler, 2010), as well as the unique consequences it has for communities of color (Roberts, 2004). The ubiquity of imprisonment in some urban neighborhoods has grown so entrenched that it has become accepted as an intrinsic, defining characteristic in itself (Fagan, 2004; Wacquant, 2001).

The quickness with which the criminal justice system is willing to imprison people from disadvantaged communities (Rodriguez, 2013) compels neighborhood destabilization. High incarceration rates in neighborhoods of color disrupt interpersonal relationships, negatively impacting families, community organization, social networks, and political efficacy (Clear, 2008; Lynch and Sabol, 2004; Roberts, 2004). Research also suggests that high county-level incarceration rates lead to worse community health outcomes, including more teen pregnancies and reports of STD infections (Thomas and Torrone, 2006). In contrast to its stated goal of reducing crime by removing offenders from society, excessive incarceration can result in a proliferation of crime (Rose and Clear, 1998). Once local incarceration reaches a certain "tipping point," additional forced removal of residents becomes destabilizing, resulting in increased crime (Clear et al., 2003; Renauer et al., 2006). The fallout of this is not only the obvious risks to neighborhood residents but also reifying societal perceptions of the association between criminality and the racialized Other (Agozino, 2000; Wacquant, 2001).

When prisoners are released, the onus of reentry falls on the same communities from which they came. Analyses of where prisoners' homes are and where they return upon release have highlighted how few communities shoulder this responsibility. At a national level, nearly half of all prisoners released during the year 1998 came from only five states (Lynch and Sabol, 2001). Studies of states and cities have yielded similar patterns (LaVigne et al., 2003; Lynch and Sabol, 2001; Solomon, Thomson, and Keegan, 2004; Visher, LaVigne and Travis, 2004; Watson et al., 2004). For example, in a single year in Ohio, 20% of the state's prisoners came from only 3% of the census block groups that constitute the city of Cleveland (Lynch and Sabol, 2001). Similarly, fully one-quarter of prisoners released from the Texas Department of Criminal Justice in 1 year returned to a single county (Watson et al., 2004). Once the geographic inequality of mass incarceration is considered, it becomes clear that prisoner reentry is not an evenly distributed societal burden, but rather a community one.

Until we begin conceptualizing sentencing, mass incarceration, and prisoner reentry as localized and spatially dependent processes, we will continue to underestimate the negative impacts they have on Black and Latino communities and fail to understand how inequality at each stage of the criminal justice system is derived from and contributes to inequality in other stages. In order to do this, court and sentencing scholars must extend their research beyond examining individuals as the unit of analysis and acknowledge how neighborhood context influences and is influenced by decisions made in the courtroom. On the front end, this means recognizing and taking seriously how neighborhood context, including racial and ethnic composition and levels of disadvantage, influence sentencing decisions. Likewise, on the back end, evidence of acute geographic concentration of criminal justice processes across the system suggests that more attention should be directed at how sentencing disrupts communal processes and maintaining racial and ethnic inequality. Reacting to neighborhood-oriented policing initiatives, including community and hot spots policing, scholars have already begun to acknowledge the significance of neighborhoods to the study of trends in urban law enforcement. In the following section, we provide an overview of the findings of this literature and how it has contributed to our understanding of the consequences of policing.

Why Is Studying Neighborhoods Important? Learning From the Study of Policing

Time and again, studies have documented that the outcomes of encounters with police are worse for Black and Latino individuals than they are for Whites. Analyses of traffic stop data reveal that Black and Latino motorists are more likely to be arrested, have their vehicle towed, or a record check conducted (Engel and Calnon, 2004; Alpert, Dunham, and Smith, 2007), as well as to be searched and frisked (Carroll and Gonzalez, 2014; Ryan, 2016). Despite the greater likelihood of being searched or frisked subsequent to a traffic stop, data suggest that contraband is equally or less likely to be found on or in the car of people of color (Engel and Calnon, 2004; Gumbhir, 2007; Ryan, 2016). Studies of pedestrian stops have yielded similar results. In New York City, Black individuals are disproportionately stopped by police when compared to their total numbers in the local population (Evans, Maragh, and Porter, 2014), a pattern that remains true even when taking into account differential crime participation rates across races and ethnicities (Gelman, Fagan, and Kiss, 2007). In that same city, Blacks who are stopped are more likely than people of other races and ethnicities to be frisked, searched, treated with force, or receive further punishment (Ferrandino, 2015). In a meta-analysis examining arrest decisions, Kochel, Wilson, and Mastrofski (2011) concluded that race is consistently a strong predictor of arrest, even when taking into account many other situational factors.

The overarching finding of these studies, that people of color fare worse in encounters with police than do their White counterparts, is an important one. However, examining individual outcomes has its limitations. First, each police-civilian encounter is considered in isolation, thus failing to account for the later consequences of repeated stops, both across an individual's life and throughout a community. Focusing on individual outcomes leaves no room for exploring the expansive ripple effects of police stops on a neighborhood. Second, many of these studies have an underlying assumption that racially disparate outcomes arise from conscious or subconscious discrimination on the part of individual police officers. The functioning and corollaries of implicit bias in police work have been theoretically elaborated (Smith and Alpert, 2007) and empirically bolstered through experimental studies (Eberhardt et al., 2004; Correll et al., 2007; Sadler et al., 2012). Although it is certainly possible that implicit or explicit discrimination is at play, assuming that it is the primary culprit in producing racial inequalities ignores the influence of larger organizational policies and practices.

Given that poor neighborhoods of color suffer from higher crime, they also tend to be policed more heavily than White neighborhoods (Evans et al., 2014). This fact is often treated as a truism, that more crime necessitates stricter law enforcement. Having limited resources, policing agencies must choose how to most effectively allocate them across the cityscape. For example, in 2003 the New York City Police Department launched a program known as Operation Impact. The goal of Operation Impact is to "reduce crime throughout the city by deploying more officers to high-crime hot spots" (New York City, 2010: 1). Although there is no publicly stated goal of targeting neighborhoods of color, Black and Latino neighborhoods bear the brunt of this "hot spots" policing strategy.

Researchers have demonstrated that these "color-blind" policing policies, those that have no explicit racial intent, can and do result in higher surveillance of and worse criminal justice outcomes for Black and Latino people. Lynch's (2011a) examination of selective drug law enforcement in Cleveland sheds light on how the seemingly race-neutral decision to focus policing efforts on crack resulted in differentially problematic outcomes for Black residents, despite the known racial and ethnic diversity of illicit drug users in the city. Choosing to police certain types of spaces may also result in racial consequences in aggregate numbers. Because public housing is usually found in predominantly non-White neighborhoods (Massey and Kanaiaupuni, 1993), Operation Impact's stated goal of focusing on this type of residence necessarily implicates racial and ethnic groups of color. The privatization of space associated with neoliberal schemes of development have additionally driven less advantaged city residents, especially Blacks, to outdoor spaces, leaving them exposed to and easy targets of police surveillance (Stuart, 2011). For example, Beckett, Nyrop, and Pfingst (2006) discovered that a policing initiative in Seattle focused on outdoor, as opposed to indoor drug, markets exacerbated racial disparities in arrests. Even among outdoor drug markets, they found, the Seattle police devoted substantially more resources to racially diverse markets compared to predominantly White ones. It is important to point out that policing agencies have the ability to choose how they police (Beckett, 2012) and are making formal or informal policy decisions to target certain communities in this manner. To a large degree, then, these patterns of sentencing and incarceration are driven by the concentration of policing.

Some scholars rationalize this type of intensive neighborhood-based policing using the deployment hypothesis (Engel, Smith, and Cullen, 2012). According to this perspective, the inequitable policing of communities of color is not driven by racial animus, but rather an unintended consequence of deploying more officers to areas with higher crime rates (Tomaskovic-Devey, Mason, and Zingraff, 2004). However, local crime rates cannot always account for the different amounts of policing that occur across neighborhoods. In New York City, Geller and Fagan (2010) concluded that street-stops aimed at uncovering marijuana occurred disproportionately in Black neighborhoods, a relationship that persisted even when taking neighborhood crime rates into account. Similarly, Beckett et al. (2005) noted that the Seattle Police Department's focus on policing crack does not appear to be related to the frequency of sales of that specific drug or to crack-related violence.

It seems, then, that the extent of policing in communities of color cannot be entirely accounted for by the concentration of crime. An alternative, or perhaps complementary, perspective proposes that policing agencies focus their efforts on poor communities of color in part because of the meanings that are attached to those spaces and the people who live in them. The organized policing of racial and ethnic minorities has a long history in the United States that can be traced back to the era of slavery (Bass, 2001). Today, crime control, including policing, is to such a great extent associated with Black and Latino people that Van Cleve and Mayes (2015) suggest that criminal justice has become a primary social practice involved in constituting beliefs about and attitudes towards those racial and ethnic minorities. Non-White neighborhoods are assumed to be rife with crime, thus necessitating extreme law enforcement tactics. The bad reputation of these neighborhoods is consequently projected onto the residents, who are often viewed as "morally deficient" (Vera Sanchez and Rosenbaum, 2011). Ethnographic studies of Los Angeles's notorious Skid Row, for example, have revealed that patrol officers moralistically stereotype the neighborhood's residents. Bittner (1967) found that police officers viewed Skid Row residents as living in-the-moment, without regard for future consequences of that lifestyle. More recently, Stuart (2014) observed that police view the perpetually homeless on Skid Row as bad decision-makers. From the police officer's perspective, supportive services are readily available to those in need. Therefore, those who remain homeless must be actively choosing that lifestyle. Broadly speaking, the intense policing of neighborhoods of color is justified by drawing on stereotypes that portray Blacks and Latinos as criminal and otherwise lacking in what are deemed admirable values.

The policing of urban spaces in which poor people of color live has become a prominent issue of concern across American cities over the last few decades due to processes of "urban revitalization." A century ago, the residential areas within a city were primarily inhabited by disadvantaged populations (Park and Burgess, 1925). More recently, the development of a modern, global economy, where financial and commercial activity is concentrated in large city centers, has led to renewed interest among the wealthier classes in urban living (Sassen, 2001). The result is a cleaning up processes, whereby rundown buildings are demolished and replaced and problematic populations are vanished to other parts of the city (Beckett and Herbert, 2008). The meaning of this for policing is evidenced in selective drug law enforcement in San Francisco, where the desire for urban development has encouraged proactive policing of disadvantaged communities in gentrifying neighborhoods and promoted containment of "problematic" populations in informally designated parts of the city (Lynch et al., 2013).

Not only can the location and traits of a neighborhood influence agency-level policy decisions, but neighborhood characteristics have also been demonstrated to influence how police officers conduct their work (Klinger, 1997). These differences in policing outcomes are frequently detrimental to non-White citizens and disadvantaged communities. Decision-making processes of police differ across neighborhoods, with the likelihood of "downgrading" a situation greater in areas with a larger Black population (Lum, 2011). Reports of police misconduct are positively related to neighborhood structural disadvantage (Kane, 2002), and officers are more likely to use force against citizens in primarily Black or racially mixed neighborhoods than in those that are predominantly White (Smith, 1986). One explanation for these neighborhood-level differences in policing is that, while patrol officers exercise a great deal of discretion in determining the trajectory of an encounter with a citizen, that discretion tends to be practiced through routinization processes, where decisions are made using a broad brush strategy, rather than through individual treatment (Portillo and Rudes, 2014; Fagan and Geller, 2015).

While it is easy to believe that these practices affect mainly so-called "criminals," in reality they infiltrate the lives of all people who live in heavily policed communities. In part this is the product of a criminal justice strategy that emphasizes the management of unruly groups of people, rather than rehabilitating individuals (Feeley and Simon, 1992). Order maintenance policing, widely adopted across American cities, assumes that disadvantaged neighborhoods are inhabited by disorderly people who require supervision; left to their own devices they will engage in behaviors that degrade their communities. In this way, the character of assumed criminality is imposed upon all people who reside in the boundaries of a designated problem area (Roberts, 1999). Furthermore, because the primary target of order maintenance policing is minor offenses, an inordinate segment of the population is implicated, including many people who would, under normal circumstances, never be considered "criminal" (Howell, 2009).

Law enforcement is so pervasive in some urban neighborhoods that police encounters serve as the primary, if not the only, point of contact with the government (Lerman and Weaver, 2014). This is a troubling pattern because of the negative community-level consequences that are associated with heightened police contact and aggressive policing tactics. For adolescents, simply being stopped by a police officer is a predictor of later delinquency, even if no arrest results from the stop (Wiley, Slocum, and Esbensen, 2013). At the neighborhood level, high rates of searches and use of force negatively impact the civic engagement of community members (Lerman and Weaver, 2014). Through mechanisms such as these, intensive policing practices cultivate inequality, not only for offenders, but for the residents of the impacted communities more generally.

These lessons from the neighborhoods and policing literature should be better accounted for in sentencing research because police stops and arrests represent the first stage of the criminal justice funnel. Sentencing decisions are not made in a vacuum. The cumulative disadvantage observed in court processes is fundamentally tied to the racial and ethnic inequalities that pervade urban policing, which themselves are rooted in structural disadvantage. Because criminal justice outcomes are so tightly tied to neighborhood characteristics, and neighborhoods remain highly racially segregated, researchers in courts and sentencing must reconfigure how they think about and conceptualize race as a mechanism that produces inequality in sentencing outcomes.

Therefore, scholars interested in racial inequality should better account for the defendants' community context. This may include other formally "race-neutral" ways in which neighborhood characteristics are racialized, particularly socioeconomic status. Although judges and prosecutors are not present in disadvantaged neighborhoods in the same way as police, they pervade defendants' communities through punishment decisions in a similarly powerful manner.

Moving Forward With Sentencing Research: Considering the Complexities of Racial Inequality

Although the Drug War may be in the beginnings of a retrenchment, its impact on racial inequality in the criminal justice system and on communities of color is still as relevant as ever. Although research on race and the law has elucidated the subtle and indirect ways that racism occurs, many scholars studying the criminal justice system quantitatively still treat the system as race-neutral, and racism as aberrant rather than natural (Murakawa and Beckett, 2010; Van Cleve and Mayes, 2015). This is often because scholars focus on the final sentencing stage alone and ignore pre-sentencing stages that "themselves result from discretionary charging, plea-bargaining, and fact-finding processes" (Starr and Rehavi, 2013: 2). These processes, as well as the policing practices that bring defendants into the system, are vastly understudied as a whole. Consequently, sometimes research finds only small racial disparities in sentencing (Baumer, 2013), despite large-scale racial inequalities in the prison system.

The inability of researchers to empirically capture the presence of racial discrimination in the criminal justice system may also be due, in part, to the traditional focus on individual-level processes and outcomes. This tendency has characterized research on a broad range of social inequalities and, because individual instances of discrimination are difficult to ascertain, inhibited the detection of systemically situated injustices (Feagin and Eckberg, 1980; Quillian, 2006). An individualized approach to studying the existence and maintenance of inequality is misguided because inequality is an inherently aggregate and relational process. The harsher punishment of a Black individual relative to a White individual after controlling for all (presumably race-neutral) "legally-relevant characteristics" does not constitute inequality alone. Rather, Black and Latino *communities* disproportionately bear the burdens of harsh and lengthy sentences, relative to White communities. Although individuals may be the ones directly affected by discriminatory processes, it is the aggregate effects of these experiences that result in inequality across groups (Krivo et al., 2013; Reskin, 2012). This is a vital distinction to make because group-level disparities need not be the outcome of discrimination, as understood in a traditional causal sense (Feagin and Eckberg, 1980; Stewart, 2008). Criminal justice procedures, including sentencing practices, may perpetuate inequality through mechanisms not easily captured in individual cases. If this is the situation, attempts to quantitatively verify that inequality exists by predicting individual outcomes are futile (Hipp, 2007). Therefore, researchers must develop theoretical and empirical models that accurately reflect the societal level at which the phenomena they study actually function.

In taking institutional racism and inequality seriously in sentencing, we suggest two additional avenues of research for sentencing and punishment scholars. First, as others have suggested, scholarship should consider both pre-sentencing stages and how these stages contribute to a larger court process of inequality rather than simply focusing on sentencing outcomes in isolation (Starr and Rehavi, 2013; Zatz, 1987). This will allow us to better understand how inequality may accumulate over multiple stages, occur indirectly, and occur under ostensibly "race-neutral" prosecutorial and sentencing formal and informal decisions. Early efforts examining cumulative disadvantage represent one area of research in this vein, but other research and other conceptual models would also help expand this burgeoning literature. In other words, we might start refocusing our research questions on understanding racial/ethnic, gender, socioeconomic, and other inequalities over the criminal justice system and see sentencing simply as the last stage in a broader punishment process. These questions might explore how much cumulative disadvantage there is over a process and how cumulative disadvantage happens. For example, does cumulative disadvantage represent inequality over a process that is greater than the sum of its parts and, if so, how? Are there certain decision points in criminal justice processing that might be particularly consequential for sentencing outcomes, and why? What are the mechanisms that link inequality at one stage of the criminal justice system to those before and after it?

Secondly, in drawing from the neighborhoods and crime literature, punishment and sentencing scholars should also consider how neighborhood and community context may matter, particularly in terms of how drug crimes are brought into the criminal justice system in the first place. It is unclear as to how much of the massive inequality observed in the system is due to policing versus court decisions or how policing contributes to sentencing and punishment outcomes. There is a tendency for big dataset sentencing scholarship to assume (or be unable to control for) how disparities occur uniformly, with similar mechanisms, over vastly different court contexts, courtroom workgroups, and defendant populations. More than just modeling context as a secondary consideration to individual-level characteristics or controlling contextual variation through fixed effects, research questions might explore context more centrally and, in particular, neighborhood ones: How does geographic context impact cumulative disadvantage? How do differences in sentencing perpetuate geographically situated inequality? In other words, what consequences does cumulative disadvantage in the criminal justice system have for communities of color?

These questions might require rethinking current data sources and methods as well. There has been a limited amount of qualitative scholarship examining the mechanisms and practices of racial inequality in these local sites. Lynch (2011b) argues that, in addition to legislative changes, one of the areas of change in mass incarceration occurs on-the-ground in localized legal sentencing and punishment practices. Recent qualitative work conducted recently in the courts has examined questions of how local racialized practices operate on the ground in different federal (Lynch, 2016) and state (Van Cleve, 2016) courts to create mechanisms of inequality. For example, Van Cleve (2016) finds that Chicago court actors practice everyday racism through "degradation ceremonies" of defendants. Although the federal system is in theory a unified criminal justice system, Lynch (2016) contrasts the diverse caseloads and court actors' practices in several federal courtrooms. For example, a federal court in the Northeastern District often processes low-level drug cases, where defendants of color were often caught through "buy and busts," while at the same time court actors' use high rates of departures in order to sentence below the guidelines. This court operates in contrast to a court in the Southeast, which prosecutes a high rate of crack mandatory minimum cases and therefore have relatively long sentences, and a court in the Southwest, which is a district that focuses little on proactively prosecuting "state" drug cases and instead processes high volumes of immigration and drug trafficking cases that cross the border. While these studies highlight the importance of local practices and actors, there may also be larger mechanisms of inequality that can be conceptualized theoretically across different sites.

In quantitative research, scholars might approach these questions in three primary ways that advance inequality research: by examining different dependent and independent variables related to inequality; by conceptualizing different types of models; and by bringing in additional multistage, historical, geographic, and contextual data. In terms of variables, researchers should reconceptualize race as a situated, dynamic, and interactive process rather than a passive, fixed characteristic (James, 2008; Stewart, 2008). This means, at a minimum, not treating race as an atheoretical "control" variable where differences are presumed to be rooted as a characteristic of the groups themselves, but rather examining social underpinnings of presumed racial differences (James, 2008). This might include examining racial/ethnic inequality in policing or prosecutorial decision-points at an aggregate level as a dependent variable or estimating multilevel models with cross-level interaction terms with race/ethnicity as independent variables to examine interactive processes that produce racial inequality in the criminal justice system.

In traditional models, regression-based methodology is used to isolate the source(s) of inequality, net of other characteristics (Stewart, 2008). While some recent work has made advancements in this area (e.g. Kutateladze et al., 2014; Sutton, 2013), highlighting the importance of place (Johnson, Ulmer, and Kramer, 2008; Kautt, 2002; Lynch, 2012; Lynch and Omori, 2014; Wu and Spohn, 2008), future analyses might further build from these examples. In addition to employing multilevel models to consider context, researchers might model process using structural equation modeling with path models to highlight inequalities in different stages or perhaps using growth curve modeling to estimate racial inequality over the criminal justice system process (for an additional discussion and possible solutions, see Stewart, 2008).

Finally, data advances might help quantitative scholars on this front as well. While previous scholarship has done excellent work with existing courts data sources and, in particular, the Federal Justice Statistics Program and the State Court Processing Statistics, future research might connect these sources with other types of contextual demographic, political, and economic data, as well as collecting other local administrative data from single jurisdictions to answer some of these questions. With the increased accessibility of electronic administrative policing and court data in local jurisdictions, scholars might be able to better access data for multiple pre-sentencing stages of the system, as well as geographic information, to identify how neighborhoods drive inequality in criminal punishment, and how criminal punishment furthers inequality in neighborhoods.

Ultimately, our goal in moving the scholarship on criminal justice and race forward should be to the break down the "illusion of racial neutrality while exacerbating racial disproportionality" (Van Cleve and Mayes, 2015: 406). These two developments will help broaden the empirical scope of how punishment and sentencing scholars consider racial inequality in the criminal justice system. They will also help shift our conceptual and analytical frameworks to be in line with more recent research on racism and racial inequality.

References

Agozino, B. (2000). Theorizing otherness, the war on drugs and incarceration. *Theoretical Criminology, 4*(3), 359–376.

Albonetti, C. A., Hauser, R. M., Hagan, J., & Nagel, I. H. (1989). Criminal justice decision making as a stratification process: The role of race and stratification resources in pretrial release. *Journal of Quantitative Criminology, 5*(1), 57–82.

Albonetti, C. A., & Hepburn, J. R. (1996). Prosecutorial discretion to defer criminalization: The effects of defendant's ascribed and achieved status characteristics. *Journal of Quantitative Criminology, 12*(1), 63–81.

Alexander, M. (2010). *The new Jim Crow: Mass incarceration in the age of colorblindness*. New York: The New Press.

Alpert, G. P., Dunham, R. G., & Smith, M. R. (2007). Investigating racial profiling by the Miami-Dade police department: A multimethod approach. *Criminology & Public Policy, 6*(1), 25–55.

Bass, S. (2001). Policing space, policing race: Social control imperatives and police discretionary decisions. *Social Justice, 28*(1), 156–176.

Baumer, E. (2013). Reassessing and redirecting research on race and sentencing. *Justice Quarterly, 30*(2), 231–261.

Beckett, K. (2012). Race, drugs, and law enforcement. *Criminology & Public Policy, 11*(4), 641–653.

Beckett, K., & Herbert, S. (2008). Dealing with disorder: Social control in the post-industrial city. *Theoretical Criminology, 12*(1), 5–30.

Beckett, K., Nyrop, K., & Pfingst, L. (2006). Race, drugs, and policing: Understanding disparities in drug delivery arrests. *Criminology, 44*(1), 105–137.

Beckett, K., Nyrop, K., Pfingst, L., & Bowen, M. (2005). Drug use, drug possession arrests, and question of race: Lessons from Seattle. *Social Problems, 52*(3), 419–441.

Bittner, E. (1967). The police on skid-row: A study of peace keeping. *American Sociological Review, 32*(5), 699–715.

Blau, P. M., & Duncan, O. D. (1967). *The American occupational structure*. London, Sidney: Wiley.

Bonilla-Silva, E. (2006). *Racism without racists: Color-bind racism and the persistence of racial inequality in the United States* (2nd ed.). Oxford: Roman and Littlefield Publishers, Inc.

Brickley, K. (1995). Criminal mischief: The federalization of American criminal law. *Hastings Law Journal, 46*, 1135–1174.

Buckman, W. H., & Lamberth, J. (2001). Challenging racial profiles: Attacking Jim Crow on the interstate. *Rutgers Race & Law Review, 3*, 83.

Bursik, R. J., & Grasmick, H. G. (1993). *Neighborhoods and crime: The dimensions of effective community control*. Lanham, MD: Lexington Books.

Bushway, S. D., Johnson, B., & Slocum, L. (2007). Is the magic still there? The use of the Heckman two-step correction for selection bias in criminology. *Journal of Quantitative Criminology, 23*(2), 151–178.

Bushway, S. D., & Piehl, A. M. (2007). Social science research and the legal threat to presumptive sentencing guidelines. *Criminology & Public Policy*, *6*(3), 461–482.

Caravelis, C., Chiricos, T., & Bales, W. (2011). Static and dynamic indicators of minority threat in sentencing outcomes: A multi-level analysis. *Journal of Quantitative Criminology*, *27*(4), 405–425.

Carroll, L., & Gonzalez, M. L. (2014). Out of place racial stereotypes and the ecology of frisks and searches following traffic stops. *Journal of Research in Crime and Delinquency*, *51*(5), 559–584.

Chen, E. (2008). Cumulative disadvantage and racial and ethnic disparities in California felony sentencing. In B. Cain, J. Regalado, & S. Bass (Eds.), *Racial and ethnic politics in California* (Vol. 3). Berkeley, CA: Institute of Governmental Studies Press.

Clear, T. R. (2002). The problem with 'addition by subtraction': The prison-crime relationship in low-income communities. In M. Chesney-Lind & M. Mauer (Eds.), *Invisible punishment: The collateral consequences of mass imprisonment* (pp. 181–194). New York: The New Press.

Clear, T. R. (2007). *Imprisoning communities: How mass incarceration makes disadvantaged neighborhoods worse*. Oxford: Oxford University Press.

Clear, T. R. (2008). The effects of high imprisonment rates on communities. *Crime and Justice*, *37*(1), 97–132.

Clear, T. R., Rose, D. R., & Ryder, J. A. (2001). Incarceration and the community: The problem of removing and returning offenders. *Crime & Delinquency*, *47*(3), 335–351.

Clear, T. R., Rose, D. R., Waring, E., & Scully, K. (2003). Coercive mobility and crime: A preliminary examination of concentrated incarceration and social disorganization. *Justice Quarterly*, *20*(1), 33–64.

Correll, J., Park, B., Judd, C. M., Wittenbrink, B., Sadler, M. S., & Keesee, T. (2007). Across the thin blue line: Police officers and racial bias in the decision to shoot. *Journal of Personality and Social Psychology*, *92*(6), 1006–1023.

Dannefer, D. (2003). Cumulative advantage/disadvantage and the life course: Cross-fertilizing age and social science theory. *The Journals of Gerontology Series B: Psychological Sciences and Social Sciences*, *58*(6), S327–S337.

Dannefer, D., & Schutt, R. K. (1982). Race and juvenile justice processing in court and police agencies. *American Journal of Sociology*, *87*(5), 1113–1132.

Demuth, S. (2003). Racial and ethnic differences in pretrial release decisions and outcomes: A comparison of Hispanic, Black, and White felony arrestees. *Criminology*, *41*(3), 873–908.

Demuth, S., & Steffensmeier, D. (2004). The impact of gender and race-ethnicity in the pretrial release process. *Social Problems*, *51*(2), 222–242.

DiPrete, T. A., & Eirich, G. M. (2006). Cumulative advantage as a mechanism for inequality: A review of theoretical and empirical developments. *Annual Review of Sociology*, *32*, 271–297.

Eberhardt, J. L., Goff, P. A., Purdie, V. J., & Davies, P. G. (2004). Seeing black: Race, crime, and visual processing. *Journal of Personality and Social Psychology*, *87*(6), 876.

Engel, R. S., & Calnon, J. M. (2004). Examining the influence of drivers' characteristics during traffic stops with police: Results from a national survey. *Justice Quarterly*, *21*(1), 49–90.

Engel, R. S., Smith, M. R., & Cullen, F. T. (2012). Race, place, and drug enforcement. *Criminology & Public Policy*, *11*(4), 603–635.

Engen, R. (2008). Have sentencing reforms displaced discretion over sentencing from judges to prosecutors? In J. L. Worrall & M. E. Nugent-Borakove (Eds.), *The changing role of the American prosecutor*. Albany, NY: State University of New York Press.

Evans, D., Maragh, C. L., & Porter, J. (2014). What do we know about NYC's stop and frisk program? A spatial and statistical analysis. *Advances in Social Sciences Research Journal*, *1*(2), 130–144.

Fagan, J. (2004). Crime, law, and the community: Dynamics of incarceration in New York city. In M. Tonry (Ed.), *The future of imprisonment* (pp. 27–59). New York: Oxford University Press.

Fagan, J., & Geller, A. (2015). Following the script: Narratives of suspicion in "Terry" stops in street policing. *The University of Chicago Law Review*, *82*(1), 51–88.

Farrell, R. A., & Swigert, V. L. (1978). Prior offense record as a self-fulfilling prophecy. *Law and Society Review*, *12*, 437–453.

Feagin, J. R., & Eckberg, D. L. (1980). Discrimination: Motivation, action, effects, and context. *Annual Review of Sociology*, *6*, 1–20.

Feeley, M. M. (1979). *The process is the punishment: Handling cases in a lower criminal court*. New York: Russell Sage Foundation.

Feeley, M. M., & Simon, J. (1992). The new penology: Notes on the emerging strategy of corrections and its implications. *Criminology*, *30*(4), 449–474.

Fernandez-Mateo, I. (2009). Cumulative gender disadvantage in contract employment. *American Journal of Sociology*, *114*(4), 871–923.

Ferrandino, J. (2015). Minority threat hypothesis and NYPD stop and frisk policy. *Criminal Justice Review*, *40*(2), 209–229.

Geller, A., & Fagan, J. (2010). Pot as pretext: Marijuana, race, and the new disorder in New York City street policing. *Journal of Empirical Legal Studies*, *7*(4), 591–633.

Gelman, A., Fagan, J., & Kiss, A. (2007). An analysis of the New York City police department's "stop-and-frisk" policy in the context of claims of racial bias. *Journal of the American Statistical Association*, *102*(479), 813–823.

Gumbhir, V. K. (2007). *But is it racial profiling? Policing, pretext stops, and the color of suspicion*. New York: LFB Scholarly Publishing.

Hagan, J. (1974). Parameters of criminal prosecution: An application of path analysis to a problem of criminal justice. *The Journal of Criminal Law and Criminology*, *65*, 536–544.

Hagan, J. (1975). The social and legal construction of criminal justice: A study of the pre-sentencing process. *Social Problems*, *22*(5), 620–637.

Hagan, J. (1989). Why is there so little criminal justice theory? Neglected macro- and micro-level links between organization and power. *Journal of Research in Crime and Delinquency*, *26*(2), 116–235.

Haney Lopez, I. F. (2000). Institutional racism: Judicial conduct and a new theory of racial discrimination. *The Yale Law Journal*, *109*, 1717–1884.

Heydebrand, W. V., & Seron, C. (1990). *Rationalizing justice: The political economy of federal district courts*. Albany, NY: State University of New York Press.

Hipp, J. R. (2007). Block, tract, and levels of aggregation: Neighborhood structure and crime and disorder as a case in point. *American Sociological Review*, *72*(5), 659–680.

Howell, B. (2009). Broken lives from broken windows: The hidden costs of aggressive order-maintenance policing. *New York University Review of Law & Social Change*, *33*, 271.

James, A. (2008). Making sense of race and racial classification. In T. Zuberi & E. Bonilla-Silva (Eds.), *White logic, white methods: Racism and methodology* (pp. 31–45). Plymouth, UK: Rowman and Littlefield Publishers.

Johnson, B. D. (2005). Contextual disparities in guidelines departures: Courtroom social contexts, guidelines compliance, and extralegal disparities in criminal sentencing. *Criminology*, *43*, 761.

Johnson, B. D., Ulmer, J. T., & Kramer, J. H. (2008). The social context of guidelines circumvention: The case of federal district courts. *Criminology*, *46*(3), 737–783.

Kane, R. J. (2002). The social ecology of police misconduct. *Criminology*, *40*(4), 867–896.

Kautt, P. (2002). Location, location, location: Interdistrict and intercircuit variation in sentencing outcomes for federal drug-trafficking offenses. *Justice Quarterly*, *19*(4), 633–671.

Kautt, P., & Spohn, C. (2002). Crack-ing down on black drug offenders? Testing for interactions among offenders' race, drug type, and sentencing strategy in federal drug sentences. *Justice Quarterly*, *19*, 1–35.

Kerckhoff, A. C., & Glennie, E. (1999). The Matthew effect in American education. *Research in Sociology of Education and Socialization*, *12*(1), 35–66.

Klinger, D. A. (1997). Negotiating order in patrol work: An ecological theory of police response to deviance. *Criminology*, *35*(2), 277–306.

Kochel, T. R., Wilson, D. B., & Mastrofski, S. D. (2011). The effect of suspect race on police officers' arrest decisions. *Criminology*, *49*(2), 473–512.

Kramer, J. H., & Ulmer, J. T. (2009). *Sentencing guidelines: Lessons from Pennsylvania* (pp. 90–101). Boulder, CO: Lynne Rienner Publishers.

Krivo, L. J., Washington, H. M., Peterson, R. D., Browning, C. R., Calder, C. A., & Kwan, M. (2013). Social isolation of disadvantage and advantage: The reproduction of inequality in urban space. *Social Forces*, *92*(1), 141–164.

Kutateladze, B. L., Andiloro, N. R., Johnson, B. D., & Spohn, C. C. (2014). Cumulative disadvantage: Examining racial and ethnic disparity in prosecution and sentencing. *Criminology*, *52*(3), 514–551.

LaVigne, N. G., Mamalian, C. A., Travis, J., & Visher, C. A. (2003). *A portrait of prisoner reentry in Illinois*. Washington, DC: Urban Institute.

Lerman, A. E., & Weaver, V. (2014). Staying out of sight? Concentrated policing and local political action. *The ANNALS of the American Academy of Political and Social Science*, *651*(1), 202–219.

Liska, A. E., & Tausig, M. (1979). Theoretical interpretations of social class and racial differentials in legal decision-making for juveniles. *The Sociological Quarterly*, *20*(2), 197–207.

Lum, C. (2011). The influence of places on police decision pathways: From call for service to arrest. *Justice Quarterly*, *28*(4), 631–665.

Lynch, J. P., & Sabol, W. J. (2001). *Prisoner reentry in perspective* (Vol. 3). Washington, DC: Urban Institute.

Lynch, J. P., & Sabol, W. J. (2004). Assessing the effects of mass incarceration on informal social control in communities. *Criminology & Public Policy*, *3*(2), 267–294.

Lynch, M. (2011a). Crack pipes and policing: A case study of institutional racism and remedial action in Cleveland. *Law & Policy*, *33*(2), 179–214.

Lynch, M. (2011b). Mass incarceration, legal change, and locale. *Criminology & Public Policy*, *10*(3), 673–698.

Lynch, M. (2012). Theorizing the role of the 'war on drugs' in US punishment. *Theoretical Criminology*, *16*(2), 175–199.

Lynch, M. (2016). *Hard bargains: The coercive power of drug laws in federal court*. New York: Russell Sage Foundation.

Lynch, M., & Omori, M. (2014). Legal change and sentencing norms in the wake of Booker: The impact of time and place on drug trafficking cases in federal court. *Law & Society Review*, *48*(2), 411–445.

Lynch, M., Omori, M., Roussell, A., & Valasik, M. (2013). Policing the 'progressive' city: The racialized geography of drug law enforcement. *Theoretical Criminology*, *17*(3), 335–357.

Manza, J., & Uggen, C. (2006). *Locked out: Felon disenfranchisement and American democracy*. Oxford: Oxford University Press.

Massey, D. S., & Kanaiaupuni, S. M. (1993). Public housing and the concentration of poverty. *Social Science Quarterly*, *74*(1), 109–122.

Mauer, M. (1999). *Race to incarcerate*. New York: The New Press.

Merton, R. K. (1973). *The sociology of science: Theoretical and empirical investigations*. Chicago: University of Chicago press.

Merton, R. K. (1988). The Matthew effect in science, II: Cumulative advantage and the symbolism of intellectual property. *Isis*, *79*(4), 606–623.

Murakawa, N., & Beckett, K. (2010). The penology of racial innocence: The erasure of racism in the study and practice of punishment. *Law and Society Review*, *44*(3/4), 695–730.

New York City. (2010). *Best practice: Using data to target high-crime areas*. Retrieved from www.nyc.gov/html/ia/gprb/downloads/pdf/NYC_Safety%20and%20Security_OperationImpact.pdf.

Omori, M. (2014). *Cumulative racial inequality of drug defendants*. Unpublished doctoral dissertation, University of California, Irvine, Irvine, CA.

Omori, M. (2016). Spatial dimensions of racial inequality: neighborhood racial characteristics and drug sentencing. *Race and Justice*, *7*(1), 35–58.

Osgood, D. W., & Chambers, J. M. (2000). Social disorganization outside the metropolis: An analysis of rural youth violence. *Criminology*, *38*(1), 81–116.

Pager, D. (2008). *Marked: Race, crime, and finding work in an era of mass incarceration*. Chicago: University of Chicago Press.

Park, R.E., & Burgess, E.W. (1925). The growth of the city: An introduction to a research project. In *The City* (pp. 47–62). Chicago: University Chicago Press.

Peterson, R. D., & Krivo, L. J. (2012). *Divergent social worlds: Neighborhood crime and the racial-spatial divide* (2nd ed.). New York: Russell Sage Foundation.

Portillo, S., & Rudes, D. S. (2014). Construction of justice at the street level. *Annual Review of Law and Social Science, 10*, 321–334.

Provine, D. M. (2011). Race and inequality in the war on drugs. *Annual Review of Law and Social Science*, 7, 41–60.

Quillian, L. (2006). New approaches to understanding racial prejudice and discrimination. *Annual Review of Sociology, 32*, 299–328.

Reinarman, C., & Levine, H. G. (1997). *Crack in America: Demon drugs and social justice*. Berkeley, CA: University of California Press.

Renauer, B. C., Cunningham, W. S., Feyerherm, B., O'Connor, T., & Bellatty, P. (2006). Tipping the scales of justice the effect of overincarceration on neighborhood violence. *Criminal Justice Policy Review, 17*(3), 362–379.

Reskin, B. (2012). The race discrimination system. *Annual Review of Sociology, 38*(1), 17–35.

Roberts, D. E. (1999). Foreword: Race, vagueness, and the social meaning of order-maintenance policing. *The Journal of Criminal Law and Criminology, 89*(3), 775–836.

Roberts, D. E. (2003). The social and moral cost of mass incarceration in African American communities. *Stanford Law Review, 56*, 1271.

Roberts, D. E. (2004). The social and moral cost of mass incarceration in African American communities. *Stanford Law Review, 56*(5), 1271–1305.

Rodriguez, N. (2007). Juvenile court context and detention decisions: Reconsidering the role of race, ethnicity, and community characteristics in juvenile court processes. *Justice Quarterly, 24*(4), 629–656.

Rodriguez, N. (2010). The cumulative effect of race and ethnicity in juvenile court outcomes and why preadjudication detention matters. *Journal of Research in Crime and Delinquency, 47*, 391–413.

Rodriguez, N. (2013). Concentrated disadvantage and the incarceration of youth examining how context affects juvenile justice. *Journal of Research in Crime and Delinquency, 50*(2), 189–215.

Rose, D. R., & Clear, T. R. (1998). Incarceration, social capital, and crime: Implications for social disorganization theory. *Criminology, 36*(3), 441–480.

Ross, C. E., & Wu, C. L. (1996). Education, age, and the cumulative advantage in health. *Journal of Health and Social Behavior, 37*(1), 104–120.

Ryan, M. E. (2016). Frisky business: Race, gender and police activity during traffic stops. *European Journal of Law and Economics, 41*(1), 65–83.

Sadler, M. S., Correll, J., Park, B., & Judd, C. M. (2012). The world is not Black and White: Racial bias in the decision to shoot in a multiethnic context. *Journal of Social Issues, 68*(2), 286–313.

Sampson, R. J., & Groves, W. B. (1989). Community structure and crime: Testing social-disorganization theory. *American Journal of Sociology, 94*(4), 774–802.

Sampson, R. J., & Loeffler, C. (2010). Punishment's place: The local concentration of mass incarceration. *Daedalus, 139*(3), 20–31.

Sampson, R. J., Raudenbush, S. W., & Earls, F. (1997). Neighborhoods and violent crime: A multilevel study of collective efficacy. *Science, 277*(5328), 918–924.

Sassen, S. (2001). *The global city: New York, London, Tokyo* (2nd ed.). Princeton, NJ: Princeton University Press.

Schlesinger, T. (2005). Racial and ethnic disparity in pretrial criminal processing. *Justice Quarterly, 22*(2), 170–192.

Schlesinger, T. (2007). The cumulative effects of racial disparities in criminal processing. *Journal of the Institute of Justice and International Studies*, 7, 261.

Schlesinger, T. (2013). Racial disparities in pretrial diversion: An analysis of outcomes among men charged with felonies and processed in state courts. *Race and Justice, 3*(3), 210–238.

Shaw, C. R., & McKay, H. D. (1942). *Juvenile delinquency and urban areas*. Chicago: University of Chicago Press.

Shihadeh, E. S., & Flynn, N. (1996). Segregation and crime: The effect of black social isolation on the rates of black urban violence. *Social Forces*, *74*(4), 1325–1352.

Smith, D. A. (1986). The neighborhood context of police behavior. *Crime and Justice*, *8*, 313–341.

Smith, M. R., & Alpert, G. P. (2007). Explaining police bias a theory of social conditioning and illusory correlation. *Criminal Justice and Behavior*, *34*(10), 1262–1283.

Solomon, A. L., Thomson, G. L., & Keegan, S. (2004). *Prisoner reentry in Michigan*. Washington, D.C.: Urban Institute, Justice Policy Center.

Spohn, C. (2009). Race, sex, and pretrial detention in federal court: Indirect effects and cumulative disadvantage. *Kansas Law Review*, *57*, 879–901.

Starr, S. B., & Rehavi, M. M. (2013). Mandatory sentencing and racial disparity: Assessing the role of prosecutors and the effects of *Booker*. *Yale Law Journal*, *123*, 2.

Steffensmeier, D., Ulmer, J., & Kramer, J. (1998). The interaction of race, gender, and age in criminal sentencing: The punishment cost of being young, Black, and male. *Criminology*, *36*(4), 763–798.

Stewart, Q. T. (2008). Swimming upstream. In T. Zuberi & E. Bonilla-Silva (Eds.), *White logic, white methods: Racism and methodology* (pp. 111–126). Plymouth: Rowman & Littlefield Publishers.

Stolzenberg, L., D'Alessio, S. J., & Eitle, D. (2013). Race and cumulative discrimination in the prosecution of criminal defendants. *Race and Justice*, *3*(4), 275–299.

Stuart, F. (2011). Race, space, and the regulation of surplus labor: Policing African Americans in Los Angeles's skid row. *Souls*, *13*(2), 197–212.

Stuart, F. (2014). From 'rabble management' to 'recovery management': Policing homelessness in marginal urban space. *Urban Studies*, *51*(9), 1909–1925.

Sutton, J. (2013). Structural bias in the sentencing of felony defendants. *Social Science Research*, *42*, 1207–1221.

Thomas, J. C., & Torrone, E. (2006). Incarceration as forced migration: Effects on selected community health outcomes. *American Journal of Public Health*, *96*(10), 1762–1765.

Tomaskovic-Devey, D., Mason, M., & Zingraff, M. (2004). Looking for the driving while black phenomena: Conceptualizing racial bias processes and their associated distributions. *Police Quarterly*, 7(1), 3–29.

Tomaskovic-Devey, D., Thomas, M., & Johnson, K. (2005). Race and the accumulation of human capital across the career: A theoretical model and fixed-effects application. *American Journal of Sociology*, *111*(1), 58–89.

Ulmer, J. (2012). Recent developments and new directions in sentencing research. *Justice Quarterly*, *29*, 1–40.

Ulmer, J., & Johnson, B. D. (2004). Sentencing in context: A multilevel analysis. *Criminology*, *42*, 137–177.

Ulmer, J., Painter-Davis, N., & Tinik, L. (2016). Disproportional imprisonment of Black and Hispanic males: Sentencing discretion, processing outcomes, and policy structures. *Justice Quarterly*, *33*(4), 642–681.

Van Cleve, N. G. (2016). *Crook county: Racism and injustice in America's largest criminal court*. Palo Alto, CA: Stanford University Press.

Van Cleve, N. G., & Mayes, L. (2015). Criminal justice through "colorblind" lenses: A call to examine the mutual constitution of race and criminal justice. *Law & Social Inquiry*, *40*(2), 406–432.

Vera Sanchez, C. G., & Rosenbaum, D. P. (2011). Racialized policing: Officers' voices on policing Latino and African American neighborhoods. *Journal of Ethnicity in Criminal Justice*, *9*(2), 152–178.

Visher, C., LaVigne, N., & Travis, J. (2004). *Returning home: Understanding the challenges of prisoner reentry. Maryland pilot study: Findings from Baltimore*. Washington, DC: Urban Institute.

Wacquant, L. (2001). Deadly symbiosis when ghetto and prison meet and mesh. *Punishment & Society*, *3*(1), 95–133.

Wakefield, S., & Uggen, C. (2010). Incarceration and stratification. *Annual Review of Sociology*, *36*, 387–406.

Wang, X., & Mears, D. P. (2010). A multilevel test of minority threat effects on sentencing. *Journal of Quantitative Criminology*, *26*(2), 191–215.

Ward, G., Farrell, A., & Rousseau, D. (2009). Does racial balance in workforce representation yield equal justice? Race relations of sentencing in federal court organizations. *Law and Society Review, 43*(4), 757–805.

Watson, J., Solomon, A. L., LaVigne, G., Travis, J., Funches, M., & Parthasarathy, B. (2004). *A portrait of prisoner reentry in Texas.* Washington, DC: Urban Institute.

Western, B. (2006). *Punishment and inequality in America.* New York: Russell Sage Foundation.

Wiley, S. A., Slocum, L. A., & Esbensen, F. A. (2013). The unintended consequences of being stopped or arrested: An exploration of the labeling mechanisms through which police contact leads to subsequent delinquency. *Criminology, 51*(4), 927–966.

Wooldredge, J. (2007). Neighborhood effects on felony sentencing. *Journal of Research in Crime and Delinquency, 44*(2), 238–263.

Wooldredge, J., Frank, J., Goulette, N., & Travis, L. (2015). Is the impact of cumulative disadvantage on sentencing greater for Black defendants? *Criminology & Public Policy, 14*(2), 187–223.

Worrall, J. (2008). Prosecution in America: A historical and comparative account. In J. L. Worrall & M. E. Nugent-Borakove (Eds.), *The changing role of the American prosecutor.* Albany: State University of New York Press.

Wu, J., & Spohn, C. (2008). Interdistrict disparity in sentencing in three U.S. district courts. *Crime and Delinquency, 56*(2), 290–322.

Zatz, J. (1987). The changing forms of racial/ethnic biases in sentencing. *Journal of Research in Crime and Delinquency, 24*(1), 69–92.

Zatz, M. S. (1984). Race, ethnicity, and determinate sentencing. *Criminology, 22*(2), 147–171.

Zuckerman, H. (1977). *Scientific elite: Nobel laureates in the United States.* New York: The Free Press.

5

"ESCAPE" FROM PUNISHMENT

Exploring the Sealing of a Criminal Record and Potential Disparities in Its Application

Megan C. Kurlychek and Heather M. Washington[1]

Introduction

The criminal justice literature has a long tradition of studying sentencing as the final form of punishment meted out by the criminal justice system including both empirical studies of large administrative data sets to explore trends in sentencing and localized ethnographic accounts that detail how judges and court-room work groups work together to determine sentencing outcomes as a form of punishment. From early studies by Eisenstein and Jacob (1977) that detail the intricate dance between prosecutor, defense attorney, and judge to determine "going rates" at sentencing, to an explosion of literature in the 1980s forward that focuses more specifically on the potential for resulting gender and racial biases at sentencing outcomes (see Mitchell, 2005, Ulmer, 2012, and Zatz, 2000, for reviews of the literature), criminological literature is indeed rich in studies of judicial decision-making at the sentencing stage.

More recently, however, there has been growing awareness that focusing only on judicial discretion at sentencing may indeed paint a picture that is missing many of its primary colors. That is, judicial decisions at sentencing are only the end result of a much longer and richer process that involves multiple system actors and decision-making points. This series begins with the potential for an initial police contact and progresses through arrest, charging, the plea bargain or conviction stage, sentencing, and even parole decisions. While it is difficult for any one study or even a series of studies to encompass this complete picture of system processing, we dare here to challenge the borders even a bit further by adding yet another nuance—discretionary decision-making that leads to differential application of the criminal record seal or expungement.

The ability to have a record sealed or expunged has broad consequences that reach far beyond immediate criminal justice system outcomes. In today's world where employers, landlords, and even colleges and universities want to know if a person has a criminal record before opening up an opportunity for him or her, the ability to have a record sealed or expunged can truly be a life-altering event. The criminal sentence, which is so vastly studied in the empirical literature, has a distinct beginning and an end—the time you enter jail, prison, or probation for example and the day you successfully complete the sentence. Yet, the stigma of the criminal record restricts an individual's movement through life like shackles that have no key. These shackles can limit multiple aspects of an individual's life by hindering opportunities for employment, for earning a college degree and, in some states, even the right to vote for the rest of one's life.

Having a record sealed or expunged may truly be the only key to release the shackles and allow an individual to have his/her debt to society finally paid. All states and the federal government allow for the sealing and/or expungement of criminal records in certain circumstances. Yet, as with most criminal justice policy, there is little rhyme or reason as to why only some individuals are granted sealing or expungement when comparing these policies across jurisdictions except that they are ultimately tied to 1) the charge at arrest and/or conviction and 2) in many cases time since the arrest and/or conviction.

In this chapter, we first review the ways in which race has been found to influence other key decision-making points in the criminal justice system. We then explore these state and federal sealing policies and discuss how prosecutorial and judicial decision-making in charging and plea bargaining/conviction could greatly impact the demographics of those individuals eligible to have their record sealed. We then specifically test the possibility of such racial and gender bias using data from one state, New York, on a cohort of young offenders who have perhaps the most to lose from the lifelong sentence of a criminal record. Finally, we use these examples to suggest pathways for future research to further explore the intricate ways in which prosecutorial and judicial discretion may impact the "punishment" of having a permanent criminal record.

Discretion and Bias: A Step-by-Step Review

Police Contact

Minority citizens' contact with the police has received much attention and scrutiny in recent years. The Rodney King beating stood out in the 1990s as the go-to example of the disparaging treatment of minority citizens by police officers. Today, instances like the Michael Brown and Eric Garner killings now occupy the minds of many Americans as contemporary examples of the kinds of disadvantageous treatment African Americans receive from police officers and, more broadly, the criminal justice system. These instances, along with the Rodney King beating, have resulted in angry reactions among minority citizens toward the police and added to the long history of police distrust among minority group members (Lundman and Kaufman, 2003; Tyler and Huo, 2003; Weitzer and Tuch, 2002; Slocum et al., 2010).

A long body of research documents the narrative currently playing out in our country: that African Americans and other minority group members have dissimilar rates of police contact when compared to their White counterparts and that police interactions with minority group members do not mirror the kinds of interactions police have with White citizens. Examples of disparate contact and treatment can be found in both the literature traffic (i.e. "driving while black") and pedestrian stops (Gelman, Fagan, and Kiss, 2007; Lundman and Kaufman, 2003).

Regarding traffic stops, research stemming from two surveys using nationwide probability samples revealed two important findings: 1) African Americans are far more likely than other citizens to be stopped by the police and 2) African American-police encounters on the highway are more likely to lead to tickets, arrests, handcuffing, searches, and the use or threat of physical force when compared to traffic stops with other race citizens (Langan et al., 2001; Durose, Schmitt, and Langan, 2005). Other research corroborates and adds to these findings by showing that, in general, African American and Hispanic motorists are disproportionately stopped by the police and that, when stopped, they are often searched and/or arrested (Cole, 1999; Veneiro and Zoubeck, 1999; Harris, 1999; Gross and Barnes, 2002; Meehan and Ponder, 2002; Petrocelli et al., 2003: 1–11; Warren et al., 2006).

Stop-and-frisk policies have made pedestrian stops a common experience among black and brown citizens in many American locales. Stemming from the New York City Police Department (NYPD), stop-and-frisk polices allow police to "temporarily detain," question, and search pedestrians for a wide variety of crimes on the grounds of "reasonable suspicion" (Spitzer, 1999). Multiple complaints have been levied against police departments, and the NYPD in particular, for perceived discriminatory practices toward African American and Hispanic citizens who complain that police harass them on the street (Spitzer, 1999) and use aggressive stop-and-frisk tactics (see Kelvin Daniels et al. v. City of New York, 2004).

Recent research supports citizens' concerns about the NYPD's stop-and-frisk policies. Gelman, Fagan, and Kiss (2007) found that African Americans and Hispanics were disproportionately represented among citizens who are stopped and frisked in New York City with African Americans representing 53% of stops and Hispanics representing 33% of stops. When compared to Whites, African Americans and Hispanics were stopped 23% and 39% more often, respectively. This pattern held even when controlling for characteristics of the precincts where the stops occurred and across offense types for which the stop was initiated.

Another contentious issue is the police use of force during such stops and arrests. With recent police shootings and deaths of minority suspects resulting from alleged police misuse of force including such renowned incidents as the deaths of Trayvon Martin, Michael Brown, and Freddie Gray, just to name a few, we are seeing race riots against police in a manner not experienced in this country since the civil-rights movement in the 1960s and the widely publicized police beating of Rodney King in the 1990s. One recent study by Legewie (2016), however, might alarmingly suggest that such brutality sets itself up as a vicious circle. In this analysis of over 3.9 million police encounters in New York City, the author finds that police abuse of force against minorities, particularly African Americans, increases after an incident in which an African American suspect shoots a police officer. The same effect, however, did not hold true if a White suspect shot a police officer. Combined, this research shows that minorities are, at the very front end of the system, more likely to experience differential treatment from traffic-stops, to stop-and-frisk policies, to the use of potentially excessive force during such encounters.

Arrest

Given the high likelihood of police contact among minority citizens, it is not surprising that African Americans and Hispanics are also more likely to be arrested than Whites. In 2010, the Federal Bureau of Investigation (FBI) found that arrest rates among African Americans were 2.2 times higher than that of Whites (FBI, 2011). Using data from the National Longitudinal Survey of Youth 1997, Brame and colleagues (2012, 2014) confirm that arrest is not evenly distributed across race/ethnic groups. While 25%–41% of youth have been arrested by the age of 23 (Brame et al., 2012), rates of arrest are significantly higher for African American youth. The authors reported that about 30% of African American youth have experienced at least one arrest by age 18 compared to 22% for White males. This pattern of arrest remained consistent to age 23 with 49% of African American males being arrested compared to 38% of White males being arrested by age 23 (Brame et al., 2014).

Charging/Plea Bargains

A growing body of research investigates racial disparities in prosecutorial discretion, with particular concern regarding charging and plea bargaining. The area on racial and ethnic disparities in the charging of criminal defendants focuses largely on prosecutors' decision-making behavior. This is true, in part, because prosecutors are often afforded full discretionary power to dismiss a case, to reduce criminal charges, to enhance criminal charges, and to negotiate with defendants via plea-bargaining.

Recent research focusing on prosecutorial discretion in the application of mandatory sentences and sentence enhancements reveals racial disparities. The bulk of research in this area shows that African American and Hispanic men are more likely than Whites to receive mandatory terms and sentence enhancements (Caravelis et al., 2011; Crawford, Chiricos, and Kleck, 1998; Crow and Johnson, 2008; Farrell, 2003; Ulmer et al., 2007). This is particularly true among men who are convicted of drug and property crimes (Caravelis et al., 2011; Crawford, Chiricos, and Kleck, 1998; Crow and Johnson, 2008; Farrell, 2003; Ulmer et al., 2007).

Studies investigating racial disparities in plea bargaining reveal dissimilar treatment for racial and ethnic minorities when compared to their White counterparts. In particular, this body of research suggests that prosecutors are less likely to engage in charge bargaining with African American and Latino defendants than with White defendants, even when defendants share similar legal characteristics (Bjerk, 2005; Bushway and Piehl, 2007; Shermer and Johnson, 2010; Kutateladze et al., 2014). So, not only are minority men more likely to be charged with offenses that are eligible for mandatory terms and sentence enhancements, they are also less able to reduce or evade these charges through plea-bargaining.

Conviction

Research on racial disparities in the likelihood of criminal conviction has focused largely on jury decision-making regarding judgments of guilt and sentencing recommendations. The results of this body of work have been mixed; some studies point to disparate treatment of African Americans by jurors, while a handful report no differences in jury behavior by defendants' race/ethnicity (e.g., Pfeifer and Ogloff, 1991; Williams and Holcomb, 2001). Nevertheless, the bulk of the research in this area supports narratives of racial discrimination in the American criminal justice system by showing that jury members are no less influenced by defendants' race than are other actors in criminal court. Whether intentional or unintentional, the literature regarding jury members' decision-making suggests that race matters in decisions about a defendant's guilt or innocence.

Several studies on the decision-making of "mock" jurors show that African Americans are more likely to be found guilty than Whites, especially in cases involving rape or homicide (see Sommers and Ellsworth, 2001, for a review). Not only are African Americans more likely to be convicted by these mock juries, but they are also treated more harshly than White defendants when it comes to jurors' sentencing recommendations. More recently, a meta-analysis revealed that race is predominant in the majority of studies on jury decision-making as the marker for guilt and as a criterion for punishment and that the influence of defendants' race becomes more pronounced when jury members' race/ethnicity is considered (Mitchell et al., 2005).

Sentencing

Much research on racial disparities in the criminal justice system focuses on the final stage in criminal justice processing: sentencing. Decades of research have been devoted to understanding judicial decision-making with regard to the sentencing of criminal defendants (Kramer and Steffensmeier, 1993; Peterson and Hagan, 1984; Steffensmeier, Ulmer, and Kramer, 1998). While this area of research has received more attention than other areas, the research findings regarding race and ethnic disparities in sentencing have led to several different conclusions (for a full analysis see reviews by Zatz, 2000; Spohn, 2000; Mitchell, 2005; and Ulmer, 2012).

Some research suggests that African Americans are sentenced more harshly than their white counterparts (Demuth and Steffensmeier, 2004; Poe-Yamagata and Jones, 2000; Pope and Feyerherm, 1995; Pope, Lovell, and Hsia, 2002). These studies report racial differences in sentencing even when other relevant factors related to the case such as offense seriousness and prior criminal history are taken into account (Albonetti, 1997; Crawford, Chiricos, and Kleck, 1998; Kramer and Steffensmeier, 1993). Such findings are further supported by a meta-analysis of 71 published and unpublished studies on sentencing disparities by race in which Mitchell (2005) found that overall, African Americans are sentenced more harshly than their White counterparts. These disparities in sentencing can be found across a wide variety of crimes. For example, a 2000 report by Human Rights Watch showed that, although drug usage rates are virtually equivalent for African Americans and Whites, African American drug users were 13 times more likely to be sentenced to jail than White drug users. Other research found that African Americans are four times more likely than White defendants to receive the death penalty (Baldus et al., 1998) and that a death sentence and execution is all the more likely if the defendant is African American and the victim is White (Baldus et al., 2002; Paternoster et al., 2003; Jacobs et al., 2007; Paternoster and Brame, 2008).

Other research suggests that African Americans are treated more leniently than Whites when sentencing decisions are made (Bernstein et al., 1977; Myers and Talarico, 1986). Still, other studies have found the race of the defendant to play no role in sentencing outcomes among criminal defendants (Engen and Gainey, 2000). Williams and Holcomb's (2001) work, for example, revealed no race/ethnic differences in the likelihood that a defendant would receive the death penalty.

The Hidden Punishment

Up to this point we have been reviewing what the literature tells us about distinct decision-making points in the criminal justice system from a police officer's initial decision to stop and question and individual, through arrest, charging, and ultimately sentencing a defendant—and, at all these points, showing how such decisions can disadvantage minorities. However, there is a punishment that is meted out by the criminal justice system that can be as costly and far more long-lasting than the result of any of these encounters—except of course those leading to death or a sentence of death. To what are we referring? For the remainder of this chapter, we would like to draw your attention to the undeniable fact that the mere existence of a criminal record—be it evidence of a police encounter, a formal arrest, a conviction, or a period of incarceration—can follow and impact the life of an individual long after the formal criminal justice system has lost its authority.

The main premise of our argument in this chapter is that a key decision point that has been missing in the above studies is the decision to allow a criminal record to be sealed. This decision can actually come in many different forms. For example, it could be in the decision to charge with, or allow the individual to plea to, a "sealable" offense. In many instances a seal can later be applied for after a given period of time or in some cases may even be automatic based upon conviction charge and time since the charge. In such cases the ability to obtain the seal/expungement is determined by the final conviction charge and thus is inherently tied to charging and plea bargaining decisions. In other instances, there is an additional element of judicial discretion in which the judge determines if the seal is granted—yet another unstudied area of judicial discretion that has meaningful lifelong consequences for the accused. Because of the lifelong collateral consequences of a criminal record, which range from inability to secure student loans and the inability to gain employment, to even the inability to obtain housing, we propose that the inability to have a record sealed or expunged is indeed another form of punishment meted out by the criminal justice system. While it is beyond the scope of this chapter to review each state's sealing policies and the total extent of the collateral consequences of a criminal record, in the following section, we briefly describe the practice of either sealing or expunging criminal records, provide a brief overview of national sealing/expunging policies, and review why these policies are of such great consequence at this particular time in history.

A General Review of Sealing and Expunging Policies

In general, sealing a criminal record refers to an instance in which an arrest, the following court proceedings, and final disposition are all made inaccessible to the public and, in many instances, to criminal justice agencies as well. Most simply, the record exists somewhere, but it is sealed so that most, if not all, cannot access the record. One might be most familiar with this term as it relates to juvenile records as most states maintain strict confidentiality laws regarding juvenile proceedings. For example, an arrested juvenile would not have his/her name released to the public or media, and the juvenile court proceeding and all its transcripts would be maintained at the courthouse but not released to the public. Thus, although the record exists and could be viewed by local law enforcement for justice purposes, to the rest of the world, the youth would not appear a criminal. Expungement on the other hand typically refers to a process by which the entire record is actually destroyed or in today's terms, deleted. In some instances the immediate record only is destroyed, and in other cases, the individual's fingerprints, DNA, or any other collected information is also destroyed. Therefore, no one, not even internal justice workers, could attach a specific name/identifier to a given person. This is also a common practice with juveniles. For example, many states offer full expungement of juvenile records upon request after the youth has remained crime free for a given period of time, thus providing a true second chance.

Sealing and expungement are not exclusive to juvenile records however. A survey conducted by SEARCH in 2010 found that 33 states maintain at least some mechanism by which an individual can have a criminal record sealed or expunged under specific circumstances. Trying to provide a national overview of these policies is tricky as they vary vastly by jurisdiction. Here we elect only a few criteria to compare that we believe might be useful to the reader. Overall, 16 states maintain policies for sealing adult criminal records in some circumstances, and 27 states report allowing for the full expunging of records, with Colorado noting that this option is only available for juveniles (SEARCH, 2010). In some instances the seal is automatic based on a non-conviction or the charge of conviction. In other cases, it is applied for and granted at a later date via judicial discretion.

Also, in many states, the ability to receive a seal is not only linked to age and time since offense but also the type or level of offense. For example, while seals or expungement are available in 33 states, only 11 of the 33 states offer expungement for felonies while 16 of the 33 states extend it for misdemeanor charges. Thus, it seems the less serious the immediate criminal court outcome, the more likely one is to later receive the benefit of expungement. For example, Illinois offers the ability to seal misdemeanors and lower-level felonies (class 3 and 4 felonies) after the sentence is completed. There is a 3-year waiting period to seal felonies (e.g. waiting period is tied to level of charge), and the waiting period can be waived if the individual completes high school or higher education (e.g. another factor that may be linked with disadvantage and race in American society). The individual must apply and pay for the sealing of the record after the waiting period, but it is still not automatic; the request is reviewed by and granted by a judge.

Because many states have these practices available, we believe it is important for research on discretion in the criminal justice system to take a close look at how the original charge and any charge reduction offered in a plea bargain impact the potential for the record to be sealed or expunged either immediately or at a later date. Moreover, in states where the sealing or expunging decision is later granted by a judge, we believe it is equally important to study the judicial decision-making criteria that impact the granting or denial of the seal or expungement.

Importance of Sealing/Expunging a Criminal Record

As hinted at in the introduction, the ability to conceal a criminal record in today's technological age is quite difficult. Anyone who has surfed the internet, perhaps even just searching for the name of an author, has been bombarded with website advertisements to run criminal background checks on that person for a fairly low fee (e.g. instantcheckmate.com, beenverified.com, goodhire.com, and intellius.com, just to name a few that routinely pop up on our own computers), and this is just the tip of the iceberg. Criminal background checks have become popular among employers and others because they are now easy to perform. As early as 2004, upwards of half of all companies surveyed indicated they performed a criminal background check before hiring an individual (Holzer, Raphael, and Stoll, 2004), and almost 80% of the nation's largest companies reported performing such checks (Burke, 2004). Even when compared to other traditionally stigmatized labor market groups, such as individuals on welfare, those with less than college education, or job applicants with gaps in employment, employers express the strongest aversion to hiring individuals who have criminal records (Holzer, Raphael, and Stoll, 2006). One overview by the Center for Economic and Policy Research suggests that criminal records cost the United States about 0.4 to 0.5 percentage points of GDP in 2008, or roughly $57 to $65 billion in economic output, as a result of lower employment. Moreover, this literature also points to further racial disparities in the impact of a criminal record at employment. For example, an audit study examining the behavior of employers faced with similar resumes except for the fact that one set of resumes indicated a criminal record and the other did not found that the mark of the criminal record served as more of a hindrance to employment for minority males when compared to White males (Pager, 2003). In fact, in this particular study, none of the minority males with a criminal record indicated on the application received an interview.

Beyond employment, it is well documented that having a criminal record, particularly for a felony offense, can restrict numerous life opportunities by limiting the probability of high school completion and eligibility for federal financial aid for college (Kirk and Sampson, 2013); limiting housing options (Thatcher, 2008); and even the right to vote (Uggen and Manza, 2004). With so much at stake for someone carrying the burden of a criminal record, it seems timely and important to understand the mechanisms by which such a record may be sealed from public view, or even entirely purged from file to offer these individuals a second chance at life. In the following sections, we take a more detailed look at one state's sealing policies; the number of individuals impacted (e.g. given a second chance) through such policies; and ultimately how sealing might be a hereto yet unstudied point of judicial discretion that holds the potential to either correct for, or exacerbate, systemic bias against minorities and males.

New York Example: Three Types of Seals

In this section, we provide an overview of what the population of visible offenders might look like regarding age, gender, and race when considering all records versus only unsealed records. We then explore the factors that relate to an individual receiving the benefit of a sealed record with a particular focus on race and gender. For this exercise, we selected New York State as it has some of the most liberal sealing policies in the nation. New York also has very stringent regulation of its sealed records to that to ensure that not only employers or private entities conducting a background investigation are barred from viewing the record, but also that even the FBI and other criminal justice entities are barred from viewing the record.

New York also has three distinct types of seals that we will explore here that represent three decision points in the system. The first is the decision to convict. New York seals all arrests that do not lead to conviction immediately without any needed application on part of the accused individual. Moreover, if the individual does not have any prior record or other open arrests, the fingerprints are destroyed so that the individual cannot be connected back to that arrest. Second, New York also has a policy that automatically seals all convictions reduced to violations or infractions.[2] Furthermore, similar to the above case, if the individual had no prior convictions, the fingerprints are destroyed, so that no future arrest can be linked to this individual. Finally, New York statute provides one additional opportunity for sealing that places more discretion directly in the hands of the judge known as the Youthful Offender seal. If the offender was under the age of 19 at the time of the offense, and the conviction is not for a Class A Felony offense, the judge, upon conviction, may designate the individual a "youthful offender," which seals the criminal record and mitigates possible punishments at sentencing. However, for a "youthful offender" seal, the personal identifier is not destroyed and is maintained in the New York criminal history file along with all charge, conviction, and disposition information. Thus, a quick examination of sealed and unsealed records in New York can provide an overview of how decisions to convict, to plea to lesser offenses, and to apply direct judicial discretion can impact the population of individuals with a formal criminal record.

Data/Sample

For the following analysis, we utilize a sample of youth arrested in New York State in 2001. This data was collected by the Bureau of Justice Statistics as part of the

"Adult Trajectories of Juvenile Offenders Processed in Adult Court" data series, which includes three cohorts of arrestees in New York (1987, 1994, and 2001). In particular, this population is useful as it involves only very young offenders who are unlikely to have significant criminal record at the time of entrance into the study that would prevent them from being eligible for a seal, and because of age, they are indeed eligible for all three types of seals noted above. We chose to focus on the most recent cohort, the 2001 cohort, for this analysis.

The data were provided to the Bureau of Justice Statistics by the New York Division of Criminal Justice Services and represents a "top charge" file that includes the most serious arrest and disposition offense for each system cycle. A cycle in New York is defined as a set of charges resulting from one arrest event. For example, if an individual committed a breaking and entering, vandalized a building, and assaulted a tenant, the assault would be recorded in the top charge file. However, the seal indicator is available at both the individual charge and the cycle levels. For this analysis we include as "sealed" those instances in which the entire cycle is sealed rather than just specific charges within a cycle.

The original file had 33,859 initial arrest events that were connected to 33,503 unique individuals. For these 33,503 individual/event combinations, we applied coding provided by the New York Division of Criminal Justice Services to determine whether the event was sealed and found that only 4,275, or 12.8%, were *not* sealed. Table 5.1 presents a basic breakdown of sealed and unsealed records based on legal and extralegal factors such as gender, race, offense severity, and prior record.

The first thing that might jump out at the reader is that, of the original 33,503 individuals arrested, only 1 individual was charged with a violation or infraction at arrest.[3] That is because, in general, a violation or infraction is not a fingerprintable offense and, thus, does not get entered into the state's official repository. This original sample of arrested youth is almost equally represented between White and Black youth (41% to 40%) and is about 17% Hispanic. As might be expected, the sample is predominately male (78%), only a small portion of the sample (less than 5%) has any type of prior record, and the primary offense at arrest is classified as a Misdemeanor A (51%). The most popular type of crime is a property crime (37%), followed by violent offenses (24%).

Table 5.1 also divides the sample into sealed and not-sealed portions. What is most surprising at first glance based on the prior literature is that, after sealing, the visible sample appears much more White than Black with White youth now representing 51% of the non-sealed sample and Black youth representing only 36%. However, it is important to remember this is a simple bivariate comparison. Thus, in the later sections, we employ multivariate analysis to further examine and understand the factors that influence sealing and thus the population of "offenders" visible to law enforcement and/or the public.

We then also divided the sealed records into three categories representing the three types of seals available: 1) sealed at arrest due to non-conviction (n = 16,602); 2) application of a youthful offender (YO) seal upon adjudication (n = 5,856); and (3) sealed at disposition due to a plea to a violation/infraction (n = 7199).[4] Table 5.2 provides a breakdown of our sample by type of seal.

As depicted in Table 5.2, the samples for the different types of seals seem to differ considerably; in fact, every factor examined was different at a statistical significance

Table 5.1 Sample Descriptive Statistics

	Full Sample		*Not Sealed*		*Sealed*		*Sig.*
	#	%	#	%	#	%	
	33503	100.00%	4257	12.71%	29246	87.29%	
Male	26173	78.12%	3552	83.44%	22621	77.35%	***
Race							***
White	13612	40.63%	2181	51.20%	11431	39.09%	
Black	13312	39.73%	1540	36.18%	11772	40.25%	
Asian	760	2.27%	82	1.93%	678	2.32%	
Unknown	8	0.02%	2	0.05%	6	0.02%	
Missing	5811	17.34%	452	10.62%	5359	18.32%	
Ethnicity							***
Hispanic	5790	17.28%	456	10.71%	5334	18.24%	
Prior Record							***
Prior Felony	778	2.32%	218	5.12%	560	1.91%	
Prior YO Felony	847	2.53%	322	7.56%	525	1.80%	
Prior Misdemeanor	435	1.30%	233	5.47%	202	0.69%	
Prior YO Misdemeanor	989	2.95%	400	9.40%	589	2.01%	
Charge Seriousness Arrest							***
Felony A	91	0.27%	40	0.94%	51	0.17%	
Felony B	2493	7.44%	552	12.97%	1941	6.64%	
Felony C	2002	5.98%	305	7.16%	1697	5.80%	
Felony D	3637	10.86%	500	11.75%	3137	10.73%	
Felony E	2254	6.73%	353	8.29%	1901	6.50%	
Misdemeanor A	17089	51.01%	1907	44.80%	15182	51.91%	
Misdemeanor B	5556	16.58%	356	8.36%	5200	17.78%	
Unclass. Misdemeanor	380	1.13%	243	5.71%	137	0.47%	
Violation/Infraction	1	0.00%	1	0.02%	0	0.00%	
Crime Type							***
Violent Crime	7972	23.79%	1022	24.01%	6950	23.76%	
Property Crime	12517	37.36%	1428	33.54%	11089	37.92%	
Drug Crime	6691	19.97%	665	15.62%	6026	20.60%	
Other Crime	6323	18.87%	1142	26.83%	5181	17.72%	

Note: *** = 0.001, significance level 2; ** = 0.01, significance level 1; * = 0.05.

level of .001 or higher. Some of the more major differences seem to be that the YO sealed sample is more likely than the other samples to be White males charged with more serious and violent offenses at arrest that the samples of individuals receiving seals through non-conviction or plea to a violation or infraction. Seals through non-conviction or pleas were more likely for those with some sort of prior record, where the YO seal was rarely given to individuals with a prior record.

Table 5.2 Sealed Sample by Seal Type

	Arrest Seal		*YO Seal*		*Violation Seal*	
	#	%	#	%	#	%
Male	12496	75.27%	4717	80.55%	5517	76.64%
Race						
White	5824	35.08%	2860	48.84%	2855	39.66%
Black	6996	42.14%	1989	33.97%	2807	38.99%
Asian	400	2.41%	127	2.17%	153	2.13%
Unknown/Missing	3382	20.37%	606	10.35%	1384	19.22%
Ethnicity						
Hispanic	3369	20.29%	599	10.23%	1371	19.04%
Prior Record						
Prior Felony	262	1.58%	98	1.67%	201	2.79%
Prior YO Felony	275	1.66%	34	0.58%	216	3.00%
Prior Misdemeanor	77	0.46%	43	0.73%	83	1.15%
Prior YO Misdemeanor	22	0.13%	161	2.75%	206	2.86%
Charge Seriousness Arrest						
Felony A	25	0.15%	22	0.38%	4	0.06%
Felony B	756	4.55%	959	16.38%	228	3.17%
Felony C	655	3.95%	829	14.16%	213	2.96%
Felony D	1266	7.63%	1257	21.47%	623	8.65%
Felony E	748	4.51%	691	11.80%	475	6.60%
Misdemeanor A	9066	54.61%	1636	27.94%	4633	64.36%
Misdemeanor B	4122	24.83%	126	2.15%	964	13.39%
Unclass. Misdemeanor	24	0.14%	62	1.06%	59	0.82%
Violation/Infraction						0.00%
Crime Type						
Violent Crime	3631	21.87%	1653	28.23%	1694	23.53%
Property Crime	6136	36.96%	2092	35.72%	2921	40.58%
Drug Crime	4234	25.50%	763	13.03%	1038	14.42%
Other Crime	2601	15.67%	1074	18.34%	1546	21.48%

Because each type of seal is necessarily influenced by different factors, we chose not to perform a multinomial logistic regression but chose to divide our sample into three separate samples that compare those receiving each type of seal. For the first analysis, which assesses differences in individuals receiving a "seal" because the arrest does not lead to a conviction, the sample consists of all arrests with the outcome being conviction or no conviction. For the remaining two analyses, which examine those receiving a seal because 1) the final charge is reduced to a violation/infraction or 2) the judge orders a Youthful Offender seal upon conviction regardless of the seriousness of the offense charge, the sample consists of only those arrests that ultimately lead to a conviction.[5]

Modeling Strategy

Our primary independent variables of interest are gender, race, and ethnicity. New York measures Hispanic ethnicity separately from race. Our race/ethnicity variables thus include White (reference), Black, Asian, American Indian, and Other, while we also have a non-mutually exclusive variable for Hispanic ethnicity (1 = Hispanic, 0 = not Hispanic). Gender is measured on the traditional categories of male and female as this is what is captured in the data.

Because this research builds upon the extensive body of research reviewed above addressing disparity at other decision-making points, we draw upon that literature to inform a selection of control variables. First, we control for seriousness of offense with a 10-point scale ranging from a Felony A, the most serious classification in New York, being coded as "10" and a law infraction/violation, the least serious classification in New York coded as "1." We also divide offenses out by tradition types: violent, drug, property (reference), and other.

Prior record was examined several ways, and because much of the sample had no record, we selected a series of dichotomous measures rather than a continuous count. These dichotomies are: any prior felony (1 = yes, 0 = no), any prior misdemeanor (1 = yes, 0 = no), any prior YO seal for a felony (1 = yes, 0 = no), and any prior YO seal for a misdemeanor (1 = yes 0 = no). Even given this simplified version of counting a criminal record, the model for YO adjudication would not converge with this measure in the model. This is likely because having a prior felony or misdemeanor is one of the criteria judges use to "disqualify" a youth from this type of seal.

We also explored contextual factors and determined that there was not much variance at level 2 except for between New York City and its Boroughs and the rest of the state.[6] Thus, we would not have power at level 2 to perform a multi-level model. To be conservative, however, we perform fixed effects models that include dummy variables for New York City and its Boroughs versus the rest of the state. Each table will present findings with and without this control as it proves to significantly alter one's conclusions about the impact of race/ethnicity.

Results

Seal at Arrest: Non-Conviction

Table 5.3 provides the results for the logistic regression predicting a seal based on non-conviction. Here, we first note that conviction may largely be tied to the strength of evidence and capabilities of attorneys, which are concepts that cannot be measured with an administrative data set. Therefore, these results may encompass factors beyond charging and prosecutorial and judicial discretion.

Table 5.3 Sealed at Arrest—No Conviction

	Model 1				*Model 2*			
	Coef.	*Std. Err.*	*Odds Ratio*	*Sig.*	*Coef.*	*Std. Err.*	*Odds Ratio*	*Sig.*
Male	−0.359	0.052	0.698	0.000	−0.400	0.052	0.670	0.000
Black	0.049	0.045	1.050	0.275	−0.390	0.049	0.677	0.000
Asian	0.163	0.136	1.177	0.233	−0.251	0.142	0.778	0.077
Other Race	0.648	0.351	1.912	0.065	0.255	0.310	1.290	0.411
Hispanic	−0.160	0.351	0.852	0.648	−0.583	0.310	0.558	0.060
Felony B	1.227	0.225	3.410	0.000	1.342	0.229	3.828	0.000
Felony C	1.983	0.234	7.266	0.000	2.114	0.238	8.282	0.000
Felony D	2.227	0.230	9.270	0.000	2.368	0.234	10.675	0.000
Felony E	2.279	0.235	9.770	0.000	2.474	0.239	11.873	0.000
Misdemeanor A	2.539	0.225	12.663	0.000	2.740	0.229	15.488	0.000
Misdemeanor B	3.090	0.228	21.970	0.000	3.157	0.232	23.508	0.000
Misdemeanor U	−0.151	0.255	0.860	0.554	0.134	0.258	1.144	0.603
Violent	−0.031	0.053	0.969	0.560	−0.126	0.054	0.882	0.020
Drug	0.095	0.071	1.100	0.182	−0.052	0.072	0.950	0.474
Other Crime	−0.263	0.055	0.769	0.000	−0.282	0.055	0.754	0.000
Trial	−1.820	0.237	0.162	0.000	−1.683	0.238	0.186	0.000
Other Disposition	−3.420	0.053	0.033	0.000	−3.259	0.054	0.038	0.000
NewYork/Boroughs					1.146	0.054	3.145	0.000
Constant	0.353	0.231	1.423	0.126	0.133	0.234	1.142	0.569
LL	9600				9461			
Pseudo R^2	0.24				0.258			

	Coef.	*S.E.*	*Odds Ratio*	*Sig.*
Male	−0.609	0.057	0.544	0.000
Black	−0.629	0.059	0.533	0.000
Asian	−0.331	0.160	0.718	0.038
Race Missing	−0.123	0.345	0.884	0.721
Other Race	Omitted			
Hispanic	−0.476	0.345	0.622	0.168
Felony B	1.144	0.280	3.139	0.000
Felony C	1.716	0.287	5.560	0.000
Felony D	1.999	0.283	7.380	0.000
Felony E	2.079	0.288	7.999	0.000
Misdemeanor A	3.218	0.279	24.973	0.000
Misdemeanor B	3.773	0.282	43.494	0.000
Unclass. Misdemeanor	−0.340	0.359	0.712	0.344
Violent	−0.025	0.061	0.976	0.686
Drug	−0.206	0.080	0.814	0.010
Other Crime	−0.221	0.060	0.801	0.000
Constant	−1.916	0.310	0.147	0.000

In Model 1, Table 5.3, we find that Black youth are more likely to receive a sealed record because the arrest did not lead to a conviction. However, the effect is not large (odds ratio of 1.05) and does not reach significance. For Hispanic youth, however, the effect is negative with an odds ratio of .85 and significant. When fixed effect controls are added in for New York City and its boroughs in Model 2, the effect for the city itself is positive and significant, meaning less youth are likely to be convicted in the metropolis than the rest of the state. This is important as almost half of all arrests happened in the city. Also, when controlling for this, the effect for being Black is negative and substantially large (odds ratio of .677, p = .000) and the effect for being Hispanic is also much larger (odds ratio .558, p = .000). This may indicate that more Black youth are subject to false arrest in New York City, or it could reflect more leniency on part of the court, or it could be a function of workload. The point of this chapter is not to identify causality, however, but to examine how sealing policies impact youth of color and Hispanic origin. Thus, from Table 5.3, we can conclude that this type of seal is less likely to be given to Hispanic youth across the state and less likely to be applied to black youth outside of New York City and its boroughs.

Seal at Conviction: Plea to Violation/Infraction

Because essentially no one in the original sample was charged with a violation or infraction (e.g. this are traditionally non-fingerprintable offenses and would not make it into an official criminal history database), those convicted of such an offense are essentially the result of a charge bargain determined during the plea or conviction stage. Table 5.4 provides the results of the logistic regression analysis predicting this type of seal for all those eventually convicted of at least one of the original arrest charges in the criminal history cycle. It should be noted that, in this model, the charges are also charges at arrest as the conviction charge level (violation/infraction) is the dependent variable thus capturing charge bargaining/reduction. Also, prior record and type of disposition (plea, trial, other) are included in this model as well.

As Table 5.4, Model 1, shows, being Black increases the likelihood of this type of seal with an odds ratio of 1.5 (p = .000), and being Hispanic reduces the odds with an odds ratio of .53 although it does not reach significance. However, again, when controlling for the impact of New York City and its boroughs in Model 2, the effects change. In fact, for Black youth, the coefficient changes direction so that being Black now reduces the likelihood of receiving this type of seal (odds ratio of .884) with the impact approaching significance (.067). The impact for being Hispanic again increases reducing the odds to .410 and reaches significances at the p = .05 level (p = .035).

Having any type of prior record explored in this analysis significantly reduces the likelihood of this type of seal and crime severity is inversely related to the odds of receiving this type of seal. However, neither type of crime (violent, drug, property, other) nor type of disposition (plea bargain, trial, other) reached significance in this model.

Table 5.4 Seal at Disposition: Plea to Violation/Infraction

N = 11,127	*Model 1*				*Model 2*			
	Coef.	*Std. Err.*	*Odds Ratio*	*Sig.*	*Coef.*	*Std. Err.*	*Odds Ratio*	*Sig.*
Male	−0.212	0.069	0.809	0.002	−0.259	0.071	0.772	0.000
Black	0.436	0.061	1.546	0.000	−0.123	0.067	0.884	0.067
Asian	0.281	0.184	1.325	0.127	−0.221	0.191	0.802	0.247
Other Race	1.452	0.454	4.272	0.001	0.952	0.423	2.590	0.025
Hispanic	−0.368	0.453	0.692	0.416	−0.891	0.423	0.410	0.035
Felony B	1.777	0.541	5.912	0.001	1.770	0.544	5.868	0.001
Felony C	2.444	0.547	11.523	0.000	2.482	0.550	11.970	0.000
Felony D	3.205	0.542	24.653	0.000	3.295	0.545	26.965	0.000
Felony E	3.483	0.546	32.554	0.000	3.665	0.549	39.049	0.000
Misdemeanor A	4.183	0.539	65.539	0.000	4.415	0.542	82.704	0.000
Misdemeanor B	4.374	0.543	79.379	0.000	4.552	0.546	94.835	0.000
Misdemeanor U	1.551	0.565	4.717	0.006	1.858	0.568	6.411	0.001
Prior Felony	−0.573	0.109	0.564	0.000	−0.801	0.114	0.449	0.000
Prior YO Felony	−1.155	0.104	0.315	0.000	−1.299	0.110	0.273	0.000
Prior Misd.	−1.051	0.111	0.350	0.000	−1.175	0.114	0.309	0.000
Prior YO Misd.	−1.246	0.094	0.288	0.000	−1.174	0.096	0.309	0.000
Violent	−0.073	0.070	0.929	0.297	−0.141	0.072	0.869	0.050
Drug	−0.068	0.094	0.934	0.472	−0.232	0.097	0.793	0.017
Other Crime	−0.321	0.071	0.726	0.000	−0.354	0.073	0.702	0.000
Trial	−1.571	0.388	0.208	0.000	−1.386	0.384	0.250	0.000
Other Disp.	−5.238	0.173	0.005	0.000	−5.052	0.173	0.006	0.000
New York/Boroughs					1.410	0.077	4.095	0.000
Constant	−2.477	0.543	0.084	0.000	−2.685	0.546	0.068	0.000
LL	−4607.000				−4506.000			
Pseudo R^2	0.310				0.390			

Seal at Adjudication: Youthful Offender Seal

The last type of seal considered is the Youthful Offender seal, which reduces the conviction to an "adjudication," and as such seals the record from public view as one would for a juvenile. This type of seal is rather unique to New York as New York is one of only two states (three at the time of this data collection) that processed all 16- and 17-year-olds in adult court. Even though this policy appears harsh, the state does offer this Youthful Offender seal that helps to reduce the lifelong impact of a criminal record. This particular seal, as noted above, is not as charge specific as it is offered upon conviction for any type of offense other than a Felony A (murder, non-negligent manslaughter). And, even in the case of a Felony A conviction, the judge has the authority to offer the seal if it will benefit the administration of justice in the view of the court.

As Table 5.5, Model 1, reveals, for this type of seal, race is a significant predictor even without controlling for the New York City/state variance. Here we find that with the discretion being more specifically in the hands of the judge, the difference is an odds ratio of .78 for Blacks (p = .000) and .57 for Hispanics (p = .06). When controlling for

Table 5.5 Seal at Conviction—Youthful Offender Designation

N = 9,976	*Model 1*				*Model 2*			
	Coef.	*Std. Err.*	*Odds Ratio*	*Sig.*	*Coef.*	*Std. Err.*	*Odds Ratio*	*Sig.*
Male	−0.121	0.060	0.886	0.044	−0.124	0.060	0.883	0.039
Black	−0.247	0.051	0.781	0.000	−0.297	0.054	0.743	0.000
Asian	0.047	0.154	1.048	0.762	0.002	0.155	1.002	0.987
Other/Unknown Race	0.297	0.302	1.346	0.324	0.249	0.302	1.282	0.410
Hispanic	−0.569	0.302	0.566	0.060	−0.638	0.303	0.528	0.035
Felony B	1.166	0.271	3.208	0.000	1.181	0.271	3.259	0.000
Felony C	1.469	0.279	4.345	0.000	1.499	0.279	4.478	0.000
Felony D	1.385	0.275	3.995	0.000	1.426	0.276	4.163	0.000
Felony E	1.128	0.280	3.089	0.000	1.179	0.281	3.252	0.000
Misdemeanor A	0.242	0.272	1.273	0.375	0.300	0.273	1.350	0.272
Misdemeanor B	−0.522	0.287	0.593	0.069	−0.465	0.288	0.628	0.107
Misdemeanor U	−0.887	0.311	0.412	0.004	−0.826	0.312	0.438	0.008
Violent	0.071	0.059	1.073	0.232	0.054	0.059	1.056	0.361
Drug	−0.057	0.081	0.944	0.481	−0.069	0.081	0.934	0.398
Other Crime	−0.100	0.062	0.905	0.104	−0.111	0.062	0.895	0.073
Trial	−0.261	0.247	0.770	0.290	−0.261	0.247	0.771	0.291
Other Disp.	3.646	0.296	38.308	0.000	3.652	0.296	38.534	0.000
New York Boroughs					0.173	0.065	1.189	0.007
Constant	−0.290	0.278	0.748	0.297	−0.336	0.278	0.715	0.228
LL	1371.000				1378.000			
Pseudo R^2	0.100				0.101			

New York City and its boroughs in Model 2, the effect is slightly larger for Black youth with an odds ratio of .74 (e.g. a 26% versus a 22% reduction in the odds of receiving this type of seal as compared to a white youth) and for Hispanic youth as well with an odds ratio of .53 (e.g. a 47% versus a 43% reduction in the odds versus White youth) and the impact for Hispanic youth now reaches significance ($p = .03$).

Connections With the Literature

We began this chapter with two basic notions: 1) that race and ethnicity have been found to impact all stages of the criminal justice process and 2) that the ability to seal a criminal record is one particular aspect of the criminal justice process that has to date been unexplored as it may relate to bias in punishment. What is significantly different here is that the ability to seal a criminal record has consequences that reach far beyond the bounds of the criminal justice system and while many speak of the "collateral consequences" of a criminal record, scholars have been slower to speak of this as an actual punishment applied by the system. We hope to have first highlighted in this chapter that due to the lifelong nature of a criminal record and the increased use of such a record to limit social mobility and opportunity, it should indeed be viewed as part of the punishment inflicted by the criminal justice system.

Second, we propose that the discretion of police and prosecutors in charging with sealable/expungable offenses and the discretion of judges in accepting pleas to lesser offenses or directly applying a seal to a record are hereto unstudied areas of potential bias in the criminal justice system.

We began with a step-by-step review of the literature as it applied to different stages of the criminal justice process and decision-making for a reason—each step is inherently tied to and influences the others, just as each step is inherently tied to an influences the potential of having a criminal record sealed or expunged. In this chapter we are particularly concerned with the potential impact of each stage on influencing the likelihood of such a seal or expungement as well as judicial discretion in the final stages of choosing to seal or not seal a criminal record.

We started with literature that suggests that police might be more likely to stop and arrest minorities as compared to White youth (Spitzer, 1999). Our findings here cannot causally support that statement, but they do reveal that Black and Hispanic youth are disproportionally represented in the arrest statistics. For example, according to estimates from the U.S. Census, the population of New York State is about 18% African American and 17% Hispanic, yet African Americans made up almost 40% of the original arrest sample.

If racial bias is inherent in all stages of the system, we would have expected that, when we originally divided the sample into those cases with sealed and not-sealed records, we would find more African Americans having non-sealed records as well. That is, their proportion in the sample would increase to above 40%. However, the opposite was true as it decreased to 36% while the visible population of White offenders grew to over 50%.

To understand the implications of this, we further explored the three reasons an individual might have their record sealed up front: 1) an arrest not leading to a conviction, 2) a plea to a sealable offense, and 3) a Youthful Offender seal specifically applied by the judge at conviction.

First, we find that almost half of the original sample has the event sealed because it does not lead to a conviction. Thus, this type of seal is the "most popular" in our data. We also find that, not controlling for New York City (the site of much research on police stop-and-frisk policies), it appears that race has a positive impact on sealing with African American youth more likely to have an arrest that does not lead to a conviction. Once we control for the impact of New York City, the effect for being African American switches direction, however. Our interpretation of this interesting finding is that indeed in New York City there appear to be many more arrests of African Americans that are later not substantiated by conviction. The two explanations for this findings could be 1) the system is "correcting" itself for the disproportional arrest rate at later stages through leniency towards minority youth or 2) the police are simply arresting Black and Hispanic youth with less probably cause/evidence than White youth, and therefore, their cases are less likely to result in a conviction. If this is the case, the impact at the arrest stage seems to be largely limited to New York City with minority youth in this jurisdiction much more likely to receive an acquittal or dismissal of charges thus leading to the arrest record being sealed.

One very important point to make here is that New York is fairly unique in its seal of all arrests that do not lead to convictions. In fact, we could not find any other state that automatically sealed such arrests, let alone destroyed identifiers. Thus, if this same effect holds true in other key metropolitan areas such as Chicago, Philadelphia, and Washington, D.C. for example, regardless of the conviction status, the individual would maintain a rap sheet with the arrest visible to the public. Thus, while New York City may "auto-correct" in some fashion for disproportionate minority arrests due to state sealing policy, this is not a benefit that is extended elsewhere.

Second, we find a small but significant effect for plea bargaining with the impact in the direction anticipated. That is, being a minority youth reduces the likelihood of a plea that automatically seals the criminal record. When not controlling for the New York City effect, it appears Black youth are more likely to receive this type of plea. However, when you control for New York City and its boroughs the effect reverses direction again, although here it only approaches significance for black youth. Hispanic youth are less likely to receive this type of plea in both models explored, with and without New York City controls. Similar to a possible "over-arresting" impact at the initial arrest stage, this plea distinction in New York City could be related to initial charging decisions. If prosecutors are more likely to initially charge Black youth with a non-sealable offense (a Misdemeanor A or higher), then it is important that they are able to plea down to this level to have a record sealed. What our data cannot capture is the number of youth and their race/ethnic distribution who are initially charged with a sealable offense (e.g. a violation or infraction) as these are traditionally non-fingerprintable offenses that are not recorded in the state criminal history file. It may or may not be the case that White youth are originally more likely to be charged with these offenses.

Regarding the last type of seal, the Youthful Offender seal, in which the decision lies more directly in the hands of the judge to apply the seal, we find the most consistent evidence of racial and ethnic disparity in both models. Regardless of controls for New York City and its boroughs, Black and Hispanic youth are less likely to have this final type of seal applied at the conviction stage. This is also important not only for collateral consequences, but for immediate sentencing outcomes as well as being designated a Youthful Offender reduces the possible punishment that can be meted out by the judge. For example, a Felony B conviction for an adult is punishable by up to 10 years in prison, but this is reduced to 4 years for an individual designated a Youthful Offender. We did not explore actual sentencing outcomes in this chapter as our focus was directly on the seal itself but exert this as another area of possible study. To our knowledge, only one study by Peterson (1988) was conducted that examined punishment by Youthful Offender status, and in this work, minority youth were still found to receive more significant punishment even if they were awarded Youthful Offender status (e.g. more likely to receive prison or jail sentence as compared to white youth).

Finally, as we acknowledge that these findings are exploratory and descriptive and not causal in nature, we boldly call for more attention to be given to specific state and federal sealing policies and the stages of system discretion that ultimately impact whether or not an individual receives a seal or expungement. While we focus on only one state and a population of young offenders as an example, future research in this area should explore differences in outcomes based on the nature of state sealing policies to make recommendations about which practices lead to more or less disparity. We also believe it will be important for such research to consider the causal interplay of legal and extralegal factors such as race, ethnicity, gender, and even socioeconomic class. Because a criminal record is truly seen as a "punishment with no end" (Evans, 2014), we hope our brief exercise in this chapter will bring much-needed attention to the lifelong consequences of a criminal record and to the realization that the ability to escape its stigma is subject to the same disparities that have long been acknowledge at other stages of system decision-making.

Notes

1 This project was made possible through a grant from the U.S. Department of Justice, Bureau of Justice Statistics, award #2013R2CXK052. The data was provided by the New York State Division of Criminal Justice Services (DCJS). The opinions, findings, and conclusions expressed in this publication are those of the authors and not those of DCJS or the U.S. Department of Justice. Neither the federal government, New York State nor DCJS assumes liability for its contents or use thereof.
2 There are several exceptions to this rule with convictions for violations of domestic violence and harassment among others not qualifying for the automatic seal.
3 A violation or infraction is not a fingerprintable offense in New York. Thus, an individual originally charged with this low level of offense is not entered into the main administrative data set used for this analysis which is based upon fingerprints.
4 There were 137 individuals in the data for which it indicated both a YO seal and a seal due to a plea to a violation/infraction. For the included analysis, these 137 individuals were included in both samples in Table 5.2; thus the total *n* does not equal the full sample *n* of 33,503. Supplementary analyses were done eliminating these 137 individuals, and the overall trend of results was unchanged.
5 We note that 141 individuals had a seal that included both a YO seal granted by a judge and a plea to a violation/infraction. We chose to include these individuals in our analysis of both types of seals but performed sensitivity analysis to ensure that excluding them from either sample did not alter results, and it did not.
6 We also conducted fixed effect models controlling for county of arrest and conviction, the results from these models are almost identical to the ones presented herein and are available from the authors upon request.

References

Albonetti, C. A. (1997). Sentencing under the federal sentencing guidelines: Effects of defendant characteristics, guilty pleas, and departures on sentencing outcomes for drug offenses, 1991–1992. *Law and Society Review*, *21*(4), 789–822.

Baldus, D., Woodworth, G., Grosso, C., & Christ, A. (2002). Arbitrariness and discrimination in the administration of the death penalty: A legal and empirical analysis of the Nebraska experience (1973–1999). *Nebraska Law Review*, *88*, 486–753.

Baldus, D., Woodworth, G., Zuckerman, D., Weiner, N. A., & Broffitt, B. (1998). Racial discrimination in the death penalty in the post-Furman era: An empirical and legal review, with recent findings from Philadelphia. *Cornell Law Review*, *83*, 1638–1770.

Bernstein, I. N., Kick, E., Leung, J. T., & Schulz, B. (1977). Charge reduction: An intermediary stage in the process of labeling criminal defendants. *Social Forces*, *56*(2), 362–384.

Bjerk, D. (2005). Making the crime fit the penalty: The role of prosecutorial discretion under mandatory minimum sentencing. *The Journal of Law and Economics*, *48*, 591–625.

Brame, R., Bushway, S. D., Paternoster, R., & Turner, M. G. (2014). Demographic patterns of cumulative arrest by ages 18 and 23. *Crime and Delinquency*, *60*(3), 471–486.

Brame, R., Turner, M. G., Paternoster, R., & Bushway, S. D. (2012). Cumulative prevalence of arrest from ages 18–23 in a national sample. *Pediatrics*, *129*, 21–27.

Burke, M. E. (2004). *Reference and background checking survey report*. Alexandria, VA: Society for Human Resource Management.

Bushway, S., & Piehl, A. M. (2007). Social science research and the legal threat to presumptive sentencing guidelines. *Criminology and Public Policy*, *6*, 461.

Caravelis, C., Chiricos, T., & Bales, W. (2011). Static and dynamic indicators of minority threat in sentencing outcomes: A multi-level analysis. *Journal of Quantitative Criminology*, *27*, 405–425.

Cole, D. (1999). *No equal justice: Race and class in the criminal justice system*. New York: New Press.

Crawford, C., Chiricos, T., & Kleck, G. (1998). Race, racial threat, and sentencing of habitual offenders. *Criminology*, *36*, 481–512.

Crow, M. S., & Johnson, K. A. (2008). Race, ethnicity, and habitual-offender sentencing. *Criminal Justice Policy Review*, *19*, 63.

D'Alessio, S. J., & Stolzenberg, L. (2003). Race and the probability of arrest. *Social Forces*, *81*(4), 1381–1397.

Demuth, S., & Steffensmeier, D. (2004). Ethnicity effects on sentence outcomes in large urban courts: Comparisons among White, Black, and Hispanic defendants. *Social Science Quarterly*, *85*, 994–1011.

Durose, M. R., Schmitt, E. L., & Langan, P. A. (2005). *Contacts between police and the public: Findings from the 2002 national survey*. NCJ 207845, Bureau of Justice Statistics, U.S. Department of Justice.

Eisenstein, J., & Jacob, H. (1977). *Felony justice: An organizational analysis of criminal courts* (p. 21). Boston, MA: Little, Brown.

Engen, R. L., & Gainey, R. R. (2000). Modeling the effects of legally relevant and extralegal factors under sentencing guidelines: The rules have changed. *Criminology*, *38*, 1207–1225.

Evans, D. (2014). *Punishment without end*. Research and Evaluation Center. John Jay College of Criminal Justice. New York, New York: City University of New York.

Farrell, J. (2003). Mandatory minimum firearm penalties: A source of sentencing disparity? *Justice Research and Policy*, *5*, 95–116.

Federal Bureau of Investigation. (2011). *Crime in the United States, 2010*. Washington, D.C.: United States Department of Justice.

Gelman, A., Fagan, J., & Kiss, A. (2007). An analysis of the New York City police department's "stop-and-frisk" policy in the context of claims of racial bias. *Journal of the American Statistical Association*, *102*(429), 813–823.

Gross, S. R., & Barnes, K.Y. (2002). Road work: Racial profiling and drug interdiction on the highway. *Michigan Law Review*, *101*, 653–754.

Harris, D. A. (1999). The stories, the statistics, and the law: Why 'Driving While Black' matters. *Minnesota Law Review*, *84*, 265–326.

Holzer, H. J., Raphael, S., & Stoll, M. A. (2004). Will employers hire ex-offenders? Employer checks, background checks, and their determinants. In M. Pattillo, D. Weiman, & B. Western (eds.), *Imprisoning America: The Social Effects of Mass Incarceration*. New York: Russell Sage Foundation.

Holzer, H. J., Raphael, S., & Stoll, M. A. (2006). Perceived criminality, criminal background checks, and the racial hiring practices of employers. *Journal of Law and Economics*, *49*, 451–480.

Jacobs, D., Qian, Z., Carmichael, J. T., & Kent, S. (2007). Who survives death row? An individual and contextual analysis. *American Sociological Review*, *72*, 610–632.

Kelvin Daniels et al. v. City of New York. (2004). Stipulation of settlement, 99 Civ 1695 (SAS), ordered January 9, 2004; filed January 13, 2004.

Kirk, D. S., & Sampson, R. J. (2013). Juvenile arrest and collateral educational damage in the transition to adulthood. *Sociology of Education*, *86*(1), 36–62.

Kramer, J., & Steffensmeier, D. (1993). Race and imprisonment decisions. *Sociological Quarterly, 34*, 357–376.

Kutateladze, B. L., Andiloro, N. R., Johnson, B. D., & Spohn, C. C. (2014). Cumulative disadvantage: Examining racial and ethnic disparity in prosecution and sentencing. *Criminology, 52*(3), 514–551.

Langan, P., Greenfeld, L. A., Smith, S. K., Durose, M. R., & Levin, D. J. (2001). *Contacts between police and the public: Findings from the 1999 national survey*. NCJ 184957, Bureau of Justice Statistics, U.S. Department of Justice.

Legewie, J. (2016). Racial profiling and use of force in police stops: How local events trigger periods of increased discrimination. *American Journal of Sociology, 122*(2), 379–424.

Lundman, R. J., & Kaufman, R. L. (2003). Driving while black: Effects of race, ethnicity, and gender on citizen self-reports of traffic stops and police actions. *Criminology, 41*, 195–220.

Meehan, A. J., & Ponder, M. C. (2002). Race and place: The ecology of racial profiling African American motorists. *Justice Quarterly, 19*(3), 399–430.

Mitchell, O. (2005). A meta-analysis of race and sentencing research: Explaining the inconsistencies. *Journal of Quantitative Criminology, 21*(4), 439–466.

Mitchell, T. L., Haw, R. M., Pfeifer, J. E., & Meissner, C. A. (2005). Racial bias in mock juror decision-making: A meta-analytic review of defendant treatment. *Law and Human Behavior, 29*(6), 621–637.

Myers, M., & Talarico, S. (1986). The social contexts of racial discrimination in sentencing. *Social Problems, 33*, 236–251.

Pager, D. (2003). The mark of a criminal record. *American Journal of Sociology, 108*, 937–975.

Paternoster, R., & Brame, R. (2008). Reassessing race disparities in Maryland capital cases. *Criminology, 46*(4), 971–1008.

Paternoster, R., Brame, R., Bacon, S., Ditchfield, A., Beckman, K., & Frederique, N. (2003). *An empirical analysis of Maryland's death sentencing system with respect to the influence of race and legal jurisdiction*. College Park, MD: University of Maryland.

Peterson, R. (1988). Youthful offender designations and sentencing in New York criminal courts. *Social Problems, 35*(2), 111–130.

Peterson, R., & Hagan, J. (1984). Changing conceptions of race: Towards an account of anomalous findings of sentencing research. *American Sociological Review, 49*, 56–70.

Petrocelli, M., Piquero, A., & Smith, M. R. (2003). Conflict theory and racial profiling: An empirical analysis of police traffic stop data. *Journal of Criminal Justice, 31*(1), 1–11.

Pfeifer, J. E., & Ogloff, J. R. P. (1991). Ambiguity and guilt determinations: A modern racism perspective. *Journal of Applied Social Psychology, 21*, 1713–1725.

Poe-Yamagata, E., & Jones, M. A. (2000). *And justice for some*. Washington, DC: Youth Law Center.

Pope, C. E., & Feyerherm, W. (1995). *Minorities and the Juvenile justice system*. Office of Juvenile Justice and Delinquency Prevention. Washington, DC: U.S. Department of Justice.

Pope, C. E., Lovell, R., & Hsia, H. M. (2002). *Disproportionate minority confinement: A review of the research literature from 1989 through 2001*. Juvenile Justice Bulletin, NCJ 198428. U.S. Department of Justice, Office of Juvenile Justice and Delinquency Prevention, Washington, DC.

SEARCH. (2010). Survey of state criminal record sealing and expungement practices, 2010. www.search.org/files/pdf/Criminal_record_sealing_expungement_survey_March_2010.pdf

Shermer, L., & Johnson, B. (2010). Criminal prosecutions: Examining prosecutorial discretion and charge reductions in US federal district courts. *Justice Quarterly, 27*, 394–430.

Slocum, L. A., Taylor, T. J., Brick, B. T., & Esbensen, F. (2010). Neighborhood structural characteristics, individual-level attitudes, and youths' crime reporting intentions. *Criminology, 48*(4), 1063–1100.

Sommers, S. R., & Ellsworth, P. C. (2001). White juror bias: An investigation of prejudice against Black defendants in the American courtroom. *Psychology, Public Policy, and Law*, 7, 201–229.

Spitzer, E. (1999). *The New York City police department's "stop and frisk" practices."* Office of the New York State Attorney General.

Spohn, C. (2000). Thirty years of sentencing reform: The quest for a racially neutral sentencing process. *Criminal Justice, 3*, 427–501.

Steffensmeier, D., Ulmer, J., & Kramer, J. (1998). The interaction of race, gender, and age in criminal sentencing: The punishment cost of being young, black, and male. *Criminology*, *36*(4), 763–798.

Thacher, D. (2008). The rise of criminal background screening in rental housing. *Law & Social Inquiry*, *33*(1), 5–30.

Tyler, T. R., & Huo, Y. J. (2003). *Trust in the law*. New York: Russell Sage.

Uggen, C., & Manza, J. (2004). Voting and subsequent crime and arrest: Evidence from a community sample. *Columbia Human Rights Law Review*, *36*, 193.

Ulmer, J. T. (1995). The organization and consequences of social pasts in criminal courts. *Sociological Quarterly*, *3*, 587–605.

Ulmer, J. T. (2012). Recent developments and new directions in sentencing research. *Justice Quarterly*, *29*(1), 1–40.

Ulmer, J. T., Kurlychek, M. C., & Kramer, J. H. (2007). Prosecutorial discretion and the imposition of mandatory minimum sentences. *Journal of Research on Crime and Delinquency*, *44*(4), 427–458.

Veneiro, P., & Zoubeck, P. H. (1999). *Interim report of the state police review team regarding allegations of racial profiling*. Office of the New Jersey State Attorney General.

Warren, P., Tomaskovic-Devey, D., Smith, W., Zingraff, M., & Mason, M. (2006). Driving while Black: Bias processes and racial disparities in police stops. *Criminology*, *44*(3), 709–738.

Weitzer, R., & Tuch, S. A. (2002). Perceptions of racial profiling: Race, class, and personal experience. *Criminology*, *50*, 435–456.

Williams, M., & Holcomb, J. (2001). Racial disparity and death sentences in Ohio. *Journal of Criminal Justice*, *29*, 207–218.

Zatz, M. S. (2000). The convergence of race, ethnicity, gender, and class on court decision making: Looking toward the 21st century. *Criminal Justice*, *3*(1), 503–552.

6

DISCRETION IN THE ABSENCE OF GUIDELINES

Charge Bargaining and Sentencing for Felony Defendants in New York[1]

Shi Yan, Shawn D. Bushway, and Allison D. Redlich

Introduction

Sentencing guidelines represent the pursuit of formal rationalization of law, in its aim to enhance consistency in sentences and limit judicial discretion at individual cases (Savelsberg, 1992). However, scholars have argued that the resulting decline of judicial power has left room for prosecutors to manipulate the charges and, therefore, to exert stronger influence over the case outcomes, a phenomenon known as the "hydraulic displacement of discretion" (McCoy, 1984; Miethe, 1987; Reitz, 1998). Although it is hard to study prosecutorial discretion because of data limitations, recent studies have shown that substantial prosecutorial discretion is present in strict sentencing guidelines systems, by examining the movement of the charges from arrest to conviction (Piehl and Bushway, 2007; Rehavi and Starr, 2014). Moreover, this discretion appears to be used in a way that is correlated with race, leading to harsher sentences for Black defendants (Rehavi and Starr, 2014).

Meanwhile, the majority of U.S. states still do not have sentencing guidelines, and judges maintain a relatively large amount of discretion. Less is known about how prosecutors affect case outcomes in these situations. Moreover, data tend to be even less available in non-guidelines states, since it is usually the movement towards guidelines that requires the collection of administrative sentencing and case processing data (for a more comprehensive discussion on the availability of sentencing data, see Miller, 2005). To address this problem, we collected our own data from prosecutor files, for over 500 cases that started as felony filings in two counties in New York State. Our analysis found that the absence of guidelines does not translate into an absence of charge bargaining. In fact, there was substantial charge reduction in the two New York counties. As suggested by the literature, we found considerable racial disparity in the probability of incarceration when we used the information at conviction in the standard criminological sentencing model. However, our estimate of racial disparity decreases when we account for charges at arrest and filing instead of charges at conviction.

Literature Review

Studies conducted using data from single guidelines jurisdictions, especially those with presumptive rather than voluntary guidelines, consistently conclude that guidelines have successfully reduced extralegal disparity at the sentencing stage (e.g. Engen and Gainey, 2000; Tonry, 1996; Wooldredge, 2009). A more recent cross-jurisdiction study further found that compared with voluntary guidelines or the absence of guidelines, presumptive guidelines reasonably diminished racial disparity in sentencing (Wang et al., 2013; see also Bushway and Piehl, 2001). On the other hand, those findings triggered concerns that disparity may have simply been displaced to the prosecution stage rather than eliminated, a phenomenon known as the *hydraulic displacement of discretion* (McCoy, 1984; Miethe, 1987; Reitz, 1998).

Reitz (1998, 2005) argued that legislative attempts to concentrate the power to determine individual cases—the enactment of sentencing guidelines—would lead to a decrease in judicial impact on individual case outcomes but an increase in prosecutorial power. Consider the two extreme hypothetical cases. In a system that allows judges to have unlimited discretion on the sentence (i.e., any sentence can be imposed on any defendant), prosecutors will have no impact on the sentence through charging and charge bargaining, because there is no established relationship between the charge and the sentence. Meanwhile, we can expect a considerable amount of extralegal disparities when we run regression analyses of the sentence. Many variables that correlate with both the extralegal variables and the sentence, such as the legal representation and socio-economic status, are simply hard to collect (and is particularly the case for administrative data collected by state and local agencies). As a result, the effect of these variables will instead be reflected as the correlation between the sentence and the extralegal variables. The other extreme case is a sentencing system that prescribes one single fixed sentence for each crime, which resembles a computer program that gives back the result as soon as the judge enters the charge. Reitz predicted that such system would not eliminate discretion at individual level. Instead, all efforts to influence case outcomes would be around the charge. Prosecutors, in lieu of judges, would gain control over the sentence by manipulating the charge. In those cases, the goal of sentencing guidelines—to promote consistency across cases—may be undermined, particularly when the charging practice is correlated with extralegal factors such as the race of the defendant.

Obviously, neither of the two extreme systems actually exist in the United States. Instead, all state sentencing systems, as well as the federal sentencing system, fall somewhere in between the two ends regarding the control over judicial discretion. In general, non-guidelines jurisdictions are closer to the first example mentioned above, and presumptive guidelines jurisdictions are closer to the second (Reitz, 1998, 2005; see also Kauder and Ostrom, 2008). Following the logic presented above, Reitz predicted that prosecutors would exert more influence over case outcomes in jurisdictions with strict and presumptive guidelines and less influence in jurisdictions with voluntary guidelines or no guidelines.

Another fact that cannot be neglected is that the vast majority of criminal cases in the United States are now resolved by plea bargaining in lieu of court trials (Cohen and Kyckelhahn, 2010). It is typical to consider plea bargaining as the combination of two components, charge bargaining and sentence bargaining (Spohn, 2009). Charge bargaining refers to the shift of the charges between filing and disposition and typically exists in the form of charge reduction. Sentence bargaining refers to the negotiation over the sentence within the statutory range prescribed for a given charge. Sentence bargaining can still occur, and is found to exist substantially, in guidelines jurisdictions (Ulmer, 1997). Yet according to Reitz's (1998) theory, the power of charge bargaining would increase as states move towards presumptive and restrictive guidelines. Moreover, compared with sentence bargaining, charge bargaining is more visible. It is easy to see whether a defendant's charges moved between filing and disposition, but it can be hard to tell how much a defendant's sentence departs from the appropriate level or a reasonable counterfactual, particularly when the statutory range is broad (like the situation in New York detailed below). While we have no intention of denying the impact of sentence bargaining, the focus of this chapter is on charge bargaining (or charge reduction) and its impact on sentencing for both the theoretical and practical reasons presented above.

There has been evidence that both judges (D'Alessio and Stolzenberg, 1995; Stolzenberg and D'Alessio, 1992) and prosecutors (Bjerk, 2005; Engen and Steen, 2000) proactively circumvented the laws that limit judicial discretion. As a result, decisions related to charging, that is, the filing and reduction of charges, have become more important to the sentences. Recent studies generally confirmed this pattern using data in guidelines jurisdictions. In the federal system, which features highly restrictive sentencing guidelines, Shermer and Johnson (2010) found that for some crime types, White defendants had a higher probability of receiving charge reductions than Black and Hispanic defendants, which were associated with 23% shorter recommended sentences. The influence of charging decisions can also exist in the form of mandatory minimums. Also in the federal system, Rehavi and Starr (2014) found Black defendants received longer sentences than White defendants, a result that that they traced back to Black defendants' higher probability of receiving a mandatory minimum charge at indictment, holding the arrest charge constant. In Pennsylvania, another guidelines state, Ulmer, Kramer, and colleagues also found an association between extralegal variables and the use of mandatory minimums (Kramer and Ulmer, 2009; Ulmer, Kurlychek, and Kramer, 2007).

There is limited support for Rehavi and Starr's (2014; see also Ulmer et al., 2007) finding that prosecutors are using their power to negatively affect minorities in some earlier studies conducted at the county level, in non-guidelines jurisdictions. For example, Spohn, Gruhl, and Welch (1987) examined the dismissal and charge reduction decisions among felony defendants in Los Angeles. They found Black defendants were significantly less likely to have their charges reduced to misdemeanors but had similar probabilities of having their case dismissed. Similar to Rehavi and Starr, Barnes and Kingsnorth (1996) found that Black drug defendants in Sacramento County, California faced longer sentences than White defendants if convicted. Even though Black defendants had a higher probability to have their cases dismissed, they had a lower chance of having their charges reduced to misdemeanors. Holmes, Daudistel, and

Farrell (1987), on the other hand, found in Delaware County, Pennsylvania, that Black robbery and burglary defendants were more likely to receive charge reductions, which subsequently resulted in them receiving less harsh sentences.[2]

The larger body of literature on prosecutorial decision in state systems focused on the effectiveness of guidelines and was therefore on states that had relatively well-structured guidelines, such as Minnesota (Miethe, 1987; Stolzenberg and D'Alessio, 1992) and Pennsylvania (Kramer and Ulmer, 2009; Ulmer and Kramer, 1996). Relatively less attention has been paid to prosecutorial behaviors in states without presumptive guidelines, or to how prosecutors behave in jurisdictions under different sentencing systems from a comparative perspective. One example of the latter type is a study conducted by Piehl and Bushway (2007), using data from two counties in Maryland (a state with voluntary guidelines) and one county in the State of Washington (a state with presumptive guidelines). They found that, in keeping with the predictions of Reitz (1998), there was more discretion at the pre-conviction stage in the county in Washington, where the guidelines were stricter than their counterparts in Maryland. They also found more unexplained racial differences in the charge bargaining process in the county in Washington. In general, however, we are not aware of published studies that have replicated Rehavi and Starr's (2014) approach using data from guidelines jurisdictions. In other words, there do not seem to be many studies that use a standard sentencing model and controlling for both charges at conviction and charges at arrest and indictment.

Finally, there has been little focus on what happens in states without sentencing guidelines. However, sentencing guidelines, as of recently, are still the exception rather than the norm. As of 2008, 21 of the 50 states have adopted guidelines (Kauder and Ostrom, 2008). Over a half of the states, including the five most populous ones (California, Texas, New York, Florida, and Illinois), have not adopted sentencing guidelines. In the next section, we detail the sentencing system in New York, where we were able to collect our own data from prosecutor files for over 500 cases that started as felony charges in two counties. This dataset is much smaller than most datasets used in recent published studies but has the advantage of having information on charges at all three stages we were interested in: arrest, original filing, and conviction. It is therefore possible to study the sentence at conviction, like typical sentencing studies, and then analyze the pattern when we control for the arraignment and arrest charges instead of the conviction charge.

Sentencing in New York

Judges in New York have very broad discretion in determining the sentence. As of 2016, the state has still not established sentencing guidelines and prescribes wide sentence ranges in the Penal Law. In 2006, felonies in New York were divided into five classes, denoted by letters A to E; class A being the most serious and class E being the least serious.[3] Within each class, crimes were divided into three categories: violent, drug, and non-violent-non-drug (which we refer to as "general").[4] The intersection of classes and categories resulted in a total of 14 "cells" in the sentencing charts.[5]

The sentence for felonies in New York was unique in that determinate and indeterminate sentences existed at the same time. Determinate sentences were prescribed for violent and drug felonies, and indeterminate sentences were prescribed for general felonies. Within each cell, the available choices covered a broad range. For instance, a defendant convicted of a class B drug felony may be sentenced to a determinate term at any length between 2 and 9 years. Another example is for a defendant convicted of a class B general felony, the law allows from an indeterminate sentence for 1 to 3 years, to an indeterminate sentence for 8.33 to 25 years, or a sentence of any length in between. Moreover, apart from prison terms, the statute allowed judges to sentence defendants convicted of a class C felony or below to alternative sanctions, such as probation or community service, so long as the defendant did not have prior felony convictions within the past 10 years, and such sentences would not be in conflict with the goals of justice. Therefore, the sentence for a defendant convicted of class C general felony may be either an indeterminate term with the upper limit being any length between 3 and 15 years or alternative sanctions only with no incarceration at all. These ranges were much wider than in the sentencing guidelines of the federal jurisdiction as well as of many states.

The sentences for misdemeanors were simpler. Misdemeanors were categorized into two classes, A and B, with class A being more serious. The statutory maximum sentences were 1 year in jail or 3 months in jail, for the two classes respectively. There were also unclassified misdemeanors defined in laws other than the penal law (such as driving while intoxicated, DWI, which was defined by the vehicle and traffic law). For these crimes, the sentence was directly prescribed in the law defining such crimes and could be no longer than 1 year in jail. Alternative sanctions were also authorized for defendants convicted of misdemeanors.

Although the laws of New York did limit the extent of charge bargaining, particularly for defendants charged with more serious crimes, such limitations only apply to defendants indicted by a grand jury.[6] In practice, defendants may avoid grand jury indictments by opting to be prosecuted by the Superior Court Information (SCI) or by having the case transferred to local (city, town, or village) courts, which made charge bargaining possible even for those charged with serious crimes.[7] Moreover, although alternative sanctions were, as stated above, not authorized for defendant with predicate felony convictions, our data demonstrate that the predicate criminal records could be negotiated in plea bargaining. Therefore, alternative sanctions could, in practice, be given to defendants with predicate histories on their rap sheets.[8]

Both prosecutors and judges under the New York system appeared to have substantial discretion over the case outcomes. On the one hand, judges had substantial discretion in deciding whether to incarcerate, the margin on which we will focus. On the other hand, prosecutors also had high levels of freedom in determining the charges, and the final charge could impose some limitations on the sentence. Although we do not have sufficient information to generate a strong hypothesis for New York, Reitz's (1998) theoretical model leads us to expect that movement from charge to conviction will have less impact on sentencing outcomes than in the federal system. We also expect to find less racial disparity at the earlier stage of the process relative to the sentencing stage.

Data and Methodology

We obtained permission to code district attorney files for cases filed as felonies in two counties in New York State (for confidentiality, the counties are named County A and County B hereinafter). County A was a mostly rural county (population less than 50,000), and County B was a county with mixed urban and suburban areas (population higher than 100,000). Both counties, nonetheless, were smaller counties relative to the counties examined in the studies described above (e.g., Barnes and Kingsnorth, 1996; Holmes et al., 1987; Piehl and Bushway, 2007; Spohn et al., 1987).

Sampling

To select the cases to code, multiple factors were taken into consideration. First, we examined cases filed in 2005 and 2006 to ensure that the cases were closed in 2012 (the time of data collection). Second, we only coded cases that were initially charged as an adult felony (in New York, 16 years was the age of majority for criminal responsibility). The entire population of available eligible cases in County A were coded (n = 243). For County B, a sample of 259 cases was collected out of the population of more than 2,000 eligible cases using a stratified sampling approach. Specifically, we first selected and coded all available cases that went to trial (n = 8). For plea and dismissal cases, we drew samples based on the mode of prosecution (i.e., whether the court case stayed in superior court or was transferred to local court). A total of 105 superior court cases were randomly selected from the arrest list. Local court case files were stored in boxes at the basement of County B's courthouse. We counted the total number of eligible cases in each box, then randomly selected one case out of each box as our sample.

The analytical sample of this study was further limited to cases that met all the criteria below. First, only cases ended up as criminal guilty pleas (n = 411) were selected to rule out potential confounds brought in by trial cases. By limiting our cases to criminal guilty pleas, we also excluded cases that ended as civil violation convictions (which were not considered as crimes in New York). Second, to ensure the consistency of sample across analyses, we selected only the cases that had no missing data in any variable used (variables to be detailed below). The final analytical sample consisted of 384 cases (76.5% of the entire sample).

Weighting

We used a simple strategy to calculate the analytic weight we used in this study. First, we had the sampling weight for all the cases, that is, the number of cases each case in our dataset represented.[9] The size of case population in County B was almost ten times as large as County A. Therefore, if we applied the sampling weight directly to estimate the statistics of the whole sample, all results would be driven by cases from County B. To solve this problem, we devised the analytic weight for County B, which enabled the weighted sample size of County B to be roughly the same size as County A while still reflecting the stratified sampling nature of County B.[10] In this study, all results are reported with the analytic weights applied.

Dependent Variables

To examine the sentencing outcomes, we used two dependent variables on the incarceration status of defendants. We decided to focus on the in/out decision rather than sentence length, because the relative low severity of crimes in our sample resulted in a large number of defendants receiving alternative sanctions rather than incarceration. In addition, as explained above, there was a great deal of discretion on this margin. The two dependent variables indicate whether the defendant received *any incarceration sentence* (i.e., including time-served) and whether the defendant received *any post-sentencing incarceration sentence* (i.e., excluding time-served), respectively.

Independent and Control Variables

The current study used five groups of independent and control variables. Demographics recorded the defendant's race, gender, and age. *Race*, as our main independent variable, was coded as a dummy variable indicating whether the defendant was non-Hispanic White. Whites constituted the majority of our sample (higher than 70%), and none of the non-White race (Hispanic, Black, Asian, etc.) had a sufficiently large proportion to be coded separately. *Gender* was coded as a dummy variable indicating whether the defendant was male. Defendants' *age* was coded into five groups: less than 20 years old, 20–29 years old, 30–39 years old, 40–49 years old, and 50 years and above. We also considered the *county* in which the cases were processed to control for the possible variation in local context between the counties.

Because criminal record is a strong predictor of sentence outcome (Mitchell, 2005; Ulmer, 2012), we made efforts to capture this information of the defendants as completely as possible. We obtained the defendants' criminal history record information (CHRI) from the Federal Bureau of Investigation (FBI), which documented the prior history of arrest, conviction, and sentences reported to FBI from state-level agencies. We carefully matched the identifying information (name, social security number, FBI and state-agency ID, race, location of arrest records, etc.) to confirm they were the correct match to the defendants in our sample.[11] We did not get a credible match for 18 out of 384 defendants and treated those defendants as if they had no criminal record. Moreover, for the defendants who had CHRI information, a non-trivial proportion of their arrest records came with missing disposition information. Several possibilities may account for the missing information. The identifying information we supplied to the FBI may have been insufficient or wrong. The disposition records may be sealed in accordance with state laws. It is also possible that those records were simply not sent to the FBI by the local and state agencies. Nevertheless, if the prosecutor's office checked the defendants' criminal history in the manner we did, they should not have found those records for the defendants either. This issue should therefore not negatively affect our analysis.

Instead of coding criminal history solely based on the defendants' number of arrests or convictions, we created a scale that took into account all the previous arrests, convictions, and prison sentences by assigning different weights for each component to preserve the different nature of the crimes and outcomes. Based on the raw score, defendants were then coded into one of the four *history* classes: clean history, minimal history, moderate history, and serious history.[12]

The severity of charges at two stages were coded: *statutory classes of the most serious initial charge* and *the most serious conviction charge*, both of which were coded as a group of dummy variables representing each class. Class A and B felonies were combined into one category in our analyses because they were relatively rare events. To control for crime type, we coded *the type of most serious initial charge*. We used the type of the initial charge rather than the conviction charge as the control variable in all the regression models to rule out the possible impact of charge bargaining. Finally, the *crime types* included violent (murder, rape/violent sexual crime, robbery, assault, other violent crimes); property (burglary, larceny, forgery, fraud, and other property crimes); drug (drug sale, drug possession); and public order crimes (weapons crimes, driving crimes and other public order crimes).

Statistical Models

To directly study the mechanism of sentencing and charge bargaining, we compared models that control for the conviction charge to those that control for the initial charge. We estimated probit regression models to explain the probability of incarceration for defendants in our sample and focused on what variables explained the variation among incarceration outcomes at each stage. We were especially interested in whether there were racial disparities in the in/out decision.

Results and Discussion

We present the descriptive statistics in Table 6.1. Among defendants in the sample, 55% were incarcerated at any point, and 42% were incarcerated post-sentencing. The vast majority of the sample was White and male, and approximately two thirds of them had some type of prior record.

In addition to the descriptive statistics, we also present the flow of cases throughout the system. Figure 6.1 shows the case processing flow in the 75 largest U.S. counties in 2006, produced using State Court Processing Statistics (SCPS, see Cohen and Kyckelhahn, 2010), and is the base of the comparison to our counties in New York.

Figures 6.2 and 6.3 depict the typical case processing pipeline for White and non-White defendants in our data separately.[13] At the pre-prosecution stage, defendants in our sample were more likely to be detained than those in the 75 largest counties. However, this higher probability of detention may be an artifact due to the different definition of pretrial detention between SCPS and our data. SCPS considered a defendant detained only if he/she was detained during the entire pretrial period, and we adopted a more liberal definition of pretrial detention due to the missing information in our data.[14] Nevertheless, among defendants in our sample whose pretrial detention status was available, non-Whites faced higher probability of pretrial detention than Whites. This observed disparity in detention has a significant implication for our regression analysis results.

Table 6.1 Descriptive Statistics

Variable	*Prop.*
Any incarceration	0.551
Post-sentencing incarceration	0.419
White	0.784
Male	0.869
Age	
Less than 20	0.210
20–29	0.331
30–39	0.240
40–49	0.155
50 and above	0.064
County B	0.510
Criminal history	
Clean	0.334
Minimal	0.259
Moderate	0.192
Serious	0.215
Conviction charge	
A or B felony	0.009
C felony	0.028
D felony	0.223
E felony	0.175
Misdemeanor	0.565
Initial charge	
A or B felony	0.155
C felony	0.086
D felony	0.342
E felony	0.417
Crime type	
Violent	0.147
Property	0.396
Drug	0.202
Public order	0.255
n	384
Number of cases represented	393.78

Comparing the prosecution and sentencing stage reveals that defendants in our sample were 18 to 19 percentage points more likely to be prosecuted (which essentially guaranteed conviction given the overwhelming prevalence of guilty pleas) and less likely to be dismissed. The implication of these patterns is complex. On the one

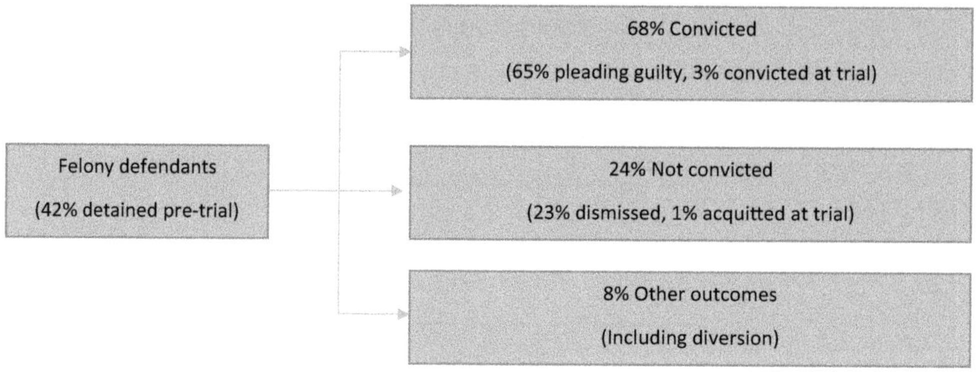

Figure 6.1a Case Processing Outcome of Felony Defendants in 75 Largest U.S. Counties, 2006

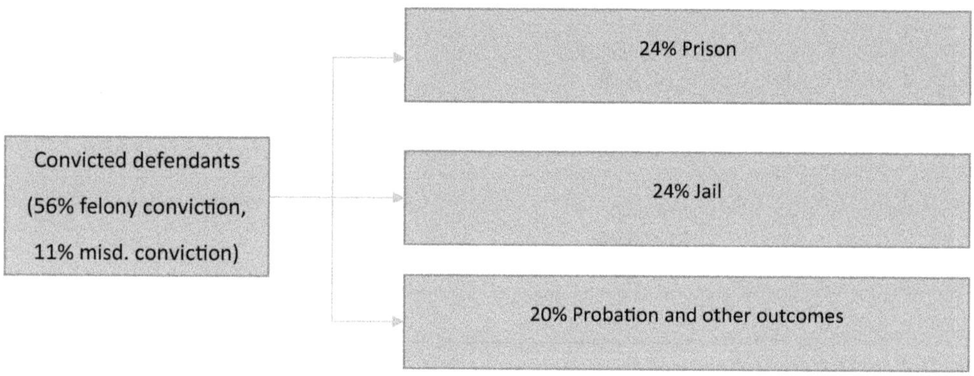

Figure 6.1b Sentencing Outcome of Felony Defendants in 75 Largest U.S. Counties, 2006

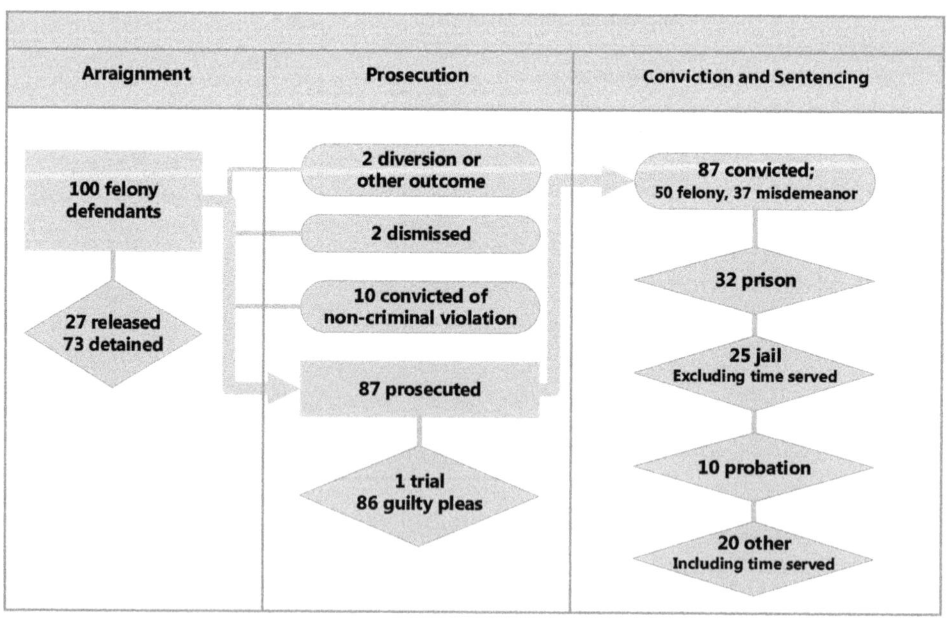

Figure 6.2 Typical Case Processing Outcome of 100 Non-White Felony Defendants in Our Sample of Two Counties, 2005–2006

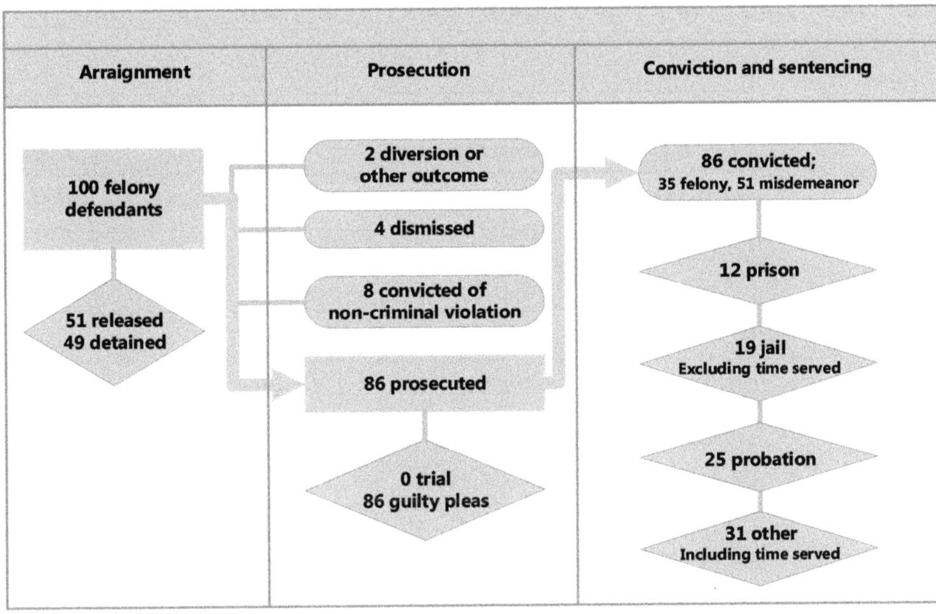

Figure 6.3 Typical Case Processing Outcome of 100 White Felony Defendants in Our Sample of Two Counties, 2005–2006

hand, the higher probability of prosecution and conviction may indicate that defendants in our sample faced more punitive disposition. On the other hand, it may also be due to the higher standard of arrest decisions among police officers in the smaller counties, which ruled out the weaker cases that would have resulted in dismissals. It is also important to note that White and non-White defendants appeared similar in their prosecution stage outcomes (86% of Whites and 87% of non-Whites were prosecuted).

A noteworthy pattern at the conviction stage is that, although all defendants in SCPS and in our data started with felony charges, defendants in our sample were much more likely to be convicted of misdemeanors. Among the convicted defendants, more than a half (55%) pled down to a misdemeanor. Even among defendants who were still convicted of a felony, there was a considerable amount of charge bargaining. As shown in Table 6.1, nearly a quarter of these defendants faced the top charge of a class C felony (which was punishable by a maximum prison term of 15 years for general and violent crimes and 5.5 years for drug crimes) or above. However, less than 4% of the cases eventually ended up as a class C felony conviction or above; the rest all pled down to less serious felonies and misdemeanors. Clearly, a great deal of charge bargaining happened in our sample. The question of interest for us is how the charge bargaining process affected the sentencing outcomes.

We next move on to the regression analysis. The first and second columns of Table 6.2 present the probit models on any incarceration and post-sentencing incarceration. The single most influential independent variable on incarceration was the class

Table 6.2 Probit Regression Models Explaining Incarceration Outcomes for Guilty Plea Defendants

	(1)	(2)	(3)	(4)
	Any Incarceration	*Post-Sentencing Incarceration*	*Any Incarceration*	*Post-Sentencing Incarceration*
White	−0.708***	−0.486**	−0.501**	−0.335
	(0.238)	(0.212)	(0.222)	(0.206)
Male	−0.0148	0.224	−0.0690	0.182
	(0.207)	(0.217)	(0.218)	(0.228)
Age (less than 20 as reference)				
20–29	−0.215	0.0777	−0.0368	0.132
	(0.224)	(0.240)	(0.223)	(0.228)
30–39	−0.399	−0.152	−0.132	−0.0386
	(0.257)	(0.270)	(0.248)	(0.252)
40–49	−0.447	−0.129	−0.346	−0.145
	(0.326)	(0.291)	(0.300)	(0.286)
50 and above	−0.495	−0.406	−0.387	−0.413
	(0.351)	(0.408)	(0.358)	(0.372)
County B	0.236	0.0277	0.195	−0.0153
	(0.170)	(0.167)	(0.159)	(0.156)
Criminal history (clean history as reference)				
Minimal	0.390*	0.436*	0.460**	0.557***
	(0.216)	(0.223)	(0.205)	(0.205)
Moderate	0.871***	0.835***	1.041***	1.042***
	(0.241)	(0.235)	(0.228)	(0.220)
Serious	1.541***	1.266***	1.542***	1.337***
	(0.270)	(0.251)	(0.257)	(0.237)
Conviction charge (A or B felony as reference)				
C felony	−3.507***	−4.099***		
	(0.661)	(0.453)		
D felony	−3.956***	−4.351***		
	(0.311)	(0.265)		
E felony	−4.404***	−4.824***		
	(0.404)	(0.351)		
Misdemeanor	−5.642***	−5.906***		
	(0.337)	(0.304)		
Initial charge (A or B felony as reference)				
C felony			−1.145***	−1.300***
			(0.381)	(0.373)
D felony			−1.459***	−1.321***
			(0.326)	(0.325)
E felony			−1.541***	−1.401***
			(0.338)	(0.343)

	(1)	(2)	(3)	(4)
	Any Incarceration	*Post-Sentencing Incarceration*	*Any Incarceration*	*Post-Sentencing Incarceration*
Crime type (Violent as reference)				
Property	−0.963***	−0.767***	−0.907***	−0.655***
	(0.240)	(0.238)	(0.244)	(0.245)
Drug	−1.350***	−1.163***	−1.413***	−1.213***
	(0.309)	(0.291)	(0.334)	(0.336)
Public order	−0.886***	−0.909***	−0.548*	−0.559*
	(0.270)	(0.273)	(0.281)	(0.285)
Constant	6.193***	5.465***	2.043***	1.028**
	(0.526)	(0.506)	(0.492)	(0.496)
n	384	384	384	384
F	53.83	69.56	6.27	5.62

Standard errors in parentheses.

*** $p < 0.01$, ** $p < 0.05$, and * $p < 0.1$.

of the conviction charge. The probability of incarceration generally decreased with the charge severity, although defendants convicted of a class D felony were slightly more likely to be convicted than those convicted of a class C felony. Criminal history also predicted the probability of incarceration, as more serious criminal history predicted significantly higher probability of incarceration. Compared with defendants charged with violent crimes, property, drug, and public order crime defendants were all less likely to be incarcerated. There was no significant correlation between the sentence and the gender, county, and age of the defendant.

Our most striking finding is that there was a large and significant racial disparity on the likelihood of incarceration. The disparity we found is much larger than those found in most analyses (Mitchell, 2005). The model for post-sentencing incarceration found basically the same story. We predicted the probability of incarceration for each individual based on the coefficients estimated by the models; the predictions indicate that White defendants were 28 percentage points less likely to be incarcerated (.360 vs. .641) when time-served was excluded, and 32 percentage points less likely to be incarcerated when time-served was included (.482 vs. .803).

There are two possible explanations of this large race disparity. The first is that unstructured sentencing systems lead to greater racial disparity than the structured guidelines systems. The second is that most datasets used in the literature have more control variables than we do, precisely because the guidelines mandate the collection of more systematic data on the legal factors that drive sentencing. It is not possible to differentiate between these two possibilities in this chapter. From these models, we could contend that sentences in the counties in New York were meted out in a more individualized manner than in guidelines jurisdictions, although additional evidence would be necessary to conclude that any systematic bias existed against non-White defendants.

One lesson from Rehavi and Starr's (2014) study is that if the charging practice differs for White and non-White defendants, a different pattern of racial disparity may emerge after controlling for an earlier stage. Specifically, if prosecutors in the New York counties treated non-White defendants less favorably in either charging or charge bargaining, the observed large racial disparity would increase when the charges at earlier stages were included in the model.

We estimated a second group of models, using the class of the initial charge, rather than the class of the conviction charge. All other variables remained unchanged. We show the models in the third and fourth columns of Table 6.2, for incarceration and post-sentencing incarceration respectively. The coefficients for legal variables and extra-legal control variables were similar to those in the models using the conviction charge. The observed racial disparity, however, was contrary to Rehavi and Starr's (2014) findings. We found in both models an impressive decrease for the coefficient of race. Moreover, the coefficient for race in the post-sentencing incarceration model was no longer significant. These findings indicate that for the same arrest charge, non-White defendants still faced higher probability of incarceration. However, such disparity was because non-White defendants were more likely to be sentenced to time-served terms than White defendants. The more frequent use of time-served terms on non-White defendants is not surprising considering that non-White defendants were more likely to be detained (Figures 6.2 and 6.3).

Another interesting finding emerges when we compare model (2) and model (4). Instead of being processed equally throughout the system, non-White defendants received more favorable outcomes in charge bargaining, but less favorable outcomes at sentencing. The apparent non-disparate outcome in sentencing was because prosecutors' decision to reduce charge and judges' decision to sentence worked in opposite directions.

The finding that non-White defendants received more charge bargaining seems counterintuitive. One lesson we learned from Rehavi and Starr's (2014) study is that federal prosecutors may be more likely to add charges on non-White defendants *between arrest and filing*, in the form of either mandatory minimums or more serious charges. If this also happened in the two sampled counties, it could partly explain the larger charge discounts we found for non-White defendants. This actually did not seem to be the case in our sample. Only 3% of our cases' top charge class had become more serious from arrest to filing, and there did not seem to be a racial disparity in this upward charge movement. The lack of charge movement between arrest and filing in our data may be explained by two factors. First, most initial charges documented were the arraignment charges, which by their nature would not differ much from the arrest charges. Second and more importantly, the freedom in both charge bargaining and sentencing in New York, as well as the lack of power to influence sentence through charging decisions, eliminated prosecutors' motivation to manipulate the charges like their federal counterparts did.

Conclusion

Our statistical analysis demonstrates that both prosecutors and judges in the two counties in New York had a great deal of flexibility in their decisions. As a result, the prosecutorial power did not appear to be as important on the sentence as it is in stricter guidelines systems (cf. Rehavi and Starr, 2014; Shermer and Johnson, 2010). At the very least, we found no evidence that racial disparity was created at earlier stages of the process. In contrast, we found substantial extralegal racial variation in the probability of getting an incarceration sentence after controlling for legal factors, variation that is much larger than those reported in most standard studies of the in/out decision. This result is in striking contrast to Rehavi and Starr's findings. Rather than viewing this as a contradiction of their work, we view it as an extension. Even though our research question and analytic technique were similar to theirs, our data were obtained from a very different setting. Compared with defendants in the federal system, defendants in New York were in general charged with less serious crimes. Plus, there were no sentencing guidelines in New York, which stood in contrast with the presumptive and rigorous guidelines of the federal jurisdiction.

The picture is even more interesting if we compare the case processing statistics of the large counties across states. The percentage of felony defendants who were eventually convicted of misdemeanors ranged from 24% to 52% in the five counties in New York State sampled in 2006 SCPS. However, no county sampled in California had over 4% of the felony cases pleading down to misdemeanors, and only one county each in Florida and Texas had this rate over 10% (Cohen and Kyckelhahn, 2010, Appendix Table 21). All of the four states were non-guidelines states, leaving the picture of New York to look more like the exception than the rule. In our sample from two counties, 57% of felony defendants pled down to misdemeanors, which hinted that smaller counties in New York may share the pattern found in larger counties as well.

The results present an interesting puzzle. Reitz's (1998) theory predicts that, in the absence of serious downstream constraints, much plea bargaining should occur around the sentence. There should be little charge bargaining because of the lower correlation between the charge and the sentence. The SCPS statistics show that counties in many non-guidelines states, such as California, Florida, and Texas, did appear to have this pattern, in the sense that only a small proportion of felony defendants would plead down to misdemeanors. To the contrary, we found substantial charge bargaining in our data. Why did prosecutors in New York still offer these large charge discounts, even though the final outcome was largely unconstrained by the charge?

Both focal concerns perspective and organization efficiency perspective predict that, in addition to the characteristics of the case and the defendant, practical constraints can also play an important role in determining the sentence (Engen and Steen, 2000; Steffensmeier, Ulmer, and Kramer, 1998). To cope with these constraints such as caseload, prosecutors may induce defendants to plead guilty by offering them substantial charge discounts. Another possible explanation is the cases that pled down to misdemeanors would have been filed initially as misdemeanors in other non-guidelines states. Not only do non-guidelines states differ in case processing from guidelines states, but they differ from each other as well. More advanced analytical techniques, as well as datasets that have detailed case information across a variety of states, would be necessary to move a step further in estimating and explaining the differences.

Our study has several limitations. First, the sample size was small. Even though small sample size may lead to concerns on the statistical power of the models, we still found large and statistically significant racial disparity when using the information at conviction. Second, the fact that the data came from only two counties limits the generalizability of our conclusions. Third, although we aimed to collect an extensive body of case information, some variables that might critically affect the case outcomes, such as type of defense counsel or pretrial detention status, were missing in a large proportion of the sample. Fourth, there were no in-depth interview data. Collecting first-hand qualitative data from prosecutors and judges may substantially help explain the patterns we found. Despite these limitations, this study fills a research gap on sentencing and prosecution in small counties and non-guidelines jurisdictions, which is relatively understudied compared with guidelines jurisdictions, or populous counties in non-guidelines states. We believe the findings of this study would be especially helpful when serving as a base of comparison for studies in similar-sized counties in other states.

Proponents of sentencing guidelines argued that guidelines would be capable of reducing extralegal disparity in sentencing. According to Savelsberg (1992), sentencing guidelines represent the pursuit of formal rationalization of law, whereas a system like New York emphasizes substantive rationalization. We have no intention to contend here that either goal is inherently superior over the other, nor do we think either judicial or prosecutorial discretion naturally deserves tighter control over another. Before conclusions about the ideal design of sentencing systems can be drawn, more studies on prosecutorial and judicial behavior, particularly on non-guidelines states, are needed. To achieve such a goal, it will be important for researchers to continue to create datasets (and estimate models) that include information in stages earlier than conviction on non-guidelines jurisdictions that, to date, have largely been unavailable.

Notes

1 This project was supported by Award No. 2009-IJ-CX-0035, awarded by the National Institute of Justice, Office of Justice Programs, U.S. Department of Justice. The opinions, findings, and conclusions or recommendations expressed in this publication are those of the authors and do not necessarily reflect those of the Department of Justice. The authors thank Jeffrey Ulmer for his constructive comments, and Karissa Pelletier for her help in copyediting. Correspondence concerning this article should be addressed to Shi Yan, School of Criminology & Criminal Justice, Arizona State University, 411 N. Central Ave, Ste 600, Phoenix, AZ 85004. Email: shiyan@asu.edu.

2 Holmes et al.'s (1987) study included cases closed between 1976 and 1977, which was before Pennsylvania adopted the guidelines.

3 Description of the laws refers to the situation as of the legislative year 2006, which applies to the cases we collected.

4 It is noteworthy that "violent felonies" in New York are prescribed by the New York State Penal Law and do not necessarily overlap with the criminological understanding of "violent crimes."

For instance, first- and second-degree burglaries are considered violent felonies in the Penal Law but are usually considered as property rather than violent crimes in the criminology literature. To the contrary, robbery in the third degree is not considered a violent felony in the Penal Law but is usually considered a violent crime in criminology. This chapter uses the term "violent felony" in statutory sense as part of background knowledge of New York's sentencing system and uses the term "violent crime" in the same way as in the criminological literature.

5 The 5 classes and 3 categories should have resulted in a total of 15 cells. However, there were no class A violent felonies because non-drug class A felonies were by definition serious violent crimes: murder, terrorism, kidnapping in the first degree, etc.

6 For instance, the statute allowed defendants indicted of a class B (if unarmed) or class C violent felony to plead down to a class D violent felony. Defendants indicted of a class B general felony, on the other hand, were allowed to plead down to a class E general felony. No limitation was imposed on defendants charged with a non-violent felony at class C or lower.

7 In New York, although superior courts (county courts) had statutory jurisdiction over all felonies and misdemeanors, misdemeanor cases were generally processed in local courts. Defendants (with the exception of defendants being charged with class A felonies) may waive their right of being indicted by grand jury and opt to be instead prosecuted using a written document, known as the SCI.

8 This practice was confirmed by a former district attorney in New York State during a conversation in the course of the project.

9 In County A, all cases were self-representative and had a weight of 1 because we coded the population of cases. In County B, the weight of cases depended on the outcome and type of prosecution. For plea cases, all superior court cases had a weight of 9.64, which equals the total number of superior cases (excluding trials) divided by the number of cases coded. Each local court case, as described in the sampling method above, had a weight that equals the total number of eligible cases in the box from which it was drawn (ranging from 1 to 22).

10 Analytic weight for County B = the sampling weight of each case (see Note 9) × 259 (total number of cases sampled in County B) / total number of eligible cases in County B (slightly over 2,000).

11 Because of the small sample size, we were able to review all matches manually. All three authors participated in the reviews to ensure that the matches were accurate to the best of our knowledge.

12 First, each defendant received two points for each prior felony conviction. He/she received one additional point for each felony conviction that resulted in a prison sentence (but no point for jail sentence). Next, he/she received one point for each prior misdemeanor conviction. Defendants were limited to receive up to four points for misdemeanor convictions. Finally, half of one point was added for each arrest record with missing disposition mentioned above in data description. An upper limit of two points was set for this part of their history. No point was counted for the arrests that resulted in known non-conviction (i.e., a disposition clearly marked as "dismissed" or "acquitted" on the CHRI feedback). To account for the possible non-linearity between history and disposition, we broke the defendants' criminal history into four categories: clean history (score was 0); low history (score higher than 0 but less than 3, equivalent to any crime less than one felony conviction with prison sentence); medium history (score greater than or equal to 3 but lower than 6, equivalent to one felony conviction with prison sentence or higher, but lower than two felony convictions with prison sentence); and serious history (score equal to or greater than 6, equivalent to two felony convictions with prison sentence or higher).

13 These figures are produced using weighted statistics for all defendants in the dataset whose dispositions were known (n = 474), rather than our analytic sample, because the latter sample includes only defendants who pled guilty.

14 In the case files, information about pretrial detention was spotty. Our pretrial detention status was estimated using the following method. In the standard New York State arrest report, there is a cell "arrestee status," if the defendant was marked as "held," we considered the defendant detained. If the defendant was not marked held in the arrest report, but had a date in the case

file indicating he/she was booked into jail, we considered the defendant detained as well. A large number of missing values existed in both variables. In approximately a third of the cases, both variables were missing (in Figures 6.2 and 6.3, we considered this information to be missing at random and computed the detention percentage using only cases that had non-missing arrestee status information). Knowing the effect of pretrial detention shown in our study could have very different implication and risky reliability, we eventually decided not to include it in the regression analyses.

References

Barnes, C. W., & Kingsnorth, R. (1996). Race, drug, and criminal sentencing: Hidden effects of the criminal law. *Journal of Criminal Justice, 24*(1), 39–55.

Bjerk, D. (2005). Making the crime fit the penalty: The role of prosecutorial discretion under mandatory minimum sentencing. *Journal of Law and Economics, 48*(2), 591–625.

Bushway, S. D., & Piehl, A. M. (2001). Judging judicial discretion: Legal factors and racial discrimination in sentencing. *Law & Society Review, 35*(4), 733–764.

Cohen, T. H., & Kyckelhahn, T. (2010). *Felony defendants in large urban counties, 2006.* Washington, DC: Bureau of Justice Statistics.

D'Alessio, S. J., & Stolzenberg, L. (1995). The impact of sentencing guidelines on jail incarceration in Minnesota. *Criminology, 33*(2), 283–302.

Engen, R. L., & Gainey, R. R. (2000). Modeling the effects of legally relevant and extralegal factors under sentencing guidelines: The rules have changed. *Criminology, 38*(4), 1207–1230.

Engen, R. L., & Steen, S. (2000). The power to punish: Discretion and sentencing reform in the war on drugs. *American Journal of Sociology, 105*(5), 1357–1395.

Holmes, M. D., Daudistel, H. C., & Farrell, R. A. (1987). Determinants of charge reductions and final dispositions in cases of burglary and robbery. *Journal of Research in Crime and Delinquency, 24*(3), 233–254.

Kauder, N. B., & Ostrom, B. J. (2008). *State sentencing guidelines: Profiles and continuum.* Williamsburg, VA: National Center for State Courts.

Kramer, J. H., & Ulmer, J. T. (2009). *Sentencing guidelines: Lessons from Pennsylvania.* Boulder, CO: Lynne Rienner.

McCoy, C. (1984). Determinate sentencing, plea bargaining bans, and hydraulic discretion in California. *The Justice System Journal, 9*, 256–275.

Miethe, T. D. (1987). Charging and plea bargaining practices under determinate sentencing: An investigation of the hydraulic displacement of discretion. *Journal of Criminal Law and Criminology, 78*(1), 155–176.

Miller, M. L. (2005). A map of sentencing and a compass for judges: Sentencing information systems, transparency, and the next generation of reform. *Columbia Law Review, 105*(4), 1351–1395.

Mitchell, O. (2005). A meta-analysis of race and sentencing research: Explaining the inconsistencies. *Journal of Quantitative Criminology, 21*(4), 439–466.

Piehl, A. M., & Bushway, S. D. (2007). Measuring and explaining charge bargaining. *Journal of Quantitative Criminology, 23*(2), 105–125.

Rehavi, M. M., & Starr, S. B. (2014). Racial disparity in federal criminal sentences. *Journal of Political Economy, 122*(6), 1320–1354.

Reitz, K. R. (1998). Modeling discretion in American sentencing systems. *Law & Policy, 20*, 389–428.

Reitz, K. R. (2005). The enforceability of sentencing guidelines. *Stanford Law Review, 58*(1), 155–173.

Savelsberg, J. J. (1992). Law that does not fit society: Sentencing guidelines as a neoclassical reaction to the dilemmas of substantivized law. *American Journal of Sociology, 97*(5), 1346–1381.

Shermer, L. O., & Johnson, B. (2010). Criminal prosecutions: Examining prosecutorial discretion and charge reductions in US federal district courts. *Justice Quarterly, 27*(3), 394–430.

Spohn, C. (2009). *How do judges decide? The search for fairness and justice in punishment*. Thousand Oaks, CA: Sage.

Spohn, C., Gruhl, J., & Welch, S. (1987). The impact of ethnicity and gender of defendants on the decision to reject or dismiss felony charges. *Criminology, 25*(1), 175–191.

Steffensmeier, D., Ulmer, J., & Kramer, J. (1998). The interaction of race, gender and age in criminal sentencing: The punishment cost of being young, black, and male. *Criminology, 36*(4), 763–798.

Stolzenberg, L., & D'Alessio, S. J. (1992). Sentencing and unwarranted disparity: An empirical assessment of the long-term impact of sentencing guidelines in Minnesota. *Criminology, 32*(2), 301–310.

Tonry, M. (1996). *Sentencing matters*. New York: Oxford University Press.

Ulmer, J. T. (1997). *Social worlds of sentencing: Court communities under sentencing guidelines*. Albany, NY: SUNY Press.

Ulmer, J. T. (2012). Recent developments and new directions in sentencing research. *Justice Quarterly, 29*(1), 1–40.

Ulmer, J. T., & Kramer, J. H. (1996). Court communities under sentencing guidelines: Dilemmas of formal rationality and sentencing disparity. *Criminology, 34*(3), 383–408.

Ulmer, J. T., Kurlychek, M. C., & Kramer, J. H. (2007). Prosecutorial discretion and the imposition of mandatory minimum sentences. *Journal of Research in Crime and Delinquency, 44*(4), 427–458.

Wang, X., Mears, D. P., Spohn, C., & Dario, L. (2013). Assessing the differential effects of race and ethnicity on sentence outcomes under different sentencing systems. *Crime & Delinquency, 59*(1), 87–114.

Wooldredge, J. (2009). Short- versus long-term effects of Ohio's switch to more structured sentencing on extralegal disparities in prison sentences in an urban court. *Criminology & Public Policy, 8*(2), 285–312.

7

PERSPECTIVES INFORMING DEFENSE ATTORNEY EFFECTS ON CRIMINAL CASE OUTCOMES

John Wooldredge, James Frank, and Natalie Goulette

Empirical research on extra-legal disparities in criminal case outcomes has recently incorporated a greater focus on the role of prosecutors (relative to judges) in shaping these disparities. We believe there should also be greater attention paid to defense attorneys given their roles in shaping charge reductions and guilty plea submissions. Arguments are presented favoring such a focus, and these arguments are then used to build a preliminary bi-level framework. A partial test of this framework using data from an urban jurisdiction is provided to encourage more research on defense attorneys, with the caveat that all related designs should incorporate a qualitative component in order to place any statistical findings in proper context.

For decades, empirical studies of extra-legal disparities in case processing and outcomes focused primarily on judges' roles in shaping disparities in sentencing decisions involving imprisonment and the length of prison terms (as discussed by Kim, Spohn, and Hedberg, 2015). More recently, this body of research has paid more attention to the role of prosecutors in the sentencing process (e.g., Kim et al., 2015; Kutateladze et al., 2014; Wooldredge et al., 2015; but see Albonetti's [1987] early empirical research on prosecutorial discretion). Greater focus on prosecutors relative to judges makes sense given that the vast majority of convictions are obtained via guilty pleas and plea "negotiations" in which judges are not permitted to participate or are discouraged from participating in most states (Batra, 2015; Redlich, Bushway, and Norris, 2016). Less attention seems to be paid to the role of defense attorneys, however, perhaps because of academic perceptions of prosecutors as more powerful officers of the court (for exceptions, see Abrams and Yoon, 2007; Anderson and Heaton, 2012; Cohen, 2014; Edkins, 2011; Hartley, Miller, and Spohn, 2010; Hoffman, Rubin, and Shepherd, 2005; Williams, 2013). Yet, a greater focus on pretrial dispositions such as charge reductions, in recognition of the role these decisions ultimately play in shaping imprisonment for a defendant (Kutateladze et al., 2014; Schlesinger, 2007; Sutton, 2013), also demands consideration of how defense attorneys contribute to these decisions. For example, defense attorneys may differ in terms of whether they primarily initiate the negotiation process or simply respond to plea offers by prosecutors, and may also differ in their investment in these "bargains." In short, defense attorneys can directly impact disparate treatment in terms of how they influence the magnitude of charge reductions for their clients.

To encourage greater focus on defense attorneys in related empirical research, this chapter addresses three questions regarding the role of defense attorneys in shaping extra-legal disparities in case processing and outcomes. First, why is empirical research on defense attorneys less popular relative to research on prosecutors? Second, what observations can be identified in the courts literature that suggest defense attorneys might have a greater role in disparate outcomes than a focus on prosecutors would convey? Finally, how might the observations identified for question 2 inform a framework for understanding defense attorneys' influences on these decisions? Towards the end of advancing related frameworks and as encouragement for further research, the second part of this chapter offers an exploratory bi-level analysis of guilty pleas and charge reductions in a large urban court, with defendants nested within defense attorneys.

Here we define "plea bargaining" as a process involving communication and negotiation between defense counsel and prosecutors that ultimately lead to an agreement, subject to judicial approval, whereby a defendant agrees to plead guilty in exchange for one or more reduced charges. Our focus here is on *charge bargaining*, which occurs when the charges in the indictment are reduced in severity and result in a reduced sentence (e.g., second-degree homicide reduced to manslaughter). *Sentence bargaining* is less common and involves a more lenient sentence relative to what the penal code dictates for the indicted charge(s) and is only possible in states with sentence ranges for specific felony levels. A number of defendants also plead guilty to the indictment without any real negotiation, but even then, the sentences might be reduced (for reasons described in this chapter).

Understanding the Limited Focus on Defense Attorneys in Empirical Research

A synthesis of ethnographies on courtroom workgroups in state trial courts clearly portrays defense attorneys as culpable yet less powerful participants relative to prosecutors in the plea bargaining process (e.g., Alschuler, 1983; Casper, 1972: Eisenstein and Jacob, 1977: Eisenstein, Flemming, and Nardulli, 1988; Flemming, Nardulli, and Eisenstein, 1992; Heumann, 1978: Nardulli et al., 1988; Ulmer, 1997). This portrayal is consistent with the broader image of prosecutors as the most influential court actors (e.g., Lynch, 1998; Wooldredge et al., 2015; Wright and Miller, 2003). Some ethnographies published before the mid-1980s even portray judges as more powerful negotiators relative to defense counsel, but this changed after most states either prohibited or discouraged active participation by judges in plea negotiations. (Nine states still allow and encourage judicial participation, however [Batra, 2015]. Even in states that disallow or discourage judicial participation, attorneys learn through experience the recommended charge reductions that are acceptable to particular judges in certain types of cases.) Today, "judges serve as mere functionaries, only occasionally supervising the determination of guilt, and maintaining a somewhat larger voice at sentencing" (Wright and Miller, 2003, p. 1409).

An assumption that prosecutors consistently maintain the upper hand in plea negotiations relative to defense counsel would lead to the expectation that they are primarily responsible for extra-legal disparities in sentences associated with guilty pleas, and therefore the *level* of disparity in an attorney's caseload is more likely to differ by prosecutor rather than by defense attorney. This would explain why multi-level analyses of pretrial dispositions typically involve nesting defendants within prosecutors or prosecutor/judge dyads (e.g., Kim et al., 2015; Kutateladze et al., 2014; Wooldredge et al., 2015) but not within defense attorneys.

The plea bargaining literature is filled with verbiage conveying a much larger role of prosecutors in plea negotiations. The most obvious example is how often phrases such as "plea offers by prosecutors" are used in court ethnographies (noted above), implying that defense counsel is usually at the whim of prosecutors' willingness to reduce charges and initiate negotiations. In their classic work on courtroom workgroups in three urban jurisdictions, Eisenstein and Jacob (1977) observed that Chicago prosecutors actually "offered" less attractive plea bargains as trial dates approached and defense counsel delayed responses to earlier offers (Eisenstein and Jacob, 1977). Consistent with this image of prosecutors as holding the upper hand in plea negotiations, Alschuler (1975) described some public defenders as impatient and so invested in moving cases that they often settled for less attractive plea offers by prosecutors. Although Alschuler (1975) commented on how these offers seemed more attractive as the odds of conviction declined in certain cases, this observation still portrays prosecutors as having the upper hand because defense counsel cannot act until an offer is actually put forth.

But what about situations when defense counsel are confident about acquittal at trial? Even then, according to Alschuler (1975), there were some defense attorneys who would encourage their clients to plead guilty when prosecutors offered very large concessions relative to what the laws dictated in such cases (also see Schulhofer, 1992). Similarly, Eisenstein and Jacob (1977) also described how any weaknesses in a state's case against a defendant led some prosecutors to initiate negotiations very early in the process, even before formal charges were filed, so that the prosecution could gain a conviction with insufficient evidence for conviction at trial. More recent research supports the idea that even self-proclaimed innocent defendants will sometimes plead guilty although "innocents" are less likely than guilty defendants *in general* to accept plea bargains (e.g., Tor et al., 2010). Prosecutors also have an upper hand by being able to schedule cases for trial in order to persuade defense attorneys to accept their offers (Alschuler, 1975).

Eisenstein and Jacob's (1977) observations of Detroit's system as "bureaucratic plea bargaining" sounds very much like legal scholars' commentaries on plea bargaining in the 21st century (e.g., Stuntz, 2004). Eisenstein and Jacob observed that both prosecutors *and* judges in Detroit encouraged negotiations when there was little ambiguity regarding guilt and/or defendants wanted to avoid trials, regardless of defense attorneys' interests. This type of system seems even more prevalent today, with the exception that the active role of judges has been virtually eliminated in most states. Stuntz (2004: 2548) summed up this system as follows: "litigants in criminal cases do not bargain in the shadow of the law. Rather, they bargain in the shadow of prosecutors' preferences, budget constraints, and political trends. Law's shadow disappears." A theme that has emerged in the courts literature over time is that prosecutors in particular have much more of a role in the sentencing process than previously thought due to (a) the much higher rate at which defendants plead guilty rather than go to trial, and (b) their seemingly greater control over initiating negotiations and holding out for outcomes that they perceive as desirable.

Casper's (1972) interviews with criminal defendants echoed the last point above in addition to suggesting that judges, even prior to the 1980s when they played an active role in plea bargaining in all states, were not independent of prosecutors' interests and acted only as a rubber stamp on sentences recommended by prosecutors. Defendants indicated that the prosecutor "runs the show" (Casper, 1972: 17) instead of the judge, who simply follows the prosecutor's recommendation. Judges had the authority to dismiss formal charges brought by prosecutors and to override their plea agreements, but such judicial actions were very rare. Defendants perceived judges as figureheads who delegated power to prosecutors and relied on them to take care of business. This same observation was highlighted by Worden (1995) over 20 years after Casper's study. She discussed the willingness of judges to accept the sentence recommendations of prosecutors.

Consistent with the above, the courts literature more broadly describes the sheer amount of power prosecutors maintain over case processing, with some scholars arguing that they are more powerful than judges because there is less oversight on their decisions and they operate with relative autonomy because their decisions are less visible to the public compared to judges (e.g., Albonetti, 1987; Lynch, 1998; Wright and Miller, 2003). All of this portrays prosecutors as more powerful than defense attorneys in terms of their ability to control case outcomes, and this could have much to do with scholars' primary foci on prosecutors and judges in research on disparate sentencing. Yet, the same ethnographies of courtroom workgroups are also replete with more subtle suggestions of how defense attorneys might be just as culpable as prosecutors and judges for shaping case outcomes, and some of these observations have been (selectively) borne out in more recent empirical research.

Arguments Favoring a Larger Role of Defense Counsel in Disparate Sentencing

This section includes some discussion of how *type* of defense counsel might shape case outcomes, so we begin with a brief overview of defense attorney types. The origins of these types emanate from the fact that the U.S. Supreme Court (USSC) never specified in their landmark cases how defense counsel services must be made available to poor defendants (*Powell v. Alabama*, 287 U.S. 45 [1932]; *Gideon v. Wainwright*, 372 U.S. 335 [1963]; *Argersinger v. Hamlin*, 407 U.S. 25 [1972]).

Over 80 percent of felony suspects are indigent and must be assigned defense counsel (Davies and Worden, 2009; Wolf-Harlow, 2000). These defendants are likely to be represented by an attorney through one of three types of programs. First, a defendant may be represented through assigned counsel where local courts create a list of private attorneys available for appointment to represent indigent defendants when needed. These attorneys may be paid an hourly rate or a flat fee for their services (Cohen, 2014). A limitation to the assigned counsel system is that courts may rely on attorneys who lack the experience and skills to defend their clients. This occurs when young, inexperienced attorneys ask to be included in order to gain more experience or to earn extra money (Beck and Shumsky, 1997; Gist, 1989–1990; Iyengar, 2007; Neubauer and Fradella, 2011; Spangenberg and Beeman, 1995).

Second, and similar to the assigned counsel system, an indigent defendant may be represented by a contract attorney. Under this system, the government enters into a financial agreement with private attorneys, law firms, or bar associations to represent defendants for a negotiated period of time (Davies and Worden, 2009; Spangenberg and Beeman, 1995). Opponents argue that these attorneys may provide subpar services if the overall rate of pay is negotiated too low between the government and a particular law firm (Cohen, 2014).

Assignment of counsel to indigent defendants through a public defender's office is a third system adopted by many urban jurisdictions across the U.S. Public defenders are full-time employees of a public or private non-profit organization or are direct employees of the government (Cohen, 2014). While it has been argued that public defenders handle high caseloads and may not provide all clients with the necessary time and attention (Williams, 2013), proponents argue that they are more experienced and skilled than assigned or contract attorneys (Cohen, 2014). They often have stronger professional relationships with other members of the courtroom workgroup, giving them the ability to negotiate for more favorable outcomes (Flemming et al., 1992; Hartley et al., 2010; Heumann, 1978).

Finally, defendants who have the ability to do so may hire a private attorney. While public defenders might feel the pressure from their colleagues to quickly resolve cases, private attorneys may not feel this pressure as they are not regularly working with the same prosecutors and judges (Bowen, 2009; Hartley et al., 2010). They may also not be motivated to resolve cases quickly since they are often paid based on the number of appearances in the court process. However, without the working relationship between these courtroom actors, private attorneys may not have the ability to secure as favorable outcomes for their clients, sometimes skipping the plea negotiations entirely and sending the case to trial (Champion, 1989; Feeley, 1992; Flemming et al., 1992; Hartley et al., 2010).

The plea bargaining literature focuses primarily on public defenders and private attorneys although we think it is important to separate all types in any empirical analysis due to nuances between them that might generate differences in case outcomes for similarly situated clients. Now returning to the purpose of addressing the second question posed at the beginning of the chapter, aside from the observations of court scholars underscoring the greater control of prosecutors over plea negotiations, many of these same scholars have also commented on ways in which defense attorneys have equal sway in the process.

Sudnow (1965) conducted one of the first ethnographic studies of defense attorney decision making, specifically focusing on public defenders (PDs). At the time of his study, Sudnow observed that PDs represented over two-thirds of all indigent defendants across the United States. Given the heavy workloads relative to their pay, PDs were more concerned with moving their caseloads rather than providing their clients with the best possible legal defense (recently echoed by Williams, 2013). Alschuler (1975) made a related observation that the only way a defense attorney could be financially successful, aside from being an excellent trial attorney, was to handle large numbers of clients. The incentive to avoid time-consuming trials might lead PDs to accept less than desirable plea offers for their clients, thus generating a link between sentencing and attorney type, as well as between sentencing and a defendant's socio-economic status (SES) because PDs handle indigent defendants. A defendant's SES, in turn, is sometimes tied to a defendant's race or ethnicity in areas where minorities are over-represented in the poverty class. Empirical studies of whether guilty plea rates vary by type of attorney suggest that clients of public defenders are much more likely to plead guilty than defendants who are represented by a private attorney (Anderson and Heaton, 2012; Champion, 1989; Gitelman, 1971; Taylor et al., 1973).

Similar to discussions of focal concerns (Steffensmeier, Ulmer, and Kramer, 1998) and uncertainty avoidance (Albonetti, 1987), which emphasize how prosecutors and judges might stereotype certain types of offenders (e.g., young black men) as greater threats to public safety, Sudnow observed that PDs also stereotyped their clients (see also Lyon, 2012, for a more recent discussion of Chicago PDs' racial stereotypes of defendants). However, Sudnow's perspective leads to a prediction of greater *benefits* to poor and minority defendants, unlike recent research findings indicating harsher sentences for minorities (see Kim et al., 2015, for some extant findings).

According to Sudnow, PDs would act on stereotypes of persons arrested for large-volume crimes, which helped them to expedite case processing when they lacked the time to carefully review the circumstances of every offense. Particular types of plea agreements became commonplace based on stereotypes of "typical" offenders and their crimes (i.e., commonly committed crimes committed in poor neighborhoods by persons living in poverty). These plea bargains became "going-rate" plea agreements that, in reality, involved very little communication and actual negotiation (also see Flemming et al., 1992; Heumann, 1978; Nardulli, Eisenstein, and Flemming, 1988). Prosecutors would have to agree to these going rate deals, and Sudnow discussed how prosecutors shared these offender stereotypes. As for a defendant's willingness to accept the offer, the typical plea bargain would be described by the PD to the defendant, often with an added "threat" of what might happen if the defendant took a chance at trial (conviction and sentencing on the original charge, a jury would not be as sympathetic, etc.). This standard procedure would actually generate more lenient sentences for lower SES defendants, but the argument underscores comparable roles of defense attorneys and prosecutors in shaping case outcomes via guilty pleas.

Sudnow examined only PDs, so he could not speak to whether the magnitude of these plea bargains varied by attorney type. More recent research has addressed this issue, and Anderson and Heaton (2012) found that PDs in Philadelphia obtained prison sentences in murder cases that were three-fourths in length (on average) compared to court-appointed private attorneys. Although not large-volume crime, the findings (based on random assignments of cases to attorneys) are consistent with the idea that PDs might obtain greater leniency for their clients (see an overview of the literature by Hartley et al., 2010). In separate studies, both Cohen (2014) and Roach (2010) also found harsher sentences among defendants with assigned counsel versus a PD, although their research designs were not as rigorous as Anderson and Heaton's (2012) design (also see Hanson et al. [1992] and Wice [2005], for null findings related to differences between PDs and assigned counsel). At the federal level, Iyengar (2007) concluded that clients represented by public defenders in federal district courts received more lenient prison sentences than defendants represented by court-appointed counsel.

Regarding possible differences between PDs and private attorneys, early empirical research suggested that being represented by a private attorney decreased an offender's likelihood of being sent to prison (Gitelman, 1971; Hermann, Single, and Boston, 1977; National Center for State Courts, 1992) or that prison sentences were shorter for clients of private attorneys (Silverstein, 1965; but see Hoffman et al., 2005, for more recent evidence favoring this conclusion). However, some recent research suggests otherwise. In their analysis of felony offenders in Chicago, Hartley et al. (2010) found that PDs were more likely than private attorneys to keep their clients out of prison when those defendants obtained pretrial release. PDs also secured more lenient trial outcomes, with defendants represented by private attorneys being sent to prison more often and for longer periods (46 months longer, on average) (Hartley et al., 2010). When assessing differences between PDs, assigned counsel, and private attorneys, other researchers suggest that assigned counsel is actually the least successful in obtaining favorable outcomes for defendants (Beck and Shumsky, 1997; Champion, 1989). All of these studies highlight the theme that case outcomes might vary by defense attorney and, in particular, by type of attorney.

Alschuler (1975) provided a different set of observations to suggest that case outcomes might vary by type of defense attorney. He observed that prosecutors maintained greater trust of public defenders based on their greater familiarity with the PD's office. Therefore, even defendants who received less attention from their PD may have still fared better in plea bargains relative to the clients of private defense lawyers, suggesting that PDs might have a greater influence on recommended sentences via plea agreements relative to private attorneys. On the other hand, but also related to differences in case outcomes by attorney type, Casper (1972) observed that defendants with private attorneys might fare better than those with PDs because the former were in a position to buy a better defense. They typically paid private attorneys a small fee up front and later paid another fee based on the severity of the outcome (i.e., more money for less severe sentences with the highest amount paid for an acquittal or dismissal). Paying for private counsel also changes the tone of the attorney/client relationship by placing a defendant in greater control of the situation. Even Alschuler (1975) noted that attorney/client relationships were more antagonistic among public defenders relative to private attorneys because indigent defendants did not have the luxury of choosing their attorneys, and more antagonistic relations may have contributed to generally higher odds of bargaining among public defenders if they were generally less interested in their client's welfare.

Returning to the issue of a defendant's race, recent research underscores the power of defense attorneys for shaping case outcomes differently for minority and white defendants and also suggests that case outcomes might vary among defense attorneys based on differences in the extent to which they apply racial stereotypes to their clients. Edkins (2011) found that defense attorneys were more likely to accept plea offers with longer sentences for minority clients compared to white clients and were also more likely to accept jail time for minority clients. Lyon (2012) provided a commentary of racial attitudes among PDs in Cook County (Chicago), in which she served as a PD and supervisor of other attorneys. Lyon observed more disrespectful attitudes of certain attorneys toward minority clients, arguing that a predominantly white male staff can bias against minority defendants due to implicit and subconscious biases emanating from "race loyalty" (Smith, 2008). Although not a quantitative analysis, the concept of race loyalty might play a role in how PDs approach plea negotiations with minority versus white clients to produce the differences in case outcomes found by Edkins (2011).

On the other hand, perhaps the key segment of Lyon's commentary was her description of the vastly white male staff of PDs, which might feed a culture of unconscious bias when no one is willing to step forward with reports of unequal treatment. This observation must be tempered with the possibility that her observations based on limited personal encounters might not be borne out in a statistical analysis of a representative cross-section of defense attorneys. Nonetheless, in a study of federal sentences, Farrell, Ward, and Rousseau (2009) found that the racial composition of the prosecutorial workforce mattered most for shaping the effects of defendant's race on sentence severity, where race group differences in case outcomes were more significant in court environments with larger proportions of black prosecutors. Important to note, however, is that the racial composition of defense attorneys did *not* matter in this regard. Still, a synthesis of the evidence that defense attorneys contribute to race effects on case outcomes with the earlier discussion of possible links between type of attorney and case outcomes as well as between type of attorney and a defendant's race opens up the possibility of significant between-attorney differences in race effects that might be explained by type of counsel.

Alschuler (1975) offered an additional set of observations that differ from those above but also suggested that defense attorneys hold a fair amount of control over the bargaining process and that sentencing disparities might vary across defense attorneys. Contrary to research indicating a greater use of guilty pleas by public defenders (Anderson and Heaton, 2012; Champion, 1989; Gitelman, 1971; Taylor et al., 1973), Alschuler observed that both private attorneys and public defenders used guilty pleas to the same degree but that each group had different motivations to encourage defendants to plead guilty. Private attorneys pursued guilty pleas to expedite case processing in order to make more money. By contrast, PDs dealt with more socially and economically disadvantaged defendants who often had prior records, and so defense counsel sometimes pursued plea bargains in order to reduce the odds of more severe sentences at trial resulting from the defendant's criminal histories and/or from potential biases held by some jurors toward poor, minority defendants. Therefore, in contrast to the cited research suggesting harsher outcomes for minority clients, both Alschuler's and Sudnow's arguments, while different from each other, imply that minorities might obtain more lenient sentences relative to whites through plea bargaining. On the other hand, a focal concerns perspective (Steffensmeier et al., 1998) would suggest that prosecutors still pursue harsher sentences for minority defendants relative to white defendants even in plea negotiations (Wooldredge et al., 2015).

Contrary to Eisenstein and Jacob (1977), Alschuler (1975) also observed that defense attorneys received *better* offers from prosecutors with the passage of time because witnesses became impatient with so many court appearances, their memories faded, and they sometimes backed out of the process altogether. As the odds of conviction declined, the prosecutor's plea bargains became more attractive. The passage of time was also linked to defense counsel's stubbornness to engage in negotiations with the prosecution, according to Alschuler. This is yet another of Alschuler's discussions suggesting that defense counsel might have more control over plea bargaining than Eisenstein and Jacob might concede.

In short, the classic literature on courtroom workgroups simultaneously underscored the power of prosecutors in plea negotiations while providing separate sets of observations that can be used to form a compelling argument that defense attorneys still maintain substantial control over the plea bargaining process and, in turn, sentencing. These observations can also be used to build a framework for understanding defense attorney effects on guilty pleas and sentencing.

Framing Defense Attorney Effects on Case Outcomes

The relevance of defense attorney factors for shaping case outcomes via the magnitude of charge reductions through the guilty plea process lies in both the main effects of defense attorney characteristics on case outcomes as well as in possible interaction effects (i.e., how defense attorney characteristics might *condition* defendant effects on case outcomes). The appropriate way to study such effects is with multi-level modeling, where defendants are nested within defense attorneys, similar to recent multi-level studies of defendants nested within judges (e.g., Johnson, 2006), or defendants nested within prosecutors (e.g., Wooldredge, 2012), or even defendants nested within pairs of judges and prosecutors (Kim et al., 2015). This section presents a bi-level framework of defense attorney effects on case outcomes, consistent with the evolution of thought on disparate sentencing.

The Most Relevant Actors for Shaping Disparate Outcomes

A synthesis of observations regarding the seemingly greater power of prosecutors relative to defense attorneys in plea negotiations with observations of how defense attorneys might "take control" of plea negotiations in certain types of cases suggests that both prosecutors *and* defense attorneys are important contributors to disparities in case outcomes via guilty pleas. However, we perceive a greater contribution from prosecutors in this regard if only because they shape the initial charges and appear to be the most likely to initiate negotiations with the defendant and the defense. When comparing attorneys to each other, both within and between these groups, we would expect to find significant differences in case outcomes among defense attorneys and among prosecutors, but with more dramatic differences among the latter. It seems intuitive to expect that, for example, *any* between-prosecutor differences in charging practices or approaches to initiating negotiations would generate important differences in the end result and perhaps would be more important than between-counsel differences in trial delays (for example) because the latter is subject to more control by the court. On the other hand, and consistent with an expectation of significant differences in case outcomes between defense attorneys, Abrams and Yoon (2007) found substantial heterogeneity among defense attorneys in case outcomes for their clients even when controlling for case selection through random assignments of defendants to attorneys.

Aside from determining whether the variance in case outcomes is significant among defense attorneys, it is also important to establish whether extra-legal effects (defendant's race and SES) on these outcomes vary significantly between defense attorneys and whether the variance in these effects is larger among prosecutors versus defense attorneys. If the magnitude of extra-legal effects differs more between prosecutors, this would suggest that individual prosecutors contribute more to extra-legal disparities in case outcomes relative to defense attorneys.

Comparing prosecutors to defense counsel in terms of between-attorney differences in case outcomes and defendant effects on these outcomes only speaks to individual differences rather than actual attorney "effects" on these outcomes. For example, significant between-counsel differences in case outcomes, even if smaller in magnitude compared to between-prosecutor differences, would raise the question of whether specific attorney characteristics matter for shaping these differences. There seem to be four factors relevant to defense attorneys that have been most frequently identified in the court literature as impacting these differences *directly* (as *main* effects): type of attorney (public attorney, assigned counsel, private attorney); caseload demand; caseload composition or types of cases processed; and time to final disposition. This is not to say that other factors have not been mentioned or that other factors are not related to these four in particular, but that these four are the most commonly discussed and may, therefore, account for all of the significant between-counsel differences in case outcomes.

Type of Defense Attorney, Cases Processed, and Processing Time

As discussed in the last section, type of attorney (public defender, assigned/contract counsel, or private attorney) might impact the recommended sentences accompanying plea agreements due to differences in experience, familiarity with prosecutors and judges, and/or in quality of the legal defense provided. For example, guilty plea sentences might be more severe for clients of PDs and assigned counsel relative to similar cases handled by private attorneys. Such a thesis would be supported with Sudnow's (1965) observation that PDs appeared more interested in moving their caseloads versus providing the best possible legal defense, in conjunction with Casper's (1972) discussion of how private attorneys have economic incentives to work harder for their clients who also have greater control over their defense. Related to Casper's discussion, Alschuler (1975) also observed that attorney/client relationships involving PDs were more volatile and that these attorneys might be less vested in their client's welfare as a result. Yet, a caveat to this thesis emerges from a separate discussion by Alschuler (1975) regarding how PDs might fare *better* than private attorneys because of greater familiarity with and trust of PDs by prosecutors, and recent research (cited earlier) suggests that PDs fare better than assigned counsel in case outcomes for their clients.

Defense attorneys' workloads might also influence charge reductions if greater caseload demands lead them to become less diligent in championing for the best possible outcomes for their clients. To some extent this could also be linked to type of attorney, as Sudnow (1965) observed that PDs were often overworked because their pay was insufficient, and this could lead to higher odds that PDs agree to less desirable sentences accompanying plea agreements. However, caseload demands could impact any type of attorney with the same end result. Extant research on an empirical link between caseload "pressure" and plea bargaining is extremely rare, limited primarily to studies from the 1970s and 1980s (Wooldredge, 1989), but the general theme from that research is that there is no meaningful empirical relationship between these factors (Meeker and Pontell, 1985). However, relatively small samples in conjunction with limited statistical controls and relatively crude statistical analyses prohibit placing much confidence in this theme.

The types of cases predominantly handled by a defense attorney could also impact attorney differences in case outcomes via guilty pleas. Sudnow's (1965) discussion of large volumes of certain crimes for which "going rate" charge reductions became the norm in plea agreements suggests that certain low-level drug crimes (e.g., possession and low-level distribution) and property crimes (e.g., residential burglaries in poor neighborhoods) might coincide with greater leniency. Attorneys with higher-than-average proportions of these types of cases, therefore, might obtain generally better outcomes for their clients. Also related to this point, attorneys with larger proportions of clients who fit the offender stereotypes for these types of crimes (e.g., persons from poorer neighborhoods) might also obtain generally better outcomes for their clients.

Lastly, attorneys who generally take longer to close their cases via guilty pleas might gain less desirable outcomes for their clients relative to those who move their cases more quickly. This thesis is consistent with Eisenstein and Jacob (1977), who observed that defense attorneys who delayed case dispositions were offered less appealing plea bargains by prosecutors. They also noted that prosecutors were slower to initiate negotiations when the state had a strong case and that charge reductions were not as dramatic in stronger cases favoring the state. Therefore, both processes might contribute to a positive correspondence between time to conviction and sentence severity in plea agreements. Once again, Alschuler (1975) offered an exception to this thesis, where his observations suggested *better* offers from prosecutors with the passage of time because witnesses became impatient with so many court appearances, their memories faded, and they sometimes backed out of the process altogether.

Aside from the possible main effects of the four factors described above on defense attorney differences in plea outcomes, no less relevant to the subject is how type of attorney might *condition* defendant effects on charge reductions and sentences. Alschuler (1975) observed that PDs dealt with more socially and economically disadvantaged defendants who often had prior records, and so defense counsel sometimes pursued plea bargains in order to reduce the odds of more severe sentences at trial resulting from the defendant's criminal histories and/or from potential biases held by some jurors toward poor, minority defendants. Therefore, extra-legal disparities in sentencing that reflect harsher sentences for persons reinforcing stereotypes of more dangerous offenders (e.g., young black males) might be more of a phenomenon among PDs rather than private attorneys or assigned counsel.

A Partial Test of the Proposed Model

To encourage further discussion and refinement of the framework presented above, we conducted a partial test of our perspective using data from a large urban jurisdiction in a mid-Atlantic state. We treat this as a "partial" test because the data examined were not compiled specifically for this purpose. These data are limited in the number of defense attorneys available for analysis in addition to the absence of more specific measures of the factors described above for proper model specification.

Samples and Data

Samples for the analysis presented here included 1,989 defendants indicted on felony charges who either pled guilty or opted for trial (including 1,890 who pled guilty) nested within 110 defense attorneys. The jurisdiction has a public defenders' office in addition to an assigned counsel system with private attorneys available for appointment to represent indigent defendants when needed. Therefore, in terms of type of attorney, the analysis was restricted to PDs, assigned counsel, and private (for hire) attorneys while excluding contract attorneys. The defendants and attorneys examined here came from a larger study of extra-legal disparities in case processing funded by the county's prosecutors office, including 3,459 suspects referred to their office for felony crimes in 2009 (reflecting all such referrals during the calendar year; see Wooldredge et al., 2015, for a description of the larger study). There were 496 defense attorneys responsible for the full sample of 3,459 suspects, but we selected attorneys with at least 5 cases for the analysis described here because of the bi-level model examined and the need to have non-zero variance in case factors for each attorney. Also excluded were Latino suspects given their relatively small representation (less than 1 percent).

The prosecutors' office provided access to a non-public database for most of the data examined, and a public database provided the remaining data. We supplemented this information for the present analysis with qualitative survey data from 20 of the original 110 defense attorneys working in the county in 2009. An electronic survey was used to this end, and the passage of time made it possible to locate working email addresses for only 45 attorneys from the original pool who still practiced as defense attorneys in the jurisdiction under study. (Sixty-eight addresses were found, but only 45 addresses were active.) Selected comments from these surveys are presented to provide some context to the quantitative findings and, more importantly, to offer insight into the court culture under study and a more qualitative assessment of our framework. We do not claim that these 20 defense attorneys are a representative cross-section of the original sample of attorneys because there is no way to quantitatively evaluate this claim and because of the differences between individuals who remain practicing attorneys in the same jurisdiction versus those who moved to different areas or quit the profession altogether.

Measures

All defendant (level 1) and attorney (level 2) measures for the analysis are described in Table 7.1. Most of these measures are intuitive although some need explanation, and we also note where more precise measures are needed for a more reliable assessment. The outcomes for the analysis included whether a felony defendant pled guilty (n = 1,989) and the magnitude of charge reductions for those defendants who pled guilty (n = 1,890). The measure of *charge reductions* is the difference in charges between indictment and conviction. Felony and misdemeanor levels were scored 1 through 9 for every count a person was indicted on and for every count a defendant was convicted on. These values ranged from 1 (Misdemeanor 4) through 9 (Felony 1). Scores were summed across all counts per defendant at both indictment and conviction, and the difference between these sums reflects the magnitude of charge reductions accompanying a guilty plea. This measure is somewhat crude, and a thorough critique is provided in Wooldredge et al. (2015). The primary drawback worth noting here is that a defendant indicted on a very large number of less serious charges might be scored comparable to (if not higher than) a defendant charged with homicide at either indictment or conviction. Nonetheless, a focus on the *difference* between these two raw scores for each defendant rather than the absolute magnitude of each raw score should capture the more important differences in charge reductions across defendants. The square root of the difference in raw scores was taken to remove the skewed distribution on the original scale in order to conform to the assumptions of generalized least-squares regression (Fox, 2016: 61).

The defendant measures of primary interest included those reflecting race, SES, type of offense, prior record, and days between referral and final disposition. The last measure reflects one of our four main effects of primary interest, namely, the link between case processing time and the magnitude of charge reductions. Type of offense is another main effect of interest, although primarily at the attorney level, and so how the offense measures were centered for the analysis is important for interpretation (described later in this section). All of these defendant measures, except number of days between referral and final disposition, are of interest as cross-level interactions

Table 7.1 Description of Measures for the Analysis of Defense Attorneys

Measures	*Mean*	*SD*
Level 1: Felony defendants (pled guilty or opted for trial) (N_1 = 1,989)		
Outcomes		
Pled guilty (N_1 = 1,989)	0.95	0.22
Charge reductions (square root) (N_1 = 1,890)	2.61	2.45
Demographics		
African American male 18–29	0.32	0.47
Social disadvantage of street block population (range: −1.37–2.52)	0.00	1.00
% street block pop. same address > 1 year (range: 34–98)	79.8	11.7
Legal factors and case characteristics		
Indicted for . . .		
Drug crime(s)	0.11	0.32
Domestic violence	0.03	0.17
Prior prison term	0.46	0.50
# days to outcome (square root) (range: 1–23)	10.5	3.83
Most serious charge indicted . . .		
Felony 1	0.20	0.40
Felony 2	0.18	0.38
Felony 3	0.17	0.38
Felony 4	0.15	0.36
Felony 5 (reference)	0.26	0.44
Total indicted charges (square root) (range: 1–3)	1.70	0.53
# victims of violence (range: 0–4)	0.27	0.62
Pretrial detention	0.33	0.47
Uncooperative with prosecutors	0.02	0.15
Level 2: Defense attorneys (N_2 = 110)		
Type of attorney . . .		
Public defender	0.32	0.47
Assigned by court	0.55	0.50
Hired (reference)	0.12	0.32
# felony cases handled in county during 2009 (range: 6–48)	17.2	7.53
Proportion caseload consisting of		
Felony 1 charges	0.21	0.13
Felony 2 charges	0.19	0.11
Felony 3 charges	0.18	0.10
Felony 4 charges	0.16	0.10
Felony 5 charges (reference)	0.27	0.14
Proportion caseload with African American defendants	0.74	0.15

and whether the magnitude of these effects on the outcome measures varies by type of attorney.

Rather than focus more generally on a defendant's race, we focused specifically on African American males 18 to 29 because this subgroup is more consistent with our earlier discussion of demographic effects on case outcomes and extant studies to date have produced considerable evidence that this subgroup is treated more severely than any other by the criminal courts. Exclusion of the more traditional demographic measures necessarily prohibits us from examining more general demographic effects, but this was a necessary compromise due to the restricted numbers of cases nested within the attorney sample and the loss in degrees of freedom associated with including all additive and multiplicative terms in the model. Still, a focus on this subgroup is consistent with court scholars' discussions of high volume crimes.

The absence of available defendant data on SES led us to create related measures for the street blocks in which these defendants resided. The availability of residential addresses allowed us to locate census data on street blocks, including the percentage of African American residents, female-headed households, vacant residences, renters, and the percentage of residents living at the same address for at least 1 year. The residential "stability" measure did not correlate strongly with the other four, and so it was treated separately in the model. A principal components analysis of the first four measures produced a single factor for the model (Cronbach's alpha = .81). Although not a scale of SES per se, we examined the correlation between this factor and a more traditional factor created at the tract-level including the above four items in addition to the percentages of unemployed civilians, residents living at or below the poverty level, residents receiving public assistance, and adults without high school degrees. The correlation between the two factors examined at the tract-level was 0.74 (r). The use of street block indicators of social disadvantage rather than individual-level measures highlights yet another shortcoming of our model.

Our interest in type of offense stems from the discussion of charge reductions related to large-volume crimes. We initially explored measures of drug crimes, theft, fraud, and domestic violence because these were the four "large-volume" felony crimes defendants were referred for in the sample examined. Only two of these measures (drugs and domestic violence) were retained for the models presented here, however, due to the null main effects of theft and fraud on both outcomes in addition to the absence of significant between-attorney variance in these effects. Ideally, we would have kept all four measures in these models if the average number of cases per attorney had been much larger. Measures of more specific types of drug offenses would have also been preferred, including drug use versus possession versus sale, in addition to parsing these out by type and amount.

Several other case factors were also included in the analysis as statistical controls based on prior research indicating their significant effects on case dispositions and/or outcomes. Defense of these particular measures can be found in Wooldredge et al. (2015) and so are not elaborated on here given our focus on defense attorney effects. Still, it is important to note that the binary measure of pretrial detention compares persons who were released (bond posted or released on their own recognizance) to those detained prior to trial (no bond posted or denied release).

In addition to the level 2 (defense attorney) measures listed in Table 7.1, we also explored the effects of attorney's sex, race/ethnicity, and years as an attorney on the outcomes for a subset of 61 attorneys for which this information was available. None of these effects were significant in either model, and so they were excluded from the multivariate models in order to maximize sample size. Regarding *# felony cases handled*, a weakness of this measure is that attorneys could have also handled other non-felony cases in 2009. We were unable to determine the numbers of these other cases, so the measure might be a crude proxy for an attorney's actual caseload.

Statistical Analysis

Multi-level modeling with HLM7 was used for the analysis. The first stage of the analysis involved comparisons of defense attorneys and prosecutors in the level 2 variance in each outcome measure (*pled guilty*, *charge reductions*), and in the level 2 variance in each level 1 effect of interest (*African American male 18–29*, *social disadvantage*, *street block pop. same address > 1 year*, *drug crime*, *domestic violence*, and *prior prison term*). These specific comparisons are described in the next section, but it is important to note here that significant variance in each outcome measure was established for defense attorneys at $p < .01$, indicating that the proportion of an attorney's caseload resulting in guilty pleas and the average amount of charge reductions associated with guilty pleas differed significantly across the 110 defense attorneys. These significant estimates permitted modeling the level 2 effects on both outcomes.

The level 2 variance estimates were compared between the two groups of attorneys to determine whether the estimates were larger for prosecutors. The number of prosecutors ($N_2 = 117$) was comparable to the number of defense attorneys ($N_2 = 110$), and so the small difference in sample size alone should not have contributed to substantive differences in these estimates between the two groups of attorneys. As previously discussed, larger variance estimates in the level 2 outcomes for prosecutors might reflect their greater control over pleas and charge reductions relative to defense counsel, presumably through greater control over plea negotiations. Also, if the level 2 variance in each of the level 1 effects noted above was larger for prosecutors, this would suggest that they contribute more to disparities in case outcomes based on these factors relative to defense attorneys.

The second part of the analysis focused on modeling both main and cross-level defense attorney effects on guilty pleas and charge reductions. Binary logistic (Bernoulli) regression was used to estimate the model of guilty pleas, and generalized least squares regression was used for the model of charge reductions. (Level 1 PRE estimates cannot be derived from multi-level Bernoulli models based on the information provided in HLM7 although they can be computed for models estimated with generalized least squares. Both models permit estimation of level 2 PRE estimates.) As noted, significant level 2 variance in guilty pleas and in charge reductions was established at $p < .01$, thus permitting estimation of the main effects of defense attorney characteristics on the level 2 outcomes. Similarly, significant level 2 variance in each of the level 1 effects of *African American male 18–29*, *street block pop. same address > 1 year*, and *prior prison term* was established at $p < .05$, indicating that the magnitude of these defendant effects differed across attorneys. This permitted analysis of whether type of attorney might have influenced the magnitude of these effects (e.g., whether *African American male 18–29* was a stronger influence on charge reductions for PDs relative to private attorneys).

All defendant measures were grand mean-centered in each model in order to control for compositional differences in attorney caseloads that might have correlated with attorney characteristics (e.g., PDs might have had higher proportions of lower SES defendants in their caseloads, and both type of attorney and defendant SES might impact the magnitude of charge reductions). In contrast to group-mean centering, centering the level 1 measures around their grand means also allows the level 1 predictors to explain between-attorney differences in the outcomes at level 2, which is our primary interest in the measures of *drug crime* and *domestic violence*, as noted above.

Findings

It is important to first highlight certain characteristics of the jurisdiction under study in order to place some of our findings in proper context. The county's rank on racial segregation is high, with over half of the population living in racially homogeneous zip code areas. Editorials in the main local newspaper have highlighted public criticisms of the police and prosecutors' office for the disproportionate overrepresentation of African Americans in arrests and indictments. Table 7.1 reveals that African American males 18 to 29 constituted nearly one-third of the sample of indictments. The city faced a very high home foreclosure rate back in 2008, only 1 year prior to our study period. Even before the Great Recession, less than 15 percent of census tracts in the city limits were gentrified.

In this jurisdiction, whether arrested for a misdemeanor or a felony, the initial appearance (where bond is usually set) occurs in municipal court with the exception of the most severe grade of felonies which immediately move to the trial court of general jurisdiction. If not waived by the accused, the subsequent preliminary hearing (where bond is continued or might be set) also takes place in municipal court, again with the exception of the most severe felonies. Once a felony case is bound over, jurisdiction shifts from municipal court to the trial court of general jurisdiction. The state adopted sentencing guidelines, but they are voluntary only and include fairly broad sentence ranges relative to other guideline states.

The jurisdiction does not operate under bail guidelines. Whereas suspects who hire their own attorneys prior to the initial appearance are joined by those attorneys at initial appearance, one supervisor from the public defenders' office is present for all other suspects, and there is no assignment of PDs or assigned counsel to specific cases until *after* the initial appearance. At initial appearance, the supervisor enters a "not guilty" plea, asks for reasonable bond, requests a PD or assigned counsel for indigent defendants and, on rare occasions, requests a preliminary hearing although the grand jury will almost always indict before the preliminary hearing can be held in this county. Indigent felony defendants with odd last-digit case numbers are appointed the public defenders' office. All even last-digit cases receive court-appointed assigned counsel off of an approved list. Once assigned to a case, the attorney sees the case through to its conclusion (plea, trial, diversion program, suppression, or dismissal). There are over 30 PDs assigned to felony cases in this jurisdiction, with over 70 PDs in the entire office.

The assignment of counsel after the initial appearance is important because bond amounts are usually set at the initial appearance. Although these amounts are ultimately set by judges and are influenced by bond schedules, in the jurisdiction examined here, they are also influenced by the recommendations of prosecutors. This could give prosecutors the upper hand in plea bargaining with PDs and assigned counsel if higher bond amounts incentivize defendants to settle more quickly on particular offers. On the other hand, as explained to us by some of the defense attorneys, bail amounts are also informed by "usual amounts," state law and agency rules, and a risk assessment instrument. As explained to suspects, a judge sets the bond amount based on the severity of the arrest charge(s), the suspect's criminal record, and the suspect's community ties. In short, there appears to be some room for discretion in these decisions. Bail investigators are used to help make recommendations to judges, and they consult with attorneys to this end. Therefore, while prosecutors play some role in bail decisions, their ultimate influence on amounts that might lead some defendants to be more eager to accept plea offers might be limited.

Quantitative Results

The analysis began with a comparison of differences between defense attorneys and prosecutors in (a) proportion of guilty pleas in pool of felony defendants who either pled guilty or went to trial, and in (b) average charge reductions accompanying pleas for defendants who pled guilty. Between-attorney differences in the proportions of convictions obtained with guilty pleas were greater for prosecutors (τ = 0.15, $p <$ .001, χ^2 = 170, df = 116) than defense attorneys (τ = 0.11, $p < .05$, χ^2 = 132, df = 109). Although both estimates are statistically significant, the comparison suggests that defense attorneys are more similar to each other in rates of plea negotiations relative to prosecutors. On the other hand, differences among defense attorneys in mean charge reductions was more significant than guilty plea rates (τ = 0.26, $p < .001$, χ^2 = 190, df = 109) even though between-prosecutor differences in charge reductions were also considerably larger (τ = 2.54, $p < .001$, χ^2 = 537, df = 116). As much as 32 percent of the variance in charge reductions actually fell between prosecutors in this court compared to 4 percent between defense attorneys. The larger differences in guilty plea rates and mean charge reductions across prosecutors relative to defense attorneys might indicate greater control over plea negotiations by prosecutors, assuming that larger between-attorney differences actually reflect a manifestation of individual differences in preferences for guilty pleas and charge reductions. Such findings would be expected in order to corroborate Casper's observation that prosecutors seemed to "run the show" (1972: 17). On the other hand, it is possible that these findings simply reflect greater heterogeneity among prosecutors in attorney-level factors linked to these processes.

We were also interested in comparing these groups of attorneys on the effects of a defendant's demographics on guilty pleas and charge reductions (i.e., whether these effects vary more significantly among one group versus the other). The effect of being a young African American male on the odds of pleading guilty did not vary significantly among either group of attorneys. On the other hand, the demographic subgroup effect on charge reductions varied significantly among attorneys in each group but with a considerably larger variance for prosecutors ($\tau = 3.87, p < .001, \chi^2 = 210, df = 115$) relative to defense attorneys ($\tau = 0.22, p < .05, \chi^2 = 123, df = 108$). This difference suggests that while defense attorneys might be culpable for a certain level of demographic disparities in case outcomes, prosecutors might have the dominant influence on shaping these disparities among convicted defendants who plead guilty.

A similar theme emerged for the block-level indicators of social disadvantage and residential stability. The effects of disadvantage on guilty pleas and charge reductions did not vary significantly among defense attorneys, yet both of these effects varied significantly among prosecutors (guilty pleas: $\tau = 0.12, p < .01, \chi^2 = 130$; charge reductions: $\tau = 0.83, p < .001, \chi^2 = 222$). The effect of residential stability on both outcomes, by contrast, varied significantly among both defense attorneys and prosecutors. Differences in residential stability effects on guilty pleas were comparable for both groups, yet residential stability effects on charge reductions varied more dramatically for prosecutors ($\tau = 0.01, p < .001, \chi^2 = 300$) relative to defense attorneys ($\tau = 0.001, p < .05, \chi^2 = 137$). Overall, the more substantive differences among prosecutors in the magnitude of defendant's demographic effects on charge reductions suggest that prosecutors play a heavier hand than defense attorneys in shaping extra-legal disparities in sentencing.

Turning to the analysis of defense attorney effects on case outcomes, Table 7.2 displays both defendant and defense attorney effects on whether a defendant pled guilty (from the pool of defendants who either pled guilty or went to trial). The most important finding in this table is related to the null effects of attorney type on guilty pleas. It does not appear that public defenders or assigned counsel maintain higher rates of guilty pleas compared to hired attorneys (the reference group), which is consistent with Alschuler's observation that PDs and private attorneys are just as likely to engage in plea bargaining. On the other hand, defense counsel with higher proportions of their caseloads consisting of more serious felony referrals (Felony 1s and Felony 2s) had lower guilty plea rates, perhaps indicating greater reluctance by the prosecution and/or the defense to negotiate in these cases. Consistent with this finding is the significant inverse effect of F1 at level 1, suggesting that offense severity matters at both the individual and attorney levels for influencing mode of case disposition.

More interesting is the significant inverse effect of *proportion caseload with African American defendants*, where higher proportions coincided with lower guilty plea rates. Note also the negative coefficient for *African American male 18–29* at level 1, although the effect is null. However, both inverse effects could reflect less zeal to either negotiate or to accept plea offers in cases involving young black men (at level 1), and in cases

Table 7.2 Bi-Level Bernoulli Models of Guilty Pleas

Level 1: Felony Defendants (N_1 = 1,989)	β	se_β	e^β
African American male 18–29	−0.10	0.21	0.91
Social disadvantage of city block population	−0.17	0.10	0.85
% city block pop. same address > 1 year	*−0.004*	*0.01*	*1.00*
Prior prison term	*−0.06*	*0.19*	*0.94*
Most serious charge indicted . . .			
Felony 1	−0.90**	0.28	0.41
Felony 2	−0.23	0.29	0.79
Felony 3	−0.23	0.31	0.80
Felony 4	−0.53*	0.28	0.59
Total indicted charges (square root)	0.65**	0.24	1.91
Indicted for . . .			
Drug crime(s)	0.92*	0.39	2.51
Domestic violence	2.22**	0.62	9.17
# victims of violence	0.06	0.16	1.07
Pretrial detention	0.50*	0.20	1.64
Uncooperative with prosecutors	−3.68**	0.46	0.03
# days to outcome (square root)	−0.11**	0.02	0.90
Level 2: Defense Attorneys (N_2 = 110)	γ	se_γ	e^γ
Type of attorney . . .			
Public defender	0.31	0.21	1.37
Assigned by court	0.26	0.19	1.30
# felony cases handled 2009 in county	−0.002	0.01	1.00
Proportion caseload consisting of			
Felony 1 charges	−1.56*	0.71	0.21
Felony 2 charges	−1.46*	0.65	0.23
Felony 3 charges	−0.50	0.78	0.61
Felony 4 charges	−1.41	0.77	0.24
Proportion caseload with African American defendants	−1.36*	0.72	0.65
Intercept	4.41		
Level 2 variance (τ_{00})—null model	0.11*		
Level 2 variance (τ_{00})—full model	0.09*		
Level 2 proportionate reduction in error	0.138		

** $p < .01$ and * $p < .05$.

Italicized coefficients reflect significantly varying effects across defense attorneys ($p < .05$).

involving African Americans in general, whether this reluctance falls primarily on the prosecution or the defense or equally on both. Also noteworthy is that, contrary to the case pressure thesis, the number of felony cases handled by an attorney in 2009 was not related to the proportion of guilty pleas in an attorney's caseload. Overall, there remained significant variance in guilty plea rates across defense attorneys in the full model, suggesting need for improvement in level 2 model specifications.

A few of the level 1 findings are also relevant to our framework and provide some support for ideas mentioned earlier. Specifically, defendants referred for drug crimes and domestic violence (particularly the latter) were more likely to plead guilty than other defendants, providing support for the idea that cases involving large-volume crimes are more likely to be pled out (Sudnow, 1965). The inverse effect of *# days to outcome*, where guilty pleas were less likely to occur with longer spans between court referral and sentencing, might only reflect the fact that cases set for trial (with certainty by both sides) take longer to process. However, this relationship is consistent with Alschuler's (1975) observation that the passage of time is linked to defense counsel's stubbornness to engage in negotiations with the prosecution. Ruling out the first possibility can only be accomplished with a more rigorous analytical design than what we offer here.

In contrast to the findings for guilty pleas, the model of charge reductions (Table 7.3) produced more interesting evidence in favor of our framework. First and foremost, type of attorney was a significant predictor of charge reductions, with the magnitude of charge reductions being lower (on average) for both PDs and assigned counsel relative to private attorneys. The larger coefficient for PDs relative to assigned counsel also suggests even smaller charge reductions for PDs. These findings appear contrary to Sudnow's (1965) discussion of PDs and more in line with Casper's (1972) observations about defendants with private attorneys faring better than those with PDs because the former were in a position to buy a better defense. Alschuler (1975) noted that attorney/client relationships were more antagonistic among public defenders relative to private attorneys because indigent defendants did not have the luxury of choosing their attorneys, and more antagonistic relations may have contributed to generally higher odds of settling for smaller charge reductions.

Defense attorneys also seem to fare better in general when their caseloads consist of more serious felony referrals. The significant findings for F1s, F2s, and F3s might also reflect the state's sentencing guidelines and recommended prison sentences for F1s and F2s, with community sanctions recommended for F4s and F5s, and F3s falling somewhere in the middle. Similarly, note the significant positive effects of the four felony levels included in the level 1 model. Both sets of findings might be considered intuitive in that the ability to experience larger charge reductions demands more serious charges, but it also indicates that prosecutors are willing to offer substantial reductions in the most serious cases.

Attorneys who handled larger proportions of African American clients experienced *lower* levels of charge reductions, which counters the idea that minority defendants might receive more substantive reductions if they fit attorneys' stereotypes of "typical" offenders involved in large-volume crimes (Sudnow, 1965). Even so, the level 2 finding is compatible with the level 1 significant inverse effect of *African American male 18–29* indicating less dramatic charge reductions for young black men. Both findings are more in line with focal concerns theory and a racial threat perspective and, in conjunction with the significantly varying race effect among prosecutors mentioned above, might reflect stronger contributions to demographic disparities in case outcomes among prosecutors.

Table 7.3 Generalized Least Squares Model of Charge Reductions

Level 1: Felony Defendants (N_1 = 1,890)	β	se_β
African American male 18–29	*−0.22⋆*	*0.10*
Social disadvantage of city block population	0.10⋆	0.05
% city block pop. same address > 1 year	*−0.002*	*0.004*
Prior prison term	*−0.04*	*0.10*
Most serious charge indicted . . .		
Felony 1	1.28⋆⋆	0.18
Felony 2	0.75⋆⋆	0.13
Felony 3	0.55⋆⋆	0.12
Felony 4	0.31⋆⋆	0.10
Total indicted charges (square root)	2.91⋆⋆	0.15
Indicted for . . .		
Drug crime(s)	−0.19	0.16
Domestic violence	−0.58⋆⋆	0.18
# victims of violence	0.35⋆⋆	0.08
Pretrial detention	−0.37⋆⋆	0.11
# days to outcome (square root)	0.03	0.02
Level 2: Defense Attorneys (N_2 = 110)	γ	se_γ
Type of attorney . . .		
Public defender	−0.51⋆	0.20
Assigned by court	−0.36⋆	0.19
# felony cases handled 2009 in county	−0.01⋆	0.005
Proportion caseload consisting of		
Felony 1 charges	3.17⋆⋆	0.57
Felony 2 charges	2.27⋆⋆	0.66
Felony 3 charges	2.74⋆⋆	0.72
Felony 4 charges	1.45	0.82
Proportion caseload with African American defendants	−0.90⋆	0.44
Intercept	2.25	
Level 1 variance (σ)—null model	6.04⋆⋆	
Level 2 variance (τ_{00})—null model	0.26⋆⋆	
Intraclass correlation (ρ)	0.04	
Level 1 variance (σ)—full model	2.71⋆⋆	
Level 2 variance (τ_{00})—full model	0.05	
Level 1 proportionate reduction in error	0.55	
Level 2 proportionate reduction in error	0.82	

⋆⋆ $p < .01$ and ⋆ $p < .05$.

Italicized coefficients reflect significantly varying effects across defense attorneys ($p < .05$).

(Although the minority composition of an attorney's caseload was also linked to lower guilty plea rates, the finding for charge reductions cannot be linked to the finding for guilty pleas because the former applies only to defendants who pled guilty.)

The number of felony cases handled by an attorney in 2009 was significantly and inversely related to the magnitude of charge reductions. This empirical relationship could reflect time constraints on defense attorneys that interfere with their ability to obtain the best possible outcomes for their clients. Alschuler (1975) described some defense attorneys as impatient and so invested in moving cases that they often settled for less attractive plea agreements relative to those secured by other attorneys who more actively argued and negotiated with prosecutors. However, it might not be impatience so much as time constraints that lead defense attorneys to settle for less.

Two additional level 1 findings are worth noting in favor of our framework. First, greater social disadvantage coincided with significantly larger reductions in charges. Although the inverse effect of *African American male 18–29* counters Sudnow's idea of offender stereotypes and "normal" crimes, the effect of social disadvantage is consistent with his idea and provides some merit to his thesis after all (especially given that the racial composition of a defendant's block population was one component of this factor). The significant inverse effect of *African American male 18–29* might not necessarily counter Sudnow given the specific demographic subgroup examined. This subgroup, in turn, might better reflect the stereotypes of "more dangerous" offenders held by prosecutors who pursue the focal concern of crime control.

Finally, defendants referred to court for domestic violence received *smaller* charge reductions in general, which counters the idea of larger reductions to facilitate pleas in large-volume crimes. However, the finding that these defendants were still much more likely to plead guilty (Table 7.2) still offers support for Sudnow's (1965) original thesis and suggests that more dramatic charge reductions are not necessary for encouraging domestic violence offenders to plead out. Perhaps this is due to the already fairly lenient sentences for felony domestic violence in the jurisdiction examined.

The final stage of our statistical analysis involved examination of whether the magnitude of significantly varying defendant effects on each outcome differed between PDs and other defense attorneys. As noted earlier, the level 1 effects of *prior prison term* and *same address > 1 year* on both guilty pleas and charge reductions varied significantly between defense attorneys, as did the effect of *African American male 18–29* on charge reductions. The level 2 variance in each of these effects and the cross-level interaction involving public defender are displayed in Table 7.4. None of these effects were significant, suggesting that type of defense attorney had no influence on the strength of these factors for shaping case outcomes. This counters our prediction that public defenders would obtain *better* outcomes for more disadvantaged defendants and those with more serious criminal histories relative to other types of attorneys. The null effects in the model of charge reductions, however, are consistent with the smaller charge reductions obtained by PDs *in general* relative to other attorneys (Table 7.3).

Emerging Themes and Corroboration from Attorneys

The statistical analysis provided evidence favoring aspects of our framework for understanding defense attorney effects on guilty pleas and accompanying sentences, but with some important exceptions. These "themes" are identified below. Here we provide select comments from some of the attorneys that serve to corroborate particular

Table 7.4 Cross-Level Effects of Public Defender Status on Level 1 Coefficients

	Guilty Plea		*Charge Reductions*	
	Coeff.	*se*	*Coeff.*	*se*
Level 1 main effect: African American male 18–29	—	—	−0.23*	0.12
Level 2 variance (τ_{01})	—		0.22*	
Cross-level effect of public defender	—	—	0.17	0.16
Level 1 main effect: % city block pop. same address > 1 year	0.01	0.01	0.002	0.01
Level 2 variance (τ_{01})	0.003**		0.001*	
Cross-level effect of public defender	0.01	0.01	−0.004	0.009
Level 1 main effect: prior prison term	−0.01	0.10	0.03	0.15
Level 2 variance (τ_{01})	0.55*		0.46*	
Cross-level effect of public defender	0.16	0.17	−0.24	0.18

** $p < .01$ and * $p < .05$.

themes and provide insight into a more realistic framework for future research. The comments presented in this section came from 16 attorneys including a variety of PDs, assigned counsel, and private attorneys.

Theme 1

Attorney differences in guilty plea rates and mean charge reductions are apparent among both defense attorneys and prosecutors, even when controlling for differences in caseload composition, but these differences are much more pronounced for prosecutors.

Empirical studies of extra-legal disparities in case dispositions and outcomes to date focus primarily on judges and prosecutors, with far less attention paid to defense attorneys. The dominant focus on prosecutors is warranted, based on our findings, but the significant and substantive differences in charge reductions between defense attorneys in our sample suggest that their potential impact on the disparate treatment of defendants should be investigated. Not only is this consistent with early observations by Sudnow (1965), Casper (1972), and Alschuler (1975), it is consistent with the observations of attorneys in this jurisdiction. Several of them commented voluntarily about how, in this particular jurisdiction, it is customary for a defendant to initiate a proposal for a plea bargain after arraignment and that prosecutors will generally not initiate negotiations. This might have to do with the more formal process of plea bargaining:

> In our County, individual prosecutors are not given authority to negotiate a plea on his/her own. They must go to a "File Marker," one of five supervisors, for approval. . . . I will say that I frequently see/hear defense counsel request a plea offer of the prosecutor without having spoken to his/her client. Pretrial discussions in our Court occur in the open lobby area of each floor.

On the other hand, the political climate of the prosecutors' office might play a role in restricting what defense attorneys can actually request in this particular jurisdiction:

> The prosecutors' office in ***** County . . . is mostly populated with a very conservative staff. The lens it has viewed criminal defendants has been very right or wrong with not much room for nuance. The floor prosecutors have almost no control on the plea bargaining process and supervisors, in order to maintain their positions, generally have little give on plea bargains.

So even the "File Markers" mentioned by the first attorney ("supervisors" above) are conservative in their discretion. Another attorney commented about the substance of bargaining itself:

> There is never really "negotiations." I ask for a specific plea, the prosecutor either accepts my offer or counters and his counter is the plea—there is no negotiating other than refusing the plea and going to trial.

This orientation of prosecutors might also explain, in part, the greater between-prosecutor variance in charge reductions relative to defense attorneys if the prosecutor counters the defense's proposal only once and is unwilling to accept anything else. This might also reflect prosecutors' understanding of the charge reductions judges are willing to tolerate in particular types of cases, discussed at length by Eisenstein and Jacob (1977). As two attorneys commented,

> Knowing how a judge sentences defendants is probably the primary motivator and encompasses all of the other factors. Having knowledge of the prosecutor and his/her position on certain offenses is important. . . .
>
> Who the Judge is may alter how to approach a case. Some Judges you will know a prison sentence is likely, while another Judge you know that probation is the likely outcome.

Still, the ability of counsel to formulate and initiate a proposal still gives them some control over the process whereby prosecutors work off of the counsel's proposal. This could ultimately produce significant (albeit more modest) between-defense differences in charge reductions.

Theme 2

The effects of defendant demographics and residential stability on charge reductions vary among both defense attorneys and prosecutors, but these differences are more pronounced for prosecutors.

Although residential (in)stability was never a theme that emerged in attorneys' observations, one individual made a comment suggesting that case outcomes via plea bargains varied by a defendant's race and SES:

> Often our white suburban clients (which are few) get much better plea deals than our inner-city minority clients (the majority of our clients).

This attorney conflated race with SES, which is not surprising for a highly segregated jurisdiction (described earlier). Although this particular observation does not speak to possible differences in the extent to which defense and prosecutors each consider defendant demographics, in conjunction with the observation above regarding a conservative prosecutors' office, it leads one to suspect that these extra-legal disparities might have more to do with prosecutorial preferences.

Theme 3

Defendants referred for large-volume crimes such as drugs and domestic violence are more likely to plead guilty than defendants charged with smaller-volume crimes.

An important qualification to this theme is that large-volume crimes were related only to the odds of pleading guilty as opposed to the magnitude of charge reductions. However, given the comments of some of these attorneys, we believe that the null effects on charge reductions might have had more to do with how we operationalized each type of crime. For example, all drug crimes were grouped into a single category, yet attorneys typically referred to less serious drug cases as those resulting in the most favorable deals. Some of this has to do with the fact that, because these crimes are committed at such high rates, the county implemented formal mechanisms to expedite case dispositions:

> Low-level drug felonies often receive favorable plea outcomes due to access to intervention programs such as Intervention in Lieu of Conviction, Early Intervention Program, Drug Court, etc. Many of the remaining low-level drug cases that do not qualify for diversion programming receive a community control sanction such as probation and treatment.
>
> In a felony drug possession case involving a first offender where guilt is conceded: Most will be given an option of Intervention in Lieu of Conviction, a diversion program where a conditional guilty plea is entered, followed by a term of treatment, if necessary, and supervision. The case is dismissed (and arrest records eligible for expungement) at the conclusion of the program.

However, there was no question that there was very little (if any) negotiating that actually occurred in these types of cases:

> A typical example of a case with no "negotiation" is a low level drug case. Defendant is stopped in a car with a small amount of cocaine/heroin etc. He'll

> be charged with three counts—possession, trafficking (under the subsection that prohibits transport of drugs) and PCT (Possession of Criminal Tools) for having anything in his possession that could possibly be used to facilitate a drug transaction (phone, money, etc., regardless of any evidence of it actually being used for that purpose). If a defendant has no record, he'll be offered an intervention program to avoid a felony. *If* he has been through that already or has a lengthy history, he'll be offered one count of possession, the state will drop the other two charges and he has to forfeit the seized property. It's the most pro forma plea in the system. You could have a mannequin stand in as the attorney and get the same result as a 30 year veteran. There is zero negotiation. It's basically the system functioning on auto-pilot. And it happens every single day.

> In routine cases such as low level drug charges, often the prosecutor will propose a "standard offer" (i.e., one level reduction as a plea offer).

> Typically, a first time drug offender is going to get a reduction of charge or sentence with little work by me.

One attorney specifically referred to domestic violence in addition to drug charges:

> [I]f a defendant has a prior felony conviction and/or prior felony of the same type, a one-level reduction is given without much discussion between defense and prosecutor. Example, F-3 DV (2 prior DVs) or F-3 Drug case may be reduced to an F-4 level. Obviously, there are exceptions, such as suppression issue.

Also related to domestic violence, another attorney noted, "Domestic violence cases often receive unfavorable pleas and a high percentage result in prison sentences." This practice could have contributed to the null effect of felony domestic violence charges on the magnitude of charge reductions even though proportionately more of these cases were disposed with guilty pleas.

On the other hand, prosecutors in this jurisdiction place a heavy emphasis on a defendant's criminal history, sometimes more so than on the type of crime and unique circumstances:

> Often, a plea discussion will begin with the prosecutor asking "what is his record?" and not focusing on the specific details of the case we are specifically addressing. . . . Having such a policy, regardless of the specific details of a case, results in fundamental feelings of unfairness to defendants.

> An offender's record or lack of a record will impact again how "good" a plea offer is and whether your client is exposed to a prison sentence.

Although prior imprisonment had no bearing on the outcome measures in our statistical analysis, the consideration of priors might be more nuanced than simply having served a previous term of imprisonment. Consistent with the court ethnographies cited earlier, attorneys in this jurisdiction seem to place heavier emphasis on the *length* of a defendant's criminal history:

> [G]etting a significant reduction for a client with a lengthy criminal record will be far more beneficial to him or her, and satisfactory to me, than getting a minimal reduction for a client with little or no criminal history.
>
> In my opinion, a plea offer should mostly rest on what the state can prove, and the issue of whether to give a defendant a "break" should rest with his or her record. But the two considerations are commonly conflated, so a defendant with a lengthy history is faced with going to trial and risking more time, or taking a plea that is probably worse than it should be.

Theme 4

Certain case processing factors can have unanticipated effects on the odds of pleading guilty and/or on the magnitude of charge reductions, such as pretrial detention (more likely to plead guilty yet smaller charge reductions), longer periods of time between court referral and final disposition (less likely to plead guilty), and being uncooperative with prosecutors (less likely to plead guilty).

The influence of uncooperative defendants might be greater relative to other jurisdictions based on the informal procedure of defendants initiating the negotiation process, as described above. The simple act of not submitting a proposal can dramatically increase the odds of a trial in this county.

Theme 5

Caseload size and offense/client composition influence attorneys' guilty plea rates and mean charge reductions, where more serious caseloads coincide with lower guilty plea rates yet larger charge reductions (on average), proportionately more African American clients correspond with lower guilty plea rates and smaller charge reductions, and more cases correspond with smaller charge reductions. At the individual level, consistent with the level 2 race effects, charge reductions are smaller in magnitude for African American males ages 18 to 29. Also at the individual level, consistent with offense composition at level 2, more serious cases are less likely to result in guilty pleas yet correspond with larger charge reductions.

Considering only the pool of defendants who plead guilty, larger charge reductions in more serious cases is likely a consequence of the greater "play" in charge reductions possible with F1s and F2s versus F4s and F5s. For example, in this jurisdiction it is common to see F1s drop to F3s (two felony grades), and to see F5s drop to M1s (one felony grade). One attorney actually noted that dropping a 2nd degree felonious assault to a 1st degree misdemeanor assault was nearly as common as dropping a 4th degree felony drug possession to a 5th degree "attempted" drug possession. The finding of larger reductions in more serious cases is not necessarily inconsistent with the lower guilty rates in more serious cases, given that this last finding applies to the larger sample including defendants who opted for trials. Larger proportions of defendants indicted on more serious charges might be more likely to take their chances at trial because a plea might still involve prison time in this relatively conservative court. One attorney described the contributing factors to a prison sentence in these types of cases:

> [T]he more serious felony cases generally receive heightened scrutiny and resources from law enforcement and judges. These cases usually involve a serious injury or serious risk of harm to the community. I don't want any of my clients to go to prison, but obviously prison is more likely depending on the seriousness of the offense and the criminal history of the client, and whether or not the client has multiple pending cases, and whether the client is already under supervision by a probation or parole authority.

The other findings related to caseload size and proportion of African American clients seem to reinforce the idea put forth earlier that defense counsel may not be as zealous in obtaining the best possible outcomes for their clients if they are more concerned with moving their caseloads and if white counsel maintain conscious biases toward minorities, or even subconscious biases emanating from race loyalty (Lyon, 2012). The vast majority of defense attorneys in this jurisdiction are white whereas most defendants are African American.

Theme 6

Public defenders and assigned counsel obtain smaller charge reductions, on average, compared to private (for hire) attorneys.

None of the attorneys provided insight into this theme although it is consistent with Casper's (1972) argument that paying for private counsel changes the tone of the attorney/client relationship by placing a defendant in greater control of the situation, perhaps benefitting plea negotiations. Alschuler (1975) also observed more conflict between PDs and their clients relative to private attorneys, possibly fueling attorneys' disrespect of uncooperative clients as well as motivating attorneys to close these cases quickly.

Theme 7

All significant variance in charge reductions at level 2 can be explained by type of attorney, number of cases processed, felony caseload composition, and proportion minority clients.

This theme is relevant to proper model specification and suggests that we may have captured all of the substantive influences on differences in the magnitude of charge reductions among defense attorneys. Future research will help to determine whether this is an accurate assessment of our model or whether these particular factors merely proxy other, more proximate effects on charge reductions. In particular, more specific measures of caseload composition will identify the specific offenses most responsible for linking caseload composition to the magnitude of charge reductions.

Conclusions

Our primary goal with this discussion is to stimulate more research on how defense attorneys shape case outcomes for defendants. Although we did not focus specifically on sentencing per se, the very high rates of guilty plea convictions across trial courts of general jurisdiction in conjunction with the courtroom workgroup literature suggest that the most important influence of defense attorneys on case outcomes lies in their ability to secure substantive charge reductions after indictment. This is especially true in jurisdictions such as the one examined here since PDs and assigned counsel do not really shape the odds of pretrial detention aside from a supervisor requesting "reasonable bond" for every case coming before a municipal judge on a particular day. Charge reductions might therefore be the more meaningful focus when studying how defense attorneys impact case outcomes for the vast majority of convicted defendants. Future research might also address case dismissals, which were not examined here, because reduced charges necessarily include dropped charges.

In light of the evidence we found of significant differences among defense attorneys in the magnitude of charge reductions as well as some of the specific attorney effects on these reductions, a broader understanding of extra-legal disparities in case outcomes might be achieved with more research attention paid to defense attorneys. The caveat to this call for research is that prosecutors still appear to have greater control over charge reductions, based on our findings, and so greater attention to prosecutors is still warranted. Along these lines, researchers with the ability to examine very large samples might also consider looking at prosecutor/defense counsel dyads in studies of guilty pleas and charge reductions, similar to the method employed by Kim et al. (2015) in their study of prosecutor/judge dyads.

The rudimentary framework presented here was introduced more as a suggestion for how to think about related empirical models grounded in the courts literature and not as a comprehensive paradigm for the subject. Similarly, the statistical analysis served only as a partial test and should be treated as preliminary to what will hopefully become a substantive body of rigorous empirical research grounded in more fully developed theoretical frameworks. To this end, the findings from our analysis revealed several themes that might be used to guide both the conceptual and empirical development of related frameworks. Most relevant to the topic of extra-legal disparities in case outcomes is the theme incorporating lower guilty plea rates and smaller charge reductions for attorneys with higher portions of African American clients, even after controlling for felony level composition. Similarly, the significant variance in the level 1 effect of *African American male 18–29*, in conjunction with the overall significant inverse effect, indicates that individual differences in attorneys manifest themselves, in part, as differences in demographic biases in charge reductions.

Perhaps the most important caveat to our presentation lies in the analysis of a single and perhaps unique urban jurisdiction. As scholars have pointed out time and again since Eisenstein and Jacob (1977), different jurisdictions sometimes produce different observational *and* empirical findings. For example, some recent research suggests that sentences are generally more lenient for PDs relative to private attorneys or even assigned counsel (Beck and Shumsky, 1997; Champion, 1989; Hartley et al., 2010), yet we found more dramatic charge reductions for private attorneys even when controlling for caseload composition. Closer inspection of the court culture revealed a fairly conservative prosecutors' office in addition to political tensions between this office and the public defenders' office, and this could have contributed to a greater stubbornness by prosecutors to accept the initial plea offers of PDs. (The tension between the two offices is the reason why we were unable to compile SES data at the individual level, because this information was available only in PSI reports available through the defenders' office and because staff were unwilling to provide the information precisely because we were hired by the prosecutors' office to conduct the larger study.) This observation highlights an important link between quantitative and qualitative assessments of extra-legal disparities in case outcomes, and expanding quantitative research on defense attorneys demands the addition of qualitative components to these research designs in order to place findings in proper context and to explain between-study differences in these findings.

References

Abrams, D. S., & Yoon, A. H. (2007). The luck of the draw: Using random case assignment to investigate attorney ability. *The University of Chicago Law Review, 74*, 1145–1177.

Albonetti, C. A. (1987). Prosecutorial discretion: The effects of uncertainty. *Law and Society Review, 21*, 291–313.

Alschuler, A. (1975). The defense attorney's role in plea bargaining. *Yale Law Journal, 84*, 1179–1314.

Alschuler, A. (1983). Implementing the criminal defendant's right to trial: Alternatives to the plea bargaining system. *University of Chicago Law Review, 50*, 931–1050.

Anderson, J. M., & Heaton, P. (2012). How much difference does the lawyer make? The effect of defense counsel on murder case outcomes. *Yale Law Journal, 122*, 154–217.

Batra, R. R. (2015). Judicial participation in plea bargaining: A dispute resolution perspective. *Ohio State Law Journal, 76*, 565–597.

Beck, J., & Shumsky, R. (1997). A comparison of retained and appointed counsel in cases of capital murder. *Law and Human Behavior, 21*, 525–538.

Bowen, D. M. (2009). Calling your bluff: How prosecutors and defense attorneys adapt plea bargaining strategies to increased formalization. *Justice Quarterly, 26*, 2–29.

Casper, J. (1972). *Criminal courts: The defendant's perspective*. Washington, DC: National Institute of Law Enforcement and Criminal Justice.

Champion, D. (1989). Private counsels and public defenders: A look at weak cases, prior records, and leniency in plea bargaining. *Journal of Criminal Justice, 17*, 253–263.

Cohen, T. H. (2014). Who is better at defending criminals? Does type of defense attorney matter in terms of producing favorable case outcomes. *Criminal Justice Policy Review, 25*, 29–58.

Davies, A. L. B., & Worden, A. P. (2009). State politics and the right to counsel: A comparative analysis. *Law & Society Review, 43*, 187–219.

Edkins, V. A. (2011). Defense attorney plea recommendations and client race: Does zealous representation apply equally to all? *Law and Human Behavior, 35*(5), 413–425.

Eisenstein, J., Flemming, R., & Nardulli, P. (1988). *The contours of justice: Communities and their courts*. Boston, MA: Little, Brown.

Eisenstein, J., & Jacob, H. (1977). *Felony justice: An organizational analysis of criminal courts*. Boston, MA: Little, Brown.

Farrell, A., Ward, G., & Rousseau, D. (2009). Race effects of representation among federal court workers: Does black workforce representation reduce sentencing disparities? *Annals of the American Academy, 623*, 121–133.

Feeley, M. (1992). *The process is the punishment: Handling cases in a lower criminal court*. New York: Russell Sage Foundation.

Flemming, R., Nardulli, P., & Eisenstein, J. (1992). *The craft of justice: Politics and work in criminal court communities*. Philadelphia, PA: Pennsylvania University Press.

Fox, J. (2016). *Applied regression analysis and generalized linear models*. Thousand Oaks, CA: Sage.

Gist, N. (1989–1990). Assigned counsel: Is the representation effective? *Criminal Justice, 4*, 16–48.

Gitelman, M. (1971). The relative performance of appointed and retained counsel in Arkansas felony cases: An empirical study. *Arkansas Law Review, 24*, 442–452.

Hanson, R., Ostrom, B., Hewitt, W., & Lomvardias, C. (1992). *Indigent defenders get the job done and done well*. Williamsburg, VA: National Center for State Courts.

Hartley, R., Miller, H., & Spohn, C. (2010). Do you get what you pay for? Type of counsel and its effect on criminal court outcomes. *Journal of Criminal Justice, 38*, 1063–1070.

Hermann, R., Single, E., & Boston, J. (1977). *Counsel for the poor: Criminal defense in urban America*. Lexington, MA: Lexington Books.

Heumann, M. (1978). *Plea bargaining: The experiences of prosecutors, judges, and defense attorneys*. Chicago, IL: The University of Chicago Press.

Hoffman, M., Rubin, P., & Shepherd, J. (2005). An empirical study of public defender effectiveness: Self-selection by the marginally indigent. *Ohio State Journal of Criminal Law*, 3, 223–255.

Iyengar, R. (2007). *An analysis of the performance of federal indigent defense counsel*. Cambridge, MA: National Bureau of Economic Research, Harvard University.

Johnson, B. (2006). The multilevel context of criminal sentencing: Integrating judge and county level influences in the study of courtroom decision making. *Criminology, 44*, 259–298.

Kim, B., Spohn, C., & Hedberg, E. (2015). Federal sentencing as a complex collaborative process: Judges, prosecutors, judge-prosecutor dyads, and disparity in sentencing. *Criminology, 53*, 597–623.

Kutateladze, B., Andiloro, N., Johnson, B., & Spohn, C. (2014). Cumulative disadvantage: Examining racial and ethnic disparity in prosecution and sentencing. *Criminology, 52*, 514–551.

Lynch, M. (1998). Waste managers? The new penology, crime fighting, and parole agent identity. *Law and Society Review, 32*, 839–869.

Lyon, A. (2012). Race bias and the importance of consciousness for criminal defense attorneys. *Seattle University Law Review, 35*, 755–768.

Meeker, J. W., & Pontell, H. N. (1985). Court caseloads, plea bargains, and criminal sanctions: The effects of section 17 P.C. in California. *Criminology, 23*, 119–143.

Nardulli, P., Eisenstein, J., & Flemming, R. (1988). *Tenor of justice: Criminal courts and the guilty plea process*. Urbana, IL: University of Illinois Press.

National Center for State Courts (1992). *Indigent defenders: Get the job done and done well*. Washington, DC: National Center for State Courts.

Neubauer, D., & Fradella, H. (2011). *America's courts and the criminal justice system*. Belmont, CA: Wadsworth.

Redlich, A. D., Bushway, S. D., & Norris, R. J. (2016). Plea decision-making by attorneys and judges. *Journal of Experimental Criminology, 12*, 537–561.

Roach, M. (2010). Explaining the outcome gap between different types of indigent defense counsel: Adverse selection and moral hazard effects. *SSRN Working Paper Series*.

Schlesinger, T. (2007). The cumulative effects of racial disparities in criminal processing. *Journal of the Institute of Justice and International Studies*, 7, 268–285.

Schulhofer, S. J. (1992). Plea bargaining as disaster. *Yale Law Journal, 101*, 1979–2009.

Silverstein, L. (1965). *Defense of the poor in criminal cases in America state courts: A field study and report*. Chicago, IL: American Bar Association.

Smith, C. (2008). Unconscious bias and "outsider" interest convergence. *Connecticut Law Review, 40*, 1077–1086.

Spangenberg, R., & Beeman, M. (1995). Indigent defense systems in the United States. *Law and Contemporary Problems, 58*, 31–50.

Steffensmeier, D., Ulmer, J., & Kramer, J. (1998). The interaction of race, gender, and age in criminal sentencing: The punishment cost of being young, black, and male. *Criminology, 36*, 763–797.
Stuntz, W. J. (2004). Plea bargaining and criminal law's disappearing shadow. *Harvard Law Review, 117*, 2548–2569.
Sudnow, D. (1965). Normal crimes: Sociological features of the penal code in a public defender office. *Social Problems, 12*, 255–276.
Sutton, J. (2013). Structural bias in the sentencing of felony defendants. *Social Science Research, 42*, 1207–1221.
Taylor, J. G., Stanley, T. P., DeFlorio, B. J., & Seekamp, L. N. (1973). An analysis of defense counsel in the processing of felony defendants in San Diego, California. *Denver Law Journal, 49*, 233–275.
Tor, A., Gazal-Ayal, O., & Garcia, S. (2010). Fairness and the willingness to accept plea bargain offers. *Journal of Empirical Legal Studies, 7*, 97–116.
Ulmer, J. (1997). *Social worlds of sentencing: Court communities under sentencing guidelines*. Albany: SUNY Press.
Wice, P. (2005). *Public defenders and the American justice system*. Santa Barbara: Praeger.
Williams, M. R. (2013). The effectiveness of public defenders in four Florida counties. *Journal of Criminal Justice, 41*, 205–212.
Wolf-Harlow, C. (2000). *Defense counsel in criminal cases*. United States Department of Justice. Bureau of Justice Statistics. Washington, DC: Author.
Wooldredge, J. (1989). An aggregate-level examination of the caseload pressure hypothesis. *Journal of Quantitative Criminology, 5*, 259–283.
Wooldredge, J. (2012). Distinguishing race effects on pre-trial release and sentencing decisions. *Justice Quarterly, 29*, 41–75.
Wooldredge, J., Frank, J., Goulette, N., & Travis, L. III (2015). Is the impact of cumulative disadvantage on sentencing greater for black defendants? *Criminology and Public Policy, 14*, 187–223.
Worden, A. (1995). The judge's role in plea bargaining: An analysis of judges' agreement with prosecutors' sentencing recommendations. *Justice Quarterly, 12*, 257–278.
Wright, R., & Miller, M. (2003). Honesty and opacity in charge bargains. *Stanford Law Review, 55*, 1409–1418.

Legal Cases

Argersinger v. Hamlin, 407 U.S. 25 (1972).
Gideon v. Wainwright, 372 U.S. 335 (1963).
Powell v. Alabama, 287 U.S. 45 (1932).

PART III

Disparities in Punishment Outcomes

8

FOCAL CONCERNS THEORY AS CONCEPTUAL TOOL FOR STUDYING INTERSECTIONALITY IN SENTENCING DISPARITIES

Focus on Gender and Race Along With Age

Darrell Steffensmeier and Noah Painter-Davis

Our general goal in this chapter is to advance theory and research on the application of intersectionality as a framework for studying sentencing or punishment outcomes, with focus on gender and race (and age) effects. An intersectional approach involves examining how gender and race influence sentencing outcomes through their interactions with, not only one another, but also with other defendant characteristics, such as defendant's age or social class, along with other legal and social factors that shape the sentencing process. Intersectional approaches are increasingly prominent in social science writings for examining how gender or race *in combination with each other or with other social characteristics* affects inequality outcomes. Relatedly, some research in criminology has also been concerned with how the intersection of gender or race with other defendant characteristics (e.g. age) may affect sentencing outcomes.

Intersectional approaches recognize that social statuses like gender and race do not simply operate in social life independently but intersect with each other and with other status characteristics and therefore cannot be studied fully in isolation (Burgess-Proctor, 2006; McCall, 2005). The recognition is perhaps strongest among feminist sociologists and criminologists that "experiences are not the same, even among people of the same gender or race, and that scholarship must address the direct and interactive effects of social and demographic characteristics" on various inequality outcomes or behavioral practices (Gaub and Holtfreter, 2015: 299; Browne and Misra, 2003; Choo and Ferree, 2010; Davis, 2008; McCall, 2005).

Our specific aims in this chapter are: first, to clarify the notion of intersectionality and the sorts of questions it raises about the effects of gender and race on sentencing; second to elucidate the *focal concerns of sentencing* as a conceptual framework for studying intersectionality, with particular focus on how the framework helps to theorize and guide research about the intersection of gender, race, and age effects on the sentencing of criminal defendants; and third to illustrate the advantages of intersectionality by presenting findings of sentencing practices in Pennsylvania. These findings clarify that defendants' gender and race do not simply influence sentence outcomes independently but intersect with each other and with defendants' age and therefore these forms of stratification or social differentiation need to be studied in relation to each other. Fourth, this chapter outlines some directions for advancing research on the application of intersectional approaches to the study of sentencing.

Intersectionality as Framework or Approach

Both feminist and general sociological writings on gender and race have projected the importance of intersectional analyses for studying these two prominent social statuses. Feminist scholarship in particular has embraced the call for intersectional analyses but largely left the specifics of what it means indistinct, leading Davis (2008) to call "intersectionality" a theoretical "buzzword" with as yet unrealized analytic bite. There has been disagreement concerning what "intersectionality" actually means and how it can or should be applied in feminist or social inquiry (Choo and Ferree, 2010; Davis, 2008; McCall, 2005). Feminist overviews of the concept of intersectionality have multiplied in recent years as theorists have attempted to grasp what it actually means to those who use it to study the intersection of gender and race, on one hand, and the intersection of multiple social statuses, on the other hand (Davis, 2008; see also: Choo and Ferree, 2010; McCall, 2005; Prins, 2006; Hancock, 2007). These reviews highlight three prominent dimensions of theorizing that have become part of what "intersectionality" signifies.

One, unlike some feminist theory where the focus *per se* was on women's social marginalization, intersectional approaches project that gender cannot be studied in isolation from various socio-demographic factors such as race, sexuality, and class (Belkhir and Barnett, 2001; Lorde, 1984; Collins, 1993). Rather, these individual traits may converge in ways that produce distinct outcomes, experiences, and degrees of marginalization for women (or men) that cannot be understood by adding the individual effects of each variable (Collins, 1993). Consistent with the notion that "women experience oppression in varying configurations and in varying degrees of intensity" (Lengermann and Niebrugge, 2008: 478), a fundamental concern of feminist intersectionality and scholarship involves the acknowledgement of *differences among women* along with the importance of an *intersectional approach* for uncovering and explaining these differences.

A second dimension singles out the importance, in particular, of including the perspectives of multiply-marginalized people, especially women of color. As introduced by Kimberle Crenshaw (1989), this approach sees the experiences and struggles of women of color as falling between the cracks of both feminist and anti-racist discourse. Thus, the need to consider how both gender and race interact to shape the multiple dimensions of Black women's experiences. Specifically applicable to the legal system, Collins (1993: 34) uses the intersectionality approach to emphasize that women of color differ from White women in their relationship to White male authority. Hegemonic masculinity and the historically privileged position of White Americans as compared to racial minorities culminate in inequitable treatment under the law for African American females.

A third approach to intersectionality is broader in scope and draws heavily from traditional sociological theorizing as regards the intersection of race, gender, and other social statuses on social phenomena. This approach represents an analytic shift toward a broad conceptualization of intersectionality to refer to any scholarship that presents race, gender, class, age, and other social characteristics as closely intertwined and argues that these forms of stratification or social differentiation need to be studied in relation to each other (Choo and Ferree, 2010; Crenshaw, 1991). As exemplified in McCall's (2005) *inter-categorical* approach—intersectionality includes, but does not exclusively focus on, intersectionality as constituting an emphasis on differences among women (Crenshaw, 1991) or giving voice to the experiences of multiply-marginalized persons and groups such as women of color (Collins, 1999; Phoenix and Pattynama, 2006). Instead, this approach to intersectionality goes beyond original feminist concerns of prioritizing gender and women to approach intersectionality as having to do with broader characteristics of the social world, as applying to all social phenomena, not just the inclusion of a specifically subordinated group (McCall, 2005; Yuval-Davis, 2006).

We draw on all these approaches to intersectionality, but our main emphasis is with its broader conceptualization as it has been manifest recently in some feminist writings and historically in sociological theorizing and research. These approaches to intersectionality raise several questions about gender and race effects on the sentencing of criminal defendants. Does gender or does race have a greater effect on sentencing outcomes, net of legal factors that are intended as the basis for sentencing decision making? Do these prominent social statuses interact or intersect to influence sentencing outcomes? How does age or other social statuses intersect with gender and race to affect punishment decisions? The combinations and possibilities for diverse interactive outcomes increase quickly when considering gender, race, and age effects along with ethnicity and class. Very little research or theory have dealt *rigorously* with this complexity. One main reason for this, it appears, has been the limitation of databases that include simultaneous information about the effects of these status characteristics relative to sentencing outcomes and with a large enough sample representing each status sufficient to conduct rigorous meaningful analyzes. In addition to these combinations of defendant characteristics, intersectional assessments of gender and race effects on sentencing might be extended to include their intersection with the social characteristics (e.g. gender or race) of both the victims of crime (e.g. gender or race) and of the court actors who decide or prosecute the case, characteristics of the crime (e.g. atypical crimes), or with social context indicators such as urban versus rural or time period. We return to these considerations later.

Prior Sentencing Research on Intersection of Gender and Race Along With Age

There is an abundance of research examining the main effects of both gender and race on sentencing outcomes, and there also exists a fairly sizable volume of research investigating the joint effects of gender and race on sentencing. Overall, the main findings from this large and growing body of sentencing studies include the following. First, the legal variables of defendants' offense conduct and criminal history are the most robust predictors of sentencing outcomes. Nonetheless, it is also the case that there is a fair amount of leftover variation that remains to be explained beyond the reach of the legal indicators. Second, overall race effects are fairly small and found fairly consistently across studies, with Blacks sentenced more harshly than Whites. Third, the main effects of gender are fairly robust and persistent in the empirical literature on sentencing, with females sentenced more leniently than males. The gender effect is stronger and more persistently found than is a race effect. Fourth, studies examining the intersection of gender and race effects on sentencing generally find a small or negligible race effect when looking only at female defendants as compared to a small to moderately large race effect when considering male defendants, with Black males sentenced more harshly than White males and all female defendants. Most notable here are the small differences, if any, in sentencing outcomes between Black and White females as compared to the much larger racial gaps in sentencing outcomes among men. The latter findings signify the importance of applying intersectionality to the study of gender and race effects on sentencing. They also are supportive of feminist (and sociological) perspectives emphasizing that analysis based exclusively on men may lead to inaccurate, even misleading, conclusions regarding the process of gender or racial stratification. However, the much larger racial gap in sentencing outcomes among men than among women contradicts the expectation that Black women will suffer a "double disadvantage."

Although quantitative empirical research on sentencing that goes beyond the intersection of gender and race (White/Black) effects remains sparse and underdeveloped, one important advance in recent years has involved research on the role of age in influencing the effects of gender and/or race on sentencing outcomes. Besides advancing sentencing research, the study of age effects on criminal punishment has also contributed more broadly to feminist inquiry and long-standing sociological interests in main and interactive effects of two or *multiple* configurations of social characteristics on social phenomena. A matter of concern to many aging and life-course scholars (Pampel, 2008), it is also the case that age is generally ignored in broader intersectional work.

Two seminal studies in the 1990s by Steffensmeier and colleagues were instrumental for establishing the importance of considering defendants' age in sentencing research and in studies of gender and race disparities in particular. The first was the 1995 study in *Justice Quarterly* (Steffensmeier, Kramer, and Ulmer, 1995) that examined the main effects of age on sentencing and revealed considerable complexity in how age influences sentencing outcomes. The key finding of their study was that age has a curvilinear relationship to sentencing with offenders in their 20s and early 30s sentenced most harshly, while offenders in their 50s or older received especially lenient sentences. Falling between these two extremes were teen-adults (18–20) and offenders in their late 30s and 40s. In identifying this age-curvilinearity, the study (1) helped explain the anomalous findings in statistical studies of sentencing whereby age, when used as a linear control variable is found to have only negligible effects on sentencing outcomes, and (2) projected the possible importance of age as having influential effects on sentencing outcomes in combination with other social statuses such as gender or race.

The second study extended the *Justice Quarterly* article with an assessment of how age interacts with gender and race to influence sentence outcomes. Published in *Criminology* (Steffensmeier, Ulmer, and Kramer, 1998), this analysis of sentencing practices in Pennsylvania revealed that age combines with race and gender to form an important source of sentencing disparity. Focusing in particular on how race and gender effects were conditioned by defendants' age (18–29, 30–49, 50+), the researchers found that race and gender differences were smaller among older defendants and greater among younger defendants, with young Black males (ages 18–29) sentenced more harshly than other groups. Several subsequent studies have confirmed this prominent finding that young minority males are sentenced particularly harshly compared to other race-gender groups (Doerner and Demuth, 2010; Kramer and Ulmer, 2009; Warren, Chiricos, and Bales, 2012).

The 1998 study is important for at least two reasons: one empirical, the other theoretical. The main empirical lesson of the 1998 article is the importance of going beyond the traditional approach of studying the intersection of gender and race on sentencing to also consider how age might condition the effects of each status, singly or in combination. The 1998 article is also important theoretically because it contained an elaboration of a *focal concerns theory* (FCT) of sentencing that we see as well suited for studying intersectionality in sentencing. The statement of focal concerns theory, as outlined below, draws from both the 1995 and 1998 articles along with a recent article published in *Sociological Perspectives* (Steffensmeier, Painter-Davis, and Ulmer, 2017). The 2017 study is noteworthy, also, because it incorporates a fuller specification of age effects (e.g. teen-adults, ages 18–20) and their interactive relationships with gender, race, and Hispanic ethnicity. For parsimony, although some consideration of Hispanic effects on sentencing is offered, we focus our discussion on gender and race (White, Black) along with age and consider how taking into account age effects provides a fuller and richer understanding of how gender and race intersect to influence sentencing outcomes.

Focal Concerns Theory as Intersectional Framework

In this section we expound a *focal concerns theory of sentencing and court-actor decision making* that we see as inherently well suited for studying and theorizing about the intersectionality of social statuses, such as gender and race, on sentence outcomes along with consideration of age and by extension other factors that might affect sentencing such as defendants' social class or judge or victim characteristics. We build on the focal concerns' conceptual framework of court-actor decision making that, as mentioned earlier, represented a central contribution of the Steffensmeier et al. (1998) article and that we further articulated in a recent assessment of gender, race/ethnicity, and age effects on sentencing (Steffensmeier, Painter-Davis, and Ulmer, 2017). A central aim of this article was to better elucidate the underlying theoretical postulates of the focal concerns framework, its connection to broader sociological themes such as stratification, culture, and social typing, *and its strong affinity with the notion of intersectionality*. Notably, FCT proposes mechanisms by which social statuses combine and interact to influence criminal justice punishment decisions, advantaging some and disadvantaging others.

The core conceptual elements of focal concerns theory (FCT) of sentencing are diagrammed in Figure 8.1. The roots of this theory were articulated in Steffensmeier's early work on sentencing (Steffensmeier and Terry, 1973; Steffensmeier and Faulkner, 1978; Steffensmeier 1980) and later expanded on by Steffensmeier and colleagues (Steffensmeier, Kramer, and Streifel, 1993; Steffensmeier, Ulmer, and Kramer, 1998; Steffensmeier and Demuth, 2001, 2006; Ulmer and Johnson, 2004). The development of focal concerns theory also draws from the court community perspective (Eisenstein, Flemming, and Nardulli, 1988; Kramer and Ulmer, 2009; Ulmer and Kramer, 1996), which focuses on the interactional dynamics of courtroom workgroups and views courts as communities of action and communication based on participants' shared workplace; interdependent working relations between key sponsoring agencies (prosecutor's office, bench, defense bar); and local legal and organizational culture. Our

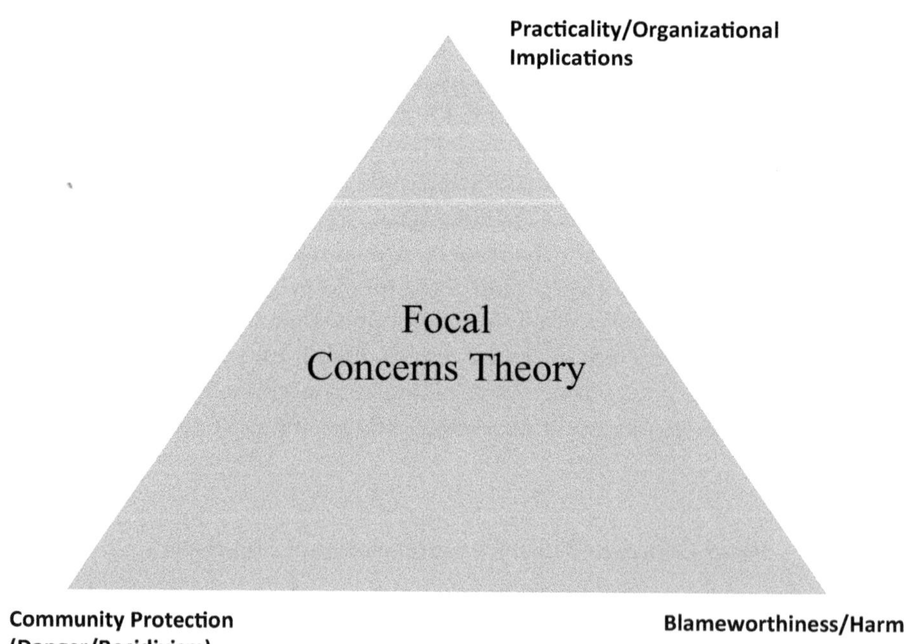

Figure 8.1 Focal Concerns Theory of Sentencing

application here of FCT to the intersectionality/sentencing issue draws in particular from a recent analysis (Steffensmeier, Painter-Davis, and Ulmer, 2017) in which we examined the joint effects of age, gender, and race/ethnicity on sentencing outcomes.

As highlighted in Figure 8.1, FCT outlines three focal concerns that are important to judges and other criminal justice actors in reaching sentencing decisions: *blameworthiness*, *protection of the community*, and *practical-organizational implications* of the resulting decision. Blameworthiness is associated with defendant culpability and having the punishment fit the crime or "harm" it has caused. Protection of the community draws on similar concerns but emphasizes the goals of incapacitation and general deterrence and emphasizes assessments about offenders' future behavior such as dangerousness or recidivism. Practical constraints and consequences relate to how sentencing decisions might be influenced by the circumstances of individual offenders and their families and communities and by how sentence outcomes might be seen as impacting the functioning of the criminal justice system.

Importantly, the defendant's present offense and prior criminal conduct are expected to play the most prominent role in the assessment of blameworthiness and community protection and in determining sentences (Steffensmeier et al., 1998). Offense factors that shape perceptions of blame and risk include: the extent of harm that was caused, such as the amount of property damage or extent of victim injury; the vulnerability of the victim as indicated by victim characteristics, such as gender or age, that may shape the perceived severity of the crime in violent cases; the weight and type of illegal substance in drug cases; and the offender's role in the offense (e.g. instigator versus accomplice, dealer versus carrier). Prior criminal history, such as repeated involvement in crime or failed efforts to reform through more moderate interventions (parole, treatment programs), has a major impact on assessments of risk as well.

As compared to blameworthiness and community protection, the focal concern of practicality and organizational constraints is perhaps less obvious. The constraints would include, on one hand, concerns about the individual offender's ability to "do the time," such as health conditions and special needs, and the potential disruption of incarceration to the offender's children (Daly, 1987; Doerner, 2015; Steffensmeier and Faulkner, 1978; Steffensmeier 1980; Steffensmeier, Kramer, and Ulmer, 1995; Steffensmeier and Motivans, 2000). On other hand, organizational influences on sentencing decisions might include concerns about maintaining working relationships among courtroom actors, ensuring the stable flow of cases, being sensitive to local and state correctional crowding and resources, local availability and financing of alternative punishment programs (e.g. drug treatment), and potential impact of offender recidivism on the court's standing in the public's eye (Eisenstein et al., 1988; Steffensmeier et al., 1998; Ulmer, 1997; Kramer and Ulmer, 2009). Moreover, organizational cultures within the courts and the correctional system may also shape the assessment of definitions of blameworthiness and community protection both broadly and in connection with the defendant's present offense and prior criminal conduct that are expected to play the most prominent role in determining sentences (Steffensmeier et al., 1998). Importantly, for purposes of considering intersectionality of social statuses in influencing sentencing decisions, all of these focal concerns may be influenced by the offender's *multiple* positions in the social structure in ways that contribute to disparate treatment of some status categories relative to others and to disparate treatment of some status configurations in particular.

Several key features of FCT are worth highlighting. First, FCT is an integrative rather than competing framework for incorporating insights from various perspectives on court decision making. Although particular theoretical treatments differ (e.g. conflict theory, racial or group threat theory, organizational efficiency theory), most focus on assessing the likelihood that criminal punishment may reflect (1) inequalities of class, status, or power in the larger society and (2) various organizational interests and practical concerns of justice officials. A focal concerns perspective (FCP) integrates such theoretical treatments.

Second, FCT draws broadly on sociological theory and research on the etiology of bias and on key tenets from attribution and labeling theories in particular. Attribution theory and social-cognitive research argue that individuals almost automatically characterize others into "groups" leading to possible bias or distortion in information processing and decision making (Higgins and Molden, 2003). Labeling theory has generally argued that stereotypes about criminals within social control agencies can influence the applications of formal criminal labels (Farrell and Holmes, 1991; Steffensmeier and Terry, 1973). Expectancies and scripts linking types of actors with classes of legitimate or illegitimate behaviors are a primary basis of social control by police or courts. To accommodate the often sizable and conflicting information, we are exposed to, we primarily simplify that information into a series of heuristics, generalizations, stereotypes, and theories that we use to make decisions and navigate our way through life (Hayes, 1962). We interpret our perceptions in light of these features of our cognitive landscape, and this strongly shapes how we react and make decisions. These cognitive shortcuts are common in organizational behavior and decisions (Scott, 2008), such as those of court actors. Through the interpretive process that psychologists refer to as "motivated cognition" (Higgins and Molden, 2003), organization officials see what they want to see and hear what they want to hear—i.e. they are not so much deciders but rather primarily perceivers or construers.

Third, as applied to sentencing, FCT accounts for a decision-making environment that is repetitive yet characterized by considerable uncertainty and complexity (Farrell and Holmes, 1991; Steffensmeier, 1980). The sentencing environment is repetitive in the sense that court caseloads tend to be sizable and dominated by "routine" cases involving conventional crimes or offenders (e.g. assault, theft). The ambiguity and complexity stem mainly from the multiple and sometimes conflicting sentencing goals faced by judges (see focal concerns above), from the difficulty inherent in predicting the risk and seriousness of recidivism, and by conflicting conceptions of justice and punishment philosophy held by court actors. Added uncertainty may arise because there sometimes is little definitive information on the background and character of the defendant (Albonetti, 1991). However, FCP argues that this is not the only or main source of uncertainty, nor the necessary or important cause of reliance on attributions, stereotypes, and other perceptual shortcuts.

It also appears that even with greater information about defendants and cases, judges, and other court actors cannot easily digest the information that they do have at their disposal (Steffensmeier and Demuth, 2006). Detailed pre-sentence reports or information brought out at trial may in fact produce an overload of information that is difficult to cognitively process, prioritize, or use (Wilkins, 1980). Also, court settings that have small caseloads, plentiful time to adjudicate, and typically abundant information about the defendants—such as rural courts—tend to generate greater gender and race disparities in sentencing outcomes as compared to urban courts where time restrictions and limited information about defendants are most at play (Lu, 2015). According to focal concerns theory, whatever the level of information at their disposal (a little or a lot), judges and other criminal justice actors make situational imputations and attributions about defendants' character and expected future behavior and assess the implications of these imputed attributes for three focal concerns: blameworthiness, community protection, and practical implications.

Fourth, FCP posits that court actors develop cognitive filters—a "perceptual shorthand"—to manage the uncertainty and competing pressures that characterize the sentencing environment by utilizing stereotypes and typescripts linked to case and defendant characteristics (Steffensmeier et al., 1998: 768). It is reasonable to assume that judges, both as citizens and as elected officials, may share in the general stereotyping in the community and that group-based attributions (e.g. based on race, ethnicity, gender, or age) will intertwine with the focal concerns outlined above to influence judges' sentencing decisions. Scripts or attributions, for example, associating certain demographic groups as more/less crime prone (e.g. young Black males vs. older White females) may lead to greater/lesser sentence severity by triggering emotions of fear or sympathy in ways that heighten/lessen concerns about the danger the defendant poses and the perception that he/she is more deserving of punishment and control. In effect, judges (and prosecutors, other court actors) make situational imputations about defendants' character and expected future behavior and assess the implications of these imputations for the focal concerns described above.

Applying FCT to Race-Gender Effects

In the abstract, the use and reliance of these focal concerns in sentencing decisions are said to be universal, but the meaning, relative emphasis and priority, and situational interpretation of them is shaped not only by legally relevant factors but also, among other factors, by the defendants' social statuses such as gender and race and age that are the focus of our discussion. Notably, FCT would predict that these prominent social statuses shape sentencing outcomes both singly and in combination—that is, by way of their intersectionality.

Regarding gender, a persistent finding in the sentencing literature is that female defendants are treated more leniently than male defendants (Doerner, 2015). In the context of societal and court concerns about crime and public safety and given the known greater proneness for crime among men, women are viewed as lower risks for recidivating and more deserving of leniency than men (Doerner and Demuth, 2014; Steffensmeier, 1980; Steffensmeier et al., 1993). Also women may be sentenced more leniently because court actors view females as less dangerous than males, tend to see women's crimes as an outgrowth of their own victimization (e.g. by coercive men or drugs), and believe the social costs of detaining women are higher since they are more likely than males to have child care responsibilities and mental or health problems that could not be treated in a jail setting (Steffensmeier, 1980; Steffensmeier et al., 1993; Brennan and Spohn, 2009). Also, women are perceived to maintain community ties more so than males (e.g. with parents) and are more closely bonded to conventional institutions that also serve to reduce the likelihood of recidivism.

Concerning race, harsher sentences are likely to be imposed on Black than White defendants because of court actors' beliefs that Blacks are more dangerous, more likely to recidivate, and more adaptable to prison. Research reveals that court officials (and society-at-large) often view Black offenders as violence prone, threatening, disrespectful of authority, and more criminal in their lifestyles (Bridges and Steen, 1998; Rios, 2011; Steen et al., 2005). Of relevance here is Bonilla-Silva's (1997: 476) concept of "racialized social systems," which helps explain how racial ideologies (e.g. seeing minority males as more likely to recidivate) may become "embedded in normal operations of institutions" (such as courts) in ways that foster racially charged actions, even if the motivations of decision makers are race-neutral. Also, Black defendants are more likely than Whites to lack the resources to thwart the imposition of sanctions.

Bringing in Age Effects in Gender and Race Intersectionality Research

As we observed earlier, there is evidence that age has important effects on sentencing both singly and in combination with gender and race and that these effects have been largely overlooked in prior sentencing research. Prior sentencing research has typically controlled for defendant's age as a continuous variable and assumed that age is inversely related to sentence severity, but few studies make age the focus of their analysis. Steffensmeier, Kramer, and Ulmer (1995) were the first to discover a curvilinear relationship between age and sentencing demonstrating that offenders in their 20s and early 30s were sentenced most harshly, while offenders in their 50s or older receive especially lenient sentences; falling between these two extremes are the youngest offenders (ages 18–20) and offenders in their late 30s and 40s. It appears that judges see very young or "*teen-adult*" offenders (ages 18–20) as more impressionable and more likely to be harmed by imprisonment than "young adult" offenders (i.e. ages 21–29), while they see older offenders as less dangerous and less risky prospects for release into the community.

Teen-adult defendants (ages 18–20), it seems, may generate some sympathy and leniency by being seen as lacking in maturity needed to recognize consequences of their actions and as more likely to be harmed by incarceration (Bernard and Kurlycheck, 2010; Steffensmeier et al., 1995). Judges may be more forgiving toward youthful offenders than offenders in their 20s or 30s, seeing them as prone to peer pressure and going through a phase they will outgrow. These attributions of "immaturity" and "proneness to peer pressure" are consistent, of course, with nationwide under-age drinking and under-age DUI laws that apply to this age group and define them as more like "teens" than full-fledged adults. Moreover, it continues to be the case today that some states (e.g. Florida, Alabama, and Georgia; Pennsylvania until the mid-1980s) have youthful offender statutes whereby younger offenders (i.e. usually under 21) can be given more lenient sentences, including alternatives to incarceration (Florida State Law, Title XLVII, Chapter 958).

Drawing from FCT, it also can be assumed that older offenders are likely to benefit from judges seeing them as less dangerous and as less likely to recidivate. Also, doing time in prison may be perceived as harsher punishment for older offenders because time for them may be seen as a diminishing, exhaustible resource wherein the future becomes increasingly valuable. Practical constraints may be salient, too, as older offenders present the likelihood of greater health care costs that would be borne by correctional facilities. On the other hand, young-adult offenders in their 20s and 30s are more likely to be linked to notions of dangerousness and recidivism, seen as more responsible for their actions (e.g. versus teen-adults), and viewed as less likely to be harmed by prison.

Since publication of the 1995 and 1998 studies by Steffensmeier and colleagues that established the importance of main and interactive effects of age on sentencing, several studies have explored how age might influence sentencing in combination with gender and race (see earlier review). Overall, while these studies represent significant advances in research on sentencing disparities, they nonetheless lacked sufficient differentiation across age groupings to definitively evaluate how defendants' age might intersect with gender and race to influence sentencing outcomes. Owing largely to the difficulty of obtaining a large enough defendant population for meaningful analysis, the standard approach has been to collapse defendants' age into broad groupings, such as under versus over age 30 (e.g. Kramer and Ulmer, 2009; Warren et al., 2012), that do not take into account the potentially unique *teen-adult* (ages 18–20) or elder (50+) effects. In similar fashion, the 1998 Steffensmeier et al. article *also* did not distinguish the teen-adult category in its age disaggregation. Instead, the 1998 study's widely-reported finding that *young Black males* received especially harsh sentences was in reference to *ages 18–29*.

Taking advantage of a very large multi-year sample of criminal defendants from Pennsylvania, a recent paper of ours remedied this age-disaggregation limitation by separating teen-adult effects in order to better take into account the main and interactive effects of age, gender, and race on sentencing outcomes. Our 2017 study drew on FCT and also on previous research on the effects of these social statuses on sentencing. We sought to extend our earlier research in the 1995 article on age effects *but which did not consider intersectionality* and in the 1998 article on race-gender-age effects *but which did not take teen-adult effects into account*. Our analysis sought to clarify the potentially varied ways in which defendants' age may contextualize race (also ethnicity) and gender effects on sentencing outcomes.

We theorized that the three focal concerns are shaped by the intersection of these statuses such that the influence of a particular status on sentencing outcomes, such as race, is likely to be conditioned by *both* age and gender. The stereotypes associated with one status category may heighten or soften the labels associated with another status category in ways that influence the application of the focal concerns. Likewise, certain status categories may combine (e.g. teen-adult Black males vs. teen-adult Black females) to prioritize or trigger focal concerns that are unique or less emphasized than when status categories are encountered independent of other defendant characteristics (Ghavami and Peplau, 2013). Research has shown, for example, that Black men—especially young Black men—are stereotyped as "aggressive" or "quick to anger," but this stereotype is not salient for older Blacks or for Black women overall (Ghavami and Peplau, 2013; Oliver, 2003).

Regarding sentencing, it appears that labels of dangerousness and crime proneness attributed to Blacks are shaped by gender—i.e. amplified for males (considered more blameworthy, higher recidivism risk) but mitigated for females (lower recidivism risk, etc.). These stereotypes may be further shaped by age. Youth and its associated attributions tend to heighten stereotypes of Black males, with those in their 20s and early 30s perceived as dangerous and as less likely to be harmed by prison. The public's fear of crime seems especially linked to young minority males, including those in their teens, who are portrayed in the media as hostile, aggressive, violent, and dysfunctional (Rios, 2011). By contrast, it appears that these fears of crime are more muted among older Black men where advanced age seems to temper stereotypes of dangerousness and risk to the community.

Likewise, FCP helps to theorize about the "teen-adult effect" and how in particular it may interact with gender and race to influence sentencing. Teen-adult female defendants may generate added leniency by being seen as more easily swayed by male companions and as likely to be harmed by incarceration (Steffensmeier, 1980). Historically, young female offenders have been treated as "status" offenders and sentenced less strictly (Bernard and Kurlychek, 2010), owing apparently to notions of chivalry and paternalism defining them as needing protection and as likely to benefit from alternative punishment. An exception to the leniency granted to teen-adults may be young minority male defendants (ages 18–20) because they, like their young-adult counterparts (21 to early 30s), might be perceived as dangerous, recidivism-prone, and easily adaptable to incarceration.

Robust evidence for intersectionality in effects of gender, race, and age on sentencing decisions is displayed in Figure 8.2. Of note, the figure also includes Hispanic male and female defendants as an added benchmark. Several findings stand out for elaboration. First, the gender effect of greater leniency for female defendants is pronounced and consistent for both the in/out and length decisions. It also persists across both race and age comparisons, with female defendants sentenced more leniently than their same-race male counterparts and similarly-aged minority males. Second, a substantial race effect on sentencing exists, but this applies mainly to male defendants. Younger Black male defendants (ages 18–20, 21–34) receive the harshest sentences, along with Hispanic male defendants who receive the harshest sentences overall (i.e. across all age groups as a whole). Third, *age curvilinearity* is strongly in evidence and age conditions the effects of membership in specific race-gender subgroups in different ways. A core feature of the curvlinearity is that young adults (21–34) are consistently sentenced more harshly than teen-adults (18–20). The partial exception is for Black males where for the in/out decision teen-adults are sentenced on par with young-adults. Age also

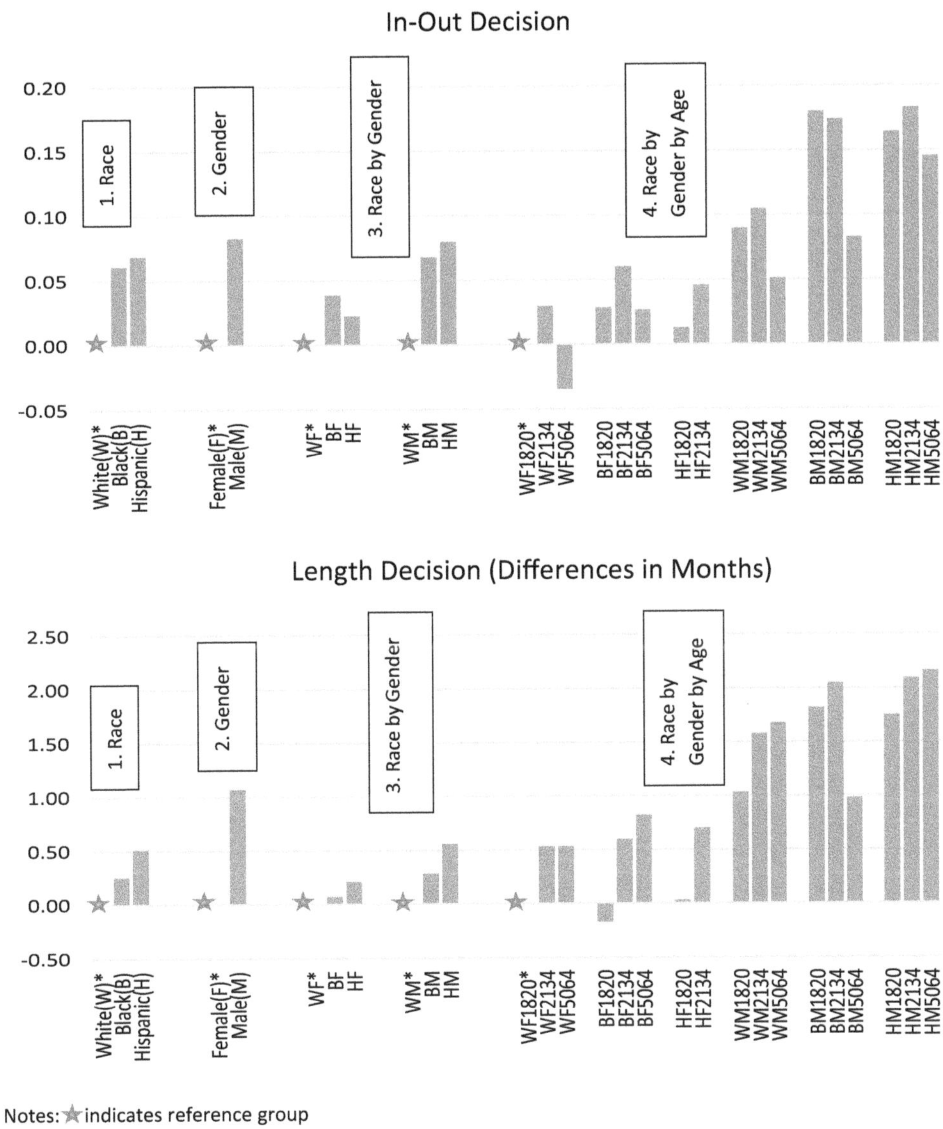

Figure 8.2 Differences in Predicted Probabilities of Incarceration (Top Panel) and Predicted Sentence Length (Bottom Panel) (In Order of Presentation): 1. Race; 2. Gender; 3. Race × Gender; 4. Race × Gender × Age

Note: To reduce clutter in Figure 8.2, we do not show the Race by Gender by Age results for groups aged 35–49.

conditions the effects of defendant's social statuses in ways that contribute to lighter sentencing of some subgroups compared to others. For example, teen-adult females receive more lenient sentences overall and for length of term in particular. Fourth, as the in/out and length differences in Figures 8.2 illustrate, substantial disparities in sentence severity exist when comparisons are made between the most dissimilar groups. For example, young-adult minority males (Black, Hispanic) have a roughly 25% greater probability of incarceration than the oldest White female defendants and a 30% greater probability than the youngest White, Black, and Hispanic females. Taken together, this is strong confirmation for the importance of intersectionality in studying the effects of defendant social statuses, singly and in combination, on sentencing decisions.

That racial gaps in sentencing are prominent for men but muted for women is consistent with extant research on other inequality outcomes (e.g. Mandel and Semyonov, 2016). These findings run counter to the "double disadvantage hypothesis" frequently cited by intersectional scholars that racial/ethnic disparities may be sharper among females than males (see Belkhir and Barnett, 2001; Browne and Misra, 2003). That the extent of racial disparities varies by gender also illustrates that the process of racial and gender stratification may be misunderstood when analysts focus on one gender group. Last, that the extent of racial disparities varies simultaneously by gender and age signals the importance of including age in statistical and theoretical inquiries of intersectionality.

These statistical findings were buttressed by qualitative evidence from interviews with sentencing judges in Pennsylvania. These comments from several veteran trial court judges confirm the importance of studying age as it intersects with gender and race to influence the interpretation and prioritization of the focal concerns (Steffensmeier et al., 2017: 24).

> An 18 or 19 year old in one sense is less mature, more inclined to peer influence. But in another sense is more apt to get into trouble again and so is more of a threat to the community, to prey on their neighborhoods. So you have to balance this. I'm talking mostly about male defendants now. The females I see in court, the threat and the danger aspect really isn't there—no matter their age. Unless she a main pusher or dealer [in drugs].
>
> If [as you say] older African-American men seem to do okay with their sentences, it likely would have to do with the judge's thinking that he isn't a threat to his neighborhood, isn't part of the drug problem, or maybe he has really serious health problems; whereas the judge's worry would lean otherwise with the [Black] defendant who is younger.

The focal concerns perspective is based on a relatively complex decision-making process in which judges take into account multiple factors and consequences of sentencing decisions. These considerations may or may not conflict with one another, and how *judges and other court actors interpret or prioritize the focal concerns may vary as well.* This complexity seems to be most strongly in play in the case of age effects and their intersection with gender and race. Drawing from our statistical findings and qualitative interviews, it seems, on the one hand, that some judges view youth as a protective factor for offenders and downplay their culpability because of a perceived lack of maturity and strong peer pressures prodding their criminal involvement. On other hand, other judges may focus on the practical issue of whether older offenders are able to do time in prison because of possible health issues but ignore or don't prioritize the possible negative consequences of incarceration for young offenders. Adding gender to the mix, judges may view female offenders overall as less culpable because of victimization or exploitation by male offenders, and especially in cases involving older female offenders, as less of a threat to society (e.g. violent recidivism) and less able to "do the time." Also, some judges may view younger female defendants with greater sympathy because they see them as more "salvageable" or amenable to treatment, or they may see young women's law violations as due to victimization or association with male offenders during a vulnerable life stage. On the other hand, when assessing potential risk to the community, some judges may link age with other status characteristics whereby young Black males elicit more fear and are projected as more dangerous or crime prone, and viewed as the group, that warrants added sentence severity.

Future Directions

The application of an intersectional approach to the study of sentencing in the context of gender and race, along with age, is a crucial direction for moving the field forward. Building on our earlier work as well as Ulmer's recent review of sentencing research (2012), there are numerous added ways that an intersectional approach can advance the study of sentencing and other forms of officially-sanctioned punishment as well. Space constraints prevent a full treatment, so we limit our recommendations to four main ways that seem most promising.

(1) Broader Coverage of Race Categories in Gender-Age Intersectional Analysis

Research is needed that replicates and extends the intersectional approach to study race/ethnicity groups more broadly. Are the effects of gender and age similar/different for Hispanics or Native Americans or Asians? Some intersectional research on Hispanic defendants does exist, though it is still sparse. Notably, our research showed that the penalty disadvantage for Hispanic males was strong and persistent at all ages including older ages, in contrast to penalty declines for older Black males, which created sentencing disparities between these groups at the older age ranges. Steffensmeier and Demuth (2000) suggest in the context of heated debate about immigration and perceptions linking it to social problems such as diminished employment opportunities and drug-trade networks, Hispanics may be viewed as more "culturally dissimilar and threatening than either Blacks or Whites" (p. 278). However, this greater sentence severity seems to apply mainly to Hispanic males. Black and Hispanic females were sentenced somewhat more harshly than White females, but the differences were small and due largely to harsher sentencing of older Black and Hispanic females. Notably, as was the case with White and Black teen-adult female defendants, the youngest Hispanic females were sentenced most leniently. The small number of Hispanic females at older ages prevents a fuller treatment of age effects, so this remains a topic for future research. Particularly scarce are studies that incorporate Hispanics and females into the analysis and that also cover the full range of ages to take into account likely age-curvilinear effects.

In light of the robust growth in Hispanic peoples in recent decades, there is a significant need to develop databases with information about the sentencing of Hispanic defendants in which there are sufficient numbers of (1) Hispanic females and (2) Hispanics disaggregated by country of origins for meaningful statistical analysis of intersectionality. For example, sentencing practices involving Cuban Hispanic Americans may differ from that of Mexican or Puerto Rican defendants both overall and in intersection with gender or age. It also is important to incorporate other racial groups into an intersectional analysis such as Native Americans and Asians. Some studies (e.g. Johnson and Betsinger, 2009) show that Asian defendants benefit from more lenient sentencing as compared to other racial groups, but whether or how this might vary by age or gender is unknown.

(2) Race and Gender of Judges (and Prosecutors)

Relative to the sizable empirical literature on the effects of the defendant's gender and race on sentencing, research on the influence of the gender and race of judges in criminal courts is rare (see review in Johnson, 2014). Research to date suggests that judge's gender and race have minimal impact on punishment decisions in criminal courts (e.g. see Johnson, 2014; Spohn, 1990; Steffensmeier and Britt, 2001; Steffensmeier and Hebert, 1999). Overall, these studies found that that the effects of judges' gender and/or race (White/Black) were relatively small or, as Steffensmeier and Britt (p. 749) concluded: "the job, not so much the individual, apparently makes the judge." The powerful forces of selective recruitment and judicial socialization, it is argued, result in a fairly uniform "subculture of justice" among jurists (Frazier and Bock, 1982; Steffensmeier and Britt, 2001; Steffensmeier and Hebert, 1999). Despite the overall consistency of findings showing considerable similarity in sentencing outcomes between male versus female and Black versus White judges, three cautions in particular are important as regards the empirical literature on the topic.

First, there is a scarcity of research which examines the intersectionality of judge characteristics (e.g. Black female judges) because, on one hand, databases with the requisite information are often lacking (i.e. judicial characteristics as connected to sentence outcomes) and, on other hand, adequate numbers of Black or women judges for meaningful statistical analysis is only a recent development. Second, even scarcer are databases that allow for research considering the intersection of judges' gender and race effects *disaggregated* by offenders' gender and race. Third, very little, if any, research has studied judges' effects disaggregated by *type of offense* or by *victim characteristics*. The focal concerns perspective implies that the effects of defendant social statuses on sentencing decisions may be conditioned by victim characteristics such as gender or race or age. Some research also suggests that this might be the case (Spohn, 2009). But not much is known definitively, due largely to the lack of readily-available data. Sentencing commissions and centralized court record keeping systems typically collect little if any data on victim characteristics. Drawing from focal concerns theory, we might expect some judge effects—including for gender and race—on sentence severity depending on whether the offender is being sentenced for a sexual assault committed by a male defendant against a female victim or an aggravated assault involving two males stemming from a barroom dispute. In brief, in light of scarce empirical research, it is premature to draw firm conclusions about the intersection of judges' characteristics such as gender and race on sentencing decisions and how this might vary by type of offense or by victim characteristics.

An added research agenda, and one even more understudied, is the intersection of prosecutors' gender and race on sentencing outcomes both overall and as disaggregated by defendants' characteristics such as gender, race, and age. Prosecutors are highly influential to the sentencing decision as they have direct influence on charging, imposition of mandatories, and the formation of plea agreements (Ulmer, Kurlycheck, and Kramer, 2007). As noted by Ulmer (2012: 4), "prosecutorial discretion is highly consequential and pervasive, and yet much less visible than judicial sentencing discretion." Building datasets that track the multiple decision points in the justice process (charge, conviction) and that are linked to prosecutor characteristics is an important task for increasing the visibility of prosecutorial decision making and for studying intersectionality of multiple social statuses on sentencing disparities.

(3) Extension of Intersectionality Approach and FCT to Other Arenas of Official-Punishment

The focal concerns framework we applied and elaborated on, along with our findings, may also be useful for gaining a better understanding of decision-making processes in other areas of social control in which individuals are labeled and sanctioned. Indeed, some researchers (e.g. Higgins et al., 2012) have begun to apply the focal concerns framework to other actors or officials within the criminal justice system (e.g. police, probation, parole, prosecution, juvenile court, corrections); as well, the framework would seem to have applicability to a number of non-criminal justice institutions that are central to both social control and stratification (e.g. military tribunals, adoption agencies, visa review boards, and school disciplinary boards).

(4) Need for Qualitative Inquiries

As a number of sentencing researchers have noted (e.g. Spohn, 2009; Ulmer, 2012) to fully unpack and test the intersectional approach and the hypothesized mechanisms articulated in FCT requires measuring how or what judges and other court actors actually think about defendants representing these status characteristics and how such thoughts might influence their sanctioning decisions. Our research has contributed to that effort, as have others, but much more in the way of qualitative and contextual information is needed. Of added value would be research connecting these thoughts, as well as judges' penal philosophies, to their sanctioning decisions. Such a study would require considerable resources and access. Useful incremental steps, however, might involve observing sentencing hearings for a sample of defendants or selecting a sample of defendants and interviewing judges afterwards about their sentencing decisions and punishment philosophies. Then, one would analyze the judges' narratives for evidence of each of the focal concerns and evaluate whether their assessments help to mediate the effects of defendant status characteristics on sentencing decisions. Along these lines, Bridges and Steen (1998) analyzed probation officers' written attributions for delinquency involvement for evidence of racial stereotyping and then examined whether these characterizations mediated the influence of race on sentencing recommendations. The use of mock judge or jury trials, followed by post-hoc experimental assessments, represents another strategy for assessing how "judges" views of defendant status characteristics, both singly and in combination, might be linked to sanctioning decisions. Finally, *we advocate FCT* as a conceptual template and research guide for framing questions and observations in which the aim is to better uncover how court-actors (and other official sanctioning agents) both balance and prioritize the themes of blameworthiness, community protection, and practicality contingencies in rendering and justifying the consequential, possibly life-altering, decisions they make.

Conclusion

Returning to the importance of intersectionality for studying sentencing and other social phenomena that provided the point of departure for this review, we highlight the need for more research and theorizing on the interactive effects of gender, race, and age on sentencing decisions. How much and in what ways these defendant status characteristics shape criminal punishment has still been understudied in law and the social sciences. Particularly scarce are studies that cover the full range of ages to take into account likely age-curvilinear effects. Our treatment in this chapter provided a statement of the focal concerns theory of court actor decision making and a review of results from a recent analysis of sentencing practices in Pennsylvania, a large and diverse state. The findings confirm the importance of intersectionality and are consistent with the focal concerns perspective that argues that legal decision making is organized around concerns of blameworthiness, dangerousness/protection of the community, and other practical constraints. While the primary determinants of sentencing decisions are the past and present criminal behaviors of defendants, our findings are consistent with the notion that legal attributions of culpability, criminal risk, and practical considerations are influenced by commonly held perceptions of membership in various racial/ethnic, gender, and age categories, both singly and in combination with one another. These social statuses and their intersectionality are not just individual attributes but cultural categories that shape the distribution of sanctions and criminal punishment.

Racialized scripts such as the association of Hispanic males with the drug trade or young Black males with violence and crime may enhance punishment because they trigger negative emotions such as fear, anger, or anxiety that intensify punitive responses. On the other hand, scripts about young female defendants as generally law-abiding but vulnerable to male influence or adverse situational contingencies may soften criminal punishment because they trigger emotions of sympathy, chivalry, or tolerance. These sorts of scripts and social typing processes help to explain the strong main effects we observed in our analysis for gender (lenient sentencing of females) and age (lenient sentencing of youngest and oldest defendants across most gender and race categories), as well as the even stronger effects of specific status constellations on sentence severity. Notably, we also observe particularly harsh sentences for Hispanic men overall, as well as harsh sentencing of younger Black men (but not older Black men) as compared to especially lenient sentences for the youngest female defendants regardless of race/ethnicity. The joint constellations of certain offender characteristics, therefore, resulted in compounded sentence severity for some defendants but greater leniency for others.

Gender, race/ethnicity, and age are primary social statuses that are a prominent core of sociological as well as criminological and feminist analyses, and a persistent theme of interest covering essentially all substantive areas within these and other social science disciplines. Our findings demonstrate that these statuses cannot be studied alone but rather interact to produce disparate outcomes by gender and race/ethnicity and age simultaneously, and they show that intersectionality effects are apt to be dynamic in response to fluctuations and oscillations in cultural context of social differentiation. Our findings also emphasize the underutilized potential of the concept of intersectionality for scholars and researchers in criminology, legal studies, sociology, and the social sciences more generally. Tests for intersectionality should be extended to also examine the effects on sanctioning decisions of these social statuses in combination with added contextual factors such as: judge and prosecutor characteristics, time, locality, etc. We project that the focal concerns perspective might serve as a template for future intersectional studies that seek to integrate and understand the complex ways in which membership in these social categories, both singly and in combination, shapes variability in the application of criminal punishment and other types of official social control.

References

Albonetti, C. A. (1991). An integration of theories to explain judicial discretion. *Social Problems, 38*(2), 247–266.

Belkhir, J. A., & Barnett, B. M. (2001). Race, gender and class intersectionality. *Race, Gender Class*, 8(3), 157–174.

Bernard, T. J., & Kurlychek, M. C. (2010). *The cycle of juvenile justice* (2nd ed.). New York: Oxford University Press.

Bonilla-Silva, E. (1997). Rethinking racism: Toward a structural interpretation. *American Sociological Review, 62*(3), 465–480.

Brennan, P. K., & Spohn, C. (2009). The joint effects of offender race/ethnicity and sex on sentence length decisions in federal courts. *Race Social Problems, 1*, 200–217.

Bridges, G. S., & Steen, S. (1998). Racial disparities in official assessments of juvenile offenders: Attributional stereotypes as mediating mechanisms. *American Sociological Review, 63*(4), 554–570.

Browne, I., & Misra, J. (2003). The intersection of gender and race in the labor market. *Annual Review of Sociology, 29*, 487–513.

Burgess-Proctor, A. (2006). Intersections of race, class, gender, and crime: Future directions for feminist criminology. *Feminist Criminology, 1*(1), 27–47.

Choo, H.Y., & Ferree, M. M. (2010). Practicing intersectionality in sociological research: A critical analysis of inclusions, interactions, and institutions in the study of inequalities. *Sociological Theory, 28*(2), 129–149.

Collins, P. H. (1993). Toward a new vision: Race, class, and gender as categories of analysis and connection. *Race, Sex, and Class, 1*(1), 25–45.

Collins, P. H. (1999). *Black feminist thought: Knowledge, consciousness, and the politics of empowerment* (2nd ed.). New York: Routledge.

Crenshaw, K. (1989). Demarginalizing the intersection of race and sex: A Black feminist critique of antidiscrimination doctrine, feminist theory, and antiracist politics. *University of Chicago Legal Forum, 1*, 139–167.

Crenshaw, K. (1991). Mapping the margins: Intersectionality, identity politics, and violence against women of color. *Stanford Law Review, 43*(6), 1241–1299.

Daly, K. (1987). Discrimination in the criminal courts: Family, gender, and the problem of equal treatment. *Social Forces, 66*(1), 152–175.

Davis, K. (2008). Intersectionality as buzzword: A sociology of science perspective on what makes a feminist theory successful. *Feminist Theory, 9*(1), 67–85.

Doerner, J. K. (2015). The joint effects of gender and race/ethnicity on sentencing outcomes in Federal Courts. *Women & Criminal Justice, 25*(5), 313–338.

Doerner, J. K., & Demuth, S. (2010). The independent and joint effects of race/ethnicity, gender, and age on sentencing outcomes in U.S. Federal Courts. *Justice Quarterly, 27*(1), 1–27.

Doerner, J. K., & Demuth, S. (2014). Gender and sentencing in the Federal Courts: Are women treated more leniently? *Criminal Justice Policy Review, 25*(2), 242–269.

Eisenstein, J., Flemming, R., & Nardulli, P. (1988). *The contours of justice: Communities and their courts*. Boston, MA: Little, Brown.

Farrell, R. A., & Holmes, M. D. (1991). The social and cognitive structure of legal decision-making. *The Sociological Quarterly, 32*(4), 529–542.

Florida Youthful Offender Act. In F. Legislature (Ed.), XLVII.

Frazier, C. E., & Bock, E. W. (1982). Effects of court officials on sentence severity: Do judges make a difference? *Criminology, 20*, 257–272.

Gaub, J. E., & Holtfreter, K. (2015). New directions in intersections, inequality, and sentencing. *Women and Criminal Justice, 2015*(25), 298–312.

Ghavami, N., & Peplau, L. A. (2013). An intersectional analysis of gender and ethnic stereotypes testing three hypothesis. *Psychology of Women Quarterly, 37*(1), 113–137.

Hancock, A-M. (2007). When multiplication doesn't equal quick addition: Examining intersectionality as a research paradigm. *Perspectives on Politics, 5*(1), 63–79.

Hayes, J. (1962). *Human data processing limits in decision-making*. Bedford, MA: Operational Applications Lab, Air Force Electronics, Systems Division.

Higgins, E. T., & Molden, D. (2003). How strategies for making judgments and decisions affect cognition: Motivated cognition revisited. In G. V. Bodenhausen & A. J. Lambert (Eds.), *Foundations of social cognition*. Mahwah, NJ: Lawrence Erlbaum.

Higgins, G. E., Vito, G. F., & Grossi, E. L. (2012). The impact of race on the police decision to search during a traffic stop: A focal concerns theory perspective. *Journal of Contemporary Criminal Justice, 28*, 166–183.

Johnson, B. (2014). Judges on trial: A reexamination of judicial race and gender effects across modes of conviction. *Criminal Justice Policy Review, 25*(2), 159–184.

Johnson, B. D., & Betsinger, S. (2009). Punishing the "model minority": Asian-American sentencing outcomes in Federal District Courts. *Criminology, 47*(4), 1045–1090.

Kramer, J. H., & Ulmer, J. (2009). *Sentencing guidelines: Lessons from Pennsylvania*. Boulder, CO: Lynne Rienner Publishers.

Lengermann, P. M., & Niebrugge, G. (2008). Contemporary feminist theory. In G. Ritzer (Ed.), *Sociological theory* (pp. 450–498). Boston, MA: McGraw Hill.

Lorde, A. (1984). *Sister outsider*. Freedom, CA: The Crossing Press.

Lu, Y. (2015). *Rural and urban differences in gender-sentencing patterns of Pennsylvania*. Presented at the annual meeting of American Society of Criminology, November 18. Washington, DC.

Mandel, H., & Semyonov, M. (2016). Going back in time? Gender differences in trends and sources of the racial pay gap, 1970 to 2010. *American Sociological Review, 81*(5), 1039–1068.

McCall, L. (2005). The complexity of intersectionality. *Signs, 30*(3), 1771–1800.

Oliver, M. B. (2003). African American men as "criminal and dangerous": Implications of media portrayals of crime and "criminalization" of African American men. *Journal of African American Studies, 7*, 3–18.

Pampel, F. C. (2008). *Aging, social inequality, and public policy*. Thousand Oaks, CA: Pine Forge Press.

Phoenix, A., & Pattynama, P. (2006). Intersectionality. *European Journal of Women's Studies, 13*(3), 187–192.

Prins, B. (2006). Narrative accounts of origins: A blind spot in the intersectional approach? *European Journal of Women's Studies, 13*(3), 277–290.

Rios, V. (2011). *Punished: Policing the lives of Black and Latino boys*. New York: New York University Press.

Scott, R. (2008). *Institutions and organizations*. Thousand Oaks, CA: Sage Publications.

Spohn, C. (1990). The sentencing decisions of Black and White judges: Expected and unexpected similarities. *Law and Society Review, 24*(4), 1197–1216.

Spohn, C. (2009). *How do judges decide? The search for fairness and justice in punishment* (2nd ed.). Thousand Oaks, CA: Sage.

Steen, S., Engen, R. L., & Gainey, R. R. (2005). Images of danger and culpability: Racial stereotyping, case processing, and criminal sentencing. *Criminology, 43*(2), 435–468.

Steffensmeier, D. (1980). Assessing the impact of the women's movement on sex-based differences in the handling of adult criminal defendants. *Crime and Delinquency, 26*, 344–357.

Steffensmeier, D., & Britt, C. L. (2001). Judges' race and judicial decision making: Do Black judges sentence differently? *Social Science Quarterly, 82*(4), 749–764.

Steffensmeier, D., & Demuth, S. (2000). Ethnicity and sentencing outcomes in U.S. Federal Courts: Who is punished more harshly? *American Sociological Review, 65*(5), 705–729.

Steffensmeier, D., & Demuth, S. (2001). Ethnicity and judges sentencing decisions: Hispanic-Black-White comparisons. *Criminology, 39*(1), 145–178.

Steffensmeier, D., & Demuth, S. (2006). Does gender modify the effects of race-ethnicity on criminal sanctioning? Sentences for male and female, White, Black, and Hispanic defendants. *Journal of Quantitative Criminology, 22*, 241–261.

Steffensmeier, D. J., & Faulkner, G. L. (1978). Defendant's parental status as affecting judges behavior: An experimental test. *Psychological Reports, 42*, 939–945.

Steffensmeier, D., & Hebert, C. (1999). Women and men policymakers: Does the judge's gender affect the sentencing of criminal defendants? *Social Forces*, 77(3), 1163–1196.

Steffensmeier, D., Kramer, J., & Streifel, C. (1993). Gender and imprisonment decisions. *Criminology, 31*(3), 411–446.

Steffensmeier, D., Kramer, J., & Ulmer, J. (1995). Age differences in sentencing. *Justice Quarterly, 12*(3), 583–602.

Steffensmeier, D., & Motivans, M. (2000). Older men and older women in the arms of the criminal law: Offending patterns and sentencing outcomes. *Journals of Gerontology, 55*(3), 141–151.

Steffensmeier, D., Painter-Davis, N., & Ulmer, J. (2017). Intersectionality of race, ethnicity, gender, and age on criminal punishment. *Sociological Perspectives, 60*(4), 810–833.

Steffensmeier, D., & Terry, R. M. (1973). Deviance and respectability: An observational study of reactions to shoplifting. *Social Forces, 4*(51), 417–426.

Steffensmeier, D., Ulmer, J., & Kramer, J. (1998). The interaction of race, gender, and age in criminal sentencing: The punishment cost of being young, Black, and male. *Criminology, 36*(4), 763–797.

Ulmer, J. (1997). *Social worlds of sentencing: Court communities under sentencing guidelines*. Albany: State University of New York Press.

Ulmer, J., & Johnson, B. D. (2004). Sentencing in context: A multilevel analysis. *Criminology, 42*(1), 137–177.

Ulmer, J. T. (2012). Recent developments and new directions in sentencing research. *Justice Quarterly, 29*(1), 1–40.

Ulmer, J. T., & Kramer, J. H. (1996). Court communities under sentencing guidelines: Dilemmas of formal rationality and sentencing disparity. *Criminology, 34*(3), 383–408.

Ulmer, J. T., Kurlycheck, M. C., & Kramer, J. H. (2007). Prosecutorial discretion and the imposition of mandatory minimum sentences. *Journal of Research in Crime and Delinquency, 44*(4), 427–458.

Warren, P., Chiricos, T., & Bales, W. (2012). The imprisonment penalty for young Black and Hispanic males: A crime-specific analysis. *Journal of Research in Crime and Delinquency, 49*(1), 56–80.

Wilkins, L. (1980). World crime: To measure or not to measure? In G. Newman (Ed.), *Crime and deviance*. Beverly Hills, CA: Sage Publications.

Yuval-Davis, N. (2006). Intersectionality and feminist politics. *European Journal of Women's Studies, 13*(3), 193–209.

9

RACIAL AND ETHNIC DISPARITIES AMONG FEMALE OFFENDERS ADJUDICATED IN FEDERAL COURTS

Explicating the Patterns of Disparities Using a Path Model

Cassia C. Spohn, Pauline K. Brennan, and Byungbae Kim

Sentencing research has evolved significantly over the past several decades due in large part to post-conviction data that became available in the late 1980s and early 1990s for cases at the federal level and for cases in many states with guidelines-based sentencing structures (e.g., Pennsylvania, Washington State). These data have allowed researchers to assess punishment disparities while controlling for the effects of legally-relevant variables with sophisticated statistical techniques. In most studies, female offenders are found to receive more lenient sentences than male offenders (Daly and Bordt, 1995; Doerner and Demuth, 2014; Steffensmeier, Kramer, and Streifel, 1993; Spohn, 2009; Spohn and Brennan, 2013). Research also reveals that African American and Hispanic offenders are more likely to be incarcerated than white offenders (Baumer, 2013; Mitchell, 2005; Spohn, 2000; Ulmer, 2012). Disparity appears to be particularly large for young male African American and Hispanic offenders (Spohn, 2000).

Although scholars have added to the body of literature on the effects of race and ethnicity and gender on sentencing outcomes (Spohn, 2009; Ulmer, 2012), much work still needs to be done (Baumer, 2013). Among the important but underexplored topics is whether sentences are racially and ethnically disparate among female offenders, because the vast majority of sentencing studies have focused on male offenders or have merely included offender sex as a control variable in their examinations of data sets comprised largely of male offenders—the so-called "add sex and stir" approach. Thus, our understanding of the intersectionality of race and gender is narrow and the limited empirical evidence is mixed (see Steffensmeier, Ulmer, and Kramer, 1998; Griffin and Wooldredge, 2006; Spohn and Brennan, 2013). That said, findings from most studies suggest that minority women and white women receive similar sentences (Bickle and

Peterson, 1991; Brennan, 2009; Crew, 1991; Farnworth and Teske, 1995; Kruttschnitt, 1984; Spohn and Beichner, 2000; Spohn and Spears, 1997; Steffensmeier and Demuth, 2006); fewer find that white women receive more lenient sentences than minority women (Steffensmeier et al., 1993, 1998). This overall body of evidence seems to be at odds with literature reporting the persistence of negative racial and ethnic stereotypes for women of color (Brennan, 2002; Landrine, 1985) and official statistics that highlight the disproportionate rates of imprisonment for minority women (Carson, 2014; Human Rights Watch, 2008).

Sentencing disparities among women, however, may be obscured if sufficient attention is not given to the potentially important moderating influence of offense type; sentencing disparities among women may materialize only for certain types of offenders. For example, Crawford (2000) found that among those convicted of drug offenses, minority women received harsher sentences than white women. In line with these findings, Kautt and Spohn (2002) and Steen and colleagues (2005) found preferential treatment for white women, but not for African American women, convicted of drug offenses. Indeed, many have argued that sentencing outcomes are likely to be particularly severe for minority drug offenders (Brennan and Spohn, 2008; Demuth and Steffensmeier, 2004; Mitchell, 2005; Steffensmeier and Demuth, 2000). But, most studies on the issue of racial and/or ethnic disparities in the sentencing of drug offenders do not allow for comparisons to be made between African American, white, and Hispanic females (for a review of these studies, see Brennan and Spohn, 2008). This is unfortunate because, as Steen and colleagues (2005) have suggested, attitudes toward drug offending and perceptions of drug offenders are likely to be influenced by stereotypes about gender *and* race/ethnicity.

Another limitation of prior research about the effect of race and ethnicity on sentencing outcomes among females is that most studies do not adequately consider crucial decisions that are made prior to the sentencing outcome. It may be that a race or ethnicity effect among female offenders would not be captured if focus is placed solely on the tightly regulated final sentencing stage, especially under sentencing guidelines. The effect may be more subtle and may materialize through what Zatz (1987) called the *cumulative disadvantage* that results from disparate outcomes at earlier stages in the process (for evidence of this, see Kutateladze et al., 2014). In other words, what we know about sentencing disparity would be enhanced if researchers focused more of their attention on upstream outcomes, especially bail and pretrial detention and the pre-conviction decisions made by prosecutors. More work of this sort is needed because the punishment decision does not occur in isolation.

The need for research to move in this direction was stressed by attendees and speakers who participated in the *Symposium on the Past and Future of Empirical Sentencing Research*, sponsored by the National Science Foundation and hosted by the University at Albany in 2010, and in three recent publications where scholars provided commentaries and reviews linked to the Symposium (Bushway, 2013; Bushway and Forst, 2013; Ulmer, 2012). One should not interpret this to mean that scholars have completely ignored earlier stages in the process, as there is a substantial amount of research on pretrial detention and the actions taken by prosecutors (see for example Hartley, Maddan, and Spohn, 2007; Kim, Spohn, and Hedberg, 2015; Shermer and Johnson, 2010; Sorensen and Wallace, 1999; Spohn and Holleran, 2001). However, most researchers have not empirically linked theses outcomes to imposed punishments.

As Baumer (2013) recently noted, "the vast majority of studies in the modal research tradition on race and sentencing forge ahead with a focus on estimating either main or interactive effects, neither of which address the many indirect pathways through which race may influence sentencing outcomes" (p. 249; see also Frase, 2013; Ulmer, 2012). One of the few exceptions, and one noted in Baumer's (2013) review, is Brennan's (2006) study of female misdemeanants sentenced in New York City. Upon analyzing outcomes for a sample of persons arrested in 1989 she found indirect, but not direct, effects between defendant race and ethnicity and the sentencing outcome. African American and Hispanic females were more likely than white females to receive jail sentences due to differences in socio-economic status, community ties, prior record, earlier case processing, and charge severity (Brennan, 2006). These differences would have been masked had she merely controlled for the effects of important mediators.

We agree that a failure to consider indirect effects is problematic given the inherent mediating nature of earlier case processing outcomes. We expect that the effects of race and ethnicity will manifest themselves in less closely regulated, intermediate decision-making stages of court processing, including decisions related to pretrial detention and, at the federal level, motions for substantial assistance departures. We also expect that the effects of race and ethnicity will be especially pronounced among females convicted of drug offenses. We use path analysis and data on female offenders adjudicated in U.S. District Courts to test for the direct and indirect effects of offender race and ethnicity. In addition, we examine whether crime type moderates the effects of race and ethnicity. Our study thus provides a more robust consideration of the potential sources of sentencing disparity among female offenders and responds to calls for examinations of sentencing in the context of earlier case processing decisions (Baumer, 2013; Blumstein et al., 1983; Spohn, 2000; Ulmer, 2012).

Literature Review

The primary theoretical perspective guiding this study is *critical race feminism*, sometimes called *black feminist criminology* (Potter, 2006; Belknap, 2014). Black feminist scholars direct our attention to racist ideologies that affect perceptions of minority women and their treatment. Such scholars argue that the perceptions and experiences of white women are quite distinct from those of African American or Hispanic women. Whereas white women may suffer primarily from the effects of sexism, minority women experience "double and multiple marginality" where "racism and sexism are combined with each other" to influence perceptions and treatment by others (Belknap, 2014; Chesney-Lind and Morash, 2011).

Stereotypes for minority women are more negative than stereotypes for white women (Brennan, 2002, 2006; Castro, 1998; Healey, 1997; Landrine, 1985; Madriz, 1997; Portillos, 1998; Young, 1986). Landrine (1985: 71–72), for example, found that, whereas white women were more likely to be stereotyped as "competent, dependent, emotional, intelligent, passive . . . and warm," African American women tended to be stereotyped as "dirty, hostile, and superstitious." Furthermore, African American women are often depicted as aggressive or dangerous (Brennan, 2002, 2006; Irwin and Chesney-Lind, 2008; Farr, 1997; Madriz, 1997; Young, 1986). Other researchers have found that minority females are stereotyped as "hyper sexed" (Farr, 2000: 55; see also Young, 1986) and as "welfare queens" (Hurwitz and Peffley, 1997: 393).[1] This body of research, then, suggests that stereotypical conceptions of "femininity" more closely fit white women than African American or Hispanic women (Klein, 1995). Such notions of femininity may affect how women are treated by the criminal justice system. Rafter (1990), for example, has documented the harsh treatment of women slaves in the United States and explained that such women were viewed as quite distinct from their white counterparts and, hence, not "worthy" of chivalrous treatment.

With regard to sentencing outcomes, many scholars emphasize the role that stereotypes and causal attritions play in decision-making. For example, Albonetti's (1991, 1997) discussion of "uncertainty avoidance/causal attribution" suggests that, when individuals are forced to make decisions without all of the relevant information, they attempt to reduce uncertainty by relying upon both prior experience and stereotypes. Judges and prosecutors, she argues, rely on stereotypes of African Americans and Hispanics as more dangerous, more threatening, and more likely to recidivate to help them achieve rational outcomes in the face of limited information. "Focal concerns" theorists similarly argue that judges have limited case information and, therefore, develop a "perceptual shorthand" based on stereotypes linked to an array of offender characteristics, including race, ethnicity, and gender (Engen et al., 2003; Spohn and Holleran, 2000; Steffensmeier et al., 1998; Ulmer and Johnson, 2004). These offender characteristics (along with offense type and prior record) influence sentencing outcomes because attributions of dangerousness and threat connect them to groups thought to be poor risks for rehabilitation, potentially dangerous, and more culpable (Steffensmeier and Demuth, 2000). Therefore, assessments of blameworthiness and dangerousness that incorporate negative racial and ethnic stereotypes may lead to harsher sentences for African Americans and Hispanics.

The tenets of critical race feminism notwithstanding, the empirical evidence regarding racial/ethnic disparities in sentencing outcomes among female offenders is not necessarily consistent with the theory's notion of double marginality for women of color. Although some researchers reported race effects favoring white females (Steffensmeier et al., 1993, 1998; Kruttschnitt, 1982; Crawford, 2000; Albonetti, 2002), others identified differences that favored African American females (Koons-Witt, 2002; Griffin and Wooldredge, 2006). To further complicate the situation, a number of studies found that race and ethnicity did not directly affect sentence outcomes for women (Brennan and Spohn, 2009; Bickle and Peterson, 1991; Spohn and Spears, 1997; Spohn and Beichner, 2000; Spohn and Brennan, 2011; Steffensmeier and Demuth, 2006). The fact that some of the evidence is inconsistent with the primary theoretical perspective guiding research in this area suggests that the effects of race and ethnicity among female offenders may be subtle and nuanced rather than overt and obvious. In this chapter, we attempt to tease out these possible more nuanced effects.

We begin, as have previous researchers, by testing for the direct effects of race and ethnicity on sentencing outcomes for female offenders. In line with previous discussions of negative racial and ethnic stereotypes and their link to assessments of culpability, threat, and reform potential, we expect that race and ethnicity will directly affect the sentences given to female offenders. We expect that stereotypes of women of color as "aggressive," "unfeminine," "hyper-sexed," and "welfare queens" will influence prosecutors' and judges' assessments of their culpability, threat, and potential for rehabilitation. Therefore, our first hypothesis is:

> H (1): Race and ethnicity will directly affect sentence outcomes for female offenders.

A Consideration of the Indirect Effects of Race and Ethnicity

It is possible, however, that race and ethnicity may not directly affect sentencing outcomes given restrictions placed on judicial discretion under Federal Sentencing Guidelines. The absence of a direct race or ethnicity effect would not necessarily provide proof of a racially unbiased sentencing process (Baumer, 2013; Brennan, 2006; Spohn, 2000; Ulmer, 2012; Zatz, 2000). Indeed, Zatz (1987: 72) argued that subtle racial and ethnic differences at earlier stages of case processing could accumulate and that cumulative disadvantage could have significant effects on sentence severity. One outcome that has both immediate and long-term consequences is whether the defendant is released or in custody before the sentence is imposed. As a case proceeds, the defendant's failure to gain release gives the impression that she is a flight risk and a danger to society (Albonetti et al., 1989; Bernstein et al., 1977; Demuth, 2003). Researchers have shown that the effects of race and ethnicity influence the pretrial release decision (Holmes et al., 1996; Demuth, 2003; Demuth and Steffensmeier, 2004; Schlesinger, 2005) and that pretrial detention adversely affects sentencing outcomes (Albonetti, 1998a, 1999; Chiricos and Bales, 1991; Lizotte, 1978; Spohn and DeLone, 2000; Spohn, Gruhl, and Welch, 1981–82). And, when considering both decisions, some have found that the effects of race and ethnicity operate indirectly through pretrial release to affect sentence outcomes (Lizotte, 1978; Schlesinger, 2005; Spohn, 2009). Although the above findings are informative, little is known about the indirect effects of race and ethnicity on the sentences given to female offenders because only two studies tested for such effects, and these two studies produced contradictory findings (Spohn, 2009; Brennan, 2006). We expect that the negative stereotypes about women of color will affect this more *loosely regulated* case outcome, producing a higher likelihood of pretrial detention for African American and Hispanic female offenders. Thus, our second hypothesis is:

> H (2): African American and Hispanic female offenders will be less likely than white female offenders to be released prior to sentencing and will, consequently, receive harsher sentencing outcomes than white female offenders.

Yet another potentially important mediating variable in the federal system is whether a defendant is granted a guidelines departure for providing substantial assistance in the prosecution and conviction of another offender. A motion for substantial assistance may only be filed by a U.S. Attorney; moreover, the decision to do so is highly discretionary and generally unreviewable. Researchers have found that offender race, ethnicity, and gender affect both the likelihood of a substantial assistance departure and the magnitude of the sentence discount given to offenders who receive departures (Albonetti, 1997, 2002; Everett and Wojtkiewicz, 2002; Hartley et al., 2007; Johnson, Ulmer, and Kramer, 2008; Kempf-Leonard and Sample, 2001; Maxfield and Kramer, 1998; Steffensmeier and Demuth, 2000; Stacey and Spohn, 2006). Overall, this body of research raises concerns about "the equal application of the law and the wherewithal of the sentencing guidelines in reducing sentencing disparities of any kind" (Steffensmeier and Demuth, 2000: 725). These concerns appear to remain when one examines the influence of substantial assistance departures among female offenders. In Albonetti's (2002) study of federal drug offenders, the offender's sex and race/ethnicity worked jointly to condition the effects of a substantial assistance departure; white females received the greatest benefit from this type of downward departure. Hartley and his colleagues (2007) came to a similar conclusion in a later examination of federal drug offenders. Among offenders facing a guidelines sentence for a powder cocaine charge, both African American and Hispanic females were less likely than white females to receive substantial assistance departures.[2] These findings suggested that "prosecutors' discretionary decisions regarding departures for substantial assistance [were] re-introducing unwarranted disparity into the federal sentencing process" (Hartley et al., 2007: 404). Taken together, these studies suggest that African American and Hispanic women will be perceived as less sympathetic and salvageable (Nagel and Schulhofer, 1992) relative to their white counterparts, due to the negative stereotypes, and therefore will be disadvantaged in this process, which in turn will lead to more severe sentencing outcomes. Thus, our third hypothesis is as follows:

> H (3): African American and Hispanic female offenders will be less likely than white female offenders to receive a substantial assistance departure and will, consequently, receive harsher sentencing outcomes than white female offenders.

The Moderating Effect of Crime Type

The examination of racial/ethnic disparities among female offenders is further complicated when the image of drug offenders is taken into consideration (Daly and Tonry, 1997). Many argue that minority offenders have been disproportionately affected by punitive sentencing policies that materialized as a result of the Reagan/Bush "War on Drugs" (American Civil Liberties Union, 2004; Mauer and King, 2007; Tonry, 1995). Given the assertion that the "*war on drugs has translated into a war on women*" (Chesney-Lind, 1995: 111), minority females convicted of drug crimes may now be facing even harsher treatment, compared to their white counterparts. On average, across the country in 2003 African American women were incarcerated for drug offenses at a rate that was 4.8 times higher than the rate for white women (Human Rights Watch, 2008: 19, Table 13). Some have argued that the overrepresentation of African Americans among those in the criminal justice system for drug offenses reflects a "racialized conception of 'the drug problem'" (Beckett et al., 2005: 436). Thus, it is highly plausible that minority females convicted of drug crimes will be more likely to receive severe punishments, because of negative racial/ethnic stereotypes linked to perceptions of the drug problem and/or aggressive drug policies directed towards minority communities.

However, the empirical evidence concerning disparity in sentencing of drug offenders is mixed. Kruttschnitt (1980–81, 1982) and Crawford (2000) reported that African American women convicted of drug crimes were treated more severely than similarly situated white women. By contrast, Brennan and Spohn (2009) and Spohn and Brennan (2011) found no differences in sentence length and or in the odds of receiving a substantial assistance departure for white, African American, and Hispanic women convicted of drug offenses in federal courts. In the present study, we expect that direct and indirect effects of race and ethnicity will be greater among females convicted of drug offenses, given previous research on stereotypes regarding the association between racial and ethnic minorities and drug crimes and punitive drug policies that target minorities.

> H (4): Race and ethnicity will have a direct effect on sentence outcomes for female offenders convicted of drug offenses (compared to female offenders convicted of non-drug offenses) and the indirect effects of race and ethnicity will be greater for female offenders convicted of drug offenses than for female offenders convicted of non-drug offenses.

To summarize, our goal in this chapter is to determine if the disconnect between the tenets of critical race feminism and the empirical evidence regarding the effects of race and ethnicity on sentences for female offenders can be attributed to the fact that most research tests for direct, rather than indirect, effects. Although we, like prior researchers, do test for the direct effects of race and ethnicity, our primary focus is on determining whether race and ethnicity affect sentence outcomes indirectly through their effects on pretrial detention and substantial assistance departures and whether these effects are moderated by crime type.

Research Design and Methodology

This study uses United States Sentencing Commission (USSC) data on offenders convicted in U.S. District Courts during fiscal years 2006 and 2007. The original data file included 19,055 female offenders adjudicated in 94 district courts, but we excluded cases for several reasons. First, following prior research on sentencing in federal courts (Johnson et al., 2008; Ulmer, Light, and Kramer, 2011), all immigration cases (N = 2,543) and the cases adjudicated in five districts (Puerto Rico, Guam, Virginia Islands, the District of Columbia, and Northern-Mariana Island) (N = 292) were deleted from the analysis. Second, consistent with our arguments, this study focuses on the differences in the sentences imposed on African American, Hispanic, and white female offenders. Thus, other offenders from other racial groups were removed from the analysis (N = 961). After excluding these cases, the final data file included 15,299 female offenders who were sentenced in 89 district courts.

Descriptive statistics for all of the variables are presented in Table 9.1. There are two dependent variables: whether the offender was sentenced to prison and the length of the prison sentence. Imprisonment is measured using a binary variable, which indicates whether an offender received a prison sentence or not (imprisonment = 1, other sentences = 0). The length of the prison sentence was originally measured in actual months. Following prior studies (U.S. Sentencing Commission, 2010; Ulmer et al., 2011), we made two adjustments to this variable. We capped sentence length at 470 months and then logged the variable due to its skewed distribution.[3] Our models include two mediating variables, both of which measure case processing outcomes that occur prior to sentencing. We include whether the offender was in custody prior to sentencing (in custody = 1, released = 0) and whether the offender received a downward departure for providing substantial assistance (SA) in the prosecution and conviction of another (other) offender(s) (yes = 1, no = 0).[4] The primary independent

Table 9.1 Descriptive Statistics

		Frequency	*%*	*Min*	*Max*	*Mean*
Dependent Variables	Imprisonment	10,374	68.70	0	1	
	No imprisonment	4,727	31.30			
	Sentence length (ln)	10,250		−3.51	6.15	2.85
Mediating Variables	Detained	6,160	42.99	0	1	
	Non-detained	8,170	57.01			
	SA departure	2,977	20.47	0	1	
	No SA	11,563	79.53			
Independent Variables	White (reference)	6,607	45.56	0	1	
	African American	4,274	29.47			
	Hispanic	3,621	24.97			
Control Variables	Age (ln)	14,920		2.77	4.44	3.52
	Education	4,711	33.14	0	1	
	Dependents	8,678	60.59	0	1	
	Non-citizen	1,887	12.98	0	1	
	Pled guilty	14,597	96.49	0	1	
	Mandatory minimum	3,656	25.12	0	1	
	FY2007	7,588	50.14	0	1	
	Violent crimes (reference)	332	2.19	0	1	
	Drug offense	6,001	39.67			
	Fraud offense	5,647	37.33			
	Firearms offense	546	3.61			
	Others	2,602	17.20			
	Presumptive sentence (ln)	14,539		−2.30	6.15	2.29
	Multiple counts	2,834	18.73	0	1	
	Final criminal history score	14,617		1	6	1.66

variable is the offender's race/ethnicity, which is measured using a set of dummy variables (African American, Hispanic, white), with white offenders as the reference category. Moving on to control variables, age is a continuous variable, which was log transformed due to its skewed distribution. Education is measured using a binary variable (some college or above = 1). We also control for whether the offender had any dependents (yes = 1), was not a U.S. citizen (yes = 1), whether the offender pled guilty (plea = 1), whether the offender faced a mandatory minimum sentence (yes = 1), and whether the case was adjudicated in FY 2007 (FY2007 = 1). Crime type is also controlled using a set of dummy variables, with violent crime as the reference category (drug, fraud, firearm, and others). The presumptive sentence is included and is adjusted in the same way as the dependent variable. Finally, we control for whether the case involved multiple counts of conviction and the offender's final criminal history score.

Analytic Strategy

Given our hypotheses, which focus on the direct and indirect effects of race and ethnicity on sentencing outcomes, we use path analysis as the main data analysis technique. Path analysis is not only capable of estimating a model in which mediating relationships are considered but also allows for the simultaneous estimation of direct, indirect, and total effects (MacKinnon, 2008). However, there are two important issues that must be addressed when using this technique in the current study. First, both of our mediating variables are measured as binary variables, which prevented us from using traditional path analysis based on ordinary least squares (OLS) regression. For this reason, we use M-plus 6 with the estimator of WLSMV along with the theta parameterization to estimate our path models (Muthén and Muthén, 1998–2011).[5] We use probit regression to analyze the binary mediating variables as dependent variables and OLS regression to analyze the continuous dependent variable. The second issue is potential clustering in the data; because individual offenders are nested within one of the 89 federal district courts included in the analysis, there is the possibility of intraclass correlation. To account for this, we use the "type = complex-cluster" option provided by M-plus, which specifies that the data are clustered in groups and that corrections in standard errors should be made based on group dependency—in this case, clustering within districts (MacKinnon, 2008).[6]

To test our hypothesis regarding the moderating effect of the type of conviction charge (drug versus non-drug), we employ multiple group comparisons, which allows us to examine whether the direct and indirect effects of race and ethnicity are invariant across the two sub-groups (Bollen, 1989; Edwards and Lambert, 2007). In other words, we are interested in determining (1) whether the direct path coefficients from race and ethnicity to sentencing outcomes are different for drug and non-drug offenders (moderated direct effect) and (2) whether the two hypothesized indirect effects of race and ethnicity differ across drug and non-drug offenders (moderated mediation). To that end, we estimate separate path models, using the grouping option offered by M-plus. We then use the chi-square difference test with the method of equality constraint in structural parameters to test for differences in the paired path coefficients from the two sub-groups. We begin the analysis by estimating a baseline model where all of the independent variables are included and all of the paths are specified. Then we estimate a trimmed model from which non-significant paths are fixed at zero to identify a more parsimonious model.

Findings

The Direct, Indirect, and Total Effects of Race and Ethnicity on the Imprisonment Decision

As noted above, the first step is the analysis to estimate a baseline model of the decision to incarcerate (and of the likelihood of pre-sentence detention and receipt of a substantial assistance departure). The results, which are presented in Table 9.2, indicate that the model fit the data well ($x^2 = 2.768$, $d/f = 1$, $p = 0.0962$, RMSEA = 0.011, and CFI = 0.999) and that most of the findings are consistent with the results from previous research. Significant predictors of the imprisonment decision include the presumptive sentence, the offender's criminal history, and whether the offender pled guilty or went to trial. The three outcomes also are affected by the offender's race and ethnicity, but not necessarily as predicted. Finally, the two mediating variables (pretrial detention and substantial assistance departure) have strong effects on the likelihood of incarceration, which raises the possibility that a portion of the race and ethnicity effect may be mediated through these variables.

To obtain more accurate estimates of the direct and indirect effects of race and ethnicity, we re-estimated the baseline model with the non-significant paths fixed at zero. The results of the final trimmed model are presented in Figure 9.1. The goodness-of-fit measures indicate that the final trimmed model fits the data well ($x^2 = 18.537$, $d/f = 19$, $p = 0.4869$, RMSEA = 0.000, and CFI = 0.999). We expected that race and ethnicity would directly affect the odds of imprisonment (Hypothesis 1). The results provide partial support for the hypothesis, but not in the manner anticipated; whereas there were no differences in the odds of imprisonment between African American female offenders and white female offenders, Hispanic female offenders faced substantially *lower* odds of imprisonment, compared to their white counterparts ($b = -0.179$, $p = 0.023$).

With respect to the indirect effects of race and ethnicity on the probability of imprisonment, our second hypothesis predicted that race and ethnicity would increase the odds of imprisonment via presentencing detention (i.e., African American/Hispanic (+) $\rightarrow$ detention (+) $\rightarrow$ imprisonment). The results presented in Figure 9.2 offer mixed support for this hypothesis. In line with our expectations, Hispanic female offenders were more likely than white female offenders to be detained prior to sentencing ($b = 0.234$, $p = 0.000$) and, consequently, faced higher odds of receiving a prison sentence (indirect effect = 0.111, $p = 0.000$). Contrary to our expectations, however, African American females were less likely than white females to be detained prior to sentencing ($b = -0.163$, $p = 0.000$) and thus were less likely to be imprisoned compared to white female defendants (indirect effect = −0.077, $p = 0.000$).

Table 9.2 Baseline Model for the Imprisonment Decision

Variables	*Endogenous Variables*		
	Detention (Model-1)	*SA Departure (Model-2)*	*Imprisonment (Model-3)*
Black	**−0.142****	**−0.020**	**−0.111**
	(0.041)	**(0.055)**	**(0.062)**
Hispanic	**0.235*****	**−0.230****	**−0.183***
	(0.046)	**(0.068)**	**(0.079)**
Age	−0.352***	−0.366***	−0.367***
	(0.035)	(0.073)	(0.093)
College	−0.201***	0.028	0.034
	(0.025)	(0.036)	(0.046)
Dependent	−0.137***	0.019	0.041
	(0.036)	(0.036)	(0.036)
Non-citizen	0.969***	−0.064	0.173*
	(0.103)	(0.068)	(0.097)
Multiple count	0.101**	−0.069	0.033*
	(0.034)	(0.064)	(0.073)
Criminal history	0.297***	−0.032*	0.120***
	(0.013)	(0.015)	(0.023)
Presumptive sentence	0.091***	0.407***	0.652***
	(0.009)	(0.033)	(0.034)
Drug	−0.166	0.284**	0.038
	(0.135)	(0.106)	(0.206)
Fraud	−0.653***	0.163	0.044
	(0.102)	(0.121)	(0.160)
Firearms	−0.296*	0.376*	−0.553**
	(0.134)	(0.154)	(0.196)
Other crimes	−0.443***	0.128	−0.424**
	(0.100)	(0.135)	(0.163)
FY2007	0.006	0.012	−0.012
	(0.034)	(0.031)	(0.041)
Plea		1.722***	0.364**
		(0.140)	(0.137)
Minimum	0.302***	0.128	0.809***
	(0.076)	(0.071)	(0.122)
Pretrial detention		**−0.186*****	**0.464*****
		(0.024)	**(0.039)**
Substantial assistance			**−0.615*****
			(0.046)
R-square	0.392	0.469	0.765

Coefficients are unstandardized.

Standard errors provided in parentheses.

* $p < 0.05$, ** $p < 0.01$, and *** $p < 0.001$.

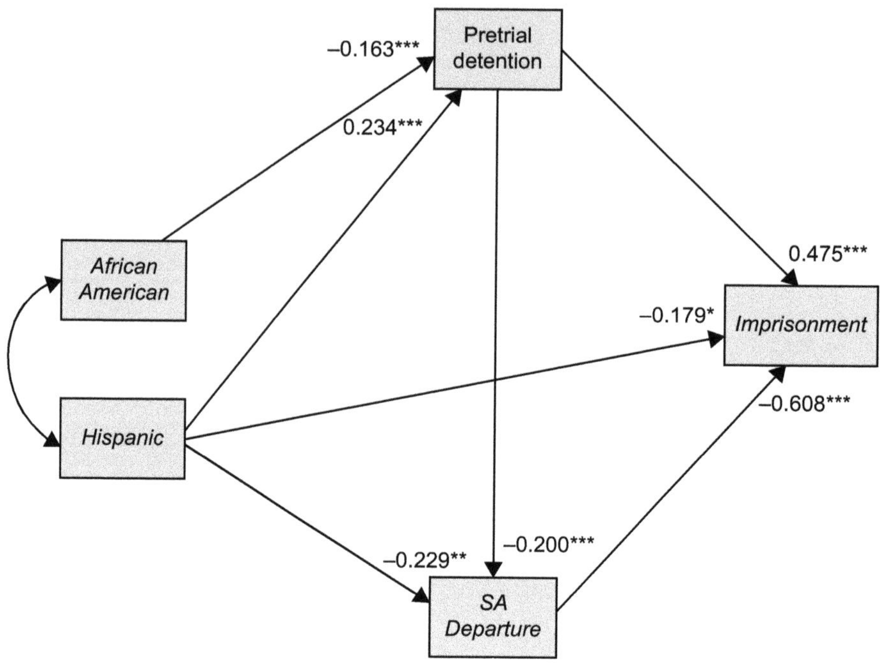

Figure 9.1 Final Trimmed Model for the Imprisonment Decision

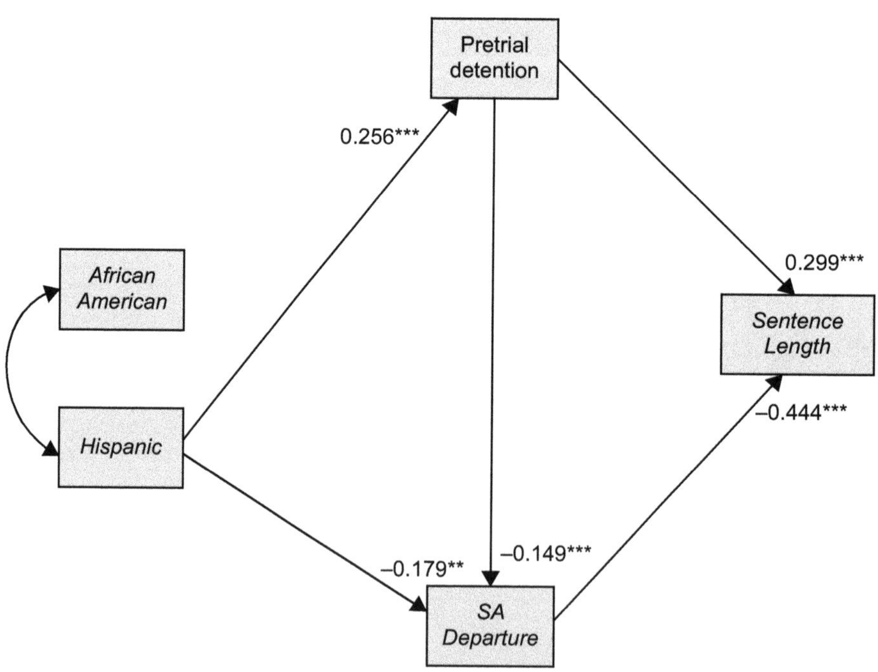

Figure 9.2 Final Trimmed Model for the Sentence Length Decision

Moving on to Hypothesis 3, we predicted that African American and Hispanic female offenders would be less likely than white female offenders to receive a substantial assistance departure and would, as a result, be subject to higher odds of imprisonment. The hypothesized path was African American/Hispanic (−) → SA departure (−) → imprisonment. As reflected in Figure 9.1, we found only partial support for this hypothesis. The likelihood of receiving an SA departure did not vary by race, but Hispanic female offenders were less likely than white female offenders to receive this type of departure ($b = -0.229, p = 0.001$) and, as a result, faced higher odds of imprisonment than white female offenders (indirect effect = $0.139, p = 0.001$).

The results discussed thus far illustrate that the offender's race and ethnicity have complex relationships on our outcomes of interest, not all of the observed relationships were consistent with our predictions. Therefore, we calculated the total effects to ascertain whether African American and Hispanic female offenders were disadvantaged overall. For African American females, we found a statistically significant total race effect that suggested that African American females were at an advantage (not a disadvantage) compared to their white counterparts (total effect = $-0.097, p = 0.000$). As shown by Figure 9.1, this effect operated through presentence detention status.[7] However, for Hispanic female offenders, the relationship was much more complex; there were two statistically significant indirect effects that worked to the disadvantage of Hispanic females, but there was also a strong negative direct effect that worked to favor Hispanic females. These contrasting effects produced a total effect that was not statistically significant (total effect = $0.099, p = 0.291$); the direct and indirect effects, in other words, canceled out each other. In summary, ethnicity did not exert a statistically significant overall (total) effect on the likelihood of incarceration, but African American female offenders were statistically less likely to be incarcerated than white females.

The Direct, Indirect, and Total Effects of Race and Ethnicity on Sentence Length

We also estimated the direct and indirect effects of the offender's race and ethnicity on the length of the prison sentences. The results for our baseline model, which are provided in Table 9.3, reveal that the model fit the data well (x^2 = 1.755, d/f = 1, p = 0.1852, RMSEA = 0.009, and CFI = 0.999). The overall results are largely congruent with the findings of prior research; legally relevant variables have statistically significant effects on our endogenous variables, and the offender's race and ethnicity also have varying effects on our two mediating variables and sentence length. Finally, our two mediating variables have relatively strong effects on sentence length, which points to the possibility that some of the race and ethnicity effects may be mediated through these variables.

Employing the same approach we took with the estimation of the in-out decision, we re-estimated our baseline model for sentence length. The results of the final trimmed model are presented in Figure 9.2. The goodness-of-fit measures demonstrate that the final trimmed model fits the data well (x^2 = 26.852, d/f = 24, p = 0.3114, RMSEA = 0.004, and CFI = 0.998).

Table 9.3 Baseline Model for the Sentence Length Decision

Variables	*Endogenous Variables*		
	Detention (Model-1)	*SA Departure (Model-2)*	*Sentence Length (Model-3)*
Black	**−0.103***	**−0.064**	**−0.030**
	(0.049)	**(0.059)**	**(0.049)**
Hispanic	**0.261*****	**−0.200****	**−0.082**
	(0.049)	**(0.070)**	**(0.090)**
Age	−0.391***	−0.304***	0.137*
	(0.038)	(0.082)	(0.056)
College	−0.198***	0.017	0.028
	(0.029)	(0.042)	(0.029)
Dependent	−0.139***	0.022	0.029
	(0.038)	(0.037)	(0.031)
Non-citizen	1.073***	−0.106	−0.186*
	(0.107)	(0.077)	(0.077)
Multiple count	0.120**	−0.074	0.100*
	(0.038)	(0.063)	(0.050)
Criminal history	0.295***	−0.013	0.043*
	(0.013)	(0.017)	(0.021)
Presumptive sentence	0.023	0.465***	0.842***
	(0.013)	(0.033)	(0.027)
Drug	−0.208*	0.191	−0.008
	(0.102)	(0.106)	(0.115)
Fraud	−0.769***	0.071	−0.130
	(0.093)	(0.128)	(0.105)
Firearms	−0.173	0.052	−0.107
	(0.133)	(0.139)	(0.116)
Other crimes	−0.390***	−0.030	−0.055
	(0.090)	(0.145)	(0.104)
FY2007	0.033	0.025	0.017
	(0.039)	(0.034)	(0.026)
Plea		1.739***	0.308**
		(0.149)	(0.107)
Minimum	0.244***	0.202***	0.294***
	(0.063)	(0.064)	(0.069)
Pretrial detention		**−0.124*****	**0.300*****
		(0.026)	**(0.026)**
Substantial assistance			**−0.454*****
			(0.022)
R-square	0.347	0.392	0.556

Coefficients are unstandardized.

Standard errors provided in parentheses.

* $p < 0.05$, ** $p < 0.01$, and *** $p < 0.001$.

Our first hypothesis was that the offender's race and ethnicity would directly affect the length of the prison sentence. Inconsistent with our hypothesis, we found that the sentences imposed on African American female offenders and Hispanic female offenders did not differ from those imposed on white female offenders. Hypothesis 2 predicted that race and ethnicity would positively affect sentence length via presentence detention. The results presented in Figure 9.2 offer only partial support for this hypothesis. Hispanic female offenders were more likely than white female offenders to be detained prior to sentencing ($b = 0.256, p = 0.000$) and, consequently, received longer prison terms than white female offenders (indirect effect $= 0.077, p = 0.000$).[8] By contrast, the offender's race did not have a significant effect on sentence length through presentence detention.[9]

We also hypothesized that African American and Hispanic female offenders would be less likely than white female offenders to receive a substantial assistance departure and would, as a result, receive longer prison terms than white female offenders (H-3). As reported in Figure 9.2, we found only partial support for this hypothesis. The likelihood of receiving a substantial assistance departure did not vary by race, but Hispanic female offenders were less likely than white female offenders to receive this type of departure ($b = -0.179, p = 0.016$) and, as a result, received longer prison terms than white female offenders (indirect effect $= 0.079, p = 0.011$).

Moving on to our estimation of the total effects, there was no statistically significant race effect, since none of the paths for African American females were statistically significant. By contrast, a unique overall Hispanic effect emerged, which was evident by a statistically significant total effect (total effect $= 0.173, p = 0.000$) that manifested as a result of two statistically significant and positive indirect effects from ethnicity through pretrial detention and substantial assistance departures. These findings suggest that ethnic disparities exist at earlier case processing stages and that these earlier case outcomes have spillover effects on sentencing severity.

The Moderating Effect of a Drug Offense in the Imprisonment Decision

Our fourth hypothesis predicted that the direct and indirect effects of race and ethnicity on the likelihood of incarceration would vary by whether the offender was convicted of a drug offense or a non-drug offense. To test this hypothesis, we conducted a multigroup path analysis, the results of which are summarized in Table 9.4. The results for the baseline model indicated that there was a good fit to the data ($x^2 = 3.998$, $d/f = 2$, $p = 0.135$, RMSEA $= 0.012$, CFI $= 0.999$).

The first three rows of Table 9.4 indicate that offense type moderates the effect of race. To elaborate, there is a direct race effect that favors African American females convicted of drug crimes (but not those convicted of non-drug crimes). In addition, African American females convicted of drug offenses were less likely than white females convicted of drug offenses to receive substantial assistance departures and thus faced higher odds of imprisonment than white females offenders ($b = 0.091, p = 0.022$), but this pattern was not found for those convicted of non-drug offenses. The difference in the observed coefficients was statistically significant (x^2 difference: $7.362, p = 0.024$). In

Table 9.4 Two-Group Comparisons for the Imprisonment Decision

Paths	*Drug*	*Non-Drug*	X^2 *Difference*/d.f.
(a) AA → Detention → Imprisonment	−0.055	−0.090***	3.334/2
	(0.034)	(0.025)	
(b) AA → SA Departure → Imprisonment	0.091*	−0.053	7.362/2*
	(0.041)	(0.041)	
(c) AA → Imprisonment	−0.347**	0.008	5.725/1*
	(0.133)	(0.069)	
(d) Hispanic → Detention → Imprisonment	0.152***	0.059*	4.994/2$^+$
	(0.035)	(0.029)	
(e) Hispanic → SA Departure → Imprisonment	0.193***	0.027	6.941/2*
	(0.051)	(0.048)	
(f) Hispanic → Imprisonment	−0.109	−0.138	1.006/1
	(0.135)	(0.103)	

Path coefficients are unstandardized, and standard errors are in parentheses.

$p < .10$, * $p < 0.05$, ** $p < 0.01$, and *** $p < 0.001$.

short, compared to white female drug offenders, African American females convicted of drug offenses had a lower likelihood of incarceration (direct effect), but they also had a lower likelihood of receiving a substantial assistance departure, which resulted in a higher likelihood of imprisonment (indirect effect). These results were masked by our pooled-data analyses in the previous section.

The results of the two-group comparisons for Hispanic female offenders, which are presented in rows of (d), (e), and (f) of Table 9.4, also reveal interesting moderation effects across crime type. First, and most notably, the indirect effect of ethnicity through receipt of a substantial assistance departure varied significantly by conviction charge (x^2 difference = 6.941, p = 0.031). These results indicate that the positive indirect effect of ethnicity on imprisonment through a substantial assistance departure in the pooled model (Table 9.2 and Figure 9.1) was largely due to the effect of ethnicity among drug offenders. Second, the indirect effect of ethnicity on imprisonment through presentence detention also varied by type of conviction charge (at a p-value of .10, x^2 difference = 4.994, and p = 0.081). Among offenders convicted of drug offenses, Hispanic females were substantially more likely than white females to be detained prior to sentencing and, as a result, had a greater likelihood of being incarcerated. This pattern was observed to a lesser degree for the sample of non-drug offenders. Taken together, these findings indicate that the indirect effects we observed for the pooled-sample were confined to drug offenders.

The Moderating Effect of a Drug Offense in the Sentence Length Decision

The results for the multi-group analyses of sentence length are summarized in Table 9.5. Our baseline model reveals a good fit to the data (x^2 = 3.239, d/f = 2, p = 0.1980, RMSEA = 0.011, CFI = 0.999). The results presented in Table 9.5 are

Table 9.5 Two-Group Comparisons for the Sentence Length Decision

Paths	*Drug*	*Non-Drug*	X^2 *Difference*/d.f.
(a) AA → Detention → Length	−0.016	−0.076**	21.276/2***
	(0.016)	(0.027)	
(b) AA → SA Departure → Length	0.088**	−0.040	9.383/2**
	(0.032)	(0.031)	
(c) AA → Length	−0.060	0.050	1.576/1
	(0.046)	(0.073)	
(d) Hispanic → Detention → Length	0.066***	0.079	20.937/2***
	(0.014)	(0.041)	
(e) Hispanic → SA Departure → Length	−0.136***	−0.024	11.598/2**
	(0.034)	(0.036)	
(f) Hispanic → Length	−0.118	0.068	1.609/1
	(0.096)	(0.111)	

Path coefficients are unstandardized, and standard errors are in parentheses.

$p < 0.1$, * $p < 0.05$, ** $p < 0.01$, and *** $p < 0.001$.

largely congruent with the results reported in Table 9.4 and indicate that indirect effects for race and ethnicity are found primarily among drug offenders.

Turning first to the results for African American female offenders, the data presented in Table 9.5 reveal that the direct and indirect effects of race on sentence length varied somewhat by the type of conviction charge. African American females convicted of drug offenses received more severe sentences than white females because they were less likely to be granted substantial assistance departures (x^2 difference: 9.383, $p = 0.009$). This pattern was masked in our analyses of the pooled data. Table 9.5 further shows that, among non-drug offenders, however, African American females received shorter sentences as a result of a decreased likelihood of presentence detention.

The results for Hispanic female offenders, shown in rows (d), (e), and (f) of Table 9.5, also reveal an interaction between ethnicity and type of crime: the indirect effects of ethnicity on sentence length were confined to drug offenses (for pretrial detention, x^2 difference: 20.937, $p = 0.000$; for substantial assistance departure, x^2 difference: 11.598, $p = 0.003$). Among offenders convicted of drug offenses, Hispanic females were more likely than white females to be detained prior to sentencing and were less likely than white females to receive a substantial assistance departure. Consequently, Hispanic female drug offenders received longer prison sentences than their white counterparts. However, these relationships were not observed among non-drug offenders. In line with our findings of the imprisonment decision, all of the disadvantages we observed in our pooled-sample analysis can be attributed to the effects resulting from the drug offender sample.

Summary and Discussion of Findings

The purpose of this study was to move beyond an examination of the direct effects of race and ethnicity on sentencing outcomes for female offenders adjudicated in federal district courts and, in so doing, to identify more precisely the mechanisms by which race and ethnicity may influence sentencing decisions. Our objective was, first, to determine whether the effect of an offender's race or ethnicity was mediated by the offender's presentence status or by the receipt of a substantial assistance departure and, second, to ascertain whether the direct and indirect effects of race and ethnicity on sentence severity differed for drug offenders and non-drug offenders. Table 9.6 provides a summary of our findings.

As shown in Table 9.6, we found mixed support for our hypotheses. Inconsistent with Hypothesis 1, race and ethnicity did not directly affect sentence length; the prison sentences imposed on African American and Hispanic female offenders did not differ from those imposed on white female offenders. In addition, there were no differences in the odds of imprisonment for African American offenders and white females. By contrast, the offender's ethnicity had a negative effect on the likelihood of incarceration, but, inconsistent with critical race feminism, Hispanic females were *less likely* than similarly situated white females to be sentenced to prison.

Support for Hypotheses 2 and 3 regarding the indirect effects of race and ethnicity was found only among Hispanic offenders. Hispanic female offenders were less likely than white female offenders to be released prior to sentencing and to receive a downward departure for providing substantial assistance; as a consequence, they had higher odds of incarceration and received longer prison sentences than white female offenders. With regard to the effects of offender race, we found no indirect effects in the expected direction for the pooled sample of cases. The offender's race did not indirectly affect the likelihood of incarceration through its effect on substantial assistance departures and exerted an indirect effect on the odds of incarceration through presentence detention that was contrary to our expectations (African American females received shorter sentences than white females as a result of a lower odds of pretrial detention).

Our conclusions, however, differed when we considered the moderating effect of the type of conviction charge. Our offense-specific analyses revealed that most of

Table 9.6 Summary of Support for Each Hypothesis

Hypotheses	*Likelihood of Incarceration*		*Length of Prison Sentence*	
	African American	*Hispanic*	*African American*	*Hispanic*
Race/ethnicity will have a direct effect on sentence severity (H-1).	No	Yes	No	No
Minority offenders will be less likely to be released before sentencing and will, consequently, receive more severe sentences (H-2).	No	Yes	No	Yes
Minority offenders will be less likely to receive an SA departure and will, consequently, receive longer prison terms (H-3).	No	Yes	No	Yes
Being convicted for a drug offense moderates the effects of race/ethnicity on sentence severity (H-4).	Yes	Yes	Yes	Yes

the indirect effects of the offender's race and ethnicity on both sentence outcomes were largely confined to drug offenders. When we examined the moderating effect of offense type, we found that African American females convicted of drug offenses (but not non-drug offenses) were less likely to receive substantial assistance departures than white females and were, consequently, given lengthier prison terms than white female drug offenders. In addition, the adverse indirect effects that resulted from presentence detention and receipt of a substantial assistance departure for Hispanic females were confined to drug offenders.

Several of our findings merit further comment. Our results highlight the importance of testing for indirect as well as direct effects. When we analyzed the full sample (i.e., all cases pooled together), we found that only ethnicity had a direct (and negative) effect on the likelihood of imprisonment and that neither race nor ethnicity had a direct effect on sentence length. Further analysis revealed that ethnicity (and to a lesser extent, race) influenced the two sentencing outcomes through their effects on earlier case processing decisions. Contrary to our expectations, we found that African American females were less likely to be incarcerated than white females because they were less likely to be detained prior to the sentencing hearing. But, consistent with our predictions, Hispanic females had a higher odds of incarceration and received longer sentences than white females due to the fact that they were more likely than white females to be held in custody prior to the sentencing hearing and because they were less likely than white females to receive substantial assistance departures (see Schlesinger, 2005, for similar findings). A Hispanic female's increased likelihood of pretrial detention also served to decrease her chances of receiving a substantial assistance departure, which served to lengthen her prison sentence. Traditional statistical approaches that focus only on direct effects could not have teased out these more subtle effects of race and ethnicity.

Our results also underscore the importance of separately analyzing outcomes for drug offenders and non-drug offenders adjudicated in federal district courts. Doing so revealed that the direct effects of race and ethnicity were masked in the analyses of the overall sample and that the indirect effects found for the pooled sample were in fact operating in ways that worked to the disadvantage of Hispanic drug offenders in particular. With respect to the indirect effects of race and consistent with our predictions, we found that race affected both the imprisonment and sentence length decisions via substantial assistance departures among drug offenders but not among non-drug offenders. That is, compared to white female drug offenders, African American drug offenders were less likely to receive such departures, which increased their likelihood of imprisonment and also resulted in longer prison sentences. We found a similar pattern of results for both sentencing outcomes when the indirect effects of ethnicity were examined; the indirect effects of ethnicity on sentence severity via presentence detention and receipt of a substantial assistance departure were confined to drug offenders. Overall, our moderated mediation analyses allowed us to tease out important sources of disparity and showed that the disparate outcomes for Hispanic females largely resulted from disparate treatment of Hispanic drug offenders.

The finding that ethnicity had a negative direct effect on the odds of imprisonment when the pooled sample of cases was analyzed and that race had a negative direct effect on the likelihood of imprisonment among drug offenders is somewhat puzzling. Consistent with critical race feminism and the focal concerns perspective, which posits that judges' attributions of dangerousness, reform potential, and culpability are linked in predictable ways to race and ethnicity, we expected that offender race and ethnicity would result in harsher sentences. The fact that we found the opposite suggests that race and ethnicity may affect judges' attributions of dangerous and threat in different ways for female offenders and/or that judges' concerns about the practical constraints, or social costs, of sentencing may work to the advantage of some types of minority female offenders. Although we can only speculate, the shorter sentences stemming from the direct effects of race and ethnicity for African American and Hispanic female offenders might reflect the fact that these offenders played more minimal roles than white females in the offenses for which they were convicted or were more likely than white females to have been involved in the offense as a result of a relationship with a male relative or an intimate partner. If this were the case, judges might view African American and Hispanic female offenders as less blameworthy and threatening than white females. Alternatively, the shorter sentences meted out to minority female offenders in some circumstances might reflect the fact that these offenders were more likely than white females to be the sole caretakers of young children. Although we controlled for whether the offender had dependent children, we could not control for whether the offender was the sole caretaker of her child/children. These explanations also might help explain our rather counter-intuitive finding that African American females convicted of non-drug offenses had a lower likelihood of incarceration and received shorter sentences than white females as a result of their lower likelihood of presentence detention. These issues clearly merit further research.

Our finding that Hispanic female drug offenders were sentenced more harshly than white female offenders as a result of their higher odds of presentence detention and lower probability of receiving a substantial assistance departure also merits further comment. The fact that Hispanic female offenders were more likely than white female offenders to be in custody prior to the sentencing hearing is not due to an immigration/deportation dynamic, as we excluded immigration cases and controlled for the offender's citizenship status. Rather, this finding may reflect the possibility that judges, in deciding whether an offender should be detained or released, take the offender's "stakes in conformity" into account. In fact, under the Bail Reform Act of 1984, federal judges are allowed to detain a defendant as a means of insuring the safety of the community and the appearance of the defendant in court. Section 3142(g) specifies the factors that judges must take into consideration in making decisions regarding pretrial release or detention; included in the list of factors is the "history and characteristics of the defendant" (18 U.S.C.§ 3142(a)(3)(A) (2006)) (U.S. Government Publishing Office, n.d.). Our results suggest that judges' assessments of the "history and characteristics of the defendant" may lead them to conclude that Hispanic female drug offenders pose a greater risk than do white female drug offenders which would warrant their detention. The fact that Hispanic female drug offenders had a lower likelihood than white female drug offenders of receiving substantial assistance departures also is interesting. Hispanic females' lower odds of receiving such a departure could reflect prosecutors' unwillingness to offer these departures to Hispanic females and/or the inability or reluctance of Hispanic females to provide evidence against intimate partners, family members, or friends.

Although this study provided insight into the direct and indirect effects of race and ethnicity on sentence severity for female offenders and whether these effects were conditioned by the type of offense committed, some limitations should be noted. We did not investigate whether there were inter-district variations in the effects of our variables of interest. Prior research has shown that sentencing outcomes vary by the district in which the case was adjudicated and we suspect that the direct and indirect effects of race and ethnicity for female offenders might similarly vary. We therefore recommend that future researchers attempt to model inter-district variation in the direct and indirect effects of race and ethnicity using multi-level path analysis (Bauer, Preacher, and Gil, 2006).

The results of our study on the sentences imposed on African American, Hispanic, and white female offenders convicted of drug and non-drug offenses in federal district courts illustrate the complexities inherent in attempting to specify the roles that race and ethnicity play in the sentencing process. Our results reiterate that merely asking whether race and ethnicity matter at sentencing is theoretically and methodologically unsophisticated; it is overly simplistic to assume that racial minorities will receive harsher sentences than whites regardless of crime type or the types of outcomes rendered at earlier stages of case processing. As the results of our study reveal, the more interesting question is "*When* does race/ethnicity matter?"

Notes

1 In line with these arguments, studies of the influence of race on media portrayals of female offenders provide further support for the expectation that white women will receive more favorable treatment by the criminal justice system. An overarching conclusion derived from these studies is that white women are more likely than minority women to have their criminal behavior excused in some way by the media, which deems them worthy of a "mad" or "sad" label instead of a "bad" label (Brennan and Vandenberg, 2009; Bond-Maupin, 1998; Farr, 1997; Huckerby, 2003).

2 These results are, however, somewhat at odds with those of Kempf-Leonard and Sample (2001), who found that non-white female drug offenders were as likely as white female drug offenders to be granted guidelines departures.

3 A potentially important issue could be the possibility of a sample selection bias, since female offenders who were sentenced to prison were not randomly selected (Heckman, 1976). To account for this problem, we calculated the inverse Mills ratio (Bushway, Johnson, and Slocum, 2007) and attempted to include the correction term in the model as one of the exogenous variables. But the lamda term was highly correlated with the presumptive sentence ($r = -0.89$), thus creating a multi-collinearity problem. For that reason, we present the results from the non-corrected model.

4 Our decision to use only an SA departure as an intermediate variable warrants a brief explanation. We reason that an SA departure constitutes an important earlier case processing variable

because prosecutors have sole discretion to file a motion for an SA departure and judges have limited control over who gets an SA departure (even though it is finally granted by judges). In contrast, we argue that a judicial departure is a simultaneous part of the sentencing decision and is therefore not an earlier case processing variable. Along the same line, it is important to note that we did not attempt to control for departure status in the model. By not controlling for departures, the effect of race/ethnicity captures any disparity of race/ethnicity occurring at the final sentencing decision both within the guidelines range and outside the guidelines ranges (Starr and Rehavi, 2012).

5 Maximum likelihood (ML) estimation is most commonly used in a path analytic approach. ML estimation assumes that the variables are normally distributed. However, the binary nature of our mediating variables did not lend themselves to a ML approach. Oftentimes WLS (weighted least squares) has been relied upon as an alternative approach (see Albonetti, 1998b). However, Muthén, DuToit, and Spisic (1997) reported that WLS was found to be inferior to WLSMV (weighted least squares with robust standard errors and mean- and variance-adjusted chi-square) estimation. With regard to the use of the theta parameterization, M-plus provides two kinds of tests for the significance of indirect effects: the delta and the theta tests. Theta parameterization must be selected when categorical endogenous variables are employed (Muthén and Muthén, 1998–2011).

6 We use the cluster robust standard error approach rather than estimating a multi-level path model, as the focus of our study is not on modeling between-district variation in the mediating and outcome variables. In addition, it should be also noted that M-plus currently does not allow one to use 88 fixed effects dummies for each district to take into account the clustering issue.

7 It is important to note that the magnitude of the total effect (−0.097) does not exactly correspond to the indirect effect we reported earlier (−0.077). A careful reading of Figure 9.1 would reveal that there is another path, which we did not consider as one of our hypotheses (African Americans → Detention → SA departure → Imprisonment). However, when calculating the total effect, we considered both of these indirect effects. Thus, the overall effect is larger than that shown by Figure 9.1.

8 The calculation of an indirect effect is not straightforward conceptually since one of the regression coefficients is a probit coefficient and the other one is a regular OLS coefficient. However, M-plus treats the ordinal variable as a latent continuous response variable in this case and provides the indirect effect by multiplying two coefficients (Muthén and Muthén, 1998–2011).

9 The insignificant indirect race effect warrants a brief explanation; the results from the trimmed model suggest that once we fixed some of covariates at zero in pretrial detention model, the effect of African American on presentence detention, which was significant at the p value of 0.037, became statistically non-significant ($p = 0.059$), and thus, the indirect effect was also rendered insignificant (indirect effect $= -0.029, p = 0.061$).

References

Albonetti, C. A. (1991). An integration of theories to explain judicial discretion. *Social Problems, 38*, 247–266.

Albonetti, C. A. (1997). Sentencing under the federal sentencing guidelines: Effects of defendant characteristics, guilty pleas, and departures on sentence outcomes for drug offenses, 1991–1992. *Law & Society Review, 31*, 789–822.

Albonetti, C. A. (1998a). The role of gender and departures in the sentencing of defendants convicted of a white collar offense under the federal sentencing guidelines. In J. T. Ulmer (Ed.), *Sociology of crime, law, and deviance* (pp. 3–48). Greenwich, Connecticut: JAI Press.

Albonetti, C. A. (1998b). Direct and indirect effects of case complexity, guilty pleas, and offender characteristics on sentencing for offenders convicted of a white-collar offense prior to sentencing guidelines. *Journal of Quantitative Criminology, 14*, 353–379.

Albonetti, C. A. (1999). The avoidance of punishment: A legal—bureaucratic model of suspended sentences in federal white-collar cases prior to the federal sentencing guidelines. *Social Forces*, *78*, 303–329.

Albonetti, C. A. (2002). The effects of the "safety valve" amendment on length of imprisonment for cocaine trafficking/manufacturing offenders: Mitigating the effects of mandatory minimum penalties and offender's ethnicity. *Iowa Law Review*, *87*, 401–433.

Albonetti, C. A., Hauser, R. M., Hagan, J., & Nagel, I. H. (1989). Criminal justice decision making as a stratification process: The role of race and stratification resources in pretrial release. *Journal of Quantitative Criminology*, *5*, 57–82.

American Civil Liberties Union (2004). *Sanctioned bias: Racial profiling since 9/11*. New York: Author. Retrieved March 7, 2016, from www.aclu.org/sites/default/files/FilesPDFs/racial%20profiling%20report.pdf

Bauer, D. J., Preacher, K. J., & Gil, K. M. (2006). Conceptualizing and testing random indirect effects and moderated mediation in multilevel models: New procedures and recommendations. *Psychological Methods*, *11*, 142–163.

Baumer, E. P. (2013). Reassessing and redirecting research on race and sentencing. *Justice Quarterly*, *30*, 231–261.

Beckett, K., Nyrop, K., Pfingst, L., & Bowen, M. (2005). Drug use, drug possession arrests, and the question of race: Lessons from Seattle. *Social Problems*, *52*, 419–444.

Belknap, J. (2014). *Invisible women: Gender, crime, and justice* (4th ed.). Stamford, CT: Cengage Learning.

Bernstein, I. N., Kick, E., Leung, J. T., & Schultz, B. (1977). Charge reduction: An intermediate stage in the process of labeling criminal defendants. *Social Forces*, *56*, 362–384.

Bickle, G., & Peterson, R. (1991). The impact of gender-based family roles in criminal sentencing. *Social Problems*, *38*, 372–394.

Blumstein, A., Cohen, J., Martin, S. E., & Tonry, M. H. (1983). *Research on sentencing: The search for reform* (Vol. 1). Washington, DC: National Academy Press.

Bollen, K. A. (1989). *Structural equations with latent variables*. New York: Wiley.

Bond-Maupin, L. (1998). That wasn't even me they showed: Women as criminals on America's Most Wanted. *Violence Against Women*, *4*, 30–44.

Brennan, P. K. (2002). *Women sentenced to jail in New York City*. New York: LFB Scholarly Publishing.

Brennan, P. K. (2006). Sentencing female misdemeanants: An examination of the direct and indirect effects of race/ethnicity. *Justice Quarterly*, *23*, 60–95.

Brennan, P. K. (2009). The joint effects of offender race/ethnicity and sex on sentencing outcomes. In M. D. Krohn, A. J. Lizotte, & G. P. Hall (Eds.), *Handbook of crime and deviance* (pp. 319–347). New York: Springer Science and Business Media.

Brennan, P. K., & Spohn, C. (2008). Race/ethnicity and sentencing outcomes among drug offenders In North Carolina. *Journal of Contemporary Criminal Justice*, *24*, 371–398.

Brennan, P. K., & Spohn, C. (2009). The joint effects of offender race/ethnicity and sex on sentence length decisions in federal courts. *Race and Social Problems*, *1*, 200–217.

Brennan, P. K., & Vandenberg, A. L. (2009). Depictions of female offenders in front-page newspaper stories: The importance of race/ethnicity. *International Journal of Social Inquiry*, *2*, 141–175.

Bushway, S. D. (2013). Special issue on sentencing research introduction. *Justice Quarterly*, *30*, 195–198.

Bushway, S. D., & Forst, B. (2013). Studying discretion in the processes that generate criminal justice sanctions. *Justice Quarterly*, *30*, 199–222.

Bushway, S., Johnson, B. D., & Slocum, L. A. (2007). Is the magic still there? The use of the Heckman two-step correction for selection bias in criminology. *Journal of Quantitative Criminology*, *23*, 151–178.

Carson, A. E. (2014). *Prisoners in 2013*. Washington, DC: U.S. Department of Justice, Bureau of Justice Statistics.

Castro, D. O. (1998). "Hot blood and easy virtue": Mass media and the making of racist Latino/a stereotypes. In C. R. Mann & M. S. Zatz (Eds.), *Images of color, images of crime* (pp. 134–144). Los Angeles, CA: Roxbury Publishing Company.

Chesney-Lind, M. (1995). Rethinking women's imprisonment. In B. R. Price & N. J. Sokoloff (Eds.), *The criminal justice system and women: Offenders, victims, and workers* (2nd ed., pp. 105–117). New York: McGraw-Hill.

Chesney-Lind, M., & Morash, M. (2011). *Feminist theories of crime*. Surrey: Ashgate Publishing Limited.

Chiricos, T. G., & Bales, W. D. (1991). Unemployment and punishment: An empirical assessment. *Criminology, 29*, 701–724.

Crawford, C. (2000). Gender, race, and habitual offender sentencing in Florida. *Criminology, 38*, 263–280.

Crew, K. B. (1991). Sex differences in criminal sentencing: Chivalry or patriarchy? *Justice Quarterly, 8*, 59–84.

Daly, K., & Bordt, R. (1995). Sex effects and sentencing: An analysis of the statistical literature. *Justice Quarterly, 12*, 141–175.

Daly, K., & Tonry, M. (1997). Gender, race, and sentencing. In M. Tonry (Ed.), *Crime and justice: A review of research* (pp. 201–252). Chicago: University of Chicago Press.

Demuth, S. (2003). Racial and ethnic differences in pretrial release decisions and outcomes: A comparison of Hispanic, black, and white felony arrestees. *Criminology, 41*, 873–907.

Demuth, S., & Steffensmeier, D. (2004). Ethnicity effects on sentence outcomes in large urban courts: Comparisons among white, black, and Hispanic defendants. *Social Science Quarterly, 85*, 994–1011.

Doerner, J. K., & Demuth, S. (2014). Gender and sentencing in the federal courts: Are women treated more leniently? *Criminal Justice Policy Review, 25*, 242–269.

Edwards, J. R., & Lambert, L. S. (2007). Methods for integrating moderation and mediation: A general analytical framework using moderated path analysis. *Psychological Methods, 12*, 1–22.

Engen, R. L., Gainey, R. R., Crutchfield, R. D., & Weis, J. G. (2003). Discretion and disparity under sentencing guidelines: The role of departures and structured alternatives. *Criminology, 41*, 99–130.

Everett, R. S., & Wojtkiewicz, R. A. (2002). Difference, disparity, and race/ethnic bias in federal sentencing. *Journal of Quantitative Criminology, 18*, 189–211.

Farnworth, M., & Teske, R. H. (1995). Gender differences in felony court processing: Three hypotheses of disparity. *Women & Criminal Justice, 6*, 23–44.

Farr, K. A. (1997). Aggravating and differentiating factors in the cases of white and minority women on death row. *Crime & Delinquency, 43*, 260–278.

Farr, K. A. (2000). Defeminizing and dehumanizing female murderers: Depictions of lesbians on death row. *Women & Criminal Justice, 11*, 49–66.

Frase, R. S. (2013). *Just sentencing: Principles and procedures for a workable system*. New York: Oxford University Press.

Griffin, T., & Wooldredge, J. (2006). Sex-based disparities in felony dispositions before versus after sentencing reform in Ohio. *Criminology, 44*, 893–924.

Hartley, R. D., Maddan, S., & Spohn, C. (2007). Prosecutorial discretion: An examination of substantial assistance departures in federal crack-cocaine and powder-cocaine cases. Justice Quarterly, 24, 382–407.

Healey, J. F. (1997). *Race, ethnicity, and gender in the United States: Inequality, group conflict, and power*. Thousand Oaks, CA: Pine Forge Press.

Heckman, J. (1976). The common structure of statistical models of truncation, sample selection and limited dependent variables and a simple estimator for such models. *Annals of Economic and Social Measurement, 5*, 475–492.

Holmes, M. D., Hosch, H. M., Daudistel, H. C., Perez, D. A., & Graves, J. B. (1996). Ethnicity, legal resources, and felony dispositions in two Southwestern jurisdictions. *Justice Quarterly, 13*, 11–30.

Huckerby, J. (2003). Women who kill their children: Case study and conclusions concerning the differences in the fall from maternal grace by Khoua and Andrea Yates. *Duke Journal of Gender Law & Policy, 10*, 149–172.

Human Rights Watch. (2008). *Targeting blacks: Drug law enforcement and race in the United States*. New York: Author.

Hurwitz, J., & Peffley, M. (1997). Public perceptions of race and crime: The role of racial stereotypes. *American Journal of Political Science, 41*, 375–401.

Irwin, K., & Chesney-Lind, M. (2008). Girls' violence: Beyond dangerous masculinity. *Sociology Compass, 2/3*, 837–855.

Johnson, B. D., Ulmer, J. T., & Kramer, J. H. (2008). The social context of guidelines circumvention: The case of federal district courts. *Criminology, 46*, 737–784.

Kautt, P. M., & Spohn, C. (2002). Cracking down on black drug offenders? Testing for interactions between offender race, drug type, and sentencing strategy in federal drug sentences. *Justice Quarterly, 19*, 1–36.

Kempf-Leonard, K., & Sample, L. (2001). Have federal sentencing guidelines reduced severity? *Journal of Quantitative Criminology, 17*, 111–144.

Kim, B., Spohn, C., & Hedberg, E. C. (2015). Federal sentencing as a complex collaborative process: Judges, prosecutors, and judge-prosecutor dyads and disparity in sentencing. *Criminology, 53*, 597–623.

Klein, D. (1995). The etiology of female crime: A review of the literature. In B. R. Price & N. J. Sokoloff (Eds.), *The criminal justice system and women: Offenders, victims, and workers* (pp. 30–53). New York: McGraw-Hill.

Koons-Witt, B. (2002). The effect of gender on the decision to incarcerate before and after the introduction of sentencing guidelines. *Criminology, 40*, 297–328.

Kruttschnitt, C. (1980–1981). Social statuses and the sentences of female offenders. *Law & Society Review, 15*, 247–265.

Kruttschnitt, C. (1982). Women, crime, and dependency: An application of the theory of law. *Criminology, 19*, 495–513.

Kruttschnitt, C. (1984). Sex and criminal court dispositions: The unresolved controversy. *Journal of Research in Crime and Delinquency, 21*, 213–232.

Kutateladze, Besiki L., Nancy R. Andiloro, Brian D. Johnson, & Cassia C. Spohn (2014). Cumulative Disadvantage: Examining Racial and Ethnic Disparity in Prosecution and Sentencing. *Criminology, 52*, 514–551.

Landrine, H. (1985). Race x class stereotypes of women. *Sex Roles, 13*, 65–75.

Lizotte, A. J. (1978). Extra-legal factors in Chicago's criminal courts: Testing the conflict model of criminal justice. *Social Problems, 25*, 564–580.

MacKinnon, D. P. (2008). *Introduction to statistical mediation analysis*. Mahwah, NJ: Erlbaum.

Madriz, E. (1997). Images of criminals and victims: A study on women's fear and social control. *Gender & Society, 11*, 342–356.

Mauer, M., & King, R. S. (2007). *Uneven justice: State rates of incarceration by race and ethnicity*. Washington, DC: The Sentencing Project.

Maxfield, L. D., & Kramer, J. H. (1998). *Substantial assistance: An empirical yardstick gauging equity in current federal sentencing practice*. Washington, DC: U.S. Sentencing Commission.

Mitchell, O. (2005). A meta-analysis of race and sentencing research: Explaining the inconsistencies. *Journal of Quantitative Criminology, 21*, 439–466.

Muthén, B. O., DuToit, S. H. C., & Spisic, D. (1997). Robust inference using weighted least squares and quadratic estimating equations in latent variable modeling with categorical and continuous outcomes. Unpublished technical report.

Muthén, L. K., & Muthén, B. O. (1998–2011). *Mplus user's guide* (6th ed.). Los Angeles, CA: Authors.

Nagel, I. H., & Schulhofer, S. J. (1992). A tale of three cities: An empirical study of charging and bargaining practices under the federal sentencing guidelines. *Southern California Law Review, 66*, 501–566.

Portillos, E. L. (1998). Latinos and Latinas: Latinos, gangs, and drugs. In C. R. Mann & M. S. Zatz (Eds.), *Images of color, images of crime* (pp. 156–165). Los Angeles, CA: Roxbury.

Potter, H. (2006). An argument for black feminist criminology. *Feminist Criminology, 1*, 106–124.

Rafter, N. H. (1990). *Partial justice: Women, prisons, and social control.* New Brunswick, NJ: Transaction Publishers.

Schlesinger, T. (2005). Racial and ethnic disparities in pretrial criminal processing. *Justice Quarterly, 22*, 170–192.

Shermer, L. O., & Johnson, B. D. (2010). Criminal prosecutions: Examining prosecutorial discretion and charge reductions in US federal district courts. *Justice Quarterly, 27*, 394–430.

Sorensen, J., & Wallace, D. H. (1999). Prosecutorial discretion in seeking death: An analysis of racial disparity in the pretrial stages of case processing in a Midwestern county. *Justice Quarterly, 16*, 559–578.

Spohn, C. (2000). Thirty years of sentencing reform: The quest for a racially neutral sentencing process. In J. Horney (Ed.), *Policies, processes, and decisions of the criminal justice system: Volume 3* (pp. 427–501). Washington, DC: National Institute of Justice.

Spohn, C. (2009). Race, sex and pretrial detention in Federal Court: Indirect effects and cumulative disadvantage. *Kansas Law Review, 57*, 879–902.

Spohn, C., & Beichner, D. (2000). Is preferential treatment of female offenders a thing of the past? A multi-site study of gender, race, and imprisonment. *Criminal Justice Policy Review, 11*, 149–184.

Spohn, C., & Brennan, P. K. (2011). The joint effects of offender race/ethnicity and gender on substantial assistance departures in federal courts. *Race and Justice, 1*, 49–78.

Spohn, C., & Brennan, P. K. (2013). Sentencing and punishment. In C. M. Renzetti, S. L. Miller, & A. R. Gover (Eds.), *Routledge international handbook of crime and gender studies* (pp. 213–230). New York: Routledge.

Spohn, C., & DeLone, M. (2000). When does race matter? An analysis of the conditions under which race affects sentence severity. *Sociology of Crime, Law, and Deviance, 2*, 3–37.

Spohn, C., Gruhl, J., & Welch, S. (1981–82). The effect of race on sentencing: A re-examination of an unsettled question. *Law and Society Review, 16*, 71–88.

Spohn, C., & Holleran, D. (2000). The imprisonment penalty paid by young, unemployed Black and Hispanic male offenders. *Criminology, 38*, 281–306.

Spohn, C., & Holleran, D. (2001). Prosecuting sexual assault: A comparison of charging decisions in sexual assault cases involving strangers, acquaintances, and intimate partners. *Justice Quarterly, 18*, 651–688.

Spohn, C., & Spears, J. W. (1997). Gender and case processing decisions: A comparison of case outcomes for male and female defendants charged with violent felonies. *Women &Criminal Justice, 8*, 29–59.

Stacey, A. M., & Spohn, C. (2006). Gender and the social costs of sentencing: An analysis of sentences imposed on male and female offenders in three U.S. district courts. *Berkeley Journal of Criminal Law, 11*, 43–76.

Starr, S. B., & Rehavi, M. M. (2012). Racial disparity in the criminal justice process: Prosecutors, judges, and the effects of United States v. Booker. *University of Michigan Law & Economic Research Paper Series, Paper No. 12–021.* University of Michigan School of Law, Ann Arbor, MI.

Steen, S., Engen, R. L., & Gainey, R. R. (2005). Images of danger and culpability: Racial stereotypes, case processing, and criminal sentencing. *Criminology, 43*, 435–468.

Steffensmeier, D., & Demuth, S. (2000). Ethnicity and sentencing outcomes in U.S. Federal Courts: Who is punished more harshly?' *American Sociological Review, 65*, 705–29.

Steffensmeier, D., & Demuth, S. (2006). Does gender modify the effects of race-ethnicity on criminal sanctioning? Sentences for male and female white, Black, and Hispanic defendants. *Journal of Quantitative Criminology, 22*, 241–261.

Steffensmeier, D., Kramer, J. H., & Streifel, C. (1993). Gender and imprisonment decisions. *Criminology, 31*, 411–446.

Steffensmeier, D., Ulmer, J. T., & Kramer, J. H. (1998). The interaction of race, gender, and age in criminal sentencing: The punishment cost of being young, black, and male. *Criminology, 36*, 763–798.

Tonry, M. (1995). *Malign neglect: Race, crime, and punishment in America.* New York: Oxford University Press.

Ulmer, J. T. (2012). Recent developments and new directions in sentencing research. *Justice Quarterly, 29,* 1–40.

Ulmer, J. T., & Johnson, B. D. (2004). Sentencing in context: A multilevel analysis. *Criminology, 42,* 137–177.

Ulmer, J. T., Light, M. T., & Kramer, J. H. (2011). The liberation of federal judges' discretion in the wake of the Booker/Fanfan decision: Is there increased disparity and divergence between courts? *Justice Quarterly, 28,* 799–837.

United States Government Publishing Office (n.d.). *United States code, 2006 edition, supplement 5, title 18—crimes and criminal procedure.* Washington, DC: Author. Retrieved October 30, 2016, from www.gpo.gov/fdsys/pkg/USCODE-2011-title18/pdf/USCODE-2011-title18-partII-chap207-sec3142.pdf

United States Sentencing Commission (2010). *Demographic differences in federal sentencing practices: An update of the Booker report's multivariate regression analysis.* Washington, DC: Author.

Young, V. (1986). Gender expectations and their impact on black female offenders and victims. *Justice Quarterly, 3,* 305–327.

Zatz, M. S. (1987). The changing forms of racial/ethnic biases in sentencing. *Journal of Research in Crime and Delinquency, 24,* 69–92.

Zatz, M. S. (2000). The convergence of race, ethnicity, gender, and class on court decision —making: Looking toward the 21st century. In J. Horney (Ed.), *Policies, processes, and decisions of the criminal justice system: Vol. 3* (pp. 503–552). Washington, DC: National Institute of Justice.

10

STUDYING ETHNIC DISPARITIES IN SENTENCING

The Importance of Refining Ethnic Minority Measures

Hilde Wermink, Sigrid van Wingerden, Johan van Wilsem, and Paul Nieuwbeerta

An important question in sociology and criminology is whether sources of inequality occur in criminal punishment. Shared notions of equal justice and the promise of equal punishments for equal cases are underlying the majority of Western sentencing contexts. Punishments that vary systematically with individually ascribed characteristics, such as race and ethnicity raise fundamental questions about fairness and equity in the criminal justice system. In the sentencing research tradition, perhaps the most attention has been devoted to the study of racial and ethnic disparities. Traditionally, different punishment outcomes are theorized to be the result of judges relying on stereotypical attributions associated with race and ethnicity (Albonetti, 1991; Steffensmeier, Ulmer, and Kramer, 1998). Much of the literature, though, is restricted to black and white differences in the United States and, to a lesser extent, to black/white/Hispanic comparisons (Johnson and Betsinger, 2009). Other minority groups remain largely overlooked and research in other Western countries is scarce (Lee, Ulmer, and Park, 2011; Ulmer, 2012).

Similar to classic immigration countries such as the U.S., Australia, and Canada, countries in Western Europe have experienced a marked influx of immigrants over the past decades. Moreover, distinct minority groups are overrepresented in prison statistics in diverse Western countries (Haen Marshall, 1997; Tonry, 1997; Killias, 2011; Delgrande and Aebi, 2009), such as in England (Smith, 1997); France (Pager, 2008); Italy (Colombo, 2013); Germany (Mansel and Albrecht, 2003); Denmark (Holmberg and Kyvsgaard, 2003); Sweden (Martens, 1997); and Finland (Salmi, Kivivuori, and Aaltonen, 2015) as well as in the Netherlands (Blom et al., 2005; Engbersen, Leerkes, and Snel, 2014). This overrepresentation in prison populations may be the result of disproportionate involvement of some ethnic groups in (more serious) criminal offenses, but it may also be a sign of discriminatory treatment by the criminal justice system (Oberwittler and Höfer, 2005). As immigrant groups grow in Europe, constituting a sizable incarceration population, (quantitative) research on the criminal processing of immigrant groups in Europe is timely and needed.

In this chapter, we focus on ethnic disparities among first- and second-generation immigrants. We contribute to the existing literature on racial/ethnic disparity in three ways. First, we assess the generalizability of this well-researched topic in the criminological literature, by looking at ethnic disparities in an underexplored context: the Netherlands. As noted by Ulmer (2012: 31) a "key gap in the literature is that almost all of the research on sentencing is limited to the contemporary North American—particularly the US—context." He argued persuasively that research in more diverse sentencing contexts "would broaden knowledge of sentencing and sentencing disparity as related to larger patterns of social stratification" (Ulmer, 2012: 32). Thus, from a theoretical and empirical perspective, it is important to examine whether patterns observed earlier equally apply to the Dutch context. For instance, it could be that ethnic or racial disparity, which seems to exist in the U.S. context (Mitchell, 2005), is not present in sentencing patterns in the Netherlands to the same degree—because of supposed lower levels of racism. In contrast, high levels of discretionary freedom in the Netherlands may also allow for larger disparities in punishment.

Second, we try to make methodological contributions. Our data include information on personal circumstances and is therefore well suited for the proposed analysis. Including these characteristics is of great importance because ethnicity may be proxying other factors, such as socioeconomic status. Ideally, information about personal circumstances (and legally relevant factors) should be included to disentangle some of the racial/ethnic effects (Zatz, 2000). Studies that fail to do so may find inflated direct effects of race/ethnicity on sentence severity (Wooldredge, 2012). Unfortunately, though, studies that disentangle situational factors, such as socioeconomic factors, from effects of race/ethnicity are typically scarce in the sentencing literature (Ulmer, 2012). Although it is always difficult to control for all relevant factors that explain differences between cases (Pina-Sánchez and Linacre, 2014), our study does provide a relative strong test of possible ethnic disparities in punishment.

Third, we are the first to examine disparities in punishment decisions for first-generation immigrants and second-generation immigrants. Immigration to the U.S. and Western Europe has led to the establishment of ethnic groups who produced an adult second-generation (Alba, 2005). Currently, a sizable number of children of postwar immigrants in Europe and in the U.S. enter Western criminal justice systems, which opens a unique opportunity to study distinct immigrant generations. From a theoretical perspective, this is important because first-generation immigrants and second-generation immigrants differ in their level of social and economic integration (Junger-Tas, 2001; Algan et al., 2010), potentially leading to different punishment outcomes.

In this study, we rely on three distinct data sources that include information on the country of birth of the defendant and/or parents of the defendant and imprisonment decisions. The current study, thereby, specifically addresses the call for additional investigations incorporating more diverse minority groups in other sentencing contexts

(Sampson and Lauritsen, 1997; Ulmer, 2012). The first data source contains information on all defendants convicted in 2007. The second data source contains information on all offenders of whom a sentencing report was available prior to the punishment decision in 2005–2007. The third data source combines nationwide survey data with administrative data to examine punishment outcomes for suspects who entered pretrial detention between October 2010 and March 2011. These three datasets complement each other on the selection of defendants and the depth of information on the characteristics of the offender. The dataset from 2007 contains all defendants, but only includes basic background information on defendants. In contrast, the other two datasets have a more specific offender population—and thus might suffer more from selection effects in prior stages of the criminal proceedings—but have extremely detailed information on offender's personal circumstances.

The Netherlands as Context: Immigrants and Punishment Practices

Punishment Practices

In the Netherlands, as well as in most other Western countries, imprisonment is taken to be the most severe form of punishment. The Netherlands, long known for its humane and liberal penal policies, witnessed a prison growth rate comparable to the U.S.: its prison population grew almost fourfold between 1975 and 2005 (Tonry and Bijleveld, 2007), after which the prison population decreased. Prison sentences in the Netherlands are typically much shorter compared to the U.S. The majority of the defendants in the Netherlands receive a sentence up to 3 months (65%), and only a few receive prison sentence longer than 3 years (4%) (Statistics Netherlands, 2013). In contrast, three quarters of the federal prisoners in the U.S. were sentenced to more than 5 years of imprisonment (United States Sentencing Commission, 2015).

Sentences in the Netherlands are exclusively imposed by professional judges who enjoy broad levels of discretionary power at sentencing: the minimum prison sentence is 1 day for all offenses and maximum sentences are broadly defined by offense type, e.g., 12 years for violent theft. During the trial, the prosecutor requests a specific punishment for the defendant, but the judge is by no means bound to it. For some offenses, the judge can consult orientation points, but these are only available for some frequently occurring offense types and are non-binding.

The relative broad discretionary powers make the Dutch criminal justice system a highly relevant context to study offender-based disparities in sentencing because sentencing practices may be more susceptible to subjective influences. Within the boundaries of the law, offender characteristics can unrestrictedly affect the sentencing decision, and effects of ethnicity are thus not constrained by guidelines. Moreover, because Dutch judges rarely belong to one of the minority groups, subjective influences based on stereotypical attributions regarding "dangerous other" ethnic groups may enter courtroom decision-making.

Immigrant Groups in the Netherlands

Unlike the U.S., the Netherlands never was a country of immigration, until the immigration waves in the late 1960s and early 1970s. In the 1960s, so-called "guest workers," mostly from Turkey and Morocco, immigrated to the Netherlands. Although these guest workers were supposed to stay only temporarily, many of them never remigrated and instead had their families reunified in the Netherlands. Besides guest workers and their families, another prominent category consists of immigrants from the former Dutch colonies in the Caribbean. After the independence of Surinam, nearly 300,000 Surinamese, almost one-third of the Surinamese population, migrated to the Netherlands. A new wave of postcolonial migration began in the late 1980s, when residents of the Netherlands Antilles arrived. Because the Netherlands Antilles are still part of the Kingdom of the Netherlands, Antilleans are Dutch nationals (Engbersen, Leerkes, and Snel, 2014). In the 1990s asylum seekers from countries like former Yugoslavia, former Soviet Union, and Iraq, came to the Netherlands, and during recent years, the open borders of the EU brought new immigrant groups from East European countries like Poland and Bulgaria, but these groups are still quite small (Van Tubergen, 2013). Recently a new migration wave is occurring related to refugees, from Syria for example.

Over the last 25 years, the attitude towards migrant groups has changed dramatically. Although the Netherlands used to have a reputation as a tolerant and multicultural country in which migrant groups were supposed to integrate "while maintaining the migrants 'culture,'" Dutch multiculturalism was in fact not so much a choice for "equal recognition" but a pragmatic pacification strategy instead (De Zwart, 2011). In the 1970s and 1980s, persisting inequalities between ethnic groups gave rise to new policy based on affirmative action, with preferential treatment for migrant groups to improve their level of education, employment, and social integration. From the 1990s on, however, integration policy was gradually linked to social problems of public order and crime, leading to widespread support for anti-immigrant politicians who pointed out the "multicultural drama." That caused the policy that emphasized preservation of the cultural identity of the minority groups to be replaced by a policy emphasizing assimilation and active citizenship (Engbersen, Leerkes, and Snel, 2014). Even though the Netherlands was once seen as the most tolerant of the West European countries, there is now a harsher climate regarding migrants.

Nowadays, over 20 percent of the Dutch population is non-native. The immigrant population consists of an almost identical number of first-generation immigrants who are born abroad and second-generation immigrants who are born in the Netherlands but who have at least one parent who is born abroad (StatLine, 2013). And although they often have Dutch or dual citizenship, it is still common practice to label all generations by their country of origin, e.g., Surinamese, Antilleans, Turkish, or Moroccans (Bovenkerk and Fokkema, 2016).

These four main migrant groups differ in the extent to which they are integrated in Dutch society. The Caribbean immigrants are better integrated than the Mediterranean immigrants, perhaps because Surinamese and Antillean immigrants had been exposed to Dutch culture during the colonial period, being familiar with the Dutch language and often Christians, like the Dutch. An important difference with the Dutch is that colonial immigrants more often have a fatherless family structure. The Mediterranean immigrants, on the other hand, differ culturally more from the Dutch: they have not yet been exposed to Dutch culture, they did not speak the Dutch language, and they are overwhelmingly Muslim. Furthermore, Turks and Moroccans originated from more disadvantaged socioeconomic backgrounds: the guest workers that were needed for low-skilled labor were recruited from the lowest socioeconomic strata in their home countries. But despite the similarities among Mediterranean immigrants, Crul and Doomernik (2003) also note a difference between Turks and Moroccans: Moroccans are modern individualists, whereas Turks are old-fashioned collectivists. Hence, the social integration of second-generation Moroccans is proceeding more rapidly than that of the Turks: the Turks adhere more to the norms and values of their own ethnic community (Crul and Doomernik, 2003).

The level of integration differs, not only between the four minority groups, but also between the two generations. Classic assimilation theory assumes that every next generation is integrated better in society than prior generations (Maliepaard and Alba, 2016). But Tonry (2014: 2) points out that second-generation migrants are caught between two worlds: "they have the same material aspirations as natives but lack sufficient social and personal capital to achieve them easily." Because of a process of "segmented assimilation," second-generation immigrants might move on a downward pathway of assimilation, with prejudice and discrimination that stimulate a reactive and defiant assertion of ethnic minority status (Maliepaard and Alba, 2016).

Despite the differences in levels of integration, all ethnic minority groups have in common that they generally have lower socioeconomic positions than the native Dutch and that they are overrepresented in crime statistics. In 2013, 1 percent of the native Dutch were officially registered as a suspect of a crime, compared to 3 percent of the Turks, 3 percent of the Surinamese, 5 percent of the Moroccans and 6 percent of the Antilleans (Statistics Netherlands, 2014). With the exception of the Antilleans, second-generation migrants have higher crime rates than the first generation. The overrepresentation of the minority groups in crime statistics can partly be explained by demographic and socioeconomic differences, but a lack of parental supervision and informal control within ethnic communities, specific cultural traits regarding respect and codes of masculinity, street culture in certain urban areas, and selectivity in law enforcement might also be at play (Engbersen, Leerkes, and Snel, 2014), just as selectivity in sentencing outcomes.

Prior Research

The presence of sentencing disparities along the lines of ethnicity/race has attracted immense scholarly attention, with most attention devoted to the preferential treatment of White versus Black defendants at sentencing in the U.S. (Bridges and Steen, 1998; Britt, 2000; Pratt, 1998; Radelet, 1981; Sampson and Lauritsen, 1997; Steffensmeier et al., 1998; Thomson and Zingraff, 1981; Ulmer and Kramer, 1996). Recently, a growing literature also focuses theoretically and empirically on Hispanic defendants in the U.S. to provide for White-Black-Hispanic comparisons (e.g., Steffensmeier and Demuth, 2001; Warren, Chiricos, and Bales, 2012). On the whole, effects of race and ethnicity tend to be small and, in certain contexts, affect judges' decisions in sentencing only indirectly or in combination with other offender characteristics, such as age, employment, and sex (Steffensmeier et al., 1998; Spohn and Holleran, 2000).[1] As suggested by Spohn (2009: 190) about this work,

> The fact that . . . African Americans and . . . Hispanics were more likely than whites to be sentenced to prison, even after taking crime seriousness and prior criminal record into account, suggests that racial discrimination in sentencing is not a thing of the past.

Limited work on other minority groups, such as Native American offenders (e.g., Alvarez and Bachman, 1996) or Asian offenders (Johnson and Betsinger, 2009), and work in other contexts, such as Australia and Canada (Bond and Jeffries, 2011; Roberts and Doob, 1997; Snowball and Weatherburn, 2007; Williams, 1999; but see Welsh and Ogloff, 2008) reaches similar conclusions. Also in Europe, a long research tradition focuses on sentencing. In particular, scholars have focused on normative issues surrounding aggravating and mitigating factors in sentencing (e.g., Roberts, 2011; Schuyt, 2014); public opinions regarding sentencing practices (Hough and Roberts, 1999; Larrauri and Varona, 2011); and consistency and discretion within criminal justice systems (De Keijser, 2000; Kirby and Jacobson, 2014; Pina-Sánchez, 2015; Plesničar, 2013). But, in Europe, with its unique immigrant groups, quantitative multivariate research on the effects of race or ethnicity on punishment decisions is virtually non-existent.[2] Research is impeded by the lack of available data on offenders' ethnicity (Tonry, 2014). Although it is common knowledge that some immigrant groups are overrepresented in European prisons, it is unclear whether this is caused by differential involvement or by differential treatment.

Our review of Dutch judicial sentencing research revealed 14 studies that incorporated diverse ethnic groups. The findings of early descriptive (Berghuis, 1992; Berghuis and Mak, 2002; Bosma, 1985; Jongman and Schilt, 1976; Timmerman, Bosma, and Jongman, 1986) and early multivariate sentencing research (Van der Werff and van der Zee-Nefkens, 1978) suggest that sentencing outcomes are more severe for some ethnic minority groups than for native Dutch. Jongman and Schilt (1976) for instance showed that 42 percent of the Surinamese defendants received a prison sentence relative to 23 percent of the Dutch defendants. Recent Dutch multivariate work on juveniles (Komen and Van Schooten, 2006, 2009) and on homicide offenders (Johnson, Van Wingerden, and Nieuwbeerta, 2010; Van Wingerden and Nieuwbeerta, 2006, 2010) also found that some ethnic minority groups are sentenced more severely. Johnson and colleagues (2010), for instance, found that non-European homicide offenders received prison sentences that were approximately 1 year longer than Dutch offenders. On the whole, the existing research in Europe and the Netherlands has been limited mainly to univariate or bivariate analyses of race/ethnicity and sentencing that do not adequately account for other sentencing factors that might (legitimately) explain racial/ethnic disparities, or is focused exclusively on specific offense types and particular time periods, thereby raising questions about generalizability.

Recently, the authors of this chapter have tried to improve this situation by conducting a number of multivariate studies on the determinants of sentencing (Van Wingerden, Moerings, and Van Wilsem, 2011; Van Wingerden, Van Wilsem, and Johnson, 2016; Wermink, De Keijser and Schuyt, 2012; Wermink et al., 2015; Wermink et al., 2017). Each of these studies, however, relied on a single specific dataset, consisting of either a very large population with limited background information or a more selective population with detailed information on the defendants. Furthermore, none of these studies specifically focused on ethnic disparities in sentencing. The current study concentrates specifically on ethnic sentencing disparity and incorporates all three different datasets that were used in these prior studies to gain more insight into the role of ethnicity at sentencing. Moreover, data were extended providing the unique opportunity to distinguish between first and second immigrant generations.

Two Perspectives to Explain Ethnic Disparity in Sentencing

In the literature, various theoretical frameworks have been used to provide for explanations for ethnic disparity in sentencing. In an attempt to summarize this extensive literature, we identified two approaches to explain why ethnic differences in sentencing may exist: ethnicity may either indirectly or directly influence sentencing decisions.

Sociological and criminological theories have suggested that the overrepresentation of ethnic minority offenders in prison may mirror differences in offending behavior between different ethnic or racial groups (Engen, Steen, and Bridges, 2002; Hagan, 1974; Hindelang, 1978; Spohn, 2009). From this perspective, the overrepresentation of some ethnic minorities in Dutch prison is not due to discrimination at sentencing but is rather caused by *differential involvement*. This approach is also sometimes referred to as the "no discrimination" camp (see e.g., Zatz, 1987). Scholars using this approach stress that legal factors weigh heavily in sentencing decision-making, and explain sentencing outcomes from a formal legal/consensus perspective that emphasizes that sentencing decisions are technically rational and the formal legal rules are equally applied to ethnic minority groups (Dixon, 1995; Weber, 1954). Besides differences in criminal involvement, other scholars have stressed that some ethnic groups are socially and economically disadvantaged, and ethnic minority groups may be punished more severely because of *unfavorable personal circumstances* (Spohn, 2009; Van Wingerden, Van Wilsem, and Johnson, 2016; Wooldredge, 2012). To the extent that a) certain personal circumstances are tied to race or ethnicity, and b) these personal circumstances exert independent influences over sentencing decisions ethnic biases at sentencing will be produced. As such, ethnic disparity in sentencing exist though a process of indirect differential treatment (Spohn, 2009). As argued by Zatz (1987: 70), "these disparities reflect more subtle biases, but still fall within the purview of discrimination if they favor one group over another." Based on the arguments of differential involvement and indirect differential treatment one would expect the following:

> Hypothesis 1: All ethnic minority groups will be sentenced equally after controlling for various legal characteristics and social circumstances of the offender.

Other sentencing scholars have adopted the theoretical standpoint that effects of ethnicity or race may affect sentencing outcomes even after taking into account various legal characteristics and other personal circumstances. As argued by Tonry (1998: 61), "higher minority crime rates lead to stereotypes about minority groups, . . . which leads to harsher sentences." Criminal justice actors may rely on aggregate group characteristics at sentencing to evaluate individual personal characteristics. As such, the overrepresentation of ethnic minority groups in the prison population may be the result of *direct differential treatment*. In the literature, different underlying mechanisms are outlined to explain why ethnicity may directly influence sentencing decisions. Early scholars addressed the issue of sentencing disparity from a conflict perspective derived from classical Marxist conceptions of the significance of social classes (Chambliss and Seidman, 1971; Quinney, 1970). Here racial differentials are often discussed in the same context as social class differentials, and racial disparity is expected to be the result from the interest of the dominant class to maintain power over the powerless or subordinate segments of the population. Deviant acts by the powerless may represent a threat to the existing structure of authority. To the extent that subordinate groups grow in population size and have more socioeconomic resources, fear of competition by the dominant group will grow (Blalock, 1967).

Although, the conflict perspective has been widely used, current sentencing scholars usually refer to recent theoretical perspectives within the direct differential treatment approach. These theories posit that ethnic disparities at sentencing occur because decision-making processes are guided by ethnic based attribution processes (Albonetti, 1991; Steffensmeier et al., 1998). Because judicial decision-making is complex and limited by time and information constraints, judges—either consciously or unconsciously—handle these constraints by using uncertainty avoidance techniques for assessing the culpability and dangerousness of the offender. These techniques include decision-making shortcuts, cognitive heuristics, and stereotypical beliefs that can tie offender's ethnicity to assessments of culpability and dangerousness. These patterned responses are based on simplification, exaggeration, and generalization. Supposed characteristics of the social group are assigned to the individual. In the Netherlands, in particular Moroccans have very negative stereotypes attached to them. These negative stereotypes are mostly grounded in public feelings of unsafety caused by the young Moroccans that hang around on the streets. Moroccans are frequently labeled as a "problem group," not only in society, but in politics as well. When young Moroccans kicked a soccer arbiter to death in 2013, right-wing politicians called for a "debate on the integration problems of Moroccans," also known as "the Moroccan debate." One of these politicians also asked his supporters in 2014: "Do you want more or fewer Moroccans in the Netherlands?" When the crowd shouted, "Fewer! Fewer!" he replied: "Then we'll take care of that." He proposes to expel all criminal Moroccans to Morocco. Moroccans are thus often linked to very negative attributions, but other ethnic groups suffer from negative stereotypes as well, since they also have low rates of education and employment and high rates of being beneficiaries of social welfare and crime. If judges unconsciously rely on such stereotypical beliefs when an offender from a particular ethnic minority group is punished, a direct effect of ethnicity on sentence outcomes is established. From the direct differential treatment approach, we therefore expect:

> Hypothesis 2: Ethnic minority groups will be punished more severely after controlling for various legal and offender circumstances.

Data and Methods

Data

We empirically examine our research question using three data sources that will be analyzed separately. The *2007-cohort* contains information on all adult suspects of whom their case was registered at the Public Prosecutor's Office in 2007, and were subsequently sentenced by a judge (N = 89,147). This data source was made available by the Research and Documentation Centre (WODC) of the Netherlands Ministry of Justice.[3] The data include the full registered conviction history, age, gender, country of birth, index offense, court, pretrial detention, and sentencing information.

Additionally we make use of the *RISc-data* in which data from the Public Prosecutor's Office are combined with pre-sentencing report data from the Probation Service for the years 2005–2007 (N = 20,841). Typically, a pre-sentencing report is completed when a defendant is detained pretrial, or when the Probation Service is involved with the execution of the expected sentence, such as community service or suspended sentence with special conditions. This results in an underrepresentation of minor offenses in these data (for more information, see Van Wingerden, Van Wilsem, and Johnson, 2016). Although this is a more selective sample, important advantages of these data are that a) first- and second-generation immigrants can be distinguished and b) detailed information on offender's personal circumstances is included.

The third data source is collected within the *Prison Project:* a nationwide study in which detailed data were gathered from suspects who entered a Dutch pretrial detention facility for a minimum of three weeks between October 2010 and March 2011, were born in the Netherlands, and were between 18 to 65 years old. These data were further extended with multiple types of administrative data including information on offense, criminal histories, and other life circumstances. Information about punishment outcomes was retrieved from data administered at the Public's Prosecution Office in September 2012 (N = 1,506).

Dependent Variables

Using the *2007-cohort* and the *RISc-data*, we examine whether or not an offender is imprisoned (in/out) and if so, for how long. This approach is consistent with prior research.[4] Incarceration is measured with a dichotomous variable coded 0 for non-incarceration and 1 for incarceration, and the length of the prison sentence is a continuous measure capturing the total days of confinement ordered by the judge.[5] The in/out decision is not analyzed using the *Prison Project* data because the vast majority of the suspects in this sample received a prison sentence (94%) (see also Johnson et al.,

2010; Ulmer, Eisenstein, and Johnson, 2010). Instead, we examine whether or not the unsuspended length of the imposed prison sentence exceeds the time served in pretrial detention.[6] For the subgroup of offenders who receive "extra time," we examine the length of this extra term of imprisonment, and for the full sample, the full length of the prison sentence is measured.

Among the total *2007-cohort*, 18 percent are incarcerated, with a mean term of imprisonment of 226 days. A prison sentence is imposed in 47 percent of the cases in the *RISc-data*, and the average prison term is 345 days. Of all offenders in the *Prison Project*, 61 percent receives a prison length at sentencing that exceeds the term of pretrial detention, with an average "extra term" of 418 days. The full prison length is approximately 370 days.

Differences in the above described results are caused by differences in population and measurement between datasets. Important differences are related to the extent through which defendants have been selected through the criminal justice system: the *2007-cohort* includes all suspects, the *RISc-data* only those with a pre-sentencing report, and the *Prison Project* includes pretrial detained offenders only. Consequently, when the results of ethnic disparities in sentencing are presented, it is especially valuable to pay attention to differences *within* datasets rather than *between*.

The dichotomous sentencing outcomes are modeled with logistic regression. For those incarcerated, sentence length outcomes are transformed logarithmically and modeled with OLS regression. The log transformation normalizes the skewed distribution and addresses the fact that additional days of incarceration may have different meaning for different sentence lengths. Also, it allows for more convenient interpretation of the sentence lengths in terms of their proportional increase associated with a unit increase in each explanatory variable. The regression coefficients are exponentiated to provide for proportional increases in the logged sentence length models.

Ethnicity

Ethnicity is determined by the country of birth of the suspect and the country of birth of the parents of the offender. We distinguish between seven groups: Dutch, Moroccans, Antilleans, Surinamese, Turks, other Western, and other non-Western.[7] In all datasets, the Dutch serve as the reference category. This reference is strategically selected to allow comparison of each immigrant group to Dutch offenders. In the *2007-cohort*, we use the categories to examine possible differences in sentencing between first-generation immigrants and Dutch offenders, in the *Prison Project* for second-generation immigrants, and in the *RISc-data* for first- and second-generation immigrants. First-generation immigrants are foreign-born, and second-generation immigrants are born in the Netherlands who at least have one parent who is foreign-born. In the *2007-cohort*, 69 percent is Dutch-born; in the *RISc-data*, 59 percent is native; and in the *Prison Project*, 68 percent. A summary of all other variables in the analysis capturing the severity of the offense and the characteristics and local life circumstances of the offender are shown in Appendix A.

Results

We are theoretically and empirically interested in the effects of ethnicity on the "in/out" decision and the sentence length decision. First, we examine bivariate relationships between ethnicity and the sentencing outcomes. Second, we examine descriptive statistics focusing on differences between distinct ethnic groups and various sentencing factors (offense, offender, and case). Third, we test whether ethnic disparities exist in the full sample net of statistical controls for other variables that might be highly associated with both ethnicity and sentence severity.

Bivariate Relations Between Ethnicity and Sentencing Outcomes

The bivariate models, presented in Table 10.1, represent the first step to assess whether ethnicity affects the likelihood of prison versus non-custodial sanctions, and whether it helps to explain variation in sentence length. The results for the in/out decision are unambiguous: in all data sources, all except one immigrant group are more likely to receive incarceration sentences. The magnitude of these differences is large: in the *2007-cohort* data, the imprisonment odds for the distinct ethnic minority groups range from 1.36 for Turks to 3.31 for Surinamese. Surinamese offenders are thus more than three times as likely to be sentenced to prison than Dutch offenders. In the *RISc-data*, the imprisonment odds for the four main ethnic minority groups range from 1.38 for first-generation Turks to 3.81 for second-generation Moroccans. With the exception of Antillean offenders, second-generation migrant groups are more likely to be incarcerated than their first-generation counterparts. In the *Prison Project* data, second-generation Antilleans have the highest likelihood to receive a prison sentence longer than the duration of their pretrial detention, but these effects do not reach statistical significance.

Table 10.1 also presents the bivariate results regarding the sentence length. They consistently show that all first-generation immigrant groups receive longer sentences than native offenders, with the notable exception of Moroccan offenders; their average sentence length is not significantly different from that of native offenders. In the *2007-cohort* data, offenders from the four main ethnic minority groups receive prison terms that are 19 to 29 percent longer than that of Dutch offenders. In the *RISc-data*, we found 19 to 37 percent longer prison terms for the first-generation immigrants. Ethnic sentencing disparities for second-generation offenders are much smaller. Only second-generation Surinamese receive significantly longer prison terms compared to natives. In the *Prison Project* data, the sentence length differs only significantly from that for native offenders for second-generation Antilleans. Their prison terms are 52 percent longer.

Our findings show that there is no clear pattern in ethnic effects for the distinct ethnic groups. Their effects differ for the in/out-decision compared to the decision on the sentence length. Moroccans for example are more likely to be incarcerated, but the length of their sentence is not significantly different from that of the Dutch.

Table 10.1 Bivariate Relationships Between and Ethnicity and the Likelihood of Imprisonment (Odds Ratios) and Between Ethnicity and the Sentence Length

The Netherlands	*In/Out-Decision*			*Sentence Length*			
	2007 cohort	*RISc*	*PP*[1]	*2007 cohort*	*RISc*	*PP*	*PP*[2]
	(N = *89,147)*	(N = *20,841)*	(N = *1,506)*	(N = *15,889)*	(N = *9,699)*	(N = *1,506)*	(N = *925)*
	Exp(B)	*Exp(B)*	*Exp(B)*	*Exp(B)*	*Exp(B)*	*Exp(B)*	*Exp(B)*
	Ref.	*Ref.*	*Ref.*	*Ref.*	*Ref.*	*Ref.*	*Ref.*
1st Generation							
Morocco	2.84***	2.48***	–	1.05	1.01	–	–
(former) Neth. Antilles	2.58***	2.43***	–	1.23***	1.37***	–	–
Surinam	3.31***	1.77***	–	1.29***	1.19**	–	–
Turkey	1.36***	1.38***	–	1.19**	1.31***	–	–
Other Western	2.42***	1.32***	–	0.86***	1.24**	–	–
Other non-Western	3.79***	1.58***	–	1.30***	1.10	–	–
2nd Generation							
Morocco	–	3.81***	1.13	–	1.13	1.04	1.26
(former) Neth. Antilles	–	2.38***	1.58	–	1.08	1.52*	1.92
Surinam	–	2.55***	1.16	–	1.15*	1.22	1.57
Turkey	–	2.16***	1.34	–	0.98	1.14	1.22
Other Western	–	1.40***	1.38	–	1.05	1.11	1.05
Other non-Western	–	1.90***	0.88	–	1.06	1.01	1.41

* $p \leq .05$, ** $p \leq .01$, and *** $p \leq .001$.

1 Likelihood of prison sentence longer than pretrial detention.
2 Number of days the prison sentence exceeds the length of the pretrial detention.

Furthermore, there are differences between datasets. First-generation Surinamese offenders for instance have the highest likelihood of incarceration in the *2007-cohort* dataset, but not in the *RISc-data*. And in the *Prison Project* data, many ethnic disparities do not reach statistical significance. Also, differences between immigrant generations are found: regarding the in/out decision, second-generation disparities are more pronounced, and regarding the sentence length decision, disparities are more pronounced for first-generation immigrants.

Even though a clear pattern in ethnic effects is absent, our findings clearly show that ethnic sentencing disparity exists in Dutch sentencing practices. These overall higher incarceration rates and longer prison sentences for immigrant groups may (in part) be a function of other sentencing factors, such as offense seriousness, prior criminal record, and other personal circumstances. We, therefore, now turn our attention to differences on other sentencing factors between immigrant groups.

Descriptive Information on Sentencing Factors for Different Ethnic Suspect Groups

In order to examine whether other sentencing factors are related to ethnicity, mean values of various domains (such as offense, offender, and case) were compared. Results demonstrate that sentencing factors are differently distributed across ethnic groups.[8]

The three data sources show substantial differences between ethnic groups on offense characteristics. Immigrant offenders are overrepresented in offenses that carry a higher maximum penalty (more than 6 years), while Dutch convicted offenders are overrepresented in less serious offenses that carry a maximum penalty of 1 year. Moreover, Dutch offenders are more often involved in traffic offenses, while non-Dutch immigrant groups are more often sentenced for drug offenses. Especially, Moroccan, Antillean, and Surinamese offenders are overrepresented in drug offenses. In 2007, for instance, 15 percent of the Surinamese offenders were sentenced for a drug offense compared to 1 percent of the Dutch offenders. In contrast, Turkish offenders are overrepresented in assault offenses, with no less than 40 percent of the first generation and 32 percent of the second generation sentenced for committing assault offenses.

The data further reveal pronounced differences in offender characteristics between ethnic groups. Both Moroccan and Turkish offenders are relatively less likely to be female. Moreover, relatively few non-Dutch immigrants are in the oldest age category (older than 50), and second-generation immigrants, in particular, are often relatively young (aged 18 to 30). Regarding past involvement with the criminal justice system, immigrant groups tend to have more extensive criminal histories and typically start offending at a younger age. The disadvantaged position of immigrant groups also becomes visible in comparing personal circumstances related to their conventional bonds, including income, high educational attainment, marriage, and children. Ethnic minority offenders, for instance, seem to have a lower educational attainment and are less often employed than Dutch offenders. The *RISc-data* further indicate that immigrants experience more problems on various other domains of risks for future recidivism, such as emotional wellbeing, cognition and behavior, and attitudes. In contrast, Dutch offenders experience more often problems with substance misuse.

Finally, case characteristics are also differently distributed across groups. Members of immigrant groups are more likely to be detained pretrial, and if detained pretrial, terms are relatively longer. Also, Dutch offenders are less likely to be sentenced in one of the large cities in the Netherlands: Rotterdam, Amsterdam, or the Hague. Another notable difference is that immigrants less often accept their criminal responsibility than Dutch offenders.

Taken as a whole, these comparisons suggest that offenders from ethnic minority groups tend to be convicted for more serious crimes than native offenders and that they tend to have more problematic personal and offending backgrounds. These characteristics may in turn be tied to judicial assessments of increased levels of blameworthiness or increased risks of recidivism. Because offense and offender characteristics are indeed distributed unevenly over the distinct ethnic groups, ethnicity might indirectly affect sentencing outcomes.

Multivariate Relations Between Ethnicity and Sentencing Outcomes

To test whether ethnicity *directly* or *indirectly* affects sentencing outcomes, multivariate regression analyses were conducted in which we examine whether differences in sentencing among ethnic groups persist net of statistical controls for offense, case processing, and offender characteristics. Table 10.2 reports the findings of logistic and OLS regression models for the incarceration and sentence length decision, respectively.

Table 10.2 Logistic and OLS Regression for the In/Out and Sentence Length (ln) Decision (Full Models[3])

The Netherlands	*In/Out-Decision*			*Sentence Length*			
	2007 cohort	*RISc*	*PP*[1]	*2007 cohort*	*RISc*	*PP*	*PP*[2]
	(N = 89,147)	*(N = 20,841)*	*(N = 1,506)*	*(N = 15,889)*	*(N = 9,699)*	*(N = 1,506)*	*(N = 925)*
	Exp(B)	*Exp(B)*	*Exp(B)*	*Exp(B)*	*Exp(B)*	*Exp(B)*	*Exp(B)*
	Ref.	*Ref.*	*Ref.*	*Ref.*	*Ref.*	*Ref.*	*Ref.*
1st Generation							
Morocco	1.65***	1.30	–	1.06*	1.00	–	–
(former) Neth. Antilles	1.29***	1.26	–	1.08**	1.08*	–	–
Surinam	1.57***	1.01	–	0.94*	1.02	–	–
Turkey	1.39***	1.04	–	1.11**	1.19***	–	–
Other Western	3.60***	1.11	–	1.07**	1.14**	–	–
Other non-Western	3.56***	1.24	–	1.19***	1.04	–	–
2nd Generation							
Morocco	–	1.35	1.50~	–	1.14**	1.16*	1.36*
(former) Neth. Antilles	–	1.62	1.35	–	1.04	1.06	1.06
Surinam	–	1.36	0.95	–	0.97	1.15	1.55*
Turkey	–	1.70**	1.58	–	1.05	1.02	0.92
Other Western	–	1.27	1.36	–	0.99	1.05	0.86
Other non-Western	–	0.93	0.72	–	1.05	1.06	1.54

* $p \leq .05$, ** $p \leq .01$, and *** $p \leq .001$.

1 Likelihood of prison sentence longer than pretrial detention.
2 Number of days the prison sentence exceeds the length of the pretrial detention.
3 Controlled for severity of the offense (e.g. maximum penalty, type of offense, number of offenses); case processing characteristics (e.g. court district, pretrial detention); and offender characteristics (e.g. age, sex, prior criminal record, prior prison sentences). The *RISc-data* and *Prison Project-data* also controlled for social circumstances of the offender, like unemployment and drug and alcohol usage. Complete results of the full models can be requested from the authors.

In line with prior work, offense severity and case processing characteristics, such as pretrial detention outcomes, exert strong influences on sentencing outcomes. Characteristics of the offender, such as sex, criminal history, and certain personal circumstances also affect sentencing outcomes. The results further show that, despite the controls for offense, case processing, and offender characteristics, ethnic disparities still exists in both the incarceration models and in the sentence lengths models. However, effect sizes in the multivariate models are smaller in comparison with the bivariate models and some effects became non-significant, meaning that the initial ethnic disparities found are at least partly explained by including various offense, case, contextual, and other offender sentencing factors that were shown to be unevenly distributed among ethnic groups in the second step of the analyses.

In the full *2007-cohort* population, all immigrant groups are still more likely to be incarcerated compared to Dutch defendants. The imprisonment odds now range from 1.29 for Antilleans to 3.60 for other Western immigrants. The odds for Moroccans, Antilleans, and Surinamese are smaller compared to the bivariate model, yet the reduction is relatively small. Ethnic disparities can thus only partly be explained by case characteristics and indicators of differential involvement.

The *RISc-data* includes more detailed offender information compared to the 2007 cohort. The results of the multivariate analyses show that, when offense, case processing, and offender characteristics are controlled for, the ethnic sentencing disparities in likelihood of imprisonment are no longer statistically significant for the first-generation immigrants. Of the second-generation migrants, only the Turks have a significantly different likelihood of incarceration compared to the natives: Turks are 70 percent more likely to be sentenced to prison.

The results from the *Prison Project-data* show that there are no statistically significant disparities between ethnic minority groups and natives regarding their odds of receiving a prison term that exceeds the length of the pretrial detention. This was also the case in the bivariate model.

Regarding the sentence length decision, main effects for some ethnic groups are found net of other sentencing factors in all data sources. Of all offenders sentenced in 2007, for instance, first-generation Antilleans and first-generation Turks received sentences 8 and 11 percent longer than native offenders, respectively. The Surinamese, on the other hand, receive shorter prison sentences. Moreover, where Moroccans did not receive significantly different prison terms in the bivariate model, in the final model they are sentenced to 6 percent longer prison terms.

In the *RISc-data*, ethnic disparities in length of imprisonment are smaller compared to the bivariate model, but there are still differences between ethnic groups. First-generation Antilleans receive 8 percent longer prison sentences than Dutch defendants, Turks 19 percent, and immigrants from a Western country 14 percent. Regarding second-generation immigrants, only Moroccan defendants receive relative longer prison sentences (14 percent longer).

More punitive sentencing outcomes for Moroccan offenders are also found in the *Prison Project-data:* 16 percent longer total prison sentences and 36 percent longer terms of "extra time." For second-generation Surinamese, this extra time is 55 percent longer. Antilleans received longer prison terms in the bivariate model, but once controlled for offense, case processing, and offender characteristics, their sentence length is no longer significantly different from that of native offenders.

Discussion

The purpose of this study was to explore whether the ethnicity of the offender either directly or indirectly affects sentencing outcomes. We hypothesized that sentencing disparities between ethnic groups occur because the factors that judges use to determine the sentence are unevenly distributed over distinct ethnic groups. Ethnic minority groups are differentially involved in crime (e.g. more crimes or different types of crimes) (Engen, Steen, and Bridges, 2002; Hagan, 1974; Hindelang, 1978; Spohn, 2009), and are socially and economically disadvantaged compared to the native group as well. Thus, when judges take the severity of the crime and the disadvantaged personal circumstances, such as unemployment and drug usage, into account, ethnic minority groups might receive different punishment outcomes than native offenders (Van Wingerden, Van Wilsem, and Johnson, 2016). We consider this an indirect effect: offenders do not receive harsher punishment because of their ethnicity, but because of their crimes and personal circumstances, which are more disadvantageous for ethnic minority groups.

Our findings show that ethnic sentencing disparities decrease when characteristics of the crime, case processing, and the offender are taken into account. This suggests that the observed ethnic disparities in sentencing outcomes are at least partially due to differences in case and offender characteristics and that ethnicity has an indirect influence on sentencing decisions. However, we find no clear pattern in the role of ethnicity in sentencing: where one minority group has a higher chance of imprisonment, other groups receive longer prison terms. Furthermore, a clear pattern is also absent when we compare the three datasets: there is not one ethnic minority group that is consistently punished more severely than the Dutch in all three datasets.

Even though we found support for indirect ethnicity effects on sentencing, ethnic sentencing disparities did not fully disappear when offense, case processing, and offender characteristics were controlled for. These findings thus offer only partial support for our hypothesis that ethnic sentencing disparity would disappear once offense and offender characteristics are controlled for. Because ethnic disparities in sentencing cannot fully be explained by differences in characteristics of the crime, nor by differences in characteristics or social circumstances of the offender, we also found support for our second hypothesis: ethnicity may *directly* influence sentencing decisions. Ethnic minority groups may thus receive different punishment *because of* their ethnicity. This may imply that patterns of social stratification are not limited to the U.S. context but also apply to other contexts with supposedly lower levels of discrimination. However, alternative explanations cannot be ruled out. Although we employed relatively strong controls for the severity of the offense, and for characteristics and social circumstances of the offender, other unmeasured variables that are related to ethnicity might also account for the sentencing disparity between ethnic groups. Examples are cultural differences in the tendency to deny having committed the crime and in verbal and non-verbal communication with the judges. That said, *direct* effects of ethnicity on sentencing outcomes could not be ruled out in the current study. These may be caused by the heuristic strategies of judges: at sentencing judges may unconsciously rely on negative stereotypical attributions tied to offenders that belong to a particular ethnic minority group.

Although we found both direct and indirect ethnicity effects on sentencing outcomes, it is important to note that these are most likely underestimated. An important reason for this is the measurement of ethnicity in the datasets. For instance, ethnicity in the *2007-cohort* dataset is solely based on country of birth of the offender, meaning that second-generation migrants are considered Dutch. If these second-generation migrants were considered non-Dutch, more severe sentencing disparity would probably be found. Furthermore, the *Prison Project-data* only contains offenders who are born in the Netherlands, and thus ethnic disparities could not be examined for first-generation immigrant groups using these data.

Conclusion

The current study specifically addressed the call for sentencing research that focuses on more diverse ethnic minority groups in other sentencing contexts (Sampson and Lauritsen, 1997; Ulmer, 2012). Although the Dutch sentencing context is very different from that of the U.S., similar effects of defendants' ethnicity are present. Our study shows that ethnicity both directly and indirectly affects sentence outcomes, resulting in harsher punishments for offenders from an ethnic minority group. This is consistent with prior research from the U.S.-context (Mitchell, 2005; Spohn, 2009; Zatz, 2000). Stereotypical attribution processes in punishment may does not only occur in American courts but may be more universal (Johnson, Van Wingerden and Nieuwbeerta, 2010). Future research should aim to study ethnic sentencing disparities in other national contexts in order to establish this.

Our study also contributed to the existing research by incorporating very detailed offender characteristics to study effects of ethnicity on sentencing outcomes. As Zatz (2000) notes, information about personal circumstances (and legally relevant factors) should be included in sentencing research to disentangle some of the racial/ethnic effects. Although we could not control for every possible personal circumstance, the uniquely detailed offender characteristics that we used as control variables enabled us to assess ethnicity effects more accurately than in the vast majority of previous studies.

We further enriched the sentencing literature by being the first to examine differences in sentence outcomes between first- and second-generation immigrants. Our findings reveal important differences in punishments between generations. And although clear patterns for distinct ethnic groups could not be found, it seems that second-generation migrants are more likely to be send to prison, whereas first-generation immigrants receive *longer* prison terms. Future research is needed to explore these intergeneration differences further. Our results regarding the differences between the "in/out" and sentence length decisions also underscore the importance of examining these decisions separately.

Future research should also use more accurate measures of ethnicity. Unlike in the U.S., suspects in the Netherlands are not required to fill out a form on which they indicate their ethnic group. In our study, ethnicity is determined by the country of birth of the suspect in combination with the country of birth of his parents. This measure does not fully reflect ethnicity because cultural aspects of ethnicity are not captured. Future research may benefit from improved conceptualizations of ethnicity that account for the dynamic and changing nature of racial and ethnic identity in society (Johnson and Lee, 2013), for example by using a measure where the ethnic group is self-identified. This is especially important because third-generation immigrants are currently old enough to enter crime statistics. These offenders are now registered as native Dutch offenders, but cultural differences and differences in socioeconomic status clearly exist for this specific group. In order to further disentangle ethnic sentencing disparities, more attention should be paid to the cultural aspect of the concept of ethnicity.

Disentangling interaction effects is also a worthwhile avenue for future research. Because specific combinations of offense, case processing, and offender characteristics might in particular relate to harsher punishment for certain minority groups (Spohn and Holleran, 2000), studying interaction effects can provide insight into who is punished more severely in what circumstances. Moreover, future research should also try to gain more insight into cumulative disadvantage of ethnic minority groups throughout the different stages of the criminal justice system because disparity might be caused by differential treatment in prior stages of the criminal proceedings (Spohn, 2009; Ulmer, 2012; Wermink et al., 2016). To gain more insight into *why* ethnic sentencing disparity occurs, future research should strive to incorporate other research methods, such as the interviewing of judges.

The findings of the current study provide insight into the role of the ethnicity of the offender at sentencing but may also contribute to normative discussions on the desirability or legitimacy of ethnicity as a factor that either directly or indirectly affects sentencing outcomes. It is important that judges and other court actors join this debate because there is still much uncertainty about whether offender characteristics are legitimate sentencing determinants, especially in the Netherlands where judges have broad discretionary powers. If ethnicity of the offender is indeed considered to be an illegitimate sentencing determinant, it is of utmost importance to take measures that improve consistency in sentencing.

Notes

1 Differences in the criminal justice system and racial and ethnic heritage limit the applicability of these findings to the Dutch context somewhat, so we do not review this research in detail.

2 There are some examples of European multivariate studies on sentencing: Kruttschnitt and Savolainen (2009) used Finnish data, and Pina-Sánchez and Linacre (2013, 2014) used data from

England and Wales. However, these studies don't include defendant's ethnicity. A European study focusing on the treatment of immigrants and their descendants by the criminal justice system was conducted in Denmark (Holmberg and Kyvsgaard, 2003). This study shows immigrant-based disparities in being arrested and being remanded to custody, but imprisonment decisions were not studied. Moreover, controls were not included simultaneously into their models.

3 The WODC cannot be held responsible for completeness, correctness, and the use of these data.

4 Several scholars argue that sentencing should be understood as a two-stage process, involving first a decision about whether to imprison and second, if incarceration is selected, a decision about the term length (Johnson, 2006; Steffensmeier et al., 1998; Wheeler et al., 1982). Bushway and Piehl (2001) have suggested that under highly structured sentencing guidelines, sentencing may be best modeled as a single decision-making process, but this does not characterize the Dutch context, where judges must first determine the type of punishment followed by the term length.

5 All criminal sentences involving confinement are defined as incarceration sentences. Incarceration was coded 1 if the offender was sentenced to an unsuspended prison sentence and 0 if they were sentenced to any combination of non-incarceration options (e.g. full suspended sentences, community service, or fines).

6 In the Netherlands, punished offenders are immediately released from prison when the imposed sentence length is shorter or equal to the length of pretrial detention.

7 The classification of other-Western and other non-Western offenders is made along the lines of the standard classification of Statistics Netherlands. The category "Western" consists of persons from Europe (excluding the Netherlands and Turkey), North America, Oceania, Japan, and Indonesia (including the former Dutch East Indies). The category "non-Western" includes persons with African, Asian, Turkish, and Latin American backgrounds.

8 These results are not presented in order to conserve table space. The results are available from the author upon request.

References

Alba, R. (2005). Bright vs. blurred boundaries: Second-generation assimilation and exclusion in France, Germany, and the United States. *Ethnic and Racial Studies*, *28*, 20–49.

Albonetti, C. A. (1991). An integration of theories to explain judicial discretion. *Social Forces*, *38*, 247–266.

Algan, Y., Dutmann, C., Glitz, A., & Manning, A. (2010). The economic situation of first and second-generation immigrants in France, Germany, and the United Kingdom. *The Economic Journal*, *120*, F4–F30.

Alvarez, A., & Bachman, R. (1996). American Indians and sentencing disparity: An Arizona test. *Journal or Criminal Justice*, *24*, 549–561.

Berghuis, A. C. (1992). De harde en de zachte hand—een statistische analyse van verschillen in sanctiebeleid [The hard and the soft approach—a statistical analysis of differences in sentencing policy]. *Trema*, *15*, 84–93.

Berghuis, A. C. & Mak, M. (2002). *De Straftoemeting in Nederland van 1995 tot en met 2001* [Sentencing in the Netherlands from 1995 to 2001]. Den Haag: Ministerie van Justitie.

Blalock, H. M. (1967). *Toward a theory of minority group relations*. New York: Wiley.

Blom, M., Oudhof, J., Bijl, R.V., & Bakker, B. F. M. (Eds.). (2005). *Verdacht van criminaliteit: Allochtonen en autochtonen nader bekeken* [Suspected of crime: Allochtones and autochtones further examined]. Den Haag: WODC/CBS.

Bond, C., & Jeffries, S. (2011). Indigeneity and the judicial decision to imprison: A study of Western Australia's higher courts. *British Journal of Criminology*, *51*(2), 256–277.

Bosma, J. J. (1985). Allochtonen en Straftoemeting. Straftoemeting aan allochtonen en Nederlanders voor het delict eenvoudige diefstal [Meting out punishment to allochtones and to the Dutch for the crime of simple theft]. Doctoral thesis, Rijksuniversiteit Groningen.

Bovenkerk, F., & Fokkema, T. (2016). Crime among young Moroccan men in the Netherlands: Does their regional origin matter? *European Journal of Criminology, 13*, 352–371.

Bridges, G. S., & Steen, S. (1998). Racial disparities in official assessments of juvenile offenders: Attributional stereotypes as mediating mechanisms. *American Sociological Review, 63*, 554–570.

Britt, C. L. (2000). Social context and racial disparities in punishment decisions. *Justice Quarterly, 17*, 707–732.

Bushway, S., & Piehl, A. (2001). Judging judicial discretion: Legal factors and racial discrimination in sentencing. *Law and Society Review, 35*, 733–767.

Chambliss, W. J., & Seidman, R. B. (1971). *Law, order, and power*. Reading, MA: Addison-Wesley.

Colombo, A. (2013). Foreigners and immigrants in Italy's penal and administrative detention systems. *European Journal of Criminology, 10*, 746–759.

Crul, M., & Doomernik, J. (2003). The second generation in The Netherlands. Divergent trends between and polarization within the two groups. *International Migration Review, 37*(4), 1039–1064.

De Keijser, J. W. (2000). *Punishment and purpose: From moral theory to punishment in action*. Leiden: Thela Thesis.

De Zwart, F. (2011). Het systeem van etnische categorieën in Nederland [The system of ethnical categories in the Netherlands]. *Migrantenstudies, 11*(1), 2–21.

Delgrande, N., & Aebi, M. F. (2009). Les détenus étrangers en Europe: Quelques considérations critiques sur les données disponibles de 1989 à 2006 [Foreign detainees in Europe: Some critical considerations on the available data (1989–2006)]. *Déviance et Société, 33*(4), 475–499.

Dixon, J. (1995). The organizational context of criminal sentencing. *American Journal of Sociology, 100*, 1157–1198.

Engbersen, G., Leerkes, A. S., & Snel, E. (2014). Ethnicity, crime and immigration in the Netherlands. In S. Bucerius & M. Tonry (Eds.), *The Oxford handbook of ethnicity, crime, and immigration* (pp. 766–790). New York: Oxford University Press.

Engen, R. L., Steen, S., & Bridges, G. S. (2002). Racial disparities in the punishment of youth: A theoretical and empirical assessment of the literature. *Social Problems, 49*, 194–220.

Haen Marshall, I. (Ed.). (1997). *Minorities, migrants, and crime: Diversity and similarity across Europe and the United States*. London: Sage Publications.

Hagan, J. (1974). Extra-legal attributes and criminal sentencing: An assessment of a sociological viewpoint. *Law & Society, 8*, 357–383.

Hindelang, M. (1978). Race and involvement in common law personal crimes. *American Sociological Review, 43*, 93–109.

Holmberg, L., & Kyvsgaard, B. (2003). Are immigrants and their descendants discriminated against in the Danish criminal justice system? *Journal of Scandinavian Studies in Criminology and Crime Prevention, 4*, 125–142.

Hough, M., & Roberts, J.V. (1999). Sentencing trends in Britain public knowledge and public opinion. *Punishment & Society, 1*, 11–26.

Johnson, B. D. (2006). The multilevel context of criminal sentencing: Integrating judge- and county-level influences. *Criminology, 44*, 259–298.

Johnson, B. D., & Betsinger, S. (2009). Punishing the "modal minority": Asian-American criminal sentencing outcomes in Federal district courts. *Criminology, 47*, 1045–1090.

Johnson, B. D., & Lee, J. G. (2013). Racial disparity under sentencing guidelines: A survey of recent research and emerging perspectives. *Sociology Compass, 7*, 503–514.

Johnson, B. D., Van Wingerden, S., & Nieuwbeerta, P. (2010). Sentencing homicide offenders in the Netherlands: Offender, victim, and situational influences in criminal punishment. *Criminology, 48*(4), 981–1018.

Jongman, R., & Schilt, T. (1976). Gelet op de persoon van de verdachte. . . . [Considering the suspect's personal characteristics. . . .]. *Nederlands Tijdschrift voor Criminologie, 6*, 273–287.

Junger-Tas. J. (2001). Ethnic minorities, social integration and crime. *European Journal on Criminal Policy and Research, 9*, 5–29.

Killias, M. (2011). *Immigration and crime: The European experience*. Florence: European University Institute.

Kirby, A., & Jacobson, J. (2014). Public attitudes to the sentencing of drug offences. *Criminology & Criminal Justice, 14*, 334–350.

Komen, M., & Van Schooten, E. (2006). Allochtone jongeren gemiddeld langer vast [Allochtonous youth on average longer detained]. *Nederlands Juristenblad, 25*, 1352–1355.

Komen, M., & Van Schooten, E. (2009). Ethnic disparities in Dutch juvenile justice. *Journal of Ethnicity in Criminal Justice, 7*, 85–106.

Kruttschnitt, C., & Savolainen, J. (2009). Ages of chivalry, places of paternalism. *European Journal of Criminology, 6*, 225–247.

Larrauri, E., & Varona, D. (2011). Democracy at work? Public opinion and penal reforms in Spain. In H. Kury & E. Shea (Eds.), *Punitiveness international developments* (pp. 31–52). Bochum: Brokmeyer Universitätsverlag.

Lee, M., Ulmer, J. T., & Park, M. (2011). Drug sentencing in South Korea: The influence of case-processing and social status factors in an ethnically homogenous context. *Journal of Contemporary Criminal Justice, 27*, 378–397.

Maliepaard, M., & Alba, R. (2016). Cultural integration in the Muslim second generation in the Netherlands: The case of gender ideology. *International Migration Review, 50*, 70–94.

Mansel, J., & Albrecht, G. (2003). Migration und das Kriminalpolitische handeln Staatlicher Strafverfolgungsorgane. Ausländer als polizeilich Tatverdächtige und gerichtlich Abgeurteilte [Migration and the acting of law enforcement agencies. Foreigners as police suspects and defendants in court]. *Kölner Zeitschrift für Soziologie und Sozialpsychologie, 55*(4), 679–715.

Martens, P. L. (1997). Immigrants, crime, and criminal justice in Sweden. *Ethnicity, Crime, and Immigration, 21*, 183–255.

Mitchell, O. (2005). A meta-analysis of race and sentencing research: Explaining the inconsistencies. *Journal of Quantitative Criminology, 21*, 439–466.

Oberwittler, D., & Höfer, S. (2005). Crime and justice in Germany: An analysis of recent trends and research. *European Journal of Criminology, 2*, 465–508.

Pager, D. (2008). The Republican ideal? National minorities and the criminal justice system in contemporary France. *Punishment & Society-International Journal of Penology, 10*, 375–400.

Pina-Sánchez, J. (2015). Defining and measuring consistency in sentencing. In J. V. Roberts (Ed.), *Exploring sentencing practice in England and Wales* (pp. 76–92). Basingstoke: Palgrave Macmillan.

Pina-Sánchez, J., & Linacre, R. (2013). Sentence consistency in England and Wales: Evidence from the Crown Court sentencing survey. *British Journal of Criminology, 53*, 1118–1138.

Pina-Sánchez, J., & Linacre, R. (2014). Enhancing consistency in sentencing: Exploring the effects of guidelines in England and Wales. *Journal of Quantitative Criminology, 30*, 731–748.

Plesničar, M. M. (2013). The individualization of punishment: Sentencing in Slovenia. *European Journal of Criminology, 10*, 462–478.

Pratt, T. C. (1998). Race and sentencing: A meta-analysis of conflicting empirical research results. *Journal of Criminal Justice, 26*, 513–523.

Quinney, R. (1970). *The social reality of crime*. Boston, MA: Little, Brown.

Radelet, M. L. (1981). Racial characteristics and the imposition of the death penalty. *American Sociological Review, 46*, 918–927.

Roberts, J., & Doob, A. (1997). Race, ethnicity, and criminal justice in Canada. In M. Tonry (Ed.), *Ethnicity, crime, and immigration: Comparative and cross-national perspectives* (Vol. 21, pp. 469–522). Chicago: University of Chicago Press.

Roberts, J. V. (2011). *Mitigation and aggravation at sentencing*. Cambridge: Cambridge University Press.

Salmi, V., Kivivuori, J., & Aaltonen, M. (2015). Correlates of immigrant youth crime in Finland. *European Journal of Criminology, 12*, 681–699.

Sampson, R. J., & Lauritsen, J. L. (1997). Racial and ethnic disparities in crime and criminal justice in the United States. *Crime and Justice, 21*, 311–374.

Schuyt, P. M. (2014). Bestraffing van adolescenten: Punitief of pedagogisch? *Strafblad, 6*, 39–43.

Smith, D. J. (1997). Ethnic origins, crime, and criminal justice in England and Wales. *Ethnicity, Crime, and Immigration, 21*, 101–182.

Snowball, L., & Weatherburn, D. (2007). Does racial bias in sentencing contribute to Indigenous overrepresentation in prison? *Australian and New Journal of Criminology, 40*(3), 272–290.

Spohn, C. (2009). *How do judges decide? The search for fairness and justice in punishment* (2nd ed.). Thousand Oaks, CA: Sage.

Spohn, C., & Holleran, D. (2000). The imprisonment penalty paid by young, unemployed Black and Hispanic male offenders. *Criminology, 38*, 281–306.

Statistics Netherlands. (2013). *Criminaliteit en Rechtshandhaving 2012* [Crime and law enforcement 2012]. Den Haag: Boom Uitgevers.

Statistics Netherlands. (2014). *Jaarrapport Integratie 2014* [Annual report on integration 2014]. Den Haag: CBS. Retrieved at: www.cbs.nl/-/media/imported/documents/2015/40/jaarrapport-integratie-2014-pub.pdf

StatLine. (2013). Population; sex, age, origin and generation, 1 January. Statistics Netherlands. Retrieved from: http://statline.cbs.nl/Statweb/publication/?VW=T&DM=SLEN&PA=37325ENG&D1=0-2&D2=0&D3=0&D4=0&D5=0-2&D6=l&HD=170704-1210&LA=EN&HDR=G2,G3,G4&STB=G1,T,G5.

Steffensmeier, D., & Demuth, S. (2001). Ethnicity and judges' sentencing decisions: Hispanic-Black-White comparisons. *Criminology, 39*, 145–178.

Steffensmeier, D., Ulmer, J. T., & Kramer, J. (1998). The interaction of race, gender, and age in criminal sentencing: The punishment cost of being young, black, and male. *Criminology, 36*, 763–797.

Thomson, R. J., & Zingraff, M. T. (1981). Detecting sentencing disparity: Some problems and evidence. *American Journal of Sociology, 86*, 869–880.

Timmerman, H., Bosma, J., & Jongman, R. (1986). Minderheden voor de rechter [Minorities facing the judge]. *Tijdschrift voor Criminologie, 28*, 57–72.

Tonry, M. (1997). Ethnicity, crime and immigration. In Tonry, M. (Ed.), *Ethnicity, crime, and immigration: Comparative and cross-national perspectives. Crime and justice: An annual review of research* (Vol. 21, pp. 1–29). Chicago, IL: University of Chicago Press.

Tonry, M. (1998). A comparative perspective on minority groups, crime, and criminal justice. *European Journal of Crime and Criminal Justice, 6*(1), 60–73.

Tonry, M. (2014). Race, ethnicity, crime and immigration. In S. Bucerius & M. Tonry (Eds.), *The Oxford handbook of ethnicity, crime, and immigration*. New York: Oxford University Press.

Tonry, M., & Bijleveld, C. (Eds.). (2007). *Crime and justice in the Netherlands. Crime and justice: A review of research* (Vol. 35). Chicago: University of Chicago Press.

Ulmer, J. T. (2012). Recent developments and new directions in sentencing research. *Justice Quarterly, 29*, 1–40.

Ulmer, J. T., Eisenstein, J., & Johnson, B. D. (2010). Trial penalties in federal sentencing: Extra-guidelines factors and district variation. *Justice Quarterly, 27*(4), 560–592.

Ulmer, J. T., & Kramer, J. H. (1996). Court communities under sentencing guidelines: Dilemmas of formal rationality and sentencing disparity? *Criminology, 34*, 383–408.

United States Sentencing Commission. (2015, January). *Quick facts. Federal offenders in prison*. Downloaded on June 6, 2016, from www.ussc.gov/sites/default/files/pdf/research-and-publications/quick-facts/Quick-Facts_BOP.pdf

Van der Werff, C., & Van der Zee-Nefkens, A. A. (1978). *Strafrechtelijke vervolging en bestraffing van Nederlanders en buitenlanders* [Prosecution and sentencing of Dutch and foreign suspects], WODC Onderzoek en Beleid 2. Den Haag: Staatsuitgeverij.

Van Tubergen, F. (2013). Religious change of new immigrants in the Netherlands: The event of migration. *Social Science Research, 42*, 715–725.

Van Wingerden, S.G.C., & Nieuwbeerta, P. (2006). *De vervolging en berechting van moord en doodslag in Nederland, 1993–2004* [The prosecution and sentencing of homicide and manslaughter in the Netherlands, 1993–2004]. Leiden: Nederlands Studiecentrum Criminaliteit en Rechtshandhaving.

Van Wingerden, S.G.C., & Nieuwbeerta, P. (2010). Straftoemeting bij moordenaars. De invloed van dader-, slachtoffer- en delictkenmerken [Sentencing homicide offenders: The influence of offender-, victim- and offense characteristics]. *Trema, 33*, 11–21.

Van Wingerden, S. G. C., Moerings, L. M., & Van Wilsem, J. A. (2011). *Recidiverisico en Straftoemeting* [Risk of reoffending and sentencing]. Den Haag: Raad voor de rechtspraak.

Van Wingerden S. G. C., Van Wilsem, J. A., & Johnson, B. D. (2016). Offender's personal circumstances and punishment: Toward a more refined model for the explanation of sentencing disparities. *Justice Quarterly, 33*(1), 100–133.

Warren, P., Chiricos, T., & Bales, W. (2012). The imprisonment penalty for young Black and Hispanic Males: A crime-specific analysis. *Journal of Research in Crime and Delinquency, 49*, 56–80.

Weber, M. (1954). *On law in economy and society*. Cambridge, MA: Harvard University Press.

Welsh, A., & Ogloff, J. (2008). Progressive reforms or maintaining the status quo? An empirical evaluation of the judicial consideration of Aboriginal status in sentencing decisions. *Canadian Journal of Criminology and Criminal Justice, 50*, 491–517.

Wermink, H.T., De Keijser, J.W., & Schuyt, P. M. (2012). Verschillen in straftoemeting in soortgelijke zaken: Een kwantitatief onderzoek naar de rol van specifieke kenmerken van de dader [Sentencing disparity in comparable cases: A quantitative research on the role of specific offender characteristics]. *Nederlands Juristenblad, 87*, 726–733.

Wermink, H. T., Johnson, B. D., De Keijser, J. W., Dirkzwager, A. J. E., Reef, J., & Nieuwbeerta, P. (2017). The influence of detailed offender characteristics on consecutive criminal processing decisions in the Netherlands. *Crime & Delinquency, 63*, 1279–1313.

Wermink, H. T., Johnson, B. D., Nieuwbeerta, P., & De Keijser, J. W. (2015). Expanding the scope of sentencing research: Determinants of juvenile and adult punishment in the Netherlands. *European Journal of Criminology, 12*(6), 739–768.

Wheeler, S., Weisburd, D., & Bode, N. (1982). Sentencing the white-collar offender: Rhetoric and reality. *American Sociological Review, 47*, 641–659.

Williams, T. (1999). Sentencing black offenders in the Ontario criminal justice system. In J. Roberts & D. Cole (Eds.), *Making sense of sentencing* (pp. 200–216). Toronto: University of Toronto Press.

Wooldredge, J. (2012). Distinguishing race effects on pre-trial release and sentencing decisions. *Justice Quarterly, 29*(1), 41–75.

Zatz, M. S. (1987). The changing forms of racial/ethnic biases in sentencing. *Journal of Research in Crime and Delinquency, 24*, 69–92.

Zatz, M. S. (2000). The convergence of race, ethnicity, gender, and class on court decisionmaking: Looking toward the 21st century. *Criminal Justice: The National Institute of Justice Journal, 3*, 503–552.

Appendix A
SUMMARY OF VARIABLES

	2007-Cohort	*RISc-data*	*Prison Project*
Offense Characteristics			
Offense severity	Statutory maximum penalty in 5 categories	Statutory maximum penalty in 6 categories[1]	Statutory maximum penalty (continuous)
Offense	—Type of most serious offense (20 dummy variables) —Number of charges	—Type of most serious offense (15 dummy variables) —Number of charges	—Type of most serious offense (15 dummy variables) —Number of charges —Complicity
Other Offender Characteristics			
Sex	Comparison males and females (0 = male; 1 = female)	Comparison males and females (0 = male; 1 = female)	Only males
Age	5 categories (18–21, 22–30, 31–40, 41–50, > 50)	5 categories (18–21, 22–30, 31–40, 41–50, > 50)	5 categories (18–21, 22–30, 31–40, 41–50, > 50)
Criminal history	—Continuous measure of convictions in the past five years (distinctions for property, violent, and other crimes) —Prior prison sentence	—Continuous measure of convictions in the past five years (distinctions for property, violent, and other crimes) —Prior prison sentence	—Continuous measure of convictions in the past 5 years (distinctions for property, violent, and other crimes) —Prior prison sentence —Age of onset
Personal circumstances	*n/a*	Measures collected in the Probation Office's RISc assessment (see also Van Wingerden et al., 2016): —Accommodation	—Educational attainment —Fulltime education —(Un)employment —Income —Ever active on labor market

	2007-Cohort	RISc-data	Prison Project
		—Education and employment —Financial management and income —Relationships with partner, family, and relatives —Relationships with friends —Drug misuse —Alcohol misuse —Emotional well-being —Thinking and behavior —Attitude	—Benefits —Homeless/drifting —Overall health —Chronic health problem —Serious health problem past year —Alcohol misuse —Drug misuse —Married/registered partner —Number of children
Trial Characteristics			
Trial	Pretrial detention (y/n and length)	Pretrial detention (y/n and length)	Length of pretrial detention and pretrial release
	Single sitting judge/panel of judges/court of appeal	*n/a*	Single sitting judge/panel of judges
	Sentence imposed in combination with measure	*n/a*	*n/a*
	n/a	*n/a*	Private versus public attorney
	n/a	Acceptance of criminal responsibility	Acceptance of criminal responsibility

1 This measure takes into account statutory factors such as attempted versus completed crime, complicity, and concurrence of offenses.

11

THE RELATIONSHIP BETWEEN THE GENDER OF THE PROBATION OFFICER AND JUDICIAL SENTENCING

Implications for Black Male Offenders

Michael J. Leiber, Jennifer H. Peck, Melanie Valentin Rosa, and Tayler Shreve

Connecting the minimal and maximalist perspectives of gender differences in decision-making with aspects of the courtroom workgroup model, the present study examines the impact of the gender of probation officers and judges on sentencing recommendations and actual judicial sentence (community supervision versus incarceration) of White and Black adult male offenders. Utilizing data from a District Criminal Court in a Midwestern state, we investigate the extent to which being a male or female probation officer impacts sentencing recommendations and judicial sentencing by White male judges and what these relationships entail concerning the treatment of Black male offenders compared to White male offenders. The results provide insights into the complexities of criminal justice decision-making and the potential concordance between recommendations and final sentencing outcomes as well as what roles the gender and race of decision-makers and offenders play in this process.

Both theory and prior research have attempted to better delineate the contexts of criminal court outcomes as these relate to racial/ethnic disparities (Feldmeyer and Ulmer, 2011; King and Johnson, 2016; Spohn, 2009; Sutton, 2013; Ulmer and Johnson, 2004). These efforts range from the development of labeling theory and the use of typescripts by criminal justice decision-makers (e.g., Steen, Engen, and Gainey, 2005); the emergence of attribution theory (e.g., Albonetti, 1991); the expansion of attribution theory integrating organizational and community concerns and racial stereotyping to formulate the focal concerns perspective (e.g., Steffensmeier, Ulmer, and Kramer, 1998), to the impact of community characteristics (e.g., Sutton, 2013; Wang and Mears, 2010) on the social control of offenders. These efforts have particularly focused on the explanations for why Black offenders are more likely to receive disadvantaged court outcomes compared to similarly situated Whites. Despite both theoretical and empirical advancements into understanding the factors that may fuel disparate treatment of offenders based on race, one element that has been understudied is the influence of decision-maker characteristics.

For example, the gender of the probation officer and the judge are additional factors that could contribute to potential differences in the handling of White and Black offenders. Since the probation officer makes a recommendation to the judge, and then the judge makes the final sentencing decision, there are two distinct points in time where the gender of decision-makers may influence court outcomes. The presence of race differences in sentencing outcomes has mainly been attributed to the racial composition of the offender. While more recently there has been an increased focus on organizational court contexts and community characteristics as explanations for race differences in criminal justice outcomes, little is known about the influence of the gender of the court officer on these decisions.

Concomitantly, with the processing of criminal offenders comes the potential existence for stereotypes to emerge and subsequently affect decision-making (King and Johnson, 2016). The gender of the decision-maker may be an important predictor of criminal court outcomes, especially if race stereotypes influence the treatment of male offenders differently for male and female court officers (Chodorow, 1978; Johnson, 2014; Leiber and Brubaker, 2010; Peck, Leiber, Beaudry-Cyr, and Toman, 2016; Steffensmeier and Hebert, 1999). Likewise, if gender differences exist in the case processing of offenders in the form of recommendations made by male and female probation officers, these could also translate into disparities involving actual sentences of Black and White male offenders by White male judges. This possible linkage has not been explored and serves as the impetus for the present study.

We use the maximalist and minimalist perspectives drawn from the feminist and public administration literature as a framework for exploring the possibility of gender differences in probation officer recommendations and actual judicial decision-making in the treatment of male criminal offenders (e.g., Eisenstein and Jacob, 1977; Epstein, 1988; Giele, 1988; Ulmer, 1997). Using data from a District Criminal Court in a Midwestern state, two general questions frame the current study. The first question asks: What impact does the gender of the probation officer have on sentencing recommendations and judicial sentencing outcomes by White male judges? The second question investigates if these relationships exist: What are the implications for the treatment of Black male offenders compared to White male offenders? The results from our inquiry have implications for broadening the scope of the intricacies of criminal justice decision-making.

Theoretical Background

The maximalist and minimalist perspectives are used as a theoretical framework to inquire into the possible relationships between the gender of decision-makers and the processing of Black and White male offenders. According to the maximalist approach, men and women differ in their cognitive processes, emotions, world views, and behaviors (Chodorow, 1978; Gilligan, 1982; Thompson, 1991). These gender differences are due to a varied number of biological, psychological, and other interrelated factors. Both Chodorow (1978) and Gilligan (1982) suggest that the process of gender identification occurs early in childhood and results in greater autonomy and a competitive demeanor for boys, while girls are socialized to be moralistic, sensitive to the needs of others, and considered to be problem-solvers. Mothers are believed to encourage sons to develop a sense of separate self, be less relational than daughters, and ultimately form their gender identity by becoming "not female" (Chodorow, 1978). Conversely, a daughter's primary relationship is with her mother and continues longer into the life course compared to the mother-son connection. This continued association is based on their common biological sex and her mother's unconscious desire to re-experience this nurturing relationship with her own mother (the daughter's grandmother). Due to this delayed independence, daughters openly identify and satisfy their relational needs through their mothers.

Furthermore, although some argue that most people utilize two moral reasoning orientations (an ethic of justice and ethic of care), females tend to use an ethic of care model compared to an ethic of justice (Kohlberg, 1976; Gilligan, 1982). Research has found that females tend to identify their form of moral reasoning through the ability to nurture, respond to, and protect others (Gilligan, 1982). An ethic of justice is more commonly found in males with an orientation of impartiality, fairness, and reciprocity (Simola, Barling, and Turner, 2010). When specifically focusing on female decision-makers in a criminal justice setting, some research suggests that women judges speak in a different type of moral voice compared to males. However, this variation is not due to dissimilarities in moral reasoning, but is based on gender-specific experiences (Fineman, 1994; Spohn and Hemmens, 2009). Underlying this viewpoint is the argument that women are more likely to be victims of overall violence, sexual assault, domestic violence, and sexual harassment than men. Due to notions about fear of crime and perceived or actual instances of victimization, females' attitudes and responses to criminal behavior as a decision-maker are more punitive than her male counterparts (Epstein, 1988; Steffensmeier and Hebert, 1999).

An alternative approach to the maximalist perspective is the minimalist viewpoint. Rather than explaining gender differences as inherent to male and female identities, the minimalist approach contends that, if gender differences have the potential to exist in decision-making, the disparities are attenuated by factors outside of the individual. For example, a lack of opportunities or practical constraints may be present throughout society that impact females more so than males. However, the education, training, norms, and organizational rules and procedures that both sexes learn and receive are believed to override any gender disparities in decision-making that would have existed due to inherit biological, psychological, and experiential differences (e.g., Steffensmeier and Hebert, 1999: 1165–1166; Sanborn, 1996; Singer, 1996). In the sections to follow, the effects of decision-maker gender on sentencing outcomes are reviewed in the context of both the maximalist and the minimalist viewpoints.

Literature Review

Underlying the current study is the assumption that probation officer recommendations are relied upon by judges in the determination of actual sentences. Thus, the forthcoming discussion first focuses on past research on the relationships between probation officer recommendations and sentencing by judges. Next, the discussion will cover the limited research that exists assessing the role of an offender's race in the progression from probation recommendation to final sentence. Recall that we are unaware of prior empirical research that has specifically examined how the gender of the probation officer influences his/her sentencing recommendation and subsequent sentence by a White male judge involving Black male offenders. The discussion concludes with a description of the few studies that have investigated whether female decision-makers are more alike or different than her male counterparts in regards to probation recommendations and judicial sentencing, with a specific focus on the impact these relationships may have on the court outcomes of Black offenders.

Probation Officer Recommendations and Actual Judicial Sentencing

Probation officers are an integral component of the courtroom workgroup and their role in sentencing decisions is complex in nature. Spohn and colleagues (2001) contend that judges focus on punishment issues when making decisions, while prosecutors are more likely to center on the likelihood of conviction (e.g., Leiber et al., 2011; Leiber, Beaudry-Cyr, Peck, and Mack, 2017; Leifker and Sample, 2010). Probation officers are not only supervisory agents of those placed on probation but are also involved in gathering information about the offender's prior legal history; current association with the criminal justice system; and social backgrounds/situations (e.g., employment, marital status, number of children, etc.). Probation officers also make recommendations on sentencing outcomes and possible conditions of probation (Neubauer, 2005; Walsh, 1985). In performing all of these responsibilities, probation officers also consider the possibility of future criminal offending and assess the defendant's degree of remorsefulness and cooperativeness with the court (Spencer, 1983). There is also a desire for probation officers to maintain credibility with their courtroom workgroup, especially prosecutors and judges (Rosecrance, 1985). Therefore, probation officers attempt to make recommendations and decisions that appear to be reasonable and in-line with the norms and practices of the courtroom workgroup.

The courtroom workgroup consists of probation officers, prosecutors, defense attorneys, and judges. Cooperation among decision-makers rather than conflict is emphasized and expected in their working relationships (Eisenstein and Jacob, 1977; Spohn and Hemmens, 2009; Ulmer, 1997). While the courtroom workgroup consists of various court actors and each decision-maker has his/her own set of beliefs, values, and objectives, it is believed that they are dependent on one another in regards to the court outcomes of offenders (Leiber et al., 2017; Leifker and Sample, 2010; Spohn and Hemmens, 2009; Spohn, 2009). In turn, the philosophies and norms of the courtroom workgroup play significant roles in the administration of justice (Dixon, 1995; Spohn and Hemmens, 2009).

Regardless of the cooperative assumptions of the courtroom workgroup, the sentencing literature is inconsistent in terms of the influence of recommendations by probation officers on judicial court rulings. In some instances, probation officers and judges have been found to work interdependently and rely primarily on the probation officer's presentence investigation (PSI) report to determine appropriate sentencing (Czajkoski, 1973; Walsh, 1985). The PSI report is considered to be an objective reporting tool used to document the defendant's background characteristics, risks, needs, and often contains a sentencing recommendation. Probation officers are seen as having a "quasijudicial" role where their recommendations are heavily relied upon by judges (Leiber et al., 2011). Other research reports that probation officers' recommendations to judges are not "quasijudicial" but rather are largely "ceremonial" and uninfluential in sentencing decisions (Hagan et al., 1979; Rosecrance, 1988). That is, the PSI reports are neither predictive of sentencing outcomes (Kingsnorth, MacIntosh, and Sutherland, 2002) nor as influential as plea bargaining decisions (Hagan et al., 1979). Since both prosecutors and defense attorneys confer with probation officers prior to the submission of PSI reports to judges, it has been argued that sentence recommendations are already consistent with the opinions of other court actors and therefore may not be very influential on actual judicial outcomes (Neubauer, 2005; Spohn and Hemmens, 2009).

Offender Race, Probation Officer Recommendations, and Actual Sentencing

Prior research has shown that organizational arrangements among decision-makers, such as "going rates" and/or the classification of crimes and offenders as "normal," has emerged in courtroom proceedings (Albonetti, 1991; Spencer, 1983; Sudnow, 1965). An additional discovery includes the suggestion that court actors' perceptions are influenced by racial stereotypes that characterize Black defendants as criminal, dangerous, and likely to reoffend (Steffensmeier et al., 1998; Hagan, 1975). Most of these studies, however, focused on the influence of defendant race on court outcomes involving either prosecutorial and/or judicial decision-making (e.g., Albonetti, 1991; Crawford, Chiricos, and Kleck, 1998; Crew, 1991; Feldmeyer and Ulmer, 2011; Johnson, 2006; Kautt, 2002; Spohn, Gruhl, and Welch, 1987; Steffensmeier and DeMuth, 2000). This research reveals that even though legal factors are often the strongest determinants of court outcomes, minorities and young Black male offenders are more disadvantaged than comparable White offenders (Farrell and Bishop, 2008; Mitchell, 2005).

Of the few studies that have examined the effects of offender race and probation recommendations on judicial sentencing, the evidence is inconclusive if Black defendants are subjected to biased outcomes via probation officer recommendations. For example, Hagan and colleagues (1979) failed to find an indication of differences in outcomes due to race or any significant relationships between probation officer recommendations and judicial decision-making. The authors concluded that prosecutor recommendations were more important to judicial sentencing than those made by probation officers. Likewise, Drass and Spenser (1987) also failed to find evidence of race differences in the construction of probation officer presentence recommendations.

In another study by Hagan (1975), results indicated that probation officer perceptions and evaluations of offenders in terms of the likelihood of recidivism were impacted by the race of the offender. Minority defendants were perceived as having a greater risk to fail on probation than Whites. This assumption was found to be linked to sentencing recommendations that in turn introduced bias in later judicial outcomes (Hagan, 1975). Freiburger and Hilinski (2011) discovered a high level of agreement between probation officers' recommendations and final sentencing decisions. When judges departed from these recommendations, judges sentenced defendants to a harsher ruling. Probation officers were also over three times more likely to recommend a prison sentence versus jail sentence for Black males compared to White males.

Last, Leiber and colleagues (2011) reported that probation officer recommendations were in concordance with judicial sentences involving community-based corrections, jail, prison, and overall sentence length. The results suggested a complex relationship between probation officers and judges in that judges appeared to take into account factors from presentence investigations (including sentencing recommendations) to inform decisions about the sanctioning of offenders. This reliance suggested a judicial dependence on the probation officer to possibly help reduce uncertainty revolving around defendants' degree of blameworthiness, concerns about community protection, and organizational considerations and constraints. Despite the finding of agreement between probation officer recommendations and judicial sentencing, and consistent with some prior research (Drass and Spenser, 1987; Hagan et al., 1979), offender race was not a significant determinant of probation officer recommendations but did impact judicial decisions. Black offenders had an increased likelihood of receiving a prison sentence compared to jail sentence and a lengthier sentence relative to comparable White offenders. The effect of race on sanctioning is consistent with the larger body of literature on race and judicial sentencing (Johnson, 2006; King and Johnson, 2016; Spohn and Holleran, 2000; Wang and Mears, 2010).

Gender of Decision-Makers, Offender Race, Probation Officer Recommendations, and Actual Judicial Sentencing

As previously stated, we are unaware of an empirical examination that has investigated the effects of the gender of the decision-maker on probation recommendations and judicial sentencing of adult Black defendants.[1] Horn and Evans (2000) studied the link between the gender of probation officers, the gender of offenders, and findings from PSI reports. Male and female probation officers were assigned different cases depending on the gender of the offender. Male probation officers typically wrote PSI reports for male offenders, and these cases generally reflected charges involving robbery, burglary, and drug crimes. Female probation officers were more likely to oversee female offenders and wrote PSI reports for cases usually involving fraud, forgery, and other theft crimes. Consequently, because of these differences in the kinds of cases that probation officers were assigned, male officers recommended more severe sanctions compared to those given by female officers. Leifker and Sample (2010) also studied the determinants of probation recommendations, taking into consideration the gender of the probation officer, the race of the offender, and the extent probation officer recommendations were followed by judges in the sentencing of the offender. The study did not examine what factors predicted actual sentencing outcomes. Leifker and Sample (2010) reported a 79% agreement between a sentencing recommendation and judicial sentencing. Neither the gender of the probation officer nor the offender race/ethnicity was related to probation recommendations once all factors were controlled. It is important to point out that Leifker and Sample (2010) acknowledge that, in cases involving the 21% of non-agreement with judges' sentences, "85 of these 105 cases were recommendations by female probation officers" which they indicate "may be an avenue of future research" (2010: 507).

Although still understudied, and relative to the characteristics of probation officers and sentencing recommendations, a greater number of studies have been conducted that examined whether female judges sentence differently than male judges (for review, see Spohn, 2009). This research has shown little evidence that female and male judges are different in terms of sentencing decisions (Spohn, 2009). When disparities are found, conclusions were made that female judges sentence more severely than male judges (Gruhl, Spohn, and Welch, 1981; Steffensmeier and Hebert, 1999). Gruhl and colleagues (1981) also found that when the gender of the judge influenced sentencing decisions, female judges sentenced female offenders more severely than male judges. Steffensmeier and Hebert (1999) report also that female judges sentence more harshly than male judges but this effect was evident for cases involving less serious offenses (property crimes) when the amount of discretion is greatest.

More specific, basing their research on the maximalist and minimalist perspectives, Steffensmeier and Hebert (1999) found that there was greater support for the minimalist viewpoint since male and female judges were found to be more alike than different in sentencing. Conversely, some support was also provided for the maximalist position. Black defendants received harsher sentencing outcomes by male and female judges, and the effect was larger for female judges. They also found that, while there were no gender differences concerning the treatment of White female offenders, female judges sanctioned Black male offenders, Black female offenders, and male offenders more harshly than male judges. For female judges, the effect of being Black and male on punitive sanctioning was enhanced for repeat offenders. Steffensmeier and Hebert (1999) indicate that the gender-of-judge effects, in part, were due to the belief that females are more threatened by breaking norms and laws than are men, and the young Black male repeat offender is especially threatening to female judges (1999: 1182).

Implications for the Present Study

The present research is guided by two general questions that revolve around the minimalist and maximalist perspectives for decision-making in the criminal justice system. Although a direct theoretical test of both viewpoints is not feasible due to data limitations, the perspectives are able to inform and steer both research questions. The first research question is: What impact does the gender of the probation officer have on sentencing recommendations and judicial sentencing outcomes by White male judges?

The second research question states: If relationships exist, what are the implications for the treatment of Black male offenders compared to White male offenders? In addition to the theoretical perspectives that inform the research questions (although not a specific test of either viewpoint), several expectations emerge concerning the possibility of disparities across the gender of court actors' in the exercise of social control involving Black male criminal defendants. These expectations also incorporate aspects from prior studies of decision-making that involved the gender of court actors, probation recommendations, offender race, and judicial sentencing.

More specific, the first expectation derives from an interpretation of the maximalist perspective (Chodorow, 1978) and prior research concerning the concordance or lack thereof between probation recommendations and judicial sentencing (Kingsnorth et al., 2002; Walsh, 1985). The first expectation is that, since females are more likely to adhere to an ethic of care moral reasoning (Gilligan, 1982) that emphasizes compassion and empathy, female probation officers compared to male probation officers may be more lenient in their probation recommendations and specifically how the ethic applies to Black male offenders. An alternative expectation (the second expectation) is that female probation officers will sentence more severely than their male counterparts. Underlying this prediction is the interplay between the belief that females are more moralistic and less tolerant of rule violation than males, and the lived experiences of females may involve sexual harassment, sexual assault, and other forms of violent victimization (Steffensmeier and Hebert, 1999). Some suggest that these incidents and fears of being a victim of crime shape attitudes and responses to criminal offending. Accordingly, the individual and combined impact of being male and Black would result in more severe recommendations made by female probation officers since these characteristics are often portrayed and subsequently perceived as criminal and threatening (Steffensmeier et al., 1998).

Also related to the maximalist viewpoint, a third expectation is that, due to living in a society characterized by gender and racial discrimination, female probation officers may be more sensitive to bias and discrimination and therefore more equitable in the treatment of all offenders than are male decision-makers (Leiber et al., 1995; Leiber and Woodrick, 1997; Leiber, 2000; Leiber, Peck, and Beaudry-Cyr, 2016; Leiber et al., 2017). In other words, a third possibility is that female probation officers will respond to all offenders alike, irrespective of race, but male probation officers will treat Black male offenders in a disadvantaged (biased) manner. Therefore, the race of the offender will not influence probation recommendations for female officers, but offender race will predict recommendations for male officers to the disadvantage of Black male offenders.

In all three above possibilities, judges may be faced with contrasting recommendations made by male and female probation officers that could involve biases toward Black male offenders. These contrasting recommendations would be supportive of the maximalist theoretical framework. A fourth expectation that also parallels the maximalist viewpoint is that male judges are more likely rely on sentencing recommendations made by male probation officers than those by female probation officers (Leifker and Sample, 2010). Based on the first two expectations where female probation officers will recommend more lenient outcomes due to an ethic of care moral reasoning *or* harsher due to a reliance on stereotypes of Black males, male probation officers are thought to rely more on the law (i.e., an offenders prior record, crime severity, offense type, etc.) when making decisions. Subsequently, the sentencing recommendations from male probation officers will not be biased toward the Black male offender because they relate to the ethic of justice moral reasoning more so than the ethic of care. If this assumption is valid, male judges will impose sentences in a similar neutral manner that aligns with the sanctions by male probation officers but that is in direct contrast to those put forth by female officers.

Recall back to the third expectation, where male probation officers more so than their female counterparts are expected to put forth sentencing recommendations involving disadvantaged outcomes for Black male offenders. In the third expectation, female probation officers are argued to be sensitive to discrimination issues and therefore make decisions in a race-neutral manner; however, male probation officers will recommend Black male offenders for greater social control. If this is true, then the fifth expectation (which to a degree is similar to the fourth expectation with one slight difference) argues that by relying on the racially tainted recommendations made by male probation officers, judges will sentence Black male offenders more severely than White male offenders.

The final expectation is based on the minimalist viewpoint (Chodorow, 1978; Singer, 1996) and prior research of gender differences in the decision-making process of criminal justice actors (Eisenstein and Jacob, 1977; Leifker and Sample, 2010; Steffensmeier and Hebert, 1999; Ulmer, 1997). This sixth expectation is that female and male probation officers will be similar in their probation recommendations involving Black male offenders relative to White male offenders. Likewise, probation officer recommendations will be concordant with judicial sentences and these decisions would not vary by the gender of the probation officer. Further, the race of the offender is not assumed to be a determinant of judges' sentencing decisions once legal (e.g., crime severity, offense type) and court procedural factors are taken into consideration. Overall with this final expectation, male and female probation officers and male judges would appear to be bounded by the law, legal training, and courtroom workgroup socialization in making decisions as officers of the court (Tracy, 2005). The overall premise of the present study is to examine which of these expectations can explain the possible influence of the gender of the decision-maker on court outcomes and its impact on the treatment of Black male offenders.

The Present Study

The focus of the present research is on criminal justice decision-making in a District Court that consists of 3 regional divisions within 11 counties in a Midwestern state. The District Court is the third largest in the state, with the largest county in the District having a population of 130,224 residents (United States Census Bureau, 2000). At the time of the study, 28 judges and 58 probation officers held these judicial positions in the District Court.[2] Of the 28 judges, all but 3 were male. There is variability across the gender of the probation officer and will be discussed in the following section. Over 90% of the sample contains judges and probation officers who are White, preventing the race/ethnicity of the decision-makers as predictor variables for the analyses. Thus, the sample is primarily represented by White decision-makers (i.e., probation officers and judges) with the gender of the judges being male.

Data and Sample

Due to the relatively small number of Black residents in the District Court and overall state, adult case files were identified over a 2-year period (2003 through 2004) and included all cases involving the filing of a PSI report with adults accused of criminal behavior. Simple random sampling was used to acquire the case records of White defendants into the sample, while disproportionate random sampling was used for Blacks to ensure enough statistical power in the analyses.[3] Female offenders comprised a relatively small number of the total weighted sample size (256 females). Due to this small number and the primary focus of wanting to estimate interactions between the gender of the probation officer and race of the offender on probation recommendations and actual judicial sentences, the sample for the present study was restricted to male offenders (n = 907).

Independent Variables

Table 11.1 presents the coding and distribution of the independent, control, and dependent variables. The inclusion of these variables was based on the theoretical frameworks and prior research on criminal justice sentencing (e.g., Leiber et al., 2017; Leifker and Sample, 2010; Steffensmeier and Hebert, 1999).

Fifty-six percent of the sample had a male probation officer (56%), who were largely White (78%). The control variables are represented by demographic characteristics, the geographic division of the District, prior and current involvement in the criminal justice system, and various court-specific indicators relevant to the offender. On average, the sample is approximately 32 years old, not married (77%), has children (52%), and is unemployed (54%).

Two dummy variables, "Northeast" and "Western," indicate the geographic division of the District Court, where the "Eastern" division served as the reference category.[4] In regards to prior and current history with the court, the sample averaged six prior court referrals, and 59% were currently under court authority at the time of their most recent offense. Multiple measures regarding the most recent offense of each offender was captured as well. These indicators included the number of charges, offense type, offense severity, and whether a weapon was present during the offense. The average number of charges was 1.70, and dummy variables were created to distinguish between property, person, and drug offenses. "Other" offenses constituted the reference category (e.g., disorderly conduct, resisting arrest, etc.). Most cases involved drug offenses (49%), followed by property offenses (22%), and person offenses (14%). Offense severity represented the statutory code of the crime and ranged from the least severe (simple misdemeanor) to most severe (Class A felony). The average offense severity was 4.70, which corresponded to a significant percentage of cases being classified as a Class C

Table 11.1 Coding and Distribution ofVariables (N = 907)

Variable	*Value*	N	%
Independent			
Gender of probation officer	0 – Male	509	56
	1 – Female	398	44
Race	0 – White	704	
	1 – Black	202	
Controls			
Age (low to high)	Mean = 31.6 SD = 10.6 Range = 18–67		
Not married	0 – Married	210	23
	1 – Not married	697	77
No children	0 – Children	469	52
	1 – No children	487	48
Unemployed	0 – Employed	416	46
	1 – Unemployed	490	54
Northeast division[a]	0 – No	701	77
	1 – Yes	205	23
Western division[a]	0 – No	394	43
	1 – Yes	513	57
Prior referrals (low to high)	Mean = 6.0 SD = 3.7 Range = 0–10		
Court authority	0 – No	703	78
	1 – Yes	203	22
# Charges (low to high)	Mean = 1.7 SD = 1.1 Range = 1–5		
Property offense[b]	0 – No	703	78
	1 – Yes	203	22
Person offense[b]	0 – No	782	86
	1 – Yes	125	14
Drug offense[b]	0 – No	455	51
	1 – Yes	451	49
Offense severity (low to high)	Mean = 4.7 SD = 1.8 Range = 0–6		
Weapon	0 – No	820	90
	1 – Yes	87	10
No bail	0 – Bail	328	36
	1 – No bail	579	64

(Continued)

Table 11.1 (Continued)

Variable	*Value*	N	%
Counsel	0 – No	530	59
	1 – Yes	376	41
No plea bargain	0 – Plea bargain	290	32
	1 – No plea bargain	617	68
Dependent			
Probation officer recommendation[c]	0 – Community	501	55
	1 – Incarceration	405	45
Judicial sentence[d]	0 – Community	418	58
	1 – Incarceration	320	42

a Dummy variable with eastern division as reference category.
b Dummy variable with "other" (e.g., resisting arrest) as the reference category.
c Probation recommendation treated as independent and dependent variable.
d Sample is 720 cases. Discrepancy due to 187 cases dismissed prior to or after trial.

felony. Only 10% of the cases in the sample included the presence of a weapon. In general, these distributions indicated that offenses in this sample of adult males were more severe and contained an overrepresentation of charges involving drug offenses than those reflected in national aggregate arrest statistics during the period of data collection (United States Department of Justice, 2005). Last, three court-specific procedural variables were also taken into consideration. These measures indicated whether the defendant was on bail (36%), had legal counsel (59%), or was offered a plea bargain (32%).[5]

Dependent Variables

Probation recommendation is treated not only as independent variable but also as a dependent variable. While existing literature has indicated that sentencing research should distinguish between community-based sanctions, jail, and prison outcomes (Freiburger and Hilinski, 2013), we were unable to do so as a result of the small number of offenders who received a recommendation of jail as an outcome (n = 35). Thus, the two dependent variables, "Probation recommendation" and "Judicial sentencing" were differentiated by 0 (community) and 1 (incarceration).[6] The incarceration category within both dependent variables consisted of recommendations or actual sentences involving jail or prison. Fifty-five percent of the sample had a probation recommendation that consisted of a community-based sanction, and 58% of the sample received an actual sentence of community placement.

Similarities in Cases Handled by Probation Officers

Although not shown, an examination of the distributions and comparisons of the independent variables differentiated by the gender of the probation officer showed few statistically significant differences between male and female probation officers. Contrary to results reported by Horn and Evans (2000), these similarities indicate that the assignment of cases is not dependent upon the gender of the probation officer. For example, adults charged with property offenses comprised 23% of the cases handled by male probation officers compared to 22% for female probation officers. Person offenders represented 17% of the cases for male probation officers and represented 11% of the cases for female probation officers. In terms of probation recommendations, little variability existed in suggestions of community sanctions compared to incarceration. Male probation officers recommended incarceration for 57% of their cases, while female probation officers recommended this same outcome for 54% of their cases. One difference that emerged across decision-maker gender is that female probation officers oversaw cases involving a greater percentage of people under court authority than those assigned to male probation officers (70% compared to 50%).

In addition, cases with female probation officers represented a smaller percentage of offenders receiving an actual judicial sentence of incarceration (24%) compared to her male counterparts (54%). Although bivariate in nature, these associations suggest greater nonconcordance between probation recommendations and judicial sentencing involving female probation officers. A difference of 30% emerged between incarceration recommendations and incarceration sentences for female probation officers and judges, compared to a 3% difference in recommendations and sentences of incarceration for male probation officers and judges. Despite no gender differences in probation recommendations, there is the possibility that concordance between recommendations and actual sentencing varies by the gender of the probation officer.

Results

Main Effects of the Gender of Probation Officer and Offender Race on Probation Officer Recommendations and Judicial Sentencing

Table 11.2 presents the additive (main) logistic regression results predicting probation officer recommendations (column 1) and judicial sentencing decisions (column 2). The independent variables of interest in predicting probation recommendations are the gender of the probation officer and race of the offender. These two measures are also the main predictor variables in modeling incarceration decisions; in addition to probation, recommendations become an additional independent variable in this model.

As shown in column 1, the gender of the probation officer was a significant predictor of probation recommendations. In support of the maximalist perspective (Chodorow, 1978; Thompson, 1991), female probation officers had a 38% decreased likelihood of recommending incarceration compared to male probation officers. Consistent with some research (Drass and Spenser, 1987; Hagan et al., 1979), the race of the offender did not exert a significant effect on probation recommendations, even though offender race is often a predictor of other decisions in court processing (Crawford et al., 1998; Steffensmeier and DeMuth, 2000). Being Black or White was not a determinant of how probation officers made decisions in this sample of adult offenders.

Table 11.2 Logistic Regression Results for Probation Officer Recommendations and Judicial Sentencing—Main Effects

Variable	*Probation Officer Recommendation Full Model (1)*	*Judicial Sentencing Full Model (2)*
Female probation officer	**−.48[a]****	**−1.16****
	(.17)	(.25)
	.62	.31
Black offender	.31	**.82****
	(.19)	(.26)
	1.35	2.26
Probation officer incarceration recommendation		**−1.82****
		(.22)
		.16
Controls		
Age	−.01	**.05****
	(.01)	(.01)
	1.00	1.05
Not married	−.16	−.49
	(.18)	(.27)
	.85	.62
No children	**.85****	**.64****
	(.17)	(.24)
	2.33	1.89
Unemployed	**−.40****	**.57****
	(.15)	(.22)
	.67	1.77
Northeastern division	−.14	**.63***
	(.23)	(.32)
	.87	1.87
Western division	.18	**.81****
	(.19)	(.28)
	1.20	1.87
Prior referrals	**−.15****	.03
	(.02)	(.04)
	.85	1.04
Court authority	**.40****	**−1.40****
	(.17)	(.23)
	1.49	.25
Charges	−.12	.16
	(.07)	(.09)
	.88	1.18
Property offense	**−.84****	**.76***
	(.27)	(.38)
	.43	2.14
Person offense	**−.72****	**.85***
	(.29)	(.42)
	.49	2.34

Variable	Probation Officer Recommendation Full Model (1)	Judicial Sentencing Full Model (2)
Drug offense	**−.72****	**.77***
	(.24)	(.34)
	.49	2.16
Offense severity	−.04	.01
	(.04)	(.06)
	.96	1.00
Weapon	.47	.16
	(.26)	(.35)
	1.60	1.17
No bail	−.28	.29
	(.16)	(.22)
	.76	.34
No legal counsel	**.42****	**−1.25****
	(.16)	(.24)
	1.53	.29
−2 log likelihood	1096.8	610.9
N	923	720

a Regression coefficient, Standard error (SE), Exponential B (Exp (B))

** $p < .01$, *$p < .05$

Column 2 displays the effects of the gender of the probation officer, offender race, probation officer recommendations, and control variables on actual judicial sentencing. Results indicated that cases that involved a female probation officer had a 69% decreased likelihood of being incarcerated compared to her male counterparts. The findings suggest concordance between probation officer recommendations and judicial sentencing depending on officer gender, as female probation officers were more likely to recommend community-based sanctions compared to male officers, and judges were more likely to decide a similar sentence (community sanctions) for cases with a female probation officer. Contrary to the null effect of offender race on probation recommendations, Black offenders were over two times more likely to be incarcerated compared to Whites. Therefore, even though the race of the offender did not directly impact probation recommendations, Black offenders had a higher risk of incarceration as an actual sentence than Whites (Crew, 1991; Johnson, 2006). Results also showed non-concordance between probation officer recommendations and judicial sentencing (see also Hagan et al., 1979; Rosecrance, 1985), as cases where probation officers recommended incarceration were 84% less likely to receive incarceration as their actual sentence.

Up to this point in the analyses regarding the main effects of the predictor variables on probation recommendations and judicial sentencing, the finding of leniency in probation recommendations by female officers supports the maximalist perspective and the first expectation that female decision-makers will be more lenient compared to their male counterparts. However, the minimalist perspective and the sixth expectation were not supported because the race of the offender was a determining factor in judicial sentencing to the disadvantage of Black male offenders. In addition, the concordance between probation recommendations and judicial sentencing did vary by the gender of the probation officer.

Interaction Effects of the Gender of Probation Officer and Offender Race on Probation Officer Recommendations and Judicial Sentencing

Table 11.3 presents the coefficients from 12 logistic regression models predicting probation recommendations and judicial sentencing. Each coefficient represents a separate logistic regression model, and all control variables were included in the analyses. Since the overall objective of the present study is to assess the potential joint impact between the gender of the probation officer and offender race on probation recommendations

Table 11.3 Logistic Regression Coefficients for Gender and Race Subgroup Interactions Involving Probation Officer Recommendations and Judicial Sentencing

	Probation Officer Recommendation (1)	*Judicial Sentencing* (2)
A. Comparison to male probation officer White offender		
Male probation officer Black offender	**.68[a]****	.34
	(.28)	(.36)
	1.98	1.41
Female probation officer White offender	−.28	**−1.29****
	(.20)	(.29)
	.75	.27
Female probation officer Black offender	−.55	−.48
	(.29)	(.40)
	.58	.62
B. Comparison to male probation officer Black offender		
Female probation officer White offender	**−1.10****	**−1.61****
	(.30)	(.46)
	.33	.20
Female probation officer Black offender	**−.89****	−.96
	(.38)	(.56)
	.41	.38
C. Comparison to female probation officer White offenders		
Female probation officer Black offender	.01	**2.23****
	(.28)	(.55)
	1.01	9.25

a Regression coefficient, Standard error (SE), Exponential B (Exp (B))

Note: In terms of the probation officer gender/offender race subgroups, the reference group (coded as 0) is italicized, versus the comparison group (coded as 1). For example, "comparison to male probation officer, White offender" is the reference group (coded as 0), as it relates to "Male probation officer, Black offender" (coded as 1). Each coefficient represents a separate logistic regression model. Control variables included in all models.

** $p < .01$, * $p < .05$

and actual sentencing outcomes, individual variables were constructed between each type of probation officer gender and offender race combination (e.g., male probation officer/Black offender, female probation officer/White offender, etc.). The results involving the probation officer gender/offender race subgroup comparisons in predicting probation recommendations are displayed in column 1, while column 2 presents the same comparisons and results for judicial sentencing outcomes.

As shown in column 1, approximately half of the subgroup combinations exerted a significant effect on probation recommendations. Contrary to Leifker and Sample (2010) where probation officer gender nor the race of the offender impacted probation recommendations, male probation officers supervising a Black male offender were almost two times more likely to recommend incarceration compared to cases with a White male offender. Similarly, female probation officers regardless of the race of the male offender were less likely to recommend incarceration compared to male probation officers with Black offenders. Female probation officers had a 67% and 59% decreased likelihood of recommending incarceration for White and Black male offenders (respectively), in comparison to male probation officers with Black offender cases. In other words, there was an increased likelihood for females to recommend community sanctions compared to a sentence of incarceration. No other probation officer gender/offender race combinations significantly influenced probation officer recommendations.

Column 2 displays the effects of specific subgroup combinations between probation officer gender and offender race on actual judicial sentencing. As with the earlier analyses predicting probation officer recommendations, three combinations significantly impacted judges final decisions, yet the specific combinations mostly differed from the significant subgroups that impacted probation officer recommendations. Specifically, when female probation officers recommended incarceration for White male offenders, judges were less likely to impose an actual sentence of incarceration for these offenders. In fact, White male offenders with female probation officers were 73% less likely to be incarcerated compared to White male offenders with male probation officers, and 80% less likely to be incarcerated than Black offenders with male probation officers. The largest effect that was exerted out of all three significant subgroup combinations was comparing Black male offenders with female probation officers to White male offenders with female probation officers. Judges were over 9 times more likely to sentence Black male offenders with female probation officers to incarceration compared to White male offenders with female probation officers. This finding emerged even though race did not significantly impact probation recommendations for female probation officers when comparing Black male offender cases to White male offender cases with officers who were female.

Due to the complexities of the findings based on the combination of probation officer gender, offender race, probation recommendations, and judicial sentencing as primary components of the research inquiry, supplemental regression models were estimated by examining probation recommendations for White and Black offenders, and the actual judicial sentence of incarceration. Specifically, these analyses were first conducted for White and Black cases with male probation officers, then White and

Black cases with female probation officers to predict judicial sentencing depending on the specific recommendation by each gender/race combination. By estimating these additional models, we were able to get a clearer picture of the lack of concordance probation officer recommendations and judges' decisions to incarcerate Black male offenders relative to White male offenders.

As displayed in Figure 11.1, the predominant finding that emerged is that when a female probation officer recommended a sentence of community sanctions, Black males were over 8 times more likely than White males to receive a sentence of incarceration. When a male probation officer recommended community sanctions, Black males were approximately 1.5 times more likely than White males to receive an incarceration sentence. The figure highlights the differences that probation officer gender can make on sentencing recommendations for offenders of different races and how judicial sentences can meaningfully differ than what probation officers recommend as appropriate sanctions, especially for Black male offenders.

In summary, the above findings in regards to probation recommendations by female officers confirms the conclusions made in prior analyses in support of the maximalist perspective and the first expectation that females would have a greater tendency to be lenient in making decisions compared to their male counterparts. Recall the third expectation, also based on the maximalist viewpoint, predicted that being a female probation officer would not impact recommendations involving Black male offenders.

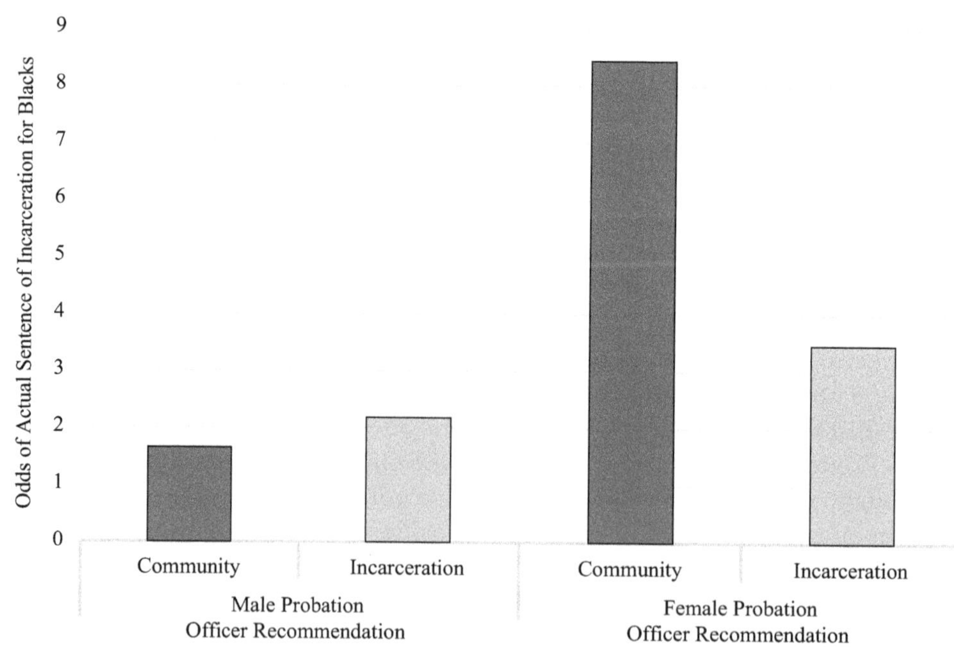

Figure 11.1 Concordance Between Probation Officer Recommendations and Judicial Sentencing of Black Male Offenders

Note: The figure represents the judicial sentence of incarceration of Black males relative to White male offenders taking into consideration the recommendation of the probation officer, differentiated by probation officer gender.

But, her male counterpart would be harsher in their recommendations for Black male offenders. Evidence emerged that male probation officers were harsher in their recommendations for Black male offenders compared to cases with White male offenders. Also confirming support for the maximalist viewpoint and the third expectation, female probation officers recommended community sanctions for both White and Black offenders compared to male probation officers with Black offender cases. In other words, the race of the offender did not impact probation recommendations for female probation officers because, irrespective of offender race, female probation officers were more lenient in their recommendations compared to male officers with Black offender cases.

Contradicting the fourth and fifth expectations, it was also discovered that male probation officers were impacted by offender race compared to all three other probation officer gender/offender race subgroups, but only in one combination did judges follow the probation officer recommendation put forth by male officers: the comparison of female probation officer/White offender to male probation officer/Black offender resulted in concordance between probation officer recommendations and final sentencing decisions. Findings also revealed that judges are overruling recommendations put forth by female probation officers with Black male cases (recall Figure 11.1) with an actual sentence of incarceration, even though female probation officers recommended community sanctions. Tied to this finding, no support was found for the minimalist perspective and sixth expectation, since offender race was predictive of judges' sentencing outcomes and results differed depending on the specific subgroup comparison. Even at times when offender race did not influence probation recommendations, certain combinations exerted a significant effect on judicial sentencing, and vice-versa.

Discussion

Based on the maximalist and minimalist viewpoints of gender differences in moral reasoning and prior criminal justice literature that has examined the role of gender and race in criminal justice decision-making, the present study investigated the extent to which the gender of the probation officer and race of the offender impacts probation recommendations and judicial outcomes for Black male offenders. We inquired about the impact of probation officer gender on sentencing recommendations and judicial sentencing outcomes by White male judges and what these relationships imply for the treatment of Black male offenders compared to White male offenders. Utilizing data from adult criminal court cases in one District Court located in a Midwestern state, two research questions consisting of six expectations based on the maximalist and minimalist perspectives detailed potential relationships between probation officers, offenders, judges, and court outcomes.

In regards to the first research question that examined the impact of probation officer gender on probation recommendations and judicial sentencing by White male judges, the gender of the probation officer was often predictive of probation recommendations. Contrary to the findings reported by Leifker and Sample (2010), and in support of the maximalist perspective, female probation officers were more lenient in their recommendations compared to males. While prior research has primarily focused on gender differences in the decision-making processes of judges rather than probation officers, the finding of lenient recommendations posed by female probation officers conflicts with earlier studies of female judges of either imposing harsher sentences than male judges and/or reporting no gender differences (Gruhl et al., 1981; Steffensmeier and Hebert, 1999).

Although speculative, we attribute this finding to differences in the socialization process of females and males, as well as females adhering to an ethic of care moral form of moral reasoning versus an ethic of justice (Gilligan, 1982). It may be that female probation officers believe that offenders have a better chance serving their sentence in the form of community supervision rather than incarceration. Components of the PSI report that include the offender's age, prior record, circumstances surrounding the offense, and other extra-legal factors may be more thought provoking for female probation officers in making recommendations, while males strictly focus on the legal aspects of decision-making. For example, female officers may recommend probation or some other form of community supervisions to a nonviolent offender who needs to provide for their family but will be unable to do so if incarcerated (see also Spohn, 2009). As argued by Goldman (1999), female decision-makers may bring a certain type of sensitivity to the decision-making process that result in lenient outcomes regardless of the race of the offender.

Also tied to the first research question was the discovery that the gender of the probation officer impacted judicial sentencing by White male judges. The concordance between recommendations and actual sentences did vary by the gender of the probation officer. Specifically, cases with female probation officers were more likely to receive community sanctions compared to cases with male probation officers. This interplay between the gender of the probation officer and gender of the judge is intriguing and provides direction for further inquiry especially since we failed to find that such differences may be the result of gender differences in the assignment of cases as reported by others (Horn and Evans, 2000).

Concerning the second research question, we discovered that the gender of the probation officer and decisions made by judges differently impacted Black male offenders compared to White male offenders. While the race of the offender by itself did not explain probation recommendations, being a Black male offender was directly related to judicial sentencing. Some of the more nuanced outcomes for Black male offenders depended on the gender of the probation officer, comparisons to White male offenders, and recommendations versus actual sentences. Across half of the instances, male probation officers recommended harsher outcomes for Black male offenders than White offenders and were more severe in their recommendations than their female counterparts.

One potential explanation for this finding could be that female officers may be more cognizant of racial discrimination in court outcomes than males, and instead of not having race impact their recommendations, females may be more likely to overcompensate for stereotypes by suggesting community sanctions and reentry back into society. Furthermore, as the current study utilized data from the early 2000s, and prior research (see Gruhl et al., 1981; Spears, 1999; Steffensmeier and Hebert, 1999) examined data on or before the early 1990s, the perception that female decision-makers recommend and subsequently sanction Black male offenders to greater social control may be shifting. Feelings of compassion may have a larger presence in the decision-making process of female court officers in more recent years, resulting in a shift from perceptions of dangerousness in the belief of what Black male offenders represent to females, to a greater overall concern for the welfare of minority offenders.

In addition, of the various combinations of probation officer gender/offender race, only for one combination did judges follow the recommendation put forth by male officers. Although prior studies have often centered on the role of offender race on prosecutorial and judicial decisions (Crawford et al., 1998; Feldmeyer and Ulmer, 2011; Steffensmeier and DeMuth, 2000), the finding that male probation officers recommended harsher sanctions for Black male offenders yet were often overruled by White male judges poses questions about the goals and orientations of the courtroom workgroup model. Overall, the findings add to the inconsistent findings of under what conditions probation officer recommendations influence actual judicial sentencing.

Further supporting the need to understand the interaction between probation officers and judges is based on the finding that White male judges overwhelmingly incarcerated Black males even after taking into consideration of a recommendation of community sanctions by female probation officers. The assumption based on the maximalist perspective and early research (Hagan, 1975; Steffensmeier et al., 1998) that female officers would recommend harsh outcomes for Black male offenders due to stereotypical perceptions tied to dangerousness, accountability, and risk of recidivism did not occur in the current study. The overruling of female probation officers compared to males in the final decisions by White male judges calls into question how probation officers make decisions that they believe align with the norms and practices of the courtroom workgroup, only to be overlooked or overruled by the judge. Consistent with other research (Rosecrance, 1985); this finding lends credence to the suggestion that probation recommendations may be purely "ceremonial" in nature rather than officers having a "quasijudicial" role in court outcomes.

Still, it must be noted that judges incarcerated Black male offenders almost twice as often as White male offenders when the recommendation was community sanctions; the discrepancy was eight-fold involving female officers. Although speculative, the gender gap may reflect once again, a "correction" factor on the part of judges who may perceive female officers as too lenient, especially toward Black male offenders. Such a practice seemed to be also in play involving male probation officers recommendations but rather than too lenient judges appear to perceive these recommendations as too harsh. Further research is needed to confirm these assumptions and to examine why the corrective relationship appears to be much stronger for cases involving female probation officers and Black male offenders and judicial sentencing relative to her male probation officer counterpart.

The current study is not without limitations. First, as introduced earlier, over 90% of the sample was comprised of judges and probation officers who were White. The inclusion of probation officers and judges who have similar racial characteristics justifies the need for future research to consider the combination of the gender and race/ethnicity of the decision-makers on probation recommendations and judicial sentences of offenders. Paralleling this limitation, the relatively small number of female offenders (n = 256) in the sample prevented the examination of how the gender of decision-makers may differently impact case outcomes for both male and female offenders. Future research would benefit from replicating the current analyses with the inclusion of female offenders to determine if similar findings emerge or if the outcomes of White and Black female offenders differ from their male counterparts based on the gender of probation officers.

Third, our conclusions are limited to interpretations from additive and interactive effects of probation officer gender and offender race on probation recommendations and judicial sentences. The use of qualitative research methods through racial priming experiments (i.e., the Implicit Association Test), open-ended interviews, and participant observations are needed to more confidently confirm or refute that male and female probation officers as well as White male judges make decisions in a different manner that result in disadvantaged outcomes for Black male offenders. While theoretical advancements have been made in the literature surrounding the maximalist perspective and courtroom workgroup model in regards to understanding the differences in male and female criminal justice staff, the use of qualitative methods could further enhance our understanding for these divergent outcomes involving Black male offenders.

Overall, the study examined a neglected topic by looking into the interrelationships among the gender and race of the offender and the decision-maker with probation recommendations and actual sentencing outcomes. The results show that the Black male offender often receives disadvantaged outcomes though the source for this may be contingent by the decision-maker and his or her gender. Further research is needed before these findings can be generalized to courts across the country.

Notes

1 A significant amount of past research has examined attitudes toward correctional orientations across male and female criminal justice personnel (e.g., Bazemore & Feder, 1997; Britton, 1997; Lambert et al., 2007; Leiber, 2000; Leiber, Woodrick & Roudebush, 1995; Van Voorhis et al., 1991). For example, Davis and colleagues (1993) examined the gender of the decision-maker in their national study of juvenile justice personnel that focused on attitudes toward delinquency causation and sentencing recommendations. Compared to their male counterparts, female juvenile justice personnel supported punishment for youth involved in serious sexual crimes. No other gender effects on attitudes towards sentencing recommendations were present. The finding involving greater punishment orientations for sexual assaults is consistent with the position that the experiences of women, especially concerning perceived and actual instances of victimization, would influence their response to delinquency in a more severe direction. Overall, evidence from prior research on gender differences in attitudes toward correctional philosophies, role orientations, and work style is mixed. Some find no differences across staff gender (Lambert et al., 2007; Poteyeva & Sun, 2009) while others report women decision-makers to be either more supportive of rehabilitation, and/or less punitive than male decision-makers (Homant & Kennedy, 1985; Ward & Kupchik, 2009).

2 Further examination of the data revealed variation in the case distributions handled by probation officers and sentenced by judges. This finding lends support to the belief that the results to be reported are not based on the practices and decision-making of a small number of probation officers and/or judges.

3 At the time of the study (2003–2004), Hispanic residents represented less than 2% of the population in this District. Hispanics accounted for a total of 23 cases or less than 1% of the cases studied. While it is possible that some Hispanics were classified as White, we feel confident that the racial/ethnic classifications and distributions are accurate.

4 Although the study is multilevel in nature (offenders within divisions within counties), the decision to not estimate a 3-level model is two-fold. First, there is a relative small number of overall cases in the sample (Level-1), especially when estimating joint relationships (i.e., subgroup comparisons) between probation officer gender and offender race on probation recommendations and judicial sentencing. Instead, we controlled for the geographic division by the use of dummy variables in each multivariate regression model to account for possible contextual differences across courts.

5 If multiple charges were associated with offense type and crime severity, the most serious charge was included in the analyses. Data were not available to discern if bail was denied, the defendant received release on one's own recognizance (ROR), or whether bail was set and the defendant could not pay. The data could not differentiate between the types of the plea bargain.

6 Objective risk assessment scales were not part of the PSI report or used in general by the court at the time of the study (2003, 2004). This state's criminal justice sentencing system operates under a minimum and maximum sentencing scheme and does not have the death penalty as a potential sentencing outcome. The court considers the facts and circumstances in imposing judgment by taking into consideration various factors such as age, prior record, circumstances of the offense, etc. The court must enumerate reasons for selecting the sentence imposed. Data was not collected to capture sentencing departures. This is an omission that future research should incorporate.

References

Albonetti, C. A. (1991). An integration of theories to explain judicial discretion. *Social Problems, 38*, 247–266.

Bazemore, G., & Feder, L. (1997). Judges in the punitive juvenile court: Organizational, career and ideological influences on sanctioning orientation. *Justice Quarterly, 4*, 87–114.

Britton, D. (1997). Perceptions of the work environment among correctional officers: Do race and gender matter? *Criminology, 35*, 85–106.

Chodorow, N. (1978). *The reproduction of mothering*. Berkeley and Los Angeles, CA: University of California Press.

Crawford, C., Chiricos, T., & Kleck, G. (1998). Race, racial threat, and sentencing of habitual offenders. *Criminology, 36*, 481–512.

Crew, B. K. (1991). Race differences in felony charging and sentencing: Toward an integration of decision-making and negotiation models. *Journal of Crime and Justice, 14*, 99–122.

Czajkoski, E. H. (1973). Exposing the quasi-judicial role of the probation officer. *Federal Probation, 37*, 9–13.

Davis, T., Severy, L., & Kraus, S. (1993). Predictors of sentencing decisions: The beliefs, personality variables and demographic factors of juvenile justice personnel. *Journal of Applied Social Psychology, 23*, 451–477.

Dixon, J. (1995). The organizational context of criminal sentencing. *American Journal of Sociology, 100*, 1157–1198.

Drass, K. A., & Spenser, J. W. (1987). Accounting for pre-sentencing recommendations: Typologies and probation officers' theory of office. *Society for the Study of Social Problems, 34*, 277–293.

Eisenstein, J., & Jacob, H. (1977). *Felony justice: An organizational analysis of criminal courts.* Boston, MA: Little Brown.

Epstein, C. (1988). *Descriptive distinctions: Sex, gender, and the social order.* New Haven, CT: Yale University Press.

Farrell, A., & Bishop, D. (2008). A review of the race and sentencing literature. In M. J. Lynch, E. B. Patterson, & K. K. Childs (Eds.), *Racial divide: Racial and ethnic bias in the criminal justice system* (pp. 83–108). New York: Criminal Justice Press.

Feldmeyer, B., & Ulmer, J. T. (2011). Racial/ethnic threat and federal sentencing. *Journal of Research in Crime and Delinquency, 48*, 238–270.

Fineman, M. A. (1994). *The illusion of equality: The rhetoric and reality of divorce reform.* Chicago: University of Chicago Press.

Freiburger, T. L., & Hilinski, C. M. (2011). Probation officers' recommendations and final sentencing outcomes. *Journal of Crime and Justice, 34*(1), 45–61.

Freiburger, T. L., & Hilinski, C. M. (2013). An examination of the interactions of race and gender on sentencing decisions using a trichotomous dependent variable. *Crime &Delinquency, 59*, 59–86.

Giele, J. Z. (1988). Gender and sex roles. In N. J. Smelser (Ed.), *Handbook of sociology* (pp. 291–323). Newbury Park, CA: Sage.

Gilligan, C. (1982). *In a different voice: Psychological theory and women's development.* Cambridge, MA: Harvard University Press.

Goldman, S. (1999). *Picking federal judges: Lower court selection from Roosevelt through Reagan.* New Haven, CT: Yale University Press.

Gruhl, J., Spohn, C., & Welch, S. (1981). Women as policymakers: The case of trial judges. *American Journal of Political Science, 25*, 308–322.

Hagan, J. (1975). The social and legal construction of criminal justice: A study of the presentencing process. *Social Problems, 22*, 620–637.

Hagan, J., Hewitt, J. D., & Alwin, D. F. (1979). Ceremonial justice crime and punishment in a loosely coupled system. *Social Forces, 58*, 506–527.

Homant, R., & Kennedy, D. (1985). Police perceptions of spouse abuse: A comparison of male and female officers. *Journal of Criminal Justice, 13*, 29–47.

Horn, R., & Evans, M. (2000). The effect of gender on pre-sentence reports. *Howard Journal of Criminal Justice, 39*, 184–197.

Johnson, B. (2006). The multilevel context of criminal sentencing: Integrating judge and county-level influences. *Criminology, 44*, 259–298.

Johnson, B. (2014). Judges on trial: A reexamination of judicial race and gender effects across modes of conviction. *Criminal Justice Policy Review, 25*, 159–184.

Kautt, P. (2002). Location, location, location: Interdistrict and intercircuit variation in sentencing outcomes for federal drug-trafficking offenses. *Justice Quarterly, 19*, 633–671.

King, R., & Johnson, J. (2016). A punishing look: Skin tone and Afrocentric features in the halls of justice. *American Sociological Review, 122*, 90–124.

Kingsnorth, R. F., MacIntosh, R. C., & Sutherland, S. (2002). Criminal charge or probation violation? Prosecutorial discretion and implications for research in criminal court processing. *Criminology, 40*, 553–577.

Kohlberg, L. (1976). Moral stages and moralization: The cognitive-developmental approach. In T. Lickona (Ed.), *Moral development and behavior* (pp. 31–53). New York: Hold, Rinehart & Winston.

Lambert, E., Paoline, E., Hogan, N., & Baker, D. (2007). Gender similarities and differences in correctional staff work attitudes and perceptions of the work environment. *Western Criminology Review, 8*, 16–31.

Leiber, M. J. (2000). Gender, religion, and correctional orientations among a sample of juvenile justice personnel. *Women and Criminal Justice, 11*, 15–44.

Leiber, M. J., Beaudry-Cyr, M., Peck, J. H., & Mack, K.Y. (2017). Sentencing recommendations by probation officers and judges: An examination of adult offenders across gender. *Women & Criminal Justice.* DOI: 10.1080/08974454.2017.1297279.

Leiber, M. J., & Brubaker, S. J. (2010). Does the gender of the intake probation officer contextualize the treatment of Black youth? *Justice Research and Policy, 12*, 51–76.

Leiber, M. J., Peck, J. H., & Beaudry-Cyr, M. (2016). When does race and gender matter? The interrelationships between the gender of probation officers and juvenile court detention and intake outcomes. *Justice Quarterly, 33*, 614–641.

Leiber, M. J., & Woodrick, A. C. (1997). Religious beliefs, attributional styles, and adherence to correctional orientations. *Criminal Justice and Behavior, 24*, 495–511.

Leiber, M. J., Woodrick, A. C., & Roudebush, E. M. (1995). Religion, discriminatory attitudes and the orientations of the juvenile justice personnel. *Criminology, 33*, 431–449.

Leiber, M., Reitzel, J., & Mack, K. (2011). Probation officer recommendations for sentencing relative to judicial practice: The implications for African Americans. *Criminal Justice Policy Review, 22*, 301–329.

Leifker, D., & Sample, L. L. (2010). Do judges follow sentencing recommendations, or do recommendations simply reflect what judges want to hear? An examination of one state court. *Journal of Crime and Justice, 33*, 127–151.

Mitchell, O. (2005). A meta-analysis of race and sentencing research: Explaining the inconsistencies. *Journal of Quantitative Criminology, 21*(4), 439–466.

Neubauer, D. W. (2005). *American's courts and the criminal justice system* (9th ed.). Belmont, CA: Wadsworth.

Peck, J. H., Leiber, M. J., Beaudry-Cyr, M., & Toman, E. L. (2016). The conditioning effects of race and gender on the juvenile court outcomes of delinquent and "neglected" types of offenders. *Justice Quarterly, 33*, 1210–1236.

Poteyeva, M., & Sun, I. (2009). Gender differences in police officers' attitudes: Assessing current empirical evidence. *Journal of Criminal Justice, 37*, 512–522.

Rosecrance, J. (1985). The probation officer's search for credibility: Ballpark recommendations. *Crime and Delinquency, 31*, 539–554.

Sanborn, J. Jr. (1996). Factors perceived to affect delinquent dispositions in juvenile court: Putting the sentencing decision into context. *Crime & Delinquency, 42*, 99–113.

Simola, S. K., Barling, J., & Turner, N. (2010). Transformational leadership and leader moral orientation: Contrasting an ethic of justice and an ethic of care. *The Leadership Quarterly, 21*, 179–188.

Singer, S. (1996). *Recriminalizing delinquency: Violent juvenile crime and juvenile justice reform*. New York: Cambridge University Press.

Spears, J. W. (1999). *Diversity in the courtroom: A comparison of the sentencing decisions of black and white judges and male and female judges in Cook County Circuit Court* (Doctoral Dissertation). Retrieved from ProQuest Dissertations and Theses Database. University of Nebraska at Omaha.

Spencer, J. (1983). Accounts, attitudes, and solutions: Probation-officer-defendants negotiations of subjective orientations. *Social Problems, 30*, 570–581.

Spohn, C. (2009). *How do judges decide? The search for fairness and justice in punishment.* Thousand Oaks, CA: Sage Publications.

Spohn, C., Beichner, D., & Davis-Frenzel, E. (2001). Prosecutorial justification for sexual assault case rejection: Guarding the "gateway to justice." *Social Problems, 48*, 206–235.

Spohn, C., Gruhl, J., & Welch, S. (1987). The impact of the ethnicity and gender of defendants on the decision to reject or dismiss felony charges. *Criminology, 25*, 175–191.

Spohn, C., & Hemmens, C. (2009). *Courts: A text/reader.* Thousand Oaks, CA: Sage Publications.

Spohn, C., & Holleran, D. (2000). Research note: The imprisonment penalty paid by young, unemployed Black and Hispanic male offenders. *Criminology, 38*, 501–526.

Steen, S., Engen, R. L., & Gainey, R. R. (2005). Images of danger and culpability: Racial stereotyping, case processing, and criminal sentencing. *Criminology, 43*, 435–468.

Steffensmeier, D., & DeMuth, S. (2000). Ethnicity and sentencing outcomes in U.S. federal courts: Who is punished more harshly? *American Sociological Review, 65*, 705–729.

Steffensmeier, D., & Hebert, C. (1999). Women and men policymakers: Does the judge's gender affect the sentencing of criminal defendants? *Social Forces, 77*, 1163–1196.

Steffensmeier, D., Ulmer, J., & Kramer, J. (1998). The interaction of race, gender, and age in criminal sentencing: The punishment cost of being young, black, and male. *Criminology*, *36*, 763–798.

Sudnow, D. (1965). Normal crimes: Sociological features of the pearl code in the public defender's office. *Social Problems*, *12*, 255–277.

Sutton, J. R. (2013). Structural bias in the sentencing of felony defendants. *Social Science Research*, *42*, 1207–1221.

Thompson, E. H. (1991). Beneath the status characteristics: Gender variations in religiousness. *Journal for the Scientific Study of Religion*, *30*, 381–394.

Tracy, P. (2005). Race, ethnicity, and juvenile justice. In D. F. Hawkins & K. Kempf-Leonard (Eds.), *Our children, their children: Confronting racial and ethnic differences in American juvenile justice* (pp. 245–269). Chicago: University of Chicago Press.

Ulmer, J. (1997). *Social worlds of sentencing: Court communities under sentencing guidelines*. Albany, NY: State University of New York Press.

Ulmer, J. T., & Johnson, B. (2004). Sentencing in context: A multilevel analysis. *Criminology*, *42*, 137–178.

United Sates Census Bureau. (2000). *Census summary file 1*. Retrieved from http://factfinder2.census.gov/faces/nav/jsf/pages/searchresults.xhtml?refresh=t

United States Department of Justice, Federal Bureau of Investigation. (October 2014). *Crime in the United States, 2005*. Retrieved from www.fbi.gov/ucr/cius2006/.

Van Voorhis, P., Cullen, F. T., Link, B. G., & Wolfe, N. T. (1991). The impact of race and gender on correctional officers' orientation to the integrated environment. *Journal of Research in Crime and Delinquency*, *28*(4), 472–500.

Walsh, A. (1985). The role of the probation officer in the sentencing process: Independent professional or judicial hack? *Criminal Justice and Behavior*, *12*, 289–303.

Wang, X., & Mears, D. P. (2010). A multilevel test of minority threat effects on sentencing. *Journal of Quantitative Criminology*, *26*(2), 191–215.

Ward, G., & Kupchik, A. (2009). Accountable to what? Professional orientations towards accountability-based juvenile justice. *Punishment & Society*, *11*, 85–109.

12

RACE, FACIAL APPEARANCE, AND THE FOCAL CONCERNS OF SENTENCING

Brian D. Johnson and Rebecca Richardson

Race is in the face. We notice it there—and notice it and notice it and notice it.

—Daniel McNeill

Contemporary approaches to the study of criminal punishment routinely emphasize the importance of social stereotypes related to offender appearance. In particular, modern sentencing theory often draws parallels between the race and ethnicity of criminal defendants and judicial attributions of culpability, dangerousness, and risk of recidivism (Albonetti, 1991; Steen et al., 2005; Steffensmeier et al., 1998). However, the primary focus of prior empirical work has been on punitive differences between members of various racial groups, leaving the criminal attributions believed to link race with punishment decisions largely unexamined. Moreover, dynamic variation exists both within and across races in other physical appearance characteristics that may also color judicial attributions of criminal threat. The current chapter explores these issues, investigating the relationship between race/ethnicity, physical appearance, and core theoretical constructs frequently invoked by contemporary sentencing theories.

The chapter offers three contributions to contemporary research on punishment disparities. First, it incorporates more proximate, appearance-based measures of the focal concerns of sentencing, including indicators of perceived dangerousness, blameworthiness, and ability to "do time" in prison. Although research often begins with theoretical assertions linking race and ethnicity to these concepts, seldom are the linkages tested or verified empirically. Second, the current work expands the focus of prior disparity research to consider the effects of various facial appearance characteristics on subjective trait impressions. Contemporary sentencing theory routinely focuses on the association between race and stereotypes, but it rarely considers other aspects of physical appearance that might also shape stereotypical attributions. Finally, this work considers the interplay between race and other physical appearance characteristics. Specifically, it examines whether or not other facial features help to explain any of the observed association between defendant race and negative social attributions related to criminal punishment.

Although a wealth of research investigates racial and ethnic disparities in sentencing (Mitchell, 2005; Ulmer, 2012; Spohn, 2000), other physical appearance characteristics, like defendant attractiveness or the presence of visible scars, represent new and intriguing dimensions of inequality that have seldom been investigated. The current chapter uses unique data collected from booking photos in a sample of convicted felons in two Minnesota counties to investigate the association between defendant race, physical features, and appearance-based stereotypes. It begins by reviewing prior work that addresses racial inequality and disparities in punishment. It then discusses the theoretical salience of race, facial appearance, and criminal stereotypes before turning to the data, methods, and findings. The chapter concludes with a discussion of fruitful directions for future research in this new and underexplored area of sentencing research.

Racial Disparity, Facial Features, and Punishment

For decades empirical sentencing research has been focused largely on the study of racial disparities in punishment (Baumer, 2013; Johnson, 2006; Kutateladze et al., 2014; Ulmer, 2012; Zatz, 1987). Although the findings of individual studies remain varied and at times equivocal, general overviews of this work suggest that defendant race exerts important effects on sentencing. Significant inequalities by race and by ethnicity are frequently reported in empirical studies, with particularly strong effects for discretionary decisions such as the type of sentence imposed (Mitchell, 2005; Spohn, 2000; Ulmer, 2012). In her classic review of this literature, Spohn (2000) concluded that the collective weight of the evidence indicates "that race and ethnicity do play an important role in contemporary sentencing decisions" (p. 458). More recently, a number of studies have shown that significant disparities also exist within racial and ethnic groups. For example, a growing sociological literature on "colorism" suggests that darker skin tone and Afrocentric facial features tend to be associated with more severe criminal punishments (Blair et al., 2004; Burch, 2015; King and Johnson, 2016; Viglione et al., 2011).

Relatively few studies, though, consider the association between other aspects of physical appearance and criminal sentencing, and what little there is has focused primarily on the influence of defendant attractiveness or baby-faced appearance. Early work by Stewart (1980) found that more attractive defendants received less punitive sentences. Similarly, DeSantis and Kayson (1997) reported that more attractive defendants were given shorter recommended punishments in fictitious burglary cases. In addition, psychological research by Zebrowitz and colleagues has found that defendants with more baby-faced appearances tend to be less likely to be found guilty and are less likely to receive harsh punishments if convicted (Berry and Zebrowitz-McArthur, 1988; Zebrowitz and McDonald, 1991). In the most recent treatment of these issues, Johnson and King (2017) showed that defendants who were more attractive or more baby-faced were less likely to receive executed prison sentences, whereas defendants with facial tattoos were more likely to be incarcerated.

Despite these interesting findings, prior studies of physical appearance and punishment remain limited in a number of ways. Previous work has been mostly restricted to small convenience samples with fictitious vignettes and hypothetical cases (e.g. Dumas and Testé, 2006). The majority of prior work uses inmate samples, which exclude offenders who are not sentenced to prison (e.g. Burch, 2015). Existing work typically examines individual facial characteristics in isolation, frequently for a single racial group (Viglione et al., 2011), and many prior studies lack controls for essential variables like offense severity and criminal history (e.g. Gyimah-Brempong and Price, 2006). Perhaps most importantly, virtually no work explicitly addresses the theoretical mechanisms that underlie the association between race/ethnicity, facial appearance, and punishment. The lone exception is the recent study by Johnson and King (2017) that links defendant facial features to perceptions of criminal threat. In that work, the authors find that African American defendants tend to be viewed as more threatening in appearance than white defendants. At the same time, more attractive or baby-faced defendants are viewed as less threatening while defendants with facial tattoos or visible scars are judged to be more threatening. The current work builds upon this recent study by investigating a broader range of social attributions related to race and physical appearance that are tied to criminal stereotypes often invoked in contemporary theoretical perspectives on sentencing disparity.

Race, Facial Features, and Criminal Stereotypes

Physical appearance has long served as a barometer of individual personality traits (McNeill, 1998). As Goldstein et al. (1984) long ago noted, facial features "function as a visible index of behavioral dispositions" (p. 549). The tendency to derive behavioral expectations from facial characteristics is both widespread and consistent across contexts, and subjective impressions tied to physical appearance have been shown to be highly reliable across independent observers (DeSantis and Kayson, 1997; McArthur and Baron, 1983; Zebrowitz, 1997). A long and sordid history recounts the evolution of physiognomic approaches to the study of crime specifically (Gould, 1981), with early scholars such as Cesare Lombroso (1911) attempting to identify the physical characteristics that were predictive of criminal behavior. Although physiological approaches to the study of crime have since largely been discredited, individual defendant appearance characteristics, including race and ethnicity, continue to play a key role in contemporary theories of criminal punishment that relate criminal stereotypes to sentencing.

Organizational actors, including judges, prosecutors, and defense counsel, are believed to rely on subconscious psychological decision-making processes that link physical appearance with impressionistic trait judgments (Albonetti, 1991; Bridges and Steen, 1998). Decades of psychological research convincingly demonstrate that subjective assessments of individual personality traits are closely tied to one's physical appearance and that this type of stereotyping occurs so quickly and automatically that we are seldom aware of it (Spencer et al., 1998). Classic work by Gordon Allport (1954), for example, long ago argued that stereotypes are endemic to human nature and that the "human mind must think with categories" as a "basis for normal prejudgment" (p. 19).

When it comes to crime and punishment, social attributions about criminal propensity are linked to the physical appearance of defendants through stereotypes about the prototypical qualities of offenders (Goldstein et al., 1984). Contemporary research demonstrates that there is strong consensus regarding stereotypes of criminal appearance (Goldstein et al., 1984; Yarmey, 1993) and that various types of stereotypical imagery are widespread in American society (Banaji and Greenwald, 2013). In particular, prior work suggests that darker skin evokes greater fear of criminality (Dasgupta et al., 1999; Maddox and Gray, 2002) and stronger impressions of criminal behavior (Dixon and Maddox, 2005). These types of negative stereotypes are often reified and reinforced in the media and in public discourse on crime and punishment (Chiricos and Eschholz, 2002; Dixon and Maddox, 2005). For instance, Weatherspoon (1998) argues that there is persistent imagery in American culture portraying young African American men as "unemployed, gang affiliated, gun toting and a menace to society" (p. 23).

Even among criminal justice actors who espouse egalitarian ideals, stereotypical notions of criminality may be inadvertently linked to race and ethnicity (Bridges and Steen, 1998; Levinson and Smith, 2012). For instance, research on jury decision-making suggests that mock jurors are more likely to interpret equivocal evidence as inculpatory when the case involves a darker-skinned suspect (Levinson and Young, 2010). In one study of trial judges, implicit racial bias was shown to affect judicial assessments of risk of reoffending as well as judicial sentencing recommendations (Rachlinski et al., 2009). Although more research is needed that focuses explicitly on the connection between race, facial appearance, and criminal stereotypes, the available evidence suggests that facial characteristics are directly related to subjective impressions that tie stereotypical notions of crime and criminality to the race of criminal defendants (Blair et al., 2004).

The Focal Concerns of Sentencing

Appearance-based social attributions play an important role in contemporary sentencing theories and may be useful for understanding the underlying causes of racial differences in punishment. Racial disparities are often theorized to result from the unintentional use of social attributions that link crime and criminality to members of certain racial and ethnic groups. According to Albonetti (1991), judges are often forced to make decisions under time constraints that preclude full knowledge of future events. In order to make decisions efficiently, they draw from past experience and from defendant stereotypes to assess the likelihood of future criminal behavior. From this perspective, race is expected to influence judicial decision-making when it is factored into cognitive shortcuts that judges use to simplify the complex calculus required to make accurate trait assessments regarding criminal propensity.

Steffensmeier et al. (1998) argue that the cognitive assessments used in judicial decision-making relate to three primary focal concerns. The first is offender blameworthiness, which encapsulates both the defendant's degree of responsibility and the harm caused to society. The second is community protection, which includes assessments of the dangerousness and the likelihood of future recidivism of the defendant. The third focal concern involves practical constraints and consequences of the punishment decision, which include broad organizational concerns as well as specific, individual defendant considerations. As Steffensmeier et al. (1998) originally noted, one important individual consideration that judges weigh is "the offender's 'ability to do time'" in prison (p. 767).

Like Albonetti (1991), Steffensmeier et al. (1998) argue that judges employ defendant stereotypes, or "perceptual short-hands" (Hawkins, 1981), to make decisions more proficiently. In particular, they suggest that young, male, and minority defendants are generally stereotyped to be "more of a threat to the community" and "not as reformable" (Steffensmeier et al., 1998: 787). Accordingly, racial disparity in criminal punishment reflects judicial reliance on stereotypical portrayals of minority defendants as more blameworthy, more threatening and dangerous, and/or more able to do "hard time" in prison (see also Steen et al., 2005: 436).

The core tenet of these theories is that there is an underlying social attribution process in which defendant appearance characteristics, like race and ethnicity, are unwittingly linked to judicial assessment of key punishment considerations, such as the culpability, dangerousness, and suitability of the defendant for imprisonment. However, the psychological processes that connect defendants' race to enhanced punishments are seldom laid out and tested. Indeed, one crucial limitation of much extant sentencing research is an inability to include direct indicators of the proximate psychological constructs thought to underlie the relationship between race and punishment. It is difficult to obtain measures of appearance-based stereotypes or other social attributions that may link defendant appearance characteristics to judicial assessments of criminal threat. Instead, rough proxies like criminal history and current offense severity are typically used under the implicit assumption that they capture underlying assessments of danger, harm, and future risk.

We propose an alternative approach that utilizes perceptual data from defendant booking photos to more directly tie defendant appearance to social attributions related to sentencing. To be clear, this approach has its own set of important limitations—it is only able to tap into perceptual assessments that are related directly to defendant appearance characteristics. Still, given psychological research indicating that appearance exerts strong influences over subjective impressions related to criminality, we believe this approach can provide new insights into the relationship between defendant race, appearance, and sentencing. As such, we capitalize on data that derive independent assessments of defendant traits and appearance characteristics from offender booking photos to examine three general research questions. First, we ask whether the race of the defendant is related to subjective assessments of blameworthiness, dangerousness, and ability to "do time" in prison. Second, we investigate whether other defendant appearance factors, including attractiveness, baby-faced appearance, facial tattoos, and visible scars, are also related to these core theoretical constructs. And finally, we consider whether any of the association between race and stereotypical assessments of the focal concerns of sentencing is attributable to other appearance-based factors or to additional considerations such as differences in defendant socioeconomic backgrounds.

Data and Methods

To explore these research questions, we analyze booking photos for a sample of male felony defendants convicted in Minnesota's Hennepin and Ramsey Counties in 2009 (see Johnson and King, 2017; King and Johnson, 2016). These two counties, which comprise the Minneapolis-St. Paul metropolitan area, account for roughly one third of felony convictions in the state and include 70% of Minnesota's racial minority population. The booking photos were linked to data from the Minnesota Sentencing Guidelines Commission (MSGC), which include additional legal and extralegal information such as defendants' age, current offenses, and criminal histories.

To create the sample, 1,200 defendants were randomly drawn from an initial sampling frame of approximately 2,500 cases that included all adult male felony defendants convicted in the two counties in 2009. Of these cases, 1,121 (93%) were successfully matched to a valid booking photo. Two defendants were removed from the sample because their booking photos clearly suggested they were female, bringing the final sample size to 1,119 defendants.

The booking photos were independently coded by a group of diverse research assistants[1] on a variety of measures, including physical characteristics, such as attractiveness and baby-faced appearance, and subjective impressions, such as perceptions of blameworthiness and dangerousness. Coders were asked to provide their initial reaction to each photograph, and they were not given any other information about the details of the research or about the individual defendants. This procedure generated perceptual measures that provide us with a rare opportunity to examine the connection between defendants' physical appearances and crime-related stereotypes in a sample of criminal defendants.

Variables

Dependent Variables

The primary dependent variables are three subjective trait assessments that align with the focal concerns of sentencing in contemporary punishment theory. For the blameworthiness construct, coders were asked to rate how blameworthy each defendant appeared to be on a seven-point scale ranging from "not at all blameworthy" to "very blameworthy." Coders were similarly asked to rate how dangerous each defendant appeared to be, from "not at all dangerous" to "very dangerous," and to rate the offender's ability to do time in prison, from "not able to do time" to "very able to do time." These ratings are averaged across the four coders to provide an overall assessment of each trait impression. Higher ratings indicate greater perceived blameworthiness, dangerousness, and ability to do time.

Independent Variables

Other defendant appearance characteristics are the primary variables of interest. Categorical race information comes from the MSGC records and is measured using a series of four dichotomous variables for African American, Hispanic, Native American, and Asian American defendants. White defendants are the reference group. The remaining appearance measures are derived from the defendant booking photos. Attractiveness was rated on a seven-point scale ranging from "very unattractive" to "very attractive." Coders also rated baby-faced appearance on a seven-point scale ranging from "mature-faced" to "baby-faced." Higher scores indicate more attractive and baby-faced appearances. The final two appearance variables include the presence of facial tattoos and visible scars. Tattoos are coded as 1 if the defendant has at least one tattoo above the neckline and 0 otherwise. A more conservative measure is used for facial scars in which scar is coded 1 if at least two coders identify a visible scar.[2]

Although the individual coders were not provided any information about the criminal defendants, we also include several control variables to explore any independent association between official case characteristics and subjective trait impressions of criminal defendants. Of primary interest is the type of attorney, which we use as a proxy for socioeconomic status. Defendants with private attorneys are coded 1 and defendants with public or appointed attorneys are coded 0. In addition, we also include the age of the defendant at the time of sentencing using a serious of ordinal dummy variables. The omitted reference category is 18–21 year olds. The severity of the offense is accounted for using a 9-point scale for offense severity based on the Minnesota Guidelines.[3] Similarly, criminal history is included using a 6-point scale that captures a defendant's prior record score under the guidelines. Finally, the type of offense is measured using dummy variables for whether the most serious conviction was for a violent, drug, or property offense, with the last the reference category.

Analytic Approach

The analysis begins with an examination of inter-rater reliabilities for variables derived from the booking photos, followed by descriptive statistics for all variables in the analysis. We then estimate a series of stepwise ordinary least squares regression models to explore the associations between defendant race, appearance, and trait impressions related to criminal punishment. First, we examine the relationship between categorical race and perceptions of the three focal concerns. Blameworthiness, dangerousness, and ability to do time are treated as continuous scales and separately regressed on race and ethnicity. Then we consider the effects of other facial characteristics, including attractiveness, baby-faced features, tattoos, and scars, on perceptions of the three focal concerns. Next, we add attorney type into the model, which serves as a proxy for socioeconomic status, and lastly, we include other relevant defendant and case controls to explore their associations with appearance-based stereotypes in sentencing. Separately including these blocks of variables allows us to assess their potential impact on any observed associations between race and our outcomes.

Findings

Descriptive Statistics

Before turning to the main findings, we briefly discuss the descriptive statistics for our variables, which are presented in Table 12.1. First, we note that alpha reliability coefficients for each of the focal concerns measures exceed .6, which is generally acknowledged as the threshold for acceptable levels of inter-rater agreement (Landis and Koch, 1977). This indicates that, even though our four independent raters knew nothing about the criminal defendants they were viewing, based only on their photographs, they generally agreed in their assessments of blame, danger, and suitability for imprisonment. Likewise, inter-rater reliabilities for defendant attractiveness, baby-faced appearance, facial tattoos, and visible scars all demonstrate moderate to high levels of inter-rater agreement. Perhaps not surprisingly, more objective qualities like facial tattoos have higher reliabilities than subjective characteristics like attractiveness.

Turning to the descriptive statistics in Table 12.1, there is clear variation in the focal concerns scales, with some offenders rated near the top and bottom of each of the 7-point indices. This suggests that offenders vary markedly in how blameworthy, dangerous, and able to do time they appear. Other defendant appearance measures also demonstrate stark variation. Defendants' attractiveness ratings average out to a relatively low 2.73 on the 7-point scale, while the mean for the baby-face scale is higher at 3.77. Roughly 10% of defendants have visible tattoos, and over one third have a scar or similar physical deformity on their face or neck. Turning to race and ethnicity, over half of the sample is African American and nearly one quarter is white. Relatively small proportions are Hispanic, Native American, or Asian American. The offender age distribution suggests that the sample is relatively young; nearly one quarter fall into the 18–21 category, and over 50% of the sample is 30 years or younger. On the 9-point offense severity scale, the average score for a defendant's current conviction is 4.42, and the average criminal history score is roughly 2 on the 6-point scale. Drug offenses are the modal crime category, followed by violent and then property offenses.

Table 12.2 further disaggregates the outcome measures by racial and ethnic group. As the table demonstrates, African American and Native American offenders are consistently rated as the most blameworthy, dangerous, and able to do time in prison. On the other hand, Asian offenders rate the lowest on these scales. Analysis of variance confirms that the means for each focal concern measure vary significantly across racial and ethnic groups. These preliminary comparisons offer some prima facie evidence for a relationship between racial and ethnic background and appearance-based criminal stereotypes in a sample of felony defendants. Next, we explore in greater detail the specific physical appearance and case processing characteristics that are associated with impressionistic stereotypes of blame, danger, and suitability for imprisonment.

Blameworthiness

Table 12.3 reports the regressions results for the first focal concern—offender blameworthiness. When only racial categories are included in the model, African American

Table 12.1 Descriptive Statistics for Dependent and Independent Variables

	Mean	*S.D.*	*Min.*	*Max.*	*Alpha*
Focal Concerns Measures					
Blameworthiness	3.90	1.05	1.25	6.5	.63
Dangerousness	3.26	.99	1	6.25	.66
Ability to "do time" in prison	3.62	1.14	1	6.75	.71
Appearance Measures					
Attractiveness	2.73	.80	1	5.25	.64
Baby-faced	3.77	1.04	1	6.75	.76
Tattoo	.10	.29	0	1	.96
Scar	.35	.48	0	1	.76
Offender Race/Ethnicity					
White	.24	.42	0	1	
African American	.54	.50	0	1	
Hispanic	.11	.32	0	1	
Native American	.06	.23	0	1	
Asian American	.06	.24	0	1	
Private Attorney	.25	.43	0	1	
Age Categories					
18–21	.24	.43	0	1	
22–25	.15	.36	0	1	
26–30	.19	.39	0	1	
31–40	.22	.42	0	1	
41–50	.15	.35	0	1	
50+	.04	.20	0	1	
Legal Factors					
Offense severity	4.42	2.28	1	9	
Criminal history	1.99	2.03	0	6	
Violent offense	.35	.48	0	1	
Drug offense	.42	.49	0	1	
Property offense	.24	.43	0	1	
Number of cases	1,119				

and Native American defendants are viewed as more blameworthy than whites, though the effect for Native Americans is only marginally significant ($p = .053$). Somewhat surprisingly, the largest effect is for Asian defendants, who, on average, were rated nearly a half point lower on the blameworthiness scale than whites. Model 2 introduces additional measures for other physical appearance characteristics. Their inclusion has little effect on the African American coefficient, but it does reduce the Native American estimate and also slightly increases the estimate for Asian Americans. These results suggest that more attractive defendants are viewed as less blameworthy and that defendants with scars or tattoos are seen as more blameworthy. In Model 3, attorney type is added, which reduces the racial effect for black defendants to non-significance. Attorney type also appears to have an independent effect on perceived blameworthiness; despite raters having no information about the type of attorney in the case, offenders who retained a private attorney are perceived to be significantly less blameworthy in appearance.

Table 12.2 Sample Means for Focal Concerns Measures by Race/Ethnicity

	Blameworthiness	*Dangerousness*	*Ability to "Do Time"*
White	3.82	3.12	3.04
(n = 264)	(1.05)	(.95)	(1.05)
African American	3.99	3.35	3.98
(n = 602)	(1.03)	(.98)	(1.02)
Hispanic	3.86	3.27	3.57
(n = 125)	(1.04)	(1.00)	(1.17)
Native American	4.10	3.47	3.64
(n = 62)	(1.01)	(1.07)	(1.21)
Asian American	3.36	2.75	2.70
(n = 66)	(1.11)	(.95)	(.99)
F-statistic	6.54***	7.75***	49.47***

Sample means with SD in parentheses. F-statistics from one-way analysis of variance tests.

N = 1,119.

† $p \leq .10$, * $p \leq .05$, ** $p \leq .01$, and *** $p \leq .001$.

Table 12.3 The Effects of Race and Other Appearance Characteristics on Subjective Assessments of Blameworthiness

	Model 1		*Model 2*		*Model 3*		*Model 4*	
	b	*SE*	*b*	*SE*	*b*	*SE*	*b*	*SE*
Intercept	3.82	.06***	4.56	.15***	4.65	.15***	5.99	.23***
Race/Ethnicity								
African American	.17	.08*	.15	.07*	.11	.07	−.01	.07
Hispanic	.04	.11	.01	.11	−.02	.11	−.13	.11
Native American	.28	.15†	.07	.14	.02	.14	−.09	.13
Asian American	−.46	.14***	−.59	.14***	−.59	.14***	−.64	.13***
Appearance								
Attractiveness			−.37	.04***	−.36	.04***	−.44	.04***
Baby-faced			.03	.03	.03	.03	−.21	.04***
Tattoos			.76	.10***	.75	.10***	.64	.10***
Scars			.29	.06***	.28	.06***	.26	.06***
Private attorney					−.24	.07***	−.25	.07***
Age								
22–25							−.04	.09
26–30							−.25	.09**
31–40							−.58	.10***
41–50							−.91	.12***
51+							−1.50	.18***
Legal Factors								
Criminal history							.02	.01
Offense severity							.01	.01
Violent offense							.23	.08**
Drug offense							.22	.07**
R-squared		.02		.16		.17		.25

N = 1,119.

† $p \leq .10$, * $p \leq .05$, ** $p \leq .01$, and *** $p \leq .001$.

The final model in Table 12.3 introduces other legal and case processing controls. Even after accounting for these additional factors, Asian defendants remain less blameworthy in appearance. Interestingly, the other appearance characteristics are not affected, though baby-faced appearance only becomes significant in the final model. Once age and legal controls are included, baby-faced defendants are perceived to be less blameworthy than mature-faced defendants. Supplementary analyses indicate that it is the addition of age, rather than the other legal controls, that drives this change. Compared to the 18–21 year old group, all groups aged 26 and older have lower levels of perceived blameworthiness. Among the legal factors, only the type of offense is related to perceptions of blame, with offenders who commit violent or drug crimes being viewed as more blameworthy than offenders who commit property crimes. The fact that type of crime is independently related to appearance-based assessments of criminal culpability is an interesting point that we return to in the discussion section of the chapter.

Dangerousness

Table 12.4 reports the regression results for the second focal concern—offender dangerousness. In Model 1, the effects of race follow a similar pattern to blameworthiness: African American and Native American defendants are perceived to be more dangerous than whites, and Asian defendants are perceived to be less dangerous. Again there is no significant difference between Hispanic and white defendants. When the other appearance characteristics are added to Model 2, the African American and Asian effects are attenuated only slightly. However, the effect of Native Americans is reduced substantially and becomes insignificant. All of the appearance characteristics have independent effects on perceived dangerousness, such that offenders who are more attractive or more baby-faced are judged to be less dangerous, while offenders with tattoos or scars are perceived to be more dangerous. The addition of attorney type to Model 3 does little to attenuate these effects, but defendants with a private attorney are judged to be less dangerous, on average, than defendants who are represented by a public defender or appointed counsel.

Findings from the full model are presented in Model 4. The addition of age and legal controls reduces the effect for African American defendants substantially, rendering it insignificant. However, Asian defendants continue to be perceived as less dangerous than whites, and all other appearance-based characteristics remain highly significant. Age also exerts an independent effect on perceived dangerousness, with older offenders being perceived as less dangerous. On average, offenders with longer criminal histories and those who committed either a violent or drug crime are also perceived to be more dangerous in appearance.

Ability to Do Time

Table 12.5 reports the regression results for the final focal concerns measure—ability to "do time" in prison. There are strong and statistically significant effects for all racial groups in Model 1. African American, Hispanic, and Native American defendants are all perceived to be more able to do time than whites, while Asian defendants are

Table 12.4 The Effects of Race and Other Appearance Characteristics on Subjective Assessments of Dangerousness

	Model 1		*Model 2*		*Model 3*		*Model 4*	
	b	*SE*	*b*	*SE*	*b*	*SE*	*b*	*SE*
Intercept	3.12	.06***	3.77	.14***	3.85	.14***	5.02	.22***
Race/Ethnicity								
African American	.23	.07**	.18	.07**	.14	.07*	.02	.07
Hispanic	.15	.11	.16	.10	.14	.10	.05	.10
Native American	.34	.14*	.21	.13	.16	.13	.04	.13
Asian American	−.38	.13**	−.32	.13*	−.32	.13*	−.37	.12**
Appearance								
Attractiveness			−.13	.04***	−.12	.04***	−.20	.03***
Baby-faced			−.12	.03***	−.13	.03***	−.34	.04***
Tattoos			.80	.09***	.79	.09***	.67	.09***
Scars			.29	.06***	.28	.06***	.26	.06***
Private attorney					−.21	.07***	−.22	.06***
Age								
22–25							−.06	.09
26–30							−.12	.09
31–40							−.39	.09***
41–50							−.85	.11***
51+							−1.48	.17***
Legal factors								
Criminal history							.04	.01**
Offense severity							.01	.01
Violent offense							.16	.07*
Drug offense							.18	.07*
R-squared		.03		.13		.14		.22

$N = 1{,}119$

† $p \leq .10$, * $p \leq .05$, ** $p \leq .01$, and *** $p \leq .001$.

perceived to be less suitable to imprisonment. Interestingly, the magnitudes of the effects are substantially larger than they were for perceived blameworthiness or perceived dangerousness. African Americans, for example, are rated nearly a full point higher than whites on perceived ability to do time.

Other appearance-based characteristics are introduced in Model 2 of Table 12.5. Their inclusion reduces the Asian American effect to non-significance, but the other groups continue to be seen as more able to do time than whites. Moreover, baby-faced defendants are viewed as less able to do time, whereas defendants with tattoos or scars are perceived to be more able to serve time. The next model shows that defendants represented by a private attorney are also judged to be less able to serve prison time, though the inclusion of this measure does little to account for the racial differences.

Lastly, Model 4 presents the full results that include age and legal controls. The race effects are reduced only modestly and remain statistically significant. They indicate that African American, Hispanic, and Native American defendants are all perceived to be more able to do time in prison, even after accounting for other legal and extralegal

Table 12.5 The Effects of Race and Other Appearance Characteristics on Subjective Assessments of Ability to Do Time in Prison

	Model 1		*Model 2*		*Model 3*		*Model 4*	
	b	*SE*	*b*	*SE*	*b*	*SE*	*b*	*SE*
Intercept	3.05	.06***	3.52	.15***	3.57	.15***	4.36	.23***
Race/Ethnicity								
African American	.93	.08***	.86	.07***	.84	.07***	.70	.07***
Hispanic	.52	.11***	.54	.11***	.53	.11***	.44	.11***
Native American	.60	.15***	.51	.14***	.48	.14***	.35	.14*
Asian American	−.34	.14*	−.19	.14	−.19	.14	−.25	.13†
Appearance								
Attractiveness			.06	.04	.06	.04	−.00	.04
Baby-faced			−.20	.03***	−.21	.03***	−.38	.04***
Tattoos			.94	.10***	.93	.10***	.81	.10***
Scars			.21	.06***	.21	.06***	.18	.06**
Private attorney					−.14	.07*	−.18	.07**
Age								
22–25							.14	.09
26–30							.01	.09
31–40							−.20	.10*
41–50							−.55	.12***
51+							−1.57	.19***
Legal Factors								
Criminal history							.05	.02**
Offense severity							.01	.01
Violent offense							.24	.08***
Drug offense							.29	.08***
R-squared		.15		.25		.25		.33

N = 1,119
† $p \leq .10$, * $p \leq .05$, ** $p \leq .01$, and *** $p \leq .001$.

factors. The effects of other appearance characteristics change only slightly and retain their direction and significance. As with the other appearance-based attributions, age is significantly related to one's perceived ability to do time in prison, with older defendants viewed as less suitable for incarceration, while defendants with longer criminal histories and those who committed a violent or drug crime are perceived as better suited to imprisonment.

Discussion and Conclusions

Contemporary theoretical perspectives on punishment suggest that judges and other court actors employ social psychological decision-making processes that link stereotypical notions of crime and criminality to defendant race and ethnicity. Despite their ubiquity, though, little empirical evidence exists to validate such claims. Direct measures that capture judicial assessments of key sentencing criteria, such as a defendant's blameworthiness, dangerousness, or suitability for imprisonment, are virtually non-existent in contemporary sentencing datasets. The current chapter attempts to address this issue by utilizing perceptional measures derived from defendant booking photos to examine the relationship between race and ethnicity, physical appearance characteristics, and criminal trait impressions associated with key focal concerns in sentencing. Several notable conclusions emerge from this endeavor.

First, we find marked consistency in independent trait assessments derived from the photographs of convicted offenders. Inter-rater reliabilities range from .63 to .96 for the various physical appearance and perceptual measures we examined. This result aligns with a well-established psychological literature on social cognition and trait impressions that finds high degrees of consistency among independent raters based on facial images. Goldstein et al. (1984) stated that "the outward appearance of the face" is often "used as an index of the inner character" such that "faces can serve as stimuli that trigger consensual stereotypical responses in observers" (p. 549). This phenomenon may be particularly acute when criminal stereotypes that can serve as adaptive mechanisms for identifying physical or social threat are involved (McArthur and Baron, 1983). Goldstein et al. (1984) showed that subjects demonstrate a high degree of consistency in separating criminals and non-criminals, and more recently, Valla et al. (2011) concluded that "participants presented with brief exposures to static cropped facial images of convicted criminals and non-criminals were able to reliably distinguish between them" (p. 81). The validity of stereotypical trait assessments remains highly controversial, but scholars generally agree that faces evoke consistent stereotypical impressions, and we find evidence for that here in our sample of convicted felons.

Second, we find partial evidence that the racial and ethnic backgrounds of legal defendants are related to stereotypical attributions theorized to affect criminal sentencing. Focal concerns theory and similar perspectives emphasize that judges and other court actors are concerned with offender blameworthiness, dangerousness, and other considerations such as ability to "do time" in prison (Steffensmeier et al., 1998). Our findings suggest that based solely on facial appearance, African American and Native American defendants are rated higher on these perceptual qualities than whites. Asian Americans, on the other hand, are rated the lowest for all three of these trait impressions. Interestingly, the largest and most consistent race effects emerged for ability to serve time in prison, suggesting that stereotypes linking certain race groups to suitability for incarceration are particularly strong. One possible explanation for this is that perceptions of defendants' ability to survive in prison have a cultural component; if prison culture is viewed as akin to minority street culture (see Wacquant, 2001), decision-makers may assume that minority defendants will be better equipped to navigate the prison social environment.

Third, our results also suggest that other physical appearance characteristics are predictive of perceptional ratings on the focal concerns scales. With few exceptions, more attractive and baby-faced individuals score lower on blameworthiness, dangerousness, and ability to "do time." Defendants with facial tattoos and visible scars, on the other hand, tend to score higher on these subjective qualities. Even after adjusting for case characteristics including criminal history and offense type, these associations remain strong and statistically significant. One implication of these findings is that trait impressions might not only be associated with race and ethnicity but also with other facial appearance characteristics; specific physical attributes may align with stereotypes about what a "criminal" looks like. This conclusion is consistent with the limited prior work that examines these influences and finds that more attractive and baby-faced defendants tend to fair better in criminal court (Stewart, 1980; DeSantis and Kayson, 1997; Johnson and King, 2017). More research is clearly needed in this area, particularly for other facial features like tattoos and scars that have received even less attention in empirical sentencing studies (Bull and David, 1986; Johnson and King, 2017; Durkin and Houghton, 2000).

Finally, we find mixed evidence for the mediating effects of other facial characteristics on the effects of race and ethnicity in our sample. For Native Americans, part of the bivariate association between race and perceptual focal concerns ratings is related to other facial features. In particular, Native American defendants in the sample are the most likely to have scars and tattoos, and they are generally rated as less attractive and less baby-faced. Accounting for these differences reduces the significant effects for blameworthiness and dangerousness to non-significance, though it does not fully account for racial differences in ability to do time. For African Americans, other facial features do little to explain the bivariate association between race and focal concerns ratings. However, legal and case processing factors do substantially account for racial differences for both blameworthiness and dangerousness. For Asian Americans, who were perceived as less blameworthy, less dangerous, and less suitable for prison, neither facial features nor legal and case factors were able to account for associations with these focal concerns concepts. The variation in mediating effects across racial groups is noteworthy and indicates that there may be different mechanisms tying each racial group to criminal stereotypes.

Interestingly, in this study actual criminal history and current offense type are consistently related to subjective trait assessments such that more experienced offenders and offenders who committed violent or drug rather than property crimes tend to score higher on appearance-based focal concerns ratings. Likewise, type of attorney appears to be significantly associated with perceptions of the three focal concerns; though this proxy for socioeconomic status does not fully explain the link between race and subjective trait impressions, the defendants in our sample who retained private attorneys are perceived to be less blameworthy, dangerous, and able to do time. These results occur despite the fact that coders had no prior knowledge of the defendants or the crimes they committed. On the surface, this offers some preliminary evidence for relationships between criminal offending patterns, socioeconomic status, and subjective trait impressions. The exact nature of the relationships, however, cannot be discerned from our data. It may be that physical appearance affects life opportunities in ways that influence socioeconomic status (Hamermesh and Biddle, 1993) and are indirectly related to criminal activity (Mocan and Tekin, 2010), or perhaps criminal experiences and social standing shape one's appearance, such as when higher SES defendants present more favorable appearances in the courtroom or when incarcerated offenders elect to get prison gang tattoos (Phelan and Hunt, 1998). Future research and more robust measures of socioeconomic status are required to better disentangle these apparent associations and determine the exact relationships between physical appearance, socioeconomic status, and criminal activity (see also Johnson and King, 2017).

Collectively, the findings from this study suggest that defendant appearance is related to stereotypical trait impressions of blameworthiness, dangerousness, and ability to do time, which, according to contemporary sentencing theories, can shape criminal punishment. Most extant sentencing data lack measures of these proximate theoretical constructs, leaving researchers to assume their role in sentencing disparities rather than demonstrate it. In this chapter we discuss a novel approach to disparity research that captures appearance-based trait impressions by relying on booking photos to begin testing this key assumption. We find that race and ethnicity are related to stereotypical attributions of key focal concerns in sentencing and that other facial features such as attractiveness and baby-faced appearance also shape these subjective assessments in consequential ways.

Although we believe this is an important conclusion, it is important not to draw inferences beyond the scope of our data. Our focal concerns measures are restricted to impressions based only on booking photos. Clearly judges and other court actors have a wealth of relevant case information that they review during the decision-making process, limiting the importance of impressions based only on physical appearance. We fully acknowledge this to be the case. In order to assess the impact of appearance in a more representative context, sentencing researchers will need to develop more nuanced focal concern measures that tap into additional considerations such as victim harm, offender intent, and other practical considerations that may affect sentencing. Furthermore, our perceptual ratings were determined by a team of research assistants; this type of research should be replicated with real-world court actors. Prior work suggests that trait impressions tend to be highly reliable across diverse populations (DeSantis and Kayson, 1997; McArthur and Baron, 1983; Zebrowitz, 1997), but this has yet to be demonstrated with prosecutors or judges. Additional mechanisms for tapping into racial stereotypes and other appearance-based cognitive biases, such as implicit association tests (Rachlinski et al., 2009), should ultimately be combined with the approach used here to further investigate the reliability and impact of these influences in criminal punishment.

Finally, although this chapter demonstrates an association between defendant appearance and stereotypical trait impressions, it stops short of investigating actual sentencing decisions. Related work by Johnson and King (2017) recently looked into this issue with a more general measure of "threatening appearance" and found little evidence that it predicts imprisonment once other legal controls are incorporated. However, these researchers did find that offender appearance was related to legal criteria, such as prior criminal record, and it was only after legal factors were controlled that the association between threatening appearance and imprisonment disappeared. This suggests that there may be complex interrelationships between defendant appearance characteristics and experiences with the criminal justice system. Moreover, no prior work considers the theoretical import of defendant appearance at earlier case processing stages, such as charging practices and pretrial detention decisions, which may have important influences on downstream punishment outcomes. Measures that are often treated as legal variables, such as the placement of offenders within sentencing guidelines grids, or the accumulation of prior criminal history records, may be influenced by the types of stereotypical attributions that are demonstrated in this work. A clear priority for future disparity research, then, is to broaden the types of perceptual measures that are examined and to extend the current line of inquiry to various stages of criminal case processing, including legal factors that are too often viewed as categorically immune from implicit biases (Bushway and Forst, 2013).

This chapter provides a valuable first step toward incorporating aspects of physical appearance other than race into criminological research and toward more directly testing the role of criminal attributions in courtroom decision-making. The furtherance of these goals has great potential for enhancing our understanding of sentencing disparities, and we hope that the chapter helps to spur new and innovative investigations into the complex relationships between defendant race, physical appearance, and other legal and extralegal case characteristics, as well as the unique contributions they make to social inequalities and unwarranted disparities in criminal punishment.

Notes

1 The four research assistants varied by racial background and gender. Two were male, and two were female. Two identified as black, one as white, and one as Hispanic.

2 Because scars were quite prevalent in the data, we reviewed a subsample of these defendants and found that, in some cases, related features such as visible cuts, bandages, birthmarks, acne, or other facial blemishes were coded as scars. We therefore use a more conservative measure that requires at least two coders to identify a scar. The empirical relationship with the focal concerns constructs are not affected by this coding decision.

3 The Minnesota Guidelines have 11 severity levels, but the top two levels are reserved for murder and these crimes were not included in the sampling frame. Therefore our severity scale ranges from 1 to 9.

References

Albonetti, C. A. (1991). An integration of theories to explain judicial discretion. *Social Problems, 38*(2), 247–266.

Allport, G. W. (1954). *The nature of prejudice*. New York: Addison.

Banaji, M. R., & Greenwald, A. G. (2013). *Blindspot: Hidden biases of good people*. New York: Bantam Books.

Baumer, E. (2013). Reassessing and redirecting research on race and sentencing. *Justice Quarterly, 30*(2), 231–261.

Berry, D. S., & Zebrowitz-McArthur, L. (1988). What's in a face? Facial maturity and the attribution of legal responsibility. *Personality and Social Psychology Bulletin, 14*(1), 23–33.

Blair, I. V., Judd, C. M., & Chapleau, K. M. (2004). The influence of Afrocentric facial features in criminal sentencing. *Psychological Science, 15*, 674–679.

Bridges, G., & Steen, S. (1998). Racial disparities in official assessments of juvenile offenders: Attributional stereotypes as a mediating mechanism. *American Sociological Review, 63*(4), 554–570.

Bull, R., & David, I. (1986). The stigmatizing effect of facial disfigurement. *Journal of Cross-Cultural Psychology, 17*(1), 99–108.

Burch, T. (2015). Skin color and the criminal justice system: Beyond black-white disparities in sentencing. *Journal of Empirical Legal Studies, 12*(3), 395–420.
Bushway, S., & Forst, B. (2013). Studying discretion in the processes that generate criminal justice sanctions. *Justice Quarterly, 30*(2), 199–222.
Chiricos, T., & Eschholz, S. (2002). The racial and ethnic typification of crime and the criminal typification of race and ethnicity in local television news. *Journal of Research in Crime and Delinquency, 39*(4), 400–420.
Dasgupta, N., Banaji, M. R., & Abelson, R. P. (1999). Group entitativity and group perception: Associations between physical features and psychological judgment. *Journal of Personality and Social Psychology*, 77(5), 991–1003.
DeSantis, A., & Kayson, W. A. (1997). Defendants' characteristics of attractiveness, race, and sex and sentencing decisions. *Psychological Reports, 81*(2), 679–683.
Dixon, T., & Maddox, K. (2005). Skin tone, crime news, and social reality judgments: Priming the stereotype of the dark and dangerous black criminal. *Journal of Applied Social Psychology, 35*(8), 1555–1570.
Dumas, R., & Testé, B. (2006). The influence of criminal facial stereotypes on juridic judgments. *Swiss Journal of Psychology, 65*, 237–244.
Durkin, K., & Houghton, S. (2000). Children's and adolescents' stereotypes of tattooed people as delinquent. *Legal and Criminological Psychology, 5*(2), 153–164.
Goldstein, A. G., Chance, J. E., & Gilbert, B. (1984). Facial stereotypes of good guys and bad guys: A replication and extension. *Bulletin of the Psychonomic Society, 22*(6), 549–552.
Gould, S. J. (1981). *The mismeasure of man*. New York: Norton & Company.
Gyimah-Brempong, K., & Price, G. N. (2006). Crime and punishment: And skin hue too? *The American Economic Review, 96*(2), 246–250.
Hamermesh, D. S., & Biddle, J. E. (1993). Beauty and the labor market. *The American Economic Review, 84*(5), 1174–1194.
Hawkins, D. F. (1981). Causal attribution and punishment for crime. *Deviant Behavior, 2*(3), 207–230.
Johnson, B. D. (2006). The multilevel context of criminal sentencing: Integrating judge- and county-level influences. *Criminology, 44*, 259–298.
Johnson, B. D., & King, R. D. (2017). "Facial profiling": Race, physical appearance and punishment. *Criminology.* DOI: 10.1111/1745-9125.12143.
King, R. D., & Johnson, B. D. (2016). A punishing look: Skin tone and Afrocentric features in the halls of justice. *American Journal of Sociology, 122*(1), 90–124.
Kutateladze, B. L., Andiloro, N. R., Johnson, B. D., & Spohn, C. (2014). Cumulative disadvantage: Examining racial and ethnic disparity in prosecution and sentencing. *Criminology, 52*, 514–51.
Landis, J. R., & Koch, G. G. (1977). The measurement of observer agreement for categorical data. *Biometrics, 33*, 159–174.
Levinson, J. D., & Smith, R. J. (Eds.). (2012). *Implicit racial bias across the law*. Cambridge: Cambridge University Press.
Levinson, J. D., & Young, D. (2010). Different shades of bias: Skin tone, implicit racial bias, and judgments of ambiguous evidence. *West Virginia Law Review, 112*, 307–350.
Lombroso, C. (1911 [2006]). *Criminal man*. Durham, NC: Duke University Press.
Maddox, K., & Gray, S. (2002). Cognitive representations of black Americans: Reexploring the role of skin tone. *Personality and Social Psychology Bulletin, 28*(2), 250–259.
McArthur, L. Z., & Baron, R. M. (1983). Toward an ecological theory of social perception. *Psychological Review, 90*(3), 215–238.
McNeill, D. (1998). *The face*. Boston, MA: Little, Brown & Company.
Mitchell, O. (2005). A meta-analysis of race and sentencing research: Explaining the inconsistencies. *Journal of Quantitative Criminology, 21*(4), 439–466.
Mocan, N., & Tekin, E. (2010). Ugly criminals. *The Review of Economics and Statistics, 92*(1), 15–30.
Phelan, M. P., & Hunt, S. A. (1998). Prison gang members' tattoos as identity work: The visual communication of moral careers. *Symbolic Interaction, 21*(3), 277–298.

Rachlinski, J. J., Johnson, S. L., Wistrich, A. J., & Guthrie, C. (2009). Does unconscious racial bias affect trial judges? *Notre Dame Law Review, 84*, 1195–1246.

Spencer, S. J., Fein, S., Wolfe, C. T., Fong, C., & Duinn, M. A. (1998). Automatic activation of stereotypes: The role of self-image threat. *Personality and Social Psychology Bulletin, 24*(11), 1139–1152.

Spohn, C. (2000). Thirty years of sentencing reform: The quest for a racially neutral sentencing process. *Criminal Justice: The National Institute of Justice Journal, 3*, 427–501.

Steen, S., Engen, R. L., & Gainey, R. R. (2005). Images of danger and culpability: Racial stereotyping, case processing, and criminal sentencing. *Criminology, 43*, 435–468.

Steffensmeier, D., Ulmer, J., & Kramer, J. (1998). The interaction of race, gender, and age in criminal sentencing: The punishment cost of being young, black, and male. *Criminology, 36*, 763–798.

Stewart, J. E. (1980). Defendant's attractiveness as a factor in the outcome of criminal trials: An observational study. *Journal of Applied Psychology, 10*, 348–631.

Ulmer, J. T. (2012). Recent developments and new directions in sentencing research. *Justice Quarterly, 29*(1), 1–40.

Valla, J. M., Ceci, S. J., & Williams, W. M. (2011). The accuracy of inferences about criminality based on facial appearance. *Journal of Social, Evolutionary, and Cultural Psychology, 5*(1), 66–91.

Viglione, J., Hannon, L., & DeFina, R. (2011). The impact of light skin on prison time for black female offenders. A research note. *The Social Science Journal, 48*, 250–258.

Wacquant, L. (2001). Deadly symbiosis: When ghetto and prison meet and mesh. *Punishment and Society, 3*(1), 95–133.

Weatherspoon, F. D. (1998). *African-American males and the law: Cases and materials*. Lanham, MD: University Press of America.

Yarmey, A. D. (1993). Stereotypes and recognition memory for faces and voices of good guys and bad guys. *Applied Cognitive Psychology, 7*(5), 419–431.

Zatz, M. S. (1987). The changing forms of racial/ethnic biases in sentencing. *Journal of Research in Crime and Delinquency, 24*(1), 69–92.

Zebrowitz, L. A. (1997). *Reading faces: Window to the soul?* Boulder, CO: Westview Press.

Zebrowitz, L. A., & McDonald, S. M. (1991). The impact of litigants' baby-facedness and attractiveness on adjudications in small claims courts. *Law and Human Behavior, 15*(6), 603–623.

13

TOWARDS THE DEVELOPMENT OF A STANDARDIZED FOCAL CONCERNS THEORY OF SENTENCING

Sean Maddan and Richard D. Hartley

Introduction

A considerable amount of scholarly research has been devoted to answering the question of how do judges decide? This corpus of research has demonstrated differences in the ways some criminal defendants are treated in relation to others. These sentencing disparities have often been attributed to the amount of discretion that is afforded to judges. As such, across various jurisdictions, many different policies have been implemented that have attempted to curb the differential treatment of criminal defendants ranging from determinate sentencing strategies to sentencing guidelines. Despite these policy adoptions, there has continued to be disparities across judicial outcomes and sentencing decisions. Multiple reasons have been proffered for the continued differences in sentencing decisions across similarly situated offenders, but the focal concerns perspective has become one of the key theoretical perspectives utilized to explain the differential treatment of similarly situated criminal defendants.

The focal concerns perspective postulates that judicial decision-making is influenced by three primary (focal) concerns: (1) an assessment of the blameworthiness or culpability of the offender; (2) a desire to protect the community by incapacitating dangerous offenders or deterring potential offenders; and (3) a concern about the practical consequences, or social costs, of sentencing decisions. The focal concerns perspective furthers that, because judges rarely have enough information to accurately determine an offender's culpability, dangerousness, or risk for re-offense, they develop a "perceptual shorthand" (Hawkins, 1981; Steffensmeier, Ulmer, and Kramer, 1998) based on stereotypes and attributions about these focal concerns that are linked to offender characteristics such as race, sex, and age. Thus, "race, age, and sex will interact to influence sentencing because of images or attributions relating these statuses to membership in social groups thought to be dangerous and crime prone" (Steffensmeier et al., 1998: 768).

Rather than explicitly testing the focal concerns perspective, the majority of past empirical studies have interpreted the results of analyses of sentencing outcomes using the focal concerns perspective. More to the point, scholars have used the focal concerns perspective to explain sentencing disparities based on the direct effects of race, ethnicity, sex, and age. Although a few scholars have attempted to formalize the focal concerns perspective into a theory comprised of assumptions and propositions which provide descriptions/suggestions of how theoretical concepts and variables might interact, very few studies have advanced the theory's empirical accuracy and scope.

For example, Hartley, Maddan, and Spohn (2007) used data on sentences imposed under the federal sentencing guidelines in 2000 to operationalize and provide a more comprehensive quantitative test of the focal concerns perspective on sentencing outcomes. While the study provided insights into the interplay between the variables, it only examined 1 year of federal sentencing data from the year 2000, and it relied on variables derived from an exploratory factor analysis. If that year had been anomalous, the theoretical model elaborated on could have limited generalizability.

The current study attempts to further the development of the focal concerns perspective in two important ways. First, this research, based on previous works (Kramer and Ulmer, 2009; Hartley et al., 2007; Steffensmeier et al., 1998), identifies some implicit assumptions and statements about the focal concerns perspective and formulates these assumptions and statements into explicit theoretical propositions and testable hypotheses. It is hoped that this attempt at a more formal theory can be used to guide future studies and aid in interpretation of the results of past studies. Second, we utilize data from the federal criminal courts from 1999 to 2005 to more fully evaluate the utility of the focal concerns theory. Our conceptual and analytic strategy begins with identification of the variables in the federal sentencing database that can be used to operationalize the three focal concerns and the concept of perceptual shorthand. We then use factor analysis to test our theoretical model and specify relationships among the independent variables. Finally, we use these underlying concepts—or "factors"—to model outcomes at two judicial decision-making stages: the imprisonment decision and the length of the prison sentence. We begin our discussion by outlining the evolution of the focal concern perspective and the research that has been conducted in this area.

Review of the Literature

The focal concerns perspective was first used by Miller (1958) in his work on lower-class delinquency. Miller suggested that the lower class was a subculture unto itself that had its own norms and values. Miller then outlined the key focal concerns of the lower-class subculture that were vital in the day-to-day interactions of group members. While the focal concerns associated with a so-called lower-class subculture have no bearing on disparities in judicial sentencing, the implications of Miller's work is that any subculture or organized group will have its own set of focal concerns that are central to group interactions as well as behavior of individuals within the group.

Although there was a dearth of theoretical frameworks to explain sentencing practices in the early 1980s (Blumstein et al., 1983; Hagan and Bumiller, 1983; Spohn,

2000), the idea of subcultural focal concerns was first introduced into the sentencing literature by Steffensmeier. Steffensmeier (1980) used the focal concerns concept to explain lenient sentences that female offenders were receiving in relation to male offenders. In this early work, Steffensmeier suggested that sentencing disparities across males and females were the result of five factors: Practicality, chivalry, naiveté, perceived permanence of behavior, and perception of dangerousness. Practicality referred to judges' "assumptions that most women defendants have young children and sending a mother to prison would be too disruptive of family life" (1980: 349). Practicality was an indication of the social position of the defendant; for instance, variables that Steffensmeier, Kramer, and Streifel (1993) would use to measure practicality would include if the defendant had a child, if the defendant was pregnant, had emotional/physical problems, and the availability of jail space. Chivalry—"the generally protective and benevolent attitudes toward women"—and naiveté—"the view that women are less capable than men of committing criminal acts"—were linked by Steffensmeier (1980: 350) as stereotypes and expectations that were deeply ingrained in society. Perceived permanence of the behavior was linked to criminal history; leniency in sentencing should favor females as males tend to have lengthier criminal histories. Steffensmeier (1980) argued that the research illustrated that judges tended to believe that females were also more susceptible to reform than males (p. 352). Finally, Steffensmeier (1980) noted that the perception of danger and the fear of male offenders was another factor involved with the more lenient treatment of female offenders (p. 352).

From this earlier work on sentencing disparities across male and female defendants, Steffensmeier and colleagues' (1993) research in Pennsylvania also helped to extend the theoretical model of focal concerns in the courts. Most important in this formulation was the first use of the concept of blameworthiness. Blameworthiness merged the perceived permanence of behavior and perceived dangerousness concepts into a single concept. Blameworthiness involves aspects of the defendant and the offense and is measured by variables such as prior criminal history, seriousness of the offense, and type of offense. Females are thought to engage in less serious crimes; these variables, therefore, would theoretically explain away the variance in sentencing outcomes across sex. Steffensemeier (1980) and Steffensmeier et al.'s (1998) efforts would eventually lead to the first formulation of the modern focal concerns perspective in 1998. None of the early works referred to, or explicitly used, the focal concerns concept, although the underlying logic (theoretical framework) was similar and evolved into the focal concerns perspective.

Steffensmeier et al. (1998) formalized the perspective by asserting that there are three focal concerns which influence judicial sentencing decisions: blameworthiness, protection of the community, and practical constraints and consequences. As stated earlier, blameworthiness is seen as the degree of the offender's culpability or the degree of injury caused. Thus, variables used to measure the blameworthiness of an offender would include measures like the seriousness of the offense and the offender's criminal history. The protection of the community is "conceptually distinct" from blameworthiness; this focal concern keys upon the need to incapacitate and/or deter offenders. While conceptually distinct, however, the variables are not necessarily distinct.

This concept involves the judge's ability to predict the future dangerousness of the offender; as such variables used to measure the protection of the community include criminal history, use of weapons in the offense, education, employment, and family history. Some have argued that perhaps the rehabilitative potential of the defendant is also important and could itself be a distinct focal concern (Kramer and Ulmer, 2009). Practical constraints and consequences (criminal justice system efficiency) pertains to organizational concerns; this includes the relationship among courtroom actors, case flow, and an awareness of state and federal correctional resources (overcrowding). Steffensmeier et al. (1998) did not initially outline any measures of practical constraints and consequences. Steffensmeier and colleagues also argued that these three focal concerns have complex interplay in the minds of judges when determining sentences for offenders.

Although the above focal concerns do not provide a formal explanation as to why defendant characteristics such as sex, race, ethnicity, and age are also influential in analytic models predicting judicial decisions, some research has uncovered empirical linkages. Ulmer (1997) and Kramer and Ulmer (2009) brought to the focal concerns perspective the incorporation of Albonetti's (1991) concept of uncertainty avoidance and attribution, and Farrell and Holmes' (1991) interpretive framework on legal decision making. Ulmer (1997) also integrated themes on how courtroom workgroup members didn't directly consider race but considered race-linked status and resource characteristics and their meaning for punishment. In 1991, Albonetti argued that structural organization theory posits that to be a "fully rational decision, [it] must be made with knowledge of all possible alternatives" (p. 248). Albonetti and others have also pointed out that, because judges rarely have complete information available (bounded rationality) for their usage when making sentencing decisions, this lack of information forces them to make decisions based on past experience, stereotypes, and prejudice (Albonetti, 1991). Because of this lack of useful information in a particular case, judges develop perceptual shorthand in the face of uncertainty about an appropriate sentence for an offender (Steffensmeier et al., 1998). This perceptual shorthand is hypothesized as the gateway for the inclusion of extra-legal factors when meting out sentence; sex, race, ethnicity, and age can then become indicators influencing sentencing outcomes. Some scholars have also argued that bounded rationality does not necessarily characterize federal sentencing as judges tend to have sufficient time and information with which to make determinations about appropriate sentences. Kramer and Ulmer (2002) and Ulmer and Bradley (2006) have also argued that it is not just lack of information that leads to uncertainty and bounded rationality; some uncertainty is inherent in the prediction of future behavior, and the focal concerns are considered even when there is rich information and time. So the lack of time and information is a sufficient but not a necessary cause of uncertainty and bounded rationality and reliance on perceptual shorthand.

Ulmer, Eisenstein, and Johnson (2010) assert that judges "make situational imputations about defendants' character and expected future behavior . . . these situational definitions of defendants in light of the focal concerns shape sentencing decisions" (p. 565–566). When these imputations are attributed to extra-legal factors, sentencing disparities can occur and discrimination can become a possible outcome. Several researchers also integrate the focal concerns perspective with the court community perspective to explain possible variation across local court communities (Kramer and Ulmer, 2009; Ulmer, 1997; Ulmer and Johnson, 2004). In general, judges are influenced by both legal and extra-legal factors, although legal factors are primary (Kramer and Ulmer, 2009), and the focal concerns perspective, with influences from the courts as communities perspective, proposes that stereotypes and status-linked attributions impact court actor's assessments of blameworthiness, dangerousness, and system constraints and that this is context dependent (Farrell and Holmes, 1991).

Kramer and Ulmer (2009), based on their analyses of local courts in Pennsylvania specifically, noted that individual courts within a judicial system may develop their own "distinctive organizational cultures and distinctive relationships to external organizations and externally imposed policies" (p. 4). Kramer and Ulmer's (2009) study indicated that the use of sentencing guidelines and the focal concerns of individual courts could vary between court jurisdictions. Therefore, apart from a case level explanation of judicial sentencing decisions, the focal concerns perspective complements the court communities/social worlds perspective where the attributions and stereotypes under the perspective may be context dependent or differentially ascribed dependent on characteristics of the court or district. Judges may make determinations of a defendant's dangerousness and risk for re-offense in part due to the types of defendants and cases they dispose of in their court (Ulmer, Eisenstein, and Johnson, 2010). In other words, focal concerns describes the decision-making process, the court community perspective describes the context. Indeed studies of sentencing outcomes have utilized an array of "complementary theoretical concepts, hypotheses, and models" (Ulmer, 2012: 9) to provide an enhanced understanding of variability in judicial decision-making.

Empirical research to date evaluating sentencing outcomes in relation to the focal concerns perspective has largely supported the theoretical perspective. The next section examines research that has evaluated judicial decision-making regarding sentencing with respect to the focal concerns perspective.

Prior Research on the Focal Concerns Perspective

Hartley et al. (2007) argued that, while the majority of the empirical studies conducted to date have provided at least partial support for the focal concerns theory, this research has had some theoretical and methodological shortcomings. First, the focal concerns theory is lacking full theoretical development by criminologists as there is no explicit thesis statement or established set of propositions that support this theoretical framework. While Kramer and Ulmer (2009) developed a theoretical model that incorporated the focal concerns perspective, their foci tended towards variation across court outcomes with respect to differential courtroom workgroups. Instead, researchers who study sentencing using the focal concerns perspective follow a set of established concepts (a heuristic model or substantively rational criteria; see for example Savelsberg, 1992), which offer some suggestions as to the variables which can measure particular concepts. This research tends to use the focal concerns as a mechanism to explain direct effects of race, sex, and ethnicity on sentencing outcomes while fewer studies have examined their interactions with legally relevant variables that might operationalize the focal concerns variables. Scholars have also noted that attributions and stereotypes influence judicial assessments of defendants in relation to the three focal concerns, but that these are less important that legally relevant factors in the determinations of an appropriate sentence and that they are context dependent (Kramer and Ulmer, 2009; Ulmer, 2012). In essence, if courts sentence with reference to the focal concerns, and certain extra-legal stereotypes exist in a particular court community, we would expect them to be linked to the focal concerns via the perceptual shorthand.

Results from empirical research over the past 25 years has with limited exceptions revealed that male and minority (Black and, to a lesser degree, Hispanic) defendants receive harsher sentencing outcomes net of controls. Further research demonstrates that the interaction of extra-legal factors may condition their effects (Spohn and Beichner, 2000; Spohn and Holleran, 2000; Steffensmeier and Demuth, 2006). Finally more recent research reports interaction effects between extra-legal defendant characteristics and case processing factors such as departures or mandatory minimums (Albonetti, 2002; Kautt and Delone, 2006; Kautt and Spohn, 2002; Hartley, Maddan, and Spohn, 2007), and legally relevant variables such as criminal history (Brennan, 2006; Tillyer, Hartley, and Ward, 2015) and offense severity, or offense type (Brennan, 2006; Ulmer and Bradley, 2006; Ulmer, Eisenstein, and Johnson, 2010). Sentencing researchers have also recently called for studies that specifically model both direct and indirect relationships in attempts to ferret out mediating variables. Furthermore, in order for the perceptual shorthand component of the focal concerns theory to be more fully developed, "the intervening theoretical mechanisms that link defendant race to sentencing (or other criminal justice) outcomes" need to be explored (Baumer, 2013: 254).

Researchers have also argued that the concepts of the focal concerns perspective are still relatively unexplored (Hartley et al., 2007; Ulmer, 2012). One issue is that the concepts that comprise the theory contain interrelated variables. As noted above, criminal history can be used as an indicator for both the blameworthiness and community safety concepts. Moreover, there is a conceptual void left by the focal concerns theory by not explaining how the various concepts work together; it is merely stated that there is a "complex interplay" between these focal concerns. This is especially problematic given the fact that concepts share variables. Thus, there is no guide for which variables should operationalize a given concept or how much variance a concept explains is accounted for by each variable. If a variable is used as an indicator for two concepts, then there is an implication that these two concepts are related, which means that different variables within each concept can potentially change the effect size of the variable in question. This theoretical shortcoming, however, may stem from the fact that in reality these acts and implementations are not as cut and dry as formal theory would dictate. For example, practically criminal history could be perceived by judges as an indicator of blameworthiness and community protection. Likewise, pleading not guilty and being convicted at trial can indicate more blameworthiness or practical constraints issues, and pleading guilty can indicate reduced blameworthiness, as well as saving time and resources (Kramer and Ulmer, 2009; Ulmer and Bradley, 2006).

Although testable hypotheses have been developed by a number of the focal concerns researchers, this theoretical framework is still in need of formal elaboration or standardized expansion to incorporate the interplay between the focal concerns and perceptual shorthand, and to account for contextual variation. Likewise, there has been little empirical effort exploring the relationship between the focal concerns and the perceptual shorthand variables. The focal concerns perspective in the majority of studies has mainly been used to explain the direct effects of perceptual shorthand variables on sentencing decisions. Finally, the concept of practical constraints and consequences has been a lesser developed feature of this theoretical perspective (Hartley et al., 2007). The primary variable operationalizing this concept has been whether or not the defendant pled guilty. Other variables that consider the court's number of cases, availability of jail space, and size of the court have been included in some analyses (Kramer and Ulmer, 2009; Johnson, 2006; Ulmer and Bradley, 2006). With this concept being relatively unmeasured, an empirical hole is left in the focal concerns perspective as to the effect of this integral concept on judicial decision-making.

A Theory of Focal Concerns in Sentencing Outcomes

With the ambiguity in conceptual relationships in prior work on the focal concerns perspective, we begin our analysis by proposing an explicit formulation of the focal concerns theory. There are several assumptions that underlie this theory. First, there are disparities in judicial decision-making across various offender characteristics. This assumption focuses on the fact that there are statistical differences in sentencing outcomes across many different groups of individuals. In and of itself, a disparity is not necessarily an indication of nefarious court processing. As such, the second assumption underlying our theoretical model is that disparities in judicial decisions can be the result of differential offending patterns, the differential treatment of offenders, or as an artifact of the data collection or policies that are in place in a given area. This assumption looks at the fact that various disparities are the result of many different things; most importantly, disparities can be the result of differential offending, differential treatment, a data collection artifact, or some combination of these factors. The third assumption is that the vast majority of judicial outcomes are not functions of overt discrimination. While there may be individual acts of discrimination in some places and at some times, most judges make conscious attempts at maintaining equitable decision-making practices. The fourth assumption is that, while mandated sentencing guidelines were declared as advisory only in 2005, the overwhelming majority of courts still adhere to sentencing guidelines as two generations of lawyers were trained under such systems. This will become important in our discussion of the data used in this study.

From these assumptions and previous research, we identified six propositions for the focal concerns theory. These are:

1. Judges when making determinations about appropriate sentences have three focal concerns: blameworthiness of the offender, community safety, and system efficiency.

2. The importance or priority of these concepts in the minds of judges is interpretive in nature and may be context dependent (i.e., district specific priorities, type of offense, caseload pressure).
3. The blameworthiness concept refers to the culpability of the defendant in terms of the current offense. The community safety concept refers to the potential risk the offender poses to the community in terms of the current offense and previous criminal history. The greater the blameworthiness of the offender, and the higher the risk the offender poses to the community, the more harsh the sentence decision will be.
4. The third focal concern guiding judicial decisions is system efficiency and is related to practical constraints. This macro level concept examines how judicial decisions impact the rest of the criminal justice system. Cases that might result in the inundation of the criminal justice system (or some other government bureaucracy) will receive more lenient judicial decisions. System resources may also drive sentencing decisions where sentences become more lenient where they are lacking.
5. Generally there is uncertainty inherent in the prediction of future behavior, and in some cases, there is an absence of information with which to make assessments of blameworthiness, protection of community, and practical constraints. As such, prosecutors and judges often make decisions via a perceptual shorthand. A perceptual shorthand allows judges to make decisions about the three focal concerns by utilizing attributions about blameworthiness of the offender, community safety, or system efficiency that are tied to extra-legal factors.
6. The variables associated with the perceptual shorthand concept should not have direct effects on judicial decision-making. Rather, all perceptual shorthand measures are mediated by one (or more) of the three primary focal concerns.

It is through the concept of the perceptual shorthand that disparity and potential discrimination can enter into judicial decisions through considerations of race, sex, ethnicity, and age.

The first proposition is largely a re-statement of the focal concerns perspective used by other researchers. The second proposition indicates that there is complexity amongst the focal concerns in the minds of judges. Thus, the nature and context of the case can have great bearing on court outcomes. The third proposition outlines the blameworthiness and community safety concepts. If an offender is considered to be more blameworthy or a greater danger to the community (i.e., at risk for re-offending), they will be more likely to be sentenced harshly by the courts. The fourth proposition focuses on the impact of judicial decision on the maintenance of criminal justice, especially the correctional and community correctional system. While a consideration, this focal concern is the least important concept; offense seriousness and perceived dangerousness to the community will dwarf the importance of system efficiency if the offender has committed a serious offense or is considered to be dangerous to the community.

The final propositions (5 and 6) revolve around the perceptual shorthand concept. The fifth proposition indicates that the perceptual shorthand will be used when there is uncertainty about future behavior, or an absence of information, needed to mete out a just sentence. The perceptual shorthand concept allows judges to utilize alternative metrics of blameworthiness, dangerousness to the community, and system efficiency. This concept is not necessarily a nefarious consideration for judges. The sixth proposition indicates that the perceptual shorthand is not independent of the three judicial focal concerns listed in the first proposition; rather, the perceptual shorthand has to be interrelated with the focal concerns. Whatever the perceptual shorthand metric, it must necessarily be related with at least one of the three focal concerns. While perceptual shorthand variables may have direct effects with judicial outcomes, any direct effect has to be theoretically/empirically mediated by focal concerns variables. Due to conflation between the perceptual shorthand variables of race sex, age, and ethnicity and the three focal concerns, sentencing disparities and potential discrimination can occur.

Two primary research hypotheses are derived from this theoretical elaboration. First, focal concerns variables will explain most of the variance in judicial outcomes independent of extra-legal factors. Second, any effects of perceptual shorthand variables will be mediated by focal concerns variables. To evaluate these hypotheses, the next section examines how we will test this theory.

Research Methods

This research expands on the previous exploratory work of Hartley et al. (2007) and recent commentary by other sentencing scholars (Baumer, 2013; Ulmer, 2012) by more fully operationalizing concepts associated with the focal concerns perspective and testing the focal concerns theory elaborated above. Data for this research was obtained from sentencing guideline data collected by the Federal Sentencing Commission (Monitoring of Federal Criminal Sentences Series) and made available on the Inter-University Consortium for Political and Social Research (ICPSR) website. Data were collected from the United States Sentencing Commission for the years 1999 to 2005 to more fully test the focal concerns perspective; originally Hartley et al. (2007) examined only data from a single year, 2000. The selection of data from 1999 to 2005 was contingent on two points. First, the data in the series became uniform in 1999; as such, it was selected as the start point. Second, the proscriptive nature of the federal sentencing guidelines was deemed to be unconstitutional by the Supreme Court in *Booker v. United States* (543 U.S. 220, 2005). Due to this fact, sentencing data after 2005 is omitted to minimize any historical threats to the validity of our test of the focal concerns theory.

Our data contain information on federal court dispositions allowing for the determination of court processing through both legally relevant variables (offense seriousness, criminal history, etc.) associated with the focal concerns concepts and extra-legal variables (race, ethnicity, sex, and age) in relation to perceptual shorthand metrics. Using multiple years of data and the information in the federal sentencing guideline databases will allow for a more complete test of the focal concerns perspective. The total number of federal criminal cases analyzed for this research was 452,454 (almost a half million subjects).

Dependent Variables

Similar to the majority of current sentencing research, there are two dependent variables used in the current research: the decision to imprison a guilty offender and the length of the prison sentence imposed. The decision to imprison an offender is coded as a dichotomous variable where no prison is coded as 0 and a prison receipt is coded as 1. The length of the prison sentence is a count variable that measures the number of months an offender received in prison. Anyone who did not receive a prison sentences in the first analytic model is omitted from the latter dependent variable (a prison sentence of 0 months); likewise, any sentences over 800 months were omitted.

The univariate statistics for the two dependent variables utilized in this research are provided in Table 13.1, which indicates that the vast majority of defendants found guilty were given a prison sentence (85.3%, or 374,367 offenders) from 1999 to 2005. As well, the average prison sentence defendants received was 52.88 months, or almost 4.5 years. For total months received in prison, there were minor issues with normality. The skew for months in prison was 2.7, which is acceptable. The kurtosis was 13.1. While an Ordinary Least Squares (OLS) regression is robust enough with this level of kurtosis, we logged this dependent variable to correct for this non-normality.

Table 13.1 Descriptive Statistics: Dependent and Independent Variables for Focal Concerns Concepts

Concepts	*Variable*	*Coding*	*Percent*	*Mean*
	Independent Variables			
	Incarceration decision	1 = Yes	85.3	
	Sentence length			52.88
	Independent Variables			
Blameworthiness	Offense seriousness score			18.46
	Criminal history score			2.38
	Number of counts			1.47
Community Safety	Violent offense	1 = Violent	3.9	
	Drug offenses	1 = Drug	39.1	
	Gun minimum	1 = Applied	3.4	
	Drug minimum	1 = Applied	23.6	
	Armed criminal	1 = Applied	0.6	
	Career criminal	1 = Applied	2.7	
	Citizen	1 = Not a U.S. citizen	31.2	
	Education	Less than HS	40.5	
		HS graduate/GED	29.0	
		Some college	15.0	
		College graduate	4.6	
		Missing	10.9	

Concepts	*Variable*	*Coding*	*Percent*	*Mean*
	Independent Variables			
System Efficiency	Disposition	1 = Plea	95.2	
	Departure	Upward	0.7	
		Downward	16.2	
		Substantial assistance	17.9	
	Accept responsibility	1 = Applied	92.1	
	Pretrial detention status	1 = In Custody	61.5	
	Number of dependents			1.57
Perceptual Shorthand	Sex	0 = Male	86.0	
		1 = Female	14.0	
	Ethnicity	0 = Non-Hispanic	59.2	
		1 = Hispanic	40.8	
	Race	0 = White	71.0	
		1 = Non-White	29.0	
	Age			34.27
Region	Northeast		13.7	
	Midwest		14.4	
	South		44.6	
	West		26.9	
	Territories		0.3	
N = 452,454				

Theoretical and Control Variables

The independent variables used in this research are a list of the usual suspects in relation to other federal sentencing studies. Based on the findings from existing studies testing focal concerns and in line with the previous research, we identify, a priori, the independent variables within each theoretical concept. Table 13.1 provides the coding, frequencies, and means associated with the dependent and independent variables utilized in the current study with respect to the focal concerns theoretical concepts. An explanation of the variables, by concept, is provided in the following subsections.

The Blameworthiness and Culpability of the Offender

As delineated in the theoretical model above, the blameworthiness and culpability concept is an important concern in sentencing decisions. If an offender is considered more culpable, they should be more likely to receive a prison sentence, one that is on average lengthier. We utilize three variables to measure the offender's blameworthiness: the offense seriousness score, the number of counts of conviction, and the offender's criminal history score. The offense seriousness score and the total number of conviction counts are indicators of an individual's blameworthiness. We include the criminal history score within this concept even though it could also be an indicator of community safety. Hartley et al.'s (2007) study did not definitively conclude if criminal history should be included as a measure of blameworthiness or community safety. This research will attempt to settle this question more completely. According to Table 13.1, the average offense seriousness score is 18.46, the average criminal history score is 2.38, and the average number of counts was just under one and a half (1.47).

Protection of the Community

The next focal concern evaluates sentencing outcomes with respect to the criminal's potential threat to community safety. If the offender is a greater threat, then that offender will receive a more severe sentence. The variables used for this concept evaluate either an overt violent threat to a community or a destabilizing force (actual or perceived) that can impact perceptions of community safety.

We used eight variables to measure community protection; six of these variables are legally relevant variables and two are extra-legal variables. The first two legally relevant variables for this concept deal with the type of crime: violent or drug. In Table 13.1, 3.9% of the cases involved violent crimes and 39.1% of cases involved drug offenses. The next two legally relevant variables deal with the application of mandatory minimum sentences that could be indicative of community safety: gun minimum and drug minimum. Table 13.1 illustrates that gun minimums were applied in 3.4% of cases and drug minimums were applied in 23.6% of cases. The final two legally relevant variables for community safety are the application of an armed career criminal and career criminal status. In this study, neither of these statuses were oft-used (armed career criminal = 0.6% and career criminal = 2.7%).

Two extra-legal variables were included for the community protection concept: citizenship status of the offender and education level. Both of these are predicted to have an impact on sentencing outcomes. With the current narco-criminal activity on the U.S.-Mexican border and the continuous threat of terrorism from Middle Eastern countries, many believe non-citizens to be an inherent threat to the community. Citizenship (0 = citizen; 1 = non-citizen) is included as a metric for community protection in relation to sentencing outcomes; Table 13.1 indicates that over 31% of offenders examined in the current study here were non-citizens. The focal concerns perspective would suggest that those who are undereducated are also more likely to pose a risk to community safety. We use education as a set of dummy variables that address if the offender had a high school diploma/GED or had a college degree (bachelor's). Table 13.1 shows that 29% of the subjects had a high school diploma or GED, and 4.6% of the subjects were college graduates.

Practical Constraints and Consequences

The third concept associated with the focal concerns theory is the practical constraints and consequences associated with sentencing decisions; this is also known as system efficiency. Ensuring the efficient flow of cases through the legal and correctional systems (or any other bureaucracies) is a consideration for judges. We identified five variables associated with the optimal functioning of the system. Disposition is whether or not the offender plead guilty (1) or opted to go to trial (0); this variable also alludes to any potential trial tax for defendants. Table 13.1 indicates that over 95% of offenders plead guilty. Departure evaluates whether the judge departed from sentencing guidelines (upward, downward, or a substantial assistance departure); Table 13.1 shows that over 65% of defendants did not receive a departure. In addition, of those who received a departure, most were for downward departures (16.2%) or substantial assistance departures (17.9%). The acceptance of responsibility by defendants also measures system efficiency. Theoretically, if the defendant accepts responsibility, fewer court and correctional resources will be expended on these individuals. In Table 13.1, 92.1% of defendants accepted responsibility for their actions. Pretrial detention evaluates if the defendant was held in jail prior to court processing of the trial. As noted in Table 13.1, almost 62% of offenders were in jail prior to the trial. We also include an extra-legal variable for this concept: number of dependents. The number of dependents can have ramifications for families of the offenders and potentially for various welfare agencies. Judges refer to this as the social costs of sentencing offenders to incarceration. The average number of children per defendant was 1.57.

Perceptual Shorthand

The focal concerns theory indicates the importance of the perceptual shorthand variables. Since judges sometimes may not have the entire complement of facts, they may need to impose a sentence in line with the above focal concerns, perceptual shorthand metrics that are associated with the focal concerns can be used to fill in the gap of missing information. These perceptual shorthand metrics are based on stereotypes and other attributions. For this study, we evaluate the perceptual shorthand variables associated with sex, ethnicity, race, and age. The first three variables are dichotomous in nature; sex is measured as male ... and females = 1, ethnicity as Non-Hispanic ... and Hispanic = 1, and race as white ... and non-white = 1. Table 13.1 indicates that 86% of the subjects are male, 40.8% of subjects are Hispanic, and only 29% of subjects are non-white. The remaining perceptual shorthand variable is age; age is a count variable in relation to years. The average age of subjects is 34.27 years.

Court Community Variables

To add a final dimension to this research, we also evaluated the federal court decisions by region as extra control variables; this allowed us to evaluate the newest form of the focal concerns perspective integration by Kramer and Ulmer (2009). Research on sentencing practices has recently focused on variation across courts within districts and circuits. The current study examines this line of inquiry by evaluating the focal concerns perspective with respect to regions. Regions were created out of the same states used by the Federal Bureau of Investigation (FBI) in their presentation of crime data in the Uniform Crime Report (UCR). As such, the variable region controls for differences in sentencing decisions across the Northeast, Midwest, South, West, and

U.S. Territories. If differences are shown here, future research should examine individual court communities by federal circuit or district. As shown in Table 13.1, the region with the highest case traffic is the South accounting for almost 50% of all cases (44.6%); this is followed by the West (26.9%), the Midwest, and the Northeast. There is little case traffic in the U.S. Territories. For higher-level analyses, this variable was broken into a series of dummy variables with the reference category being the South since the majority of cases are disposed of in this region.

Analytic Model

Our analytic model has two stages. First, to test if the focal concerns concepts and variables were statistically linked in the way the theoretical model suggests, a combination of exploratory and confirmatory factor analyses were utilized. While factor analysis is not as powerful as structural equation modeling (see below), factor analysis can statistically examine the relationships between independent variables. If relationships are found between variables, these variables can be collapsed into factors and used in either logistic or OLS regression analyses relative to the dependent variable in question.

Second, this research tests the focal concerns theory using two different statistical models: the judicial decision to imprison a defendant and the length of the prison sentence in months. Logistic regression is employed to test the effects of the focal concerns model on the decision to imprison a defendant since the decision to imprison is a dichotomous dependent variable. In line with current research on sentencing, OLS regression is used to test the effects of the focal concerns model with the total number of months (logged) a defendant received. The offenders who did not receive a prison sentence are omitted from this latter analysis.

Structural equation modeling (SEM) would be the optimal test of this theory, but sentencing data does not necessarily conform to such an analysis for two reasons. First, SEM is built around the chi-square statistic, which is highly susceptible to large sample sizes. As such, an SEM analysis with almost a half of a million subjects will undoubtedly yield statistically significant results. Second, the majority of the variables being used are dichotomous in nature. Some of these independent variables have slight issues with being kurtose. Kurtosis is a major problem for structural equation models and this dataset inherently violates one of the key assumptions of SEM, namely that variables are continuously and normally distributed (Bollen, 1989; Kline, 1998).

Analysis and Findings

We begin our analysis by conducting factor analyses of the independent variables associated with the focal concerns theory. For ease of interpretation, we have recoded some variables in the factor analyses so that all associations/loadings are positive; coding for dichotomous variables is provided in the tables and results are discussed after the table. The results of the exploratory factor analysis is provided in Table 13.2.

Table 13.2 Exploratory Factor Analysis of Full Focal Concerns Theoretical Model

Variable	*Factor 1*	*Factor 2*	*Factor 3*	*Factor 4*	*Factor 5*	*Factor 6*	*Factor 7*
Offense seriousness	0.749						
Drug offense (Yes = 1)	0.876						
Drug minimum (Applied = 1)	0.892						
Citizen (Yes = 1)		0.757					
High school grad/GED (No = 1)		0.462					
Ethnicity (Hispanic = 1)		0.808					
Pretrial detention (in custody = 1)		0.474					
Race (White = 1)		0.647					
Criminal history			0.801				
Career criminal (Yes = 1)			0.665				
Gender (Male = 1)			0.444				
Departure (Yes = 1)				0.269			
Disposition (Plea = 1)				0.867			
Accept responsibility (Yes = 1)				0.875			
College graduate (Yes = 1)					0.682		
Age					0.698		
Number of counts						0.721	
Violent offense (Yes = 1)						0.317	
Gun minimum (Applied = 1)						0.793	
Number of dependents							0.883

Rotation Method: Varimax with Kaiser Normalization.

The results of this exploratory analysis provide further support for the findings found in Hartley et al. (2007). Again, seven factors were derived from the variables. Factor 1 is an indicator of blameworthiness/culpability (offense seriousness, drug offense, and drug minimum). Factors 2, 3, and 4 are all indicators of community safety: Factor 2 (citizen, no high school diploma/GED, ethnicity [Hispanic], pretrial detention, and race [white]); Factor 3 (criminal history, application of career criminal status, and being male); Factor 4 (departure from guidelines, offender plead guilty, and offender accepted responsibility). Factor 5 is a system efficiency indicator (college education and age). Factor 6 is another indicator of community safety (number of criminal counts, offense was violent, and a gun minimum sentence was applied), and Factor 7 was another indicator of system efficiency (number of dependents).

As with previous research, variables associated with the perceptual shorthand concept did not load onto a singular factor (Hartley et al., 2007). Rather, these variables loaded onto factors associated with the three focal concerns, which is what we would expect according to contemporary interpretations of the focal concerns perspective. Race, ethnicity, and gender were all linked to community safety measures; being associated with citizenship, no high school diploma/GED, and pretrial detention. Gender (being male) was associated with criminal history and the application of career criminal status. Age factored only with college graduation which might suggest some concerns about practical constraints, although this finding could be context dependent on the type of crime, say a white-collar versus a violent or drug offense. What is important about the results of this analysis is that there is indeed interplay between the focal concerns and perceptual shorthand variables.

While the results from the exploratory factor analysis indicated support for the focal concerns perspective and our theoretical model, confirmatory factor analysis is necessary for testing the nature of the focal concerns and the propositions of the theory denoted above. Table 13.3 considers variables associated with the focal concerns theory minus the variables associated with the perceptual shorthand. Again, we modified coding of some variables for ease in interpreting the tables.

The results in Table 13.3 indicate support for the first propositions. There are three focal concerns and blameworthiness is the most important factor as it loaded first (a combination of drug minimum, drug offense, offense seriousness, and receipt of a departure). In addition, the next most important focal concern was community safety; this factor included the variables for accepting responsibility, pleading not guilty, criminal history, gun minimum application, number of counts, career criminal status, and violent offense. These results would also indicate that criminal history is in fact a measure of community safety, not blameworthiness. Lastly, the third factor was a metric of system efficiency (pretrial detention, lack of education, citizenship, and number of dependents). One interesting finding on this confirmatory analytic model is that disposition was more related to variables associated with community safety rather than system efficiency. To evaluate these variables in relation to the perceptual shorthand, Table 13.4 provides the final confirmatory factor analysis.

It is clear from the results in Table 13.4 that the inclusion of perceptual shorthand variables caused the focal concerns model to load with the same variables, but in

Table 13.3 Confirmatory Factor Analysis of Focal Concerns Theoretical Model Without Perceptual Shorthand Concepts

Variable	*Blameworthiness*	*Community Safety*	*System Efficiency*
Drug minimum (Applied = 1)	0.895		
Drug offense (Yes = 1)	0.879		
Offense seriousness	0.730		
Departure (Yes = 1)	0.155		
Accept responsibility (No = 1)		0.746	
Disposition (Trial = 1)		0.743	
Criminal history		0.550	
Gun minimum (Applied = 1)		0.403	
Number of counts		0.396	
Career criminal (Applied = 1)		0.338	
Violent offense (Yes = 1)		0.295	
Pretrial detention (Yes = 1)			0.722
High school grad/GED (No = 1)			0.629
Citizen (Yes = 1)			0.586
College graduate (No = 1)			0.453
Number of dependents			0.158

Rotation Method: Varimax with Kaiser Normalization.

Table 13.4 Confirmatory Factor Analysis of Focal Concerns Theoretical Model with Perceptual Shorthand Concepts

Variable	*System Efficiency*	*Blameworthiness*	*Community Safety*
Citizen (No = 1)	0.704		
Ethnicity (Hispanic = 1)	0.695		
Pretrial detention (In custody = 1)	0.692		
High school grad/GED (No = 1)	0.629		
College graduate (No = 1)	0.362		
Gender (Male = 1)	0.355		
Age	−0.300		
Number of dependents	0.163		
Drug minimum (Applied = 1)		0.888	
Drug offense (Yes = 1)		0.881	
Offense seriousness		0.708	
Departure (Yes = 1)		0.154	
Accept responsibility (No = 1)			0.559
Disposition (Trial = 1)			0.554
Criminal history			0.490
Number of counts			0.483
Gun minimum (Applied = 1)			0.468
Career criminal (Applied = 1)			0.413
Race (Non-White = 1)			0.406
Violent offense (Yes = 1)			0.358

Rotation Method: Varimax with Kaiser Normalization.

Table 13.5 Logit Regression on Decision to Incarcerate (Without Perceptual Shorthand Concepts)[†]

Variable	*Model 1*		*Model 2*	
	b	*Odds*	*b*	*Odds*
Blameworthiness	1.433*	4.452	1.495*	4.461
Community safety	1.962*	7.113	1.964*	7.125
System efficiency	1.447*	4.249	1.442*	4.231
Constant	3.556*	35.027	3.672*	39.341
Northeast	–	–	−0.378*	0.685
Midwest	–	–	−0.042*	0.959
West	–	–	−0.187*	0.830
χ^2	125531.624*		126136.147*	
−2 Log Likelihood	193415.388		192810.865	
Nagelkerke R^2	0.490		0.492	

* $p < 0.05$.

[†] Variable coding matches Table 13.3.

differing order. The first factor that loaded was the system efficiency concept. Ethnicity, gender, and age all loaded on this factor. This would indicate that non-citizenship, pretrial detention, lack of educational attainment, and number of dependents can be linked with a perceptual shorthand consisting of ethnicity (being Hispanic), gender (being male), and age (being young), which can lead to disparities across these three groups. While the variables associated with blameworthiness are the same, the factor itself loaded second. The third factor that loaded was community safety. The only perceptual shorthand variable to load here was race. Under this factor, being non-white could become a shorthand for not accepting responsibility, going to trial, lengthier criminal history, a larger number of counts, receiving a gun mandatory minimum sentence, committing a violent offense, and the application of a career criminal status. The findings from this table also support several propositions in our proposed focal concerns theory.

We now test the factors found in Tables 13.3 and 13.4 to evaluate the impact of the focal concerns and the perceptual shorthand factors on the decision to incarcerate. Table 13.5 provides the results from the logit regression on the focal concerns factors, while omitting the perceptual shorthand variables. (Model 2 includes the regional controls.)

Table 13.5 indicates that the model is fairly strong (Nagelkerke $R^2 = 0.49$) explaining almost half of the variance in the decision to imprison a defendant. This supports the overall focal concerns theory, and our first hypothesis. In particular, those with greater blameworthiness were over four times more likely to receive a prison sentence. Those who posed a risk to community safety were over seven times more likely to be given a prison sentence. Defendants who were more likely to place a potential strain on system resources were over four times more likely to receive a prison sentence. While these results are supportive of the focal concerns theory, in general, blameworthiness does not have the strongest impact on the receipt of a prison sentence; our results indicate that community safety is the greatest predictor of prison sentence.

Regional variables were also statistically significant in the model. Defendants in the south were more likely to get prison sentences. Unfortunately, while the regional variables are statistically significant, they indicate rather weak results; defendants in the south were slightly more likely to receive prison sentences. In addition, the overall R^2 did not change drastically from the model with and without the regional variables; both explained around 49% of the variance. This suggests that, to some degree, there is not extreme variation in court sentences meted out across the U.S. This might also suggest that in the years 1999–2005 the presumptive federal sentencing guidelines were mostly being adhered to by judges across the federal court system.

Table 13.6 provides the logit regression results for the full focal concerns model with inclusion of perceptual shorthand variables. Table 13.6 likewise indicates that regional variables added little to the ability to predict receiving a prison sentence. What is more important, however, is that the addition of the perceptual shorthand variables also added very little to our understanding of who gets a prison sentence. The effects of race, sex, ethnicity, and age are largely drowned out within the context of the focal concerns factors. This is support for our second hypothesis that perceptual shorthand variables are mediated by the focal concerns factors. Adding the perceptual shorthand variables into the model decreases the odds across focal concerns factors. This would again indicate support for our more formalized theory. While there may be disparities across groups, the perceptual shorthand variables' link to the focal concerns factors

Table 13.6 Logit Regression on Decision to Incarcerate (With Incorporation of Perceptual Shorthand Concepts)†

Variable	*Model 1*		*Model 2*	
	b	*Odds*	*b*	*Odds*
System efficiency	1.442★	4.144	1.426★	4.160
Blameworthiness	1.290★	3.631	1.289★	3.627
Community safety	1.584★	4.873	1.583★	4.867
Constant	3.315★	27.535	3.428★	30.808
Northeast	–	–	−0.419★	0.658
Midwest	–	–	0.055★	1.056
West	–	–	−0.195★	0.822
χ^2	123682.389★		124504.087★	
−2 log likelihood	188154.955		187333.297	
Nagelkerke R^2	0.495		0.497	

★ $p < 0.05$.

† Variable coding matches Table 13.4.

Table 13.7 OLS Regression on Length of Prison Sentence in Months (Without Incorporation of Perceptual Shorthand Concepts)†

Variable	*Model 1*		*Model 2*	
	b	*β*	*b*	*β*
Blameworthiness	0.629★	0.548	0.615★	0.536
Community safety	0.560★	0.502	0.551★	0.494
System efficiency	0.306★	0.251	0.324★	0.265
Northeast	–		0.140★	−0.004
Midwest	–		0.056★	0.017
West	–		−0.219★	−0.080
F	125736.489		64685.005	
R^2	0.532★		0.539★	

★ $p < 0.05$.

†Variable coding matches Table 13.3.

suggest that these disparities may not necessarily reflect overt discrimination but rather an association to the various legally relevant variables. In other words, differences in values on legally relevant variables across extra-legal factors can explain the disparity in outcomes. It may also suggest that judges attribute blameworthiness and need for community safety to these extra-legal factors, which therefore results in disparate sentencing decisions across race, ethnicity, sex, and age.

We now turn to evaluating the impact of the focal concerns factors on the length of the sentence. Table 13.7 provides the results of the focal concerns factors minus the perceptual shorthand variables.

This model is again statistically significant and explains over half of the variance in predicting the length of the prison sentence ($R^2 = 0.532$*). Due to the logging of the dependent variable, the coefficient metrics are not as easily interpretable. Since we are concerned with the effect of the variable combinations as aggregate factors, and in line with Ulmer's (2012: 8) assertion that coefficients are "merely indirect windows into sentencing processes," our analysis here focuses here on the standardized coefficient (beta). All factors were significant and interacted with the dependent variable as would be expected: the more blameworthy the criminal, the longer the sentence, the greater the threat to community safety, the longer the prison sentence, and the more impact presented to the system, the result was a longer sentence. The blameworthiness factor is the most important factor in the model followed closely by community safety; system efficiency was the weakest of the three focal concerns.

In relation to the regional variables, we find some variation in sentencing outcomes across regions. Defendants in the Northeast and Midwest receive greater average sentences than in the South; alternatively, offenders in the West are more likely to get shorter average prison sentences than those in the South. Overall, the regional variables added very little to the explained variance over just adding the focal concerns factors to the model ($R^2 = 0.539$*). This model supports our first hypothesis.

Finally, we explore the focal concerns factors with the inclusion of the perceptual shorthand variables; Table 13.8 provides the results of these analyses.

In this model, the regional variables added little to the explanation of prison sentence length (0.004 more variance explained). Likewise, the perceptual shorthand variable adds very little to our combined explanation of length of prison sentence ($R^2 = 0.538$). Again, most of the effects associated with perceptual shorthand variables are moderated via the focal concerns factors which supports our second hypothesis. With the addition of the shorthand variables, the community safety factor becomes the most important in the model rather than the blameworthiness factor, although it is still the second most important factor. This again indicates support for the focal

Table 13.8 OLS Regression on Length of Prison Sentence in Months (With Incorporation of Perceptual Shorthand Concepts)†

Variable	*Model 1*		*Model 2*	
	b	*β*	*b*	*β*
System efficiency	0.246*	0.201	0.263*	0.215
Blameworthiness	0.587*	0.523	0.576*	0.514
Community safety	0.612*	0.552	0.603*	0.544
Northeast	–		−0.018*	−0.005
Midwest	–		0.030*	0.010
West	–		−0.176*	−0.066
F	122468.447		62285.100	
R^2	0.534*		0.538*	

* $p < 0.05$.

† Variable coding matches Table 13.4.

concerns theory. Now that we have completed our analyses, we turn to a discussion of these results in relation to the focal concerns theory.

Conclusion and Discussion

The focal concerns perspective has been used by many criminologists to explain disparate sentences in relation to race, ethnicity, sex, and age. Thus, when large direct effects are found related to groups of individuals being treated differentially by the courts, criminologists suggest that this is partly an indication that the courts lack information, or have uncertainty about, a fully informed conclusion and therefore attribute blameworthiness and need for community safety to extra-legal defendant characteristics. While the focal concerns perspective is the most oft-used mechanism for explaining disparities, it has not received full development by criminologists. This research has attempted to advance its theoretical development by presenting a more comprehensive focal concerns theory of sentencing complete with a set of propositions, more developed conceptualization, and testable hypotheses. In addition, we tested this theory using federal court sentencing data from 1999 to 2005 through factor analysis and a series of regression analyses to better understand the interactions between measures of focal concerns' concepts and metrics of perceptual shorthand variables.

The factor analyses (exploratory and confirmatory) indicated that there were in fact only three focal concerns (blameworthiness of the offender, community safety, and system efficiency) supporting the hypotheses of the theory; likewise these analyses also supported the idea that the perceptual shorthand is not a focal concern in and of itself. The theoretical model we advocate also suggests that, although context dependent, blameworthiness is the most important focal concern followed by community safety and system efficiency. The factor analyses provided partial support for this. When the model was factored without perceptual shorthand variables, this prediction is correct. When the perceptual shorthand variables are introduced into the model, system efficiency becomes the key focal concern, followed by blameworthiness of the offender and community safety. This set of factor analyses indicates support for the sixth proposition and also is indicative of the interactive relationships between the three focal concerns and the perceptual shorthand variables.

The factor analyses provide valuable findings in relation to what variables should be included within the three focal concerns. The concept of blameworthiness of the offender should be measured with offense seriousness, if the offense was a drug offense, the imposition of a drug minimum, and whether a defendant received a departure from the guidelines. The concept of community safety should be measured with acceptance of responsibility by the defendant, if the defendant chose to plead guilty or go to trial, the offender's criminal history, if a gun minimum was imposed, the total number of counts, if a career criminal enhancement was applied, and whether or not the crime was violent. The system efficiency concept should be measured by pretrial detention, if the defendant was a citizen, education status (college and high school graduates in this research), and number of dependents. These conceptual variables held true with or without the presence of perceptual shorthand variables, which add further credence to the theoretical/analytic model evaluated here.

In relation to the decision to incarcerate, our theoretical model was statistically significant. Whether perceptual shorthand variables are included in the model or not, these models explained almost 50% of the variance in judicial decisions to imprison defendants. Those with greater blameworthiness had over four times higher odds of receiving a prison sentence. Those who posed a greater threat to the community were just over seven times higher odds of receiving a prison sentence. Those who would put strain on system resources were odds that were four times higher of being sent to prison; while this seems counterintuitive, the factor loadings indicate that non-citizens, Hispanics, those in pretrial custody, those uneducated, males, younger defendants, and those with more dependents will get longer sentences. With the exception of the systemic resources, these findings indicate support for our theoretical model. These results also reveal that perhaps judges are less retributive in philosophy than previously thought, and more concerned with community safety, and perhaps punishments that are more oriented toward future crime prevention.

In relation to the length of the prison sentence (in months), the theoretical model was again statistically significant. Knowing information about the focal concerns helped us to explain between 57% and 58% of the variance in sentence length. All coefficients were positive; those with greater blameworthiness received longer sentences, as did those who posed a greater threat to the community and those who would put strain on system resources. Again, with the exception of system efficiency, these findings indicate support for our theoretical model.

What is most important in these analyses is the impact of the variables associated with the perceptual shorthand. While studies generally indicate very robust and strong direct effects of race, sex, ethnicity, and age, most studies have not evaluated the interactive effects of these variables with respect to key legally relevant variables. The regression models which incorporated the perceptual shorthand variables indicated support for our remaining hypotheses: when interactions are taken into account, with one exception, the effect of perceptual shorthand variables dissipates and legally relevant variables associated with the focal concerns will mediate most of the effects of perceptual shorthand variables. In all of our analytic models, the inclusion of perceptual shorthand variables has a negligible impact on the focal concerns factors. Indeed, the net effect on the model R^2 ranged from 0.05% to 1% of the total variance explained. In addition, the metric effects of the focal concerns factors decreased with regard to their impact on the decision to incarcerate and the length of the sentence in prison when the perceptual shorthand variables were included in the factors. The one exception was that the effect of community safety on sentence length was larger ($b = 0.603$ vs. $b = 0.551$) with inclusion of the perceptual shorthand variables in the model. As such, all of the explanatory power in the direct effects of race, gender, ethnicity, and age are mediated through interactions with legally relevant variables associated with the focal concerns concepts/factors. Disparities in sentencing are reflective of a combination of legitimate and extralegal factors by courtroom actors, but our analyses indicate that legitimate factors are the driving force for case dispositions, and that extra-legal defendant characteristics are influential of outcomes via linkages with legally relevant variables that measure the focal concerns.

In addition, regional variables indicated significant results when introduced into the model, with relatively meager effects. The South and Midwest regions seemed to show a slightly greater affinity to incarceration than the other regions. However, the Midwest region handed out the longest sentence lengths in relation to the other regions. This indicates support for Kramer and Ulmer's (2009) integration of the focal concerns and court community perspectives and suggests that studies including disaggregated models by circuit and district will help to uncover further contexts for disparities in sentencing.

In that same vein, the focal concerns perspective has been utilized to explain sentencing outcomes at both the federal and state levels. While the results here indicate that the focal concerns theory we outlined fits with court outcomes at the federal level, there is likely some level of theoretical generalizability that should be observed. While the confirmatory factor analyses produced analytic concepts in line with the focal concerns perspective (composed of legally relevant and extra-legal variables), it is highly likely that the interaction amongst variables will be different at/across the state level. The importance of variables associated with blameworthiness, community safety, and system efficiency may differ from the federal level to the state level. While variable combinations associated with blameworthiness and community safety will be similar, the contexts of various court jurisdictions could lead to different variable combinations associated with different focal concerns theoretical constructs. In addition, the importance of the individual focal concerns may fluctuate due to the context of a particular jurisdiction. For instance, the system efficiency may take primacy if an area is in extreme financial exigency, as occurred in some places during the economic downturn of 2008 and many jurisdictions began to abandon policies in place for decades due to jail/prison overcrowding and overburdened resources.

When it comes to the administration of justice, the states are responsible for the majority of new incarcerations and the lion's share of the overall prison population in the U.S. Due to many inter-state differences, it is likely that each state will have its own set of focal concerns. These focal concerns across and within state court jurisdictions will be indicative of contexts associated with issues pertaining to individual or similar jurisdictions. At the federal level, our results indicate overwhelming support for our conception of the focal concerns perspective. This is likely due to stringent federal policies on incarceration and sentence length determination in the form of prescriptive sentencing guidelines and a much more limited discretion afforded federal judges, despite that today the Supreme Court has rendered them voluntary. Thus, criminologists should be careful in applying a singular focal concerns theoretical structure for all courts in the U.S. Rather, context-specific information must be integrated into focal concerns across each state, and possibly across courts within the states.

Future research in this area should continue to develop the version of the focal concerns theory that we have elaborated on here. Most importantly, the emphasis of future studies should focus on the interactions between perceptual shorthand metrics (extra-legal factors) and legally relevant variables. Since we have only explained roughly 50% of the variance through our theoretical model and the available database variables, it is incumbent that other researchers extend their analytic models to include other metrics of legally relevant variables, and possibly extra-legal variables. Future analyses might attempt the use of structural equation modeling (SEM). While we did not find the data used here to be appropriate based on the assumptions of SEM, other datasets may be capable of utilizing SEM as a test of the theory we propose here.

Future research should also examine other decision-making stages including the pre-trial detention decision and decisions related to departures (both prosecutorial and judicial). Researchers should also conduct analyses using multiple years of data, for example, data after the *Booker* decision, 2005 and subsequent. Finally, future research at the federal level should also continue to explore differences across federal circuits and districts to evaluate Kramer and Ulmer's (2009) theoretical integration of the focal concerns and court community perspectives. While the effects of just examining regions showed negligible results in this study, one caveat is that we examined over 400 thousand cases, which could mask inter-district variation in effects. Research which includes questions related to whether the three focal concerns and perceptual shorthand variables show differential impact across jurisdictions or districts would provide further contexts in which the focal concerns theory is supported or refuted.

References

Albonetti, C. (2002). The effects of the "safety valve" amendment on length of imprisonment for cocaine trafficking/manufacturing offenders: Mitigating the effects of mandatory minimum penalties and offender's ethnicity. *Iowa Law Review, 87*, 401–433.

Albonetti, C. A. (1991). An integration of theories to explain judicial discretion. *Social Problems, 38*, 247–266.

Baumer, E. (2013). Reassessing and redirecting research on race and sentencing. *Justice Quarterly, 30*, 231–261.

Blumstein, A., Cohen, J., Martin, S., & Tonry, M. (Eds.). (1983). *Research on sentencing: The search for reform*. Washington, DC: National Academy Press.

Bollen, K. (1989). *Structural equations with latent variables*. New York: Wiley.

Brennan, P. K. (2006). Sentencing female misdemeanants: An examination of the direct and indirect effects of race/ethnicity. *Justice Quarterly, 23*, 60–95.

Farrell, R., & Holmes, M. (1991). The social and cognitive structure of legal decision making. *The Sociological Quarterly, 32*(4), 529–542.

Hagan, J., & Bumiller, K. (1983). Making sense of sentencing: Race and sentencing outcomes. In A. Blumstein, J. Cohen, S. Martin, & M. Tonry (Eds.), *Research on sentencing: The search for reform* (pp. 1–54). Washington, DC: National Academy Press.

Hartley, R. D., Maddan, S., and Spohn, C. C. (2007). Concerning conceptualization and operationalization: Sentencing practices and the focal concerns perspective—a research note. *Southwest Journal of Criminal Justice, 4*, 58–78.

Hawkins, D. (1981). Causal attribution and punishment for crime. *Deviant Behavior, 1*, 207–230.

Johnson, B. D. (2006). The multilevel context of criminal sentencing: Integrating judge and county level influences in the study of courtroom decision making. *Criminology, 44*, 259–298.

Kautt, P., & Delone, M. (2006). Sentencing outcomes under competing but coexisting sentencing interventions: Untying the Gordian knot. *Criminal Justice Review, 31*(2), 105–131.

Kautt, P., & Spohn, C. (2002). Cracking down on black drug offenders? Testing for interactions among offenders' race, drug type, and sentencing strategy in federal drug sentences. *Justice Quarterly, 19*(1), 1–35.

Kline, R. B. (1998). *Principles and practice of structural equation modeling.* New York: The Guilford Press.

Kramer, J. H., & Ulmer, J. T. (2002). Downward departures for serious violent offenders: Local court "corrections" to Pennsylvania's sentencing guidelines. *Criminology, 40*, 601–636.

Kramer, J. H., & Ulmer, J. T. (2009). *Sentencing guidelines: Lessons from Pennsylvania.* Boulder, CO: Lynne Rienner Publishers.

Miller, W. B. (1958). Lower class culture as a generating milieu of gang delinquency. *Journal of Social Issues, 14*, 5–19.

Savelsberg, J. J. (1992). Law that does not fit society: Sentencing guidelines as a neoclassical reaction to the dilemmas of substantivized law. *American Journal of Sociology, 97*, 1346–1381.

Spohn, C. (2000). Thirty years of sentencing reform: The quest for a racially neutral sentencing process. In *Policies, processes and decisions of the criminal justice system* (Vol. 3). Washington, DC: U.S. Department of Justice.

Spohn, C., & Beichner, D. (2000). Is preferential treatment of female offenders a thing of the past? A multi-site study of gender, race, and imprisonment. *Criminal Justice Policy Review, 11*, 149–184.

Spohn, C., & Holleran, D. (2000). The imprisonment penalty paid by young unemployed black and Hispanic male offenders. *Criminology, 38*, 281–306.

Steffensmeier, D. (1980). Assessing the impact of the women's movement on sex-based differences in the handling of adult criminal defendants. *Crime and Delinquency, 26*, 344–357.

Steffensmeier, D., & Demuth, S. (2006). Does gender modify the effects of race-ethnicity on criminal sanctioning? Sentences for male and female white, black, and Hispanic defendants. *Journal of Quantitative Criminology, 22*(3), 241–261.

Steffensmeier, D., Kramer, J., & Streifel, C. (1993). Gender and imprisonment decisions. *Criminology, 31*, 411–444.

Steffensmeier, D., Ulmer, J., & Kramer, J. (1998). The interaction of race, gender, and age in criminal sentencing: The punishment cost of being young, black, and male. *Criminology, 36*, 763–797.

Tillyer, R., Hartley, R. D., & Ward, J. T. (2015). Differential treatment of female defendants: Does criminal history moderate the effect of gender on sentence length in federal narcotics cases? *Criminal Justice and Behavior.* doi:0093854814560624.

Ulmer, J. (2012). Recent developments and new directions in sentencing research. *Justice Quarterly, 29*, 1–40.

Ulmer, J., Eisenstein, J., and Johnson, B. (2010). Trial penalties in federal sentencing: Extra-guidelines factors and district variation. *Justice Quarterly, 27*, 560–592.

Ulmer, J. T. (1997). *Social worlds of sentencing: Court communities under sentencing guidelines.* Albany, NY: State University of New York Press.

Ulmer, J. T., & Bradley, M. S. (2006). Variation in trial penalties among serious violent offenses. *Criminology, 44*, 631–670.

Ulmer, J. T., & Johnson, B. (2004). Sentencing in context: A multilevel analysis. *Criminology, 42*, 137–177.

PART IV

Risk

Race, Age, and Social Class

14

ASSESSMENT OF OFFENDER RISK AT SENTENCING

A Potential for Disparity?

Julia A. Laskorunsky

Introduction

Scholars have documented the disproportionate representation of Black and Hispanic offenders in the criminal justice system (Alexander, 2012; Pettit and Western, 2004) and have identified the sentencing stage as one point of disparity (Mitchell, 2005; Spohn, 2000; Ulmer, 2012; Zatz, 2000). Swayed by the possibility of lowering incarceration through efficient and individualized offender management, states have increasingly begun to rely on actuarial risk assessment in the courtroom. Recent scholarship has focused on the role formal risk assessment should play in structuring sentencing decisions, with diverging opinions (Hannah-Moffat, 2013; Monahan and Skeem, 2014; Skeem and Lowenkamp, 2016; Starr, 2014). The recent push to use risk assessment instruments during criminal sentencing raises questions about the role of risk in punishment decisions and the relationship between risk and race/ethnicity. Examining the role of both actuarial and informal risk assessment in legal decision-making is important for understanding the overrepresentation of African American and Hispanic men in imprisonment. This chapter explores the implications of moving toward a sentencing model with an actuarial consideration of risk by putting risk assessment into a broader context of judicial decision-making and racial and gender sentencing disparity. I provide an overview of how risk assessment fits into structured sentencing, explain how risk assessment tools group offenders based on risk of recidivism, and explore how legal and extra-legal factors affect sentencing outcomes through both formal and informal evaluations of risk. Finally, I discuss issues of bias and disparate impact and the incongruence between sentencing guidelines and risk assessment tools. Suggestions for future research conclude the chapter.

Sentencing Policy and Disparity

A rich body of literature has established that the sentencing stage is a point of disparity for Black and Hispanic offenders and that these disparities are highly variable based on context and location (National Research Council, 1983; Mitchell, 2005; Spohn, 2000; Ulmer, 2012; Zatz, 2000). A meta-analysis of 71 published studies concluded that Black offenders were more likely to receive prison sentences compared to similarly situated White offenders (Mitchell, 2005). The study also found a small effect of race on sentence length, with Black offenders receiving slightly longer sentences (see also Ulmer, 2012). Research has also shown that gender and age have an effect on sentencing decisions (Doerner and Demuth, 2010; Steffensmeier and Demuth, 2000; Steffensmeier, Ulmer, and Kramer, 1998) and that race/ethnicity, gender, and age interact to produce more severe sentences for young, minority, offenders (Doerner and Demuth, 2010; Steffensmeier et al., 1998). Disparities in sentencing contribute to the stark racial disproportionality found in incarceration (Mauer, 2011; Tonry and Melewski, 2008).

Changes in sentencing policy, such as the adoption of sentencing guidelines, mandatory minimum laws, and use of risk assessments, have the potential to affect disproportionality in sentencing by affecting judicial discretion and through differential impact on minority groups (Ulmer, Painter-Davis, and Tinik, 2016). The effect of sentencing guidelines, which were enacted with the goal of reducing disparities in sentencing, is mixed. Some research shows that the adoption improved racial and ethnic disparity in sentencing (in Pennsylvania: Kramer and Ulmer, 2009; Ulmer et al., 2016) but that the effect was conditioned by level of judicial discretion and changed over time. On the other hand, mandatory minimum laws have had a strong and consistent effect on sentencing outcomes by increasing the length and severity of sentences and disproportionately affecting minority offenders (Fischman and Schanzenbach, 2012; Kramer and Ulmer, 2009; National Research Council, 2014). In more recent years, states have adopted policies that require the actuarial consideration of risk for criminal sentencing, which may also disproportionately affect minority offenders. This has spurred some recent scholarship on this topic (e.g., Hannah-Moffat, 2013; Skeem and Lowenkamp, 2016; Starr, 2014), but many important questions remain unanswered.

History of Risk Assessment in Sentencing

Risk assessments have been used in the criminal justice system, and in particular to determine sentence length on the back end (e.g., parole release), for over a century (e.g., see Burgess, 1928). In the 1960s and 1970s risk assessment at sentencing focused on identifying mentally ill offenders for incapacitation, with the help of clinicians and sometimes with the use of diagnostic tools (Simon, 2005). In the following decade, this practice sustained political, judicial, and academic attacks that questioned the accuracy of assessing individual risk, as well as the legality of holding persons for preventative reasons. The demise of risk assessment in sentencing also coincided with rise of "mass incarceration," as the U.S. shifted to a more retributive "backwards looking" approach to punishment (Monahan and Skeem, 2016b; Tonry, 2013). This brought in a new era in sentencing. In the mid-1970s, liberal reform movements focused on increasing sentencing uniformity and reducing the effects of extra-legal variables through the use of sentencing guidelines. The first presumptive guidelines were established in the

1970s and from 1978 to 1996, 20 states and the federal government established their own versions.

Tonry (2013) outlines the move away from indeterminate sentencing and rehabilitation that began in the 1970s. Martinson's (1974) famous "nothing works" report turned policymakers and many academics away from supporting rehabilitation, and judges and scholars criticized indeterminate sentencing for being unpredictable and giving too much power to parole officials. Without the promise of rehabilitation, it became less important to assess risk at sentencing. If the best the criminal justice system could do is incapacitate offenders, it seemed easier to increase penalties across the board instead of identifying which offenders would be better served by less punitive sentences. Starting in the mid-1980s, incarceration sentences became longer due to mandatory minimums, three-strikes laws, and an increase in life without the possibility of parole sentences (Tonry, 2013).

Since the 1990s, interest in actuarial risk assessment has steadily increased as part of the evidence-based movement in sentencing and corrections (Casey, Warren, and Elek, 2011; Etienne, 2009; Marcus, 2009). Even more recently, public support for tough-on-crime policies has fallen and risk assessment tools for general criminal offending have appeared as a potential "smart on crime" strategy to cash-strapped state legislatures. Numerous states are currently using or exploring the use of statewide sentencing risk assessment tools (e.g., Pennsylvania, Virginia, Missouri, Wisconsin, Kentucky, Ohio, Oklahoma, Arizona), while the use of risk assessments for sentencing sex offenders is almost ubiquitous (Starr, 2014).[1] The goals of risk assessment policy vary from state to state, and so do the individual tools, but all rely on offender and case characteristics to estimate the likelihood of recidivism.[2] The overarching goal of risk and needs assessment is to assist judges in identifying which offenders require more incapacitative sentences, which offenders should be matched up to community services, and which offenders can be diverted to less punitive sentences.

Modern Sentencing Risk Assessment Tools and Policies

The increased use of actuarial risk assessments at sentencing has started to receive more attention from policymakers and academics (e.g., Holder, 2014; Monahan and Skeem, 2014; Starr, 2014). Critics of this trend warn of the potential effects on racial and ethnic disparity and of constitutional challenges of using extra-legal variables such as race, gender, and age to determine sentencing decisions (Hannah-Moffat, 2013; Holder, 2014; Starr, 2014). For example, Hannah-Moffat (2013: 281) warns that "marginalized groups unavoidably score higher on risk instruments because of their increased exposure to risk, racial discrimination, and social inequality"—and this may lead to longer or more severe sentences for minorities and the poor. However, it is still not clear how the increased reliance on actuarial risk assessments has affected courtroom decision-making and what effects, if any, this will have on sentencing disparity. While several states have closely integrated risk assessment into the sentencing process, others use them in an advisory fashion or for certain offenders only. These variations in tools, policy, and the contextual and place-based differences in sentencing disparity have contributed to gaps in research on this topic (Monahan and Skeem, 2016b).

It is important to note that there is a difference between risk assessment technology, that is, the actuarial tool itself and risk assessment policy, which outlines how and for what purposes the tool should be used. Tools and policy vary from state to state—and these variations have implications for any potential effects on racial, ethnic, and gender disparity; judicial discretion; and possible constitutional challenges. Pennsylvania, Missouri, and Virginia have each created a risk assessment instrument for use at sentencing.[3] Pennsylvania's risk assessment tool relies on age, gender, and variations of criminal history markers to predict recidivism (Ruback et al., 2016). It does not use many of the questionable variables associated with structural inequality such as race, employment status, neighborhood, or level of education to determine risk. Missouri's tool includes both employment and education, but not gender (Wolff and Oldfield, 2010), and Virginia's uses gender, age, employment, and marital status (Ostrom et al., 2002). The use of criminal history and case characteristics is less controversial, and less likely to be legally challenged, than using markers that denote membership in a protected class (Starr, 2014). However, some researchers warn that the over-reliance on criminal history to predict risk may exacerbate racial inequalities found in the system (Skeem and Lowenkamp, 2016).

There is also a difference in policy between the three states. Pennsylvania's risk assessment scores are included with the sentencing guideline recommendation and generate an automatic pre-sentence report if they are on either tail end of the risk score range. They are not directly tied to sentence recommendations and are meant to give judges more information about offenders who score outside of the standard range. Missouri's risk assessment results are integrated into the voluntary sentencing guidelines: offenders who score in the "Good" range are recommended for mitigated sentences and offenders who score in the "Poor" range are recommended for aggravated sentences. Virginia's policy was implemented with the specific goal of reducing incarceration and is only used for felony, non-violent offenders. Those scoring in the low range of the scale are recommended for diversion (i.e., a non-specific, non-custodial sentence). Judges in Virginia follow these recommendations in two out of three cases (Ostrom et al., 2002). Piloted in 1997, Virginia's risk assessment policy is the best evaluated of the three; however, evaluations have not focused on disparate impact.

States interested in using risk assessment at sentencing should take note that the details of the accompanying policy are particularly important for warding off potential constitutional challenges. For example, the ACLU challenged the state of Virginia over the use of their sex offender risk assessment at sentencing, noting that it recommended longer sentencing ranges based on offender's age, employment history, and level of education—which have no bearing on the offense committed (*Brooks v. Commonwealth of Virginia*, 2012). The ACLU argued that this created a system where the most marginalized offenders also received the harshest sentences. The state won largely on the grounds that judges were allowed to ignore risk assessment recommendations, even though they usually didn't (Ostrom et al., 2002). Similarly, the Wisconsin Supreme Court (*State of Wisconsin v. Loomis*, 2016) ruled that the use of Northpointe

Inc.'s COMPAS risk assessment tool at sentencing does not violate the due process rights of a defendant as long as judges merely consider, but do not rely on, the risk assessment score to determine sentencing. Instead, the assessment can be used as an "observation" to "corroborate" the sentence imposed by the court (p. 43–44). The court agreed that handing out sentences based on improper factors, such as gender or socioeconomic status was unconstitutional, but that considering these factors for the purpose of statistical calculation was appropriate.

Risk-Needs-Responsivity Theory in the Courtroom

The psychology of risk assessment in the criminal justice system is best explained by the Risk-Needs-Responsivity (RNR) theory. This theory, developed by Andrews, Bonta, and colleagues (Andrews and Bonta, 2010; Andrews, Bonta, and Hoge, 1990) states that offenders' criminogenic characteristics (i.e., their risks and needs) should be met with the appropriate supervision and services. In the courts, that means low-risk offenders should be given less incarcerative sentences, and vice versa. It also means that offenders who score high on individual needs, such as drug addiction, are given resources to address those needs. The underlying rationale behind this principle is that high- and low-risk offenders do better when they are treated differently. Studies have shown that giving low-risk offenders a high level of supervision and giving high-risk offenders a low level of supervision results in a higher level of recidivism than if offenders were supervised in line with their risk level (Andrews and Bonta, 2010; Lowenkamp and Latessa, 2004).

Risk assessments focus on two types of data that are important to consider when making criminal justice decisions: static and dynamic predictors of recidivism (Andrews, Bonta, and Wormith, 2006). Static risk factors are offender characteristics that either do not change or change only in one direction, such as race, gender, and age. Dynamic predictors are offender characteristics that are changeable, such as levels of substance abuse, types of peer associates, employment, education, and marital status. And causal risk factors are a particular group of factors that are not only variable but have been shown, through research, to reduce the likelihood of recidivism when addressed with intervention (e.g., substance abuse problems) (Monahan and Skeem, 2014). Both static and dynamic extra-legal risk factors are already, informally, considered in courtroom decisions, on top of legally relevant factors such as offense seriousness and criminal record (Steffensmeier and Demuth, 2006; Ulmer et al., 2016). Risk assessment tools provide a standardized way for judicial actors to assess these factors as they relate to an offender's risk of recidivism.

The correctional system has relied on the RNR principle to sort offenders once they enter the system. The goals of correctional offender management pair well with the use of risk assessments because the tools are used to assign individuals to specific categories. New inmates are assessed by their risk level and matched up with the appropriate rehabilitative programming. Using this method to inform sentences is more complex. On one hand, classifying offenders earlier in the process can better reflect the RNR principle. For example, low-risk offenders that are sentenced to prison may receive a low level of inmate supervision, but they will never receive a non-custodial sentence, which may have resulted in a better outcome. On the other hand, sentencing has multiple goals beyond appropriate offender management. The consideration of risk can stand in contrast to goals of deterrence and retribution. Issues of fairness and legal ethics also play a more prominent role in the courtroom. By basing sentences on the RNR principle, punishment decisions are affected not only by unchangeable offender characteristics (e.g., gender), but also life choices that are not against the law (e.g., being unemployed, living in a poor neighborhood).

The Risk Assessment Instrument

At a basic level, risk assessment instruments determine the likelihood (i.e., risk) of an event occurring. Offenders with certain offense characteristics or demographics recidivate at unequal rates and these risk factors are identified for the purpose instrument creation. Offenders are then grouped by their risk score (i.e., the number of risk factors and the importance of those risk factors in predicting recidivism), with higher risk scores correlating to a greater chance of failure (i.e., a higher percentage of that group recidivating). These are often regrouped to make a manageable number of categories, which correlate to distinct differences in risk level. Subsequently, when this assessment is used in practice, it provides a likelihood estimate of failure for an offender based on how similarly situated offenders have behaved in the past. The output is less of a "prediction" (i.e., will fail/won't fail) and more of a "post-diction" in which offenders are classified into groups based on measures of past behavior (Auerhahn, 2006). Offenders with more risk factors have a higher chance of recidivating because they share characteristics with offenders in the research sample for whom the re-offending base rate is known. While the instrument is given individually, the predictions are based on aggregate levels of recidivism. Individual risk assessment scores are often related to terms such as low, medium, or high risk, however, there are no standards for using these terms. For example, a group with a 50% recidivism rate may be considered high risk in one jurisdiction and medium risk in another.

Sentencing risk assessments are attractive because they offer courts the ability to separate offenders based on (grouped) risk of recidivism. And while the process requires far more caveats, risk assessments have also been touted as a tool to identify offenders who are dangerous.[4] This promise may be even more important because identifying dangerous offenders assists with a major goal of the criminal justice system: protection of the community. Assessing which offenders are "dangerous" is also the consideration of risk. Monahan (1982) warns that the term "dangerous offender" confounds two different concepts: the prediction of dangerous behavior and an individual's characteristic traits. Therefore, it's more conceptually accurate to refer to the prediction of violent behavior instead of identifying which offenders are "dangerous." In other words, risk assessments can be used to predict the likelihood of general recidivism and violent recidivism. In the past, violent recidivism has been defined as the threat of physical violence or injury (Sherman and Hawkins, 1981) and serious assaultive crime (including sexual assault) (Miller and Morris, 1988), although the instrument-specific definition varies. There are no standards on what risk level for violent offending should elicit the mark of "dangerous offender," yet it is undeniably useful for courts to be able to identify offenders who have levels that are outside of the norm. Because all offenders have a non-zero chance of committing a violent crime, cut-off points will need to be jurisdiction and context specific.

Integrating Risk Assessment into Sentencing

Some proponents of using risk assessment in the courtroom hope that it will simply inform judicial decisions—without constraining discretion (Casey et al., 2011; Hyatt, Mark, and Steven, 2011; Kern and Bergstrom, 2013). For policy changes, this is a low bar, but perhaps one fraught with the least amount of controversy. In fact, many states already include both informal and actuarial risk assessment results in their pre-sentence reports, which are generally filled out for the most serious offenders. Probation officers, who are tasked with monitoring offenders on community supervision, are appropriately concerned about offenders who are at high risk for failing. Thus, the reports have a utilitarian focus—to assess an offender's likelihood of doing well with less restrictive punishment. These reports provide valuable information for judges, who take utilitarian considerations of community protection, as well as more retributive considerations, into account to arrive at a sentence. Including actuarial risk assessment results in the pre-sentence report, or as a standalone piece of information, is a way to integrate social science knowledge into judicial decision-making. By avoiding coupling risk assessment results with policies intended to affect judicial discretion, jurisdictions are likely to avoid many of the constitutional challenges associated with using extra-legal variables in sentencing.

For example, Pennsylvania's risk assessment tool was developed under a mandate from its state legislature and will be used as a way to flag high- or low-risk offenders for closer inspection. The risk assessment score, which is calculated using static administrative variables, is included with the sentence guideline range recommendations. Offenders who fall on the tail ends of the range (i.e., having few or many risk factors), will receive a comprehensive pre-sentence report for judges to look over. Once released, the Pennsylvania Commission on Sentencing will gather data to assess the effects on judicial discretion, sentencing outcomes, and effects on disparity. Preliminary research using simulated sentencing scenarios showed that the effects on judicial decisions varied based types of crime and that judges tended to over-estimate offender risk before being presented with the risk score (Ruback et al., 2016). In this way, a risk assessment score (when used in a purely advisory capacity) may be no different than any other piece of case information provided to a criminal justice professional.

In fact there are benefits to using risk assessment at the sentencing stage, which offers substantially more constitutional protections for offenders compared to parole hearings or correctional settings (McGarraugh, 2012). The sentencing stage provides a "controlled environment" in which the accuracy and the legality of using an instrument can be challenged. One proposed benefit to using risk assessment at sentencing is that instead of focusing it on identifying people for increased sentences, it can be used to divert low-risk offenders from incarceration. Research shows that incarcerating low-risk offenders, instead of providing a community-based sanction, can increase recidivism (Lowenkamp and Latessa, 2004). Still, if the ultimate result is less people in prison, focusing the risk assessment on diverting people from incarceration does not address the problem of potential disparate effects. In absolute terms this reduces the number of people behind bars, but in relative terms, it increases sentencing inequality by picking winner and losers (Oleson, 2011). These "losers," or offenders who score on the higher ends of the scale, will be disproportionately be male, younger, and of a racial/ethnic minority (DeMichele and Laskorunsky, 2014; Skeem and Lowenkamp, 2016; Skeem, Monahan, and Lowenkamp, 2016).

The structure of the risk assessment tools must be adopted to meet the sentencing goals of each jurisdiction (Heilbrun, 2009). For example, a tool designed to reduce risk will look different than one that is used to simply predict recidivism. A tool used to predict recidivism can be fairly easy to administer by using a handful of static predictors taken from official record (e.g., select demographics and criminal history). This tool would be particularly useful for identifying outliers. Offenders who score on the low ends of the scale would potentially be eligible for diversion and offenders who score high may be considered for sentences on the opposite end of the recommended range. If the goal of using a risk assessment tool is to reduce offender risk, dynamic and causal risk factors (e.g., substance abuse, unemployment) will need to be identified in order to match up offenders with services. This tool would need to be more extensive and possibly incorporate information from semi-structured interviews with offenders. The two types of approaches present tradeoffs in the areas of effectiveness and efficiency. Having an extensive questionnaire provides jurisdictions with the ability to match offenders up with services available in the community, but it also requires substantially greater agency resources. This would be a waste if the assessment results weren't closely linked to sentencing outcomes focused on addressing specific risks and needs. Because most jurisdictions have limited resources to address risk and needs through sentencing, courts have overwhelmingly focused on using risk assessment tools to predict, not decrease, recidivism.

The increasing popularity of using actuarial risk assessments in the in the courtroom has the potential to alter judicial decision-making by structuring the way judges arrive at their final assessment of the offender's risk of re-offense. The overarching purpose of considering risk at sentencing is that judges will give similarly situated lower risk offenders less restrictive sentences, and vice versa. However, as discussed in the next section, the consideration of an actuarial risk assessment tool in sentencing hardly turns the status quo on its head. Instruments that aim to predict risk of re-offense include the same legal and extra-legal factors judges already consider in determining offender risk and in making sentencing decisions (Clair and Winter, 2016; Gottfredson, 1999; Steffensmeier et al., 1998). While an actuarial instrument outperforms the unaided, clinical prediction of risk (Gottfredson and Moriarty, 2006; Meehl, 1954), ultimately judges still maintain the discretion to sentence an offender as they see fit.

Judicial Consideration in Sentencing

To assess the implications of using an actuarial risk assessment instrument at sentencing, it's important to first understand the role of offender risk in sentencing decisions. While attorneys, and, less often, juries, play an important role in determining the outcome of a case, the decision to incarcerate, and for how long, rests largely with the judge.[5] Steffensmeier, Ulmer, and Kramer (1998) outline how judges use "focal concerns"—offender blameworthiness, protection of the community, and practical constraints and consequences—to make sentencing decisions. Both legal and extra-legal considerations filter through individual beliefs and ideologies to influence the interpretation and prioritization of these concerns (Savelsberg, 1992; Ulmer and Kramer, 1996). Due to the time constraints of the judicial process and the practical constraints of gathering comprehensive information, judges rarely have complete facts about the cases they sentence. Even when time and information is more available, judges and other court community actors face uncertainty related to the likelihood of future criminal behavior (Albonetti, 1991; Kramer and Ulmer, 2009). To make up for their lack of information and other sources of uncertainty, judges develop a perceptual shorthand for assessing whether an offender is blameworthy, dangerous, or a good candidate for incarceration (Albonetti, 1991; Ulmer, Kurlychek, and Kramer, 2007). These "patterned responses" allow judges to reduce uncertainty in the face of limited information about both the crime and offender. The stereotypes are based on legal variables and on evident offender characteristics such as age, race, and gender and help explain disparities in sentencing.

The determination of offender blameworthiness is in line with a retributivist model of sentencing where the main factor concerning judges is the offender's culpability. Offense severity is a basic indicator of blameworthiness, with serious crimes eliciting a stronger response from the state. As blameworthiness increases, an offender becomes more deserving of punishment—usually in the form of a longer or a more restrictive sentence. Blameworthiness is also determined by the length and seriousness of an offender's prior record and any mitigating or aggravating circumstances, such mental capacity or relationship to victim. Risk assessment tools do not assist with determining offender blameworthiness, however; prior record and offense gravity are both important predictors of recidivism and are included in the major sentencing risk assessment in use today (Ostrom et al., 2002; Pennsylvania Commission on Sentencing, 2015).

Risk assessments can assist with more utilitarian concerns of sentencing, which focus on efficient offender management for the purpose community protection. This consideration is directly tied to an offender's risk of committing a new crime—particularly violent crime. Offenders at high risk for re-offense require more restrictive or lengthier punishment, and offenders who are perceived to have an elevated risk of committing violence may need to be incapacitated. An offender's risk of recidivism is mainly determined by the length and seriousness of their criminal history, and to a lesser extent the gravity of their current offense, and their potential to succeed using less restrictive sanctions, such as probation (Clair and Winter, 2016; Gottfredson, 1999;

Ulmer et al., 2016). Offender demographics also play a role in molding the perception of risk (Clair and Winter, 2016; Gottfredson, 1999; Steffensmeier and Demuth, 2006). For example, judges viewed younger offenders as more likely to re-offend (Gottfredson, 1999) and perceived Black offenders as more likely to fail on community sanctions (Clair and Winter, 2016). An actuarial risk assessment can take into account offender and case characteristics to inform judges about an offender's likelihood to re-offend upon release, but with more accuracy than informal prediction (Meehl, 1954; Skeem and Monahan, 2011).

Finally, each judge considers practical constraints and consequences in their sentencing decisions. As members of a larger organizational structure, judges take into account a variety of factors, such as county resources (e.g., space available to house the offender), local politics, and case flow. Judges may also be wary of incarcerating an older, sick offender or one who is the primary caretaker of children. Risk assessments assist judges with making efficient use of correctional resources by identifying the riskiest offenders for selective incapacitation. In general, offender characteristics used to inform practical concerns overlap with instrument risk predictors. For example, Ulmer and Kramer (1996) found that judges were reluctant to send White offenders to a predominantly Black prison or to incarcerate female offenders with dependents. Thus, offender demographics and case characteristics serve as indicators of multiple focal concerns. This overlap and interaction between multiple considerations makes it difficult to be definitive about how any one variable affects the sentencing decision through the perception of risk. Local variations in sentencing norms also complicate the picture (Ulmer, 2012).

The big question is how actuarial assessment of risk differs from the status quo—that is, the informal prediction of risk. While judges may consider a greater variation of offender and case characteristics than captured by a risk assessment instrument (e.g., offender demeanor), they are also less likely to be accurate about an offender's level of risk (Gottfredson, 1999; Meehl, 1954; Skeem and Monahan, 2011). Because, judges already have a broad sense of which offender characteristics are associated with future offending, risk assessments generally offer evaluations that are complementary to the clinical assessment of risk. For example, judges perceive offenders who are younger and those with a lengthy criminal record to have a higher likelihood of recidivism which are both identified as risk factors for recidivism in actuarial instruments (Gendreau, Little, and Goggin, 1996; Gottfredson, 1999). This complementary overlap can serve to confirm existing judicial perception of who should receive the most severe punishment. However, one legal factor that may be problematic is offense seriousness because, as a predictor variable, it has an inverse relationship with recidivism (DeMichele and Laskorunsky, 2014; Durose, Cooper, and Snyder, 2014). Judges view offenders who commit serious crimes as more blameworthy (Kurlychek and Johnson, 2004; Steffensmeier and Demuth, 2000) *and* more likely to recidivate (Gottfredson, 1999), yet offenders convicted of more serious crimes are less likely to re-offend than similarly situated offenders convicted of less serious crimes (DeMichele and Laskorunsky, 2014; Gottfredson, 1999). Serious offenders, particularly violent ones, are also singled out by sentencing commissions to receive the most severe sentences (Kramer and

Ulmer, 2002). In this way, retributivist sentencing goals that aim to punish the most morally culpable offenders are contrasted against utilitarian goals of sentencing (i.e., incarcerating the highest-risk offenders). If risk assessment results are is tied to sentencing recommendations, judges who view sentencing primarily as a way to impose "just deserts" style punishment may take issue with the results. As explained below, public backlash toward seemingly unjust light sentences may also become an issue.

The recent trend in sentencing has been to consider more utilitarian concerns, which may explain the renewed interest in risk assessment tools (Lawrence, 2013). While criticism of risk assessment has largely focused on the possibility of longer sentences for low income or minority offenders (Hannah-Moffat, 2013; Starr, 2014), sentences that appear too lenient for "privileged" offenders also elicit a strong public response. For example, a 2016 California rape case involving a Stanford competitive swimmer, Brock Turner, made headlines when the judge handed down a 6-month jail sentence based on the offender's likelihood of re-offending and ability to do time in prison (Stack, 2016). Siding with the probation officer's recommendation, Santa Clara County Superior Court Judge Aaron Persky declined to sentence the offender to prison because "a prison sentence would have a severe impact on him. . . . I think he will not be a danger to others." The first-time offender—a 20-year old Stanford student from a wealthy background—scored in the low to moderate range on California's sex offender risk assessment scale. While a sexual assault conviction usually garners prison time, both the probation officer and the judge felt that a period of prolonged incapacitation was unnecessary in this case. The public backlash was severe. Nationwide opinion pieces derided the "light sentence," a recall petition was formally launched, and Persky was subsequently removed from all criminal cases and transferred to civil court. In light of the outcry, the California legislature passed a mandatory sentencing law that made the minimum sentence for this type of crime 3 years in prison (Chokshi, 2016).

This illustrates what can happen when utilitarian goals of sentencing come into conflict with retributive goals of sentencing. On one hand, there has been a concerted effort to get behind "smart-sentencing" in order to divert low-risk offenders from incarcerative sentences. Proponents of utilitarian tools such as risk assessments claim that, in order to reduce unsustainable prison populations, efforts should be focuses on the lowest-risk individuals. However, this sentiment clashes with the retributive goals for sentencing. Law, and by extension the punishment for breaking it, is a reflection of the fundamental values of society (Black, 2010; Friedman, 1975). A society reifies these beliefs by punishing offenders for harming not just the victim, but also the community. Judges have a difficult job of forming these concerns into "a single value on a continuous dimension of sentencing severity" (Monahan and Skeem, 2016b: 33).

Race, Risk, and Criminal History

Simply put, race and risk are statistically correlated (Harcourt, 2015; Kopf, 2015; Skeem and Lowenkamp, 2016). On average, Black offenders score higher on risk assessment instruments because they have more risk factors of recidivism, and higher base rates (i.e., prevalence) of re-offending in the instrument development sample (Durose et al., 2014; Skeem and Lowenkamp, 2016). Race has been shown to have a weak, but not insignificant, relationship with re-arrest even when other risk factors are controlled (Skeem et al., 2016). While minority race status is not a causal factor in itself, it does serve as a stand-in for levels of exposure to structural inequality and, consequently, a variety of risk factors that are hard to control for in a risk algorithm.[6] Some scholars find that criminal history mediates the relationship between race and risk (Skeem and Lowenkamp, 2016), while others go further and claim that criminal history is a proxy for race (Harcourt, 2015).

Research shows that the seriousness of the offense and the offender's criminal history already explain most of the variation in sentencing outcomes, particularly between White and Black offenders (Mitchell, 2005; Spohn, 2000; Ulmer et al., 2016). Thus, Black offenders are more likely to be sentenced to prison because, on average, they have more substantial criminal histories and, to a lesser extent, are charged with more serious crimes (Chiricos and Crawford, 1995; Rehavi and Starr, 2014). However, it should be noted that Black offenders are more likely to be sentenced to prison, and for slightly longer terms, even when legally relevant factors are controlled (Chiricos and Crawford, 1995; Spohn, 2000; Ulmer, 2012). Judges determine whether an offender is likely to re-offend largely based on their criminal history (Monahan and Skeem, 2016b), which means that criminal history is a non-actuarial stand-in for risk (although it also affects perceptions of offender blameworthiness). Sentencing guidelines also reflect the importance of criminal history for determining the final sentence recommendation. Thus, the informal consideration of risk in sentencing already has a racially disparate impact on offenders because Black offenders tend to have more substantial criminal histories.

Measures of criminal history are ubiquitous in criminal risk assessments (Hamilton, 2015) because prior record is a consistent and significant predictor of recidivism (Gendreau et al., 1996; Monahan and Skeem, 2016b). Criminal history helps explain much of the differences in risk assessment scores between Black and White offenders. For example, Skeem and Lowenkamp (2016) found that 66% of the difference in the Post-Conviction Risk Assessment (PCRA) scores between Black and White offenders was explained by differences in criminal history. Thus, criminal history is an important factor in explaining both differences in risk score and differences in sentencing outcomes. In states that rely on risk assessments at sentencing, offenders with substantial criminal histories may experience the negative effects of being singled out by sentencing guidelines for the harshest sentence and the negative effects of having a high risk score (i.e., by being sentenced on the high end of the range). This would amplify the effect of criminal history on sentencing outcomes.

Why are there such substantial racial differences in criminal history? While exact proportions are hard to pin down, scholars agree that differential involvement in crime (Sampson and Lauritsen, 1997); the targeting of minorities for punishment (Alexander, 2012; Tonry, 1995); and differential treatment and impact at various stages in criminal justice system (Cole, 1999; Spohn, 2013) all contribute to Black/White differences in criminal history. Blacks and Hispanics are overrepresented in both violent offending and victimization due to longstanding patterns of inequality and disadvantage among communities of color (Sampson and Lauritsen, 1997). Differential exposure to structural risk factors such as concentrated poverty, racial segregation and bias, and community disorganization help explain racial differences criminal violence (Peterson and Krivo, 2005; Sampson and Wilson, 1995). Once they enter the system, studies show that Black and Hispanic offenders, particularly males, are treated slightly more punitively than similarly situated Whites (Cole, 1999; Spohn, 2013) and are disparately impacted by neutral policies, such as mandatory minimums (Tonry and Melewski, 2008). Differential selection into the criminal justice system is also a significant issue. For example, Black drivers are more likely to be pulled over by the police and both Black and Hispanic drivers are more likely to be searched (Langton and Durose, 2013). Blacks are more likely than Whites to be arrested for marijuana possession, despite having comparable rates of marijuana use (ACLU, 2013). Black students are more likely to receive official institutional punishment for the same infractions as White students (Nicholson-Crotty, Birchmeier, and Valentine, 2009; Skiba et al., 2002). And "Stop and Frisk" policies have overwhelmingly targeted minorities at rates above their involvement in crime (Gelman, Fagan, and Kiss, 2007). Selective enforcement and charging is a bigger issue among property and public order crimes where police and prosecutors have more discretion (Piquero and Brame, 2008). Differences in sentencing outcomes due to differences criminal history fall under "warranted disparity," yet the processes of how offenders come to have these variations underscore the effect of cumulative disadvantage associated with race and ethnicity (Sampson and Laub, 1997).

Risk Assessments: Disparate Impact and Bias

While risk assessment instruments have been used in a variety of criminal justice decisions for nearly a decade, criticism regarding their use in the courtroom has been particularly strong (Angwin et al., 2016; Harcourt, 2015; Holder, 2014; Starr, 2014). These criticisms focus on both the possibility of instrument bias and disparate impact on minority offenders, among other concerns relating to the legality of using extra-legal factors to make punishment decisions. For example, a recent study from the investigative outlet ProPublica (Angwin et al., 2016) looked at Northpointe's COMPAS risk/needs assessment instrument, which is used in a variety of criminal justice settings, including at pretrial and sentencing. They found that the instrument was equally as successful at predicting which offenders recidivate regardless of race. However, it incorrectly predicted failure for Black offender at about the same rate as incorrectly predicting survival for White offenders. By returning a higher rate of false positives for Black versus White offenders (at a ratio of 2 to 1), the instrument makes it likely that a higher proportion of Black offenders experience the consequences of having a higher risk score (e.g., being denied pre-trial release), despite them not offending. Angwin and colleagues were frank in their conclusions—they stated that the instrument is biased against Blacks. This conclusion was heavily contested by Northpointe's researchers (Dieterich, Mendoza, and Brennan, 2016) and the topic of rebuttal paper (Flores, Bechtel, and Lowenkamp, 2016). Both papers showed that the instrument predicts recidivism equally well for Black and White offenders, and thus, does not meet the definition on "bias." However, even an instrument without bias can have disparate impact (Chouldechova, 2016).

There are two distinct issues at play here. First, even though race is not included in COMPAS's algorithm (nor, to my knowledge, in any of the algorithms used to predict risk of recidivism in the criminal justice system), risk factors are unevenly distributed by race. To put it another way, Black offenders, on average, have more risk factors, which were identified in the study used to create the risk assessment algorithm. This results in differences in risk scores between Black and White offenders (which correlate to differences in the reoffending base rate in the development sample). Thus, Hannah-Moffat (2013) was right—minorities do inevitably score higher on risk assessment instruments, even when race is excluded from the algorithm. A second point missing from Angwin and colleagues' (2016) analysis is that the model error differences, that is the difference in the false positive and false negatives between Black and White offenders, is inevitable because of the difference in the base rate between Black and White offenders (for a more technical explanation see Imrey and Dawid, 2015). In other words, it is not possible to have equal model error tradeoffs for two groups whose risk score distribution and base rates differ (Dieterich et al., 2016; Kleinberg, Mullainathan, and Raghavan, 2016). As the base rate increases, the false positive rate increases as well, so a higher portion of Black offenders are marked as high risk regardless of whether or not they recidivate. A paper by Corbett-Davies and colleagues (2017) uses the COMPAS risk assessment and the same data as Angwin et al. (2016) to illustrate both theses points. They show that maximizing public safety (i.e., detaining all individuals deemed high risk) yields stark racial disparities—yet, statistical solutions to mitigate racial disparities result in detaining low-risk defendants while reducing public safety.

A recent study by Skeem and Lowenkamp (2016) using a matched sample showed that while Black offenders, on average, received higher scores than White offenders, the Post Conviction Risk Assessment (PCRA) instrument was equally as predictive of arrest for both races. They concluded that while the PCRA does not show test bias, it may contribute to disparate impact due to Black offenders' higher risk scores. However, the majority (66%) of the difference in the risk scores was due to differences in criminal history between Black and White offenders, meaning that legal factors already rmbedded within the guidelines contribute to most of the difference in scores. Their suggestion was to avoid the over-reliance on risk assessment instruments for which criminal history plays a major role, while maintaining predictive utility.

Given that criminal history plays a big part in risk score differences between Black and White offenders—does the consideration of actuarial risk represent a change from "the status quo"? Decades of research show us that sentencing is already a point of disparity for minority offenders (Spohn, 2000; Ulmer, 2012). For example, Steffensmeier, Ulmer, and Kramer (1998) showed that, net of controls, offenders who are young, minority, and male receive the harshest sentences—and that the interaction between these statuses is higher than the additive effects of each status (see also Nowacki, 2016). Presumably, this is because young, minority men are seen as more blameworthy and more dangerous and because judges have less constraints about sentencing them to incarceration. Similarly, gender, age, and neighborhood are used in many risk assessment instruments because they are predictive of recidivism (Gendreau et al., 1996; Oleson, 2011). A risk assessment that includes the variables of age, neighborhood, and gender would disproportionately place young, minority males in the highest risk category. A risk assessment that included only some of these variable is likely to do the same because other factors would serve as stand-ins for age, race, and gender—likely at the cost of predictive accuracy (Oleson, 2011). Thus, relying on an algorithm to predict risk of recidivism with a moderate degree of accuracy may exacerbate the disparate effects in sentencing, but it may also simply perpetuate the disparate patterns already in place. Without more research, it's impossible to come up with a universal answer to this question.

The consideration of risk, whether using actuarial risk or by relying on criminal history, creates a disparate impact on minorities. In other words, if judges are equally as accurate in their assessment of the likelihood of reoffending for both Black and White offenders, the inclusion of risk as a factor in sentencing would disproportionately impact Black offenders. Black offenders inevitably present more risk factors at sentencing and are more likely to recidivate than White offenders (Hannah-Moffat, 2013; Monahan and Skeem, 2016a; Starr, 2014). These differences are due to the divergent circumstances of racial groups in the U.S. At a minimum, the consideration of risk, actuarial or informal, reifies these longstanding patterns of inequality.

Sentencing Guidelines and Risk Assessment

One other issue requires further thought: the incongruence between sentencing guidelines and actuarial risk assessment. Sentencing guidelines were enacted in order to establish a uniform set of sentencing standards, to reduce unwarranted sentencing disparity, and to make sentencing more consistent (Ulmer, Light, and Kramer, 2011). Voluntary sentencing guidelines first appeared in multiple states in the mid-1970s (National Research Council, 1983). They were generally set by a group of judges based on past sentencing norms in that jurisdiction and were non-binding. Presumptive guidelines, which appeared later, usually involved a legislature appointed sentencing commissions and had more explicit goals—mainly to inflict "just punishment" on convicted offenders (Parent et al., 1996). In theory, the guidelines were supposed to reduce judicial discretion, thereby eliminating sentencing disparity due to subjectivity and extra-legal factors. Under the guidelines, an offender with a similar criminal record, convicted of a similar crime, should receive a similar sentence—regardless of their gender, age, or race/ethnicity. This stands in stark contrast to the purpose of using actuarial risk assessment at sentencing which differentiates between individuals based on both legal and extra-legal factors.

In reality, the widespread adoption of sentencing guidelines, has not eliminated racial, ethnic, or gender disparities in sentencing (Doerner and Demuth, 2010; Everett and Wojtkiewicz, 2002; Kramer and Ulmer, 1996), although some studies show it has had a mitigating effect (Pfaff, 2006; Stolzenberg and D'Alessio, 1994; Ulmer et al., 2016). However, research shows that judicial discretion is affected by guideline recommendations—generally that judges align their sentences to the recommendation. Pfaff's (2006) overview showed that even voluntary guidelines were successful in reducing variation in sentencing between judges and, to a lesser extent, in reducing the effects of offender sex and race. In a unique study by Bushway and colleagues (2012), judges decreased or increased their sentence to conform to voluntary guideline recommendation even when the recommendation was unknowingly calculated in error. Although, they were more likely to "correct" mistakes that erroneously recommend a harsher sentence. Will judges respond similarly to risk assessment information—giving more serious sentences to the riskiest offenders, and vice versa? Evaluations of Virginia's diversion risk assessment show that judges sentenced in accord with the risk assessment recommendation about two-thirds of the time (Ostrom et al., 2002), and other research shows that higher overall risk scores are associated with greater likelihood of receiving a custodial sentence (Carlson, Daniels, and Stein, 2015). Starr (2014) used a vignette to estimate changes in sentencing decisions given the introduction of a risk assessment score. She found that study participants (law school students) who were provided a risk score not only saw those offenders as more likely to recidivate, but also sentenced them to longer sentences. However, a similar study by Ruback and colleagues (2016) with Pennsylvania judges found substantial variation in outcomes by crime type.

Few sentencing guidelines were adopted with the explicit purpose of reducing risk of re-offense or recidivism (Kauder and Ostrom, 2008); however, some guideline states now use actuarial risk assessments at sentencing, or are in the process of adopting it. This poses a potential problem because risk assessments are in some ways antithetical to sentencing uniformity. Sentencing uniformity is achieved when similarly situated offenders are sentenced similarly *despite* their personal characteristics such as age, gender, and race. In contrast, the point of using a risk assessment at sentencing is to individualize recommendations based on an offender's risk of re-offense. The calculation of risk relies on offender characteristics and demographics for maximum accuracy (Oleson, 2011). Thus, all risk assessments that rely on extra-legal factors, such as gender or age, promote sentencing based on the very characteristics that the adoption of sentencing guidelines sought to reduce reliance on.

For example, in 1991, Virginia's sentencing guidelines were adopted with the explicit goals of reducing unwarranted sentencing disparity (Farrar-Owens, 2013). Similar to other states, the guidelines were adopted to increase consistency (predictability and proportionality) and fairness (non-discrimination) by reducing individual consideration of extra-legal variables, such as gender, age, and education (Casey et al., 2011). A report by the National Center for State Courts (Ostrom et al., 2008: 3) on the consistency and fairness of sentencing guidelines in Minnesota, Michigan, and Virginia found that "the undesirable influence of offender characteristics such as race and economic status were of negligible impact in all three states studied." In 2004, Virginia formally adopted an actuarial risk assessment into the guidelines with the purpose of diverting low-risk, non-violent offenders from incarcerative sentences. This instrument puts forth a sentencing recommendation based on the same offender characteristics that its guidelines strove to reduce the effects of (i.e., gender, age, employment status).

And while Virginia's evaluation of its risk assessment adoption showed that it reduced rates of incarceration overall, it did not look at the effects on racial disparity or disparate impact (Kleiman, Ostrom, and Cheesman, 2007). A pre- and post-implementation study would be important for answering these questions.

Sentencing guidelines, much like other structured sentencing policies, have had an indeterminate impact on criminal justice outcomes and on the behavior of local criminal justice actors (Ulmer, 2012). Each court community is a multilayered environment—with its own organizational culture, social order, and county-level contextual influences. The effect of a new policy, such as the adoption of sentencing guidelines or actuarial risk assessment, depends heavily on what was going on prior to its adoption. For these reasons, it is likely that the effects of risk assessment adoption will also be context specific. Difference in instrument construction, risk assessment policies, and local differences (i.e., the status quo) all contribute to variations in effects on disparity and recidivism reduction.

Conclusion

Risk assessment instruments are part of a broader push to embrace evidence-based sentencing, and in all likelihood, they are here to stay. A National Center for State Courts survey found that policymakers and judges are concerned with the ineffectiveness of traditional probation supervision, a lack of appropriate sentencing alternatives, and are interested in using risk and needs assessment tools to limit recidivism (Peters and Warren, 2006). Risk assessments provide a way to structure judicial decision-making by providing empirical information on an offender's risk of re-offense. Furthermore, today, few people in criminal justice are publicly supporting a model of mass incarceration. The model proved to be unsustainable and has not brought the kinds of crime prevention efforts hoped for (National Research Council, 2014). Across the board increases in the length and severity of sentences have been a major contributor to mass incarceration. As states move to send fewer offenders to prison, while still attempting to control crime, the consideration of risk will become more important.

Despite practical benefits to assessing risk at sentencing, there are still many unanswered questions about the impact this actuarial era of structured sentencing will have—the most important ones regarding the possibility of disparate impact. Both Northpointe's COMPAS and the PCRA represent a broader problem of recidivism risk assessments. On average, risk assessments will classify Black offenders as higher risk than White offenders because Black offenders tend to have more risk factors (i.e., appear higher risk to the risk assessment algorithm). Inevitably, a higher portion of Black offenders who don't re-offend will be classified as high risk as well (i.e., a false-positive). While this does not make the instruments biased, it does show the potential for disparate impact if judges use these scores to sentence high-risk offenders to longer or more incarcerative sentences than before. These issues are similar to ones that policymakers have grappled with in regards to other "racially-neutral" criminal justice policies, such as mandatory minimums and repeat offender laws. Unbiased policies can have deeply disparate effects due to the divergent circumstances of minority populations. The possibility of increasing racial disproportionality in incarceration through reliance on these instruments is a consequence worth weighing against the benefits of risk assessment. Given the interest in reducing the overrepresentation of minorities in the criminal justice system, this is a question that will require careful and thorough research. Importantly, research must take into account localized differences in sentencing practices in order to answer the question, "Compared to what?" (Skeem and Lowenkamp, 2016). This scholarship can then assist in the debate regarding both the practical and ethical implications of using actuarial risk assessments to make criminal justice decisions.

Moving forward, researchers should focus on several tangential questions as well. First, even though risk factors are unevenly distributed by race, court officials rarely understand how risk-related variables are obtained. They therefore cannot directly assess the likely complex selection processes by which offenders come to have or not have risk-related indicators such as a juvenile offending record or a violent conviction. For example, while differential offending contributes to the differences in criminal history record for Black and White offenders, we don't know how much of the difference is also the result of differential targeting and enforcement, as well as unequal treatment in the criminal justice system. We know even less about the feedback loop between differential offending, victimization, enforcement, and treatment that occurs over the life course of an offender. Second, studies have looked at how well judges conform to risk assessment recommendations and to changes in sentencing decisions due to risk assessment information, yet we know little about how prosecutorial behavior, or the behavior of other court-room actors would be affected by such policies. For example, could risk-related variables become a factor in plea bargaining? Third, we have little understanding of how risk assessment scores interact with other case and offender characteristics in shaping judicial perceptions of risk or affecting sentencing decisions. In other words, when does offender risk matter? For example, risk of recidivism may not be a decision factor for serious crimes that already garner high penalties. Qualitative research could also help explore whether judges differentiate between risk factors that are within the offender's control and those that arise from an ascribed status.

Fourth, pre-sentence reports no doubt play a role in shaping judicial perceptions of offender risk, yet we know little about how most states structure their reports; what information is included; and whether, or how closely, a judge may look at them. Do these differences have an effect on the final sentencing decisions? For example, in Pennsylvania, pre-sentence reports are not standardized and may include a variety of information that shapes the informal consideration of risk. Finally, we need more research on local differences in risk factors. A risk factor in one location may not increase the likelihood of failure in another location. For example, differences in policy dictate what constitutes as failure on probation and parole, with some offices taking a harder stance on recreational drug use than others. Thus, the presence of substance abuse issues may affect the probability of offender failure differently from location to location. This would necessitate localized risk assessment instruments.

A major goal of criminal justice reform is to reduce mass incarceration while avoiding an increase in crime and victimization. As of this writing, bipartisan support for criminal justice reform remains—particularly at the state level (Lampard, 2016). Sentencing risk assessment tools can help identify who to focus de-incarceration efforts on and barring any major constitutional challenges, their use in the courtroom will only become more common. The job of criminologists will be to point out the potential collateral consequences of using these instruments, particularly as they might affect sentencing disparity. To do this, we must produce research that goes beyond estimating potential effects. In the states that have already adopted a risk assessment, pre- and post-evaluations must be completed that focus, not only on the policy's effect on sentence outcomes, levels of incarceration, and on recidivism, but also on any changes in racial disparity. Perhaps most importantly, local differences in risk assessment policy, risk assessment instruments, and sentencing norms matter. Blanket statements about the effects of sentencing risk assessment adoption will need to be moderated by acknowledging localized differences in norms. Perhaps then, we can tackle a bigger question—can assessing risk at sentencing help us realize the goal of de-incarceration while maintaining community safety?

Notes

1 It is difficult to estimate how many jurisdictions consider risk assessments at the sentencing stage because so many use them informally. Scores obtained to assist with pretrial release or to assess probation risk often show up in a pre-sentencing reports.
2 This is commonly defined as arrest, but sometimes as a violent arrest, a felony arrest, or a new conviction post-release.
3 Most states do not create their own risk assessment tools and instead rely on "off the shelf" tools that have previously been validated in other jurisdictions (e.g., COMPAS, LSI-R).
4 It is important to note that the small base rate for violent re-offending makes the prediction of this behavior more difficult.
5 Sentencing guidelines and mandatory minimum sentencing laws have taken away some of the power of judges to make sentencing decisions. For a more thorough explanation, see Ulmer, Light, and Kramer (2011).
6 Being black (or male or young) does not *cause* crime. Correlation does not equal causation (Kopf, 2015).

References

ACLU. (2013). *The war on marijuana in Black and White*. New York: ACLU Foundation.

Albonetti, C. A. (1991). An integration of theories to explain judicial discretion. *Social Problems*, *38*(2), 247–266.

Alexander, M. (2012). *The new Jim Crow: Mass incarceration in the age of colorblindness*. New York: The New Press.

Andrews, D. A., & Bonta, J. (2010). Rehabilitating criminal justice policy and practice. *Psychology, Public Policy, and Law*, *16*(1), 39–55.

Andrews, D. A., Bonta, J., & Hoge, R. D. (1990). Classification for effective rehabilitation: Rediscovering psychology. *Criminal Justice and Behavior*, *17*(1), 19–52.

Andrews, D. A., Bonta, J., & Wormith, J. (2006). The recent past and near future of risk and/or need assessment. *Crime & Delinquency*, *52*(1), 7–27.

Angwin, J., Larson, J., Mattu, S., & Kirchner, L. (2016). *Machine bias: There's software used across the country to predict future criminals. And it's biased against blacks*. Retrieved February 6, 2017, from www.propublica.org/article/machine-bias-risk-assessments-in-criminal-sentencing

Auerhahn, K. (2006). Conceptual and methodological issues in the prediction of dangerous behavior. *Criminology & Public Policy*, *5*(4), 771–778.

Black, D. (2010). *The behavior of law*. Bingley: Emerald Group Publishing.

Brooks v. Commonwealth of Virginia. (2012). Va. App. LEXIS 397. VA Ct. App. 2012.

Burgess, E. W. (1928). Factors determining success or failure on parole. In A. A. Bruce (Ed.), *The workings of the indeterminate sentence law and the parole system in Illinois* (pp. 221–234). Springfield, IL: Illinois State Parole Board.

Bushway, S. D., Owens, E. G., & Piehl, A. M. (2012). Sentencing guidelines and judicial discretion: Quasi-experimental evidence from human calculation errors. *Journal of Empirical Legal Studies*, *9*(2), 291–319.

Carlson, E., Daniels, M., & Stein, S. (2015). The association between presentence risk evaluations and sentencing outcome. *Applied Psychology in Criminal Justice*, *11*(2), 111–125.

Casey, P., Warren, R. K., & Elek, J. (2011). *Using offender risk and needs assessment information at sentencing*. Washington, DC: National Center for State Courts.

Chiricos, T., & Crawford, C. (1995). Race and imprisonment: A contextual assessment of the evidence. *Ethnicity, Race, and Crime*, *13*, 281–309.

Chokshi, N. (2016, September 30). After Stanford case, California governor signs bill toughening penalties for sexual assault. *The New York Times*. New York.

Chouldechova, A. (2016). Fair prediction with disparate impact: A study of bias in recidivism prediction instruments. *arXiv:1610.07524*.

Clair, M., & Winter, A. S. (2016). How judges think about racial disparities: Situational decision-making in the criminal justice system. *Criminology*, *54*(2), 332–359.

Cole, D. (1999). *No equal justice: Race and class in the American criminal justice system*. New York: New Press.

Corbett-Davies, S., Pierson, E., Feller, A., Goel, S., & Huq, A. (2017). Algorithmic decision making and the cost of fairness. *arXiv:1701.08230*.

DeMichele, M., & Laskorunsky, J. (2014). *Sentencing risk assessment: A follow-up study of the occurrence and timing of re-arrest among serious offenders in Pennsylvania*. University Park, PA: Pennsylvania State University Justice Center for Research.

Dieterich, W., Mendoza, C., & Brennan, T. (2016). *COMPAS risk scales: Demonstrating accuracy equity and predictive parity*. Traverse City, MI: Northpointe.

Doerner, J. K., & Demuth, S. (2010). The independent and joint effects of race/ethnicity, gender, and age on sentencing outcomes in U.S. federal courts. *Justice Quarterly*, *27*(1), 1–27.

Durose, M., Cooper, A., & Snyder, H. (2014). *Recidivism of prisoners released in 30 states in 2005 : Patterns from 2005 to 2010. Special report*. Washington, DC: Bureau of Justice Statistics.

Etienne, M. (2009). Legal and practical implications of evidence-based sentencing by judges. *Chapman Journal of Criminal Justice*, *1*, 43.

Everett, R. S., & Wojtkiewicz, R. A. (2002). Difference, disparity, and race: Ethnic bias in federal sentencing. *Journal of Quantitative Criminology*, *18*(2), 189–211.

Farrar-Owens, M. (2013). The evolution of sentencing guidelines in Virginia. *Federal Sentencing Reporter*, *25*(3), 168–170.

Fischman, J., & Schanzenbach, M. (2012). Racial disparities under the federal sentencing guidelines: The role of judicial discretion and mandatory minimums. *Journal of Empirical Legal Studies*, *9*(4), 729–764.

Flores, A. W., Bechtel, K., & Lowenkamp, C. T. (2016). False positives, false negatives, and false analyses: A rejoinder to "Machine bias: There's software used across the country to predict future criminals. And it's biased against blacks." *Federal Probation*, *80*(2), 38–46.

Friedman, L. (1975). *The legal system: A social science perspective*. New York: Russell Sage Foundation.

Gelman, A., Fagan, J., & Kiss, A. (2007). An analysis of the New York City police department's "stop-and-frisk" policy in the context of claims of racial bias. *Journal of the American Statistical Association*, *102*(479), 813–823.

Gendreau, P., Little, T., & Goggin, C. (1996). A meta-analysis of the predictors of adult offender recidivism: What works! *Criminology, 34*(4), 575–608.

Gottfredson, D. (1999). *Effect of judges' sentencing decision on criminal careers.* Washington, DC: National Institute of Justice.

Gottfredson, S. D., & Moriarty, L. J. (2006). Statistical risk assessment: Old problems and new applications. *Crime and Delinquency, 52*(1), 178–200.

Hamilton, M. (2015). Back to the future: The influence of criminal history on risk assessment. *Berkeley Journal of Criminal Law, 20*(1), 1–57.

Hannah-Moffat, K. (2013). Actuarial sentencing: An "unsettled" proposition. *Justice Quarterly, 30*(2), 270–296.

Harcourt, B. E. (2015). Risk as a proxy for race. *Federal Sentencing Reporter, 27*(4), 237–243.

Heilbrun, K. (2009). Risk assessment in evidence-based sentencing: Context and promising sues. *Chapman Journal of Criminal Justice, 1*, 127.

Holder, E. (2014). Address at the National Association of Criminal Defense Lawyers 57th annual meeting and 13th State Criminal Justice Network Conference. Speech, Philadelphia, PA.

Hyatt, M., Mark, H., & Steven, L. (2011). Follow the evidence: Integrate risk assessment into sentencing. *Federal Sentencing Reporter, 23*(4), 266–268.

Imrey, D., & Dawid, A. (2015). A commentary on statistical assessment of violence recidivism risk. *Statistics and Public Policy, 2*(1), 1–18.

Kauder, N. B., & Ostrom, B. J. (2008). *State sentencing guidelines profiles and continuum.* Williamsburg, VA: National Center for State Courts.

Kern, R. P., & Bergstrom, M. H. (2013). A view from the field: Practitioners' response to actuarial sentencing: An "unsettled" proposition. *Federal Sentencing Reporter, 25*(3), 185–193.

Kleiman, M., Ostrom, B. J., & Cheesman, F. L. (2007). Using risk assessment to inform sentencing decisions for nonviolent offenders in Virginia. *Crime & Delinquency, 53*(1), 106–132.

Kleinberg, J., Mullainathan, S., & Raghavan, M. (2016). Inherent trade-offs in the fair determination of risk scores. *arXiv Preprint arXiv:1609.05807.*

Kopf, R. G. (2015). Federal supervised release and actuarial data (including age, race, and gender). *Federal Sentencing Reporter, 27*(4), 207–215.

Kramer, J. H., & Ulmer, J. T. (1996). Sentencing disparity and departures from guidelines. *Justice Quarterly, 13*(1), 81–106.

Kramer, J. H., & Ulmer, J. T. (2002). Downward departures for serious violent offenders: Local court "corrections" to Pennsylvania's sentencing guidelines. *Criminology, 40*(4), 897–932.

Kramer, J. H., & Ulmer, J. T. (2009). *Sentencing guidelines: Lessons from Pennsylvania.* Boulder, CO: Lynne Rienner Publishers.

Kurlychek, M. C., & Johnson, B. D. (2004). The juvenile penalty: A comparison of juvenile and young adult sentencing outcomes in criminal court. *Criminology, 42*(2), 485–517.

Lampard, R. J. (2016). *2016: A successful year for criminal justice reform and path to the future. The state factor.* Arlington, VA: American Legislative Exchange Council.

Langton, L., & Durose, M. (2013). *Police behavior during traffic and street stops, 2011.* Washington, DC: Bureau of Justice Statistics.

Lawrence, A. (2013). *Trends in sentencing and corrections.* Washington, DC: National Conference of State Legislatures.

Lowenkamp, C. T., & Latessa, E. J. (2004). Understanding the risk principle: How and why correctional interventions can harm low-risk offenders. *Topics in Community Corrections*, 2004, 3–9.

Marcus, M. (2009). Conversations on evidence-based sentencing. *Chapman Journal of Criminal Justice, 1*, 61.

Martinson, R. (1974). What works ? Questions and answers about prison reform. *The Public Interest, 35*(c), 1–33.

Mauer, M. (2011). Addressing racial disparities in incarceration. *The Prison Journal, 91*(3), 87S–101S.

McGarraugh, P. (2012). Up or out: Why sufficiently reliable statistical risk assessment is appropriate at sentencing and inappropriate at parole. *Minnesota Law Review, 97*, 1079.

Meehl, P. (1954). *Clinical versus statistical prediction: A theoretical analysis and a review of the evidence.* Northvale, NJ: Jason Aronson.

Miller, M., & Morris, N. (1988). Predictions of dangerousness: An argument for limited use. *Violence and Victims, 3*(4), 263–283.

Mitchell, O. (2005). A meta-analysis of race and sentencing research: Explaining the inconsistencies. *Journal of Quantitative Criminology, 21*(4), 439–466.

Monahan, J. (1982). Clinical prediction of violent behavior. *Psychiatric Annals, 12*(5), 509–513.

Monahan, J., & Skeem, J. (2016a). The evolution of violence risk assessment. *Violence in Psychiatry, 19*(5), 419–424.

Monahan, J., & Skeem, J. L. (2014). Risk redux: The resurgence of risk assessment in criminal sanctioning. *Federal Sentencing Reporter, 26*(3), 158.

Monahan, J., & Skeem, J. L. (2016b). Risk assessment in criminal sentencing. *Annual Review of Clinical Psychology, 11*, 1–25.

National Research Council. (1983). *Research on sentencing: The search for reform* (Vol. 2). Washington, DC: National Academies Press.

National Research Council. (2014). *The growth of incarceration in the United States: Exploring the causes and the consequences. Publications and research.* Washington, DC: National Academies Press.

Nicholson-Crotty, S., Birchmeier, Z., & Valentine, D. (2009). Exploring the impact of school discipline on racial disproportion in the juvenile justice system. *Social Science Quarterly, 90*(4), 1003–1018.

Nowacki, J. S. (2016). An intersectional approach to race/ethnicity, sex, and age disparity in federal sentencing outcomes: An examination of policy across time periods. *Criminology and Criminal Justice, 17*(1), 97–116.

Oleson, J. C. (2011). Risk in sentencing: Constitutionally suspect variables and evidence-based sentencing. *SMU Law Review, 64*, 1329.

Ostrom, B. J., Kleiman, M., Cheesman, F. L., Hansen, R., & Kauder, N. B. (2002). *Offender risk assessment in Virginia: A three-stage evaluation.* Williamsburg, VA: National Center for State Courts.

Ostrom, B. J., Ostrom, C. W., Hanson, R. A., & Kleiman, M. (2008). *Assessing consistency and fairness in sentencing: A comparative study in three states.* Williamsburg, VA: National Center for State Courts.

Parent, D., Dunworth, T., McDonald, D., & Rhodes, W. (1996). *Key legislative issues in criminal justice: The impact of sentencing guidelines.* Washington, DC: National Institute of Justice.

Pennsylvania Commission on Sentencing. (2015). *Development of a risk assessment scale by offense gravity score for all offenders.* University Park, PA: Pennsylvania Commission on Sentencing.

Peters, T., & Warren, R. (2006). *Getting smart about sentencing: Sentencing reform survey.* Williamsburg, VA: National Center for State Courts.

Peterson, R. D., & Krivo, L. J. (2005). Macrostructural analyses of race, ethnicity, and violent crime: Recent lessons and new directions for research. *Annual Review of Sociology, 31*(1), 331–356.

Pettit, B., & Western, B. (2004). Mass imprisonment and the life course: Race and class inequality in U.S. incarceration. *American Sociological Review, 69*(2), 151–169.

Pfaff, J. (2006). The continued vitality of structured sentencing following Blakely: The effectiveness of voluntary guidelines. *UCLA Law Review, 54*, 235.

Piquero, A. R., & Brame, R. W. (2008). Assessing the race-crime and ethnicity-crime relationship in a sample of serious adolescent delinquents. *Crime & Delinquency, 54*(3), 390–422.

Rehavi, M. M., & Starr, S. B. (2014). Racial disparity in federal criminal sentences. *Journal of Political Economy, 122*(6), 1320–1354.

Ruback, R., Kempinen, C., Tinik, L., & Knoth, L. (2016). Communicating risk information at criminal sentencing in Pennsylvania: An experimental analysis. *Federal Probation, 80*, 47.

Sampson, R. J., & Laub, J. H. (1997). A life-course theory of cumulative disadvantage and the stability of delinquency. In T. P. Thornberry (Ed.), *Developmental theories of crime and delinquency.* New Brunswick, NJ: Transaction Publishers.

Sampson, R. J., & Lauritsen, J. L. (1997). Racial and ethnic disparities in crime and criminal justice in the United States. *Crime and Justice: A Review of the Research, 21*, 311–374.

Sampson, R. J., & Wilson, W. J. (1995). Toward a theory of race, crime, and urban inequality. *Race, Crime, and Justice: A Reader*, 1995, 37–54.

Savelsberg, J. J. (1992). Law that does not fit society: Sentencing guidelines as a neoclassical reaction to the dilemmas of substantivized law. *American Journal of Sociology, 97*(5), 1346–1381.

Sherman, M., & Hawkins, G. (1981). *Imprisonment in America*. Chicago, IL: University of Chicago Press.

Simon, J. (2005). Reversal of fortune: The resurgence of individual risk assessment in criminal justice. *Annual Review of Law and Social Science, 1*(1), 397–421.

Skeem, J. L., & Lowenkamp, C. T. (2016). Risk, race, and recidivism: Predictive bias and disparate impact. *Criminology, 54*(4), 680–712.

Skeem, J. L., & Monahan, J. (2011). Current directions in violence risk assessment. *Current Directions in Psychological Science, 20*(1), 38–42.

Skeem, J. L., Monahan, J., & Lowenkamp, C. T. (2016). Gender, risk assessment, and sanctioning: The cost of treating women like men. *Law and Human Behavior, 40*(5), 580–593.

Skiba, R. J., Michael, R. S., Nardo, A. C., & Peterson, R. L. (2002). The color of discipline: Sources of racial and gender disproportionality in school punishment. *The Urban Review, 34*(4), 317–342.

Spohn, C. (2000). Thirty years of sentencing reform: The quest for a racially neutral sentencing. *Crime and Justice, 3*, 427–501.

Spohn, C. (2013). Racial disparities in prosecution, sentencing, and punishment. In S. Bucerius & M. H. Tonry (Eds.), *Oxford handbook of ethnicity, crime, and immigration*. New York: Oxford University Press.

Stack, L. (2016, June 6). Light sentence for Brock Turner in Stanford rape case draws outrage. *The New York Times*. New York.

Starr, S. B. (2014). Evidence-based sentencing and the scientific rationalization of discrimination. *Stanford Law Review, 66*, 803–872.

State of Wisconsin v. Loomis. (2016). WI 68, 881 N.W.2d 749, Supreme Court of Wisconsin.

Steffensmeier, D. J., & Demuth, S. (2000). Ethnicity and sentencing outcomes in U.S. Federal Courts: Who is punished more harshly? *American Sociological Review, 65*(5), 705.

Steffensmeier, D. J., & Demuth, S. (2006). Does gender modify the effects of race—ethnicity on criminal sanctioning? Sentences for male and female White, Black, and Hispanic defendants. *Journal of Quantitative Criminology, 22*(3), 241–261.

Steffensmeier, D. J., Ulmer, J. T., & Kramer, J. H. (1998). The interaction of race, gender, and age in criminal sentencing: The punishment cost of being young, black, and male. *Criminology, 36*(4), 763–798.

Stolzenberg, L., & D'Alessio, S. (1994). Sentencing and unwarranted disparity: An empirical assessment of the longterm impact of sentencing guidelines in Minnesota. *Criminology, 32*(2), 301–310.

Tonry, M. (1995). *Malign neglect: Race, crime, and punishment in America*. New York: Oxford University Press.

Tonry, M. (2013). Sentencing in America, 1975–2025. *Crime and Justice, 42*(1), 141–198.

Tonry, M., & Melewski, M. (2008). The malign effects of drug and crime control policies on Black Americans. *Crime & Justice, 37*(1), 1–44.

Ulmer, J. T. (2012). Recent developments and new directions in sentencing research. *Justice Quarterly, 29*(1), 1–40.

Ulmer, J. T., & Kramer, J. H. (1996). Court communities under sentencing guidelines: Dilemmas of formal rationality and sentencing disparity. *Criminology, 34*(3), 383–408.

Ulmer, J. T., Kurlychek, M. C., & Kramer, J. H. (2007). Prosecutorial discretion and the imposition of mandatory minimum sentences. *Journal of Research in Crime and Delinquency, 44*(4), 427–458.

Ulmer, J. T., Light, M., & Kramer, J. H. (2011). Racial disparity in the wake of the Booker/Fanfan decision. *Criminology & Public Policy, 10*(4), 1077–1118.

Ulmer, J. T., Painter-Davis, N., & Tinik, L. (2016). Disproportional imprisonment of Black and Hispanic males: Sentencing discretion, processing outcomes, and policy structures. *Justice Quarterly, 33*(4), 642–681.

Wolff, M., & Oldfield, D. (2010). Missouri risk and needs assessment at sentencing. In *National Association of Sentencing Commissions Conference*. Point Clear, AL.

Zatz, M. S. (2000). The convergence of race, ethnicity, gender, and class on court decision making: Looking toward the 21st century. *Criminal Justice, 3*, 503–552.

15

ASSESSMENT DISPARITIES AFTER FEDERAL INCARCERATION IN CANADA

Rose Ricciardelli, Michael Adorjan, and James Lant

Introduction

A central goal of Correctional Service Canada (CSC) remains the reintegration and "rehabilitation" of former prisoners as they transition from prison to community living. Although no two crimes are ever identical, sentencing in Canada is intended to be based on the principles of deterrence, incapacitation, and justice and rooted in the common law tradition (i.e., like cases are to be treated similarly and different cases differently). As such, people who commit crimes of comparable type, violence, and scope should receive similar convictions with comparable sentences. When a prisoner is eligible for release in Canada, it should be expected that individuals with similar needs (e.g., dynamic risk factors) and risks (e.g., static risk factors) are awarded comparable parole conditions and levels of supervision (i.e., meetings with their parole officer; for further background on dynamic and static risk factors, see Hannah-Moffat, 2005). In this chapter, we look at how individual scores on three dynamic risk factors—motivation to desist, accountability for prior actions, and engagement in correctional plan—and one static risk factor—clinical diagnosis—correspond to the level of supervision former prisoners experience at release. We operationalize level of supervision as both the number of parole conditions applied and frequency of imposed meetings with their parole officer. We use both qualitative and quantitative data to, first, exemplify what constitutes the different scores individuals receive on each of the variables and, second, to show any correlations between variables. In the former, our study is shaped by the research questions: What is the difference between a Low and High score on motivation or accountability? How is engagement calculated? What constitutes a clinical diagnosis of a mental illness? What disparities exist in such assessments, and how does each affect imposed level of supervision? In the latter, two hypotheses structure our analyses:

> H1: Individuals scored lower on motivation to desist and accountability for their prior actions and, as not engaged in their correctional plan, rate higher in actual level of supervision—they have to visit with their parole officer more

frequently and have more imposed conditions—in comparison to individuals who scored higher on motivation and accountability and as engaged in their correctional plan.

H2: Releasees with a clinical diagnosis rate higher in the actual level of supervision imposed on them than those without a clinical diagnosis.

Overall, we expect that people with a marked need for supervision (i.e., mental health needs, for example) receive higher levels of mandated supervision.

The chapter is structured into four sections. We begin by situating our study within the context of Canadian federal corrections and the associated ethos of rehabilitation, defined as the belief in prisoners' ability to change positively (e.g., among practitioners)[1] that, arguably, is braided into Canadian justice discourses. Next, we illuminate the disparities and role of practitioner discretion in re-entry supervision. After discussing our methods, we present the qualitative and quantitative findings. Specifically we illuminate, in a Canadian context, how assessments of motive are guiding supervision decisions rather than other factors such as level of "actual" engagement in correctional plan. This is despite qualitative data espousing the significance of holistic assessment of parolees. We conclude by outlining select implications for policy and future research.

Federal Corrections in Canada

Correctional systems in Canada operate at two different levels, with federal corrections under the governance of Correctional Services Canada (CSC). At the provincial and territorial level, adults under supervision fall under the jurisdiction of their provincial/territorial ministry of justice or public safety. Further, those remanded into custody or who violate conditions of their parole or probation spend time in provincial/territorial prison facilities. After sentencing and/or trial, whether a person is sent to federal versus provincial/territorial custody depends on the length of their awarded sentence. Anyone serving 2 or more years as an adult is sent to federal custody, while anyone serving less than 2 years does their time in a provincial or territorial facility. The only exceptions occur in provinces or territories that do not have federal institutions[2] because, if he or she qualifies, a prisoner may be eligible to serve a federal sentence in their home province/territorial in a close-custody facility.

Once federally sentenced, CSC mandates each prisoner to serve up to 90 days in "reception," which tends to be located on a maximum security range (CSC, 2012). During reception, prisoners undergo an "intake" assessment that includes a variety of diverse assessment scales (e.g., Custody Rating Scale [CRS], the Post-Sentence Community [PSC], and the Level of Service Inventory-Revised [LSI-R]) (CSC, 2012),[3] the purpose of which is to assess each prisoner's internal (i.e., the danger a prisoner is thought to pose to the prison staff and colleagues) and external (i.e., the threat he or she poses to society) security risk and needs (i.e., treatment, programing, or medical) (Department of Justice, 2013). Together, the diverse assessments are used to recommend the security classification most appropriate for the prisoner: a "penitentiary placement that will contribute to his/her timely preparation for safe integration [and] to ensure public safety as well as inmate rights while meeting the inmate's security requirements" (CSC, 2012). This information is later used by the National Parole Board (NPB, 2015) in their pre- and post-release assessment, which tend to occur when a prisoner becomes eligible for statutory release, conditional release, or accelerated parole.

In Canada, life sentences include a mandatory portion of time that must be spent in secure custody prior to being eligible for day parole or full parole. A life sentence can range from "Life-10" to "Life-25," where "Life-10" would leave the convicted person eligible for full parole after 10 years and ineligible for statutory release. However, unlike prisoners with a finite warrant expiration date (WED), "lifers" remain under the supervision of Correctional Service Canada (CSC) for their entire life; they will never be "free." Prisoners without a life sentence can qualify for accelerated parole after serving one-third of their federal sentence and, in most cases, are entitled to statutory release after serving two-thirds of their sentence. Nonetheless, most individuals in our sample were not serving life sentences and did not receive or qualify for accelerated parole. Instead, many re-entered the community on statutory release. Rather than investigating disparities associated with who receives statutory release versus accelerated parole, in this chapter, we orient our attention to unpacking disparities in the levels of supervision awarded to releasees whenever they qualify for community re-entry. The rationale being that when an individual is ready for re-entry, albeit if they served one-third or nearly their full sentence in prison, they should be assessed based on their current needs and re-entry potential. Further, more intense supervision requirements and the associated conditions of release can have a negative impact on a releasee's desistance potential given the increased possibility for breaches and requirements to navigate in the community.

The Ethos of Canadian Corrections: Positively Changing Prisoners (Rehabilitation)

Researchers have shown that, in Canada and other Western countries, there remains public support for positively changing prisoners (Meyer and O'Malley, 2005). Canadian researchers are long recognized for their role in the development and theorization of risk/need systems (see Andrews, Bonta, and Hoge, 1990; Hannah-Moffat, 2005), and the associated confidence of Canadians in the rehabilitative ethos of correctional systems and processes. Unlike in the United States and United Kingdom, where confidence in corrections took a dramatic downturn in the 1980s and early 1990s (Garland, 2001: 108), correctional practitioners in Canada maintained their commitment and long-term focus on, simply said, "positively changing prisoners" (Moore and Hannah-Moffat, 2005). This is not to suggest that such a focus failed to survive, especially in the United States and United Kingdom; rather it became subordinate to other goals such as deterrence, incapacitation, and risk management (Lo, 2003; Lynch, 2000; Garland, 2001; Hutchinson, 2006; Robinson, 2008). As Garland (2001: 62) puts it, using managerialist discourse, "rehabilitation and correctionalism did not disappear, but their stock was drastically depreciated." In essence, rehabilitation became braided with notions of punitive-ness, leaving practitioners to adapt to such change through risk classification, control, coercion, and tending to the interests of the public rather than offender needs (Lewis, 2005; Lynch, 2000; Robinson, 1999). Robert Werth (2013: 221) calls the approach of parole officers in California a "punitive tough love approach" where punitive orientations and practices are geared to meet "rehabilitative" goals. In Canada too, the rehabilitative ideal is at least in part braided with coercive practices (Meyer and O'Malley, 2005; Moore and Hannah-Moffat, 2005).

Nonetheless, for decades, the social and sociological "causes" of crime have been recognized as well as the need for welfare-oriented responses that support offenders in the process of desisting from offending behaviors (see Meyer and O'Malley, 2005; Moore and Hannah-Moffat, 2005). For example, in Ontario, Canada, Moore and Hannah-Moffat (2005) found that ongoing therapeutic programming remains in many provincial institutions. It is this welfare-oriented aspect of Canada penality—despite the penal populist rhetoric about getting "tough" on crime promoted under the former Conservative Harper government—that largely shapes practitioners and drives public recognition of the (arguably) "distinctly Canadian" approach to corrections (Meyer and O'Malley, 2005: 204–205; Moore and Hannah-Moffat, 2005). Beyond the occasional (and undeniable) neoliberal framework that has overtaken elements of the social-welfare ethos of Canadian corrections, actuarial assessments of static risk factors were *not* designed to simply orient offender management (Hannah-Moffat, 2005, 2013). The changing nature of a prisoner's risk profile over time was instead to shape offender management—particularly during community re-entry when need or dynamic risk factors are paramount to successful reintegration (Hannah-Moffat, 2005). Professional discretion, then, should always be central to practitioner responses or assessments of prisoners (or parolees); even when using actuarial assessment with finite close-ended scoring.

Disparities in Re-Entry Supervision

Offense type remains a central source of disparities in experiences of community re-entry after incarceration. This is most pronounced amongst persons convicted of sex-related offenses, where researchers have studied the implementation and use of sex offender registries, offender tracking, post-release conditions, and so on (Demichele, Payne, and Button, 2008; Gies, Gainey, and Healy, 2016; Petrunik, 2003). Other researchers have looked at prisoner re-entry and disparities in community-based social structures in specific locations (Travis and Petersilia, 2001); disparities tied to the use of electronic monitoring (Erez, Ibarra, and Lurie, 2004; Padgett, Bales, and Blomberg, 2006; Shoham, Yehosha-Stern, and Efodi, 2013); and in the experiences of re-entry for women more generally (Opsal, 2009; Sheehan, 2014). Across all studies, despite the topic of focus, parole conditions and supervision requirements are considered contentious yet needed markers of community reintegration. Turnbull and Hannah-Moffat (2009) theoretically associate parole conditions with "targeted governance." They use data from the National Parole Board of Canada to show how female parolees are deconstructed into fractured entities of "risk and need" rather than whole individuals eligible for parole. They describe parole conditions as:

> [T]echniques of targeted governance that exemplify an integrated exercise of penal power, which is simultaneously productive and repressive: conditions help prepare women prisoners for 'freedom' on parole by mobilizing particular techniques of self-governance, while at the same time operate as modes of surveillance that police the boundaries of acceptable conduct.
>
> (p. 532)

In essence, parole conditions and frequency of supervision place releasees—both male and female—in a precarious position: they must abide by their conditions to maintain their freedom and be successful in re-entry. However, what constitutes best practice (through discourse) versus what happens (actions) are not always in line with the needs of the individual in question.

Dating back to 1990, Clear and Hardyman voiced concerns about the achievability of the goals, effectiveness, and operating context for intensive supervision in the United States (see also Clear and Latessa, 1993). In 2001, Austin, noting that most prisoners pose little if any risk to public safety, argued that "re-entry should be curtailed either by eliminating supervision or greatly shortening the period of supervision" (p. 78). Then, another decade later in the United States, Georgiou (2014) compared the likelihood of reoffending for adult releasees in Washington State who shared similar risk characteristics but with different levels of post-release supervision imposed. Findings here revealed that releasees, assessed as high or low risk, who had higher levels of mandated supervision were not more likely to reoffend across types of recidivism.

Recognizing that post-release supervision often fails because it is executed in ways that lead to revocation, Klingele (2013) too suggested that community supervision after imprisonment should be structured by fewer conditions and imposed conditions should directly respond to the individual's risk of recidivism. Although her focus is not on disparities in parole conditions and length, she does further suggest that supervision should be of a minimal duration, just long enough to facilitate structured re-entry after imprisonment:

> Correctional officials must be judicious in imposing discretionary release conditions and in deciding how to respond to violations, paying attention to the purposes those sanctions are intended to serve. A great deal of injustice can be avoided and a great many resources conserved if more careful attention is given to three key decisions: whom to place on supervision; what conditions to attach to the supervisory term; and how long supervision should last. By exercising parsimony in each of these decisions, courts and correctional agencies can ensure that community supervision terms serve the purposes for which they were designed and do not end in unjustified incarceration.
>
> (p. 1054)

What resonates from Klingele's work with our own study is that fewer conditions of parole may best suit the needs of releasees. Indeed, she finds that conditions of supervision tend to result from "risk adverse" societies that pressure practitioners to impose unnecessary conditions that easily enable revocations when evaluating re-entry. Klingele (2013) actually goes so far as to state that legislation should be designed that actually limits the kind and number of conditions that can be imposed and that "courts and community corrections officials should ensure that all discretionary conditions imposed on offenders relate directly to their risk of criminal re-offense" (p. 1061).

In Canadian corrections, professional discretion, at a minimum theoretically, remains a central feature of practitioner decision making. Yet more knowledge is needed to understand the disparities in how "offenders" are scored on select variables during their risk assessment and how a persistent "rehabilitative" ethos, although enfolded in punitive discourses, accompanies these disparities and practitioner discretion. Through our study, we respond first to a lacuna in Canadian knowledge and research about how releasee scores on specific assessments correlate with their level of supervision at re-entry. Risk in the Canadian context, Maurutto and Hannah-Moffat (2006: 439) argue, has "ameliorative, productive and rehabilitative connotations" (Maurutto and Hannah-Moffat, 2006: 439). Yet our findings, which reveal evidence of a discourse of productive assessments of releasee engagement with programming and program completion, nevertheless illuminate how assessments of *statements of motive* drive release conditions (the relations are shown to be statistically significant), while other considerations of risk and need are not as relevant (again, in statistical terms). This study thus begins to create foundational knowledge to help those willing to take on the dearth of desistance research of any form in Canada.

Methods

We included the criminal records of 213 Canadian releasees from federal prison in the study. Their ages ranged from 21 to 64 (M = 35.975, SD = 10.337). Each had served time in a federal prison (i.e., sentenced to at least 2 years). Their criminal convictions for their current index crime ranged extensively from multiple murders (i.e., up to the murder of 4 individuals) to theft to robbery to sex-related offenses and drug possession and trafficking. In response, their sentences also ranged in length from just over 2 years to life with parole eligibility.

Materials

To construct the quantitative dataset, data were taken from each participant's criminal records. Specifically, we looked at the releasee's correctional plans (CORR PLAN), which consists of information pertaining to the offender's sentence length, number of convictions, commencement of sentence, warrant expiration date, statutory release date, and demographic information (e.g., date-of-birth, citizenship, and aliases). From the PLAN CORR, we examined assessments of dynamic risk factors, including ratings of the offenders' motivation to desist from crime, engagement in their correctional plan, and accountability for their actions. In addition to these variable ratings, we also examined clinical diagnosis of a mental disorder, which are outlined in the offenders' criminal file. We used the dynamic variables and clinical diagnosis variables to predict level of supervision (i.e., the frequency in which the offender must meet with their parole officer at release) and total number of parole conditions impinged upon the individual once paroled. For our qualitative analyses, we included the written assessments tied to each variable under analysis, which are also noted on the PLAN CORR and tend to consist of three to eight sentences per variable.

Variables

The dynamic variables include motivation to desist from crime, engagement in correctional plan, and accountability for past actions; the static variable is clinical diagnosis of a mental disorder. Current ratings are conducted at outtake, referring to when the prisoner is leaving the institution and re-entering the community. As dynamic factors are theorized to be subject to change, we focused on the most recent assessment of these factors. The motivation and accountability variables are ordinal: 1 = low motivation/accountability; 2 = medium motivation/accountability; and 3 = high motivation/accountability. The engagement in correctional plan and clinical diagnosis variables are dichotomous: 1 = Yes (i.e., they are engaged in their correctional plan or they have been clinically diagnosed with a mental disorder) or 2 = No (i.e., they are not engaged in their correction plan or they have *not* been clinically diagnosed with a mental disorder).

Our dependent variables were actual level of supervision and total number of parole conditions imposed on the parolee upon release. The former, actual level of supervision, refers to the number of times a releasee is required to meet with his or her parole officer and is classified into the four levels outlined by CSC (2012): once a month, twice a month, weekly, and more than once a week. We coded this variable such that 0 = once a month, 1 = twice a month, 2 = weekly, and 3 = more than once a week. The latter, total number of parole conditions, refers to the number of parole conditions imposed on the prisoner at release. Although various diverse parole conditions may be imposed on an offender, we were interested in the overall penality—the number of conditions (i.e., more conditions would open up more opportunities for a releasee to be revocated). Thus, we recoded this variable to count the number of parole conditions imposed, with total parole conditions ranging from 0 to 11 (see Table 15.1 for a description of all the variables used in the analyses).

Table 15.1 Means and Standard Deviations of Dependent and Independent Variables

Variables	*Mean*	*SD*
Actual level of supervision	1.64	1.01
Total number of parole conditions	4.39	2.89
Clinical diagnosis	.35	.48
Accountability	2.12	.57
Motivation	2.25	.63
Engagement	.85	.36
N = 213		

Procedure

Ethics approval was provided from the principle investigator's university Research Ethics Board and from Correctional Services Canada (CSC). Everyone in the sample consented to have their files analyzed during the CDRC intake processes. Their available criminal records were provided to the primary investigator through the CDRC and all identifying information was removed—without compromising the integrity of the data. We then assigned an identification code to each anonymized file. All quantifiable information from these files was then entered into a spreadsheet and coded for analysis. To ensure the data was being coded correctly and consistently, ten randomly selected files were coded by two independent researchers and compared. All other files were coded by one of five researchers.

The files that were made available to us did not always have a fully completed CORR PLAN. As smaller sample sizes can sometimes lead to violations of the assumptions underlying the statistics, we chose to recode missing data, as it did not alter the findings and it protected the sample size. Missing data for each variable was recoded to the respective mean. Analyses revealed that the findings did not change when missing data was recoded in this fashion.

First, qualitative data from the CORR PLAN, specifically where the "writer"[4] noted why the "offender" was given their specific score on the independent variables (i.e., engagement, motivation, accountability, and mental illness), underwent a preliminary analysis in a subset of files. For example, we sought to exemplify what constituted "low" versus "moderate" versus "high" motivation toward the correctional plan (or accountability for their previous actions), how being "engaged" versus not being "engaged" was described and what did versus did not constitute a "clinical diagnosis." Data constituted all of the writer's open-ended comments in the field provided on the record itself where the writer is to explain the reason for the prisoner's scores. The data are analyzed for emergent themes that correspond both across participant files and with participant scores on each variable. We present the resulting data to explain and contextualize the quantitative results from regression analyses and to provide insight into seemingly straightforward quantitative findings. A limitation must be noted that qualitative results are only preliminary at this point, do not include the full dataset and, thus, have yet to undergo a full thematic analysis. Nonetheless, such excerpts are invaluable in providing insight into assessments in the context of Canadian penality.

Results

To contextualize our quantitative findings and their interpretations, we present qualitative excerpts from the criminal records. The quotes represent emergent themes in descriptions of each variable among a subset of participants and give insight into the variables included in our analyses. For our first analysis, we examined the impact of clinical diagnosis and assessment scores for each variable on the number of times an offender must meet their parole officer. Furthermore, each underscores how the variable is expressed in legal documents—beyond official scores (e.g., motivation versus lack of motivation). Next, we present the results from a series of analyses that examine how assessment factors and clinical diagnosis predict the total number of parole conditions a releasee receives at release (i.e., level of supervision).

Dynamic Factors and Clinical Diagnoses

Motivation and Accountability

Across files, high scores on motivation were awarded to prisoners who avoid altercations in prison, complete programming, and follow their correctional plan. An individual scoring high on motivation is described as someone who:

> has successfully completed his education upgrading and his VPP-MI as well as managed to avoid becoming involved in any significant incidents or receiving any serious charges while incarcerated. His [name removed] program report indicated that he was attentive during group sessions and participated adequately during small group exercises. His written work was completed on time and contained sufficient detail and personalization. During the program, his motivation to change was difficult to accurately assess due to his quiet nature and flat presentation in the classroom setting.

Evinced in this participant's description is his attitude toward being the "ideal" prisoner and striving toward what could be viewed as "self-improvement" or movement toward parolee eligibility. An individual scored as at a moderate or medium level of motivation is presented as someone who:

> has expressed a desire to participate in his Correctional Plan and appears to possess the skills and knowledge to change his behaviour. [Name removed] has taken programming and successfully completed them. He has also maintained a few jobs and all records show that he did well, was always on time and worked hard at his job. The one concern with [name removed] is his schooling. In his initial correctional plan it had stated that [name removed] was expected to participate in educational upgrading. It was explained to him that failure to participate in educational upgrading could have a negative impact on his institutional employment and his pay level. He has not completed the [name removed] program and the writer believes that he needs to be motivated to finish school while still incarcerated.

Here, the prisoner in question is considered moderately motivated toward doing what is necessary to prepare for integration; however, his score also reflects and perhaps is hindered by his lack of educational attainment combined. Instead of documenting information about why the prisoner has not engaged in educational programming, he is scored as only moderately motivated. Levels of motivation, however, do vary over time, and this is accounted for in the records:

> [Name removed] level of motivation has fluctuated over his sentence of incarceration. While at [facility name removed] he involved himself in a major disturbance right after successfully completing the MI-VPP and thus his level of motivation was re-assessed as low.

In the prior excerpt, the writer explains that the prisoner's motivation was reassessed as low because he engaged in an alteration directly after completing a violence prevention program. This does not imply the program had no effect; instead it can also speak to the difficulties of applying lessons learned in programming at times in the prison context. His reassessment, however, may not take into account the nature of actions that led to participation in the altercation and if the prisoner truly had a choice to engage or not (see Ricciardelli, 2014). Indeed, for prisoners, prison living is very much determined by personal risk-management strategies yet, from the position of the writer, making the "right choice" in custody is determined by following institutional rules insofar as each clearly aligns with institutional discourses of self-responsibilization (Ricciardelli, 2014). Nonetheless, the effect on prisoner scoring is clear and underscores intolerance towards altercations; neither in prison nor in the community. To reveal the extent of discrepancies in what constitutes a low level of motivation—which is evident at the moderate level as well—another writer notes:

> [Name removed] may recognize a problem exists with his lifestyle and takes some accountability for his actions; however he refused to participate in programming to address his risk factors which is very concerning to his CMT. [Name removed] reported that he is willing to participate in programming in the community. Due to [name removed] refusing programming, his motivation to change his criminal mindset is currently assessed as Low until such time that he participates in programming to address his risk factors.

In a similar context, variability also exists in scoring on accountability, however central themes remain—those who score high take full responsibility for their actions and recognize the consequences of their actions. Indeed, low accountability tends to include complete denial of responsibility, affiliation, and accepting that one's personal actions led to negative consequences:

> [Name removed] acknowledged that [name removed] Police Services have identified him as being a gang member [gang name removed] but he denies any affiliation. Consultation with the SIO indicates that the [name removed] Police confirmed that he is a member of street gang [name removed]. While there is no evidence of association with gang members related to his current breach; it does appear that the offender has ties to street gangs and problems with criminal associates remain an active ongoing concern.

This writer scores the participant as Low because he is denying his gang affiliation and, in doing so and despite no direct evidence for gang involvement, is viewed as failing to take accountability for the scope of his criminal actions and offense. A possible disparity emerges here between an individual's assessment as gang-involved versus their individual perception. Specifically, in this example, it is possible that the releasee did not view himself as an actual gang member (i.e., he could have been an affiliate, associate, or held any other status), yet such gradation of membership may not be taken into account in justice processes despite being rather pronounced in prison and societal living—particularly among those with gang affiliation (i.e., it is not a status claimed arbitrarily). Thus, a disparity emerges as practitioners of justice (i.e., police, corrections, and so on) do have the agency to label and render attributes which, by definition, delimit the agency of prisoners or releasees to maintain their own definitions of self. Failing to agree to the imposed label may result (as evinced in the prior excerpt) in negative assessment due to releasees' perceived "denial" or lack of accountability. Without recognition of gang affiliation, CSC practitioners will view prisoners as unable or unwilling to take what can be considered necessary steps toward disassociating with negative peer influences and working toward securing pro-social supports, which are central to positive re-entry potential.

Providing an example of a moderate score on accountability, we see that another prisoner's behavior appears much more problematic than the aforementioned possibly gang-affiliated prisoner who was rated as low in accountability. However, by being open about the reasons underlying his negative behavior and open to treatment or support, this releasee received a better score:

> The subject takes responsibility for his actions and states he knows that his association with negative peers and substance abuse has played a negative role in his life. He understands he will need to distance himself from negative peers and quit using drugs in-order to be successful on conditional release. He knows what he did was wrong and in no way has he ever minimized his actions. Institutionally, [name removed] has recently demonstrated less than satisfactory behaviour. He has been involved in three separate documented incidents during [time removed] including an unauthorized item seized from his cell and an incident that led to three days segregation. . . . Most recently, [name removed] was named an associate of an incident involving another offender overdosing with heroin in [name removed] cell. The following day, [name removed] tested positive for THC during urinalysis testing. When challenged about his deteriorating behaviour, [name removed] divulged he was experiencing family difficulties with his ex-girlfriend and emotional difficulties including feelings of depressed mood and agitation. [Name removed] takes responsibility for his behaviour yet admits he has difficulty coping with stressful situations and requires extra support in managing his emotions. A referral to Psychology for further evaluation was initiated as a result.

As evinced in the excerpt, by divulging his concerns and taking responsibility for his poor behavioral choices (albeit once caught multiple times), the prisoner positions himself to acquire help in dealing with situations that could otherwise cause his behavior to take a negative turn. Cynicism would suggest that some prisoners may be skilled and knowledgeable about what to say during assessments, however it must still be recognized that many prisoners do intend to take responsibility and take steps toward desistance. What is clear here is that the words of this "offender" appear to have more weight in the assessment process than his prior (and very recent) behaviors. Further, this excerpt also demonstrates that the CSC writer is both trying to assist the prisoner with developing the needed tools to succeed during his future re-entry but also does not simply "write off" the prisoner in light of his deteriorating behavior. The correctional push remains *alongside* the social welfare ethos in Canadian corrections. Prisoners scoring high on accountability demonstrate an understanding of consequences and their actions, including in ways that goes beyond their convictions:

> Since release, [name removed] has shown considerable accountability for his actions, including those that were previously undisclosed and or undocumented on file. This rating continues to be appropriate in this case.

Engagement

Engagement is described in terms of a prisoner being engaged in his or her correctional plan and assessed by combining an individual's ratings on motivation, accountability, and responsivity. Writers describe those persons they consider not engaged as individuals who *express motivation* to participate but who do not follow through:

> [Name removed] demonstrated willingness to: fully and actively participate in his Correctional Plan, be free of criminal and gang activity while under sentence, display conduct that demonstrates respect, obey the penitentiary rules, lawful orders, and/or supervision requirements. *Due to [name removed] refusing to participate* in the High Intensity Program, he is currently assessed as not Engaged as it pertains to his Correctional Plan.
>
> The offender is not considered to be engaged at this time, due to his breaches during his previous release which were focused around him travelling within his restricted geographical boundary within [place removed], associating with an individual who was potentially involved in crime, and having intentions of travelling to [place removed], which was well outside of his approved travel radius [added emphasis].

Evinced here is how a lack of engagement is thought to be rooted in choosing not to participate in programming or abiding by parole conditions. An expressed intention to engage alongside evidence of program completion, however, is often rated more highly:

> [H]e is assessed as engaged in his correctional plan. As stated above [name removed] *has taken and completed programming*, has had a good record at work

> and continues to show motivation while on the [name of facility removed]. [Name removed] stated that he still wishes to take the NSAP maintenance program, is willing to attend AA, is officially considered the unit cleaner and has a plan to continue cell studies once back at a parent institution [added emphasis].

A prisoner's intention to participate in programming is understood as representative of engagement; in this context we see that the writer is willing to give the prisoner a chance to show his engagement (i.e., expressed sentiment but also experiences with programming) prior to rating him negatively. Regardless of stated sentiment, if a releasee fails to abide with the conditions of the plan, he/she would then be rated as not engaged—and vice versa if the participant was to be unengaged and then become engaged.

Clinical Diagnosis

Across criminal records, clinical diagnosis appeared to be a rather complex variable to operationalize. Perhaps surprisingly, the presence of addiction and substance abuse did not necessarily lead to a clinical diagnosis, nor did prior episodes of depression nor other mental health conditions that shaped the prisoners' medical history. We present three examples of different participants who each did not meet the criteria for a referral to psychological services for risk assessment at intake and were scored as not having a clinical diagnosis in their records:

> Therefore, his case does not meet the referral criteria for a psychological risk assessment. At this review there are no available psychiatric or psychological reports. During the intake interview on [date removed], he did not report current or past suicidal ideation or intent, and there are no mental health issues or intervention noted on file. . . . [Name removed] recent criminal behaviour is directly linked to his substance abuse and related lifestyle and associates as well as his criminal attitudes. He has yet to identify his personal triggers for his crack cocaine abuse.
>
> A Psychological Intake Assessment was conducted on [date removed] and found that [name removed] presented Criminogenic needs [that] include addressing factors related to impulsivity, substance abuse (particularly alcohol abuse), negative peers and associates, and pro-criminal values (while intoxicated). He has no significant mental health problems at this time that would prevent him from participating in and benefiting from correctional case management.
>
> In a psychiatric report dated [date removed], forensic psychiatrist, [Dr. name removed] confirms that [name removed] suffered from "at least moderately severe depression" for about one year prior to the offence. At the time of the offences he was in a state of high emotion and stress. No history of aggressive or violent [sic] was noted. Dr. [name removed] reports that [name removed]

> has "complete amnesia" for the events, and offered that it was possible that [name removed's] extreme emotions may have negated his ability to form specific intent. [Name removed] does not meet the criteria for a Psychological Risk Assessment at intake. Whether or not [name removed] meets the criteria for a discretionary Psychological Risk Assessment prior to consideration for conditional release by the Parole Board of Canada will be determined at the placement institution.

In the first excerpt, the CSC writer speaks of a prisoner who struggles with an addiction to crack cocaine, which triggers his criminal behaviors, yet the prisoner does not meet the criteria for a psychological assessment or score as having a clinical diagnosis. Similarly, the second prisoner described suffers from both substance abuse and "impulsivity" yet is described as having "no mental health problems at this time that would prevent" his participation in select activities. Despite the language used, the prisoner is rated as not having a clinical diagnosis, which reveals the strict definition of said diagnoses in the context of prisoners. The fact that the aforementioned prisoner has received a psychological assessment does suggest that there is recognition of possible mental health needs by the writer. The description of the third offender reveals the extent of the complexity of what constitutes a clinical diagnosis. The writer speaks of the offender having received a psychological assessment prior to federal incarceration, being assessed as depressed and in "a state of high emotion and stress" with "complete amnesia" about his criminal actions, yet he neither meets the criteria for psychological assessment at intake nor does he receive a clinical diagnosis. Further, it is uncertain if he will or will not undergo a psychological assessment prior to becoming eligible for parole. These excerpts that further present the complexity of this variable are representative of other prisoner files. Most often the individuals were assessed as not having a clinical diagnosis, having experienced mental illness, yet did not meet the criteria for a psychological referral for assessment:

> During interviews with his Parole Officer, [name removed] has identified that he suffers from Depression and this has impacted his relapse to substance abuse during his recent release. As per CD 712–1, [name removed] does not meet the criteria for a referral for psychological risk assessment; therefore, a professional psychiatric or psychological risk assessment has not been completed in this case.

There does not appear a clear answer to the question of what criteria and conditions would meet the criteria for further psychological assessment. Further, it should be noted (although beyond the scope of this study) that some individuals who were listed as not having a clinical diagnosis or qualifying for a psychological assessment did eventually receive a referral for assessment. Perhaps this disparity in who is assessed as having a clinical diagnosis is a consequence of the limited psychological resources available both in prison and during re-entry which may impinge upon who is assessed positively versus negatively (i.e., positive assessment may also be correlated to treatment availability and resources). If this is the case, assessment is resource driven rather than directed by practitioner discretion.

On the other hand, offenders who do receive a clinical diagnosis tended to have additional factors motivating the diagnosis or triggering the need for assessment. For example, in the case of some releasees, reports from other family members or partners about explicit mental health issues triggered psychological assessments and the related clinical diagnosis:

> [Name removed]'s mother ([name removed]) relayed that subject was rather low functioning and that he could be suffering from Fetal Alcohol Syndrome. . . . On [date removed], a Psychological Assessment was completed. . . . Actuarial risk measures indicate that [name removed] is in the high end of the Moderate range for both general and violent recidivism. His risk would be higher if he was using substances. His cognitive limitations and issues with anger also contribute to his already suspect judgement.

The writer in the prior except acknowledges the prisoner's developmental delays tied to Fetal Alcohol Syndrome as a psychological condition indicative of a clinical diagnosis. Thus, what seems to perhaps differentiate this individual from others who did not receive a diagnosis is his "cognitive limitations."[5] The presence of "corroborating others" may also be a factor facilitating the likelihood of a clinical diagnosis.

Our qualitative findings reveal the complexity of operationalizing the different variables, evidenced across those scored as ordinal or nominal categories. What did emerge in the CSC writers' assessments was that while levels of "actual" engagement (e.g., program participation and completion) mattered, the words of the prisoners seemed to matter more. For example, motivation scores increased when prisoners engaged in discourses of self-responsibilization during assessments, despite having recent histories of engaging in activities that were indicative of recidivism potential (i.e., using drugs, possessing contraband). Despite actions suggesting motivation to desist was low, when looking at the qualitative data, the narrative of motivation to change put forth to the writer was given genuine credibility and weight, particularly when it included the prisoner identifying their challenges and needs. In the same context, accountability—particularly when accompanied by narratives of self-responsibilization—can override behaviors indicating low accountability (i.e., an altercation or relapse can be given less weight in an assessment if a prisoner accepts responsibility and requests help to overcome whatever is presented as leading to said negative behaviors). Further, our qualitative findings reveal that making strides to demonstrate "self-improvement" through either actual or intended engagement in programming has some weight, or is at least considered, during assessments. Given that the words of prisoners in their narratives are considered by assessors when scoring prisoners, we turn to statistical analyses to determine which, if any, assessment scores are significant in predicting level of supervision. Said another way, we examine if these narratives of self-responsibilization, self-improvement, and accountability genuinely impact level of supervision.

Assessing Actual Level of Supervision

To answer our question, we first examined whether or not the independent variables predicted the frequency with which parolees are required to meet with their parole officers during initial community re-entry. We predicted that parolees who scored lower on motivation, scored lower on accountability, and who were not engaged in their correctional plan would rate higher in actual level of supervision than those who scored lower on these variables. However, we also predicted that having a diagnosis would lead to a higher intensity of supervision in comparison to those who did not have a clinical diagnosis. Four separate ordinal regressions were conducted, where each independent variable (motivation, accountability, engagement, clinical diagnosis) were used individually to predict the ordinal categorical dependent variable (actual level of supervision). As shown in Table 15.2, the four individual ordered logistic regressions reveal that motivation and accountability are significant. For every unit increase in motivation scores, participants were 75 percent less likely to be mandated to meet their parole officer than were those who rated as unmotivated, $z = -4.08, p = .000$. Moreover, those who were rated more accountable for their actions were 77 percent less likely to be mandated to see their parole officer than are those who were rated as not accountable for their actions, $z = 3.97, p = .000$.

We then performed a fifth ordinal logistic regression that included all the dynamic variables in a single model to examine how each variable predicts actual level of supervision when accounting for all the other variables. In this analysis, we consider together scores regarding motivation, accountability, engagement, and clinical diagnosis of a mental disorder, finding motivation significantly predicts actual level of supervision (see Table 15.2 for comparisons between the individual and grouped analyses). For every unit increase in motivation scores (those rated as more motivated), individuals were 61 percent less likely to be rated higher in actual level of supervision than were those who were rated as unmotivated, $z = -1.99, p = .046$.

Table 15.2 Ordinal Regression Analyses Predicting Actual Level of Supervision

Variables	*Single Variable Model 1 Odds Ratio*	*Single Variable Model 2 Odds Ratio*	*Single Variable Model 3 Odds Ratio*	*Single Variable Model 4 Odds Ratio*	*Full Model*
Clinical diagnosis	.706 (.238)	–	–	–	.652 (.224)
Accountability	–	.233*** (.086)	–	–	.426 (.203)
Motivation	–	–	.257*** (.086)	–	.394* (.184)
Engagement	–	–	–	.328 (.199)	1.138 (.830)
$N = 213$					

Standard error in parentheses.

* $p < .05$, ** $p < .01$, and *** $p < .001$.

Table 15.3 Regression Analyses Predicting Total Number of Condition

Variables	*Single Variable Model 1*	*Single Variable Model 2*	*Single Variable Model 3*	*Single Variable Model 4*	*Full Model*
Clinical diagnosis	−.684 (.417)	–	–	–	−.686 (.418)
Accountability	–	−.578 (.469)	–	–	.030 (.584)
Motivation	–	–	−.947* (.408)	–	−.963 (.565)
Engagement	–	–	–	−.913 (.730)	−.007 (.830)
N = 213					

Standard error in parentheses.

* $p < .05$, ** $p < .01$, and *** $p < .001$.

Our next series of analyses examine how the same independent variables predict the total number of parole conditions (Table 15.3). First, we examined each dependent variable separately and conducted regression analyses. Results from these analyses (Table 15.3) reveal that only motivation significantly predicts total number of parole conditions. Those that were rated as being motivated received significantly fewer parole conditions than did those who were rated as unmotivated, $t = 2.32, p = .021$.

We then performed a fifth regression analysis that included all the dynamic factor variables in a single model to examine how each variable predicts total number of parole conditions when accounting for all the other variables. No significant findings were revealed in this analysis.

Discussion

Our study focuses on sentencing disparities at reintegration (community corrections) for Canadian federal prisoners. Although our quantitative findings are marginal, unpacking the variables with qualitative data provides insight into the assessment processes and scoring that highlights the underpinning of sentences as tied to levels of supervision post-release. Disparities take a variety of forms, and this is the first study to our knowledge that looks at how dynamic risk factors and clinical diagnosis of mental health concerns impact disparities in conditions and the degree of parole supervision (i.e., number of times a releasee must meet with their parole officer) post release. In our first analyses, which examined the impact of clinical diagnosis and ratings of dynamic risk factors on the number of times a releasee must meet their parole officer, the results reveal marginally significant findings for two of the dynamic factor variables: accountability for their past actions and motivation to desist from crime. Specifically, individuals who were rated as being more accountable were mandated to see their probation officer less often than those who were rated as less accountable. Looking at what constitutes accountability qualitatively reveals that it accompanies acknowledgement of what must be "done" to promote desistance. Thus, more frequent parole supervision follows from the less willing one *appears* to be, in terms of taking responsibility for their previous behavior and the realities resulting in such behavior. Logically following as well, those who were rated as having high motivation to desist from crime were mandated to see their probation officer less often than those who were rated low in motivation.

In essence, our findings support Correctional Services of Canada's espoused goal of taking dynamic need into account at release and honoring diversities in need. Challenges, however, arise in the lack of significant findings related to mental health diagnosis, specifically given that one would expect that persons with recognized mental health needs would have such needs met during reintegration—specifically in the early stages of re-entry. However, looking at the complexity of the variable of clinical diagnosis and what constitutes a lack of diagnosis (i.e., substance abuse, prior experiences of depression, and so on) the fact that persons without diagnosis do receive a higher frequency of supervision as well does make sense. It would appear that individuals with or without a clinical diagnosis will require supervision, particularly when dealing with challenges that could be operationalized as mental illness if so desired (e.g., addiction, anxiety).

Our study's limitations present simultaneous opportunities for further research. The CSC reports touch upon motivation to desist from crime, but further research is needed to explore, for instance, reasons *why* offenders do not follow through with particular programming. For instance, arguably, professional discretion underscores all decisions made regarding imposed parole conditions, despite these decisions being rendered against a backdrop of actuarial logics and patterning. However, it is also unclear *how* decisions are reached regarding whether releasees receive a clinical diagnosis. Qualitative research involving interviews with CSC employees, especially ethnographic studies of the social context of decision making would contribute invaluable knowledge in this area.

Of the disparities highlighted in this chapter, we find most significant that of all the factors influencing level of supervision, only motivation was found to be statistically significant. The other factors—accountability, engagement, and clinical diagnosis of a mental disorder—did not significantly affect a releasee's level of supervision (i.e., either the number of parole conditions or the frequency of meetings with their parole officer). This appears to conflict with the qualitative reports where engagement was considered alongside stated motivation and where, as mentioned above, expressed motive seemed to have a higher correctional valence than other factors. This finding also requires further follow-up research, though we would speculate that we are observing a pattern of action which possesses logic through a neoliberal correctional context which places great emphasis on ex-prisoners internalization of the "script" of self-responsibilization. Further comparison to other institutional and organizational contexts where individuals are expected to align their "personal" motives with institutional narratives to warrant (or "deserve") services (e.g., women accessing the services of battered women shelters) would also contribute greater theoretical and comparative insights (see Dunn and Powell-Williams, 2007; Ferraro, 1982; Loseke,

1992). The question of whether or not releasees are being "authentic" regarding their pronouncements of positive motivation are, we would argue, sociologically irrelevant in explaining correctional decisions. It may be useful to think of expressions of motive as "accounts" or "social vocabularies of motive" (Mills, 1940; Scott and Lyman, 1968), which facilitate a correctional social order through micro-assessments of behavior and intention. Such theorizing may usefully direct further understanding of the social processes through which institutional actors affect individual efforts to desist from crime.

Notes

1 Given the contention surrounding the term and concept of "rehabilitation," we try to use the definition put forth by Moore and Hannah-Moffat (2005) of "positively changing prisoners" but add the emphasis on the *ethos* of rehabilitation, that is, the *perception* of prisoners' ability to change positively, instead of "rehabilitation" when possible throughout the chapter.

2 Newfoundland and Labrador, Prince Edward Island, and the territories do not have a federal prison facility.

3 Scores on assessments are recorded in the prisoner's correctional plan (PLAN CORR).

4 CSC refers to the person who completes the documentation and assessment as the "writer."

5 Additional and more comprehensive information about clinical diagnosis and treatment directives and adherence are located in the psychological assessments, which are not part of the current analyses. A noted limitation in the current study is that some persons who did not receive a clinical diagnosis did have psychological assessment that suggested otherwise. This could be a result of the timing of the PLAN CORR assessment versus psychological assessment or other factors and as such warrants further study.

References

Andrews, D., Bonta, J., & Hoge, R. (1990). Classification for effective rehabilitation: Rediscovering psychology. *Criminal Justice and Behavior*, *17*, 19–52.

Austin, J. (2001). Prisoner reentry: Current trends, practices, and issues. *Crime & Delinquency*, *47*(3), 314–334.

Clear, T., & Hardyman, P. (1990). The new intensive supervision movement. *Crime & Delinquency*, *36*(1), 42–60.

Clear, T. R., & Latessa, E. J. (1993). Probation officers' roles in intensive supervision: Surveillance versus treatment. *Justice Quarterly*, *10*(3), 441–462.

Correctional Service Canada (CSC). (2012). *Security classification and penitentiary placement commissioner's directive*. Ottawa: Correctional Service Canada.

Demichele, M., Payne, B. K., & Button, D. M. (2008). Electronic monitoring of sex offenders: Identifying unanticipated consequences and implications. *Journal of Offender Rehabilitation*, *46*(3–4), 119–135.

Department of Justice. (2013). *Information on the correctional centre building and supervision style*. Retrieved March 6, 2015, from www.justice.gov.yk.ca/prog/cor/wcc/correctional_building.html

Dunn, J. L., & Powell-Williams, M. (2007). 'Everybody makes choices': Victims advocates and the social construction of battered women's victimization and agency. *Violence Against Women*, *13*(10), 977–1001.

Erez, E., Ibarra, P., & Lurie, N. (2004). Electronic monitoring of domestic violence cases: A study of two bilateral programs. *Federal Probation*, *68*(1), 15–20.

Ferraro, K. (1982). Negotiating trouble in a battered women's shelter. *Urban Life*, 12(3), 287–306.

Garland, D. (2001). *The culture of control: Crime and social order in contemporary society*. Chicago: The University of Chicago Press.

Georgiou, G. (2014). Does increased post-release supervision of criminal offenders reduce recidivism? Evidence from a statewide quasi-experiment. *International Review of Law & Economics, 37*, 221–243.

Gies, S., Gainey, R., & Healy, E. (2016). Monitoring high-risk sex offenders with GPS. *Criminal Justice Studies, 29*(1), 1–20.

Hannah-Moffat, K. (2005). Criminogenic needs and the transformative risk subject. *Punishment & Society*, 7(1), 29–51.

Hannah-Moffat, K. (2013). Risk and punishment. In J. Simon & R. Sparks (Eds.), *The Sage handbook of punishment and society* (pp. 129–151). Los Angeles, CA: Sage.

Hutchinson, S. (2006). Countering catastrophic criminology: Reform, punishment and the modern liberal compromise. *Punishment & Society, 8*(4), 443–467.

Klingele, C. (2013). Criminal law: Rethinking the use of community supervision. *Journal of Criminal Law and Criminology, 103*(4), 1015–1070.

Lewis, S. (2005). Rehabilitation: Headline or footnote in the new penal policy? *Probation Journal, 52*(2), 119–135.

Lo, T. W. (2003). The debates and repositioning of community service orders in Hong Kong. *Hong Kong Journal of Social Work, 37*(2), 207–219.

Loseke, D. R. (1992). *The battered woman and shelters: The social construction of wife abuse*. Albany, NY: State University of New York Press.

Lynch, M. (2000). Rehabilitation as rhetoric: The ideal of reformation in contemporary parole discourse and practices. *Punishment & Society, 2*(1), 40–65.

Maurutto, P., & Hannah-Moffat, K. (2006). Assembling risk and the restructuring of penal control. *British Journal of Criminology, 46*(3), 438–454.

Meyer, J., & O'Malley, P. (2005). Missing the punitive turn? Canadian criminal justice, 'balance', and penal modernism. In J. Pratt, D. Brown, M. Brown, S. Hallsworth, & W. Morrison (Eds.), *The new punitiveness: Trends, theories, perspectives* (pp. 201–217). Devon: Willan Publishing.

Mills, C. W. (1940). Situated actions and vocabularies of motive. *American Sociological Review, 5*(6), 904–913.

Moore, D., & Hannah-Moffat, K. (2005). The liberal veil: Revisiting Canadian penality. In J. Pratt, D. Brown, M. Brown, S. Hallsworth, & W. Morrison (Eds.), *The new punitiveness: Trends, theories, perspectives* (pp. 85–100). Devon: Willan Publishing.

Opsal, T. D. (2009). Women on parole: Understanding the impact of surveillance. *Women & Criminal Justice, 19*(4), 306–328.

Padgett, K. G., Bales, W. D., & Blomberg, T. G. (2006). Under surveillance: An empirical test of the effectiveness and consequences of electronic monitoring. *Criminology & Public Policy, 5*(1), 61–91.

Parole Board of Canada. (2015). *Parole decision-making: Myths and realities. Cat. No. JF92-45/2001*. Retrieved July 24, 2016, from http://pbc-clcc.gc.ca/infocntr/myths_reality-eng.shtml

Petrunik, M. (2003). The hare and the tortoise: Dangerousness and sex offender policy in the United States and Canada. *Canadian Journal of Criminology and Criminal Justice, 45*(1), 43–72.

Ricciardelli, R. (2014). *Surviving incarceration: Inside Canadian penitentiaries*. Waterloo, Ontario: Wilfrid Laurier University Press.

Robinson, G. (1999). Risk management and rehabilitation in the probation service: Collision and collusion. *Howard Journal of Criminal Justice, 38*(4), 421–33.

Robinson, G. (2008). Late-modern rehabilitation: The evolution of a penal strategy. *Punishment & Society, 10*(4), 429–445.

Scott, M. B., & Lyman, S. M. (1968). Accounts. *American Sociological Review, 33*(1), 46–62.

Sheehan, R. (2014). Women exiting prison: Supporting successful reintegration in a changing penal climate. *British Journal of Community Justice, 12*(2), 57–66.

Shoham, E., Yehosha-Stern, S., & Efodi, R. (2013). Sociolegal characteristics and parole infractions Among Israeli released prisoners during electronic monitoring. *International Journal of Offender Therapy and Comparative Criminology, 57*(7), 864–887.

Travis, J., & Petersilia, J. (2001). Reentry reconsidered: A new look at an old question. *Crime and Delinquency*, *47*(3), 291–313.

Turnbull, S., & Hannah-Moffat, K. (2009). Under these conditions: Gender, parole and the governance of reintegration. *British Journal of Criminology*, *49*(4), 532–551.

Werth, R. (2013). The construction and stewardship of responsible yet precarious subjects: Punitive ideology, rehabilitation, and "tough love" among parole personnel. *Punishment & Society*, *15*(3), 219–246.

16

"OBJECTS OF CONCERN" OR "RISKY YOUNG OFFENDERS"?

Assessment and Intervention With Children in the Public Care and Youth Justice Systems of England and Wales

Jonathan Evans

Introduction

A major inquiry into the relationship between the public care and youth justice systems in England and Wales (Prison Reform Trust, 2016a) has, at the time of writing, recently published an executive summary of its findings (the full report is due to follow). The central question of the inquiry, chaired by Lord Laming, was to

> consider the over representation of children in care, or with the experience of care, in the youth justice system—why, for example, when only fewer than 1% of children and young people are committed to the care of local authorities, a third of boys and 61% of girls in custody are, or have been, in care . . .?
> (Prison Reform Trust, 2016b: 1)

It is perhaps also worth mentioning that 30% of young people in penal youth custody are black, and many of these are known to the care system (Bateman, 2015).

At the outset it is important to acknowledge that the impact of abuse, neglect, and various forms of family trauma can obviously have a profound effect on the cognitive and emotional development of children (Skuse and Matthew, 2015). Being placed away from a familiar home environment, even in cases where parenting has been extremely abusive or neglectful, is also disorientating for a child. All of this may well go some way to explaining why such young people are vulnerable to future contact with the criminal justice system. Nevertheless, such experiences of victimization and trauma cannot account fully for this over-representation. At the very least, it is important to ask whether there are certain aspects of these two systems—and their relationship with one another—that increase the risk of criminalization.

This chapter considers three main dimensions of the subject: disparities of assessment and intervention that arise from social class inequalities; the influence of cultural biases embedded in institutions, systems, and practices; and the role of practitioner agency in relation to clinical and actuarial assessments of risk. An overview of the social and cultural context is followed by a risk assessment of the powerful systems of welfare and justice through which so many vulnerable young people pass. In order to appreciate more fully the salient aspects of these risk assessments, it is necessary to provide some detail on the local particularities of the public care and youth justice systems of England and Wales. This is described, respectively, in the sections entitled "The Present Youth Justice Systems in England and Wales: Background and Context" and "Entry Into the Looked After Children (Public Care) System." However, it is important to emphasize the point that the underlying principles of risk-assessing the institutional processes and practices of child welfare and youth justice are transferable across different national contexts.

Historical and Cultural Influences on Prevailing Popular Attitudes Towards Young People

It is important to first understand something of the historical, social, and cultural context within which the public care and youth justice systems have developed. This has not only shaped the architecture of child welfare and juvenile justice services, but also widely held contemporary attitudes towards young people. In Britain there is a tendency to selectively sentimentalize some children while simultaneously demonizing others as folk devils. These *others*, it is contended, are the "usual suspects" drawn from the disadvantaged sections of the white workless class and those minority ethnic communities popularly perceived as feckless, ill-disciplined, or dangerously unintegrated (Phillips and Bowling, 2002). Britons thus simultaneously venerate their own little angels whilst at the same time seeking to exorcize the demons that animate the offspring of *others* (Hendrick, 1997). When children enter their teenage years, however, a less equivocal attitude is exhibited.

It has been argued persuasively that Britain is a place that does not really like youth (Haines and Drakeford, 1998). Two essentially contradictory—but simultaneously held—public attitudes in respect of young people are detected: *envy* and *fear*. In terms of the first sentiment, there is a belief that young people are having such a good time at their wild and orgiastic parties they forget to invite the rest of us. Paradoxically, this attitude is contrasted with a palpable sense of fear.

> These are the youngsters who are out of control, who do not know how to behave, who have been brought up by parents who are too soft, who congregate on street corners in order to intimidate passers-by, who have no respect and show no consideration. There is a physical menace which is never far from the surface in these encounters. These young people are dangerous. They need to be avoided or, better still, kept away.
>
> (Haines and Drakeford, 1998: 3–4)

If the above analysis is correct, it is perhaps unsurprising that the concepts of "youth" and "crime" have enjoyed such a long and intimate association in the public mind. Although the term "juvenile delinquent"—along with the concept of adolescence—is found in the 18th century (Hendrick, 1997), it was in the 19th century that the concept became firmly lodged in wider popular consciousness (Hendrick, 1990). Whilst the concept of juvenile delinquency undoubtedly gained popular currency in the 19th century, it was the creation of the administrative category of "juvenile offender" that facilitated a process of conceptual concretization. The establishment of a separate juvenile criminal justice system provided a material focus for the anxieties of a nervous middle-class public. Their "respectable fears" (Pearson, 1983) became ever more focused on the emerging "folk devil" (Cohen, 2002) of "unruly youth." As with most debates about crime, the populist "surface" discourse barely conceals public anxieties about deeper social concerns: structural changes in society, economic instability, and insecurities about personal safety.

The highly class-specific image of the "criminal," especially the young criminal, is—for the most part—accepted uncritically in populist political and cultural discourse. The same can be said for the social construction of "adolescence" as an essentially troublesome and challenging condition. The psychological and behavioral disorders that are supposed to cluster around young people in their teenage years are commonly regarded as "natural" and somehow an integral part of child and adolescent development. "Youth" and "deviancy" have thus become almost synonymous in public discourses about young people. Although most of Hall's (1905) ideas have been jettisoned, the vivid image of adolescence as a time of "*storm and stress*" with hormonally driven identity crises is one that has become embedded in "commonsense" folk wisdom. The traces of these ideas are still clearly discernible in many contemporary accounts of youth. Some of the psychological labels attached to "challenging" (a much favored epithet in "professional" parlance) young people have seeped into wider public consciousness. Moreover, the news media's concentration on youth offending (Jewkes, 2011) as opposed to other forms of crime (like tax fraud and corporate crime) ensures that the diminutive hooded figure of the juvenile delinquent looms large in the public imagination. Young people, after all, are far more visible on the streets with their distinctively "scary" haircuts, challenging music, and incomprehensible demotic street argot. Youth is highly susceptible to being represented as the dangerous "other" and "enemy within" the city walls. The challenges experienced by young people—the delayed and often fractured transitions into the labor market, for example—tend to be presented as social problems for which they themselves are personally and individually responsible (Furlong and Cartmel, 2007). Although there exist middle-class versions of youthful delinquency and rebellion involving cautionary narratives of "falling" into "bad company" (Cromer, 2004) and "descending into drug-dependent hells," for the most part the dominant constructions of juvenile delinquency are masculine and class-specific. The feral offspring of the Victorian "residuum" bear a striking resemblance to later representations of the modern "underclass" (Murray, 1984, 1990, 1994). Like their 19th century counterparts, the post-modern poor are contrasted with a noble but fast-vanishing working class. According to Pitts (2000: 4), there is nostalgia for the

> vision of a 1950s municipal housing estate where fully employed, skilled, solvent, working class artisans took care of their families and kept their children under control.

This lament for patriarchal authority needs to be understood in terms of the shifting power relationships between social class, family, and the status of children. Nineteenth century constructions of children were not mere "fabrications." These constructions were a direct response to material social phenomena. Whilst Aries' (1962) work presents a rather flawed historical account of childhood—the literalist interpretation of European art being a case in point—he correctly identifies the fact that the majority of children in Western Europe once shared the same social space as adults. This included the important public space of the workplace. It should be recognized, of course, that this remains the case for many children in "developing countries." At the beginning of the 19th century children were certainly active participants in the economy. At the time there were actually comparatively few voices raised in opposition to their entry into the newly developing forms of industrialized labor in Britain. However, according to Hendrick (2002), in the period 1780–1840, a significant shift in attitude towards child labor gathered momentum and achieved critical mass amongst the middle classes. Leaving aside the influence of evangelical Christianity and the sentimentalization of the Romantic movement's construction of childhood (Hendrick, 2002: 24–25), there was growing recognition that children were not genuinely "free" to enter into meaningful contracts with their employers. This recognition ran counter to one of the principal tenets of classical liberal economics. "Reformers" duly drew parallels between the position of factory children at home and the international slave trade. Moreover, there was some disquiet that patriarchal authority—or the proper "order of nature," as it was known—was in danger of being subverted. The prospect of children usurping a father's role as principal breadwinner risked disrupting the bourgeois "Domestic Ideal" of "natural" family life.

It was against this background that the movement to regulate child labor was duly realized in a series of Factory Acts. Whilst this development can be read on one level as humanitarian, at another it represented direct paternalistic intervention in working-class life. In the United States, Platt's (1974) analysis of the "child-saving" movement exposed the "mixed motives" underlying this liberal humanitarian mission. More recently, applying a broadly similar methodological approach to that of Platt, Ward (2012) has laid bare the "racial" dimension of the black child-saving movement in a compelling analysis: tracing the formal exclusionary practices represented by Jim Crow juvenile justice to the still clearly discernible shadow-lines of this inheritance in the penal classification processes of the contemporary U.S. justice system.

Child Welfare, Family Life, and Public Order

In 19th century Britain, the imposition of middle-class assumptions and values brought benefits to children, but it also attracted hardship. Many working-class families experienced "child-friendly" legislative measures as acts of impoverishment. The loss of children's contribution to the family income meant that many parents were required by economic necessity to compensate for the shortfall in income by working longer hours. This inevitably resulted in large numbers of children being left without adult supervision. Contemporary accounts suggest that many of these children subsisted on the margins of the formal economy (Mayhew, 2008). Begging and petty theft were also commonplace. It was not long before the increased visibility of unsupervised children on the streets was problematized in terms of crime, public order, and parental neglect. The economic displacement of young people produced the social conditions in which the "juvenile delinquent" emerged as a distinct and recognizable urban entity. That said, the alarm expressed about the crime and public order problems presented by these young people was tempered with sentiments of genuine concern for their physical and moral well-being. Thus, issues of youth crime and child welfare became conceptually conflated in early constructions of "juvenile delinquency."

One of the state's responses to the increased presence of children on the streets was the enlargement of the criminal code. This involved the problematization of certain street activities and the conversion of "public nuisances" into criminal offenses (a process later to be echoed in New Labour's construction of "anti-social behaviour" in the Crime and Disorder Act 1998 and the Anti-Social Behaviour Act 2003). It is nevertheless important to recognize that the expansion of the criminal code and the formal extension of summary jurisdiction in juvenile matters were not simply manifestations of social authoritarianism. Whilst such repressive impulses were not entirely alien to the governing classes, there was undoubtedly a clear desire in some quarters to soften the impact of the criminal justice system upon children. Peel's criminal justice reforms, for example, were intended to form part of a wider modernization project in which children and other vulnerable groups were offered some measure of protection. The explicit underlying purpose of Peel's review of the criminal law was "to look at all the offences which are now punishable by death, [and] to select those . . . which can be safely visited with a mitigated punishment" (Peel, cited in Magarey, 2002: 120).

The unintended consequence of this legislative strategy was a widening of the criminal justice net. The Vagrancy Act 1824, for example, captured many children who would hitherto not have been classified as "offenders." The statute made it a criminal offense to be "a suspected Person or reputed Thief" (Vagrancy Act 1824 in Magarey, 2002: 117) and expanded the category of "rogues" and "vagabonds" to include "every person playing or betting in any Street . . . or other open and Public places . . . at any Game or Pretended Game of Chance" (Vagrancy Act 1824, cited in Magarey, 2002: 117).

The criminalization of comparatively harmless street games clearly placed children at disproportionate risk. The subsequent Metropolitan Police Acts empowered officers to prosecute anyone loitering on the street without good reason (1829) as well as those engaged in a range of popular working-class leisure pursuits (1839). Children, once again, formed a significant proportion of this troublesome working-class constituency. Meanwhile the Malicious Trespass Act 1827 effectively outlawed many of the economic survival strategies deployed by destitute children.

Criminal justice practitioners (like magistrates, police officers, and probation officers) have always played an enormously influential role in interpreting and applying legislation. Thus, police practice in this period was an important factor in determining which offenders were prosecuted. The police not only had as their principal objective "the prevention of crime" (Magarey, 2002: 117)—a duty that might be interpreted to apply to the street activities of children—but also the responsibility of paying their own legal costs in the event of an unsuccessful prosecution. It is reasonable to suppose, therefore, that prosecutions were likely to be brought against those where a conviction was most likely to succeed. Unsophisticated defendants, like children, were thus particularly vulnerable to prosecution.

Such "net-widening" practices, like those mentioned above, continued as the century progressed. The Amending Act of 1861, for example, redefined Vagrancy as ". . . virtually any child under fourteen found begging, receiving alms, of no settled abode or means of subsistence or who frequented criminal company." (Amending Act 1861, in Shore, 2002: 167–168). The Consolidating Act of 1866 expanded the category of Vagrancy to include those in need of care because they were, by implication, on the periphery of juvenile offending. Those "at risk" included ". . . orphans, children of criminal parents and children whose parents were undergoing penal servitude." (Shore, 2002: 168).

The conceptual conflation of juvenile offenders with those "in need" was well established by the middle of the century. Indeed, the late 20th century notion of "at-risk" populations has its roots in this conceptual conflation. The outcome of 19th century net-widening exercises, as Crawford and Russell (cited in Magarey, 2002: 119) observe, was that half of the juvenile prison population was there as a result of the enlargement of the criminal code. This "criminalization of behaviour characteristic of the poor and urban young" (Magarey, 2002:118) lends support to the assertion that juvenile delinquency was, in a very real sense, legislated into existence.

The Emergence of a Discrete Juvenile Justice System and Early Explanations for Youth Crime

Nevertheless, a precondition for the birth of "juvenile delinquency" was the legal system's creation of the category of "juvenile offender." The incremental establishment of a separate justice system, despite its undoubted merits, inevitably raised the profile of juvenile crime in the collective consciousness of the public. The emerging juvenile legal system eventually culminated in the establishment of the juvenile court in 1908; a court that dealt with **both** criminal and welfare issues. The juvenile/youth court remains, to this day, an arena in which competing discourses of welfare, justice, punishment, and rehabilitation collide.

The introduction of a discrete judicial system, allied with concern about the corrupting effect of adult prisons on children, led to the establishment of separate custodial provision for juveniles. The nature of these regimes had been anticipated by the institutions established by the philanthropic societies at the turn of the century

(Shore, 2002: 163–164). Nevertheless, the philosophical ideas of these new, state-run regimes had already had over half a century in which to mature. The philosophical ideas that underpinned the Reformatory (1854) and Industrial Schools (1857) are worth considering briefly. In many respects the creation of these institutions helped to define and operationalize previously held constructions of juvenile delinquency. It is to some of these ideas and discourses to which reference will be made below.

Underlying the debate about the purpose of custody—whether to punish or rehabilitate—lay a deeper question concerning responsibilization. If children were not **fully** responsible for their offending, then punishment was both an inadequate and irrational response to the problem of youth crime. The questions of "whom" or "what" was responsible for youth crime had been debated with increasing urgency since the moral panic that engulfed metropolitan areas after the French wars. The authors of the *Report for the Committee Investigating the Causes of the Alarming Increase of Juvenile Delinquency in the Metropolis* (1816) identified four principal causes of crime:

> The improper conduct of parents.
> The want of education.
> The want of suitable employment.
> The violation of the Sabbath and habits of gambling in the public streets.
>
> (Report for the Committee Investigating the Causes of the Alarming Increase of Juvenile Delinquency in the Metropolis, 1816: 10)

In addition to these "primary" causes were auxiliaries that could be organized under three headings:

> The severity of the criminal code.
> The defective state of the police.
> The existing system of prison discipline.
>
> (Report for the Committee Investigating the Causes of the Alarming Increase of Juvenile Delinquency in the Metropolis, 1816: 11)

It is interesting to note that some of the primary and auxiliary causes are not so very distant from the contemporary academic and policy discussions around "risk factors" (Farrington, 2007) and the iatrogenic nature of the criminal justice system (McAra and McVie, 2010).

Rush (2002: 146) has suggested that there were two main ways in which 19th century reformers responded to the problem of juvenile delinquency. One involved an explanation based on the "narrative of place," in which the neighborhood was portrayed as a breeding ground for criminal activity. Solutions therefore involved improved housing, urban planning, and communications. The second explanation for crime presented a "narrative of life" that included parenting deficits, dysfunctional families, and the inculcation of poor life habits. It was to the second narrative that the Reformatory Movement responded with missionary enthusiasm. Reformatory schools set about the task of re-training and, perhaps, even re-parenting young offenders in accordance with sound Christian principles of honesty, self-discipline, and industriousness.

Mary Carpenter's horizons extended beyond those young people who broke the criminal code. The Industrial Schools Act 1857 (and the 1866 consolidating measure) was the formal embodiment of the concern felt for those young people at risk of offending: children in "need of care and protection" (1866 Act, cited in May, 1973) and those who were "beyond their parents' control" (1857 Act, cited in May, 1973). These embryonic Care Orders effectively brought a wide range of working-class children under the disciplinary control of the middle classes. Whilst the classificatory integrity of the child "in need of care and protection" and the "moral orphan" or "juvenile delinquent" needed to be maintained, it was clear that **both** categories of child were in need of comprehensive re-education. Whilst the desire to improve child welfare was undoubtedly a genuine sentiment held by many reformers, public protection (or, to express it another way, the protection of propertied interests) was an equally important consideration.

The removal of children from their parents, families, and communities actually ran counter to the classical model of liberal governance. State interference in working-class life was, therefore, justified on welfare grounds. For an imperial power, moreover, the removal of children from "inadequate" parents and morally corrosive neighborhoods was represented as a legitimate exercise in both "child salvation" and "nation-building."

Like most of her contemporaries, Mary Carpenter subscribed to a class analysis based on the organizing principle of moral hierarchy. This is well illustrated in her social taxonomy of juvenile delinquency (involving six classes of juvenile offender spread across three generic laboring classes: the "honest," "perishing," and "dangerous"). Therefore, when Carpenter spoke of raising a young offender above his class or station, she was not speaking in terms of socio-economic mobility. She was, rather, describing an almost salvational form of moral mobility.

It will be clear from the foregoing analysis that the characteristics of "juvenile delinquency"—projected as they were on to the institutionally manufactured new category of "juvenile offender"—were closely related to the perceived attributes of the generic "social" class from which they hailed. Interestingly, the growth of the human sciences—particularly psychology—contributed to a process in which such socially subordinated groups were pathologized. The new profession of social work, moreover, played an active part in promoting a conservative welfare model. According to Jones (2002), it was the profession's supine adoption of a quasi-psychodynamic casework model that helped to foster an essentially reactionary practitioner culture in which the dysfunctional working-class family was perceived to be at the root of most social problems. Even the more recent rhetoric of service-user empowerment, it is implied, is not too far removed from the Victorian belief in moral autonomy and self-help. The profession of social work, it is suggested, continues to recruit legions of willing accomplices to the cause of reactionary practice. Mullaly (1997), though, argues that there are two main traditions in social work. On the one hand, the casework oriented Charity Organisation Society in which individual, family, and moral explanations for problems are advanced. On the other hand, there is the Settlement House Movement tradition which privileges explanations based on social structure. Sometimes, though, it can be difficult to make a distinction between the two. It is perfectly possible, for example, to smuggle reactionary social work practices under cover of welfare rhetoric and the language of service user empowerment. The distinction between 21st century empowerment and the mid-Victorian self-help advocated by Samuel Smiles (Smiles, cited in Golby, 1986) is perhaps not always as clear as some would claim.

Youth Justice and the Risks of Welfarism

It would of course be a misrepresentation of the history of youth justice to suggest that some statutes, policies, and practices have not proved to be more child-friendly for young people in comparison with other measures. Nevertheless, such periods cannot necessarily be identified by whether explicit welfare principles are inscribed in the statutes of the time. One of the paradoxes of youth justice history is that those who desire to promote the welfare of children often do the most harm. Thus, for example, whilst the 1933 Children and Young Persons Act placed the welfare of the child center-stage it simultaneously created the potential for intrusive state intervention into family life on the basis of "needs" rather than "deeds." Girls and young women, moreover, may have been placed at particular risk by assorted "child-savers" intent on rescuing them from moral danger or, post-corruption, the moral threat they might pose to men and family life in general (Sharpe and Gelsthorpe, 2015). The history of the social work profession might well be represented in terms of "humanitarian ideals" and "harmful therapies" (Smith, 2003: 289). The risk posed by professional welfare to children and young people is well illustrated by the contrasting juvenile justice practices of the 1970s and 1980s. In the 1970s the road to high levels of juvenile incarceration was paved with the good intentions of liberal reformers and "child-friendly" social workers. Clarke (1985: 292) has identified two such good *intentions* underpinning the Children & Young Persons Act 1969, a statute widely regarded as the high watermark of welfarism: the first was the "anti-institutionalist and decarcerationist pressure to remove juveniles from state institutions," and the second was recognition of the "class inequalities of juvenile justice." As far as the latter is concerned, the White Papers that preceded the 1969 Act (Home Office, 1965, 1968) certainly acknowledged social problems as causative factors in criminal behavior; however, this Act was underpinned by an individualized treatment philosophy. As Brown (1998: 59–60) observes,

> [p]rimacy is given to the family and the social circumstances of the deprived and underprivileged whose circumstances caused crime, truancy, lack of control and neglect—but it should be noted that primacy was accorded to individual factors rather than structural factors such as poverty or poor housing.

The Act's language of welfare, moreover, should not distract attention from the extension of social control over children from poorer backgrounds. This was probably at its most explicit in the statute's creation of so-called "Criminal Care Orders" under Section 7/7. Thus, Care Orders were available to the Court as a criminal disposal in cases where children had offended (s.1 (3) (c) CYPA 1969). There was also the "offence clause" (s.1 (f) CYPA 1969) available as grounds for a Care Order application in civil proceedings. In 1989 these criminal routes to public care were duly closed. As Curtis (2005: 54) comments:

> The Care Order, as a criminal disposal, and the offence clause in civil proceedings, were seen as draconian and contrary to natural justice since, theoretically at least, after stealing a bottle of milk a child of 10 from difficult home circumstances could be placed in local authority care until the age of 18. Thus the consequences of their offending could last far longer for children than for those adults committing the same crime.

"Care" and "control" have long been presented, somewhat uncritically, as two sides of the social work coin (Davies, 1986). The harsh language of punishment may be abjured in favor of cozier sounding "contracts" and the maintenance of "supportive structures" or "healthy boundaries," but the actual practice may be no less draconian in effect. When this is understood it is, perhaps, unsurprising that the decarcerationist spirit of '69 should have resulted in a sharp increase in custody rates for young people in the decade that followed. In 1977 38% of convicted juveniles were sentenced to detention centers and borstals compared with only 21% in 1965 (Pitts, 2001: 179). A government report (Department of Health and Social Security, 1981), moreover, identified a fivefold increase in the juvenile custody rate between 1965 and 1980. Part of the explanation for this upward trend lay in the pitfalls of early intervention with young people considered "at risk" of offending (primarily working-class youth). In 1977, for example, some 12,000 children were participating in the first wave of community-based Intermediate Treatment (characterized by groupwork and supervised "youth work-style" activities); only 1,500 of these were actually adjudicated offenders. As Pitts (2001: 179) observes:

> [E]arly informal intervention revealed a tendency to draw youngsters further into the system as the discovery of new needs and new problems appeared to necessitate the formalization of such interventions. In consequence, larger numbers of children were appearing in the juvenile court and a higher proportion of these was receiving custodial sentences.

Whatever the noble intentions of those social workers operationalizing this legislation, the outcomes were both deleterious to the interests of young people and woefully ineffective as a crime reduction strategy. It was, indeed, very much upon the outcomes of the so-called "welfarist" movement that the slowly emerging justice movement concentrated its criticisms. The 1969 Act had delegated social workers discretionary powers of intervention in the lives of young people. This discretion—exercised in a dangerously secluded legal vacuum of professional privacy—was, arguably, scandalously misused by the "child-savers" (Thorpe et al., 1980: 6). The absence of "due process" and the deprivation of legal rights to meaningful defense effectively provided a fast track from "care" to "custody." It is often the case that when treatment appears to fail (as the "net-widening" strategy of Intermediate Treatment undoubtedly did), punishment almost invariably becomes the next destination for the young person.

What emerges from the foregoing historical narrative account is that the distinction between welfare and punishment has long been rather blurred. The conflation of the "deprived child" with the "depraved child" means that there exists a contested space at the heart of the youth justice system. Whilst laying the foundations for the modern youth justice system through the establishment of the youth court and the formal enhancement of welfare principles, the 1908 Children Act also eroded the boundaries between the old Industrial Schools (for neglected children) and the Reformatories (for young offenders). In doing this, it facilitated movement between these two populations (Stewart, 1995). Thus, there developed a more ambiguous public and professional reaction to young people in the care system. This ambiguity was, as has been mentioned, much later exacerbated by the 1969 Children and Young Persons Act which gave magistrates the power to effectively "sentence" children to Care Orders. As Hayden et al. (1999: 24) observe:

> In a direct, practical sense this was an attempt to funnel young offenders away from the juvenile justice system and into the care system. The debate on the wisdom of this approach continued throughout the subsequent decade. . . . What was certainly true was that perceptions of the care system began to change as the nature of its clientele changed. No longer was it an avenue for public sympathy for "neglected" children. As child care, particularly residential care, began to house relatively older children (fostering, adoption and preventive work catering for most of the others) and more of those who had been in trouble with the law, the nature of the stigma attaching to those in care changed. Children in care (particularly residential care) began to be seen as young criminals being given an easy ride by the courts rather than as those most deserving of public sympathy.

It could be argued that the sense of stigma described above has survived the abolition of those sentencing powers. Young people in care, particularly teenagers in residential units, perhaps still tend to be associated with trouble rather than vulnerability. Nevertheless, all of these young people will have personal welfare needs. In analyzing political and professional responses to such young people, is it really a question of choosing "welfare" ***or*** "punishment"? A Foucauldian analysis would imply that disciplinary discourse extends well beyond the prison walls and penetrates the institutions of welfare and education (Petrie, 2003) to create a "carceral society": the "clinical gaze" (Foucault, 1973, 1977) of the psychiatrist and the "welfare spotlight" of the social worker (Evans, 2010) respectively trained on the patient and welfare client. The warm words of the social worker, it could be argued, are merely an example of the "anesthetic function of political language" and "structured bad faith [which] allows indefensible forms of control to look more defensible" (Cohen, 1985: 273). Whether the whole social welfare system can legitimately be described as a "punitive archipelago" (Cohen, 1985) is a moot point, but the "dispersal of discipline" analysis (Cohen, 1979) is one that challenges the notion of a straightforward choice between "welfare" and "punishment." Whilst practitioners arguably still retain a reasonable degree of professional discretion in their daily working lives, those decisions are inescapably ambiguous, equivocal, and double-edged. Doing the "right thing" for young people in trouble with the law is a difficult business.

The Present Youth Justice System in England and Wales: Background and Context

Before proceeding to a risk assessment of the public care and youth justice systems, it is perhaps necessary to provide not only an overview of the framework and institutional architecture of the present youth justice system in England and Wales but also some background to the ideas and political forces that have shaped the contemporary landscape. A summary of the essential characteristics of the corresponding public care system is provided in the section, "Entry Into the Looked After Children System." The level of detail provided is hopefully sufficient to illuminate rather than obscure the analysis: the aim being to help the non-UK reader discern the wood rather than the trees. It is the conviction of this author that the underlying principles being described contain elements that are universal in character and can therefore be applied comparatively across national contexts.

The present youth justice system has, on the whole, remained intact since it was put in place by the New Labour governments in power between 1997 and 2010. It is helpful to understand the underlying philosophical approach of what came to be known as the "New Youth Justice" (Goldson, 2000), particularly in such areas as responsibilization and risk management. It is not necessary to detail the contours of the youth justice system which existed immediately prior to New Labour's election in 1997, but suffice to say it was characterized by a "minimum sufficient intervention" approach that embraced diversionary principles and flexible models of supervision in the community (operationalized by social work trained staff) with the result that relatively low numbers were sentenced to penal custody. It was, however, criticized by the Audit Commission (1996) for—*inter alia*—inappropriate diversion via repeat cautioning and its inefficiently sluggish court proceedings that led to too many adjournments. It should be noted, however, that the Audit Commission's analysis was open to critical challenge on methodological as well as philosophical grounds (Jones, 2001). Nevertheless, the Report—along with the strong public reaction and lurid media coverage of the murder of 2-year-old James Bulger by two boys aged 10 years (Jewkes, 2011)—prepared the ground for subsequent radical changes in the youth justice system.

Although New Labour's record in office can certainly not be read as a direct translation of Third Way political philosophy, policy action in the domain of children and young people was influenced by the concept of the *social investment state* (Giddens,

1998: 99–128). Although Labour's policy in the field of criminal justice—influenced as it was by populist punitiveness (Tonry, 2004)—detracted from the philosophical coherence of *positive welfare*, much of the child/youth social policy agenda is explicable with reference to Giddens' ideas.

This approach argues that whereas the old social democratic state was designed to protect people from the negative effects of the market, the new social investment state aimed to help integrate them into global markets through investment in human capital. Thus,

> [s]ocial democrats have to shift the relationship between **risk** and **security** involved in the welfare state, to develop a society of "responsible risk takers" in the spheres of government, business enterprise and labor markets. People need protection when things go wrong, but also the material and moral capabilities to move through major periods of transition in their lives.
>
> (Giddens, 1998: 100)

Whilst the redistributive functions of the old welfare state are not eliminated completely, it is to the "redistribution of possibilities" (Giddens, 1998: 101) to which governmental attention is focused. This is achieved primarily through education and training. However, "Although training in specific skills may be necessary for many job transitions, more important is the development of cognitive and emotional competence" (Giddens, 1998: 125). Nurturing flexible attitudes towards the labor market and employment practices was part of this policy re-orientation; particularly in relation to young people. In the United Kingdom the ultimate aim was to move away from a deficit model and re-cast welfare in more positive terms: "in place of Want, autonomy; not Disease, but active health; instead of Ignorance, education, as a continuing part of life; rather than Squalor, well-being; and in Idleness, initiative" (Giddens, 1998: 128).

New Labour's approach to young people was essentially twin-track: universal social investment alongside more targeted policies in respect of the socially excluded (Fawcett et al., 2004). Thus, for example, all children were beneficiaries of the increased investment in such areas as education. Whilst children may well have benefited immediately from such measures, the policies were clearly also designed to pay future dividends for wider society. New Labour's overall level of investment in younger children was impressive. Lister (2003) has noted that the amount of money spent on children under the age of eleven years actually doubled between 1997 and 2002. She has also pointed out, though, that older children were less favored under a regime of supportive "early years" measures. This may be due to an element of instrumentalism on the part of the Blair government; the benefits of investing in older young people being extremely difficult to evidence.

There were, however, groups of older young people who were targeted for additional resources. The Social Exclusion Unit, established when New Labour first came to power, was the government's *de facto* "Ministry for Troubled Youth." Its early reports (Social Exclusion Unit, 1998a, 1998b, 1998c, 1999, 2000, 2003, 2005) tackled such pertinent issues as truancy, teenage pregnancy, homelessness; the education of Looked

After Children; Care Leavers; and young people with complex needs. In these reports the vulnerable position of children leaving public care was highlighted. The case of care leavers was an exemplar of the targeted approach taken by New Labour. The response to this particularly vulnerable group was the Children (Leaving Care) Act 2000. The statute was a serious attempt to respond to the well-documented gaps in income maintenance and service provision (Goddard, 2001).

Those who seek to find perfect philosophical coherence in New Labour's approach to crime and welfare issues will be disappointed. Like most elected governments, New Labour's dominant ideological convictions were diluted by the pragmatic need to satisfy competing constituencies of interest. Nevertheless, the Third Way themes of risk and responsibility are discernible in certain aspects of youth justice policy and practice.

Traditionally, the English and Welsh criminal justice system has—albeit grudgingly on occasions—accorded children a special and protected status. The system has traditionally taken account of such factors as age, maturity, and social powerlessness. This was even reflected in Home Office advice during the 1990s, a decade that witnessed what Drakeford and Vanstone (2000) described as a "punitiveness auction" between the two main British political parties. At the beginning of the decade the then Conservative government's attitude towards the principle of *doli incapax*—the notion that, due to lack of maturity, children below the age of 14 years cannot be assumed to have a completely developed sense of moral agency—was described in the following terms,

> The criminal law is based on the principle that people understand the difference between right and wrong. Very young children cannot easily tell this difference, and the law takes account of this. The age of criminal responsibility, below which no child can be prosecuted, is 10 years; and between the ages of 10 and 13 a child may only be convicted of a criminal offence if the prosecution can show that he knew what he did was seriously wrong. The government does not intend to change these arrangements which make proper allowance for the fact that children's understanding, knowledge and ability to reason are still developing.
>
> (Home Office, 1990: paragraph 8.4)

Even in the middle of the decade a Conservative government gave the following advice to juvenile justice practitioners preparing court reports on young people who had been convicted of criminal offenses:

> When a pre-sentence report is being prepared on a child or young person, the report writer must take account of section 44 of the Children & Young Person's Act 1933 which requires the court to have regard to the welfare of the individual. The UN Convention on the Rights of the Child . . . also requires that all actions concerning children shall be the primary consideration. The report writer should therefore take account of the age of the young offender, his or her family background and educational circumstances.
>
> (Home Office, 1995: 2.35)

In opposition the Labour Party foreshadowed a departure from these protective principles of child welfare in the criminal justice domain: "Ultimately, the welfare needs of the individual cannot outweigh the needs of the community to be protected from the adverse consequences of his or her offending behaviour" (Labour Party Media Office, 1996: 9).

The audacious re-positioning of the Labour Party on "law and order" following the election defeat of 1992 was a crucial part of the New Labour project being constructed by a younger generation of social democratic Labour politicians. Tony Blair and his contemporaries drew selectively upon the insights developed by Left Realist criminologists (Lea and Young, 1984) as well as the experience of the "renewed" Democrats under the leadership of Clinton and Gore (Pitts, 2000). Tony Blair's assumption of the Shadow Home Affairs portfolio allowed him to use the now famous soundbite that summarized the emergent position on law and order: "*tough on crime, tough on the causes of crime*," although it could be argued that a more accurate reflection of the media management strategy was "loud on criminals, quiet on the causes of crime."

Although the election of a Labour government resulted in a number of important child-friendly policies—most notably in the area of child poverty with the introduction of various tax credits to support struggling families and community development initiatives such as Sure Start to tackle child poverty—the protected status of children in the criminal justice system was eroded by the first Blair administration. Its attitude to "young offenders" and those who allegedly administered the old youth justice system so incompetently was well encapsulated in the title of one of the first documents to emerge from the New Labour tenants at the Home Office. *No More Excuses* (Home Office, 1997) captured Labour's brand of "tough love" in this area of policy. The abolition of *doli incapax* was an important statement of intent in relation to children who offend. The presumption that children aged between 10 and 13 years do not have a fully developed sense of moral agency and, as such, cannot understand the full implications of their criminal actions was duly abandoned. This has effectively resulted in an untrammeled age of criminal responsibility that begins at the age of 10 years. Gelsthorpe and Morris (1999) regard the abolition of this ancient principle of English law as being deeply symbolic. For them *doli incapax* "was a statement about the nature of childhood, the vulnerability of children and the appropriateness of criminal justice sanctions for children" (Gelsthorpe and Morris, 1999: 213). This loss of protected status for children in the courts—along with other measures contained in the legislation (Bandalli, 2000; Haines, 2000; Monaghan, 2000)—represents a process that Goldson has described as the "responsibilisation of children" and the "adulterization of childhood" (Goldson, 2001).

The foundational statute introduced by New Labour on coming to power was the Crime and Disorder Act 1998. It has been pointed out, however, that the New Labour government's approach to youth justice did not involve *major* repeals or amendments to pre-existing legislation. As Monaghan observed at the time, "Reform in this sense is sedimentary rather than metamorphic" (Monaghan, 2000: 146). Nevertheless, there is no doubting the fact that the statute transformed the youth justice system and, to a significant extent, practitioner culture.

The aims of the Crime and Disorder Act 1998, inscribed in Section 37, state,

1. It shall be the principal aim of the youth justice system to prevent offending by children and young persons.
2. In addition to any other duty to which they are subject, it shall be the duty of all persons and bodies carrying out functions in relation to the youth justice system to have regard to that aim.

The first aim, "to prevent offending by children and young people," marked an explicit departure from the received wisdom instilled from previous decades of practice experience. The notion that most children and young people usually went through a phase of offending and subsequently "grew out of it" with minimal intervention was clearly rejected (with the predictable outcome that penal custody rates rose sharply in the decade that followed the introduction of the Act). The first aim of Section 37 is, quite clearly and very ambitiously, to *prevent* young people from committing offenses in the first place. The second aim, meanwhile, alludes to a more corporate, multi-disciplinary, and multi-agency approach to youth crime. The vehicles for delivering this corporate response are local authority *youth justice plans* (Crime and Disorder Act 1998: section 40); the coordination of comprehensive *youth justice services* (a continuum ranging from crime prevention and community safety measures, through community orders to post-custodial supervision); the establishment of multi-agency *Youth Offending Teams* (Crime and Disorder Act: Section 39); and the creation of a *National Youth Justice Board*, an independent executive body with an ostensibly arms-length relationship with government (Crime and Disorder Act 1998: Section 41 and Schedule 2) in order to oversee the direction and administration of the whole system. The creation of *both* a **corporate** *and* **multi-agency** approach to youth justice was not without inherent tensions. The priorities of the national Youth Justice Board agenda were not necessarily always those shared by the police, let alone the health service. That said, the corporate agenda was clearly privileged in the national Youth Justice Board's early *National Standards* and the promotion of "effective practice" guidance (Youth Justice Board, 2000, 2001). It is also present in Sections 5 and 6 of the statute. Section 5, for example, requires the police and local authority to design and implement local "crime and disorder strategies."

In terms of a shift in practitioner culture, it was the establishment of local Youth Offending Teams that most clearly institutionalized the principles of "joined up," multi-agency working. Whereas previously the responsibility of working with young people who committed crime rested primarily with social workers based in Social Services Departments (usually based in Youth Justice Teams), the new Act widened that responsibility across departments and relevant agencies. Social workers in the old order had obviously needed to cooperate with other agencies in the past, of course, but the "new youth justice" institutionalized such cooperative relationships and bound them together with common objectives, standards, and key performance indicators. In addition to social workers, these new youth offending teams were now required to be represented by staff seconded from the police, probation service, education, and health.

Other relevant agencies could also be co-opted. Thus, the intervening passage of time has witnessed the arrival of staff from specialist voluntary sector agencies in the fields of accommodation, substance misuse, training, and employment. As well as managing the complex inter-professional dynamics of these new institutions, it has been necessary—though in practice this has probably not happened to everyone's satisfaction—for protocols to be developed in relation to information sharing between practitioners from the different agencies. Nevertheless, youth offending teams—or youth offending services, as they are now commonly termed—are by now well-established.

Although there have been changes in the type of community-based orders available to the courts, a consistent theme in New Labour's youth justice policy and practice worthy of mention is the use of restorative justice in the system. Early evaluations suggested restorative processes tended towards a rather routinized approach, low levels of victim involvement, and unrepresentative community participation (Crawford and Newburn, 2002). Moreover, concerns were expressed that oppressive and adult-centric forms of restorative justice could simply be used as another method for responsibilizing children (Haines, 2000). The subsequent move away from the centrally-driven prescriptions of *National Standards* has, though, created opportunities for the development of creative and child-friendly restorative practices at local level.

There are, then, two legacies of New Labour's "New Youth Justice" that need to be borne in mind in relation to the focus of this chapter. The first relates to the way in which child offenders are heavily responsibilized for their actions. Secondly, the discourse of "risk" has become embedded in the processes and activities of youth justice practice. Given that the Crime and Disorder Act tasked youth offending teams to prevent offending, the need to identify those most likely to offend and/or re-offend has become central to the youth justice enterprise in England and Wales. Practice has been informed by the Risk Factor Prevention Paradigm (Farrington, 2000, 2007) and the application of an assessment tool known as *Asset*. During the summer of 2016 Asset was replaced by *Asset+*, a framework that ostensibly replaces a predictive risk-based model with one that is informed by desistance theory. Whether this new framework will actually effect a real shift in practice remains to be seen. Not only does risk-based practice seem to be inscribed in the institutional DNA of youth offending services, but it would appear the key performance indicators applied by the Inspectorate remain unchanged. Time will tell.

Since Labour lost power in 2010 the youth justice system has remained largely intact. There was an attempt by the Conservative-Liberal Democrat Coalition UK government (2010–2015) to abolish the Youth Justice Board, but this was defeated by the House of Lords. Little has therefore changed in terms of the essential architecture of youth justice, although it should be noted that the prescriptive approach of the Youth Justice Board has been less pronounced and greater discretion at the local level is now permitted. Since 2010, moreover, both Coalition and Conservative UK governments (2015-present) have been committed to shrinking the state; which means that many of the public services upon which young people depend are unable to offer the level of support previously available. This, of course, poses the question of whether there can be meaningful youth justice without a significant corresponding measure of social justice.

A Risk Assessment of the Public Care and Youth Justice Systems

There is a tendency in both social work and youth justice practice to make children the objects of risk assessment (being at "risk of harm" or "risk of re-offending") without paying at least equal attention to the risks posed to children by powerful professionals and the systems they represent. It is instructive therefore to undertake a critical risk assessment of the systems with which these children and young people have contact. Such a risk assessment should not be regarded as a completely negative exercise because—as every social work student knows—risks can also often represent positive opportunities.

When discussing systems three points need to be made. Firstly, changing a system—or more often simply tweaking it—can be more effective than focusing all of one's attention on changing the child. The old joke that asks how many sociologists it takes to change a light bulb is relevant here. The answer, of course, is that one doesn't change the individual light bulb because the whole circuit or system needs to be changed.

Secondly, although every system is driven by its own institutional logic and animus, every system is also staffed and operationalized by individual practitioners. Practitioners possess independent agency and the power to use their professional discretion in creative and positive ways, particularly at critical decision points. Even seemingly minor decisions can have significant longer-term effects. Practitioners' encounters with children are therefore of crucial importance, as are the representations made by professionals on behalf of young people. The reflexive practitioner should therefore be distinguished from the agency-competent trained operative who collaborates deferentially with the decisions of the organization.

Thirdly, the relationship between different systems must be interrogated thoroughly. Systems, even when they are supposed to cooperate closely, have different priorities, pressures, professional values, and discourses. Consequently, asynchronous systemic processes may sometimes work against the best interests of a child in conflict with the law. If a young person is at risk of being sentenced to penal custody for an offense being dealt with by the youth justice system, for example, it is probably in the best interests of the child to bring forward a Looked After Children (public care) review meeting in order to consider, *inter alia*, the criminogenic risks of the current placement and how such risks might be reduced; not least because the pre-sentence report author in the youth justice system will need to assess the risk of future offending. Thus, if a residential unit in the public care system is unstable or places the young person at risk of associating with more criminally sophisticated peers, then some kind of action plan needs to be put in place (which can duly be reported to the court). This might include a move to a more appropriate and stable placement that reduces the criminogenic risks. The ideal of "joined-up services" is therefore, quite reasonably, almost invariably considered a desirable one. However, could there sometimes be an argument for applying the principle of domain integrity maintenance (Evans, 2010)? It should be acknowledged, for example, that diagnostic labels may be helpful and appropriate in one domain, but profoundly unhelpful in another; perhaps because the original meaning and significance of an assessment is lost in translation when it migrates from one domain to another. Developing "communities of practice" (Wenger, 1988) across different occupational groups, agencies, and systems is another strategy to help address this challenge.

The sections that follow consider three main areas for risk assessment: the point of entry into the Looked After Children (public care) system; public care placements; and two examples of professional social work practice in the youth justice system—structured risk assessment forms and pre-sentence reports.

Entry Into the Looked After Children (Public Care) System

Given that there exists a strong correlation between a background in public care and involvement in the youth justice system, it is first important to understand how children enter public care in England and Wales; otherwise known as the Looked After Children (LAC) system. Although since 1999 child welfare has been devolved to the National Assembly of Wales, both countries are governed by the Children Act 1989 that established two main routes into the care system: those accommodated with the voluntary agreement of their parents/carers (Section 20); and those made subject to Care Orders (Section 31), which involves the local authority "sharing" parental responsibility with the parents/carers and in most cases results in removal of the child from the family home. As this author has written previously, "While social workers are required to work in partnership with children, families, and other agencies it is important to acknowledge that the balance of power is weighted in favour of the professional. . . . [N]o one leaves the courtroom doubting that the senior partners in this legal arrangement are social workers" (Evans, 2010: 459)

For a Care Order to be made the court must be satisfied that "the child is suffering, or is likely to suffer significant harm" (Section 31(2) (a), Children Act 1989). There are four categories of abuse used in the Anglo-Welsh legal-social work discourse: physical abuse, sexual abuse, emotional abuse, and neglect (Department for Children, Skills and Families, 2010); these categories account for two thirds of entrants to public care (Prison Reform Trust, 2016a). The concept of "significant harm" is, moreover, defined in the statute (as amended by the Adoption and Children Act 2002) as "ill treatment or the impairment of health or development." Inadequate or neglectful parenting may be the result of a wide range of reasons and circumstances, including families affected by bereavement, mental health problems, disability, and substance misuse issues. Central government guidance on child social work assessment (Department of Health, 2000) that continues to exert an influence on practice locates the young person at the center of a triangle. The three dimensions of the triangle need to be considered in terms of a dynamic relationship: the child's developmental needs; parenting capacity; and wider family and environmental factors. Thus, for example, parenting capacity—understood as the knowledge, skills, and emotional warmth of the primary caregiver/s—are inevitably affected by wider family circumstances, the practical support available, material resources, and the nature of the neighborhood within which the parent/s reside. The emotional impact on parenting of material hardship and the stresses of bringing up a child in a low-income, high-crime neighborhood needs to be considered. The logic of the much cited East African saying that "it takes a village to raise a child" suggests capacity-building in less advantaged neighborhoods is a legitimate policy objective in child safeguarding and family support work.

There is a presumption in the Children Act 1989 that children are generally best placed with their parents and families. This is consistent with Article 16.3 of the United Nations Declaration on Human Rights (UNDHR) that, "The family is the natural and fundamental group unit of society and is entitled to protection from the State." As human rights are "living instruments," of course, the definition of the family now encompasses many diverse forms. Although the family of origin is considered to be of great importance, the welfare principle of the Children Act 1989—which is entirely consistent with the United Nations Convention on the Rights of the Child 1989—privileges the welfare of the child as being paramount. Moreover, children are perceived as sentient human beings rather than "objects of concern" (Butler-Sloss, 1988: 245). Consequently, children are duly constructed as "rights bearers" just as their parents and other significant adults are charged with responsibilities to these young people. Nevertheless, because parents and other primary caregivers are recognized as being crucial to the health and well-being of the child, the state has a responsibility to support parents in the task of parenting. Section 17 of the Children Act 1989 requires local authorities to support "children in need" with services and resources that will enable such young people to reach full and healthy development. By providing such support to parents and families, children on the cusp of the "significant harm" threshold are maintained in their families of origin within the community. It is a power that prevents the extreme intervention of a Care Order and entry into the Looked After Children system. The assessment of which children qualify for "children in need" status is therefore crucial to the future trajectories of these young people; and this includes placing some of them at risk of negative outcomes, including possible exposure to the criminal justice system.

Given that environmental factors—such as family structure, housing, neighborhood, and access to material resources—impact on parenting capacity, it is unsurprising that children being admitted to the Looked After Children system are drawn overwhelmingly from low-income families (including the over-representation of certain minority ethnic communities). Nevertheless, recent research reveals interesting patterns of social work intervention that raise questions not only about differences between geographical areas, but also whether the removal of children from families necessarily follows the consistent application of social work assessment criteria across different local authority areas. If one returns to the previously mentioned assessment triangle, which dimension is privileged by practitioners and managers? Is it the behavioral aspect of parenting capacity or the structural dimension represented by the wider environment of neighborhood and social inequality?

Explanations for variations in child protection interventions fall broadly into two categories, which Bywaters et al. (2015) argue are not mutually exclusive: "bias" and "risk" (sometimes also expressed as "need") (Cram et al., 2015; Jonson-Reid et al., 2009). Another way to express this is in terms of "demand" for services and the "supply." "Demand-side" explanations for differential interventions include families' socio-economic position; culturally situated patterns of parental behavior; the influence of aspects of identity (that may be related to "race" and ethnicity); and the impact of neighborhood resources, local social capital, and community dynamics. "Supply-side" explanations, meanwhile, are explained in the following terms,

> the availability, accessibility, appropriateness and quality of services. Again the arguments run in different ways. Raised intervention rates in disadvantaged areas may result from greater surveillance if services are more concentrated, so that fewer children with needs may be missed, or in more affluent areas because services may be more plentiful relative to need and/or because disadvantaged families are more visible (and perhaps stigmatized). Raised rates for Black children may result from biased assumptions by service providers about the parenting capacity of Black parents, while lower rates amongst other minority groups may result from assumptions about enhanced extended family support or community cohesion.
>
> (Bywaters et al., 2015: 99)

In their study of a sample of 4,546 children on the Child Protection Register (10.6% of the English national total) and 7,210 children in out-of-home care (11.3% of the English national total) drawn from 13 local authorities (LAs) in the English Midlands, Bywaters and colleagues compare patterns of intervention with reference to neighborhoods, which were used as a proxy of socio-economic status. The neighborhood comparisons drew on the 2011 census and the 2010 scores of the Index of Multiple Deprivation (IMD), a measure which does not rely solely on income data and includes 7 key dimensions and 38 indicators (www.gov.uk/government/statistics/english-indices-of-deprivation-2010). Informed by an "inequities approach"—one that explains differential patterns of service delivery, intervention, and outcomes in terms of structured social inequalities (Wilkinson and Pickett, 2010)—the researchers' findings are explained in terms of an "inverse intervention law" across the social gradient.

> Firstly, local authorities (LAs) that were more affluent overall, measured by IMD (Index of Multiple Deprivation) scores, were placing a significantly larger proportion of children on CPPs (Child Protection Plans) or in out-of-home than more disadvantaged LAs, if you compare neighbourhoods with equivalent levels of deprivation. Secondly, this inverse relationship between overall LA deprivation and rates was strong and significant for White children, but not statistically significant, or even not apparent for children from Black and Asian minority ethnic groups, although the quality and size of the data set might be a factor here. Differences in the ethnic demography between more and less affluent LAs have an impact on the size of the inverse relationship in White children but are insufficient to account for it.
>
> (Bywaters et al., 2015)

The important research cited here is ongoing, so a full theoretical explanation for the reported variations in intervention cannot be presented authoritatively at this stage. Nevertheless, there is evidence that the relationship between geographical patterns of social inequality, variations in local authority budgets, and the local responses of social work services are part of that explanation (with practitioner assessment practices possibly not being immune from the influence of local social and cultural norms when determining the appropriateness of intervention with certain "types" of family).

Looked After Children Placements

Having considered some of the issues associated with the selection of children for child protection intervention and entry into the Looked After Children system, attention is now turned to those factors, practices, and processes that might be considered potentially criminogenic. Some of the practices and processes to which reference will be made are probably best identified and illustrated by qualitative inquiry, not least because they are brought into the light by case file analysis and the reading of reports by practitioners. Nevertheless, there is quantitative evidence to support some of the insights generated by documentary analysis and interviews with key informants, including young people themselves.

It is important to make the point that an estimated 94% of children in the Looked After Children system do not have contact with the youth justice system (Prison Reform Trust, 2016a, 2016b), although it should be noted that the characteristics and outcomes for care leavers in terms of accommodation stability, mental health, educational attainment, and engagement with education, training, and employment are stubbornly poor in comparison with the wider population (UK Government, 2015). 67% of Looked After Children are assessed as having special educational needs; the most common being "behavioral, emotional and social difficulties." Only around half of Looked After Children have emotional and behavioral health "that is considered normal." In 2014, a mere 12% of Looked After Children achieved five or more GCSEs (a set of public examinations typically taken at ages 15–16 years) at grades A* to C (the "pass" threshold), including mathematics and English; this compares with 52% of children not in public care (Howard League for Penal Reform, 2016). The attenuation of support when transitioning from the Looked After Children system to independent living—a perilous journey sometimes embarked upon as young as 16 years—is a continuing cause for concern (Evans, 2013).

As has been noted, the over-representation of the Looked After Children population within the youth justice system has been a longstanding policy issue in the UK. The nature, quality, and stability of LAC placements are worthy of a brief risk assessment here. One of the major issues identified has been the problem of multiple placements and frequent changes in social worker. This is disruptive to children on a number of levels, not least in terms of attachment and educational continuity (Evans, 2010). It is ironic that young people's experience of neglectful and chaotic birth families is in too many cases replicated by the neglectful and chaotic corporate parenting practices of many local authorities.

Although some children are placed with family members, most placements take two main forms: foster care and residential provision. Around 75% are placed in foster care (Howard League for Penal Reform, 2016), although many of this group will have initially experienced residential provision. Foster care is not devoid of criminogenic and other risks, but more attention has been given to the role of residential units in criminalizing children (Evans, 2010; Shaw, 2012).

With the exception of secure children's homes, residential units cannot be characterized as total institutions (Goffman, 1961); although they do share some of the characteristics of youth custodial regimes: the attenuation of family and community ties, albeit sometimes for understandable reasons; and the grouping together of young people who present complex needs, behavioral challenges and experience of victimization. As in custody, inevitably many young people will prioritize a hidden curriculum designed by anti-social peers instead of cooperating with staff (Taylor, 2006: 87). It should also be acknowledged that the quality of residential provision is variable in the mixed economy of Looked After care; approximately 73% of children's homes being located in the private sector (Prison Reform Trust, 2016a, 2016b). Although there are well-run children's homes in the private sector, local authorities can exert less influence on staff training, practice, and the general ethos of homes outside the public sector.

None of this is to suggest that there are not excellent residential units in existence, but institutional life is always replete with risks. One is that the residents are not only highly observed in a "welfare spotlight" but also their behavior is recorded in great detail (Evans, 2010). Such behavior might be the result of normative adolescent behavior involving boundary-testing or it might be context-specific (Jones, 2016), but the risk of narrative records being shaped to pathologize young people for assessment purposes—sometimes reproduced in pre-sentence reports—is one that emerges in research undertaken by this author (Evans, 2017). Shaw (2012) confirms that many social work residential staff have a tendency to decontextualize young people's behavior and view them through the prism of individual psychological or family deficits. The vulnerable and disorientated young person in the care of the local authority is thus perceived as a "dangerous, wilful and agentive child" (Such and Walker, 2005: 41).

The metamorphosis from "child protection case" to "young offender" is one that can be accomplished in the residential unit by challenging behaviors that, in the context of most family homes, would result in loss of pocket money and being "grounded" rather than a phone call to the police, prosecution, a court appearance, and criminal record. Despite the introduction of restorative practices in many children's homes, children are still being prosecuted for minor acts of vandalism, theft, and disorder (Howard League, 2016). This means that some children can, within a short period of time spent within such criminalizing placements, be categorized as "prolific offenders" following the commission of relatively minor misdemeanors. Most of these children, it should be noted, will have entered the public care system without criminal records. Such convictions, of course, increase the "risk of re-offending score" in the actuarial model of assessment used by youth offending services in England and Wales. This, in turn, makes more intrusive forms of criminal justice intervention likely. The journey from "child at risk of harm" to "risky young offender" can often be accomplished in months rather than years.

Professional Practice in the Youth Justice System: Risk Assessment Instruments and Pre-Sentence Reports

This section risk-assesses two aspects of youth justice assessment practice: the risk assessment instrument known as *Asset* and the pre-sentence report (PSR).

The methodological strengths and limitations of the risk factor prevention paradigm (Farrington, 2007) are well-known and need not be rehearsed here (Haines and Case, 2015; Garside, 2009; Case and Haines, 2009; Case, 2007, 2006). In terms of its application to youth justice practice, a few salient points should be noted. Asset (Baker, 2004) is an actuarial assessment tool that, in the core profile, scores between 0–4 in terms of practitioner-rating of the extent to which particular dynamic risk factors contribute to the risk of re-offending. These risk factors are grouped into 12 pre-configured domains: living arrangements; family and personal relationships; education, training, and employment; neighborhood; lifestyle; substance use; physical health; emotional and mental health; perceptions of self and others; thinking and behavior; attitudes to offending; and motivation to change. The global score at the end of the assessment locates a young person within the bands of high, medium, and low risk of re-offending. The recommended intensity, dosage, and areas of intervention are duly identified and calibrated in what is called a "scaled approach" (Youth Justice Board, 2010; Sutherland, 2009); which has the dubious virtue of sounding both vaguely scientific and measured. There are obvious risks if practitioners apply this approach uncritically, which they are exhorted not to do; but the gravitational pull of the risk paradigm is often palpable.

Firstly, there is a risk of over-weighting some factors more heavily than others through double-counting: "attitudes to offending" and "motivation to change" is just one example. Secondly, those with higher welfare "needs," by virtue of their structural position in society and service user status (as patients or clients of social services), will be given higher "risk" of re-offending scores. Thus two co-defendants can, theoretically and in some cases in practice, receive different levels of intervention. Looked After Children are almost by definition assessed by social workers as vulnerable and needy. The social work assessment of "need" in the Looked After Children system is mistranslated by the criminal justice practitioner as "risk of re-offending" in the youth justice system. Young people in the public care system will, for the reasons already outlined, score highly in such domains as living arrangements, family, and personal circumstances, and education. When these are then added to static risk factors such as criminal history, the young person who has been resident in a criminalizing care home is effectively ascribed an even higher risk of re-offending. It is worth noting here, too, that young black males—because they appear to be subject to institutional biases within the criminal justice system, including such practices as "stop and search" by the police, greater vulnerability to prosecution, and heavier sentences—are more likely to bring longer criminal histories to the risk assessment process (Webster, 2015; Raynor and Lewis, 2011).

As the format of the pre-sentence report requires practitioners to risk-assess the likelihood of re-offending, it is inevitable that there is a relationship between the Asset assessment and this particular section of the document. The penetration of a risk factor discourse into the more established genre of a pre-sentence report will depend on the discretion of the individual practitioner. The social construction and artful (sometimes artless) manipulation of discourses in pre-sentence reports is the subject of an article by this author (Evans, 2017), but suffice to say here that the risks of stereotyping will be apparent. It should be acknowledged, though, that the PSR author faces a number of very real dilemmas when writing about children with a background in public care. How should these young people be represented? Which information should be included and which omitted when narrating their backgrounds to the court? A detailed account will no doubt elicit sympathy for the child offender (particularly if there has been experience of abuse, neglect, and victimization), but perhaps leave the sentencer pessimistic about future prospects. How can the PSR author depict the high levels of welfare "need" presented by a young person without, at the same time, risking such an account being converted into the criminal justice system's currency of "risk of re-offending"? Conversely, glossing some aspects of personal background may lead to an under-appreciation of the influence of biographical history on offending.

Another dilemma for the PSR author from a youth offending service is deciding the extent to which s/he should expose the failings of the Looked After Children system (the number of placements, for example), particularly when the practitioner works for the very authority which is responsible for delivering these services. Leaving aside the tribal loyalties a youth justice practitioner will probably feel towards her/his colleagues in Looked After Children services, there are also tangible risks to the young person in court if the credibility of the local authority is undermined by an account of its past failures. Sentencers may be skeptical when they read about the efficacy of yet another new placement, especially when it is weighed against their legal responsibilities to protect the public.

There are, of course, no easy answers to the dilemmas faced by practitioners. It could be argued that, ultimately, the solutions are systemic. In the meantime practitioners must be "systems aware" and appreciate the risks they, as practitioners from powerful agencies, can potentially pose to young people.

Conclusion

This chapter has explored tentatively some of the possible relationships between the child protection, public care, and youth justice systems in England and Wales. In so doing it has attempted to shine a flickering light on a few of the interconnecting subterranean passageways of practice between these different domains. Further empirical research and risk analysis is required if the number of children migrating across these systems is to be reduced. To that end this chapter represents a modest exercise in cartography. Mapping the challenging terrain between the domains of child welfare and criminal justice is a navigational work in progress. It has hopefully been demonstrated that there is evidence of structural factors at work both within and between the child welfare and youth justice systems. Social class and inequality may have been foregrounded in the analysis presented in this chapter, but that is not to deny the importance of "race" (Webster, 2015), gender (Sharpe and Gelsthorpe, 2015; Shepherd, 2015), and relations between adult professionals and children (Evans, 2014, 2010) in this complex equation of discrimination. Disaggregating the significance of such variables as ethnicity and social class, for example, is challenging when certain minority communities occupy a structurally subordinate position in British society; which is evidenced in differential educational attainment levels and relationships to the labor market (White and Cunneen, 2015; Webster, 2015). Meanwhile, the lived experience of racial discrimination in the classroom, street, and court also suggest culturally embedded biases at work (Webster, 2015).

Children from low-income families and neighborhoods are clearly over-represented in both the child welfare and youth justice systems. The relationship between low-income and the intervention of child protection services is not, however, a straightforward one. More rigorous attempts to interrogate the relationship between social gradient and the granular detail of geographical disparities suggest that more complex processes are at work (Bywaters et al., 2015). The apparent operation of an "inverse intervention law" rather than a postcode lottery requires closer inspection. Why do more affluent local authorities place a significantly larger proportion of children on Child Protection Plans and in out of home Looked After Children placements than poorer local authorities? A number of possible explanations, most probably in combination, might account for this pattern. Are better resourced local authorities simply able to assess and intervene more efficiently than their poorer municipal counterparts? Alternatively, are these poor families in deprived neighborhoods more visible to the clinical gaze of local social workers and particularly if they belong to certain ethnic or religious communities? Are social workers in poorer local authorities with larger populations of low-income families in deprived neighborhoods more inured and desensititized to the corrosive influence of poverty on standards of parenting? These questions cannot be answered conclusively, but two points should be made. Firstly, that social class relations matter. Secondly, this power relationship is mediated by social work practitioners. Practitioners are therefore important; not least because they are gatekeepers to the Looked After Children system.

Once recruited to the Looked After Children system the focus then turns to how some young people are fast-tracked into the youth justice system. The quality of the public care system will, no doubt, be influenced by the resources available to the local authority; which, as has been established, can vary enormously between different areas. It is suggested in this chapter that, in addition to the destabilizing effect of multiple placements, some types of placement are inherently criminogenic and certain institutional practices can criminalize children very quickly. As soon as children are constructed as "offenders first, children second" the master identity of "criminal" converts the assessment of their welfare needs into the currency of "risk of re-offending" scores.

Once set on this course, such children are at risk of being escalated up through a sentencing tariff towards penal custody. Practitioner assessment practices and the quality of pre-sentence reports are important factors on the direction and speed of the journey.

Despite the apparent inevitability of so many young people's passage from public care to a criminal justice system destination, it is important to remember that child welfare and criminal justice practitioners possess agency and can therefore exercise professional discretion in ways that can make a profound difference to outcomes. A critical awareness of the discriminatory processes at work is a pre-requisite for effective, supportive, and diversionary interventions in young people's lives. The all too familiar trajectory from family of origin to penal custody is not inevitable. Postcode, or for that matter skin color, need not be a predictor of destiny. Practitioners possess power and should use it effectively and ethically. Empirical research should therefore further explore how some individual practitioners manage to exercise independent agency—against all the odds—within ostensibly obdurate structures, monolithic institutions, and sclerotic systems of power. Sometimes they do so with great ingenuity, creativity, and success. The lessons from these "success stories" for wider policy and practice are invaluable.

In conclusion the point needs to be made that, despite being constructed by powerful adults as "objects of concern" or "risky young offenders," children also possess agency. Despite progress being made since the United Kingdom signed the United Nations Convention on the Rights of the Child (1989), there is still more work to be done on realizing children's participation rights enshrined in Article 12. This means not only listening to what young people say in all matters that affect them directly, including the Looked After Children and youth justice systems, but also ensuring effective advocacy is in place. Their softer voices need to be amplified and made audible if they are to speak truth to power.

References

Aries, P. (1962). *Centuries of childhood*. London: Cape.

Audit Commission. (1996). *Misspent youth: Young people and crime*. London: Audit Commission.

Baker, K. (2004). Is *Asset* really an asset? Assessment of young offenders in practice. In R. Burnett & C. Roberts (Eds.), *What works in probation and youth justice—developing evidence-based practice* (pp. 70–87). Cullompton: Willan Publishing.

Bandalli, S. (2000). Children, responsibility and the new youth justice. In B. Goldson (Ed.), *The new youth justice* (pp. 81–95). Lyme Regis: Russell House Publishing.

Bateman, T. (2015). *The state of youth justice 2015: An overview of trends and developments*. London: National Association of Youth Justice.

Brown, S. (1998). *Understanding youth and crime: Listening to youth?* Buckingham: Open University Press.

Butler-Sloss, E. (1988). *Report of the inquiry into child abuse in Cleveland 1987*. London: HMSO.

Bywaters, P., Brady, G., Sparks, T., Bos, E., Bunting, L., Daniel, B., Featherstone, B., Morris, K., & Scourfield, J. (2015, October). Exploring inequities in child welfare and child protection services: Explaining the 'inverse intervention law.' *Children and Youth Services Review*, *57*, 98–105.

Case, S. (2006). Young people "at risk" of what? Challenging risk-focused early intervention as crime prevention. *Youth* Justice, *6*(3), 171–179.

Case, S. (2007). Questioning the "evidence" of risk that underpins evidence-led youth justice interventions. *Youth Justice*, 7(2), 91–105.

Case, S., & Haines, K. (2009). *Understanding youth offending: Risk factor research, policy and practice.* Cullompton: Willan Publishing.

Clarke, J. (1985). Whose justice? The politics of Juvenile control. *International Journal of the Sociology of Law, 13*(4), *18*, 407–421, reproduced in J. Muncie, G. Hughes, & E. McLaughlin (Eds.). (2002). *Youth justice: Critical readings* (pp. 284–295). London: Sage.

Cohen, S. (1979). The punitive city: Notes on the dispersal of social control. *Contemporary Crises, 3*(4), 341–363.

Cohen, S. (1985). *Visions of social control.* Cambridge: Polity Press.

Cohen, S. (2002). *Folk devils and moral panics: The creation of mods and rockers.* London: MacGibbon and Kee.

Committee Investigating the Causes of the Alarming Increase of Juvenile Delinquency in the Metropolis. (1816). *Report for the committee investigating the causes of the alarming increase of juvenile delinquency in the metropolis.* London: JF Dove.

Cram, F., Gulliver, P., Ota, R., & Wilson, M. (2015). Understanding overrepresentation of indigenous children in child welfare data: An application of the Drake risk and bias models. *Child Maltreatment, 20*(3), 170–182.

Crawford, A., & Newburn, T. (2002, Summer). Recent developments in restorative justice for young people in England and Wales: Community participation and representation. *British Journal of Criminology, 42*(3), 476–495.

Cromer, G. (2004). "Children from good homes": Moral panics about middle-class delinquency. *British Journal of Criminology, 44*(3), 391–400.

Curtis, S. (2005). The welfare principle. In T. Bateman & J. Pitts (Eds.), *The RHP companion to youth justice* (pp. 53–58). Lyme Regis: Russell House Publishing.

Davies, B. (1986). *Threatening youth: Towards a national youth policy.* Milton Keynes: Open University Press.

Department for Children, Schools and Families. (2010). *Working together to safeguard children: A guide to interagency working to safeguard and promote the welfare of children.* London: The Stationery Office.

Department of Health (2000). *Framework for the assessment of children in need and their families.* London: The Stationery Office.

Department of Health and Social Security. (1981). *Offending by young people.* London: DHSS.

Drakeford, M., & Vanstone, M. (2000). Social exclusion and the politics of criminal justice: A tale of two administrations. *The Howard Journal of Criminal Justice, 39*(4), 369–381.

Evans, J. (2010). Institutional abuse and children's homes. In F. Brookman, M. Maguire, H. Pierpoint, & T. Bennett (Eds.), *Handbook on crime* (pp. 458–479). Cullompton: Willan.

Evans, J. (2013). Care leavers and the new offender management system. *British Journal of Community Justice, 11*(2–3), 195–198.

Evans, J. (2014). Responding to youth crime: Reconnecting the disconnected. *Perspectives on Youth, 2*, 85–102.

Evans, J. (2017). Artful dodgers: The role of unreliable narrators in the production of authorized histories and assessments of young people in conflict with the law. *Deviant Behavior. 38*(9), 1042–1058.

Farrington, D. (2000). Explaining and preventing crime: The globalization of knowledge. *Criminology, 38*(1), 1–24.

Farrington, D. (2007). Childhood risk factors and risk-focused prevention. In M. Maguire, R. Morgan, & R. Reiner (Eds.), *The Oxford handbook of criminology* (pp. 602–640). Oxford: Oxford University Press.

Fawcett, B., Featherstone, B., & Goddard, J. (2004). *Contemporary child care policy and practice.* Basingstoke: Palgrave Macmillan.

Foucault, M. (1973). *The birth of the clinic: An archaeology of medical perception.* London: Tavistock.

Foucault, M. (1977). *Discipline and punish: The birth of the prison.* New York: Pantheon.

Furlong, A., & Cartmel, F. (2007). *Young people and social perspectives.* Maidenhead: Open University Press.

Garside, R. (2009). *Risky people or risky societies? Rethinking interventions for young adults in transition.* London: Centre for Crime and Justice.

Gelsthorpe, L., & Morris, A. (1999). Much ado about nothing: A critical comment on key provisions relating to children in the Crime and Disorder Act 1998. *Child and Family Law Quarterly, 11*(3), 209–221.

Giddens, A. (1998). *The third way: The renewal of radical politics.* Cambridge: Polity Press.

Goddard, J. (2001). Children (Leaving Care) Act 2000: A commentary. *Welfare Benefits, 8*(3), 25–34.

Golby, J. M. (Ed.), *Culture and society in Britain 1850–1890: A source book of contemporary writings.* Oxford: Oxford University Press.

Goldson, B. (Ed.). (2000). *The new youth justice.* Lyme Regis: Russell House Publishing.

Goldson, B. (2001). The demonisation of children: From the symbolic to the institutional. In P. Foley, J. Roche, & S. Tucker (Eds.), *Children in society: Contemporary theory, policy and practice.* Basingstoke: Palgrave.

Goffman, E. (1961). *Asylums: Essays on the social situation of mental patients and other inmates.* New York: Doubleday.

Haines, K. (2000). Referral orders and youth offender panels: Restorative approaches and the new youth justice. In B. Goldson (Ed.), *The new youth justice* (pp. 58–80). Lyme Regis: Russell House Publishing.

Haines, K., & Case, S. (2015). *Positive youth justice: Children first, offenders second.* Bristol: Policy Press.

Haines, K., & Drakeford, M. (1998). *Young people and youth justice.* Basingstoke: Macmillan.

Hall, G. S. (1905). *Adolescence: Its psychology and its relation to physiology, anthropology, sociology, sex, crime, religion and education.* New York: Appleton.

Hayden, C., Goddard, J., Gorin, S., & Van Der Spek, N. (1999). *State child care—looking after children?* London: Jessica Kingsley.

Hendrick, H. (1990). *Images of youth: Age, class and the male youth problem 1880–1920.* Oxford: Clarendon.

Hendrick, H. (1997). Constitutional reconstructions of British childhood: An interpretive survey, 1800 to the present. In A. James & A. Prout (Eds.), *Constructing and reconstructing childhood* (pp. 34–62). London: Falmer.

Hendrick, H. (2002). Constructions and reconstructions of British childhood: An interpretative sur vey, 1800 to the present. In J. Muncie, G. Hughes, & E. McLaughlin (Eds.), *Youth justice—critical readings* (pp. 22–44). London: Sage.

Home Office. (1965). *The child, the family and the young offender.* London: HMSO.

Home Office. (1968). *Children in trouble.* London: HMSO.

Home Office. (1990). *Crime, justice and protecting the public.* London: HMSO.

Home Office. (1995). *National standards for the supervision of offenders in the community.* London: HMSO.

Home Office. (1997). *No more excuses: A new approach to tackling youth crime in England and Wales,* Cm 3809. London: HMSO.

Howard League for Penal Reform. (2016). *Criminal care: Children's homes and criminalising children.* London: Howard League for Penal Reform.

Jewkes, Y. (2011). *Media and crime.* London: Sage.

Jonson-Reid, M., Drake, B., & Kohl, P. L. (2009). Is the overrepresentation of the poor in child welfare caseloads due to bias or need? *Children and Youth Services Review, 31*(3), 422–427.

Jones, D. (2001). "Misjudged youth": A critique of the audit commission's reports on youth justice. *British Journal of Criminology, 41,* 362.

Jones, D. (2002, February). Questioning New Labour's youth justice strategy: A review article. *Youth Justice, 1*(3), 15–26.

Jones, I. (2016). *De-escalating interventions with troubled adolescents.* Cardiff: Public Policy Institute for Wales.

Labour Party Media Office. (1996). *Tackling youth crime, reforming youth justice: A consultation paper on an agenda for change.* London: Labour Party.

Lea, J., & Young, J. (1984). *What is to be done about law and order?* Harmondsworth: Penguin.

Lister, R. (2003). Investing in citizen workers of the future: Transformations in citizenship and the state under New Labour. *Social Policy and Administration, 37*(5), 427–443.

Magarey, S. (2002). The invention of juvenile delinquency in early nineteenth century England. In J. Muncie, G. Hughes, & E. McLaughlin (Eds.), *Youth justice—critical readings* (pp. 115–122). London: Sage.

May, M. (1973). Innocence and experience: The evolution of the concept of juvenile delinquency in the mid-nineteenth century. *Victorian Studies, 17*(1), 7–29.

Mayhew, H. (2008). *London labour and the London poor*. London: Wordsworth Editions Limited.

McAra, L., & McVie, S. (2010). Youth crime and justice: Key messages from the Edinburgh study of youth transitions and crime. *Criminology and Criminal Justice, 10*(2), 179–204.

Monaghan, G. (2000). The courts and the new youth justice. In B. Goldson (Ed.), *The new youth justice* (pp. 144–159). Lyme Reis: Russell House Publishing.

Mullaly, B. (1997). *Structural social work—ideology, theory and practice*. Oxford: Oxford University Press.

Murray, C. (1984). *Losing ground*. New York: Basic Books.

Murray, C. (1990). *The emerging underclass*. London: Institute of Economic Affairs.

Murray, C. (1994). *Underclass: The crisis deepens*. London: Institute of Economic Affairs.

Pearson, G. (1983). *Hooligan: A history of respectable fears*. London: Macmillan.

Petrie, C. (2003). Social pedagogy: An historical account of care and education as social control. In J. Brannen & P. Moss (Eds.), *Rethinking children's care* (pp. 44–60). Buckingham: Open University Press.

Phillips, C., & Bowling, B. (2002). Racism, ethnicity, crime and criminal justice. In M. Maguire, R. Morgan, & R. Reiner (Eds.), *The Oxford handbook of criminology* (pp. 577–619). Oxford: Oxford University Press.

Pitts, J. (2000). The new youth justice and the politics of electoral anxiety. In B. Goldson (Ed.), *The new youth justice* (pp. 1–13). Lyme Regis: Russell House Publishing.

Pitts, J. (2001). Youth crime, youth justice and youth work. In F. Factor, V. Chauhan, & J. Pitts (Eds.), *The RHP companion to working with young people* (pp. 177–184). Lyme Regis: Russell House Publishing.

Platt, A. (1974). The triumph of benevolence; the juvenile justice system in the United States. In R. Quinney (Ed.), *Criminal justice in America* (pp. 356–389). Barton: Little Brown & Co.

Prison Reform Trust. (2016a). *In care, out of trouble: Executive summary*. London: Prison Reform Trust.

Prison Reform Trust. (2016b). *In care, out of trouble: Background briefing paper for meeting at Welsh government, Cardiff, Wales*. London: Prison Reform Trust.

Raynor, P., & Lewis, S. (2011). Risk-need assessment, sentencing and minority ethnic offenders in Britain. *British Journal of Social Work, 41*(7), 1357–1371.

Rush, P. (2002). The government of a generation: The subject of juvenile delinquency. In J. Muncie, G. Hughes, & E. McLaughlin (Eds.), *Youth justice—critical readings* (pp. 138–158). London: Sage Publications.

Sharpe, G., & Gelsthorpe, L. (2015). Girls, youth crime and youth justice. In B. Goldson & J. Muncie (Eds.), *Youth crime and justice* (pp. 49–64). London: Sage.

Shaw, J. (2012). Professionals' perceptions of offending in children's residential care. *Child and Family Social Work, 17*, 359–367.

Shepherd, B. (2015). Youth justice practice with girls. In J. Annison, J. Brayford, & J. Deering (Eds.), *Women and criminal justice: From the Corston Report to transforming rehabilitation* (pp. 99–118). Bristol: Policy Press.

Shore, H. (2002). Reforming the juvenile: Gender, justice and the child criminal in nineteenth-century England. In J. Muncie, G. Hughes, & E. McLaughlin (Eds.), *Youth justice—critical readings* (pp. 159–172). London: Sage.

Skuse, T., & Matthew, J. (2015, July). The trauma recovery model: Sequencing youth justice interventions for young people with complex needs. *Prison Service Journal*, 220, 16–25.

Smiles, S. (1986). Self help. In J. M. Golby (Ed.), *Culture and society in Britain 1850–1890: a source book of contemporary writings* (pp. 106–112). Oxford: Oxford University Press.
Smith, M. (2003). *Social science in question*. London: Sage.
Social Exclusion Unit. (1998a). *Truancy and school exclusion*. London: The Stationery Office.
Social Exclusion Unit. (1998b). *Rough sleeping*. London: The Stationery Office.
Social Exclusion Unit. (1998c). *Bringing Britain together again: A national strategy for renewal*. London: The Stationery Office.
Social Exclusion Unit. (1999). *Teenage pregnancy*. London: The Stationery Office.
Social Exclusion Unit. (2000). *National strategy for neighbourhood renewal: Report of the policy action team 12—young people*. London: The Stationery Office.
Social Exclusion Unit. (2003). *A better education for children in care*. London: Social Exclusion Unit.
Social Exclusion Unit. (2005). *Transitions—young adults with complex needs—a social exclusion unit final report*. London: Office of the Deputy Prime Minister.
Stewart, J. (1995). Children, parents and the state: The Children Act 1908. *Children and Society*, *9*(1), 90–99.
Such, E., & Walker, R. (2005). Young citizens or policy objects? Children in the 'rights and responsibilities' debate. *Journal of Social Policy*, *34*(1), 39–58.
Sutherland, A. (2009). 'The scaled approach' in youth justice: Fools rush in . . . *Youth Justice*, *9*(1), 44–60.
Taylor, C. (2006). *Young people in care and criminal behaviour*. London: Jessica Kingsley.
Thorpe, D., Smith, D., Green, C., & Paley, J. (1980). *Out of care—the community support for Juvenile offenders*. London; George Allen & Unwin.
Tonry, M. (2004). *Punishment and politics—evidence and emulation in the making of English crime control policy*. Cullompton: Willan Publishing.
UK Government. (2015). Retrieved from www.gov.uk/government/statistics/outcomes-for-children-looked-after-by-local-authorities
Ward, G. K. (2012). *The Black child-savers: Racial democracy and juvenile justice*. Chicago: The University of Chicago Press.
Webster, C. (2015). "Race," youth crime and youth justice. In B. Goldson & J. Muncie (Eds.), *Youth crime and justice* (pp. 31–48). London: Sage.
Wenger, E. (1988). *Communities of practice: Learning, meaning and identity*. Cambridge: Cambridge University Press.
White, R., & Cunneen, C. (2015). Social class, youth crime and youth justice. In B. Goldson & J. Muncie (Eds.), *Youth crime and justice* (pp. 17–30). London: Sage.
Wilkinson, R. G., & Pickett, K. E. (2010). *The spirit level: Why equality is better for everyone*. London: Penguin.
Youth Justice Board. (2000, April) *National standards for youth justice*. London: Youth Justice Board.
Youth Justice Board. (2001). *National standards for youth justice, Revised May 2001*. London: Youth justice Board.
Youth Justice Board. (2010). *Youth justice: The scaled approach*. London: Youth Justice Board.

INDEX

Page numbers in *italic* indicate a figure, and page numbers in **bold** indicate a table on the corresponding page.

For Product Safety Concerns and Information please contact our EU
representative GPSR@taylorandfrancis.com
Taylor & Francis Verlag GmbH, Kaufingerstraße 24, 80331 München, Germany

www.ingramcontent.com/pod-product-compliance
Ingram Content Group UK Ltd.
Pitfield, Milton Keynes, MK11 3LW, UK
UKHW050757180926
475701UK00007B/1093

9780367405168